D0846254

ATLAS OF THE 2012 ELECTIONS

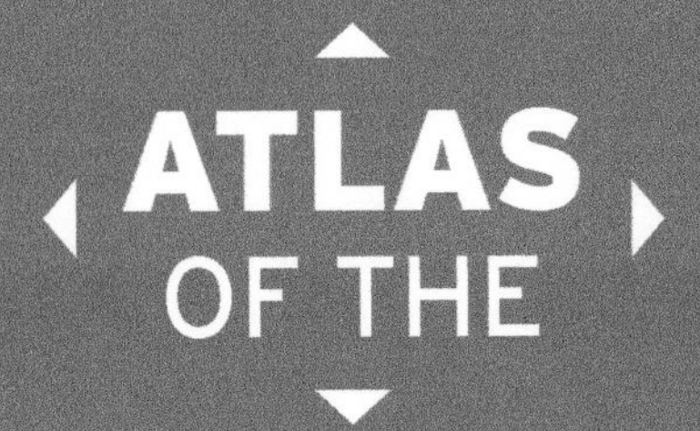

2012 ELECTIONS

EDITED BY **J. Clark Archer**
Robert H. Watrel
Fiona Davidson
Erin H. Fouberg
Kenneth C. Martis
Richard L. Morrill
Fred M. Shelley
Gerald R. Webster

CARTOGRAPHY BY J. Clark Archer and Robert H. Watrel

ROWMAN & LITTLEFIELD
Lanham • Boulder • New York • London

Published by Rowman & Littlefield
A wholly owned subsidiary of The Rowman & Littlefield Publishing Group, Inc.
4501 Forbes Boulevard, Suite 200, Lanham, Maryland 20706
www.rowman.com

16 Carlisle Street, London W1D 3BT, United Kingdom

British Library Cataloguing in Publication Information Available

Library of Congress Cataloging-in-Publication Data

Atlas of the 2012 elections / edited by J. Clark Archer [and others] ; cartography by J. Clark Archer and Robert H. Watrel.

pages cm.

"Edited by J. Clark Archer, Robert H. Watrel, Fiona Davidson, Erin H. Fouberg, Kenneth C. Martis, Richard L. Morrill, Fred M. Shelley, Gerald R. Webster."

Includes bibliographical references and index.

ISBN 978-1-4422-2583-1 (cloth : alk. paper) — ISBN 978-1-4422-2584-8 (electronic)

1. Presidents—United States—Election—2012—Maps. 2. United States. Congress—Elections, 2012—Maps. 3. Voting—United States—Maps. 4. Political campaigns—United States—Maps. 5. Elections—United States—Maps. 6. Elections—United States—Statistics. I. Archer, J. Clark, editor, cartographer.

G1201.F9A8 2014

324.973'0932—dc23 2014025512

∞™ The paper used in this publication meets the minimum requirements of American National Standard for Information Sciences—Permanence of Paper for Printed Library Materials, ANSI/NISO Z39.48-1992.

Printed in the United States of America

CONTENTS

FIGURES AND TABLES

FIGURES

TABLES

CHAPTER ONE

INTRODUCTION

In 2012, Barack Obama was reelected to a second term as president of the United States. Although his margin of victory was not as large as it had been four years earlier, Obama as the nominee of the Democratic Party defeated his Republican opponent, former governor Mitt Romney of Massachusetts, by a margin of approximately five million popular votes and by a vote of 332–206 in the Electoral College. Thus for the third consecutive time, Americans reelected an incumbent president for a second four-year term. Obama's reelection victory was notable, however, in that he was the first Democratic president to be reelected to a second four-year term with more than 50 percent of the popular vote since Franklin D. Roosevelt.

On the surface, there were few differences between the 2008 and 2012 presidential elections. In both cases, Obama defeated a Republican opponent who had been nominated following a lengthy and often bitter struggle for the Republican nomination. The two parties' campaigns highlighted the often acrimonious partisan divide facing the contemporary United States. The electoral votes of forty-eight of the fifty states went to the same party's candidate in 2012 as they had in 2008. The only exceptions were Indiana and North Carolina, which along with the Second Congressional District of Nebraska (which allocates its electoral votes by congressional district) gave electoral votes to Obama in 2008 but to Romney in 2012.

Yet the 2012 election nevertheless tells a compelling story about the present and future of US politics at the national and subnational levels. The results illustrate how partisan divides between different parts of the United States have continued to deepen. These divides are evident not only between areas dominated by the Democrats and by the Republicans but also between Republican voters in different parts of the country. Underlying these divisions are fundamental differences in voters' policy views, priorities, and visions of the future of the country. These differences are evident in the general election campaign, in the primary election campaigns used by the two parties to select their nominees, and in state and local elections throughout the country.

In this atlas, the US presidential election, along with selected state and local elections, is analyzed from a geographical perspective. This atlas contains maps of the 2012 election campaign and outcomes. Along with commentary associated with each map, the atlas provides a valuable perspective on the election that is of importance to contemporary analysts as well as to historians of the future.

THE 2012 UNITED STATES ELECTIONS

The 2012 elections took place on November 6. Although the campaign was spirited and often intense, turnout was down from the 2008 election. Approximately 126 million Americans cast ballots in 2012, as opposed to more than 130 million in 2008. Although Obama won the 2012 election less decisively than he had in 2008, he nevertheless won a comfortable victory in both the popular vote and the Electoral College.

In 2008, both parties held intense contests for their presidential nominations, after which Obama and his Republican opponent, Senator John McCain, were nominated by their respective parties. In 2012, however, Obama and his running mate, Vice President Joseph Biden, were renominated by the Democrats without opposition. Thus, only the Republicans held a contested primary campaign. Many Republicans saw their party's nomination as appealing because many regarded Obama as beatable. It was thought that a tepid economic recovery during Obama's first term, along with the passage of the controversial Affordable Care Act that was opposed strongly by many voters, would make Obama vulnerable in his quest for a second term.

The campaign for the Republican nomination lasted for more than a year. Over the course of this campaign, more than a dozen serious candidates contested for the GOP nomination. By early in the spring of 2012, after several states had held primary elections and party caucuses, the field had been reduced to four candidates: Romney, former senator Rick Santorum of Pennsylvania, former Speaker of the House of Representatives Newt Gingrich of Georgia, and Representative Ron Paul of Texas. Santorum was favored by many social conservatives, and he won primary contests in several states in the South and the Great Plains. However, he lost to Romney in several large industrial states, including Michigan, Ohio, and his native Pennsylvania. Santorum's failure to win any of the large states in the primaries helped cinch the party's nomination for Romney.

Late in the summer, both parties held their national nominating conventions. Romney selected Representative Paul Ryan of Wisconsin as his running mate, while the Democrats renominated Obama and Biden by acclamation. During the fall campaign, Romney and the Republicans blasted Obama for mismanaging the slowly recovering economy. However, public opinion polls generally showed Obama with a narrow lead over Romney. These predictions were borne out on Election Day.

Nationwide, the results of the 2012 presidential election mirrored closely the results from four years earlier. Obama's strategy was to hold onto as many of the states that he had won in 2008 as possible. The strategy succeeded in that he won every state that he carried in 2008 with the exceptions of Indiana and North Carolina. The Republicans, on the other hand, recognized that they had to capture enough states that had had Democratic majorities in 2008 to overturn Obama's Electoral College advantage. Thus, they targeted states such as Florida, Ohio, Virginia, and Colorado that had gone Democratic in 2008 but had supported Republican George W. Bush in his successful campaigns in 2000 and 2004. Although Romney would have been elected had he carried these states, he was unable to do so and thus lost the election.

The election results revealed an increasing divide between metropolitan and nonmetropolitan areas. Obama owed his victory to very high levels of support in most of the country's major cities and, in many cases, their suburbs. On the other hand, the Republicans remained strong in most rural areas. Across the United States as a whole, Romney outpolled Obama in nonmetropolitan areas. As in 2008, Obama also was supported very strongly by younger voters, whereas Romney had higher levels of support among older voters. Obama also retained very strong support among nonwhite voters, whereas Romney won a majority of white voters. After the election, it was noted that the Republicans were much more likely to be supported by older, white, rural voters. This trend was noted by Republican activists themselves as well as journalists, and it has become a matter of concern for the Republicans in that the electorate across the United States is becoming increasingly metropolitan, diverse, and nonwhite.

Meanwhile, contests were held for 33 US Senate seats and for all 435 seats in the House of Representatives. After the voters were counted, the Democrats retained their narrow majority in the Senate with a net gain of two seats. In the House, the Democrats had a net gain of eight seats, although this increase was not enough to overturn the previous Republican majority. As with the presidential election, a large majority of House districts in metropolitan areas sent Democrats to the House, whereas most rural districts elected Republicans to their congressional seats. About 90 percent of Senate and House members who sought new terms were reelected, following a recent trend in which the large majority of incumbents win their reelection campaigns. Nevertheless, several states held spirited contests for congressional seats, especially in the Senate, as illustrated by several maps in this atlas.

The results illustrate the importance of geography and territory in election outcomes. In the United States, the president and vice president are elected formally by the Electoral College. Members of the Electoral College are selected from each state, with the number of electors determined by that state's representation in Congress. Although this has happened only three times in history, it is possible for a president to be elected by the Electoral College despite having a minority of popular votes. Thus, the American system of electing presidents is fundamentally geographical in nature.

Elections for representatives in Congress, state governors, and other state and local offices are conducted by direct popular vote. However, campaigns for these offices also have strong geographical components. Each state, of course, elects two US senators. Districts for the House of Representatives, state legislatures, and other legislative offices are drawn on a geographical basis, with each legislator responsible primarily to the territorially defined district from which he or she is elected. Within this context, candidates and their backers identify areas where their supporters live, encourage these voters to turn out and cast their ballots for them, and work to identify and locate undecided voters whose decisions can often determine election outcomes.

Formally, voters do not cast their ballots for presidential nominees; rather, they vote for a slate of candidates for the Electoral College pledged to vote for their party's nominees for the presidency and vice presidency. Thus, the presidential election can be conceptualized as fifty-one separate contests for seats in the Electoral College—one for each state and one for the District of Columbia. The goal of both parties is to secure an Electoral College majority. Both parties recognize that some of the states, such as Vermont, Maryland, and Washington, are almost certain to go Democratic, whereas others, such as Oklahoma, Utah, and Mississippi, are almost certain to go Republican. Over the years, the terms "red state" and "blue state" have become synonymous with strong support for the Republicans and Democrats, respectively. These states are ignored by both parties, which concentrated their resources in the closely contested swing states or "purple states," such as Florida and Ohio, whose electoral votes are likely to decide the outcome of the election nationwide. Obama won the 2012 election by holding on to most of the swing states that he had won in 2008 but that his party's nominees had lost in 2000 and 2004.

ORGANIZATION OF THE ATLAS

The atlas is divided into nine chapters, each of which contains maps and accompanying narratives. These chapters are followed by a technical appendix that describes data sources along with cartographic and analytical procedures.

Chapter 2 deals with electoral structures and their impacts on the elections and the campaigns. The decennial US census was conducted in 2010. In accordance with the US Constitution, the results of the census were used to reallocate seats in the House of Representatives and, therefore, in the Electoral College, whose seats are allocated to each state on the basis of its total representation in both houses of Congress. These changes went into effect beginning with the 2012 elections. Reapportionment of seats following the census benefited the Republicans slightly, reflecting the general tendency over the past several decades for many Republican-leaning states to grow in population faster than many Democratic-leaning states.

At the House of Representatives level, the census results also required redrawing of district lines within states (except for the very small states such as Delaware, Vermont, and Wyoming with only one House seat each). In the 1960s, the Supreme Court held that the Fourteenth Amendment to the US Constitution, which mandates equal protection for all citizens under the law, implies that House districts must be delineated such that each has a population as equal as possible given the inevitable inaccuracies implicit in the census. Within each state, populations change at different rates, with some areas growing faster than others and some losing population. Thus, territory was added to some districts and removed from others. Some critics have suggested that the Republicans may owe their majority in the House of Representatives to gerrymandering in their favor in several states in which Republican candidates won a disproportionate share of House seats relative to their statewide shares of popular votes for these seats.

Chapter 3 deals with the Republican primary campaign. During 2011, several Republican hopefuls ran for the party's nomination, and at various times different candidates emerged as front-runners. Once the primary season began in earnest in early 2012, Romney, Santorum, and Gingrich emerged as the leading candidates, with each winning early primaries. However, Romney remained the front-runner, and after Santorum and Gingrich failed to dislodge him in later primaries, Romney won the nomination. Nevertheless, maps of the primary election results both nationwide and within individual states show deep-seated divisions within the Republican Party and within the country as a whole.

Chapter 4 is devoted to the analysis of the election campaign after the two parties formally nominated their candidates. Presidential election campaigns today are very expensive, and fund-raising becomes a very important component of any campaign. The distribution of where campaign funds are raised and where they are spent provides crucial insight into the election process and the election outcomes. Formal "debates" between the candidates have become significant in the campaign process, and comparison of domestic and foreign places mentioned by the two candidates is also insightful.

Chapter 5 focuses on the election results. It includes maps of the election results in the Electoral College, the popular vote by county, and comparisons at the state and county levels between the 2012 election and previous elections. The maps illustrate the partisan divisions between metropolitan and nonmetropolitan areas. Romney lost the election decisively despite having carried more than 85 percent of the United States' more than three thousand counties that contain more than 90 percent of the country's land area.

Comparison between the 2012 and 2008 elections at the county level also reveals subtle but nevertheless potentially significant differences. For example, Romney was the first member of the Church of Jesus Christ of Latter-day Saints, or Mormons, to be nominated for the presidency by a major party. His largest gains in the popular vote relative to McCain in 2008 were in heavily Mormon Utah and nearby southeastern Idaho, although these areas were already very heavily Republican. In a longer-run historical perspective, the geography of the 2012 election results illustrates the continuation of a trend dating back to the 1970s in which Democrats have increased their support in the Northeast and the Pacific Coast states, whereas the Republicans have been consistently strong in the South, the Great Plains states, and many of the Rocky Mountain states. However, this trend represents a sharp break from partisan differences that divided the United States politically for the century following the Civil War. Of particular note is the relationship between election outcomes and size of place, for example, in "micropolitan" areas containing small cities of between ten thousand and fifty thousand people that were less Democratic than major cities but less Republican than smaller towns and rural areas.

In chapter 6, the election results are discussed at a regional level. Seven regions of the United States—the urban Northeast, Appalachia, the South, the Rust Belt, the Great Plains, the Interior West, and the Pacific Coast states—are considered in detail. In each case, maps and analysis uncovered trends with historical significance as well as importance for the future of the two parties and their policy proposals.

Chapter 7 is devoted to breaking down different subgroups of the voting population, primarily at the state level. Previously, analyses of this sort had been done using state-by-state comparison of exit polls across all fifty states. However, in 2012 the consortium of media responsible for conducting these exit polls decided to limit their polling to only thirty-one of the fifty states, thus making such direct comparison impossible. Nevertheless, indirect analysis as illustrated by the maps in chapter 6 and the accompanying commentaries provide valuable insights.

Race and ethnicity was a crucial factor in the outcome of the election. Obama won a substantial majority of nonwhite votes, offsetting Romney's solid majority of ballots cast by white voters. As in 2008, African Americans were very solidly behind Obama. Latinos and Asian Americans also gave majorities to Obama, but these majorities were smaller. In both cases, the levels of support for both Obama and Romney varied by state and also by specific area of origin. Although various ethnic groups of Latin American and Asian origin are often linked together for purposes of analysis, Mexican Americans vote very differently than do Cuban Americans; and Indian Americans, Chinese Americans, and Vietnamese Americans also vote in very different ways relative to one another. Demography, size of place, and religion also impacted the outcome, and their geographical patterns also illustrate the degree to which Americans continue to be divided politically.

Many different issues affected how voters decided which candidate to support in the presidential election. The economy and health care were generally regarded as the most important issues. However, both the environment and foreign policy were also taken into account, with the two candidates and their supporters holding sharply contrasting views on these issues. The impacts of these issues are considered in chapter 8. The results of the elections also affected the composition of the 113th United States Congress and the distribution of votes within the new Congress on various issues of national importance.

Chapter 9 considers the geography of state and local elections. Elections for seats in the US Senate, which remains closely divided between the two major parties, were watched especially closely because partisan control of the Senate depended on their outcomes. This chapter includes maps of several of the most significant and closely contested Senate elections, including those in Indiana, Massachusetts, Montana, Virginia, and Wisconsin, all of which were won by Democratic nominees whose success allowed the Democrats to retain control of the Senate.

Chapter 9 also includes maps of gubernatorial elections in Wisconsin, where Republican governor Scott Walker was recalled and faced a second election after signing laws sharply restricting the rights of labor unions. It also considers a local election in Fort Worth, Texas. There, state senator Wendy Davis, who became a national figure in 2013 after filibustering a bill that would have enacted severe restrictions on abortion rights, narrowly defeated her Republican opponent in 2012 despite the fact that Obama lost the territory contained within her district by more than ten percentage points.

In chapter 10, ballot initiatives and referenda are considered. Two of the most controversial topics voted on directly by various electorates included the legalization of marijuana and same-sex marriage. Voters in Colorado and Washington voted to legalize marijuana, and those in Maine, Maryland, Minnesota, and Washington approved same-sex marriage. Geographical analysis of these election outcomes illustrates considerable correlation with presidential election outcomes, with Democrats tending to support legalizing marijuana and same-sex marriage and Republicans in opposition. Comparison is especially valuable in the state of Washington, in which both issues were on the ballot simultaneously. Finally, chapter 11 is devoted to discussion of technical issues, including data collection, data analysis, and mapping methods and techniques.

ELECTORAL STRUCTURES

REAPPORTIONMENT

KENNETH C. MARTIS

The 2012 elections were affected by the 2010 United States census. The United States Constitution states that every ten years a population census shall be conducted to allocate the seats to the states in the House of Representatives and, therefore, also to the Electoral College.

After the results of the census were tabulated and released, the apportionment of seats in the House of Representatives changed, with rapidly growing states gaining seats in the House at the expense of slow-growing states. In recent decades the Supreme Court's "one person, one vote" rulings mandated that even though a state may not have gained or lost a congressional seat, it must redraw its congressional and state legislative boundaries based on the new population geography. The 2014, 2016, 2018, and 2020 elections will also be held using these new numbers and districts.

Figure 2.1 is the reapportionment map resulting from the 2010 census. Twelve seats were transferred between states. As a result of these transfers, ten states lost seats and eight states gained seats. As the map shows, seats moved from the North and Northeast to the South, Southwest, and West. The reapportionment map after the 2000 census shows the same trend. In fact, this general movement has been occurring for several decades, as illustrated in *The Historical Atlas of State Power in Congress, 1790–1990.*

Of the ten states that lost seats, nine were in the North or Northeast, with Louisiana as the only exception. New York and Ohio lost two seats each, and eight other states lost one each. Texas gained four seats and Florida gained two, while six other states each gained one seat. The 2000 census regional reapportionment numbers were very similar, with New York (–2) and Pennsylvania (–2) the biggest losers among many other northern states. Four Sunbelt states—Arizona, Florida, Georgia, and Texas—gained two seats each. The reapportionments of 2000 and 2010 illustrate the continuing westward trend of American population over the past two hundred years. Many states in the South began to reverse their outward population migration in the 1960s and 1970s and, therefore, gained members in the House at the expense of the North.

FIGURE 2.1

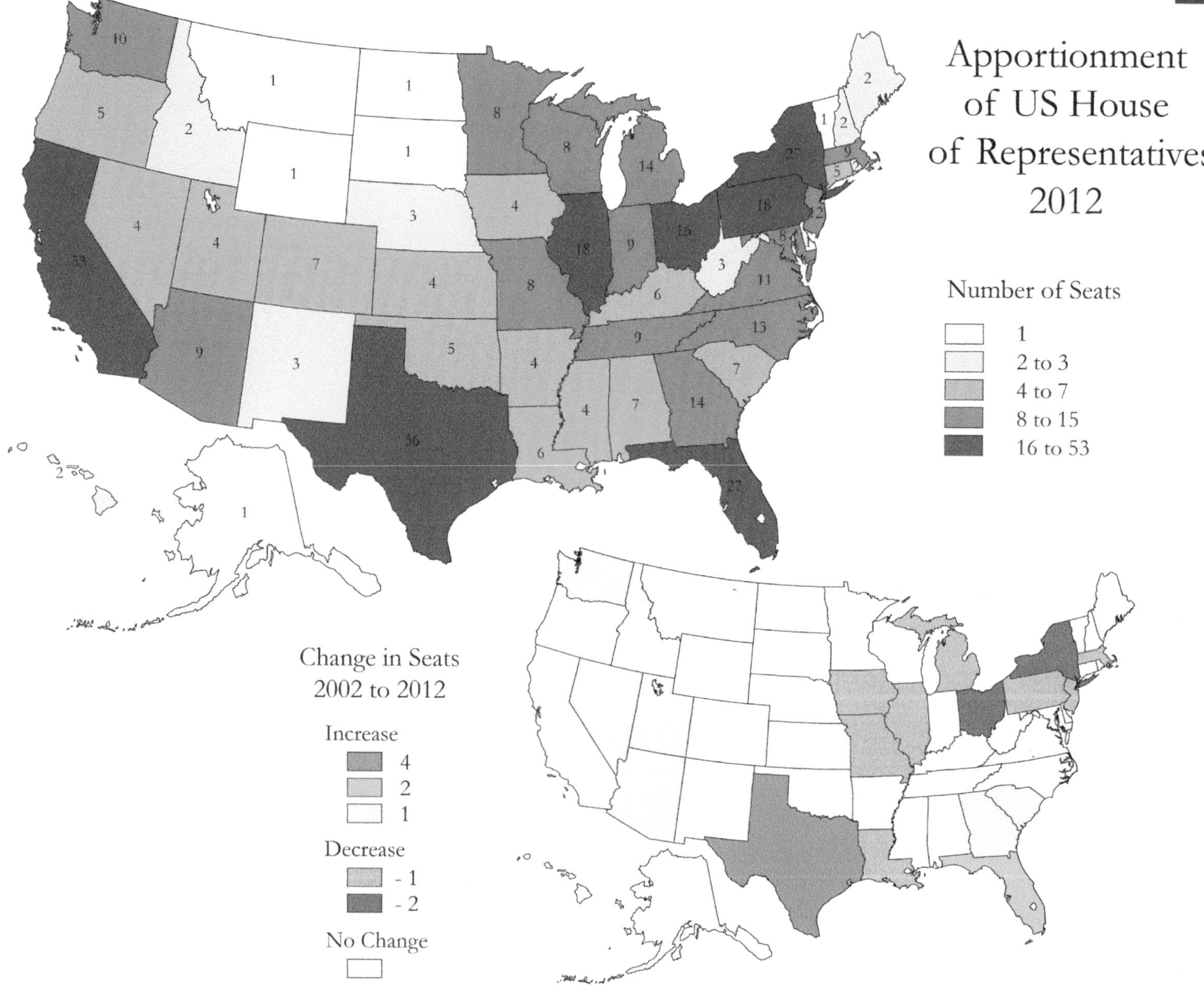

Apportionment
of US House
of Representatives
2012
Number of Seats
1
2 to 3
4 to 7
8 to 15
16 to 53
Change in Seats
2002 to 2012
Increase
4
2
1
Decrease
- 1
- 2
No Change

The combined congressional losses of the northern industrial and midwestern and Great Plains agricultural states over the past half-century are staggering. The last time that northern industrial states gained seats in reapportionment was in 1960, when Ohio, Michigan, and New Jersey each gained one seat. Ohio and Michigan each added a seat because of the post–World War II automobile industry boom. New Jersey gained a seat in response to suburbanization from New York City and Philadelphia. Since 1950, however, New York has lost sixteen seats. Pennsylvania has lost twelve seats, Ohio and Illinois have lost seven each, Massachusetts has lost five, Michigan has lost four, and New Jersey has lost two.

During the same period, of course, most of these seats lost by older industrial states in the Rust Belt were transferred to rapidly growing Sunbelt states. The biggest gainers have been the three largest states of the Sunbelt. Between 1950 and 2010, California gained twenty-three seats, Florida gained nineteen, and Texas gained fourteen. However, over the past two decades, Texas gained six seats, while Florida gained four and California gained only one. On a percentage basis, once sparsely settled states in the West have had the largest percentage gains in numbers of seats. Arizona has gained seven seats since 1950, and Nevada has gone from one seat in 1980 to four in 2010.

Since the 1960s and 1970s there has been a clear reallocation of regional power in the United States. But how has this reallocation translated into political power? Does it benefit the Republicans or Democrats? The 2012 elections are examined using the reapportionment of seats since 1960. Gains and losses are calculated based on the state's House delegation size at the time of the 1960 election versus the House size at the 2012 election, as enumerated in table 2.1. After the 1960 election, this encompasses the six census reapportionments, 1960 through 2010. During this period eighty-seven seats, that is, 20 percent of the House, were transferred between the states (including the three seats allocated to the new states of Alaska and Hawaii after the 1960 census). Only nine states did not have a net change in their House delegation during this period, including four states that kept the mandatory one representative, Alaska, Delaware, Vermont, and Wyoming. Forty-one states had their House delegation change: fifteen states gained representatives, and twenty-six lost representation.

The states are divided into three categories based on the 2012 preelection analysis, safe Republican (twenty-four), safe Democrat (eighteen), and "swing" (eight). The eight swing states are New Hampshire, Virginia, Ohio, Wisconsin, Iowa, Colorado, Florida, and Nevada. Of these states in addition to Florida, Colorado and Nevada gained three seats each and Virginia gained one. New Hampshire remained the same, and Ohio (–7), Iowa (–4), and Wisconsin (–2) all lost seats. However, Florida's gains were so large that the sum of the swing state total shows a net thirteen-seat gain, but, of course, President Obama eventually won all the swing states.

In 2012, eighteen states (and the District of Columbia) were considered safe Democrat in the presidential election. The safe Obama states are California (+23), Connecticut (–1), Delaware (0), Hawaii (0), Illinois (–7), Maine (–1), Maryland (+1), Massachusetts (–5), Michigan (–4), Minnesota (–1), New Jersey (–2), New Mexico (+1), New York (–16), Oregon (+1), Pennsylvania (–12), Rhode Island (0), Vermont (0), and Washington (+3). In the safe Democratic states, in 2012 at least, twenty-nine seats were gained over the last half-century (mostly in California), but forty-nine seats were lost, for a net loss of twenty seats. The seventeen Democratic states other than California had forty-three fewer seats and, therefore, forty-three fewer electoral votes in 2012 than they had after the 1950 census. Since the political geography of the Electoral College in recent years favors the Democrats in the North and Northeast and the Pacific Coast states, the Democrats have been on the losing end in the North but have come out ahead on the Pacific Coast.

The twenty-four states considered safe for the Republicans in the 2012 preelection analysis were Alabama (–2), Alaska (0), Arizona (+7), Arkansas (–2), Georgia (+4), Idaho (0), Indiana (–2), Kansas (–2), Kentucky (–2), Louisiana (–2), Mississippi (–2), Missouri (–3), Montana (–1), Nebraska (–1), North Carolina (+1), North Dakota (–1), Oklahoma (–1), South Carolina (+1), South Dakota (–1), Tennessee (0), Texas (+14), Utah (+2), West Virginia (–3), and Wyoming (0). At the time of the 2012 elections, the safe Republican states had gained a net of five House seats and electoral votes since 1960. These gains were mostly in Texas and Arizona, with growing southern states of Georgia and North Carolina helping. Republican losses, however, occurred in a number of Appalachia, Great Plains, and several slow-growing southern states.

Overall, these long-term trends did not appear to favor either major party, at least in presidential elections. The three large-growth pole states mentioned above are split between safely Democratic California (+23), safely Republican Texas (+14), and swing state Florida (+19). The increase in numbers the swing state Florida has made in recent decades is one of the reasons it has played a critical, and sometimes decisive, role in the election of the president. The twenty-six states won by President Obama have had a net loss of seven seats since 1950. However, the twenty-four states carried by Obama other than California and Florida lost a net total of forty-nine seats. The states carried by Governor Romney had a net gain of seven seats. However, the Republican states other than Texas and Arizona lost fourteen seats. Although Republicans have made great strides in controlling the growing South, these gains have been mitigated by population losses in the Great Plains and other places. Democrats have recently controlled the North and Northeast. This region is declining in seats/electors but still has a large population base. In addition, the Democrats have controlled the vital California vote (the 55 electors are 10.2 percent of the entire Electoral College and 20.4 percent of the 270 needed to secure the presidency) and other Pacific Coast states and have also made great inroads in some growing western areas like New Mexico, Colorado, and Nevada.

A number of political and demographic trends could alter the above alignment of safe or swing categories for both parties. For example, the Hispanic vote is growing in Arizona, Nevada, and North Carolina, and they may even be categorized as swing rather than safe Republican by the time of the 2016 or 2020 presidential election. In fact, some observers initially placed North Carolina as a swing state in 2012 since President Obama carried the state in 2008. For these reasons and more, some analysts consider the Democrats to have an "electoral lock" in the Electoral College, while for different reasons to be discussed later, the Republicans may have a lock on the US House elections. Of course, all regions in the study period have gone through voting changes since the 1960s, and a change in swing states' voting patterns or a significant realignment election could alter the 2012 election trends in the future.

TABLE 2.1. State Reapportionments, U.S. House of Representatives, Sunbelt and Snowbelt Eras, 1960–2012

Elections	AL	AK	AZ	AR	CA	CO	CT	DE	FL	GA	HI	ID	IL	IN	IA	KS	KY	LA	ME	MD	MA	MI	MN	MS	MO	MT	NE	NV	NH	NJ	NM	NY	NC	ND	OH	OK	OR	PA	RI	SC	SD	TN	TX	UT	VT	VA	WA	WV	WI	WY
1952-60	9	–[a]	2	6	30	4	6	1	8	10	–[b]	2	25	11	8	6	8	8	3	7	14	18	9	6	11	2	4	1	2	14	2	43	12	2	23	6	4	30	2	6	2	9	22	2	1	10	7	6	10	1
1962-70	8	1	3	4	38	4	6	1	12	10	2	2	24	11	7	5	7	8	2	8	12	19	8	5	10	2	3	1	2	15	2	41	11	2	24	6	4	27	2	6	2	9	23	2	1	10	7	5	10	1
1972-80	7	1	4	4	43	5	6	1	15	10	2	2	24	11	6	5	7	8	2	8	12	19	8	5	10	2	3	1	2	15	2	39	11	1	23	6	4	25	2	6	2	8	24	2	1	10	7	4	9	1
1982-90	7	1	5	4	45	6	6	1	19	10	2	2	22	10	6	5	7	8	2	8	11	18	8	5	9	2	3	2	2	14	3	34	11	1	21	6	5	23	2	6	1	9	27	3	1	10	8	4	9	1
1992-2000	7	1	6	4	52	6	6	1	23	11	2	2	20	10	5	4	6	7	2	8	10	16	8	5	9	1	3	2	2	13	3	31	12	1	19	6	5	21	2	6	1	9	30	3	1	11	9	3	9	1
2002-10	7	1	8	4	53	7	5	1	25	13	2	2	19	9	5	4	6	7	2	8	10	15	8	4	9	1	3	3	2	13	3	29	13	1	18	5	5	19	2	6	1	9	32	3	1	11	9	3	8	1
2012-20	7	1	9	4	53	7	5	1	27	14	2	2	18	9	4	4	6	6	2	8	9	14	8	4	8	1	3	4	2	12	3	27	13	1	16	5	5	18	2	7	1	9	36	4	1	11	10	3	8	1
Seats Gain/Loss	-2	0	+7	-2	+23	+3	-1	0	+19	+4	0	0	-7	-2	-4	-2	-2	-2	-1	+1	-5	-4	-1	-2	-3	-1	-1	+3	0	-2	+1	-16	+1	-1	-7	-1	+1	-12	0	+1	-1	0	+14	+2	0	+1	+3	-3	-2	0

[a] Alaska was admitted into the Union with one congressional seat in 1959 and has continued to be allocated one seat in each succeeding census (the House of Representatives was temporarily increased in size to 437 with the admission of Alaska and Hawaii).

[b] Hawaii was admitted into the Union with one congressional seat in 1959 and was allocated 2 seats in the 1960 census beginning with the 1962 election (the House of Representatives was temporarily increased in size to 437 with the admission of Alaska and Hawaii).

THE ELECTORAL COLLEGE AND THE 2012 PRESIDENTIAL ELECTION

BARNEY WARF

Contrary to the popular imagination, American voters do not directly choose a presidential candidate but instead vote for representatives to the Electoral College, the body that formally selects the new president and vice president. The college exists only for one day following the election and never meets as a unified body. Electors are obligated, but not technically bound, to vote for the candidate who wins a plurality of the popular vote in their state. If there is a tie in the Electoral College, the selection of the president falls to the House of Representatives, in which each state has one vote, an event that has occurred twice in US history.

The Electoral College acts as an intermediary between the popular vote and who is elected president. Its dynamics are complex and spatially uneven. This section of the chapter first sets it in context and then examines how Electoral College votes in the 2012 presidential election reflected and intersected with the geographies of the popular vote, including margins of victory that swing a state's electoral votes into one candidate's column or another.

Established during the constitutional convention of 1787, the Electoral College reflected fears on the part of small states that their influence in national elections would be nullified by a few populous ones. Essentially, it struck a balance between direct proportional representation, which favors large states, and equal representation by all states, which favors small ones. The number of Electoral College votes for each state equals the size of its congressional delegation (representatives and senators), with a minimum of three and the remainder allocated proportionally to its population. Thus, there are currently 538 electors corresponding with 100 senators, 435 representatives, and three representatives from the District of Columbia. To win a presidential election, a candidate must accrue a majority of Electoral College votes, that is, a minimum of 270.

The defining feature of the Electoral College is the "winner-take-all" system, in which candidates who receive a plurality of the popular vote in a state acquire *all* of its Electoral College votes. Maine, starting in 1972, and Nebraska, starting in 1991, are exceptions.

The merits and demerits of the Electoral College have been hotly debated. Defenders argue that elimination of the Electoral College would weaken the political party system, promote splinter parties, trigger interminable recounts, facilitate presidential candidates who represent narrow geographical, ideological, or ethnic bases of support, and reduce the influence of small states and rural interests (Best 1996; Hardaway 1994). Critics of the college argue that it forces presidential candidates to concentrate their campaign efforts on a few battleground states at the expense of voters elsewhere and that it is an anachronistic institution that runs contrary to the principles of democratic government by making it possible for the winner of the popular vote to lose in the Electoral College, as happened in 2000 (Abbott and Levine 1991; McCaughey 1993).

The winner-take-all system creates differences between the number of popular votes for a presidential candidate and Electoral College votes and makes the winner's proportion of electoral votes disproportionately large (Tufte 1973; Grofman 1983). The college thus has profound geographical biases: it is not simply how *many* popular votes a candidate receives that determines the outcome of the election but *where* those votes are cast. Debates over the Electoral College often point to the relative degree of influence it accords small and large states (Sterling 1981; Gelman and King 1994). Lightly populated states are frequently held to be disproportionately represented when compared to their share of the population (Abbott and Levine 1991).

Based on a simple ratio of total 2012 population to electoral votes, spatial biases are evident among states (figure 2.2), with a range of 192,000 in Wyoming to 691,000 in California. This perspective seems to affirm accusations that the Electoral College is systemically biased in favor of smaller, typically more rural states. However, the winner-take-all-strategy has also been argued to favor large, more populous states, as small margins of victory there can generate huge returns in the Electoral College. Because the margin of victory in the popular vote decides which candidate will take all of that state's Electoral College votes, its size and distribution are very important. The combinatorial mathematics of how the Electoral College creates spatial differences in the power of voters to shape national elections have been explored, most famously by John Banzhaf (1968) (see also Warf 2009).

The uneven play of the Electoral College over the nation's electoral landscape reflects the geographies of margins of victory in the popular and Electoral College votes. In the 2012 presidential election, out of 129.2 million votes cast, Obama won by a margin of 4.985 million (51 percent), or 3.86 percent. Not surprisingly, the most populous states racked up the largest absolute margins of victory in the popular vote for both candidates, including California, Texas, New York, and Illinois, but not, significantly, Florida (figure 2.3). The percentage margin of victory, which varied from .88 percent (Florida) to 83.6 percent (District of Columbia), reflects large ones in both deeply Republican and Democratic states as well as very small ones in hotly contested "battleground" states.

It is revealing to contrast the margins of victory in the popular and Electoral College votes. Such measures reflect both the geography of political sentiments and the spatially variant efficiency of both parties' campaigns. Thus, the ratio of the absolute number of votes in the margin of victory in each state to that state's Electoral College votes (figure 2.4) reveals how "hard" candidates and parties must work to put that state in their column. For example, enormous popular margins of victory in a given state are largely "wasted" in terms of their return in Electoral College votes. By this measure, Obama's large absolute margins of victory in California, New York, and New Jersey generated fewer Electoral College returns than did his victories in more closely fought states such as Ohio, Florida, Pennsylvania, and Colorado. Conversely, Romney's substantial absolute margins of victory in the popular vote in Alabama, Oklahoma, Utah, Idaho, and Kentucky were less "efficient" in generating Electoral College votes than were his efforts in Arizona, North Carolina, South Carolina, and Georgia.

Finally, the spatial distribution of the relative size of margins of victory in the popular vote also reveals the efficiency of campaigns in garnering Electoral College votes (see also chapter 5). Thus, by barely winning Florida, Obama accrued a large number of Electoral College votes in return, a strategy pursued to less effect in Ohio, Pennsylvania, and Virginia. Romney's most efficient wins were in North Carolina, Texas, and Georgia; conversely, his efforts in large numbers of lightly populated, typically rural states in the Great Plains and northern Rocky Mountains, generated relatively small proportionate returns.

Without doubt, the Electoral College continues to shape the dynamics of US presidential campaigns, elections, and their outcomes. Because the influence of the winner-take-all system is complex, it is prudent to adopt a nuanced view of this topic. Campaigns that win large absolute margins of victory in some states are largely wasting their time, effort, and resources there. Given the discrepancies between the size of the electorate in each state and its Electoral College votes, winning battleground states with small absolute margins of victory appears to be the key to electoral success. Obama's campaign in 2012 pursued this strategy to great effect, whereas the Romney campaign won decisively in lightly populated,

FIGURE 2.2

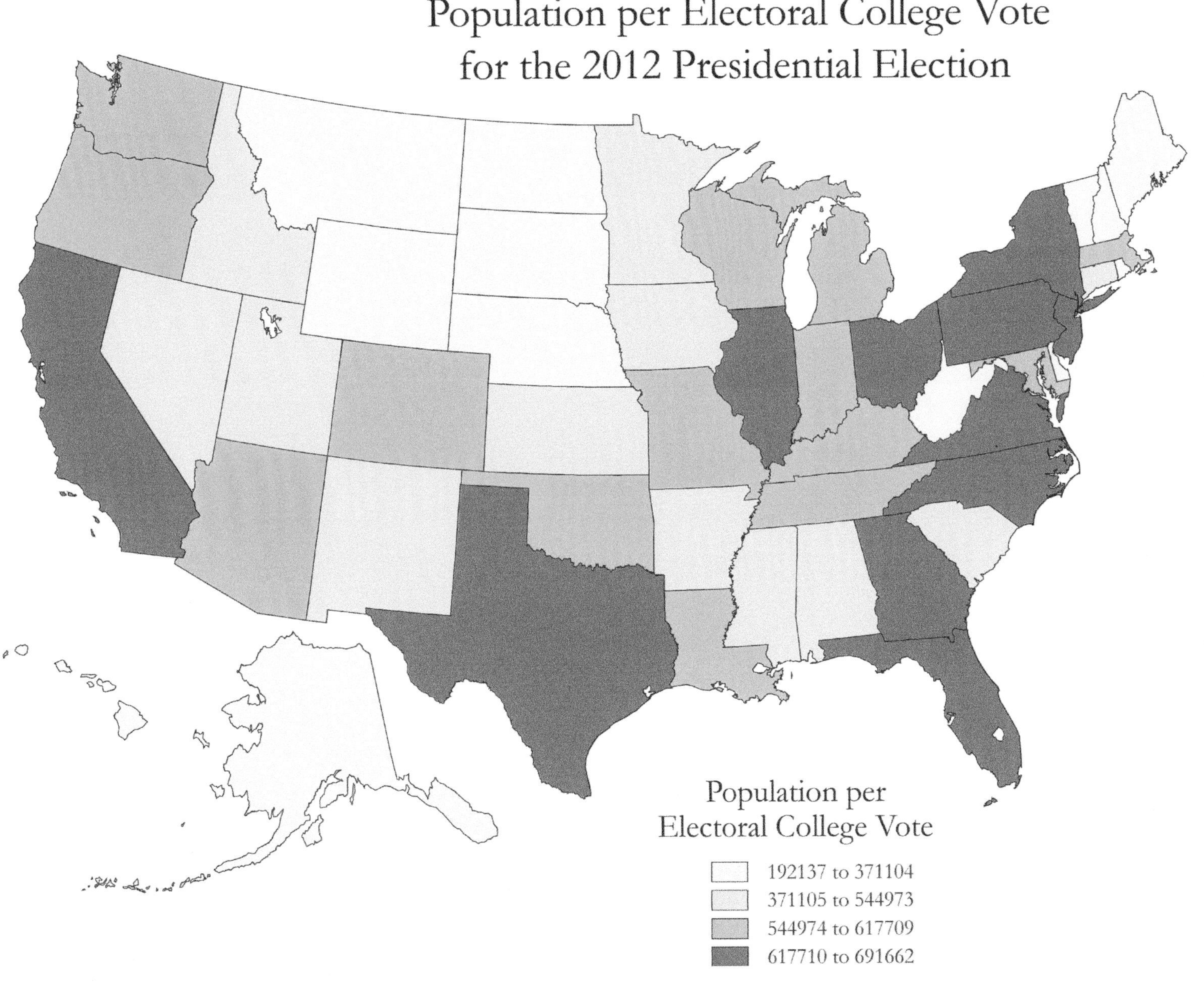
Population per Electoral College Vote
for the 2012 Presidential Election
Population per
Electoral College Vote
192137 to 371104
371105 to 544973
544974 to 617709
617710 to 691662

FIGURE 2.3

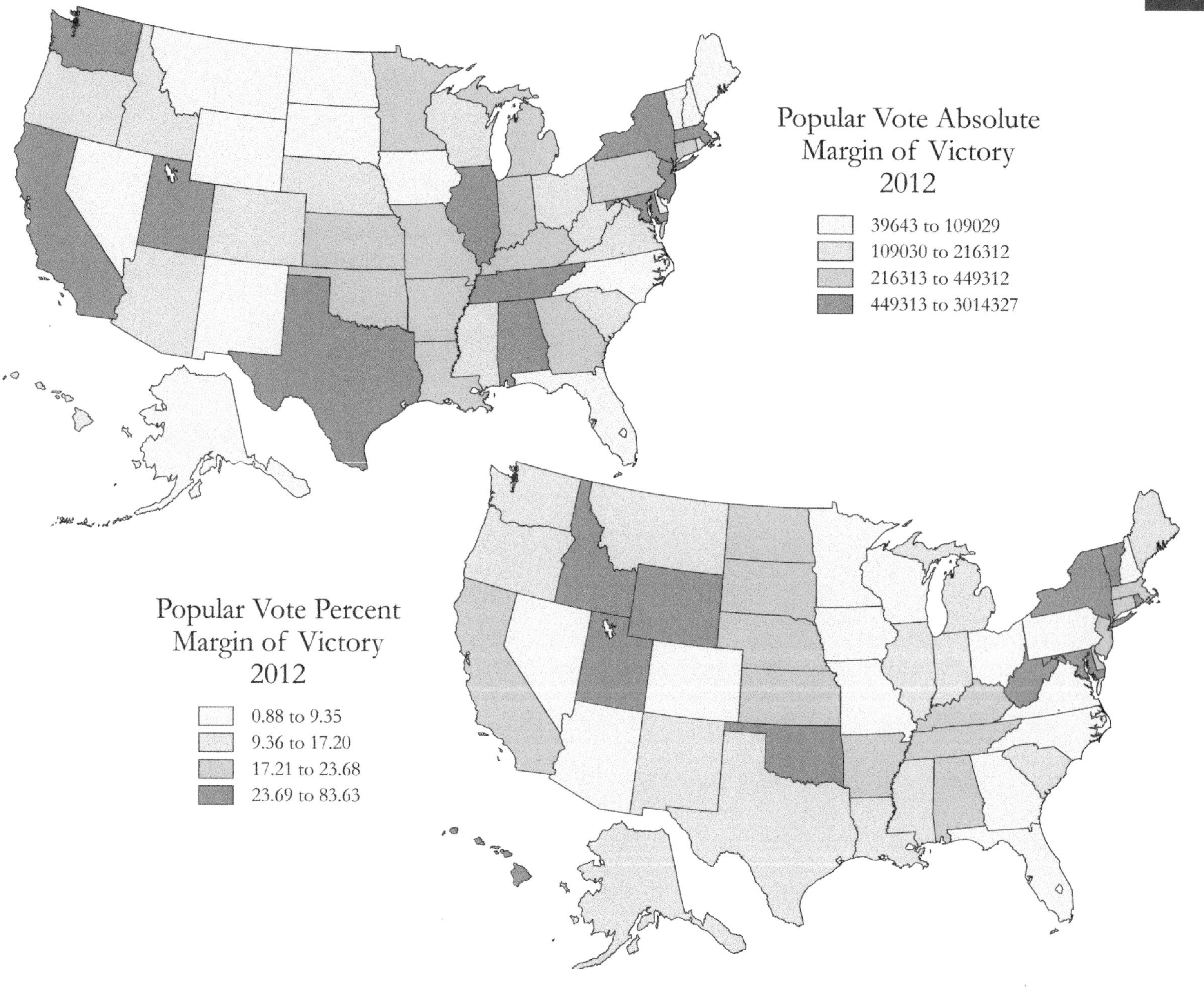

Popular Vote Absolute
Margin of Victory
2012
39643 to 109029
109030 to 216312
216313 to 449312
449313 to 3014327
Popular Vote Percent
Margin of Victory
2012
0.88 to 9.35
9.36 to 17.20
17.21 to 23.68
23.69 to 83.63

FIGURE 2.4

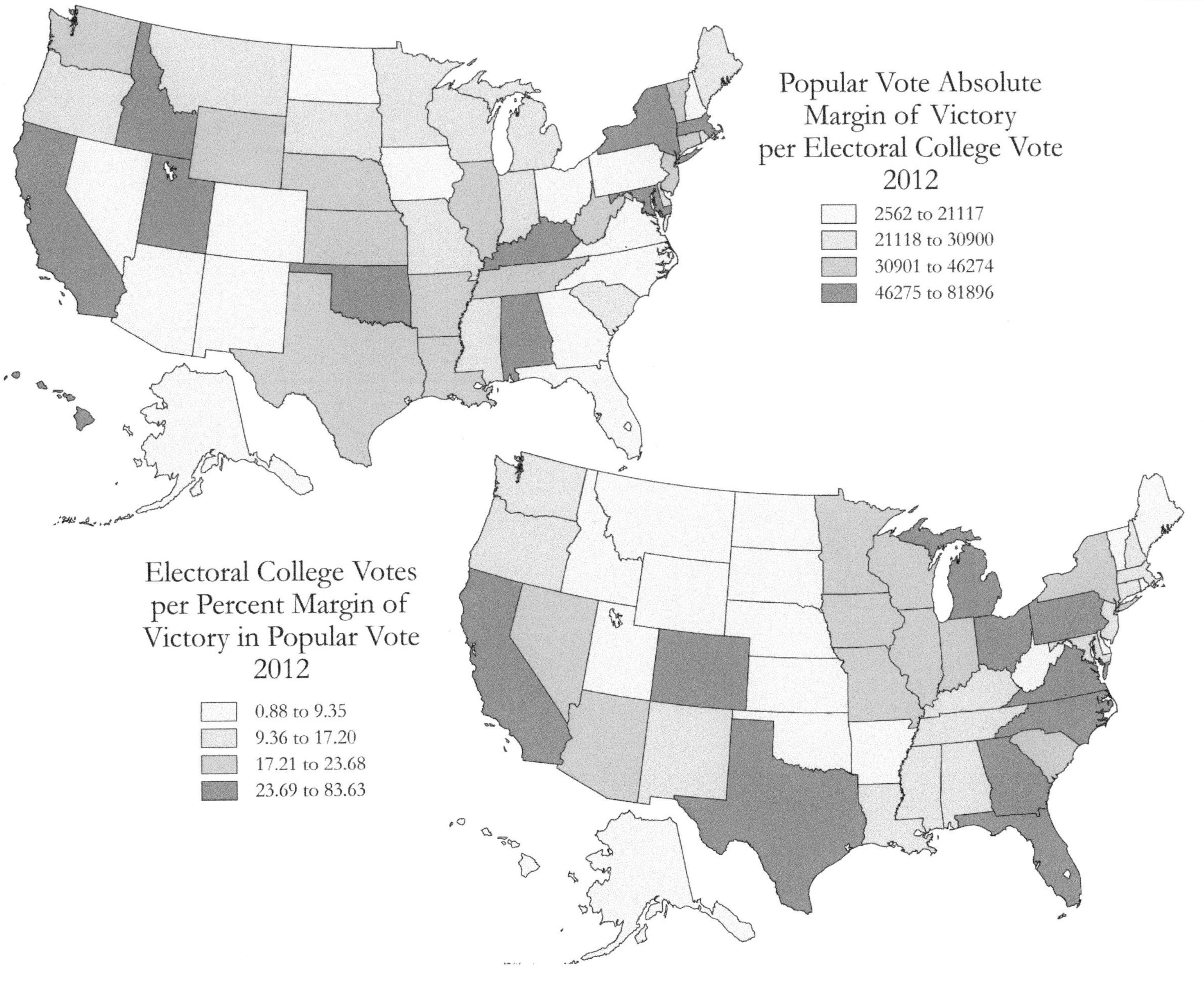
Popular Vote Absolute
Margin of Victory
per Electoral College Vote
2012
2562 to 21117
21118 to 30900
30901 to 46274
46275 to 81896
Electoral College Votes
per Percent Margin of
Victory in Popular Vote
2012
0.88 to 9.35
9.36 to 17.20
17.21 to 23.68
23.69 to 83.63

conservative states whose impacts on the Electoral College outcome were relatively minimal.

REFERENCES

Abbott, D., and J. Levine. 1991. *Wrong Winner: The Coming Debacle in the Electoral College*. New York: Praeger.

Banzhaf, J. 1968. "One Man, 3.312 Votes: A Mathematical Analysis of the Electoral College." *Villanova Law Review* 13:304–332.

Best, J. 1996. *The Choice of the People? Debating the Electoral College*. Lanham, MD: Rowman & Littlefield.

Gelman, A., and G. King. 1994. "A Unified Method of Evaluating Electoral Systems and Districting Plans." *Political Science* 12:158–67.

Grofman, B. 1983. "Measures of Bias and Proportionality in Seats-Votes Relationships." *Political Methodology* 9:295–327.

Hardaway, R. 1994. *The Electoral College and the Constitution: The Case for Preserving Federalism*. Westport, CT: Praeger.

McCaughey, E. 1993. "Democracy at Risk: The Dangerous Flaws in the Electoral College." *Policy Review* 63:79–81.

Sterling, C. 1981. "Electoral College Misrepresentation—A Geometric Analysis." *Polity* 13:425–49.

Tufte, E. 1973. "The Relationship between Seats and Votes in Two-Party Systems." *American Political Science Review* 67:540–54.

Warf, B. 2009. "The U.S. Electoral College and Spatial Biases in Voter Power." *Annals of the Association of American Geographers* 99 (1): 184–204.

REDISTRICTING: THE PROCESS

KENNETH C. MARTIS

The 2010 census enumerated new population counts and new population geographies for each state. The Supreme Court's 1960s' "one person one vote" rulings mandate that even though a state may not have gained or lost a congressional seat, they must redraw congressional and state legislative boundaries to encompass equal populations. In most cases these districts will be kept for the 2012–2020 elections, until new populations and population geographies are enumerated in the 2020 census. As discussed above in the section on reapportionment, eighteen states had the U.S. House of Representatives delegation changed by the 2010 census reallocation. For the ten states that lost seats, new districts were drawn, sometimes pitting incumbents against one another. For the eight states that gained representatives, new district boundaries were also drawn, this time with increased numbers. On the state level, virtually all legislative districts were redrawn.

Redistricting laws in each state vary so much there are in essence fifty different criteria, procedures, and processes. Nevertheless, three broad categories of redistricting methods are identified for the 2012 elections: legislative, commissions, and the courts. Seven states elected only one U.S. House representative, Alaska, Delaware, Montana, North Dakota, South Dakota, Vermont, and Wyoming, and therefore had no congressional districts drawn. However, these states are included in the discussion about the redistricting process and political party control (in these cases only for the state legislature boundaries).

The final redistricting process is also influenced by two other legal reviews and protections. First, the Voting Rights Act of 1965, and subsequent amendments, put redistricting in a number of states and smaller jurisdictions under the review of the Department of Justice. Nine states and parts of eight others, are scrutinized with respect to the drawing of districts and minority rights. Seven states in the South: Alabama, Georgia, Louisiana, Mississippi, South Carolina, Texas, and Virginia, with a history of African American disenfranchisement and district gerrymandering, and two in the West: Arizona and Alaska. with a history of Native American and/or Hispanic discrimination, are most prominent in this coverage.[1] Another influence in the drawing of congressional boundaries is the allowance for the creation of minority-majority districts. Minority-majority districts are designed to give racial or ethnic minorities legislative areas that provide that group a majority, and, therefore, a reasonable opportunity of electing one of their own. These districts first arose after the 1982 Voting Rights Act amendment and became commonplace in states with large concentrations of black and Hispanic voters. Minority-majority districts have been created in both urban and rural settings in a number of states where these concentrations exist.

REDISTRICTING METHODS

For most of American history the traditional process of redistricting was the passage of an ordinary law by both chambers of the state legislature and signed by the governor. If one political party controlled the governorship, state senate, and state house, that party could draw new district boundaries with impunity, and, of course, if needed, to their favor. Gerrymandering has been a consistent phenomenon in American politics since the first decades of the republic and redistricting for the 2012 elections is no exception. Since the control of the redistricting process is so important, the state legislative and gubernatorial elections held in 2008 and 2010 were critical in the drawing of the 2012 electoral boundaries and possible final outcome of the election.

In recent decades a new reform process for drawing congressional and legislative districts has arisen: the establishment of redistricting commissions. These commissions vary greatly in their composition, political control, and final discretionary power. Some commissions are simply advisory to the legislative process. Other commissions are put in place as a "back-up," in case of legislative deadlock, which can occur in states with split partisan control. In a few states there are political commissions made up of members of both parties, usually appointed within the legislature and/or by the governor. In seven states, Alaska, Arizona, California, Idaho, Iowa, Montana, and Washington, there are strong true independent citizen commissions holding great power in the final boundary maps. The first commission was in Iowa in 1981. Iowa is technically an advisory commission and, like most of the advisory commissions, has limited final power, but in this case has strong influential power to pass on to the legislature boundaries drawn in a fair and equitable fashion based on the criteria set out in the state election law. In most cases the independent commission process brings a high level of citizen participation and transparency not always typical in the legislative process.

In recent decades the courts have played an increasing role in arbitrating, reviewing, directing, rejecting, or, in some cases, redrawing state congressional and legislative district boundary lines. In the 1962 decision *Baker v. Carr*, the Supreme Court ruled that citizens could not only challenge a legislative redistricting law, but that it could also be adjudicated in federal and state courts. This ruling concerned malapportionment and equal population in state legislative districts. Two years later, in *Westbury v. Sanders*, the Court applied the same equal population standards to congressional districts. A flurry of court-ordered redistricting followed in the mid-1960s. In 1965 the court went further when a federal district court actually redrew the Montana congressional districts in *Roberts v. Babcock*. Since the 1960s the courts have been active in numerous court-ordered and court-drawn redistricting. The 2012 elections are no exception.

REDISTRICTING AND THE 2012 ELECTIONS

Figure 2.5 illustrates the final deciders of redistricting in each state for the 2012 elections. Twenty-nine states had their district boundaries drawn by the traditional legislative law process, with steps in the state senate, state house, and final governor's signature (noting that Nebraska has just one chamber or unicameral legislature). Twenty-one of these states were controlled by Republicans, that is, Republicans controlled the governorship and both houses of the state legislature (Texas is included in this group since although the Republicans drew the plan, it was reviewed by the court). The Republican-controlled states were geographically concentrated in the South, Midwest, and Great Plains. Significant manipulation of district boundaries occurred in many of these states, Ohio, Michigan, Wisconsin, and Pennsylvania being some of the most evident. Democrats controlled redistricting in only eight states, with noticeable gerrymandering occurring in Illinois and Maryland. Four states had split partisan power, Maine, Kentucky, Missouri, and Oregon. In nine states commissions were used to draw districts. The geography of commissions illustrated in figure 2.5 shows the western states lead in adopting this reform technique, especially with respect to the seven independent commissions. Two states—Hawaii and New Jersey—had political commissions with elected politicians or political appointees serving as the principle cartographer of district boundaries. Finally, the courts intervened in the district plans in eight different states, located in all sections of the country.

Control of the congressional redistricting process can have a great effect upon congressional election outcomes. In 2012 the final national vote for all Republican congressional candidates was 58.3 million (48.03 percent of the total vote) versus 59.7 million for the Democrats (49.16 percent).—approximately 1.4 million votes in the Democrats' favor. However, the final composition of the U.S. House was 234 Republicans (54 percent) and 201 Democrats (46 percent). The state of Wisconsin, for example, gave its electoral votes to Barak Obama, elected a Democratic senator in

FIGURE 2.5

Redistricting Process
for the 2012 Elections
Republican Controlled
Democratic Controlled
Split Control
Independent Commission
Political Commission
Court

statewide voting, and cast more votes for Democratic congressional and state legislative candidates. Nevertheless, the 2012 eight-member Wisconsin U.S. House delegation was made up of five Republicans and three Democrats because of shrewd district cartography. Similar results occurred in Illinois; this time the Democrats benefitted by drawing the districts. The above outcomes question whether the geography of partisan voters is responsible for the skewed U.S. House electoral results or the geography of district boundaries. The subsequent sections on redistricting outcomes and gerrymandering discuss in full the final results of the 2012 U.S. House elections and the roles partisan geography and partisan gerrymandering played in the final results.

NOTE

1. After the 2012 elections, the Supreme Court overturned key provisions of the 1965 Voting Rights Act with respect to Department of Justice oversight (Supreme Court of the United States, *Shelby County, Alabama v Holder, Attorney General, et al.* No. 12-96. Argued February 27, 2013, decided June 25, 2013).

REFERENCES

Iyer, Sundeep, and Keesha Gaskins. 2012. "Appendix B: Classifying Who Drew the Lines." In *Redistricting and Congressional Control: A First Look.* New York: Brennan Center for Justice.

National Conference of State Legislatures. 2009. "Redistricting Commissions: Legislative Plans." http://www.ncsl.org/legislatures-elections/redist/2009-redistricting-commissions-table.aspx.

"State Legislative and Congressional Redistricting after the 2010 Census." Ballotpedia, accessed March 25, 2013, http://ballotpedia.org/wiki/index.php/State_Legislative_and_Congressional_Redistricting_after_the_2010_Census.

US HOUSE DISTRICTS AND THE REPUBLICAN "GERRYMANDER" OF 2012

RICHARD L. ENGSTROM

In addition to the election for the US president, the November 2012 general election also entailed elections for the US Congress. These included elections of members of the Senate through statewide votes in about one-third of the states and elections for all 435 seats in the House of Representatives. Seats of the House are allocated to states based on the size of their populations. All of the House elections in states with more than one seat were held in geographical districts within which only one person is elected (single member districts, hereinafter SMDs). Prior to this election, these districts, used in forty-three states, had to be revised to keep them in compliance with the "one person, one vote" rule. This rule requires that all districts within a state have close to the same number of people within them, according to census population data.

These revisions can be, and in many states were, very politically sensitive. Areas in which voters have a distinct tendency to support candidates from a particular political party or from another type of group can be "cracked," that is, dispersed across districts in which they constitute ineffective percentages of voters, or "packed," that is, concentrated in districts with high percentages so that the winning candidates win by large margins. Both strategies are designed to waste the votes of the group. Where district lines are placed can have a direct impact on the reelection chances of incumbents, the likelihood of members of minority groups being elected, especially African Americans and Latinos, and the electoral fortunes of political parties. When it comes to the latter, these post-2010 revisions of the House districts have been dubbed a "great gerrymander" perpetrated by the Republican Party to favor its candidates over those of the Democrats. The primary reason for these allegations is that the Democratic candidates for the House across the country received a majority, albeit a slight one of 50.7 percent, of the two-party vote (those cast for either Democratic or Republican candidates), yet the Republican candidates won 53.4 percent of the House seats, leaving them with a thirty-three-seat margin over the Democrats.

State governments are responsible for adopting new congressional districts after every census (see figure 2.5). This job is typically performed by the state legislatures, with governors having veto power over their product. When one party controls the legislature and the governor is from that same party, gerrymandering in favor of that party is often expected. In this situation, it usually is not difficult for a party to draw district lines that comply with traditional districting criteria, such as contiguity, compactness, and following the lines of political subdivisions within a state (see Webster 2013), and still create districts that favor that party. Allegations of gerrymandering are common both during the districting process and after elections. This was the case with the latest round of congressional districting. But unfortunately, the perception of its presence varied greatly, depending on the eye, or party affiliation, of the beholder.

Gerrymandering has been defined as "discriminatory districting which operates unfairly to inflate the political strength of one group and deflate that of another" (Dixon 1971, 29). While this definition does seem to capture the essence of the concept, when applied in the partisan context there are arguments over how the political strength of parties should be identified, how to determine whether that strength has been inflated or deflated as a result of where the districts lines are placed, and whether the extent of that inflation or deflation reaches the point of being unfair. These are some of the reasons why the Supreme Court, which has held that partisan gerrymandering is unconstitutional under the equal protection clause of the Fourteenth Amendment, has been unable, some say unwilling, to identify an approach to identifying them.

Regardless of the definition, in the world of politics allegations of gerrymandering are commonly based on deviations from proportional representation, based on a projected consequence or the actual consequence of elections under a plan. Proportional representation occurs when the percentage of votes cast for each party's candidates results in those candidates winning that same percentage of the seats. This is certainly a common notion of fairness, even though the SMD system is not designed to produce proportional results. Gerrymandering allegedly occurs when those percentages do not match closely—the larger the difference, the more pronounced the gerrymander.

Measuring the percentage of votes received by a party's candidates is not as straightforward as one might think. Some districts are not contested by one of the major parties, typically because voters supporting the other party dominate the district. No votes are recorded for a party without a candidate, of course, but that does not mean that the party's support in the district is in fact anything close to the 0.0 percent recorded, as revealed by the votes cast in other elections on the ballot, such as a presidential or senatorial election. This is also a potential problem with using a "top two" primary system, as is used in California, Louisiana, and Washington. Under this arrangement, all candidates compete in the same primary election, regardless of their party affiliation, and the top two vote recipients compete in the general election, even if both are from the same party. (In Louisiana, a candidate winning a majority of the votes in the initial election is declared elected.) A more general complaint about relying on the votes cast for House candidates for assessing proportionality is that it assumes every vote received by a Democratic or Republican candidate is a party vote, which ignores the "personal" votes candidates receive based on their qualifications and/or issue positions.

Table 2.2 identifies the seven states widely regarded as the source of the Republican gerrymander. The first two columns in the table contain the percentage of the two-party vote won by the Republican House candidates in each, then the percentage of the districts in each state won by them, and the last column reports the disparity in those percentages. The two remaining columns provide the number of districts won by Republicans and the number won by Democrats. The last row in the table provides these figures for the seven states collectively. All of the figures are reported in

TABLE 2.2. Votes and Seats Comparisons in Selected States

	Republican % of Votes	Republican % of Seats	Republican Number of Seats	Democratic Number of Seats	Republican Seat % minus Vote %
Michigan	47.3	64.3	9	5	17.0
N. Carolina	49.1	69.2	9	4	20.2
Pennsylvania	49.2	72.2	13	5	23.0
Wisconsin	49.2	62.5	5	3	13.3
Virginia	50.9	72.7	8	3	21.8
Ohio	52.1	76.9	10	3	24.9
Florida	53.0	63.0	17	10	10.0
Totals	50.4	68.3	71	33	17.9

Source: Calculated by author.

or derived from the compilations of votes, by districts, reported by the clerk of the House of Representatives.

The redistricting of congressional seats in all of these states was under the control of the Republican Party, members who constituted a majority of each chamber of the legislature and also held the governor's office (except in North Carolina, where the governor has no veto over redistricting plans). Michigan, North Carolina, Pennsylvania, and Wisconsin are states in which the Democratic candidates won a majority of the votes but Republicans won a much larger majority of the seats. Two of the states had disparities in the Republican vote and seat share greater than 20 percentage points, Pennsylvania at 23.0 percent and North Carolina at 20.2 percent.

Pennsylvania is the state that receives the most attention by pundits. Here Republican candidates won thirteen of eighteen seats in the House, although their party won less than a majority of the statewide vote for these seats. Four of the five districts won by the Democrats were districts packed with Democratic voters. Three of them, the First, Second, and Thirteenth Districts, are adjacent districts in the Philadelphia area that Democratic candidates won with vote percentages of 84.9, 90.5, and 69.1, respectively. The districts around them were won by Republicans, at much reduced rates of 56.6, 57.1, and 59.4 percent, respectively.

Both the Democratic and Republican districts in the Philadelphia area are far from models of compactness (figure 2.6). The Fourteenth District in the Pittsburgh area is the other packed Democratic district. Democrats won that district with 76.9 percent of the vote. The two districts adjacent to it were won by Republicans, one with 51.7 percent of the vote and the other with 64.0 percent. If the Democrats had been in control of the process and also relied on bizarrely shaped districts like the Republicans did, it is highly likely that the packing would be reduced, with some Democratic areas being added to surrounding districts and facilitating the election of more Democrats.

In Virginia, Ohio, and Florida, Republicans won a majority of the votes and again a higher percentage of the districts. Ohio had the largest disparity between the vote share and seat share of all seven states, 24.9 percentage points, while Virginia had the third-highest at 21.8 percentage points. It might be surprising that as few as seven states can account for a "giant gerrymander." But as the table reveals, the first six states themselves can account for thirty-one of the Republicans' thirty-three-seat majority in the chamber (94 percent of it). When Florida is added, the seven states account for more than the Republican's nationwide margin in seats. The Republican candidates in these states collectively received just 50.4 percent of the seats but won almost 70 percent of the seats, 68.3 percent, in them. The thirty-eight-seat margin across these seven states exceeded the nationwide Republican margin of thirty-three. In addition, in six of these states, Democratic candidates won a majority of the votes in *both* the US presidential and US senatorial elections held at the same time. The exception was North Carolina, where the Republican won the presidential election and there was no senatorial election. These results illustrate how party control of the redistricting process at the state level can have a major impact on the allocation of congressional seats to a party. Only one plan, that for Illinois, is widely identified as a Democratic gerrymander. Adopted by a Democratic legislature and approved by a Democratic governor, the Democrats won 66.7 percent of the seats (twelve of eighteen) with only 55.4 percent of the two-party votes.

It has been rare for the party that wins the most votes nationally not to also win the most seats in a congressional election. But the fact that this occurred in 2012 was not a total surprise (see, e.g., Wang 2013b). The midterm "wave election" of 2010 that resulted in a new Republican majority in the House also left that party with a distinct advantage in the control of state redistricting processes. The "aggressive gerrymandering" that followed (Wing 2013) was designed, by Republicans' own admission, to provide a "Republican firewall" that would protect their seat majority from a drop in voter support for the party (Republican State Leadership Committee 2013). It worked, as the two-party vote for Republican candidates dropped 6.1 percentage points, from a majority of 53.4 percent in 2010 to a minority of 47.3 percent in 2012 but the party again won control of the chamber.

As noted above, not even a serious deviation from proportionality is considered by the US Supreme Court to be unconstitutional.

FIGURE 2.6

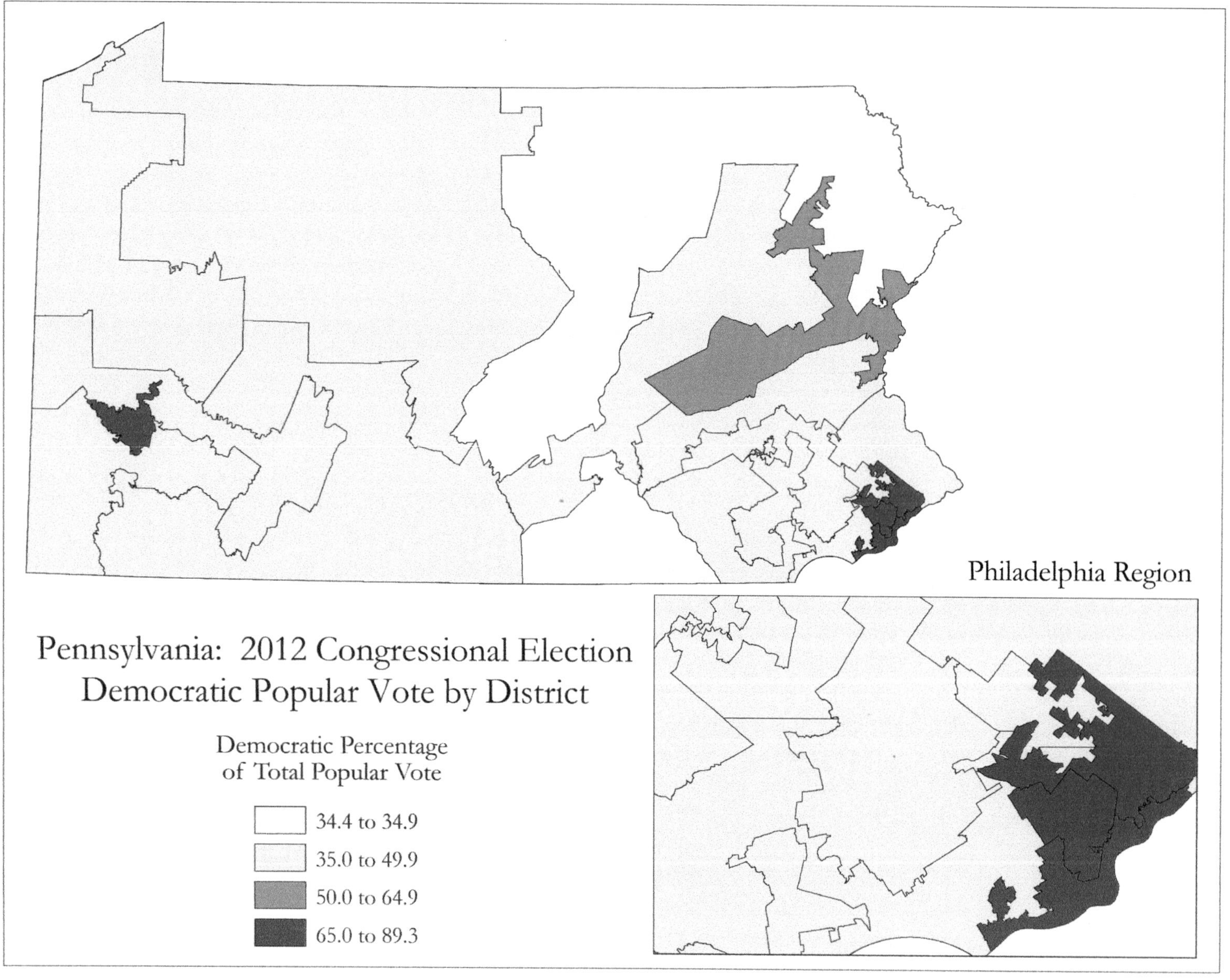
Philadelphia Region
Pennsylvania: 2012 Congressional Election
Democratic Popular Vote by District
Democratic Percentage
of Total Popular Vote
34.4 to 34.9
35.0 to 49.9
50.0 to 64.9
65.0 to 89.3

It takes more than that. But the court has been unable to decide what else needs to be shown. This no doubt is the reason why not many congressional districting plans adopted after the 2010 census have been challenged in courts on these grounds. The Wisconsin districts have been challenged as a partisan gerrymander, as have those in Illinois, Maryland, and Missouri. In each case, however, the courts have noted the absence of clear standards for adjudicating these claims and ruled against those making them. Florida's districts are also under challenge. Until the courts are capable of putting the brakes on at least the most egregious instances of gerrymandering, one can expect to see the practice continue into the future and even become more blatant and more prevalent.

REFERENCES

Dixon, Robert G., Jr. 1971. "The Court, the People, and 'One Man, One Vote.'" In *Reapportionment in the 1970s*, edited by Nelson W. Polsby. Berkeley: University of California Press.

Giroux, Greg. 2013. "Republicans Win Congress as Democrats Get Most Votes." Bloomberg.com/news/2013-03-19/republicans-win-congress-as-democrats-get-most-votes.html.

Haas, Karen L. 2013. *Statistics of the Presidential and Congressional Elections of November 6, 2012.* Washington, DC: Government Printing Office.

Meyerson, Harold. 2012. "GOP's Gerrymandered Advantages." *Washington Post*, November 13.

Republican State Leadership Committee. 2013. "2012 REDMAP Summary Report." http://www.redistrictingmajorityproject.com.

Wang, Sam. 2013a. "The Great Gerrymander of 2012." *New York Times*, February 2.

Wang, Sam. 2013b. "The House—New, with Less Democracy." Princeton Election Consortium. http://election.princeton.edu/2012/11/09/the-new-house-with-less-democracy.

Webster, Gerald. 2013. "Reflecting on Current Criteria to Evaluate Redistricting Plans." *Political Geography* 32 (2013): 3–14.

Wing, Nick. 2013. "GOP REDMAP Memo Admits Gerrymandering to Thank for Congressional Election Success." *Huffington Post*, January 17.

PHANTOM CONSTITUENTS IN THE 2012 ELECTION

PETER WAGNER AND LEAH SAKALA

The 2012 election was the first time in any state that a voter could cast a ballot for state legislative office without the weight of her vote depending on whether or not she lived next to a large prison. In anticipation of redistricting for the 2012 elections, New York and Maryland became the first two states to address a long-standing flaw in Census Bureau methodology by "ending prison gerrymandering." In the forty-eight other states, however, prison gerrymandering continued to skew the weight of every ballot cast on state affairs.

The problem of prison gerrymandering stems from the Census Bureau's method of tabulating incarcerated people at prison locations rather than at their home addresses, even though people in prison remain legal residents of their home communities and are never permitted to vote at the location where they are incarcerated. State and local governments use census data each decade to comply with the constitutional principle of "one person, one vote" by rebalancing their electoral districts after every decennial census. The integrity of this process depends on the underlying data, though, and the Census Bureau's prison miscount leads states to inflate the power of votes cast in districts that contain prisons and consequently dilute voting power everywhere else. As US incarceration rates rose to internationally unprecedented levels over the past several decades, prison gerrymandering became one of the top redistricting controversies following the 2010 census (figure 2.7).

Prison gerrymandering's impact is particularly severe on the local level. When officials in the city of McAlester, Oklahoma, redrew their city council wards in 2011, for example, more than half of the population of the city's new Fourth Ward was made up of incarcerated people whom the Census Bureau counted in the Oklahoma State Penitentiary and the Brannon Correctional Facility. As a result, the Fourth Ward had half as many actual city residents as the other wards, giving that ward's residents twice the access to city council as the residents of any other ward. In essence, simply living next to a prison doubles the weight of a McAlester resident's vote on city affairs.

Fortunately, growing public attention to this problem led many jurisdictions to take action. In April 2010, Maryland became the first state in the nation to pass legislation requiring that incarcerated people be counted at home for congressional, state, and local redistricting purposes. The new law requires the state to adjust the federal census data by collecting the home addresses of incarcerated people and reallocating them for redistricting purposes. Maryland's law resolved a key inequity from the previous 2001 redistricting cycle: 18 percent of House of Delegates District 2B (near Hagerstown) had been made up of incarcerated people. This gave every four residents of that district almost as much influence as five residents of every other district in the state.

In August 2010, after a five-year campaign, the New York state legislature followed Maryland's lead by passing its own bill to end prison gerrymandering. New York's legislation, which applies to both state legislative and local government redistricting, solved one of the clearest examples of how prison gerrymandering distorts the policymaking process. Until recently, most incarcerated people in New York came from New York City, but the majority of the state's prison cells were located in rural upstate areas. Furthermore, the state's incarcerated population was 82 percent African American or Latino, but virtually all—98 percent—of the state's prison cells were located in disproportionately white senate districts. The state was concerned that the Census Bureau's method of crediting incarcerated

FIGURE 2.7

Prison Gerrymandering

McAlester, Oklahoma City Council Wards

Oklahoma State Penitentiary
J. Brannon Correctional
Ward 4
Ward 5
Ward 1
Ward 6
Ward 3
Ward 2

Ward	Incarcerated People	City residents
1	0	3,078
2	0	3,184
3	0	3,121
4	1,755	1,295
5	0	3,038
6	0	2,962

• Incarcerated people 1 dot = 1 person
• City residents 1 dot = 1 person

Every person counted by the Census in McAlester, Oklahoma is represented by a dot, and each city council ward has about 3,000 people. But in one ward, more than half of the population is incarcerated, giving the actual residents twice the political influence of people in other wards.

Wyoming State Senate Districts

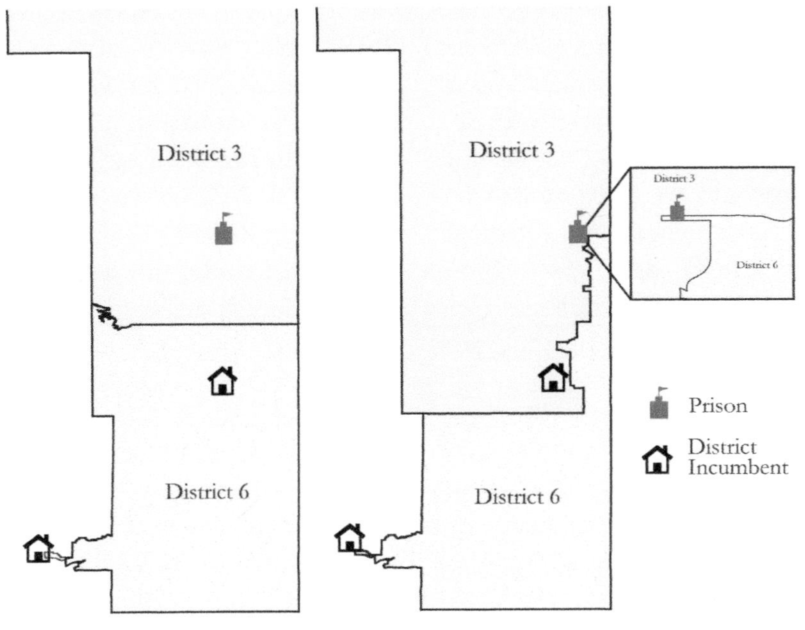

Wyoming's Committee redistricting plan would have required two incumbent senators to run against each other in Senate District 6. To avoid competition, the plan was revised with the most blatant documented prison gerrymander to date: The northern border of District 6 was lowered to shift one incumbent's house into neighboring District 3. To make up for the lost population, District 6 was extended to snake 17 miles up the Wyoming border to snag 499 people incarcerated at a state prison, plus 261 residents along the way

people to the locations of the prisons rather than to the demographic and political district communities they came from was distorting electoral and policy outcomes. Indeed, a 2002 report by the Prison Policy Initiative, *Importing Constituents: Prisoners and Political Clout in New York*, identified seven state senate districts that met minimum population requirements only because they used prison populations as padding. Representatives from these seven districts dominated the state senate's crime and codes committees and were responsible for delaying the eventual repeal of the nation's harshest ("Rockefeller") drug laws. Those extreme mandatory drug conviction sentences kept upstate prisons—and therefore the representatives' own political districts—full.

In preparation for the brief redistricting period that occurs following the decennial census, many additional states are already looking ahead to 2020. So far, California and Delaware have already joined New York and Maryland's ranks by passing legislation to abolish prison gerrymandering in the future. Similar legislation has since been introduced in other states as well, including Arkansas, Connecticut, Georgia, Illinois, Indiana, Kentucky, New Jersey, Oregon, Rhode Island, and Texas. States seeking to abolish prison gerrymandering now have the advantage of positive precedent in the courts, as both Maryland and New York's laws withstood legal challenge. In Maryland's case, the landmark law went all the way up to the US Supreme Court, where it was upheld in June 2012.

Since the 2010 round of redistricting was the first in which the problem of prison gerrymandering received national attention, it may come as no surprise that this same redistricting cycle brought the first documented example of a state legislator *intentionally* placing a prison in a district expressly to change electoral outcomes. In Wyoming, the original proposed state senate redistricting plan for the southeast corner of the state would have required two incumbent senators to run again each other in the 2012 election. To avoid the competition, one of the incumbents insisted that the Sixth District map be changed to shift his home into a separate, safe district. To make up for that population, the Sixth District would extend up the sparsely populated Wyoming-Nebraska border for seventeen miles to scoop up 499 incarcerated people whom the Census Bureau tabulated as residents of Wyoming's second-largest prison. Using prisons as political ballast was a convenient way for two Wyoming senators to avoid competition, but it dilutes the votes of all state residents who don't live near a prison.

The fact that the Census Bureau counts incarcerated people at prison locations made it tantalizingly easy for the Wyoming senator to pull off his prison gerrymandering maneuver. But, for the first time, Wyoming could have chosen to take advantage of a new data file that the Census Bureau published for the express purposes of helping state and local governments do the opposite and reject prison gerrymandering. Shortly after the 2010 census, the bureau published a separate data file that identified the location and populations for all correctional facilities in the country. As the then-director of the Census Bureau explained, "This decade we are releasing early counts of prisoners (and counts of other group quarters), so that states can leave the prisoners counted where the prisons are, delete them from the redistricting formulas, or assign them to some other locale" (Groves 2010).

Beyond New York and Maryland, hundreds of counties, municipalities, and other local governments seized the opportunity to avoid prison gerrymandering leading up to the 2012 elections. Because county and local government districts tend to be smaller than state legislative districts, a single prison has the most dramatic effect on the local level. For this reason, cities and counties generally have the most enthusiasm for addressing the Census Bureau's prison miscount. In general, the local government bodies that engage in dramatic instances of prison gerrymandering fall into one of two categories: either they are unaware of the problem and how to find solutions, or they are impeded by a state or local law that prevents them from drawing districts without engaging in prison gerrymandering.

The city council in McAlester, Oklahoma (discussed above), falls into the second category. Despite the city's long history of refusing to pad local districts with the Census Bureau's prison counts, a clause in the city's new charter unintentionally required the city to use unadjusted census data to draw skewed new districts for the 2012 elections. Local officials in Minnesota, Tennessee, and Wisconsin also frequently engage in prison gerrymandering because of unique state statutory requirements. Fortunately, the number of such states with these restrictions is shrinking. In Virginia, for example, local officials used to point to a statute that in effect required diluting the votes of one's own residents via prison gerrymandering until the Virginia General Assembly took notice and amended the problematic statute in 2012 and 2013.

Like local governments, some states also have indirect and unintentional requirements to engage in prison gerrymandering. For example, a 1990 amendment to the Massachusetts constitution that abolished the state census also unintentionally prohibits the state from passing legislation to improve federal census data for redistricting purposes. The co-chairs of the Massachusetts Special Joint Committee on Redistricting reported that the Census Bureau's prison count was one of the largest obstacles in their state legislative redistricting process. As a result, Massachusetts legislators introduced a resolution in 2013 calling on the US Census Bureau to end prison gerrymandering by tabulating incarcerated people at their home addresses in the next census.

Heightened public and policymaker concern about the problem of prison gerrymandering during the most recent redistricting cycle has placed the issue on the Census Bureau's planning agenda. If bureau officials decide to tabulate incarcerated people in their home communities in the 2020 census, the 2012 redistricting cycle will go down in history as the last one in which state, county, and municipal officials had to grapple with the problem of prison gerrymandering.

REFERENCE

Groves, Robert. "So, How Do You Handle Prisons?" Blog post on *U.S. Census Bureau Director's Blog*, March 1, 2010. http://directorsblog.blogs.census.gov/2010/03/01/so-how-do-you-handle-prisons.

PRIMARY ELECTIONS

OVERVIEW OF THE REPUBLICAN PRIMARY ELECTIONS

FRED M. SHELLEY

After several months of primary elections and caucuses in each of the fifty states, the two major parties selected their nominees for the presidency and vice presidency at the end of the summer of 2012. The Democratic Party renominated President Barack Obama of Illinois and Vice President Joseph Biden of Delaware; the Republicans selected former governor Mitt Romney of Massachusetts for president and Representative Paul Ryan of Wisconsin for vice president.

In 2008, both parties had held spirited contests for their presidential nominations. For the first time since 1952, neither the incumbent president nor the incumbent vice president was a candidate for his party's nomination in 2008. Republican president George W. Bush was ineligible for a third term and his vice president, Dick Cheney, made clear that he would not seek the Republican nomination. Eventually, the Democrats nominated Obama and the Republicans nominated Senator John McCain of Arizona, with Obama winning the general election.

In contrast to Bush, Obama was eligible for reelection in 2012. He and Biden were renominated by the Democrats without opposition. Thus, public attention focused on the contest for the Republican nomination. This contest garnered much attention, in part because many Republicans believed that Obama could be defeated in his reelection bid, given the country's sluggish economy and the unpopularity of the Affordable Care Act. Ideology and the question of which nominee was most likely to be successful in defeating Obama in the general election became major factors in the battle for the Republican nomination.

Primary elections and caucuses were held in each state to select delegates to the Republican National Convention, which took place in Tampa, Florida, in August. The contests began with precinct caucuses in Iowa on January 3 and ended with the presidential primary in Utah on June 27, 2012. In examining the outcomes in each state, it should be noted that the process of selecting convention delegates varies among the states. Some states hold closed primary elections in which voters can participate in a party's primary only if registered as a party member in advance. Others hold open primaries in which any voter can participate in either party's primary. In other states delegates are chosen by caucus rather than in primary elections. Voters in individual precincts may participate in their parties' caucuses if they desire to do so. However, caucuses are often lengthy and time consuming. As a result, caucuses tend to attract highly committed voters and party activists as opposed to casual voters. The caucus system also tends to push the Democrats to the left and the Republicans to the right, relative to the ideologies of voters in a given state in general.

Although the first formal contest was held in January 2012, various Republicans began to campaign for the party's nomination in early 2011. Several prominent Republicans, including Cheney, McCain, 2008 Republican vice presidential nominee Sarah Palin, and former Arkansas governor Mike Huckabee, who had run a strong race against McCain for the Republican nomination in 2008, chose not to run. Those who did contest the nomination along with Romney included Representative Michele Bachmann of Minnesota, business executive Herman Cain of Georgia, former Speaker of the House of Representatives Newt Gingrich of Georgia, former governor Jon Huntsman of Utah, former governor Gary Johnson of New Mexico, Representative Thaddeus McCotter of Michigan, Representative Ron Paul of Texas, former governor Rick Pawlenty of Minnesota, Governor Rick Perry of Texas, and former senator Rick Santorum of Pennsylvania. Except for Huntsman and Pawlenty, all of these candidates took positions that were to the political right of those articulated by Romney.

From the outset, Romney was regarded as the favorite for the nomination. Having run a strong but ultimately unsuccessful race for the Republican nomination in 2008, Romney enjoyed considerable name recognition relative to most of his opponents. However, many Republicans distrusted Romney and/or expressed doubts as to whether he could defeat Obama in the 2012 general election. Many conservative Republicans regarded Romney as too moderate, and others criticized him for lacking ideological conviction and for changing positions on major issues in the interests of political expediency. Other Republicans believed that the very wealthy Romney was out of touch with middle-class and working-class Americans. Still others expressed concern that Romney's Mormon faith would be a liability in the general election.

Throughout 2011 and into early 2012, Romney and his opponents campaigned vigorously and participated in several nationally televised debates. During this period, various Republican contenders emerged as significant and potentially viable challengers to Romney. The first to emerge was Bachmann, who won a nonbinding straw poll conducted in Ames, Iowa, in August 2011. Bachmann was allied with the conservative Tea Party movement and also supported by some social conservatives. Romney's opponents were encouraged by the fact that Romney finished seventh in this poll of Republican party activists behind Bachmann, Paul, Pawlenty, Santorum, Cain, and Perry. However, in subsequent debates Bachmann made several controversial and inaccurate statements that resulted in a decline in her support.

The next major candidate to emerge was Perry, whose support faded after several poor debate performances. In the fall of 2011, the charismatic and articulate Cain emerged as a strong contender after performing very well in several debates. However, Cain proved unable to defend his proposals to restructure the US economy effectively. Allegations of sexual harassment and misconduct on Cain's part emerged shortly thereafter, and he suspended his campaign on December 3. Pawlenty, McCotter, and Johnson also withdrew before the end of 2011. Johnson would eventually become the nominee of the Libertarian Party. As 2011 ended and 2012 began, Gingrich and Santorum emerged as Romney's main challengers. Paul was highly popular among a small group of supporters, but his isolationist views on international policy contrasted sharply with those of his rivals and of the mainstream of the Republican Party, and he never had a real chance to win the nomination.

The first formal contest leading up to the Republican Party's nomination was the party's precinct caucuses in Iowa, held during the evening of January 3. Santorum was highly popular among social conservatives and evangelical Christians, who make up a significant proportion of Iowa's Republican electorate. After the caucuses, Santorum emerged with thirty-four more caucus votes than did Romney. Both wound up with 24.5 percent of the votes, with Paul finishing third with 21.4 percent, followed in order by Gingrich, Perry, and Bachmann. Bachmann's sixth-place finish was a huge disappointment to her supporters, given that she was born in Iowa, had won the Iowa straw poll, and had spent considerable time campaigning in the state. Shortly after the Iowa caucuses, Bachmann withdrew from the race and filed for reelection to her seat in the House of Representatives, which she retained in November by a narrow margin.

The first primary election was the primary in New Hampshire, which was held a week after the Iowa precinct caucuses on January 10. Romney, who had served as governor of neighboring Massachusetts and owns vacation property in New Hampshire, was favored heavily to win, and he did. Huntsman had hoped to gain traction in New Hampshire, but he finished in third place and dropped out shortly after the New Hampshire primary. After Huntsman's withdrawal, Romney, Gingrich, Santorum, and Paul were the only remaining candidates for the nomination.

The focus of the race then shifted to South Carolina. Romney hoped that he could make major strides toward clinching the nomination by winning the primary election in this conservative Southern state whose population includes many evangelical Protestants within its Republican electorate. However, Gingrich won a decisive victory with 40.4 percent of the vote, with 27.9 percent for Romney, 17 percent for Santorum, and 13 percent for Paul. Gingrich carried forty-one of South Carolina's forty-four counties. Romney won three, including Charleston County, Richland County, including the wealthy suburbs of Columbia, and Beaufort County, which is also a wealthy and urbanized county along the Atlantic coast between Charleston and Savannah, Georgia. The next primary took place in Florida on January 31. The primary was seen as a potential showdown between Romney and Gingrich, who came into the race with momentum from New Hampshire and South Carolina, respectively. Romney won the primary decisively, with 46 percent of the vote to 32 percent for Gingrich, 13 percent for Santorum, and 7 percent for Paul.

Romney's Florida victory made him the front-runner for the Republican nomination once again, but on February 7 Santorum swept caucuses in Colorado, Michigan, and Missouri. In doing so, Santorum emerged as Romney's major rival, and many Republicans unhappy with the prospect of a Romney candidacy gravitated to his campaign. The next major contest was the primary in Michigan three weeks later, on February 28. Romney won a narrow victory, carrying the Detroit metropolitan area. However, Santorum carried fifty-three of the seventy-nine counties outside the Detroit region. Thus, Romney's margin in the relatively upscale and affluent suburbs of Detroit carried him to his crucial victory in Michigan.

By the end of February, the question became whether Romney could be stopped on his way to the Republican nomination. The question was settled on March 6, which was known as "Super Tuesday," when seven states held primary elections and three others held precinct caucuses. The seven states that held primary elections included Romney's home state of Massachusetts and Gingrich's home state of Georgia. Each won his home state easily, although Romney won counties containing Atlanta and Savannah in Georgia. Romney won easily in Vermont, which adjoins Massachusetts and whose Republican electorate is much more moderate than is the Republican electorate nationwide. In Virginia, neither Santorum nor Gingrich appeared on the ballot because of technicalities. Only Romney and Paul were on the ballot in the Virginia primary, which was won by Romney by a 60–40 percent margin.

The three remaining primary states on Super Tuesday were Ohio, Oklahoma, and Tennessee. Santorum won Oklahoma and Tennessee, both of which have large populations of conservative, evangelical Republican voters. Gingrich finished third in both states. Despite losing most counties in both states, Romney carried each state's largest city, Oklahoma City and Nashville. The primary getting the most attention, however, was that in Ohio. Many observers felt that Santorum needed to win Ohio in order to demonstrate his potential appeal beyond rural voters and evangelicals and to maintain the possibility that Romney could be stopped, especially given Romney's victories in the large-state primaries in Florida and Michigan. However, Romney defeated Santorum by about twelve thousand votes of more than a million cast.

After Super Tuesday, Romney emerged as the strong favorite for the nomination. Santorum won the Louisiana primary on March 24, but Romney swept eight primaries in April. All of these primaries were in northeastern states except Wisconsin, in which Romney beat Santorum by a 43–38 percent margin. In early May, Gingrich and Santorum suspended their campaigns and asked their supporters to back Romney.

What generalizations can be made about the race for the 2012 Republican nomination as well as its outcome from a geographical perspective? For several reasons, it is difficult to make direct comparisons of county-level outcomes across states. For one thing, some states select their delegates to national nominating conventions in open primary elections. Others use closed primaries, and still others use caucuses, in which turnout levels are typically much lower than in primary elections. As well, primary elections are held at different times in different states. Voters in Iowa could choose between seven candidates, whereas Bachmann, Huntsman, and Perry dropped out before the Super Tuesday primaries. Because technicalities kept Santorum and Gingrich off the primary election ballot, voters in Virginia could choose between only two candidates, Romney and Paul. Likely, some Santorum and Gingrich supporters registered their opposition to Romney by voting for Paul, although it is unlikely that these voters were any more enthusiastic about a Paul candidacy in the general election than they were about Romney's eventual candidacy.

Despite these considerations, it is useful to compare the statewide results by examining figure 3.1, which shows the candidate who received the most popular vote in each state's primary or caucuses. Romney won the Republican primaries or caucuses in thirty-seven states. Santorum won eleven, and Gingrich won the other two. This analysis might be skewed by the fact that some states held their primary elections after Romney had sewn up the Republican presidential nomination. For example, Romney won primaries in Kentucky, Arkansas, and Nebraska in May, after Santorum and Gingrich withdrew from the campaign, although it is entirely possible that Santorum would have won these primaries had he still been a viable candidate for the nomination, given that the Republican electorates in these states are conservative and contain significant evangelical populations. Nevertheless, comparison of front-runners across states is instructive.

Figure 3.1 reinforces the fact that Romney won the nomination after dominating primary elections in larger, more urbanized states. However, Romney lost many of these states in the general election. Of the thirty-seven states in which Romney finished first in the Republican primary or caucuses, he won only fourteen in the general election while Obama won the other twenty-three. On the other hand, Obama won only three (Iowa, Minnesota, and Colorado) of the thirteen states in which either Santorum or Gingrich finished first in the Republican primary or caucuses. Thus, Romney won ten states in which he lost the Republican primary to one of his rivals for the nomination.

Romney's dominance of urban areas and his lack of support in rural areas is evident from comparison between his level of support in places of different population sizes. Of the thirty largest metropolitan statistical areas by population in the United States, only five (Atlanta, Minneapolis-St. Paul, Denver, St. Louis, and Kansas City) are located in states in which Santorum or Gingrich finished first in that state's Republican primary or caucus. Romney won the states containing the other twenty-five metropolitan areas, including the eight largest metropolitan areas in the United States. Another useful measure of urban status is population density. Romney finished first in the seventeen states with the highest population densities in the United States as of the 2010 census. The most densely populated state carried by either Santorum or Gingrich was Georgia, which ranks eighteenth in population density among the fifty states. Urban status is evident within states as well; as we have seen, Romney carried the largest

FIGURE 3.1

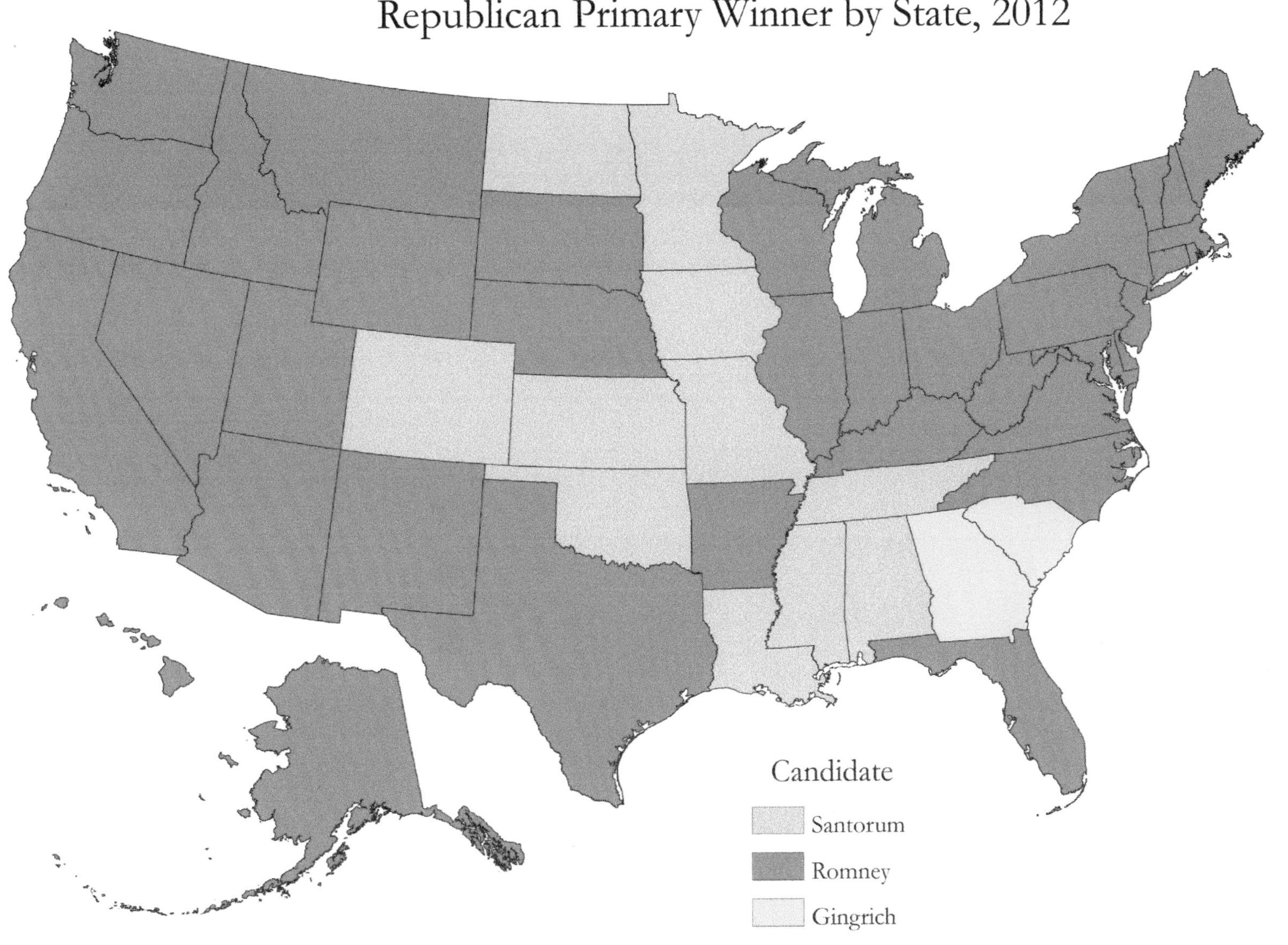
Republican Primary Winner by State, 2012
Candidate
Santorum
Romney
Gingrich

cities within most of the states that were contested closely in the Republican primaries, including Des Moines, Charleston, Miami, Tampa-St. Petersburg, Orlando, Cleveland, Columbus, Cincinnati, Oklahoma City, and Nashville.

That Romney was nominated as a result of primary votes from blue states illustrates an ongoing debate within the Republican Party. Many conservative Republicans believe that a more conservative candidate who could better define and articulate differences between the two parties' philosophies and policy proposals could have run a better race against Obama. These commentators have been particularly critical of Romney's performance in 2012 because Obama was seen as having been much more vulnerable in 2012 than he had been in his effort to succeed the unpopular George W. Bush in 2008. Their arguments may be reinforced by evidence that Romney's opponents for the Republican nomination did much better throughout the primary season in heavily Republican areas than in more Democratic regions. On the other hand, some Romney supporters argued that a more conservative nominee may have articulated positions further to the right of the mainstream of the electorate than did Romney, enhancing the Democrats' appeal to moderate voters. The political and philosophical debate between more mainstream and more conservative emphasis in Republican politics will no doubt continue as potential candidates for the party begin jockeying for position when the 2016 campaign begins.

IOWA REPUBLICAN PRECINCT CAUCUSES

FRED M. SHELLEY

Since the 1970s, the formal process for determining the Republican and Democratic nominees for president has begun with precinct caucuses in Iowa. On a designated evening, Republican and Democratic voters in every precinct in the state gather in separate caucuses—held in schools, churches, other public buildings, or private homes—associated with their respective parties. At each caucus, each participant identifies the candidate that he or she prefers for his or her party's nomination. The caucus then elects delegates to a later county convention, with the number of delegates for each candidate proportional to that candidate's support in the primary. The county conventions select delegates to congressional district conventions, which in turn select delegates to a statewide convention at which delegates to the national nominating convention are chosen.

Because the Iowa precinct caucuses represent the first test of voter support for potential presidential nominees of both major parties, candidates and journalists spend large amounts of time observing the Iowa caucus campaigns and results. The Iowa caucuses first garnered attention in 1976, when the then-little-known Jimmy Carter won the most votes across all precincts. Carter's unexpected victory provided him with media attention and publicity that led eventually to his becoming the Democratic Party's nominee and winning the presidency. Although the Iowa caucuses have not always been won by the eventual nominee, in 2008 Barack Obama won Iowa by a surprising margin, giving him a lead for the Democratic nomination that he never lost. Going into 2012, observers expected that the Iowa results would play a pivotal role in the nomination process.

While both parties held contested caucuses in Iowa in 2008, only the Republicans held contested caucuses in 2012. The caucuses took place on January 3, 2012, after several candidates for the Republican nomination had spent months campaigning in the state and airing advertisements in the mass media promoting their candidacies.

Seven major candidates—Michele Bachmann, Newt Gingrich, Jon Huntsman, Ron Paul, Rick Perry, Mitt Romney, and Rick Santorum—contested in the Iowa caucuses. More than 120,000 registered Republicans, the highest number in history, participated. After the votes were counted, Santorum emerged with a plurality of thirty-four votes over his nearest rival, Romney. (In fact, the news media reported that Romney won until an error in the tallying of ballots was discovered and corrected a few days later.) Both candidates had 24.5 percent of the vote, and Paul finished third with 21 percent, followed by Gingrich (13 percent), Perry (10 percent), Bachmann (5 percent), and Huntsman (1 percent). The results were a particular disappointment to Bachmann, who was born in Iowa and who campaigned extensively across the state.

The distribution of support at the county level within Iowa, as shown in figure 3.2, illustrates a pattern of votes that would prove to be a harbinger of results elsewhere in later primaries. Although Santorum and Romney ended up virtually tied for the overall number of votes, Santorum carried sixty-four of Iowa's ninety-nine counties as compared with only sixteen for Romney. The other nineteen counties were won by other candidates. However, Romney won pluralities in most of Iowa's urban areas, including the counties containing Des Moines, Davenport, Cedar Rapids, Iowa City, Council Bluffs, Sioux City, and Dubuque. Although these cities are predominantly Democratic in general elections, Republicans within these

FIGURE 3.2

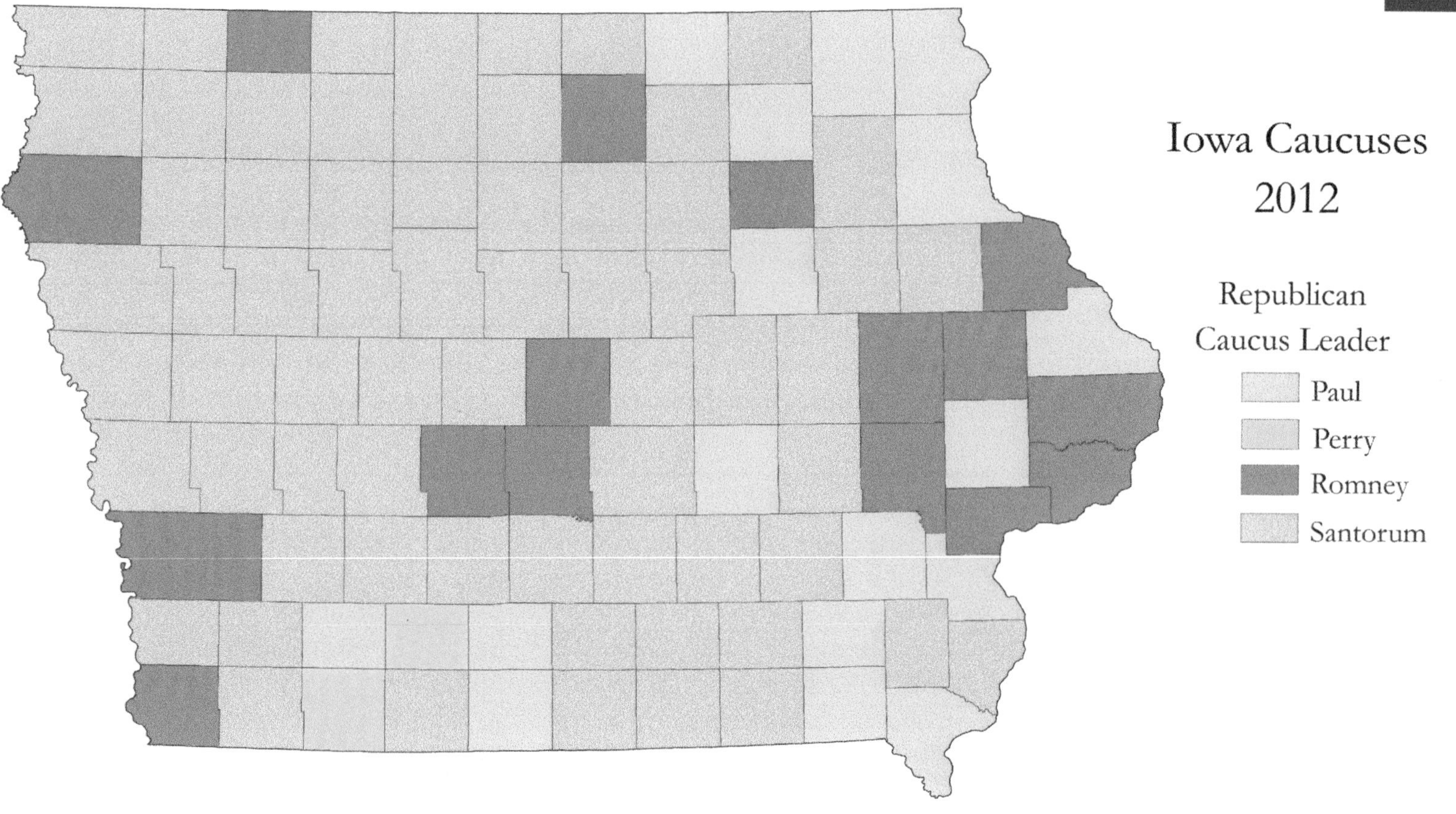
Iowa Caucuses
2012
Republican
Caucus Leader
Paul
Perry
Romney
Santorum

urban areas tend to be more moderate than are those in rural areas of Iowa.

Most of the counties won by Santorum, in contrast, are more rural and more Republican than is the case with Iowa as a whole or with the national electorate. Relative to rural voters in many other states, moderate rural Iowans are inclined to be Democrats; therefore, the rural Republican electorate is relatively conservative and dominated by evangelical voters.

The contrast between Romney's counties and Santorum's counties is evident by comparing figure 3.2 to the results of the November general election. Although Obama carried Iowa with 52.1 percent of the popular vote to 46.5 percent for Romney, Obama won only thirty-seven counties while Romney carried sixty-two. However, Obama won twelve of the sixteen counties that Romney had won in the January precinct caucuses. On the other hand, fifty-three of Santorum's sixty-four counties gave pluralities to Romney in November. Thus, in January Romney was strongest in areas that went Democratic in November, whereas Santorum did best in more heavily Republican areas that were carried by Romney. This pattern would repeat itself in later primaries and caucuses, leading many conservatives to argue that a more conservative Republican nominee would have stood a better chance to defeat Obama in November.

FLORIDA REPUBLICAN PRIMARY ELECTION

FRED M. SHELLEY

The primary election in Florida, which was held on January 31, 2012, was a pivotal event in the eventual selection of Mitt Romney as the Republican nominee for president in 2012.

Over the past few presidential elections, both parties have held their earliest primary elections and caucuses in Iowa, New Hampshire, South Carolina, and Nevada. All of these states have relatively small populations, and the fact that they are located in different regions of the country provides party leaders and observers a way to compare the relative strengths of various candidates in different areas. Florida, however, is much larger and more cosmopolitan than the early states. Its population is considerably greater than those of Iowa, New Hampshire, South Carolina, and Nevada combined, and its population characteristics, including its demography and ethnic mix, are much more consistent with those of the entire country. Also, Florida is usually one of the most closely contested states in general presidential elections. Thus, Florida is often seen as a bellwether state in primary as well as general elections.

Florida moved its primary to January 31 in order to give itself greater influence in the nomination process. However, the early date was in violation of Republican Party rules, which mandated that no states except New Hampshire and South Carolina hold a primary election before Super Tuesday on March 6 (Iowa and Nevada are exempt because these states hold caucuses as opposed to primary elections). Because Florida insisted on the early primary date, the Republican National Committee stripped the state's Republican Party of half of its delegate votes at the national convention. Eventually, fifty delegate votes were at stake in the January 31 primary.

Seven candidates for the Republican nomination had contested in the Iowa precinct caucuses held four weeks earlier on January 3. However, the three candidates who got the fewest votes in Iowa—Rick Perry, Michele Bachmann, and Jon Huntsman—dropped out before the Florida primary. This left four major candidates who contested in the Florida primary. These included Mitt Romney, who had won the New Hampshire primary and the Nevada caucuses; Rick Santorum, who had won the Iowa precinct caucuses; Newt Gingrich, who had won the South Carolina primary; and Ron Paul. The Florida race was seen as a contest between Romney and Gingrich, who was fresh off a decisive victory in South Carolina.

Many observers predicted a close race. However, Romney defeated Gingrich by a margin of 46 percent to 32 percent, followed by Santorum with 13 percent and Paul with 7 percent. The two leading candidates, Romney and Gingrich, between them carried every county. The geographical pattern of votes revealed an urban-rural split between the two candidates that had already emerged in Iowa (figure 3.3). Gingrich carried thirty-four of Florida's sixty-seven counties, whereas Romney carried the remaining thirty-three counties.

Romney carried all of peninsular Florida except for a few sparsely populated counties in the interior of the peninsula. This region contains most of Florida's major cities, including Miami, Fort Lauderdale, Tampa, St. Petersburg, Orlando, and Jacksonville. In contrast, Gingrich swept northern Florida, losing only Leon County (Tallahassee) along with upscale, resort-dominated Okaloosa County (Destin) and Bay County (Panama City). Thus, throughout Florida, as in other states, Romney won higher-income and more urbanized areas while Gingrich carried rural counties.

The pattern is illustrated also by looking at Romney's strongest and weakest counties. Romney won less than 25 percent of the vote in three counties: Hamilton, Holmes, and Jackson. All three counties are located along Florida's northern border. In combination,

FIGURE 3.3

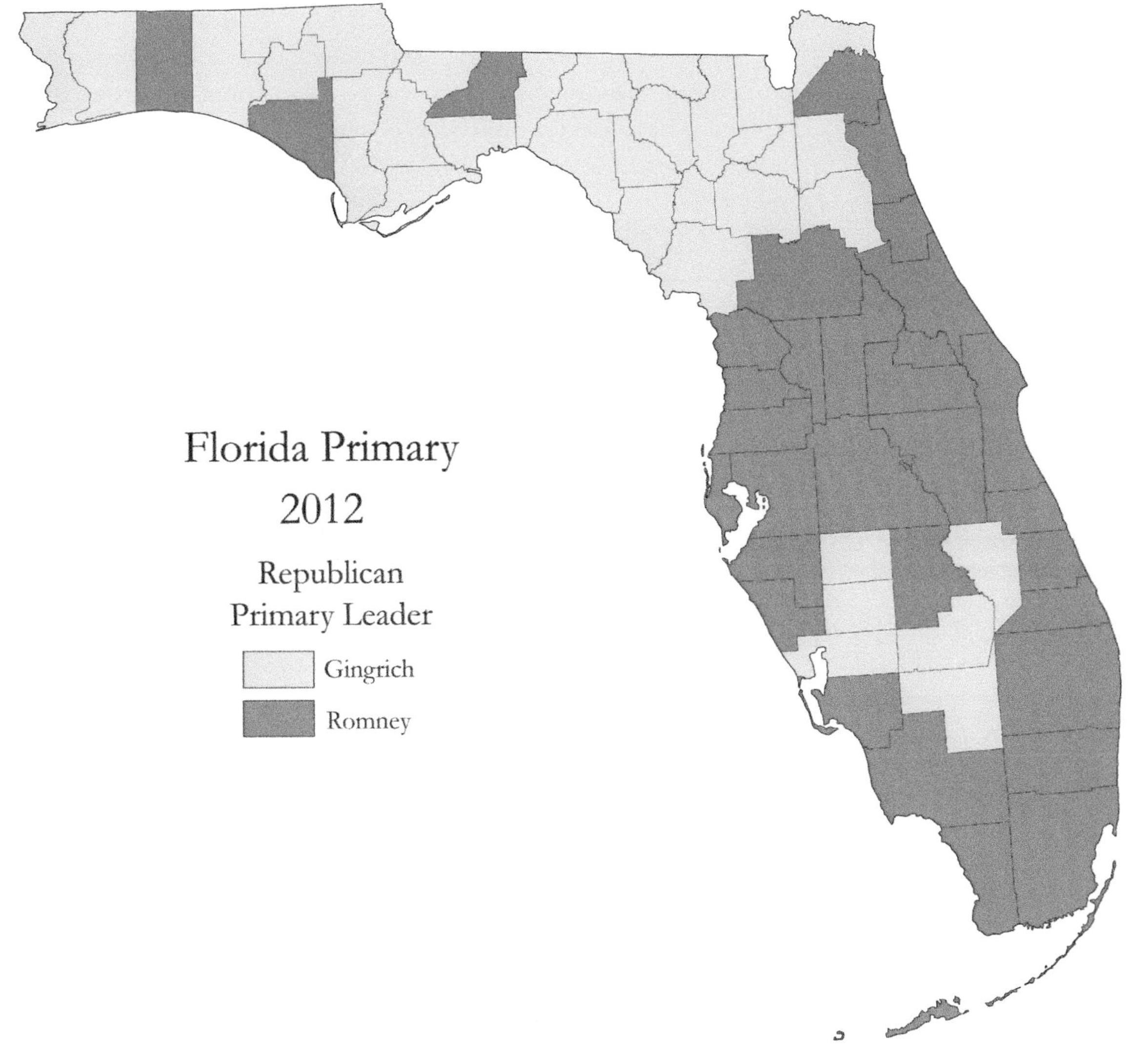
Florida Primary
2012
Republican
Primary Leader
Gingrich
Romney

these rural counties contain about 82,000 people, or 0.4 percent of the state's total population of more than nineteen million people. In contrast, Romney's strongest county was Miami-Dade, where he won 61 percent of the vote. He won 54 percent or more in three other counties: Collier County (Naples), Sumter County, on the northern fringes of the Tampa-St. Petersburg metropolitan area, and Palm Beach County, north of Miami. All of these counties contain upscale populations with substantial numbers of retirees and many well-to-do suburban dwellers.

In the general election, thirteen of Florida's sixty-seven counties gave majorities to President Obama, whereas Romney carried the other fifty-four. However, Romney won ten of these thirteen counties in the Florida Republican primary. On the other hand, Gingrich won thirty of the fifty-four counties that went for Romney in the general election. In other words, all but three counties that Gingrich carried in the primary were won by Romney in November, whereas the remaining ten counties that gave majorities to Romney in the Republican primary were carried by Obama in November (table 3.1). As elsewhere, Romney did best in the primary in those places in which he did more poorly in the general election.

TABLE 3.1. Florida Counties by Republican Primary and General Election Results

	Primary	Romney	Gingrich
General		34	33
Obama	13	10	3
Romney	54	24	30

Source: Calculated by author.

OHIO REPUBLICAN PRIMARY ELECTION

FRED M. SHELLEY

The primary election in Ohio proved to be pivotal in Mitt Romney's drive to win the Republican Party's nomination. The primary was held on March 6, 2013, or Super Tuesday, and was the headline contest among the ten primary elections held on that day.

Prior to Super Tuesday, Romney had been successful in larger, more urbanized states such as Florida. Even in more rural states such as Iowa and South Carolina, he was strongest in metropolitan areas, suburbs, and wealthy places. On the other hand, his major opponents Rick Santorum and Newt Gingrich had demonstrated strength in rural and less upscale areas. By this point, many regarded Santorum as Romney's most significant challenger. However, it was also clear that Santorum needed to show strength in more urbanized places if he was to succeed in overtaking Romney's lead for the Republican nomination.

More than 1.2 million Ohio Republicans cast ballots in the Ohio primary. Romney won the primary by a narrow margin of about twelve thousand votes over Santorum. Romney got 37.9 percent of the vote to 37.1 percent for Santorum. Gingrich trailed with 14.6 percent, followed by Ron Paul with 9.2 percent. Santorum had already lost the primary election in Michigan, and by winning in Ohio he had hoped to demonstrate that he was capable of winning a large industrial state. However, his efforts ultimately failed, and as a result Romney's campaign picked up steam as he retained his front-runner status—a lead that he would retain for the rest of the Republican primary campaign.

As shown in figure 3.4, the pattern of votes was similar to the pattern of votes in Iowa and Florida. In general, Romney carried Ohio's urban areas while Santorum carried the state's rural counties. Although he lost the primary, Santorum outpolled Romney in sixty-nine of Ohio's eighty-eight counties. However, Romney carried Ohio's three largest cities, Cleveland, Columbus, and Cincinnati, along with the counties that contain their suburbs.

As was the case in Iowa and Florida, many of Romney's counties gave majorities to Obama in the general election, while many counties carried by Santorum in the primary gave majorities to Romney in November. Although he won a popular-vote majority in Ohio, Obama carried only sixteen of Ohio's eighty-eight counties in the general election. Of the sixteen counties that Obama carried in the November general election, Romney carried ten counties in the primary while Santorum carried six. On the other hand, Santorum won sixty-three of Romney's seventy-two general-election counties in the primary. In other words, Romney lost ten of the nineteen counties that he carried in the primary to Obama in the general election. He carried only nine counties in both the primary and the general election. However, in the general election Romney won sixty-three of the sixty-nine counties that he lost in the primary, losing only six of these counties to Obama.

FIGURE 3.4

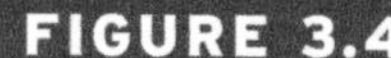

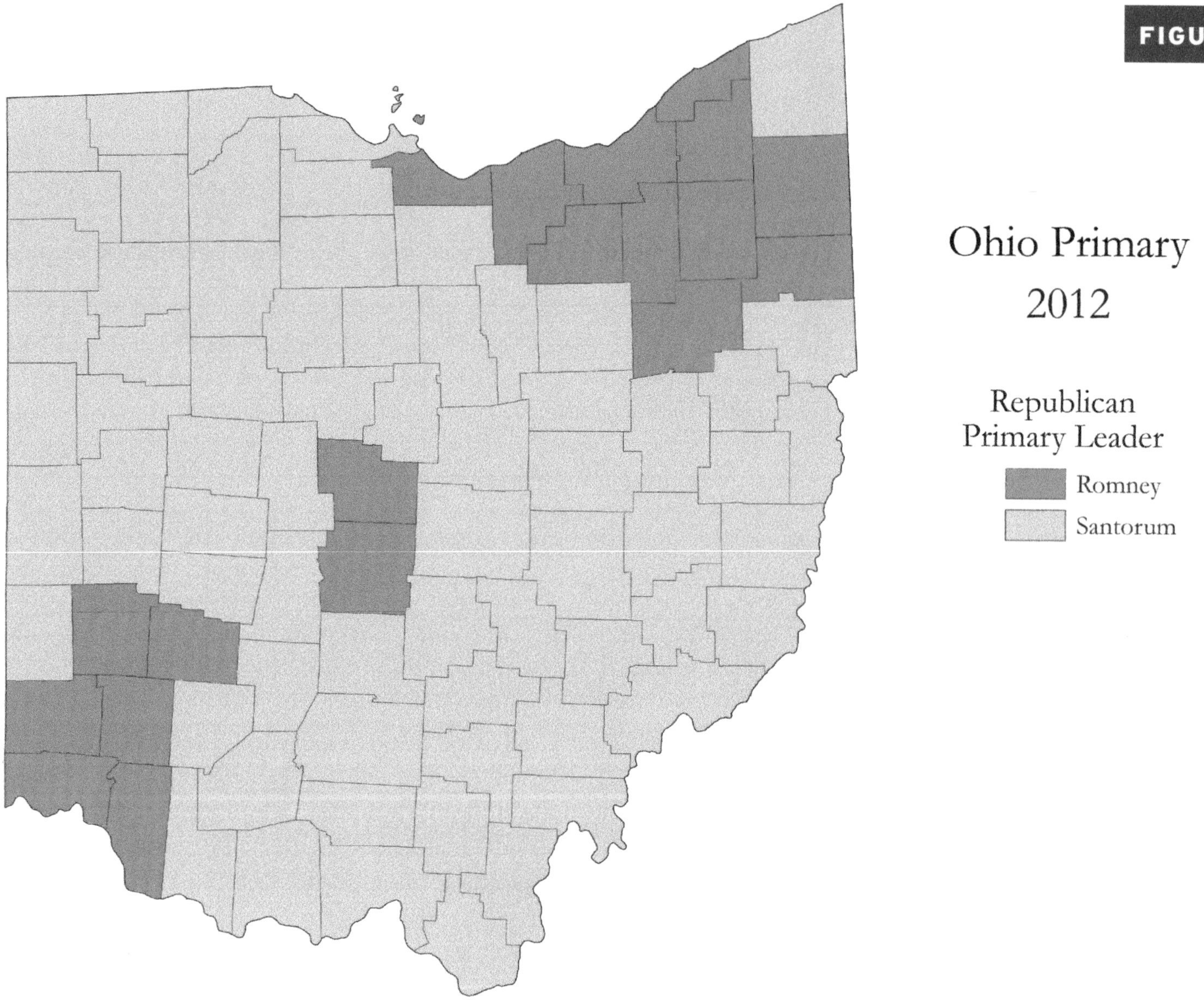
Ohio Primary
2012
Republican
Primary Leader
Romney
Santorum

THE CAMPAIGN

OVERVIEW OF THE CAMPAIGN

GERALD R. WEBSTER

The 2012 presidential campaign pitted Republican Mitt Romney, a former governor of Massachusetts, against incumbent Democratic president Barack Obama. Romney had unsuccessfully pursued the 2008 Republican presidential nomination and was therefore an experienced campaigner. Governor Romney announced his candidacy in June 2011 and was considered by many the front-runner in a crowded field of Republican candidates, which included business executive Herman Cain of Georgia, Representative Michele Bachmann of Minnesota, Governor Rick Perry of Texas, former Speaker of the House Newt Gingrich of Georgia, former senator Rick Santorum of Pennsylvania, and Representative Ron Paul of Texas, among others. Although public opinion polls indicated various front-runners as the Republican candidates vied for their party's nomination, Romney all but secured the nomination in the delegate count by late May 2012.

On August 11, Romney announced that Representative Paul Ryan of Wisconsin would be his running mate. Ryan's selection was met with substantial enthusiasm by the conservative wing of the Republican base but did not generate a significant bounce in the polls for Romney, most likely due to Ryan's conservative positions on abortion, budget cuts, support for privatizing Social Security, and turning Medicare into a voucher program. Illustrating this point, Real Clear Politics' running poll average had the president leading by 4.1 percent on August 10 and still ahead by 3.9 percent a week later on August 17, after Ryan's selection had been announced. Romney formally accepted the GOP's presidential nomination on August 30 at the Republican National Convention in Tampa, Florida. Real Clear Politics' running poll average had the president leading by 1.1 percent on August 29 but had the two candidates tied at 46.8 percent a week later on September 5.

As the incumbent, President Obama faced no serious opposition in the 2012 Democratic primaries and caucuses. The Democratic Party's convention was held in Charlotte, North Carolina, September 3–6, the week after the conclusion of the Republican convention. There Obama and Vice President Joe Biden were renominated without opposition. Most polls indicated the Democratic convention was perceived as more upbeat than the earlier Republican convention, including speeches by First Lady Michelle Obama and former president Bill Clinton. As a result, Obama enjoyed a postconvention bounce in the polls of three to four points. Real Clear Politics' rolling mean of polls had the election tied at 46.8 percent for both candidates on September 6, the last day of the Democratic convention, but had President Obama up by 3.5 percent a week later on September 12 (Silver 2012a).

There was a long list of campaign issues addressed by the two candidates, including terrorism, the environment, gun control, abortion, same-sex marriage, immigration, health care and the implementation of the 2009 Affordable Health Care Act, government spending and the deficit, and the anemic economy and jobs. Because Obama began his first term amid the worst economic crisis since the Great Depression, the economy was clearly a central issue throughout the campaign. Though the unemployment rate in October 2012 was the lowest it had been since Obama's inauguration in January 2009, it was still high at 7.8 percent. Additionally, housing values had plummeted, and the foreclosure rate had spiked between 2007 and 2009, only incrementally improving in the last three years of Obama's first term. This economic malaise led many to believe the incumbent president was vulnerable, particularly against a Republican candidate like Governor Romney, who could claim significant executive business experience. For example, a poll in early October 2012 found that 56 percent of those responding felt the country was headed in the wrong direction.

Several errors or missteps damaged the campaigns of both candidates. One of the most significant pertained to secretly recorded statements made by Governor Romney at a private fund-raising event about the 47 percent of Americans who do not pay federal income tax (Corn 2012). As the governor stated:

> There are 47 percent of the people who will vote for the president no matter what. All right, there are 47 percent who are with him, who are dependent on government, who believe they are victims, who believe that government has a responsibility to care for them, who believe they are entitled to health care, to food, to housing, to you-name-it. That that's an entitlement. . . . I'll never convince them that they take personal responsibility and care for their lives.

This statement was vetted rapidly and reported on by a number of media outlets with findings that the majority of those not paying federal income taxes are the working poor who pay federal payroll taxes as well as state and local taxes even if their incomes are too low to pay federal income taxes. Over one-fifth are retirees on social security, with the remainder including unemployed students using education loans and the disabled, including disabled military service personnel (Silver 2012c). Thus, the governor's comments could be interpreted to suggest that an elderly couple drawing social security after decades of contributions were not taking "personal responsibility" for themselves. Romney's comments also played into the image among many voters that he was an out-of-touch multimillionaire.

President Obama also made errors, likely none greater than his performance in the first of three presidential debates with Governor Romney. The first presidential debate was held in Denver on October 3, 2012, and was won decisively by Romney. A CNN poll, for example, had Romney beating the president by 67 percent to 25 percent, while a CBS poll found the gap to be 46 percent for Romney to 22 percent for Obama (Shrum 2012). Real Clear Politics' rolling poll average had Obama leading Governor Romney by 3.3 percent on October 2, the day prior to the first debate. A week after the debate, on October 10, Romney was leading Obama by 1.5 percent, nearly a five-percentage-point swing. While the president's poor performance was unexpected by many, Silver's (2012d) analysis of past presidential debates suggests the first debate oftentimes helps the challenger, leading to an average increase of 1.5 percent in the polls. The polls again tightened after Biden and Ryan debated on October 11 at Centre College in Danville,

Kentucky. A CBS poll had the vice president winning the debate 51 percent to 32 percent.

The second presidential debate occurred on October 16 at Hofstra University in Hempstead, New York. Polls indicated the debate was close in terms of performance. A CBS poll of uncommitted voters, for example, found that 37 percent thought Obama had won while 30 percent thought Romney won. In spite of the closeness of the polls, Governor Romney had a couple of missteps. The first involved his response to a question pertaining to equal pay for women, which indicated that his gubernatorial administration in Massachusetts had compiled "binders full of women" deemed qualified to serve in state government. The comment immediately went viral and led to a substantial number of parodies and jokes on late-night television with images of women being forced into three-ring binders. The second Romney misstep pertained to whether the president had stated that the attack on the US consular facility in Benghazi, Libya, was an act of terrorism. After pressing Obama on the issue, Governor Romney was corrected by moderator Candy Crowley, who confirmed that the president had in fact characterized the assault as an act of terror.

The third and final presidential debate took place on October 22 at Lynn University in Boca Raton, Florida. This debate included substantial attention to foreign affairs and policy, including trade with China, the Arab Spring, and the Syrian civil war, among other topics. A CBS poll of uncommitted voters found 53 percent thought Obama had won the debate while 23 percent thought Romney had triumphed. But a week after the last debate, Real Clear Politics' running average of polls had Governor Romney leading the president by a full percentage point.

There were several additional elements of the 2012 campaign that contrasted with past contests. First, the 2012 campaign was the first after the Supreme Court's decision in *Citizens United*, which allowed large financial contributions by corporations and unions to political candidates. Likely in part an outgrowth of increased access to campaign contributions, neither candidate accepted public funds but entirely financed their campaigns from private sources. Total private contributions from individuals topped $1.4 billion to candidates and parties in the election cycle, and that figure does not include monies contributed to super PACs. Controversy also emerged over so-called dark money from 501(c)(4) "social organizations" (Bennett 2012). These social organizations, including Crossroads GPS and Americans for Prosperity, can be involved in campaigns as long as "social welfare" is their primary purpose. Notably, such organizations do not have to disclose their donors. When all sources of campaign money are added together, the Federal Elections Commission estimated that the total cost of the 2012 presidential election exceeded $7 billion.

Another controversial issue pertained to the accuracy of the large number of polls continually measuring support for the two presidential candidates, including those taken before and after the conventions and debates. Accurate polling has become more complicated in recent cycles for a number of reasons. Traditional polls rely on live interviewers calling randomly generated lists of phone numbers, but not all such polls include cell phones. Automated polls using a single recorded voice also call randomly generated lists of phone numbers but are precluded by federal law from including cell phones. Since over a third of American households no longer have landlines, polls that do not include cell phones can produce highly inaccurate results. Silver's (2012b) analysis found that not including cell phones biases results against Democratic candidates because potential voters relying exclusively on cell phones tend to be members of Democratic-leaning groups, including young people.

The results of these polls are weighted by race, ethnicity, age, and education to determine how candidates are faring. This weighting can be problematic because the proportion of non-Hispanic whites who are likely to show up on Election Day is a critical component in the weighting process. Since the proportion of Anglos in the electorate is decreasing, pollsters must reduce their percentage of voters for each election cycle. If the percentage used is too high, the poll may underestimate support for the Democrats, and if it is too low, it will underestimate support for the Republicans. Well-known Gallup polls in particular were found to be highly biased toward the GOP, overestimating Republican strength by an average of 7.2 percent. Notably, of the twenty-three pollsters examined by Silver (2012e), nineteen had a bias toward the GOP.

Polling accuracy can be of great importance for a campaign to accurately gauge its position in an election cycle and make adjustments to its efforts. Although later analysis demonstrated that most public opinion polls overestimated Republican strength, some Republicans during the campaign had suggested the polls underestimated Republican strength, although after the election others complained that their own internal polls were flawed (Silver 2012f). There appears to have been bias in the Romney campaign's state-by-state polling. Governor Romney's internal polls in several states, including Colorado, Ohio, and Pennsylvania, had him winning, although President Obama was successful in all three (Silver 2012f). As widely reported, the Romney campaign's internal polling left them so confident they would win, the governor did not draft a concession speech until after Obama's victory was announced. In the end, Obama won reelection with over 51 percent of the total popular vote to 47 percent for Romney, and he won a comfortable majority in the Electoral College by a margin of 332 to 206 electoral votes.

DONORSHEDS: INDIVIDUAL CONTRIBUTIONS TO OBAMA AND ROMNEY

CARL T. DAHLMAN

The 2012 presidential race made history for how campaigns are financed in the United States. For the first time since 1976, both major party candidates refused public funds and relied entirely on private contributions to their campaigns. This was also the first presidential race to show the full effect of the US Supreme Court's 2010 decision in *Citizens United v. FEC* (558 U.S. 3010). Corporations and labor unions were now allowed unlimited independent expenditures for or against individual candidates through independent-expenditure-only committees, or super PACs, which technically cannot finance specific campaigns and can therefore raise funds with no limits on donations. Disclosure rules—that reveal who is funding whom—have also been weakened, shielding the identity of many super PAC contributors from public scrutiny because their funds do not directly finance candidates. These "outside" groups spent $550 million advocating for or against Obama and Romney. The national parties spent another $678 million in support of their candidates. Together, outside sources and political parties surpassed the $1.16 billion contributed directly to candidates through traditional channels.

Contributions to candidates from individual donors, though rivaled by other sources, remain an important source of funding and may be indicators of a candidate's appeal with would-be voters. Individual donors may donate up to $2,500 per election, and they remain the major source of funds controlled by the candidate's election committee. The combined total individual contributions for all candidates and parties topped $1.4 billion for the 2012 presidential race. This was 18 percent less than the record level set in the 2008 cycle, due in part to the diversion of contributions to super PACs.

Obama raised a total of $715 million from individual contributors. As in 2008, Obama's campaign was notable for the large number of small donors who gave to his campaign. These small donors contributed almost one-third of his total receipts. Romney raised $443 million from individual contributors, and only 18 percent of those contributions were from small donors.

Identifying the distribution and size of individual contributions allows us to see patterns among donors. The Federal Election Commission (2012), responsible for campaign finance rules, provides data on individual donations. These data are limited in one important way: federal disclosure laws do not require information on donors whose contributions are $200 or less. Analyzing the available data nonetheless provides us a sense of the spatial demography of campaign contributions.

Mapping "donorsheds" of where campaign contributors live reveals a pattern similar to a map of the US population weighted by income. The most important donorsheds are the wealthier neighborhoods of major metropolitan areas. These donors are a key part of national political campaigns, yet they represent a small fraction of the population and an even smaller cross-section of American communities. What is, perhaps, more surprising is how both parties' candidates have very similar donorsheds. If the candidates' major donors seem worlds apart politically, they actually live quite near one another. The smaller donor communities spread across the country are important for presidential campaigns as a whole, but individually, their resources are too limited to attract special attention from a campaign. Black-tie dinner parties with a candidate in Manhattan can raise more money than mailers to a farming community.

In general, Obama did better among urban donors and Romney among suburban donors (figure 4.1). Obama did well in most major donorsheds and raised two times more money than Romney in Silicon Valley, four times more in Chicago, six times more in San Francisco, and over seven times more in Seattle. Donors in New York City, one of the largest donorsheds in the country, also favored Obama over Romney. Obama raised $13.7 million in Manhattan from wealthy donors in the city as well as from "bundlers," middlemen who collect donations from others around the country. By contrast, Romney raised about half that much from New York City.

Romney did better in America's "1 percent" communities. For example, in Morristown, New Jersey, and Greenwich, Connecticut, Romney gathered over $5 million compared to about $2 million for Obama. Romney did very well in places like Huntington Beach, California, and in Houston and Dallas-Fort Worth, as well as in smaller cities across the Great Plains. He also did better than Obama in fund-raising in the key states of Michigan, Ohio, and Florida, although he lost those states in the popular vote. It is unclear how much conservative super PACs, such as those espousing Tea Party perspectives, might have starved Romney's campaign of much-needed resources.

Although the pattern of campaign contributions emphasizes wealthier urban and suburban communities relative to smaller and poorer communities, it nevertheless reflects geographic differences in levels of support for the Obama and Romney campaigns. How future campaigns and campaign contributions will be affected by the rise of super PACs will no doubt be an important factor in future elections.

FIGURE 4.1

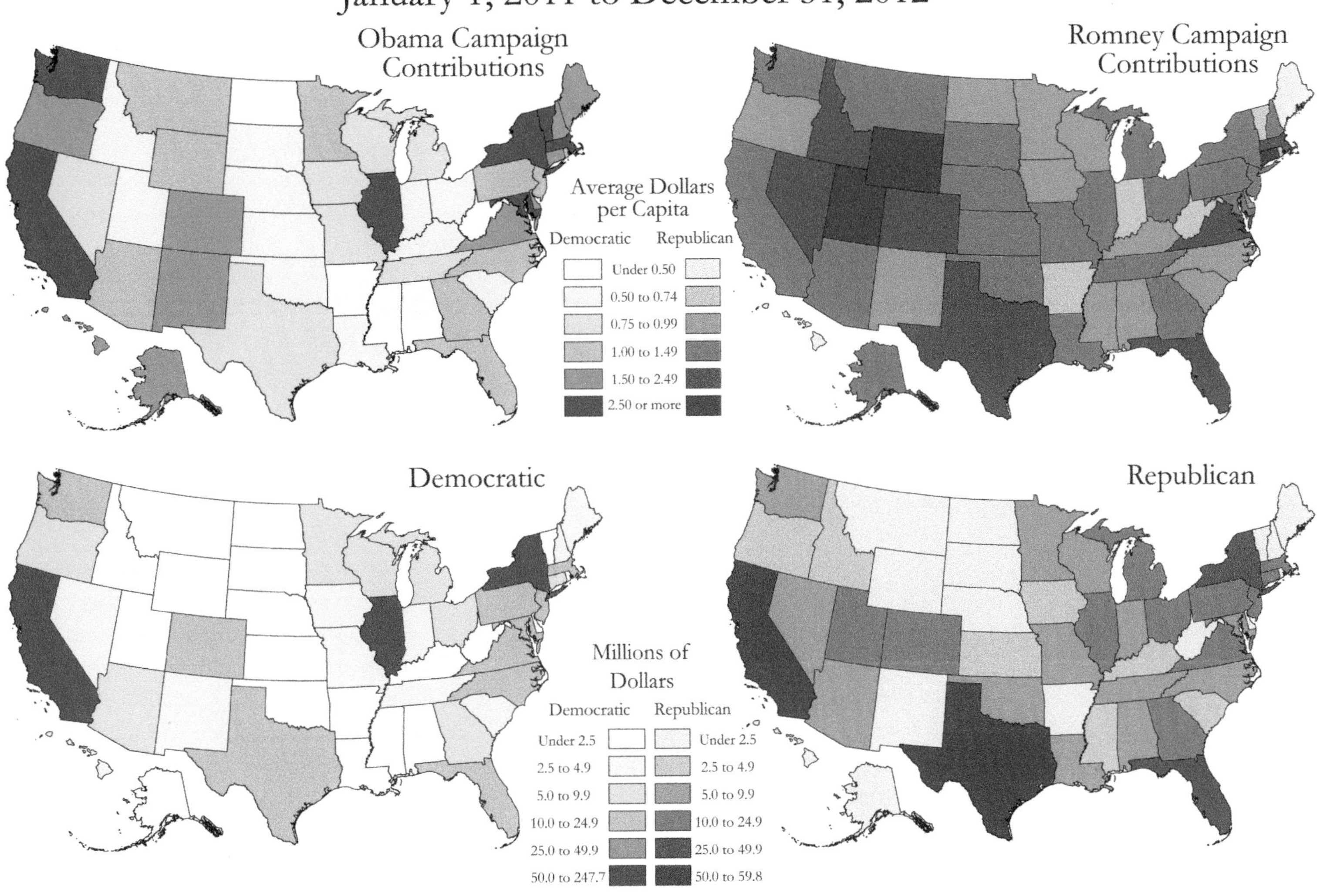
Donorsheds: Reported Campaign Contributions
January 1, 2011 to December 31, 2012
Obama Campaign
Contributions
Romney Campaign
Contributions
Average Dollars
per Capita
Democratic
Republican
Under 0.50
0.50 to 0.74
0.75 to 0.99
1.00 to 1.49
1.50 to 2.49
2.50 or more
Democratic
Republican
Millions of
Dollars
Democratic
Republican
Under 2.5
2.5 to 4.9
5.0 to 9.9
10.0 to 24.9
25.0 to 49.9
50.0 to 247.7
Under 2.5
2.5 to 4.9
5.0 to 9.9
10.0 to 24.9
25.0 to 49.9
50.0 to 59.8

CAMPAIGN EXPENDITURES IN THE 2012 ELECTION

CHRIS MAIER

Throughout history, campaign spending has played a significant role in presidential elections. Candidates need money to communicate with voters, volunteers, and other politicians. Recently, money has played an increasingly important role in elections. In the run-up to the 2012 election, many experts predicted that the presidential election would be one of the most expensive elections in American history, and this prediction proved accurate.

During the 2012 presidential election, President Barack Obama and Republican challenger Mitt Romney combined to spend $576,771,085 during the primary season and another $473,547,645 during the general election. Thus, in total the two candidates combined to spend $1,050,318,730 on the 2012 presidential election. The calculated spending totals in this essay do not include each candidate's itemized deductions, nor do they include outside spending on the presidential election from organizations such as super PACs.

President Obama spent $348,339,834 during the 2012 Democratic primaries (Federal Election Commission Obama 2012a and 2012b). As the incumbent, Obama ran a different kind of primary campaign than his Republican counterpart, Mitt Romney. Unlike his lengthy primary campaign in 2008 against Hillary Clinton, he ran unopposed in the 2012 Democratic primaries and caucuses, which allowed Obama to get a head start on the general election. Even though much of Obama's primary spending was in Washington, DC, Illinois, and Wisconsin, he spent money in all fifty states, ranging from a low of $2,926 in West Virginia to a high of $229,381,198 in Washington, DC. Nearly two-thirds of President Obama's primary and caucus spending was done in Washington, DC. The Obama campaign also spent a great deal of money in Illinois and Wisconsin. Illinois was home to Obama's campaign headquarters, which was located in Chicago's Prudential Building.

Governor Mitt Romney spent $228,431,252 during the 2012 Republican presidential primaries and caucuses (Federal Election Commission Romney 2012a and 2012b). Romney's total was significantly less than President Obama's total. He had a much different campaign in the primaries and caucuses as he faced significant competition from former senator Rick Santorum, Representative Ron Paul, and former Speaker of the House Newt Gingrich. Romney spent over half of his money ($115,770,300) in Massachusetts, which was home to Romney's campaign headquarters and where he served one term as governor. Romney also spent a significant amount of money in New Hampshire, which hosted the second primary or caucus in the Republican nominating process. After Romney lost a close race in the Iowa caucuses to Santorum, New Hampshire was a critical election for Romney. Just as President Obama did, Romney spent money in all fifty states, ranging from $2,114 in North Dakota to $115,770,300 in Massachusetts. An interesting aspect to Romney's primary spending was the lack of it in several traditional Republican states such as North Dakota. Romney's five lowest spending totals were in the small states of North Dakota, Montana, West Virginia, Delaware, and Wyoming. Out of these five states, only Delaware has a recent history of voting for the Democratic Party in the general election.

Figure 4.2 shows the expenditures for President Obama's 2012 general election campaign, which totaled $346,671,026 (Federal Election Commission Obama 2012b). The geographic pattern of Obama's largest expenditures in the general election campaign was similar to the pattern in the primary and caucuses, with large outlays in Washington, DC, and Illinois. Both places were headquarters for President Obama's reelection campaign. Along with Washington, DC, and Illinois, President Obama spent a significant amount of money in "battleground" or "toss-up" states, including Colorado, Florida, Iowa, Missouri, Ohio, Virginia, and Wisconsin. Additionally, the Obama campaign spent a substantial amount of money in California. California, a reliably Democratic state since the 1992 election, was never really in play, but it was important due to its campaign donors. President Obama spent $9,999,333 in California but raised $91,715,284, making the state central to his 2012 election fund-raising efforts.

Figure 4.2 shows Mitt Romney's expenditures in the 2012 general election campaign, which totaled $126,876,619 (Federal Election Commission Romney 2012b). Romney's pattern of expenditures was similar to those during the primaries and caucuses, with over half of the money spent in Massachusetts. Because Romney had less money to spend, the Romney campaign also had to be more selective in its expenditures. Unlike Romney's campaign during the primaries and caucuses, the Republican challenger did not spend any money in Alaska, Hawaii, Maine, North Dakota, West Virginia, and Wyoming. As was the case with Obama, Romney focused his spending on battleground or toss-up states, including Florida, Minnesota, Missouri, New Hampshire, Pennsylvania, and Virginia. Unfortunately for Romney, it was the battleground states, most of which went for President Obama, that decided the 2012 presidential election. In the end, President Obama and Republican challenger Mitt Romney combined for one of the most expensive elections in American history.

FIGURE 4.2

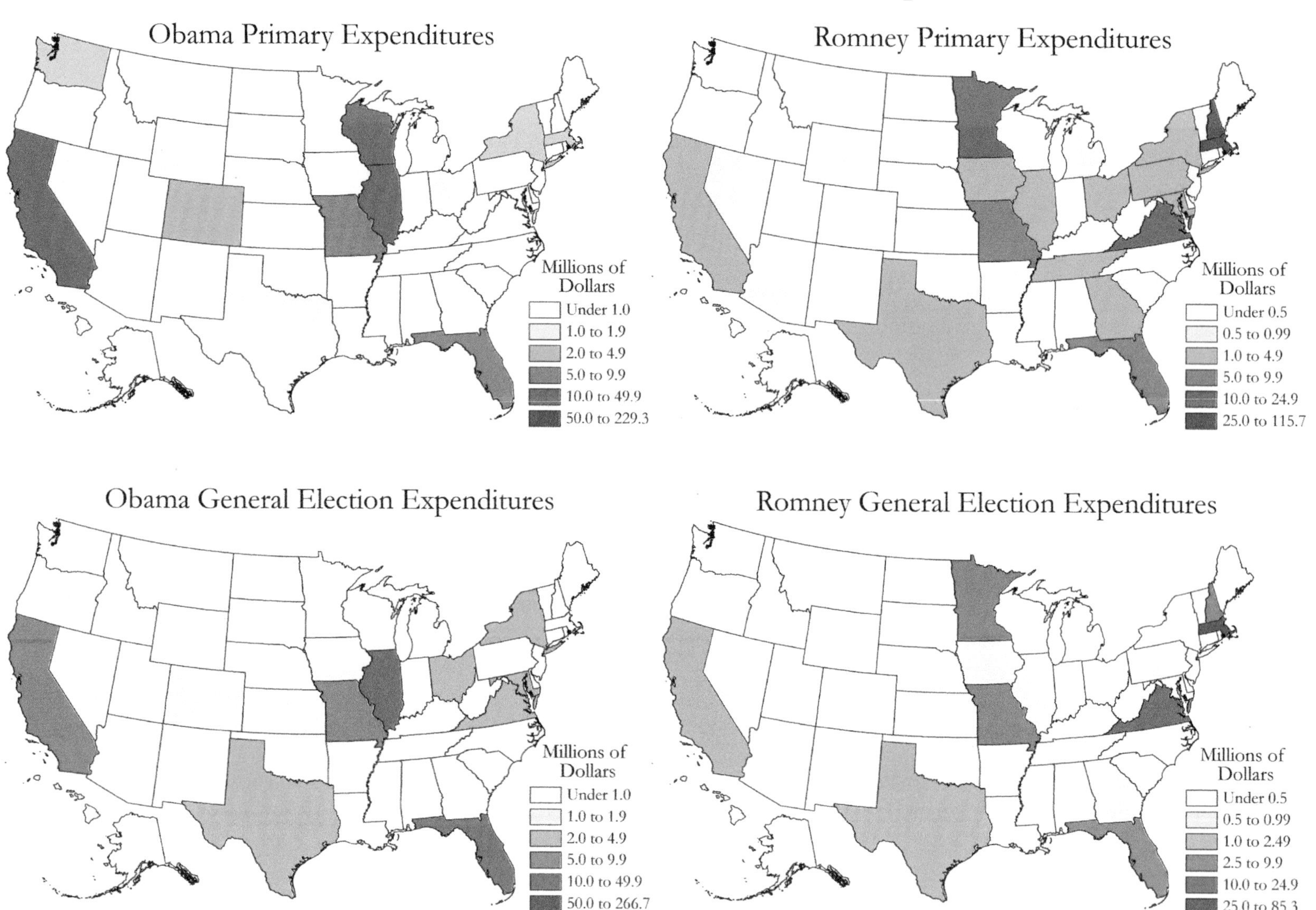
Reported Primary and General Election Expenditures
Obama Primary Expenditures
Millions of Dollars
Under 1.0
1.0 to 1.9
2.0 to 4.9
5.0 to 9.9
10.0 to 49.9
50.0 to 229.3
Romney Primary Expenditures
Millions of Dollars
Under 0.5
0.5 to 0.99
1.0 to 4.9
5.0 to 9.9
10.0 to 24.9
25.0 to 115.7
Obama General Election Expenditures
Millions of Dollars
Under 1.0
1.0 to 1.9
2.0 to 4.9
5.0 to 9.9
10.0 to 49.9
50.0 to 266.7
Romney General Election Expenditures
Millions of Dollars
Under 0.5
0.5 to 0.99
1.0 to 2.49
2.5 to 9.9
10.0 to 24.9
25.0 to 85.3

CAMPAIGN STOPS

J. CLARK ARCHER

To adopt a football metaphor, by about September 1 of every year divisible by four, all of the preseason nonconference games have been played, and the main conference contenders are beginning to confront one another in preparation for the all-important conference championship tournament at the end of the regular season. In the race for the White House, the primary elections, caucuses, and party conventions have narrowed the field to the final major party candidates for president and vice president and also focused the main issues of policy contention in the general election on the contrasting positions iterated in party platform documents. Massive amounts of campaign contributions have been collected, campaign staffs have been organized, and local efforts have begun to excite likely supportive potential voters in order to encourage them to vote. To continue the metaphor, football fields have visibly marked sidelines, end zones, and yard markers at ten-yard intervals from one end zone to the other. In presidential elections, the visibly marked boundaries of supreme importance are those which geographically demarcate each of the states in the federal union, because the crucial final Electoral College score is tallied state by state. A national popular election majority or plurality can be achieved for naught if it does not lead to an Electoral College majority. As recently as the 2000 presidential election, Democratic candidate Al Gore won the national popular vote by more than one-half million ballots but lost the crucial Electoral College vote by 271 to 266 for Republican George W. Bush.

Campaign strategists are acutely aware of the Electoral College arithmetic, which tends to make potential popular-vote supporters in some states far more valuable than potential popular-vote supporters in other states. In football, all passes that are caught out-of-bounds are "wasted plays." In presidential elections, all popular votes beyond a plurality or simple majority in a state yield what political scientists call "wasted votes," which have no value in determining the final Electoral College tally. Electoral votes are apportioned on the basis of population, so California now casts fifty-five electoral votes, while several less populous states, including Alaska, Montana, and Vermont, cast only three electoral votes in a presidential election. All but two states—excepting Maine and Nebraska, which follow a "district-level" principle—allocate all of their electoral votes to the statewide presidential popular vote leader under a winner-take-all principle. Hence, one popular vote gained in the state of California could swing 55 out of the needed total of 270 Electoral College votes required to win the presidency to a candidate, while one additional popular vote gained in Alaska, Montana, or Vermont would yield merely 3 out of the needed total of 270 Electoral College votes. Not surprisingly, not one single major party presidential or vice presidential candidate visited Alaska, Montana, or Vermont during the general election campaign in 2012.

However, it also should be noted that despite its largest-in-the-nation block of Electoral College votes, California was visited fewer than five times by a particular presidential or vice presidential candidate, while several other states were each visited more than a dozen times by one or more candidates. While a state's total population and therefore the number of Electoral College votes apportioned to it are important, a state's past election history and current election expectations also are important. It has been more than two decades since Republican Ronald Reagan—a former governor of California—won California for the Grand Old Party in 1980 and

1984. Since 1988, California has been reliably Democratic in each presidential election. So while both major presidential candidates each visited California on four occasions during the general election campaign in 2012, it is quite plausible that they went to this Pacific Coast state with much more interest in soliciting big California campaign donations than in attracting potential California voters. Obama carried California by nearly two million more popular votes than Romney in 2012.

Travel time available to major party presidential and vice presidential candidates during about the last two months of a general election campaign is among the scarcest of all of the campaign resources that can be allocated in strategic pursuit of these national offices. Greater campaign donations, more campaign workers, additional media advertising outlays, more and better speechwriters, and so on are all valuable. But no amount of money can buy any candidate more travel time to meet and greet potential voters and to generate "free media" campaign appearances in as many potentially crucial "media markets" as possible.

Because, as noted above, Electoral College votes are tallied on a winner-take-all basis state by state, national presidential politics really are "local politics" in many very important ways. Hence, numbers of campaign stops, campaign events, or campaign appearances, as these "local presidential political events" are known and reported, for presidential and vice presidential candidates during a general election campaign provide a very revealing and sensitive measure of campaign strategy decisions. Other metrics, such as media buys, print advertising outlays, get-out-the-vote mobilizing efforts, and so on are less accessible and sometimes quite difficult to measure. But candidate campaign stops are aggressively promoted by campaign workers simply because they want to attract as big and as energetic and as boisterous a crowd as possible at every single scheduled candidate appearance. This is an instance in which a very simple measure—campaign stops—can be quite revealing about presidential politics.

From September 1 to November 6, 2012, Democratic presidential candidate Obama made a total of sixty-six scheduled campaign stops, and Democratic vice presidential candidate Biden made thirty-eight stops (figure 4.3). Republican presidential candidate Romney made 104 campaign stops, and Republican vice presidential candidate Ryan made 86 campaign stops (figure 4.3). As incumbents, the Democratic candidates could depend to a somewhat greater extent on mass-media coverage of their normal governmental office-holding activities to reach potential voters and so could get by with a less frenetic campaign travel schedule than those of their Republican challengers. But while the Republican running mates Romney and Ryan made almost twice as many campaign stops from September 1 to November 6 (190 stops) than the Democratic running mates Obama and Biden (104 stops), the maps of "Presidential Campaign Stops, September–November 2012" make it obvious that they all went to essentially the same destinations (figure 4.3). Of course, they were hardly all relying on just one travel agent who could only think up one itinerary, but the maps appear as if this were the case.

Twenty-five states received no general election campaign visits at all from any of the four major party presidential or vice presidential candidates in 2012. To be sure, several of the neglected states had indeed received attention from one or more of the candidates earlier while in pursuit of primary election–based or caucus-based support at either the Democratic or Republican National Convention, but states with few electoral votes and/or which were very likely to be easily won by one or the other of the major parties in the general election fell far down the priority list when general election candidate campaign stops were chosen. While local-level campaign workers virtually everywhere undoubtedly would very much like to see their own presidential and/or vice presidential candidate in their locality, most such requests are denied simply because the candidates do not have time to visit more than a few places during a general election campaign. Campaign-stop requests from about half of the states in the Union thus end up in the "fly-over" pile during campaign strategy sessions.

During the general election campaign, fewer than a dozen states received more than a few campaign stops. As the campaign continued, the focus progressively narrowed to just a half-dozen battleground states during the last week of the campaign (figures 4.4 to 4.7). Indeed, just six states received visits from both

FIGURE 4.3

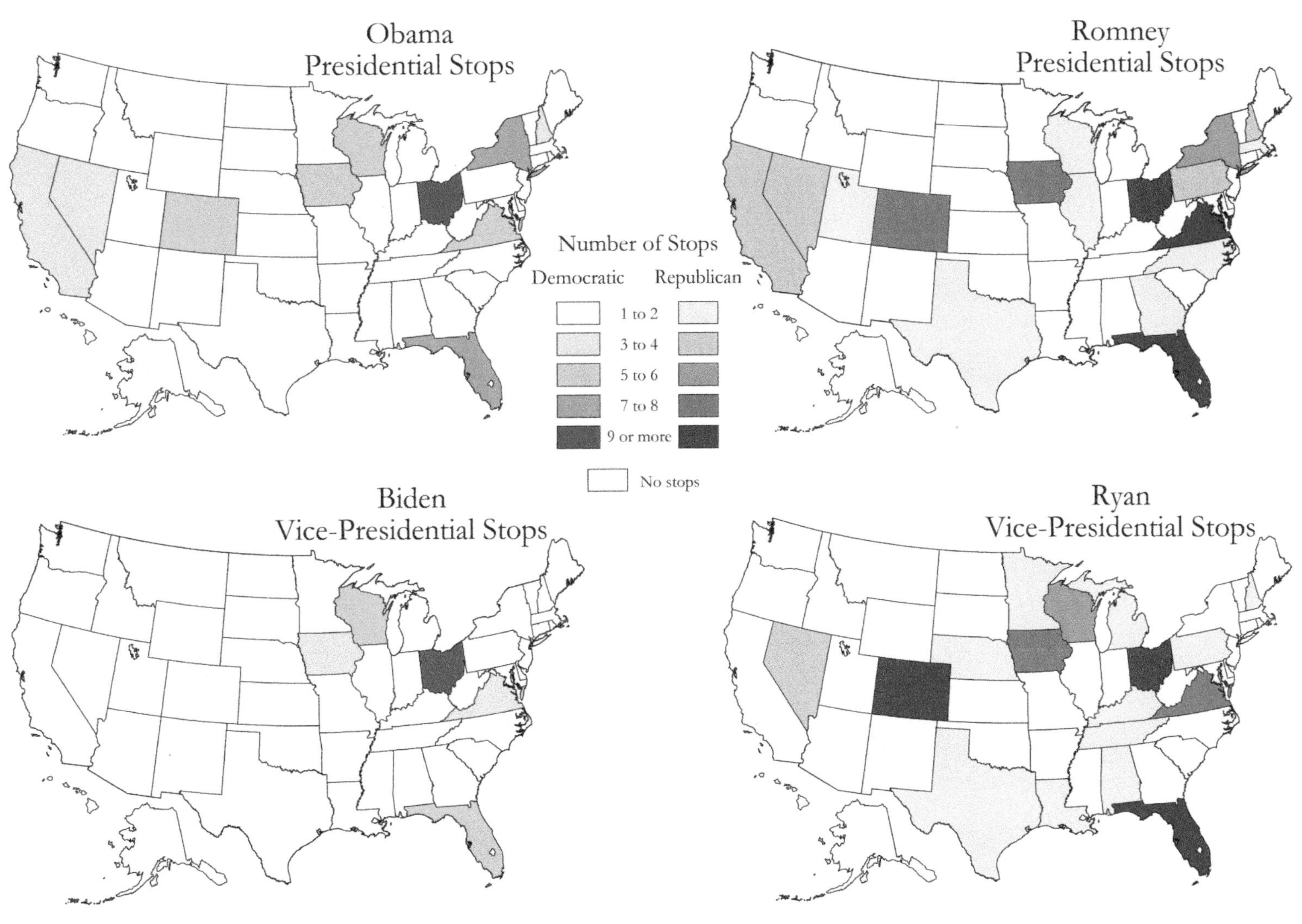

Presidential Election Campaign Stops
September - November 2012
Obama
Presidential Stops
Romney
Presidential Stops
Number of Stops
Democratic
Republican
1 to 2
3 to 4
5 to 6
7 to 8
9 or more
No stops
Biden
Vice-Presidential Stops
Ryan
Vice-Presidential Stops

FIGURE 4.4

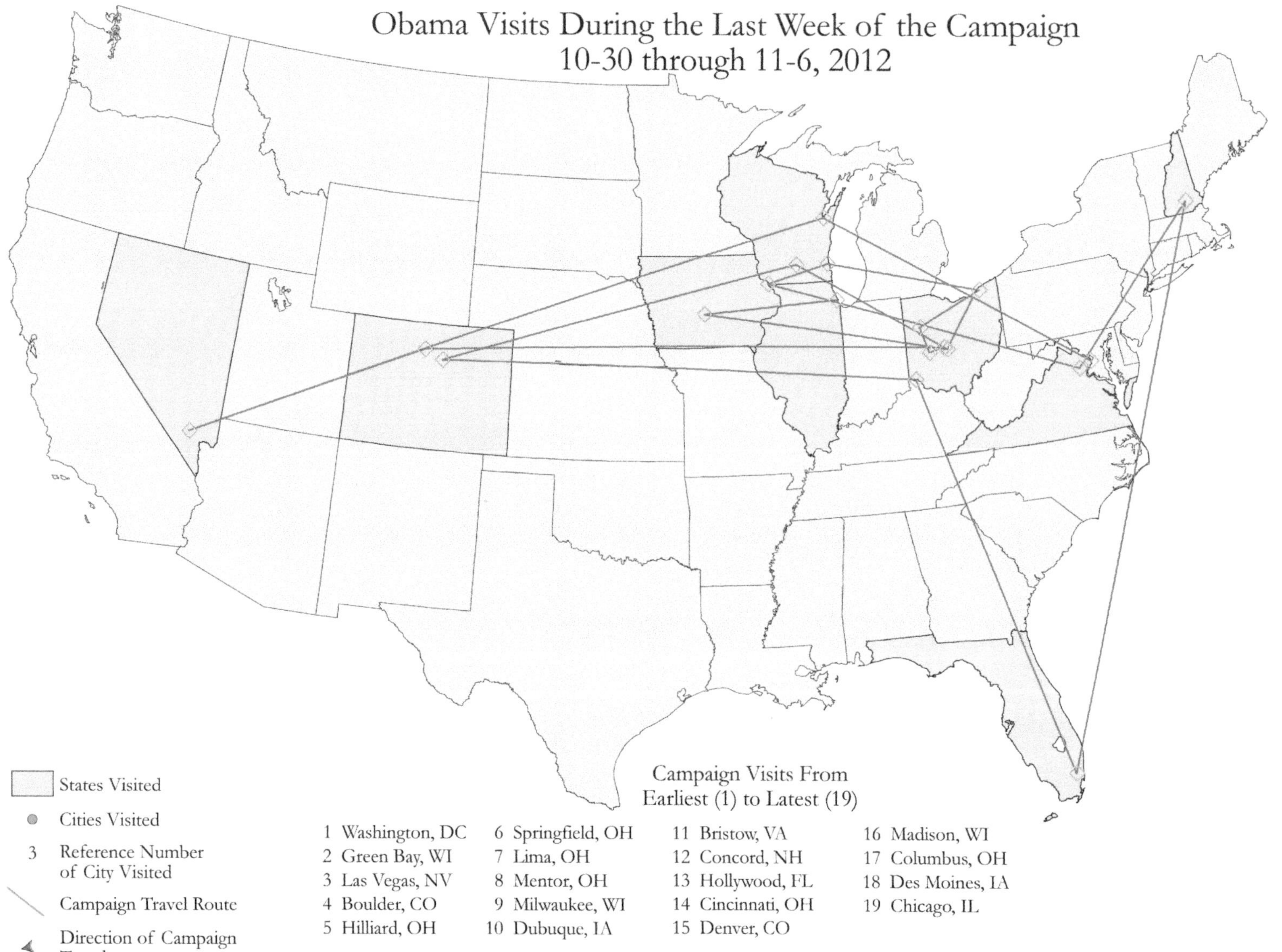

Obama Visits During the Last Week of the Campaign
10-30 through 11-6, 2012
States Visited
Cities Visited
3 Reference Number of City Visited
Campaign Travel Route
Direction of Campaign Travel
Campaign Visits From Earliest (1) to Latest (19)
1 Washington, DC
2 Green Bay, WI
3 Las Vegas, NV
4 Boulder, CO
5 Hilliard, OH
6 Springfield, OH
7 Lima, OH
8 Mentor, OH
9 Milwaukee, WI
10 Dubuque, IA
11 Bristow, VA
12 Concord, NH
13 Hollywood, FL
14 Cincinnati, OH
15 Denver, CO
16 Madison, WI
17 Columbus, OH
18 Des Moines, IA
19 Chicago, IL

FIGURE 4.5

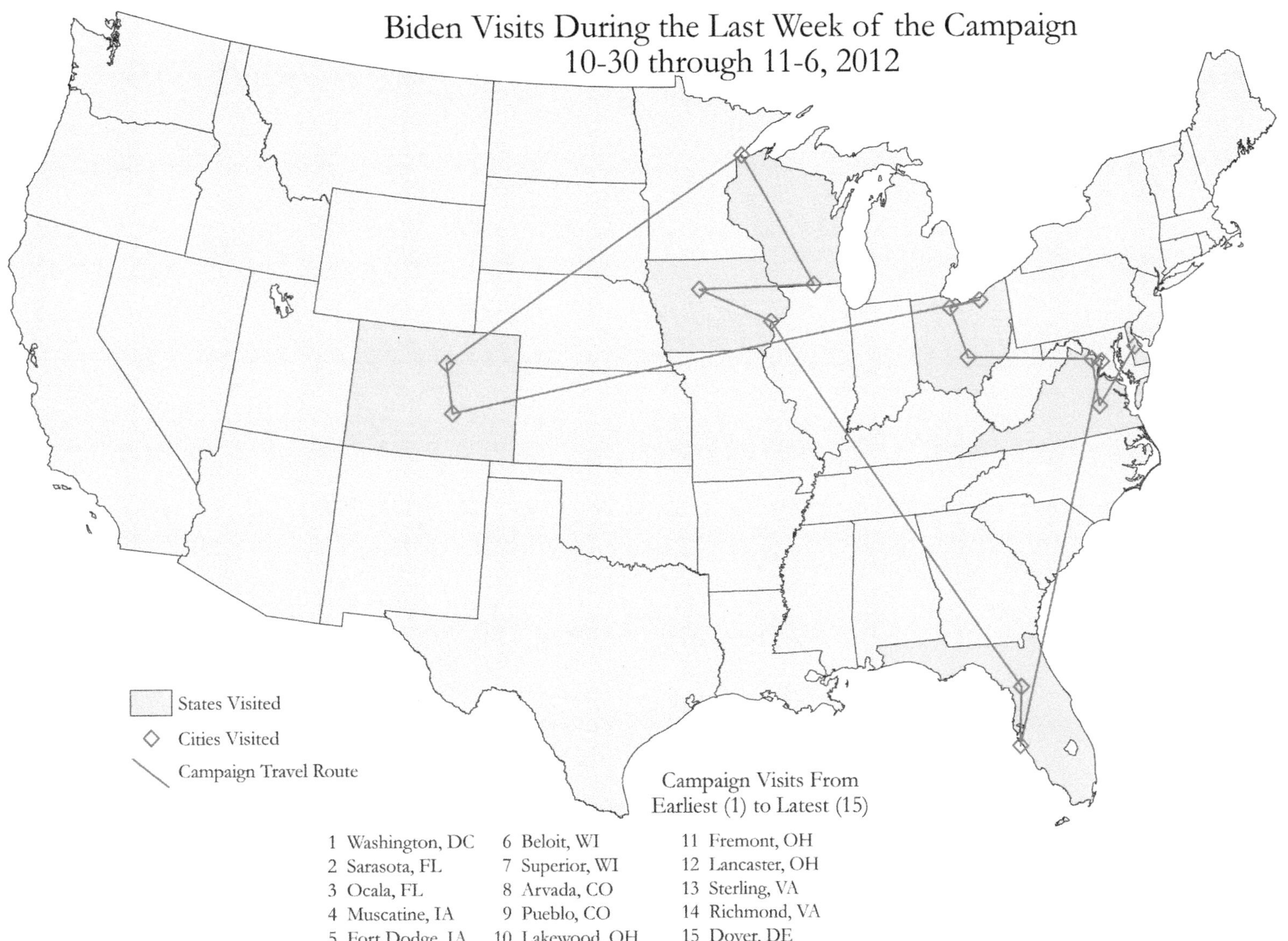
Biden Visits During the Last Week of the Campaign
10-30 through 11-6, 2012
States Visited
Cities Visited
Campaign Travel Route
Campaign Visits From
Earliest (1) to Latest (15)
1 Washington, DC
2 Sarasota, FL
3 Ocala, FL
4 Muscatine, IA
5 Fort Dodge, IA
6 Beloit, WI
7 Superior, WI
8 Arvada, CO
9 Pueblo, CO
10 Lakewood, OH
11 Fremont, OH
12 Lancaster, OH
13 Sterling, VA
14 Richmond, VA
15 Dover, DE

FIGURE 4.6

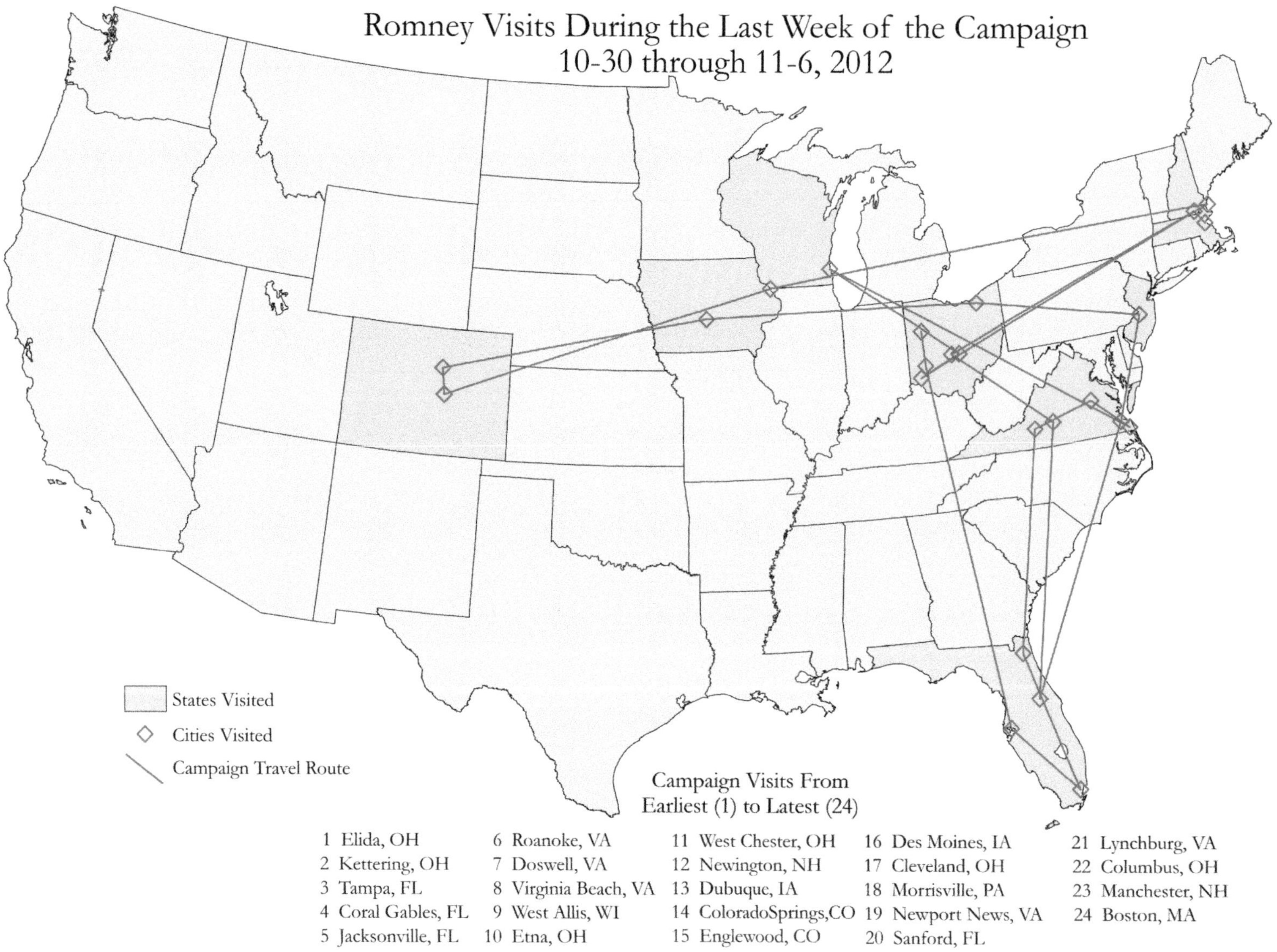
Romney Visits During the Last Week of the Campaign
10-30 through 11-6, 2012
States Visited
Cities Visited
Campaign Travel Route
Campaign Visits From
Earliest (1) to Latest (24)
1 Elida, OH
2 Kettering, OH
3 Tampa, FL
4 Coral Gables, FL
5 Jacksonville, FL
6 Roanoke, VA
7 Doswell, VA
8 Virginia Beach, VA
9 West Allis, WI
10 Etna, OH
11 West Chester, OH
12 Newington, NH
13 Dubuque, IA
14 ColoradoSprings,CO
15 Englewood, CO
16 Des Moines, IA
17 Cleveland, OH
18 Morrisville, PA
19 Newport News, VA
20 Sanford, FL
21 Lynchburg, VA
22 Columbus, OH
23 Manchester, NH
24 Boston, MA

FIGURE 4.7

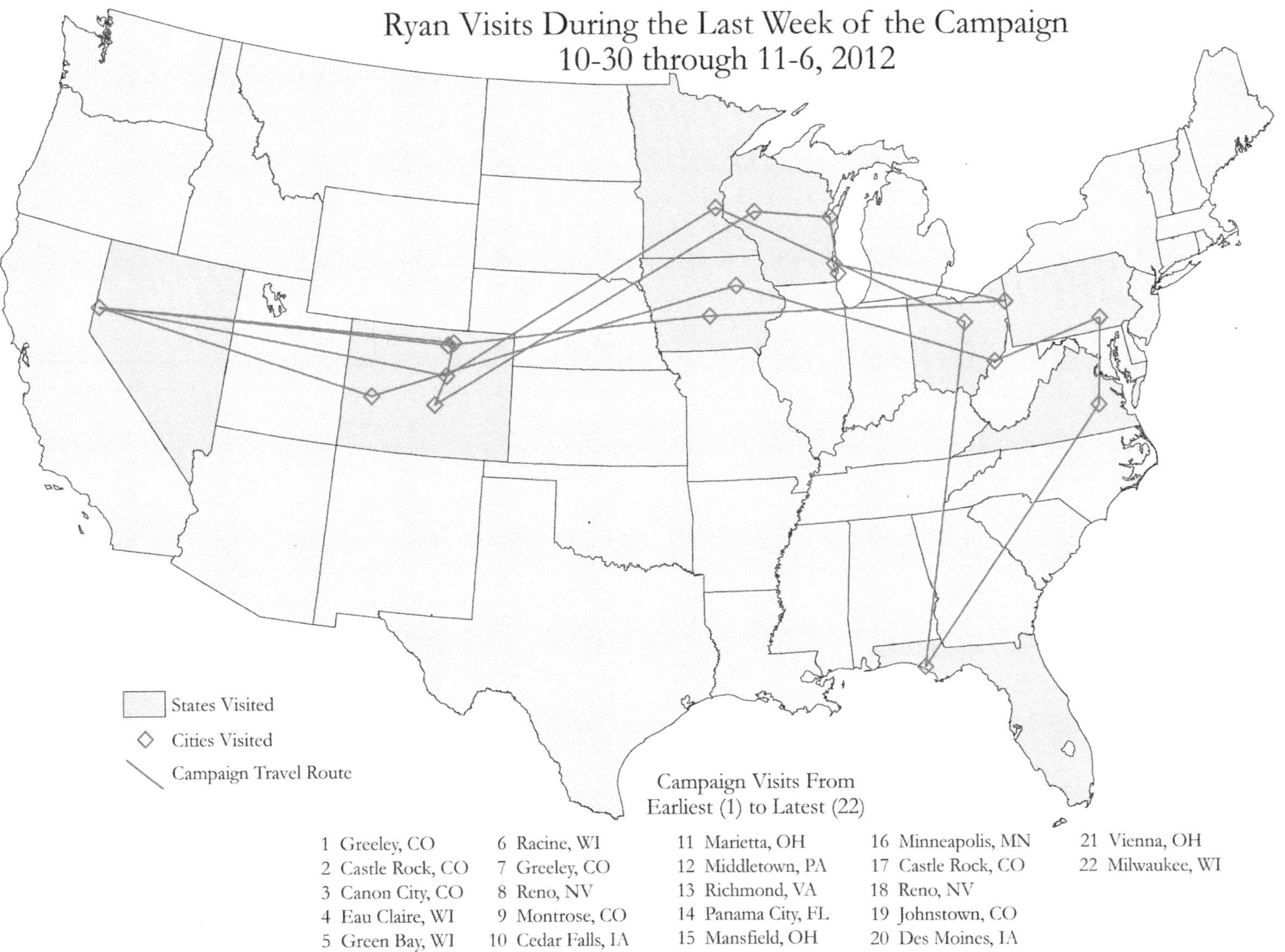

Campaign Visits From Earliest (1) to Latest (22)

1 Greeley, CO
2 Castle Rock, CO
3 Canon City, CO
4 Eau Claire, WI
5 Green Bay, WI
6 Racine, WI
7 Greeley, CO
8 Reno, NV
9 Montrose, CO
10 Cedar Falls, IA
11 Marietta, OH
12 Middletown, PA
13 Richmond, VA
14 Panama City, FL
15 Mansfield, OH
16 Minneapolis, MN
17 Castle Rock, CO
18 Reno, NV
19 Johnstown, CO
20 Des Moines, IA
21 Vienna, OH
22 Milwaukee, WI

major-party presidential candidates and also from both vice presidential candidates during the final week of the campaign, between October 30 and November 6.

Although the details remain closely guarded proprietary information, it is obvious that sophisticated models and tracking polls used by both campaigns must have pointed to just a few states that were still in play by the last stages of the campaign. Massachusetts, Nevada, and Pennsylvania each received campaign stops from one or two of the candidates during the final week, which suggests that the Democratic and Republican campaign allocation models and the Democratic and Republican tracking polls were not in total agreement with one another. But they evidently were not all that different either, since Obama and Biden on the Democratic side and Romney and Ryan on the Republican side all made at least one campaign stop each between October 30 and November 6 in Colorado, Florida, Iowa, Ohio, Virginia, and Wisconsin. In other words, there were about 85 out of an overall total of 538 electoral votes that were still sufficiently in doubt to warrant sending in both of the major parties' standard bearers for personal, on-the-ground campaign stops in each of these six states. This represents about 16 percent of all electoral votes and about 31 percent of the 270 needed to win the final Electoral College vote.

To complete the football metaphor, the Democratic Obama-Biden ticket emphatically swept the final conference championship series and won all six of the final week battleground states. Had the Romney-Ryan ticket won these states, however, the Republicans would have won the election.

GEOGRAPHIC PLACE NAME USE IN THE 2012 PRESIDENTIAL DEBATES

MATT BALENTINE, JUSTIN FRAZIER, AND GERALD R. WEBSTER

The first presidential debates were held in 1858 between Republican candidate Abraham Lincoln and Democratic candidate Stephen Douglas. The next presidential debates were not held until Democrat John F. Kennedy and Republican Richard Nixon squared off in the first televised debates in 1960. There were no debates in the presidential elections of 1964, 1968, and 1972, but since the 1976 contest between Republican president Gerald Ford and Democratic challenger Jimmy Carter, there have been televised debates in every election cycle, and they are now an expected part of the campaign process.

Presidential debates are inherently geographic from multiple perspectives. For example, candidates commonly spar over foreign policy issues discussing countries such as Iran and Mexico and world regions such as Europe or the Middle East. They also debate domestic policies that might well affect US states or regions differently. Candidates attempt to cultivate and mobilize voters in these states and regions by claiming they understand their problems and have campaign platforms to help overcome the obstacles they face (Sutherland and Webster 1994).

Given the Electoral College system, candidates commonly target those states regarded as critical to winning the election. These battleground or "swing" states include those neither candidate has an overwhelming advantage in, and they frequently determine the outcome of closely contested elections. As a result, a large share of campaign time and resources may be allocated to attempts at winning these states. Given the importance of swing states to election outcomes, it might be anticipated that they would be highlighted in nationally televised debates.

In the three debates between Democratic incumbent Barack Obama and Republican challenger Mitt Romney, nineteen different states were mentioned a total of seventy-five times (figure 4.8). Of the fifty states, eight, including Colorado, Florida, Iowa, New Hampshire, North Carolina, Ohio, Pennsylvania, and Virginia, were won by margins of 6 percent or less of the two-party vote. Notably, nineteen of the seventy-five state references in the debates were to one of these eight swing states, meaning they were mentioned one and a half times as frequently as their proportion of all states.

Obama and Romney mentioned twelve and sixteen different US states, respectively (figure 4.8). Both candidates mentioned Arizona, Colorado, Iowa, Massachusetts, Michigan, New York, Ohio, Nevada, and Pennsylvania. Thus, four of the nine states mentioned by both candidates were swing states. Interestingly, the three states mentioned most by each candidate were not swing states. President Obama's top three were Massachusetts (nine), Arizona (four), and Michigan (four). Governor Romney's top three were Massachusetts (nine), Michigan (eight), and New York (five).

Both candidates mentioned Massachusetts nine times due to Mitt Romney's previous tenure as the state's governor. Most notably, debate dialogue over health-care policy forced a discussion pertaining to Massachusetts's adoption of a universal health-care plan structured similarly to that of the health-care plan passed during President Obama's first term. Much of the conversation centered around the fact that though Governor Romney had campaigned against the Affordable Health Care Act, the Massachusetts plan was signed into state law during Governor Romney's administration with his support.

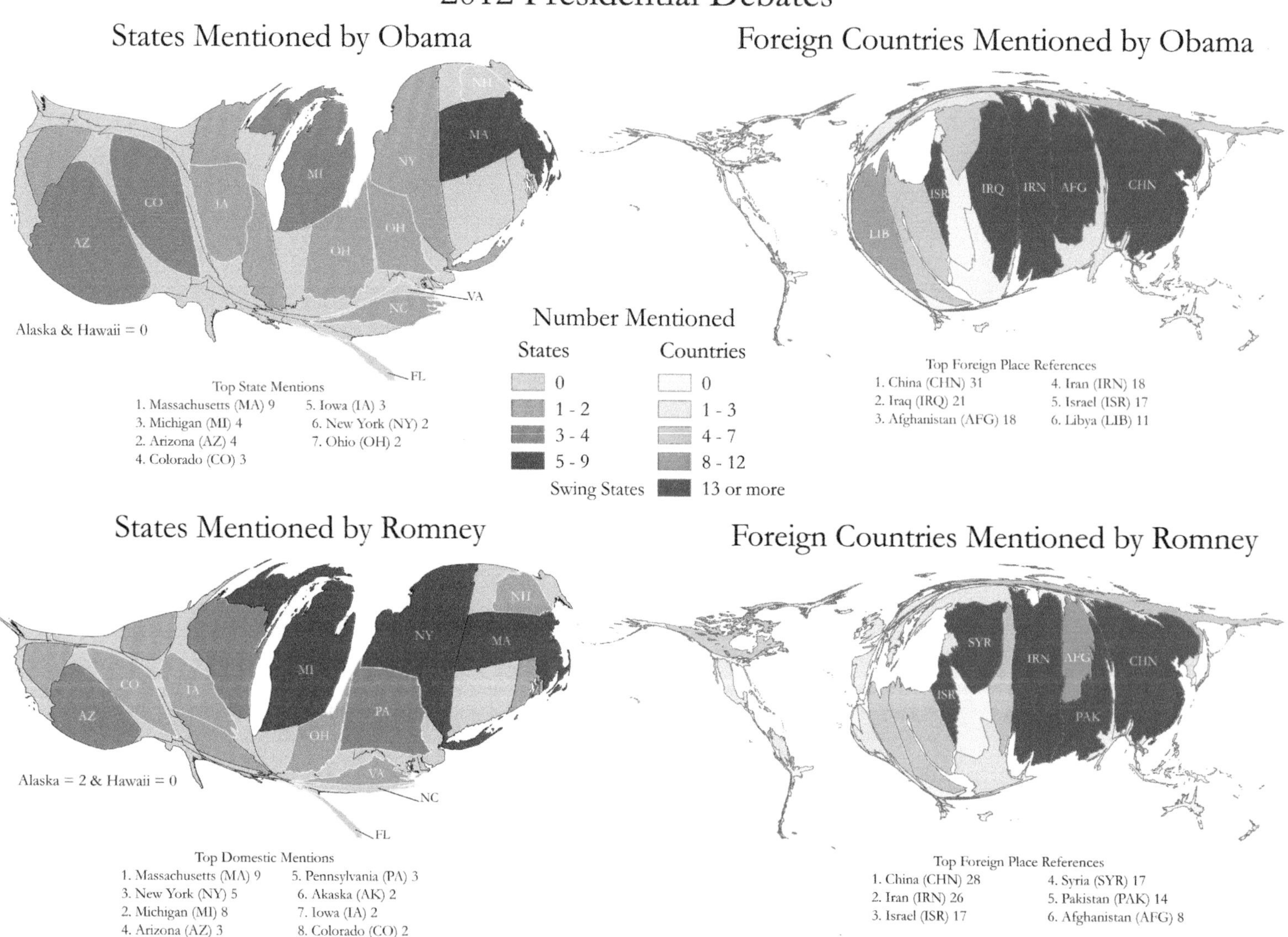
2012 Presidential Debates
States Mentioned by Obama
Alaska & Hawaii = 0
Top State Mentions
1. Massachusetts (MA) 9
3. Michigan (MI) 4
2. Arizona (AZ) 4
4. Colorado (CO) 3
5. Iowa (IA) 3
6. New York (NY) 2
7. Ohio (OH) 2
Foreign Countries Mentioned by Obama
Top Foreign Place References
1. China (CHN) 31
2. Iraq (IRQ) 21
3. Afghanistan (AFG) 18
4. Iran (IRN) 18
5. Israel (ISR) 17
6. Libya (LIB) 11
Number Mentioned
States
0
1 - 2
3 - 4
5 - 9
Swing States
Countries
0
1 - 3
4 - 7
8 - 12
13 or more
States Mentioned by Romney
Alaska = 2 & Hawaii = 0
Top Domestic Mentions
1. Massachusetts (MA) 9
3. New York (NY) 5
2. Michigan (MI) 8
4. Arizona (AZ) 3
5. Pennsylvania (PA) 3
6. Akaska (AK) 2
7. Iowa (IA) 2
8. Colorado (CO) 2
Foreign Countries Mentioned by Romney
Top Foreign Place References
1. China (CHN) 28
2. Iran (IRN) 26
3. Israel (ISR) 17
4. Syria (SYR) 17
5. Pakistan (PAK) 14
6. Afghanistan (AFG) 8

Michigan was also mentioned several times by the candidates (eight times by Governor Romney and four times by President Obama). Much of the conversation surrounding Michigan focused specifically on the downward spiral of Detroit, the country's struggling auto industry, and how the competing economic philosophies of the candidates would affect the city's interests and future. During this exchange Mitt Romney was forced to defend his controversial op-ed piece in the *New York Times* titled "Let Detroit Go Bankrupt" (Romney 2008).

Colorado, Iowa, Ohio, and Pennsylvania were the only swing states mentioned by both candidates (table 4.1). With the exception of Ohio's connection to the auto industry, none of the swing states mentioned by both candidates has much of a connection to domestic policy issues highlighted in the debates. As the examples of the Massachusetts health-care plan and Michigan's automobile industry illustrate, non–swing states may have been mentioned to illustrate important domestic policy issues. These discussions may trump efforts to identify with voters in swing states. It is also important to keep in mind that voters in the swing states will also usually receive substantial courting through multiple campaign visits as well as name-dropping in televised debates.

Debates also include discussions of United States foreign policy and relations toward different regions and countries. The use of foreign place names may be directly affected by each candidate's platform and previous international experience. For example, incumbent candidates in presidential debates have a full term of experience in foreign affairs to highlight to the electorate, whereas challengers are commonly more limited in the scope of their international experience. Incumbents may view this contrast as an advantage to be leveraged in the debates by making more foreign references than the challenger.

A review of the 2012 debates suggests only limited support for a geographic skew associated with incumbency, foreign policy experience and the use of foreign place names (figure 4.8). While both candidates emphasized China, Southwest Asia, and North Africa (see table 4.2) and their total use of foreign place references is similar, there are differences in their ratios of total foreign versus domestic place names. For example, whereas 51 percent of Governor Romney's total place references were to foreign locations, 55 percent of President Obama's total place name references were to foreign places. Obama's greater use of foreign place names may reflect an effort to emphasize Romney's lack of foreign experience, which was highlighted during his preelection trip to Great Britain, Israel, and Poland. Perhaps the most glaring mishap pertaining to international issues occurred during the second debate, when Romney's charges against President Obama about the September 11, 2012, terrorist attack on the US consulate in Benghazi, Libya, were refuted by moderator Candy Crawley.

Finally, the use of geographic place names in presidential debates may also indicate candidate worldviews or, at minimum, the central international concerns dominating the election cycle (figure 4.8). Both candidates included China, Iran, and Israel among their five most frequently mentioned countries, while Iraq, Afghanistan, Pakistan, and Syria were among the top five foreign place names used by either President Obama or Governor Romney. China was mentioned a total of fifty-nine times by the two candidates, a significantly greater number than the forty-four

TABLE 4.1. Swing State References in the 2012 Debates as a Percentage of All Domestic References

	President Obama (%)	Governor Romney (%)
Debate 1	27	23
Debate 2	27	25
Debate 3	33	14

Source: Calculated by authors.

times Iran or thirty-four times Israel was mentioned by both Obama and Romney (see table 4.2).

Presidential debates have become an expected part of the campaign cycle and can be highly suggestive of each candidate's domestic emphasis as well as his or her understanding of international affairs. The states mentioned most often in the 2012 debates included those considered electoral battlegrounds and those associated with a major campaign issue such as health care. And given the emphasis on countries in North Africa-Southwest Asia by both candidates, this part of the world was surely a central focus in the worldviews of both President Obama and Governor Romney.

TABLE 4.2. Top Foreign References for Romney and Obama in 2012 Presidential Debates

Gov. Romney's Top Foreign References	Pres. Obama's Top Foreign References
China–28	China–31
Iran–26	Iraq–21
Israel–17	Iran–18
Syria–17	Afghanistan–18
Pakistan–14	Israel–17

Source: Calculated by authors.

NEWSPAPER ENDORSEMENTS

EDWARD HEATH ROBINSON AND GERALD R. WEBSTER

The 2012 elections found the nation's print newspapers in a weakened financial position as they increasingly competed with other outlets for readership. For example, according to the Newspaper Association of America, newspaper print and online revenue fell by over 40 percent between 2008 and 2012. One method by which newspapers may attract attention from readers in election years is through their endorsement of candidates for public office, especially since newspaper endorsements typically come in the final days of the campaign and may have some effect on the eventual choices of late-deciding voters.

Although newspaper endorsements likely come too late in the campaign cycle to be formative of the national mood, they may in the aggregate reflect such sentiment. This may be the case with the 2012 elections, when presidential candidate endorsements arguably reflected a decrease in enthusiasm for President Barack Obama but not a corresponding increase in enthusiasm for Republican challenger Mitt Romney. Of the hundred daily newspapers with the largest daily circulations in the United States in 2008, Obama received sixty-five endorsements, and John McCain received twenty-five endorsements. The remaining ten newspapers did not endorse either candidate. In 2012, however, Obama received forty-one endorsements, whereas Romney received thirty-five (figures 4.9 and 4.10). Only twelve major newspapers that endorsed Obama in 2008 switched to an endorsement of Romney in 2012. Therefore, while Governor Romney was endorsed by more major dailies than McCain, his totals were still below those for Obama in both 2008 and 2012.

Perhaps surprisingly, given the long history of newspaper endorsements for political candidates, a notable trend among the major newspapers is an increasing tendency to adopt policies against the endorsement of political candidates. The number of major newspapers that did not make an endorsement in the presidential race nearly tripled over the past four years—from ten in 2008 to twenty-four in 2012. Most did not do so because they had adopted non-endorsement policies between 2008 and 2012. Among the many reasons newspapers provided for discontinuing candidate endorsements were their perceived lack of effect, a desire to decrease the perception of newspaper partisanship, and because voters are not as reliant on newspapers for direction because digital technology has given voters access to greater quantities of information about political candidates than ever before. Only one major newspaper, the *Post-Standard* in Syracuse, New York, continues to endorse candidates but deliberately endorsed neither candidate this election cycle because they felt neither was worthy of endorsement.

Eleven of the major newspapers that had endorsed Obama in 2008 chose not to endorse any candidate this election cycle. Three newspapers that had endorsed McCain in 2008 also offered no endorsement. Ten of the eleven major newspapers that had endorsed Obama in 2008 but made no endorsement in 2012 and one newspaper that had endorsed McCain in 2008 but made no 2012 endorsement did so because they adopted either a general policy against endorsing political candidates in any election or a specific policy against endorsing candidates in presidential elections. Therefore, regardless of what the historical effects of newspaper endorsements have been on electoral outcomes, a growing number of major newspapers are voluntarily deciding against future endorsements.

Newspaper endorsements seem to garner the most attention when a traditionally liberal paper endorses a conservative candidate or vice versa. Likewise, notable are those situations

FIGURE 4.9

Daily Newspaper Endorsements: Obama Campaign
2012
Daily Newspaper
Circulation
10,000
50,000
100,000
500,000
1,000,000
1,500,000

FIGURE 4.10

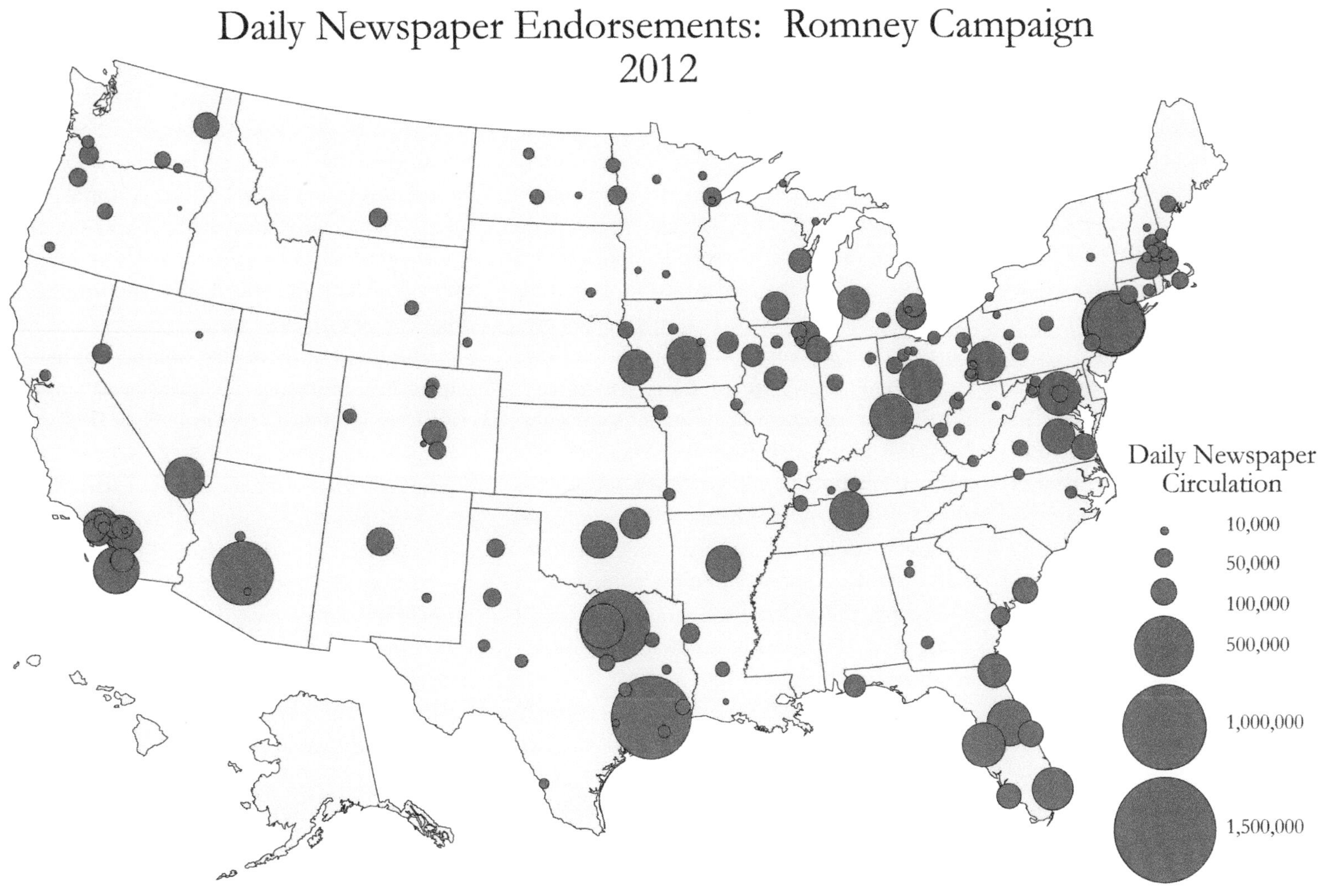

Daily Newspaper Endorsements: Romney Campaign
2012
Daily Newspaper
Circulation
10,000
50,000
100,000
500,000
1,000,000
1,500,000

in which a major newspaper in a state with which one candidate has personal ties chooses to back the other candidate. Obama was born in Hawaii but launched his political career in Chicago. Therefore, it might not be surprising that the *Honolulu Star-Advertiser* endorsed Obama in 2012 (even though the *Honolulu Advertiser*, which merged with the *Honolulu Star-Bulletin in* 2010, had not endorsed either Obama or McCain in 2008) or that the *Chicago Tribune* endorsed Obama for the second time in 2012. However, the *Chicago Sun-Times*, which had endorsed him in 2008, was one of the major newspapers to establish a new editorial policy against endorsements for the 2012 election.

Mitt Romney has many connections to Utah due to his Mormon faith and role in organizing the 2002 Winter Olympics held in that state. Despite these connections, the *Salt Lake Tribune* (which has the largest daily circulation in Salt Lake City) endorsed Obama in both 2008 and 2012. The *Deseret News*, also located in Salt Lake City and with a larger Sunday circulation than the *Salt Lake Tribune*, does not endorse political candidates as a matter of policy.

The newspapers that endorsed Governor Romney generally had smaller numbers of subscribers than those that endorsed Obama (figures 4.9 and 4.10). The mean circulation of the newspapers endorsing Romney was 185,023, and the median circulation was 331,096. In contrast, those endorsing Obama had a mean circulation of 244,268 and a median circulation of 832,605. As a result, even though in 2012 Romney had 50 percent percent more endorsements from major newspapers than McCain in 2008, these endorsements only reached 25 percent more subscribers due to the smaller size of the newspapers supporting him. Obama received 63 percent of the major newspaper endorsements in 2012 that he received in 2008, but these endorsements still reached a nearly exactly proportional 62 percent of newspaper subscribers due to the larger size of those papers supporting his reelection. In terms of total numbers, this meant that Romney's endorsements reached about 3.5 million fewer subscribers than Obama's endorsements. Moreover, given the trend toward not endorsing any presidential candidate, more subscribers received a newspaper that offered no endorsement than those who subscribed to a newspaper endorsing Romney.

The *San Antonio Express-News* was the only major newspaper that had endorsed McCain in 2008 but Obama in 2012, although some smaller papers made this switch as well. Newspapers that shifted endorsements in this manner often cited Obama's leadership on economics, health care, foreign policy, and support of the middle class. Although these papers frequently acknowledged the shortcomings of Obama's first term on these issues as well, they often argued that Romney had not sufficiently articulated consistent policies that were superior to Obama's positions. For those newspapers that endorsed Obama in 2008 but endorsed Romney in 2012, their editorial positions—particularly those with smaller circulations—generally centered on the importance of the economy and job creation and Romney's qualifications in those areas.

The trend of increasing numbers of newspapers not endorsing any presidential candidate is an interesting one in light of declining newspaper revenues and readership. In order to attract increased audience sizes and advertising revenues, other news outlets, including cable news channels, have been criticized for increasing partisanship and "infotainment" programming. Had newspapers followed this model, they might have increasingly sensationalized their endorsements in an attempt to increase readership and revenue. They appear to have selected a different approach, and it will be interesting to watch whether the general trend toward not endorsing candidates continues.

BALLOT ACCESS IN THE 2012 ELECTION

EDWARD HEATH ROBINSON AND GERALD R. WEBSTER

Voter access to the ballot box is considered one of the most fundamental constitutional rights in the United States. In spite of this view, access to the voting booth is complex in the United States because the individual states largely determine the specifics of voting procedures within certain federal constraints. As a result, the United States is a patchwork of state voting laws, regulations, and procedures that can make countrywide assessments concerning ballot access difficult. Here we briefly examine two indicators of ballot access: voter identification laws and wait times at the polls to vote.

After decades of efforts to increase voter participation in the United States, the 2012 election cycle saw an "abrupt shift in momentum" (Weiser and Norden 2011:1). Perhaps the most high-profile ballot-access issue this election cycle was an increase in the number of states that considered or approved voter identification laws, particularly those that require voters to present specific types of photo ID at the polling station prior to casting a ballot. This trend is especially notable since "[p]rior to the 2006 elections, *no* state required its voters to show government-issued photo ID at the polls (or elsewhere) in order to vote" (4).

Voter ID laws are most often proposed and enacted for the purported purpose of combating voter fraud. However, studies have found that voter fraud is uncommon, with the impersonation of an eligible voter at a polling station being particularly rare (Weiser and Norden 2011). Opponents of the laws see them as part of a voter suppression strategy targeting African American, Latino, and poor voters because they are less likely to have or be able to obtain certain forms of identification. Voter ID laws had been subject to the Voting Rights Act's section 5 preclearance process by the Department of Justice in all covered jurisdictions. For example, the preclearance process prevented a strict voter ID law from being implemented in Texas prior to the 2012 election. However, in June 2013, the United States Supreme Court struck down section 4 of the Voting Rights Act, which determined which jurisdictions were subject to preclearance. As a result, voter ID laws can now be more rapidly passed and implemented in previously covered states such as Mississippi, Texas, and Alabama since the Department of Justice no longer has the authority to block them if it determines they will have negative effects on the political positions of members of minority groups.

Voter ID laws can vary greatly among states in their requirements (figure 4.11; National Council of State Legislatures 2013). Here we group state voter ID laws into four general categories: no ID required, non-photo ID required, non-strict photo ID required, and strict photo ID required. "Non-photo ID" states such as Montana, Colorado, or Connecticut require some form of identification in order to vote, but current utility bills, bank statements, paychecks, government checks, or other government documents showing the voter's name and address are commonly accepted as identification. "Non-strict photo ID" states such as Idaho, Louisiana, and Michigan generally require some form of photo identification to vote. While driver's licenses, passports, and military IDs are acceptable, other kinds of photo identification such as student IDs, work-related IDs, or assisted living center photo IDs can also be used. States with "strict" photo ID laws such as Georgia, Indiana, and Kansas require specific types of photo ID. These generally include a passport,

FIGURE 4.11

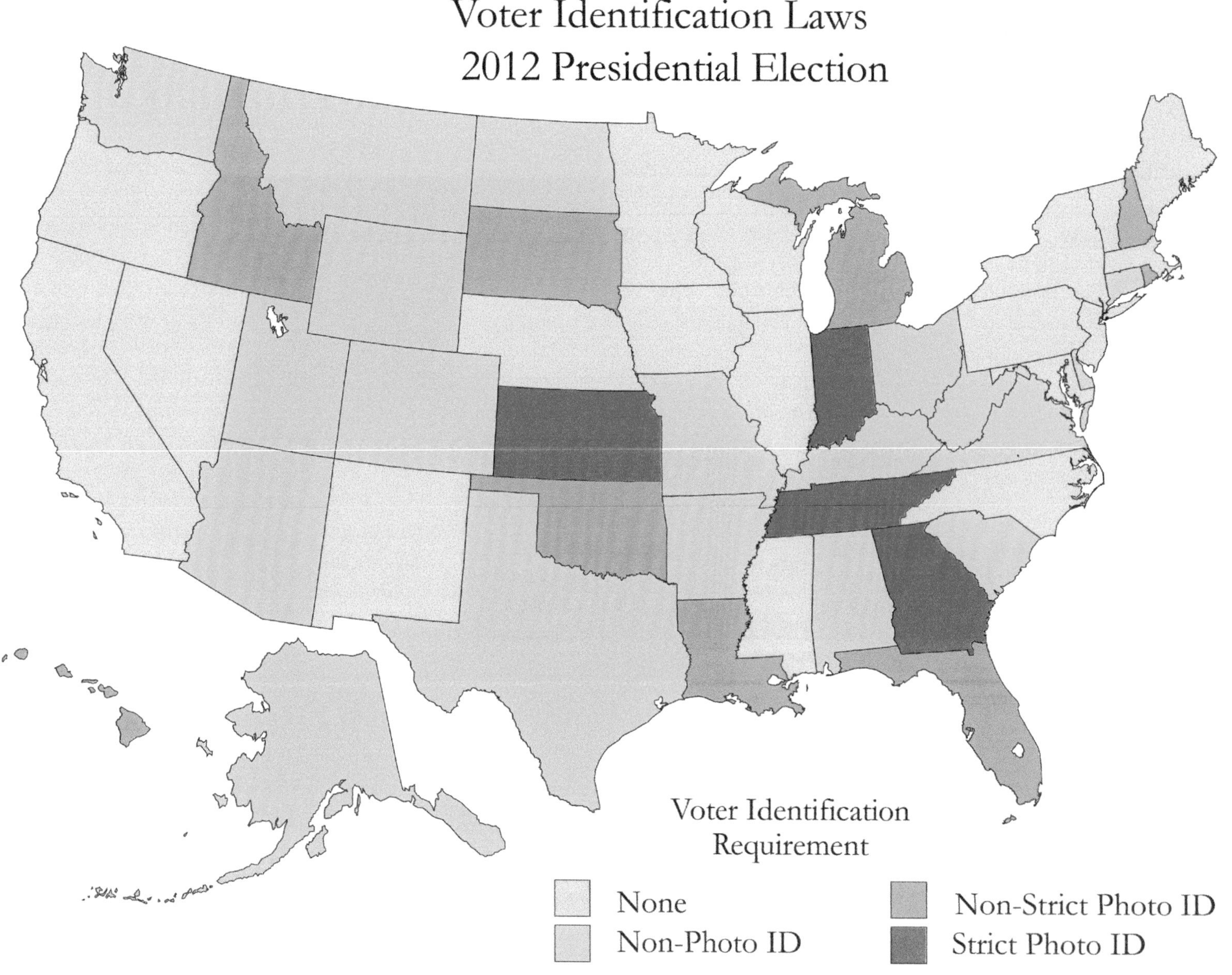
Voter Identification Laws
2012 Presidential Election
Voter Identification Requirement
None
Non-Photo ID
Non-Strict Photo ID
Strict Photo ID

a state driver's license, a state-issued identification card, or a military ID, but student IDs are generally not accepted, most particularly if they do not have an expiration date.

Disagreements about whether a particular kind of photo ID is acceptable can become highly politicized. For instance, Wisconsin's original voter ID legislation did not accept student IDs as valid for voter identification. After much controversy, an amendment was passed making student IDs acceptable if they met certain criteria. Notably, in spite of the amendment, IDs issued by the University of Wisconsin system did not meet the legal criteria for use at the polls (Averill 2011). Also, because obtaining an acceptable ID often requires a processing fee, voter ID laws have been challenged in some jurisdictions on the basis that they constitute poll taxes, which have been unconstitutional since ratification of the Twenty-Fourth Amendment in 1964. As a result, some states have established mechanisms for providing free IDs to voters for identification purposes at the polls. Providing free identification has the potential to be expensive, so some states require a person to specifically request a free ID or to sign a pledge that the ID is needed for voting purposes before waiving the fee (Weiser and Norden 2011).

Even citizens who have the appropriate identification to cast ballots may find additional obstacles to voting, such as the amount of time needed to cast a vote after arriving at the polling station (figure 4.12). Reports of long lines can dissuade voters from making the trip to the polling station and provide for provocative TV news images on election night. In 2012, President Obama acknowledged in his acceptance speech that some voters had to wait in very long lines to vote, remarking that "by the way, we have to fix that." While the average wait time to vote in the country as a whole is low, voters in different places can experience dramatically different wait times. For instance, according to Stewart's (forthcoming) analysis of wait times to cast ballots, voters in Vermont experienced an average wait time of less than two minutes, while the average wait time in Florida was nearly forty minutes. But even aggregating data by state obscures tremendous variability. The actual wait time experienced by Floridians in different counties varied between 131 minutes in Lee County to only about 6.7 minutes in St. Johns County.

According to Stewart (forthcoming), when countrywide wait times are analyzed demographically, the most determinative variable regarding average wait time is race. Nationally in 2012, African Americans waited an average of twenty-three minutes to vote, Hispanics nineteen minutes, and non-Hispanic whites twelve minutes. This, of course, fuels concern that the combined effects of increasingly restrictive ballot access measures (which not only includes voter ID laws but restrictions on voter registration drives, permanent or long-term disenfranchisement after felony convictions, reduced early voting opportunities, and restrictions on same-day and Election Day registration) disproportionally disqualify voters belonging to ethnic or racial minority groups.

REFERENCES

Averill, A. (2011). "After Months in Limbo, Voter ID Bill Will Include University Cards." *Badger Herald*, May 1, 2011. Accessed November 2, 2013. http://badgerherald.com/news/2011/05/01/after-months-in-limb/.

Bennett, J. 2012. "The New Price of American Politics." *Atlantic Monthly*, October. Accessed September 20, 2012. http://www.theatlantic.com/magazine/archive/2012/10/the/309086/.

Center for Responsive Politics. "2012 Election Spending Will Reach $6 Billion, Center for Responsive Politics Predicts." Accessed October 30, 2013. http://www.opensecrets.org/news/2012/10/2012-election-spending-will-reach-6.html.

Corn, D. 2012. "The Story Behind the 47 Percent Video." *Mother Jones*, December 31. Accessed January 13, 2014. http://www.motherjones.com/politics/2012/12/story-behind-47-video.

Federal Election Commission. 2012. 2012 Presidential Election, Contributor Data Files. Accessed

FIGURE 4.12

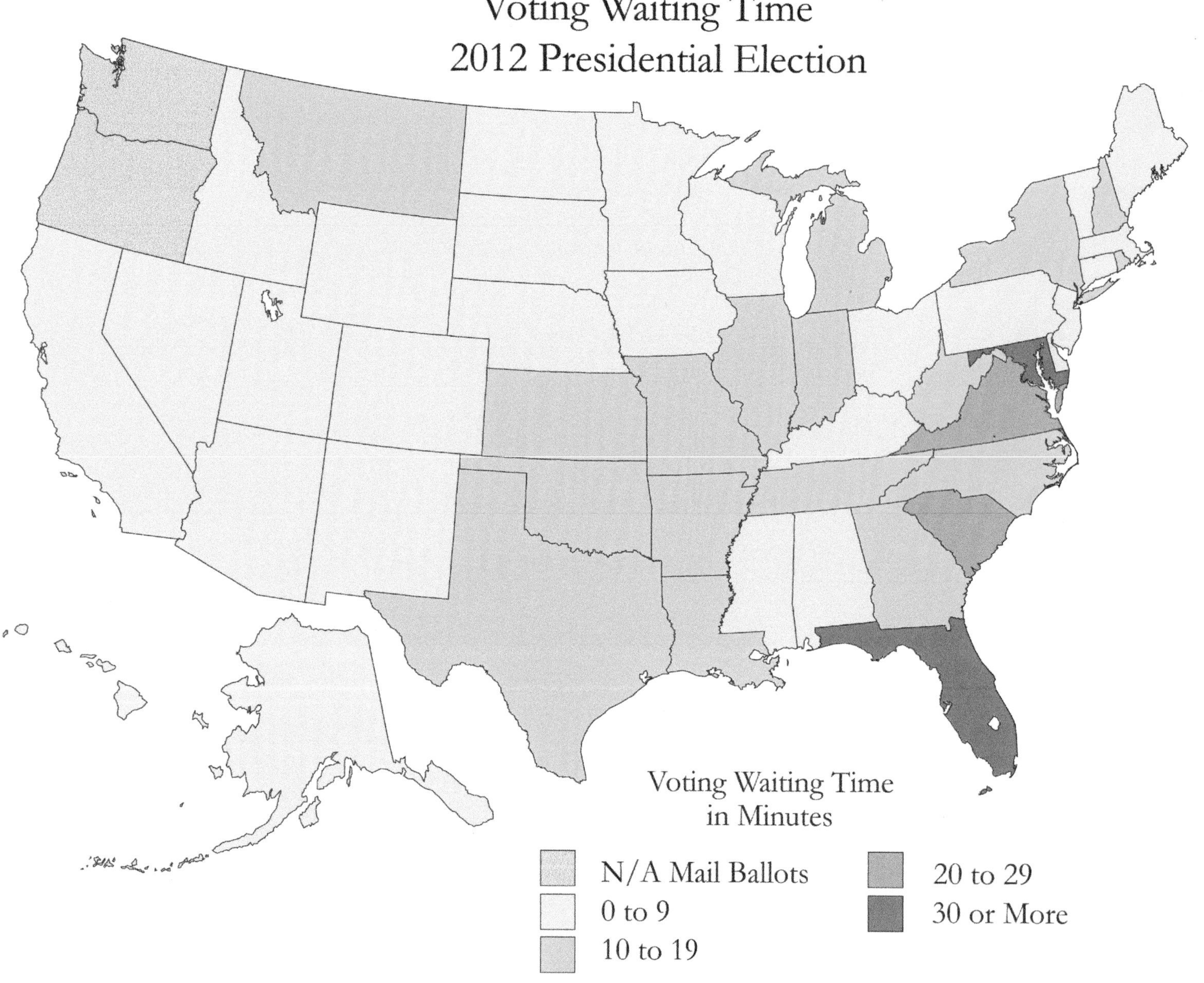

Voting Waiting Time
2012 Presidential Election
Voting Waiting Time
in Minutes
N/A Mail Ballots
0 to 9
10 to 19
20 to 29
30 or More

April 22, 2014. http://www.fec.gov/press/bkgnd/pres_cf/pres_cf_Even.shtml.

Federal Election Commission, Obama. 2012a. "Two-Year Campaign Contributions." Accessed October 30, 2013. http://www.fec.gov.

Federal Election Commission, Obama. 2012b. "Two-Year Campaign Expenditures." Accessed October 30, 2013. http://fec.gov/disclosurep/pnational.do.

Federal Election Commission, Romney. 2012a. "Two-Year Campaign Contributions." Accessed June–October 30, 2013. http://www.fec.gov.

Federal Election Commission, Romney. 2012b. "Two Year Campaign Expenditures." Accessed October 30, 2013. http://fec.gov/disclosurep/pnational.do.

Haynes, A., P. Gurian, and S. Nichols. 1997. "The Role of Candidate Spending in President Nomination Campaigns." *Journal of Politics* 59 (1): 213–25.

National Broadcast Company. 2011. "Obama 2012 HQ in Prudential Building." March 28. Accessed October 30, 2013. http://www.nbcchicago.com/news/local/Obama-Election-HQ--118764779.html.

National Council of State Legislatures. 2013. "Voter Identification Requirements." Accessed November 5, 2013. http://www.ncsl.org/research/elections-and-campaigns/voter-id.aspx.

Real Clear Politics 2012. "Obama vs. Romney Compared to Obama vs. McCain." Accessed February 13, 2014. http://www.realclearpolitics.com/epolls/2012/president/obama_vs_romney_compared_to_obama_vs_mccain.html.

Romney, M. 2008. "Let Detroit Go Bankrupt." *New York Times*, November 18. Accessed April 18, 2014. http://www.nytimes.com/2008/11/19/opinion/19romney.html?_r=0.

Shrum, R. 2012. "Romney Won the Debate but It Was No Game Changer." *Daily Beast*, October 4. Accessed October 5, 2012. http://www.thedailybeast.com/articles/2012/10/04/romney-won-the-debate-but-it-was-no-game-changer.html.

Silver, N. 2012a. "Measuring a Convention Bounce." *FiveThirtyEight*, August 29. Accessed October 10, 2012. http://fivethirtyeight.blogs.nytimes.com/2012/08/29/measuring-a-convention-bounce/?_php=true&_type=blogs&_r=0.

Silver, N. 2012b. "Obama's Lead Looks Stronger in Polls That Include Cellphones." *FiveThirtyEight*, September 19. Accessed October 10, 2012. http://fivethirtyeight.blogs.nytimes.com/2012/09/19/obamas-lead-looks-stronger-in-polls-that-include-cellphones/?_php=true&_type=blogs&_r=0.

Silver, N. 2012c. "The Impact of the '47 Percent.'" *FiveThirtyEight*, September 28. Accessed October 10, 2012. http://fivethirtyeight.blogs.nytimes.com/2012/09/28/sept-27-the-impact-of-the-47-percent/?_php=true&_type=blogs&_r=0.

Silver, N. 2012d. "First Debate Often Helps Challenger in Polls." *FiveThirtyEight*, October 3. Accessed October 6, 2012. http://fivethirtyeight.blogs.nytimes.com/2012/10/03/first-debate-often-helps-challenger-in-polls/?_php=true&_type=blogs&_r=0.

Silver, N. 2012e. "Which Polls Fared Best (and Worst) in the 2012 Presidential Race." *FiveThirtyEight*, November 10. Accessed April 1, 2013. http://fivethirtyeight.blogs.nytimes.com/2012/11/10/which-polls-fared-best-and-worst-in-the-2012-presidential-race/?_php=true&_type=blogs&_r=0.

Silver, N. 2012f. "When Internal Polls Mislead, a Whole Campaign May Be to Blame." *FiveThirtyEight*, December 1. Accessed April 1, 2013. http://fivethirtyeight.blogs.nytimes.com/2012/12/01/when-internal-polls-mislead-a-whole-campaign-may-be-to-blame/?_php=true&_type=blogs&_r=0.

Stewart III, C. Forthcoming. "Waiting to Vote in 2012." *Journal of Law and Politics.*

Sutherland, C., and G. R. Webster. 1994. "The Geography of the 1992 U.S. Presidential Debates." *Geographical Bulletin* 36(2): 83–93.

Thompson, D. 2012. "The 47%: Who They Are, Where They Live, How They Vote, and Why They Matter," *Atlantic.com*. Accessed February 13, 2014. http://www.theatlantic.com/business/archive/2012/09/the-47-who-they-are-where-they-live-how-they-vote-and-why-they-matter/262506/.

Weiser, W. R., and L. D. Norden. 2011. *Voting Law Changes in 2012*. New York: Brennan Center for Justice at New York University School of Law.

OUTCOMES

RESULTS OF THE 2012 PRESIDENTIAL ELECTION AT THE STATE AND COUNTY LEVELS

FRED M. SHELLEY

The lengthy campaign for the presidency came to an end on November 6, 2012, when ballots for the presidential election as well as state and local elections were counted. When the counting was completed, it was evident that the Democratic Party's nominee, President Barack Obama, had been reelected over his Republican challenger, former governor of Massachusetts Mitt Romney. Obama and his running mate, Vice President Joe Biden, received nearly 66 million popular votes to about 61 million for their Republican opponents, Romney and Representative Paul Ryan of Wisconsin. Thus, Obama and Biden won about 51.1 percent of the popular vote nationwide as compared with 47.2 percent for Romney and Ryan. In the Electoral College, Obama defeated Romney by a margin of 332–206. Obama and Biden carried twenty-six of the fifty states, along with the District of Columbia, while Romney carried the remaining twenty-four states (figure 5.1).

In the parlance of political scientists, the 2012 election was a maintaining election. In other words, the geographic pattern of votes in 2012 was quite similar to that of the 2008 election, in which Obama was elected to his first term. That the two elections showed similar patterns of support for the two parties is underscored by the fact that forty-eight of the fifty states cast their electoral votes for the same party in both elections. Only Indiana and North Carolina, whose electoral votes were won by Obama in 2008, gave their electoral voters to Romney in 2012. (One electoral vote in Nebraska, which allocates its electoral votes by House of Representatives district, also switched from Democratic in 2008 to Republican in 2012.)

Despite the geographic similarities between the two elections, the 2012 election is noteworthy for several reasons. Perhaps most importantly, it represented the fourth Democratic win in the six most recent elections. Democrat Bill Clinton won in 1992 and 1996 while Republican George W. Bush won in 2000 and 2004; however, Bush's 2000 win was bitterly contested, and in fact his Democratic

FIGURE 5.1

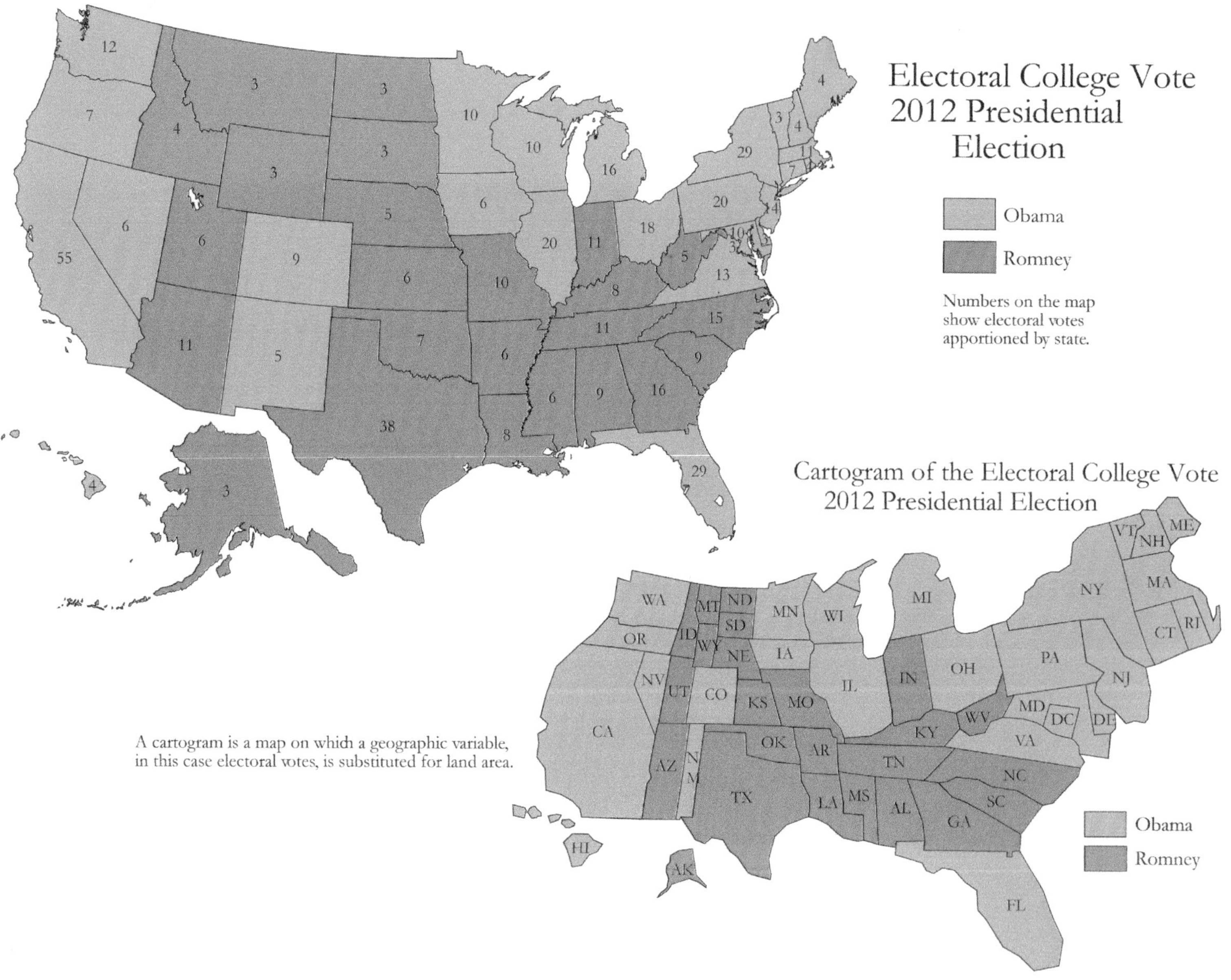

A cartogram is a map on which a geographic variable, in this case electoral votes, is substituted for land area.

opponent, Al Gore, received about half a million more popular votes that did Bush himself. Bush was reelected more comfortably in 2004, although his Electoral College and popular vote margins were less than those enjoyed by Clinton and Obama in their successful campaigns. In fact, Obama became the first Democrat to win more than 50 percent of the popular vote in consecutive elections since Franklin D. Roosevelt did so between 1932 and 1944.

Thus, the 2012 election reiterated the Democratic Party's domination of the presidency since the early 1990s. The outcome of the election was a heavy blow to Republicans who hoped that the tepid state of the national economy and the unpopularity of the Affordable Care Act (often known as "Obamacare") would swing the electorate in their favor. However, not enough voters swung from the Democrats in 2008 to the Republicans in 2012 to secure a Republican victory.

The 2012 election was also noteworthy in that three successive presidents—Clinton, Bush, and Obama—were each elected for two terms. This happened previously only in 1820, when James Monroe followed Thomas Jefferson and James Madison in winning a second term at a time when many states had not yet chosen their representatives to the Electoral College by popular vote. That Clinton, Bush, and Obama all won reelection underscores that the 2012 presidential election was a maintaining election. Although Clinton and Obama are Democrats and Bush is a Republican, in all six elections there was relatively little difference in geographic pattern. With only a few exceptions, those states that were most Republican in 1992 were, in many cases, the same states that were most Republican in 2012, and vice versa.

The 2012 election occurred also at a period in history in which American electoral politics has become increasingly polarized, both in terms of issue positions and in geographic terms. As other sections in this volume document, the Democrats have become an increasingly metropolitan-oriented party. In both 2008 and 2012, Obama owes his margin of victory to very strong support in the country's largest metropolitan areas and especially in central cities. Suburban areas were divided more evenly, and a majority of voters in nonmetropolitan and rural areas chose Romney over Obama.

Polarization is also evident along racial lines. As in 2008, African Americans gave well over 90 percent of their votes to Obama while Latinos and Asian Americans also gave him very large majorities. Meanwhile, Obama won only a minority of votes cast by white voters and, according to exit polls, he won a majority of popular votes among white voters in only nine states. Polarization on the basis of age was also evident, as in 2008. Exit polls indicate that voters under thirty supported Obama by a margin of nearly two to one, whereas older voters, and especially those age sixty-five and over, gave Romney solid majorities. The degree to which polarization was evident in the 2012 presidential election is also indicated by margins of victory. Although Obama won the popular vote over Romney by a margin of about 4 percent, in a majority of the country's counties, the candidate who won the most votes did so by a margin of more than 20 percent over his opponent.

How many people voted, and for whom did those living in different places cast their ballots? And how does this pattern compare with those of previous elections? Figure 5.2 and figure 5.3 show levels of voter turnout on a statewide and on a county-by-county basis throughout the country, respectively. According to the Center for the Study of the American Electorate, about 57.5 percent of eligible voters cast ballots in the 2012 presidential election. This turnout level was down slightly from 2008, in which 62.3 percent of eligible voters participated, and 2004, when the turnout rate was 60.4 percent. The lower turnout may help to explain why Obama's margin of victory in 2012 was less than that of 2008, because many of Obama's core constituencies, including minority and young voters, tend to be less likely to vote than is the case with other demographic groups.

As figures 5.2 and 5.3 indicate, voter turnout rates varied considerably across the United States. For decades, voter turnout rates have been highest in the northern part of the country and have tended to decline from north to south. This pattern held true in 2012, but with some exceptions. Most notably, turnout rates were higher than might have been expected

Voter Turnout
2008
2012
Percentage of Voting
Age Population
Who Voted
48.6 to 49.9
50.0 to 54.9
55.0 to 59.9
60.0 to 64.9
65.0 to 69.9
70.0 to 70.8
39.9 to 49.9
50.0 to 54.9
55.0 to 59.9
60.0 to 64.9
65.0 to 69.9
70.0 to 71.5
Change in Voter Turnout
2008 to 2012
Percent Change
0.0 to 2.5
-2.0 to -0.1
-4.0 to -2.1
-6.0 to -4.1
-8.0 to -6.1
-10.8 to -8.1

FIGURE 5.3

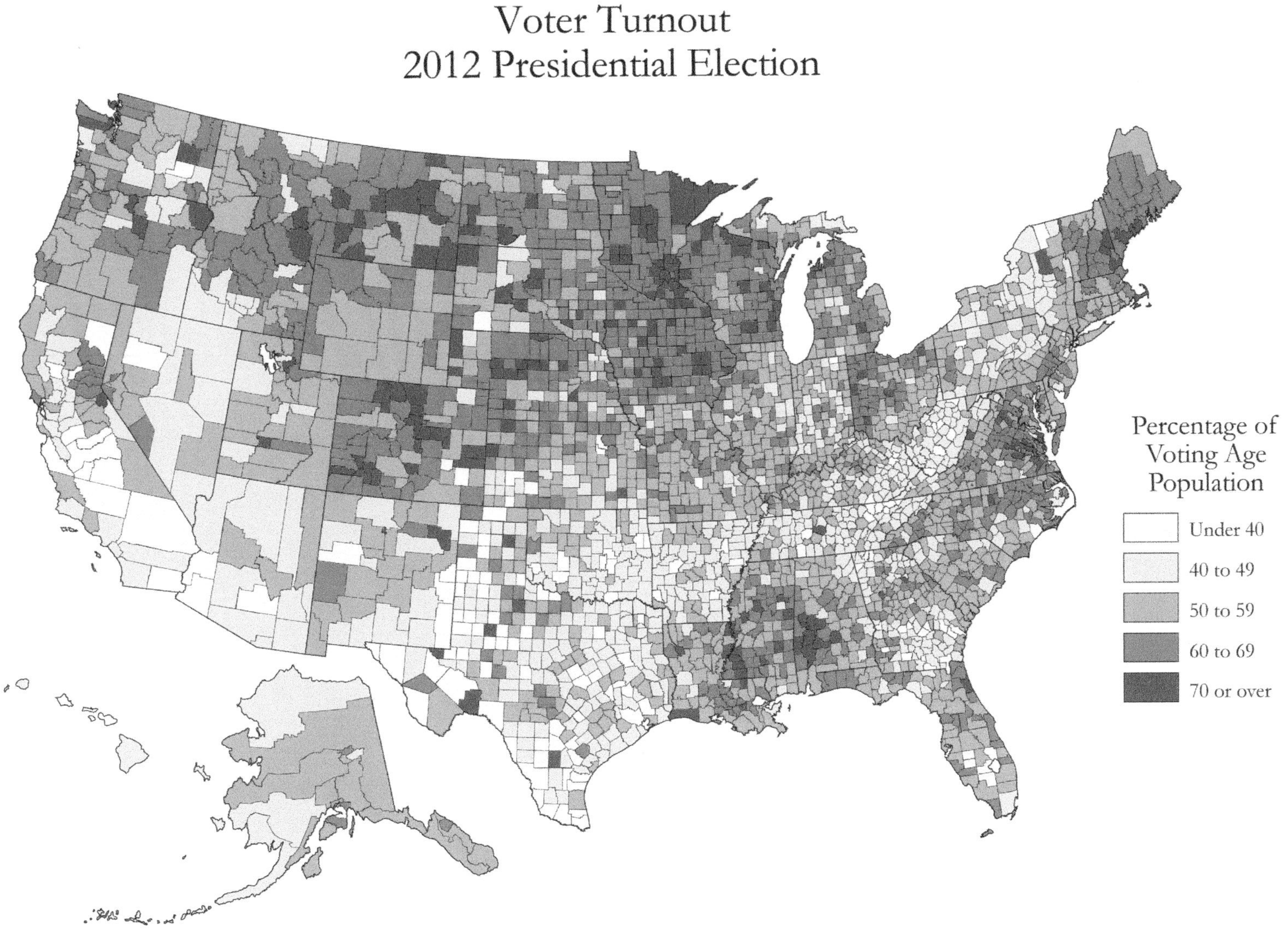

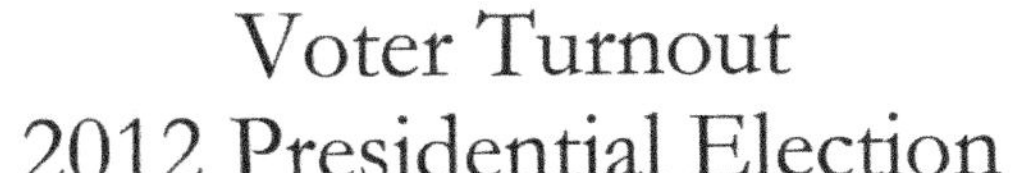

Voter Turnout
2012 Presidential Election
Percentage of
Voting Age
Population
Under 40
40 to 49
50 to 59
60 to 69
70 or over

in some of the most closely contested swing states, notably Ohio, Florida, Colorado, Virginia, and North Carolina. That turnout rates did not drop off in these states relative to others is evident from the comparison between 2012 and 2008 shown in figure 5.2. The high turnout rates in these states no doubt reflect the fact that campaigning and campaign advertising was concentrated in them because it was known that the popular vote outcomes in these places would determine the outcome of the election nationwide. Turnout rates were relatively less in states that were less closely contested. This can be observed in figure 5.3 by comparing county-level turnout rates in closely contested Colorado with those in counties in adjacent, deep-red Utah and Wyoming.

Elsewhere, the north-south pattern was evident in many parts of the country. Historically, the Upper Midwest states of Minnesota, Wisconsin, and Iowa have reported some of the highest turnout rates in the country. 2012 was no exception. Turnout rates may have been even higher there because the Republicans had some hope of carrying these states going into the fall campaign—especially Wisconsin, the home state of Romney's running mate, Paul Ryan. However, Obama ended up carrying all three of these states.

Turnout was generally lower than average in a large group of counties extending through Appalachian West Virginia and Kentucky westward through Tennessee, Arkansas, and Oklahoma. This region is the only area of the country in which Obama did worse in the popular vote than the 2004 Democratic nominee, John Kerry. Low turnout in the region in 2012 may be explained on the basis of voter distaste for both nominees (as evidenced by the fact that Romney lost most of these counties in the Republican Party primaries) and by the fact that none of these states was closely contested between the two major-party candidates. On the other hand, turnout rates were high in many counties containing large numbers of rural African Americans, notably in Louisiana, Mississippi, Alabama, and southeastern Virginia.

The overall pattern of popular vote in 2012 was strikingly similar to that in 2008, although differences between the two elections are evident at both the state and the county level. Figure 5.4 (state-level popular vote) shows the percentage of the popular vote won by Obama, who got about 51.1 percent of the popular vote nationwide, in each state. Obama's highest percentages were recorded in the District of Columbia and in his native Hawaii, in which he got more than 70 percent of the popular vote. He exceeded 60 percent in six other states: Vermont, New York, Rhode Island, Maryland, Massachusetts, and California. Importantly, Democratic nominees have carried all seven of these states in every election since 1992.

Figure 5.4 also shows the distribution of popular votes for Romney, whose strength was concentrated in smaller and more rural states. Romney got more than 70 percent of the vote in Utah and Wyoming, and he exceeded 60 percent in six other states. As with the Democrats, all eight of the states that Romney carried with more than 60 percent of the vote have gone Republican in every election since 1992. The figure also shows the distribution of votes for third-party candidates combined. These third-party candidates earned less than 2 percent of the total popular vote nationwide, but vote percentages for these third-party candidates showed meaningful geographical variation.

Although Obama won the electoral voters of twenty-six of the fifty states, he carried only a small minority of counties throughout the country. This is illustrated by figure 5.5 (county-level winner), which categorizes each of the counties on the basis of which candidate won the most popular votes. In most of the counties, either Obama or Romney won a majority of the vote, but in a few counties, neither won as much as 50 percent of the vote. In these cases, the map identifies the candidate who won a plurality of the popular vote.

Although the Democrats won popular-vote majorities in only about 15 percent of the counties nationwide, they won the election by amassing large majorities in many large and densely populated counties throughout the country. In addition to Washington, DC, Obama enjoyed very large percentages of the popular vote in large central cities. This is illustrated in figure 5.6, which shows the overall Democratic percentage of the popular vote by county across the United States. Although Obama exceeded 70 percent of the

FIGURE 5.4

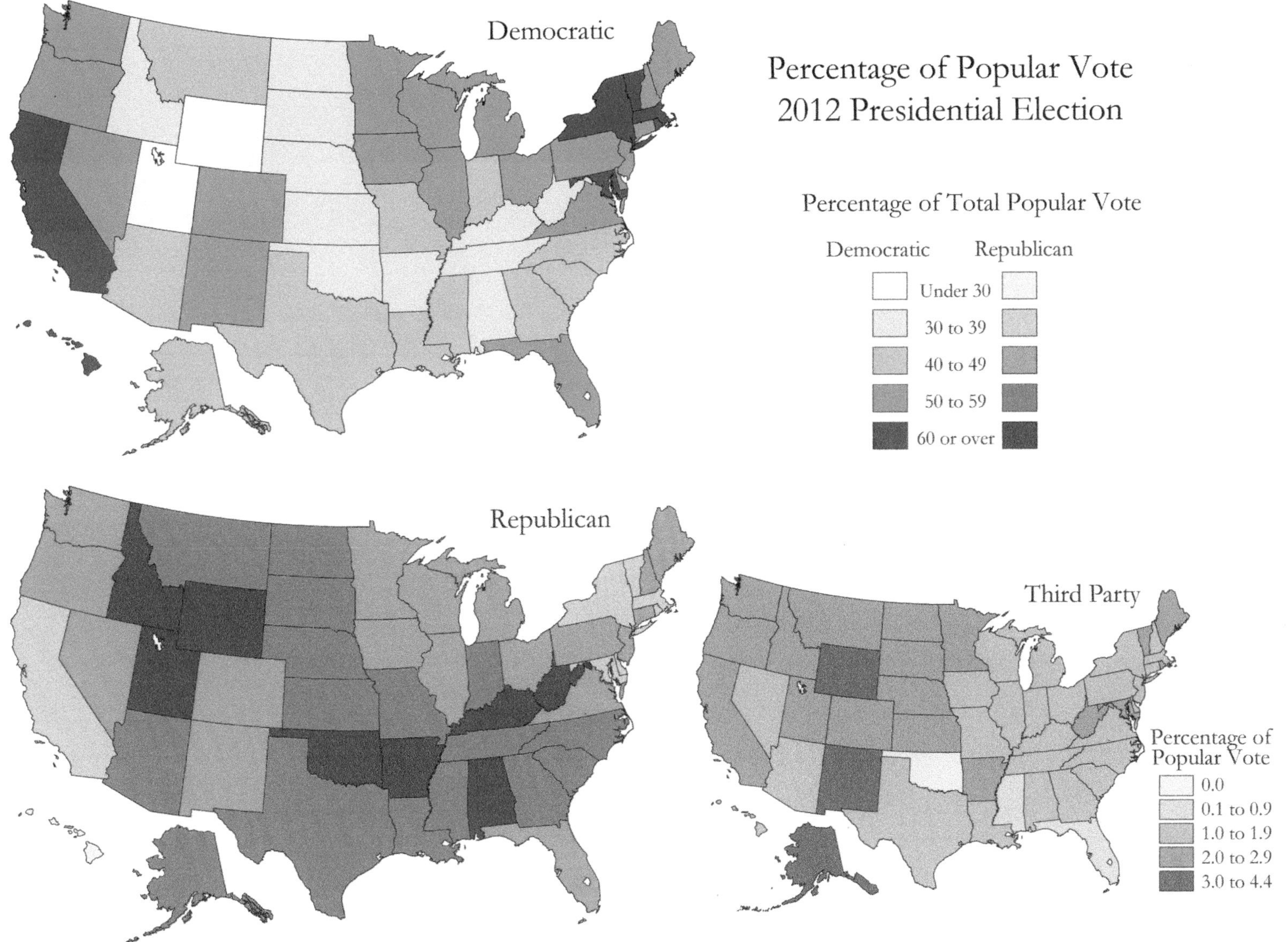
Democratic
Percentage of Popular Vote
2012 Presidential Election
Percentage of Total Popular Vote
Democratic
Republican
Under 30
30 to 39
40 to 49
50 to 59
60 or over
Republican
Third Party
Percentage of
Popular Vote
0.0
0.1 to 0.9
1.0 to 1.9
2.0 to 2.9
3.0 to 4.4

FIGURE 5.5

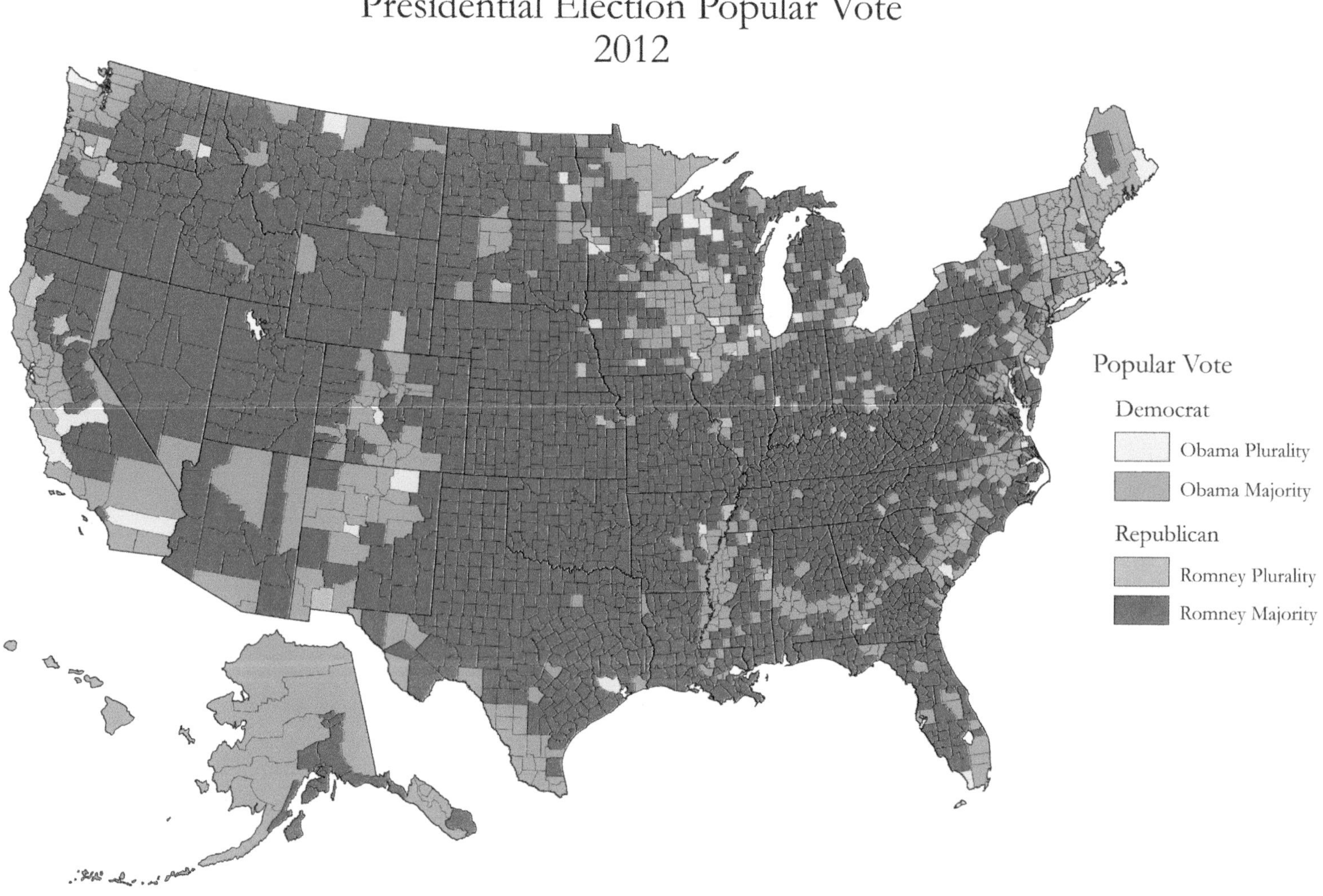
Presidential Election Popular Vote
2012
Popular Vote
Democrat
Obama Plurality
Obama Majority
Republican
Romney Plurality
Romney Majority

popular vote in only a few counties, these counties included the largest counties contained within New York City as well as Cook County, Illinois (Chicago), Wayne County, Michigan (Detroit), Suffolk County, Massachusetts (Boston), and several highly urbanized counties in the San Francisco Bay area of California. Obama won the electoral votes of several states despite losing most of those states' counties, notably Michigan, Ohio, Illinois, Florida, Pennsylvania, Nevada, Oregon, and Washington. Here as elsewhere, Obama's large margins in urban counties outweighed Romney's smaller margins in more rural territory, as evidenced by figure 5.7.

Outside of central cities, Obama's highest margins were generally found in rural counties populated by large minority communities. He won more than 70 percent of the popular vote in a group of counties extending from the Mississippi delta region of western Mississippi, northeastern Louisiana, and southeastern Arkansas extending eastward through central Alabama into eastern portions of South Carolina, North Carolina, and Virginia. African Americans make up the majority of the populations of many of these rural counties. Similarly, counties along the Rio Grande in extreme southern Texas are heavily Mexican American. Obama also did very well in counties containing American Indian reservations, most notably in North Dakota, South Dakota, and New Mexico.

Given that Obama and Romney between them won more than 98 percent of the popular vote across the United States, it is not surprising that the areas strongly supportive of Obama gave little support to Romney, and vice versa. Romney won more than 85 percent of the counties nationwide, but where did he get his highest percentages? Romney's strongest places were rural areas, as can be observed in figure 5.8 (Romney percentage by county).

As Figure 5.8 illustrates, Romney won more than 70 percent of the popular vote in a wide swath of counties across the Great Plains from western Texas northward to North Dakota and eastern Montana, with the notable exception of counties with American Indian reservations, as indicated previously. The large region containing Romney's strongest counties extended westward into the Rocky Mountain West, notably in rural areas of Wyoming, Idaho, Utah, and Nevada. However, most of these counties have small populations, and their high percentages of support for Romney had very little impact on the presidential election nationwide. For example, more than two-thirds of Nevada's people live in Clark County, which contains the city of Las Vegas and whose voters gave Obama a comfortable majority of its popular vote. Obama's margin in Clark County easily outweighed Romney's larger percentages in the rural counties, and the Democrats carried the state without difficulty.

The other region containing large numbers of counties whose voters supported Romney strongly was Appalachia, in which Romney won majorities of 60 percent or more in most of the counties in a belt from southwestern Pennsylvania and extreme western Maryland southward and westward to Tennessee, northern Alabama, and northwestern Georgia. As elsewhere, Romney did best in rural counties with primarily white populations. In Tennessee, for example, Romney lost the counties containing Nashville and Memphis, although he carried all but two of the remaining counties in the state.

That Obama won the election while losing the large majority of counties across the United States is evident also from the map showing his margin of victory by percentage (figure 5.9). As the map indicates, many of the counties that Obama carried gave him a margin of at least 20 percent of the vote—in other words, 60 percent or more of the vote. This map underscores the fact that Obama's strength in large cities was the key to his victory. Similarly, the large majority of Romney's counties gave him margins of more than 20 percent (figure 5.10). Most of these are rural counties. Thus, figures 5.9 and 5.10 also illustrate the degree to which presidential politics have become polarized nationwide.

With more than 98 percent of the voters having cast ballots for Obama or Romney, the impact of third parties on the election was negligible. However, several third-party candidates contested for the presidency, notably the Libertarian and Green Parties. The Libertarian candidates were former governor Gary Johnson of New Mexico for president and former judge James Gray of California for

FIGURE 5.6

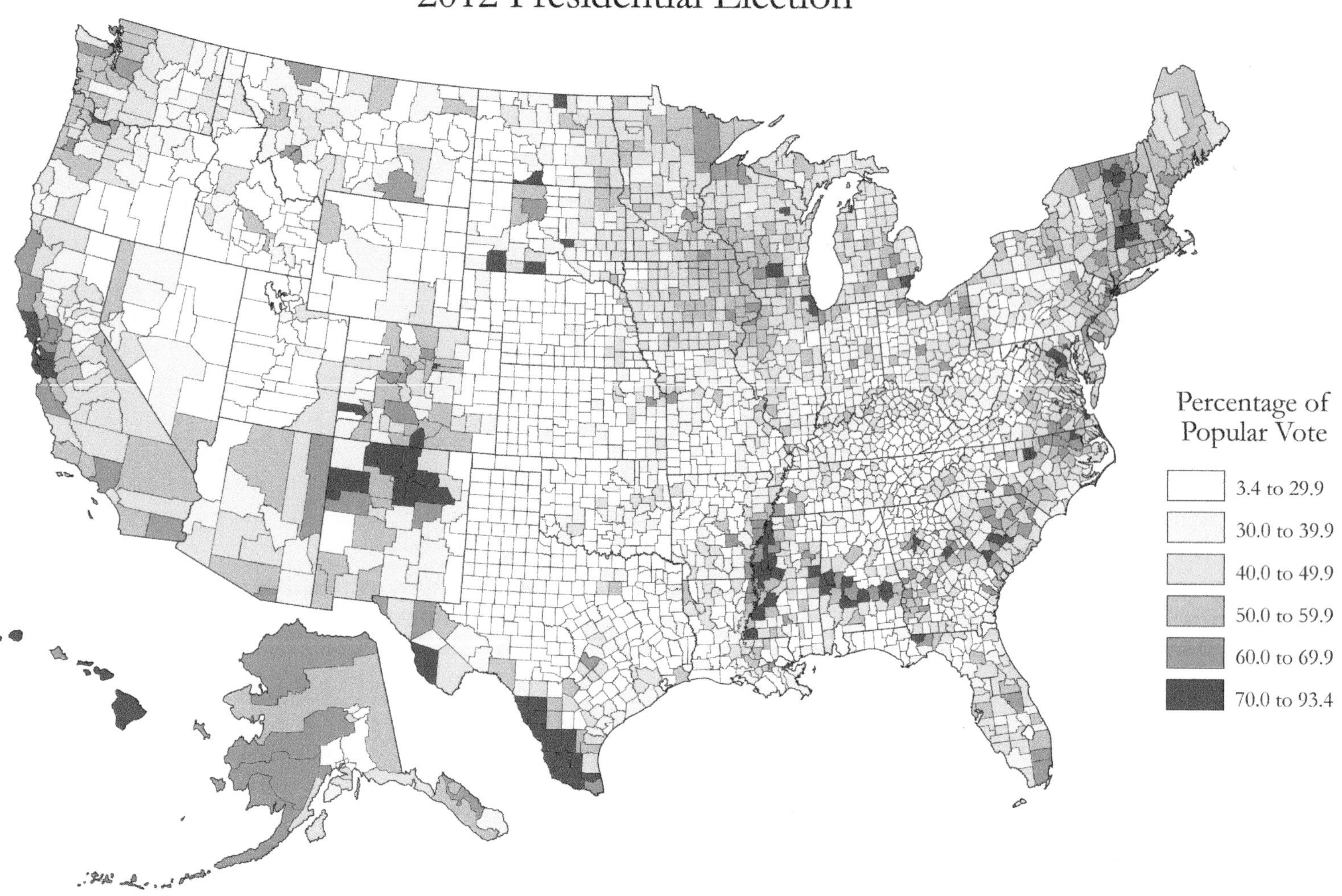
Democratic Popular Vote
2012 Presidential Election
Percentage of
Popular Vote
3.4 to 29.9
30.0 to 39.9
40.0 to 49.9
50.0 to 59.9
60.0 to 69.9
70.0 to 93.4

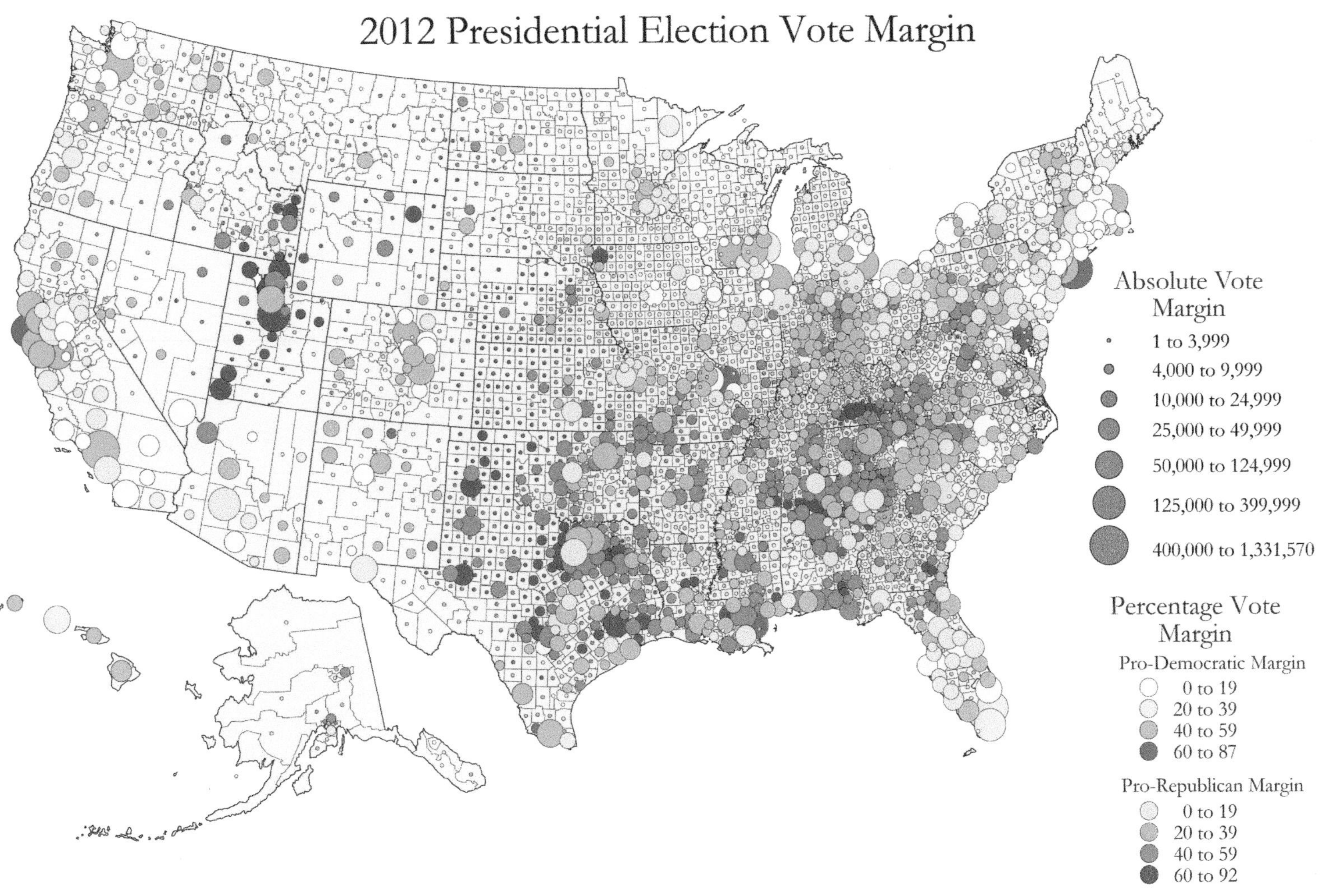
2012 Presidential Election Vote Margin
Absolute Vote Margin
1 to 3,999
4,000 to 9,999
10,000 to 24,999
25,000 to 49,999
50,000 to 124,999
125,000 to 399,999
400,000 to 1,331,570
Percentage Vote Margin
Pro-Democratic Margin
0 to 19
20 to 39
40 to 59
60 to 87
Pro-Republican Margin
0 to 19
20 to 39
40 to 59
60 to 92

FIGURE 5.8

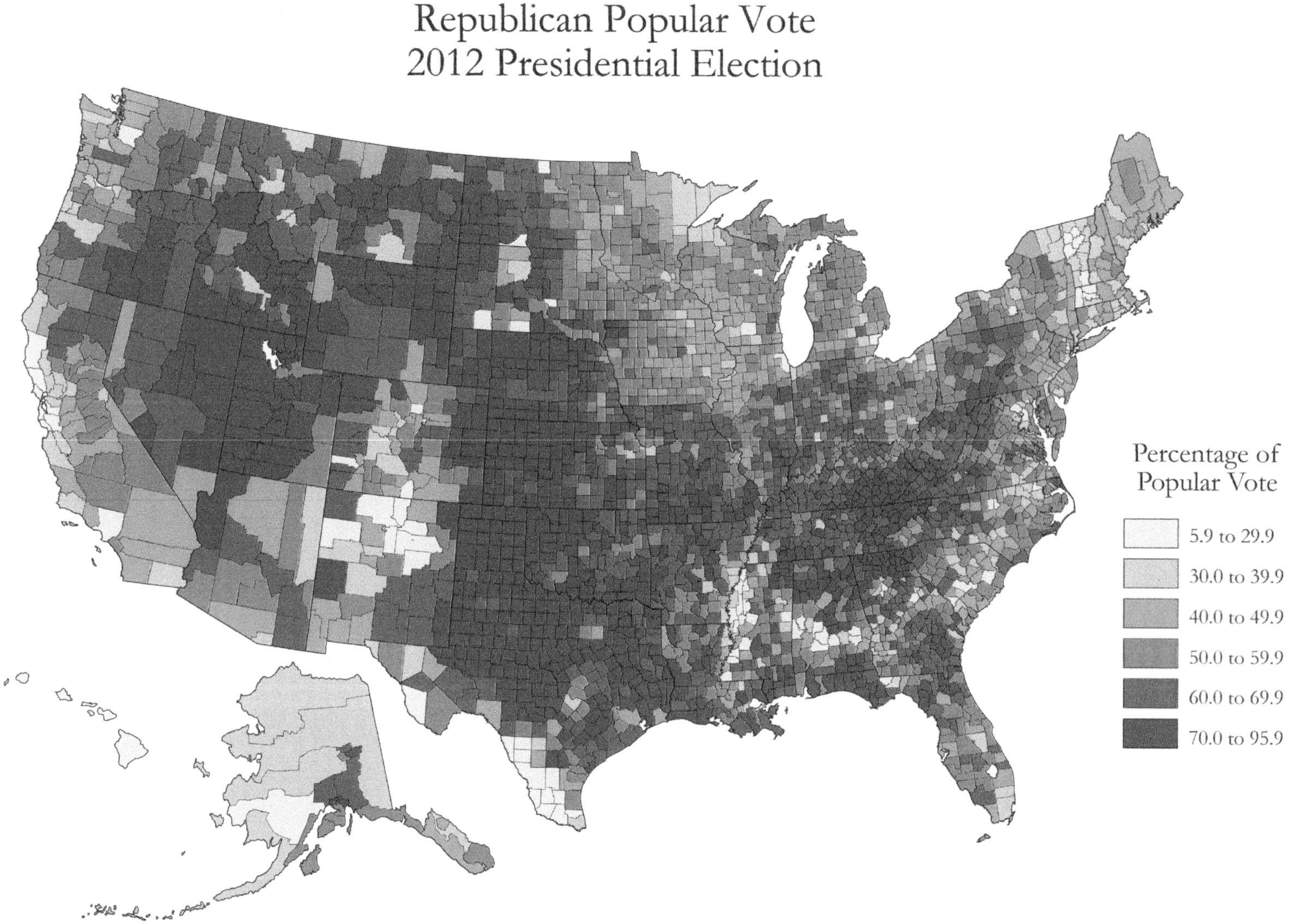

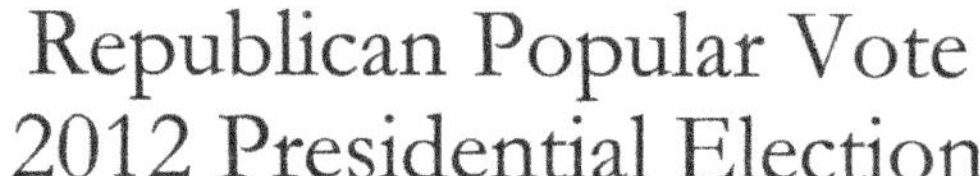

Republican Popular Vote
2012 Presidential Election
Percentage of
Popular Vote
5.9 to 29.9
30.0 to 39.9
40.0 to 49.9
50.0 to 59.9
60.0 to 69.9
70.0 to 95.9

FIGURE 5.9

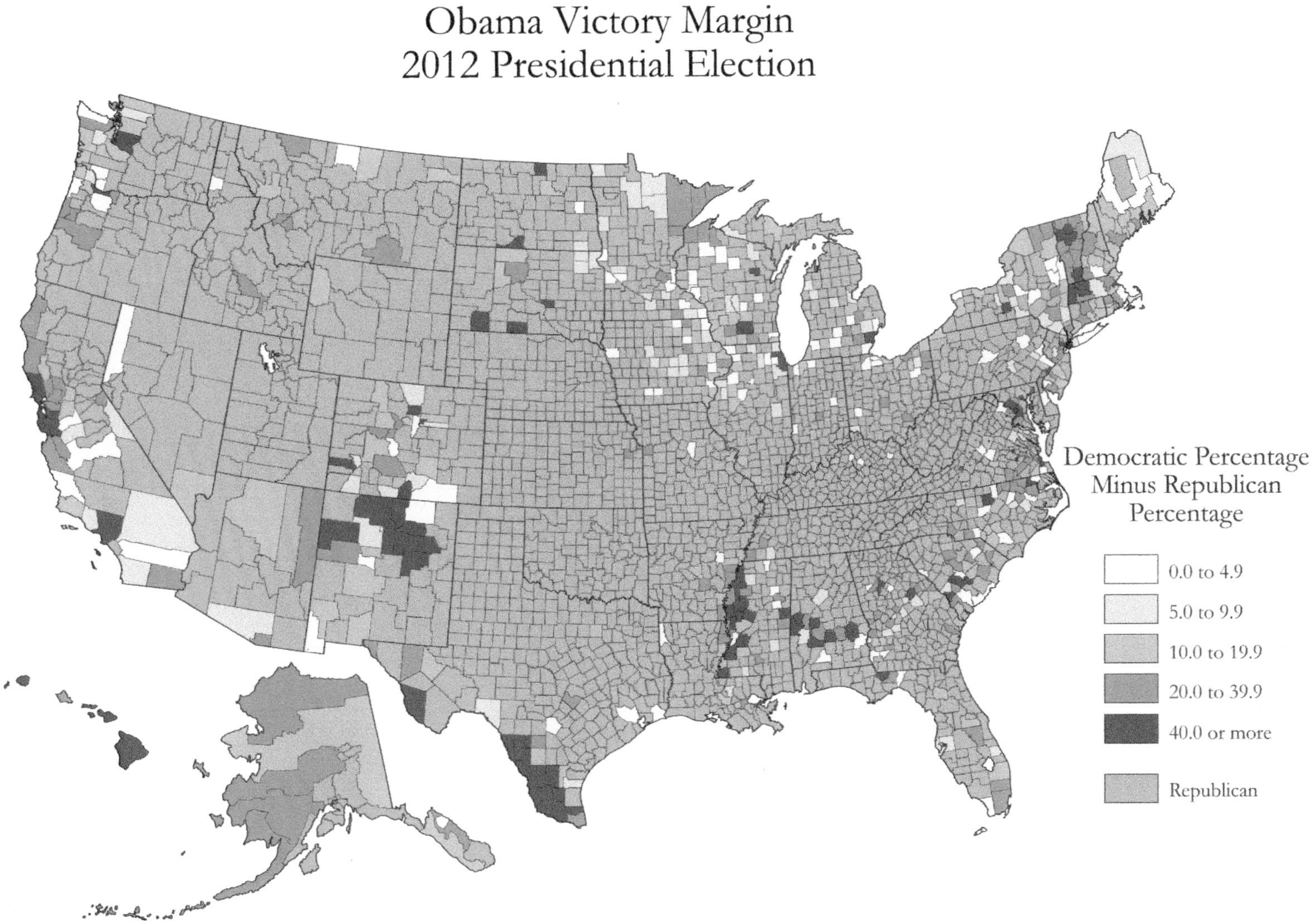

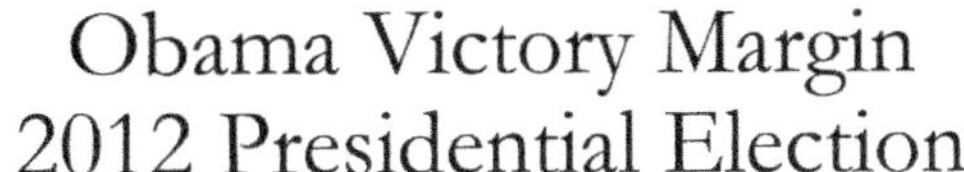

Obama Victory Margin
2012 Presidential Election
Democratic Percentage
Minus Republican
Percentage
0.0 to 4.9
5.0 to 9.9
10.0 to 19.9
20.0 to 39.9
40.0 or more
Republican

FIGURE 5.10

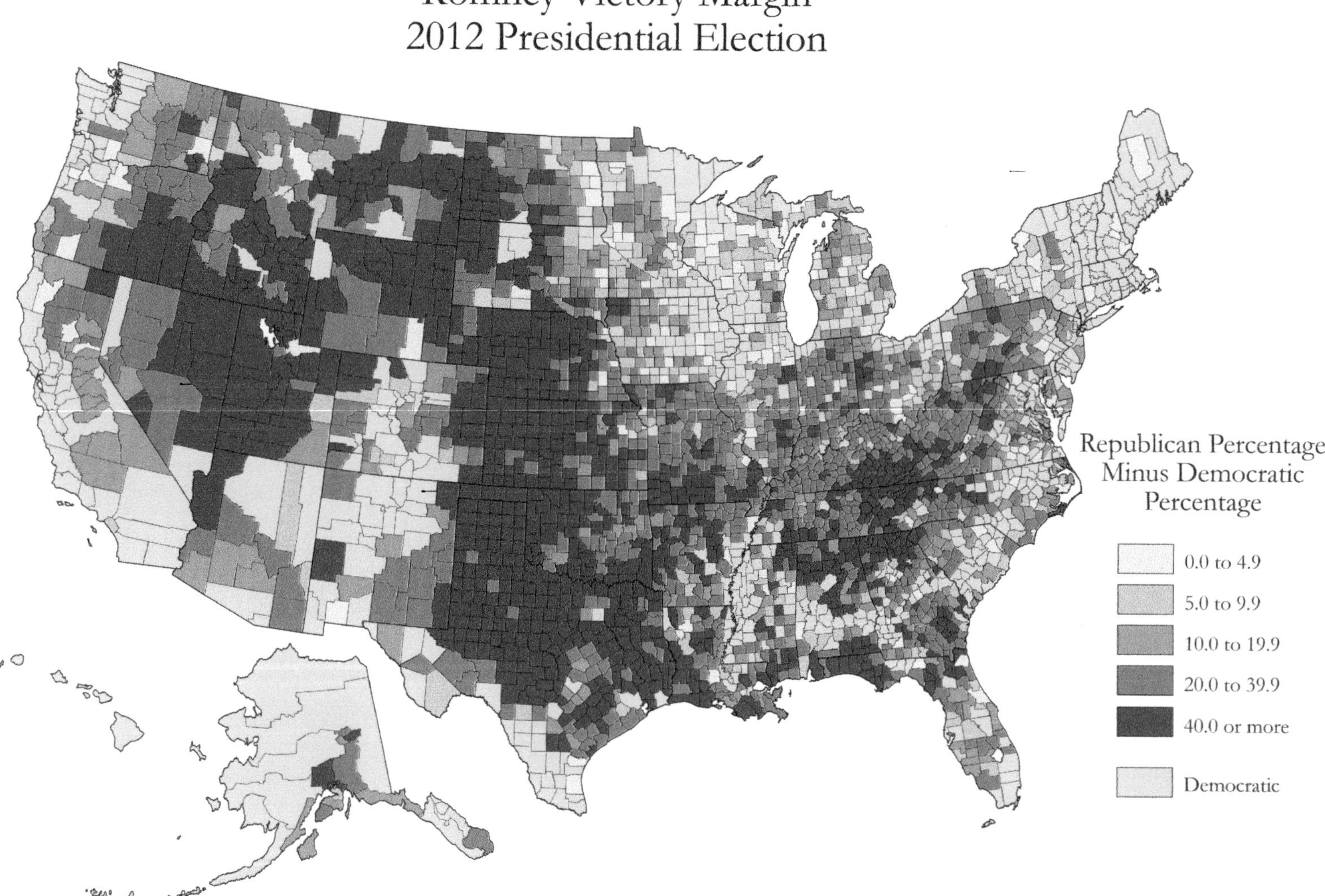
Romney Victory Margin
2012 Presidential Election
Republican Percentage
Minus Democratic
Percentage
0.0 to 4.9
5.0 to 9.9
10.0 to 19.9
20.0 to 39.9
40.0 or more
Democratic

vice president. Johnson and Gray won about 1.28 million popular votes, or just under 1 percent of the nationwide popular vote. The Green Party candidates were Jill Stein of Massachusetts, who is a practicing physician, for president, and community organizer Cheri Honkala of Pennsylvania. Stein and Honkala got about 470,000 votes, or 0.36 percent of the national total. Other third-party candidates together won about 217,000 popular votes, or less than two-tenths of 1 percent of the national popular vote.

The overall percentage of votes won by all third-party candidates together at the state level can be observed in figure 5.4 and at a county level in figure 5.11. In examining the patterns of votes for third-party candidates combined in figure 5.11, for the Libertarian Party (figure 5.12), and for the Green Party (figure 5.13) at a county level, it is important to note that their candidates' names did not appear on the ballot in several states. The Johnson-Gray ticket did not appear on the ballot in Oklahoma, where only the Democratic and Republican tickets appeared on the ballot. The Stein-Honkala ticket appeared on the ballots of only forty of the fifty states. Nevertheless, geographic differences among counties in those states in which their names did appear on the ballot are striking.

The Libertarians did best in relatively isolated rural areas, notably in outstate Alaska and in the Mountain West. Johnson did relatively well in his home state of New Mexico, which he had served as a Republican governor, as well as in Montana. In general, Libertarian support is greatest in the West and is less in the continuously settled East and South, particularly in cities. Libertarian support was relatively low in the closely contested purple states such as Ohio and Florida, where voters were no doubt admonished not to "throw away their votes" and instead to cast their ballots for a major-party candidate.

The Green Party did better along the Pacific Coast, notably in the isolated counties along the coast of northwestern California and in the Bay Area. It was weaker in the South and in general is less rural in orientation than is the Libertarian Party. Stein and Honkala exceeded their nationwide percentage also in large numbers of counties in deep-red Arkansas and West Virginia and in deep-blue Illinois and Maine, perhaps because third-party votes in these states were seen as very unlikely to affect the overall outcome of the election.

How did the percentage of votes for the two major parties vary between 2008 and 2012? This question is addressed by figure 5.14 (difference between Obama percentage in 2012 and 2008), which shows differences between the two elections at a county level. In this map, counties are classified on the basis of the difference in popular vote percentage for Obama in 2012 and 2008. Counties in which Obama did considerably worse in 2012 than in 2008 are those in which Romney did much better in 2012 relative to the performance of John McCain, the Republican nominee in 2008.

Given that Obama did not do as well nationwide in 2012 as he had done in 2008, it is not surprising that his popular vote percentage in 2012 was less than his popular vote percentage in 2008 in the large majority of the counties in the country. However, there are some notable exceptions. The largest shift toward Obama was in Alaska, where in many rural areas he improved on his 2008 percentage by more than 5 percent. This could be explained by the fact that Alaska's governor, Sarah Palin, was the Republican vice presidential nominee in 2008 but of course was not on the 2012 ballot.

Obama also improved his percentage in rural, minority-dominated counties that he won easily throughout the country. He improved also in coastal areas of New Jersey along with southeastern Louisiana and southern Mississippi. This may be due to the fact that Hurricane Sandy struck coastal New Jersey and New York a few days before the election, causing widespread damage. The Obama administration was given high marks for its timely response to this natural disaster. Voters in Louisiana and Mississippi, on the other hand, live in an area that was devastated by Hurricane Katrina in 2005. They may have noticed that the Obama administration responded effectively to Sandy, whereas the Bush administration had been criticized widely for poor and inadequate response to Katrina.

Several areas stand out as places in which swings away from Obama in 2008 to Romney in 2012 were particularly high (figure 5.15). Perhaps most notable is Utah. Here a majority

FIGURE 5.11

Third Party Popular Vote
2012 Presidential Election

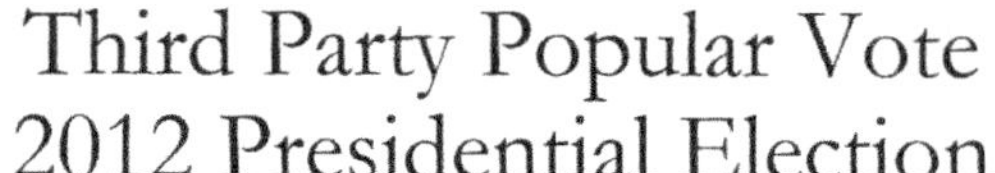

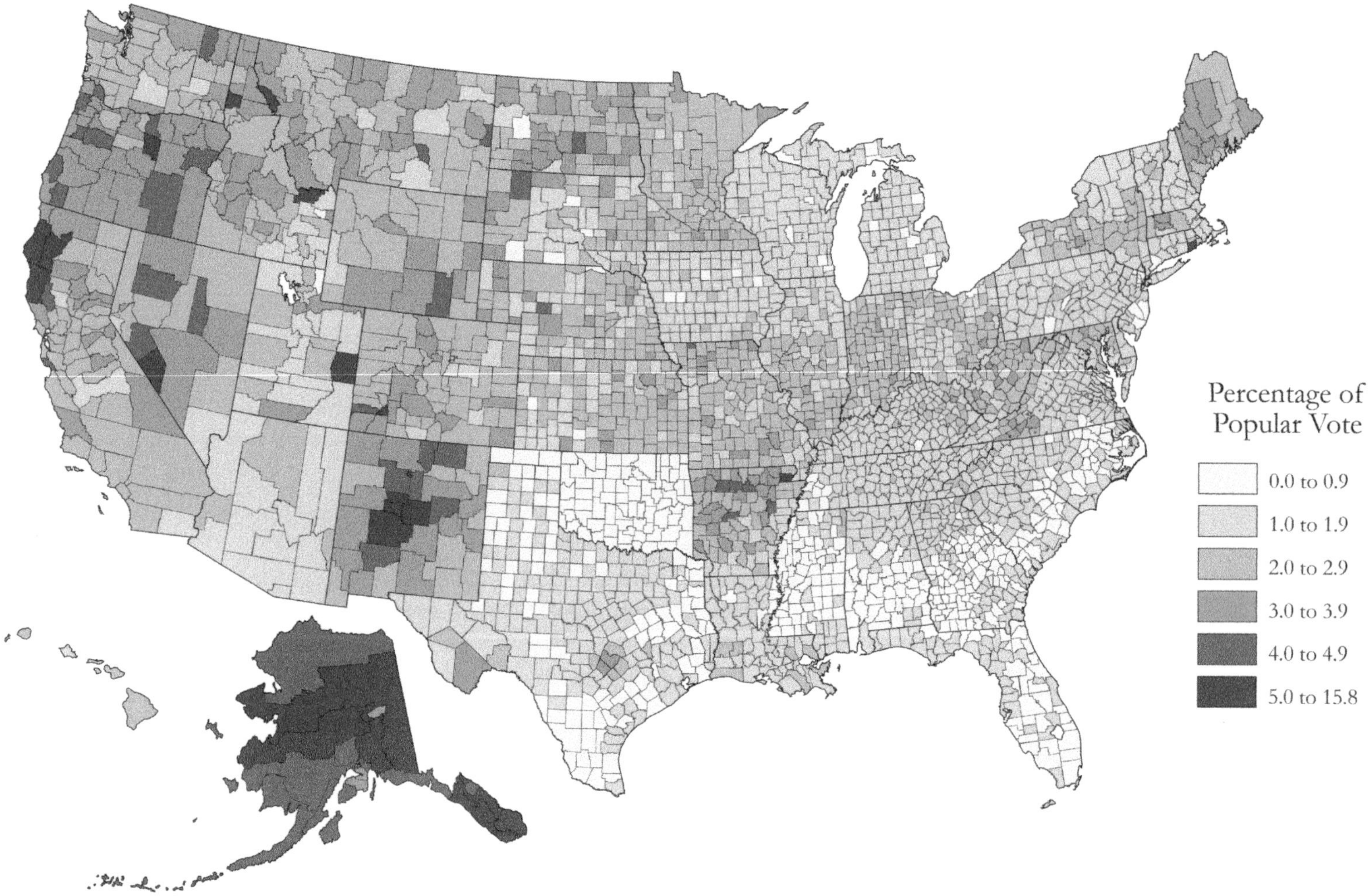
Percentage of
Popular Vote
0.0 to 0.9
1.0 to 1.9
2.0 to 2.9
3.0 to 3.9
4.0 to 4.9
5.0 to 15.8

FIGURE 5.12

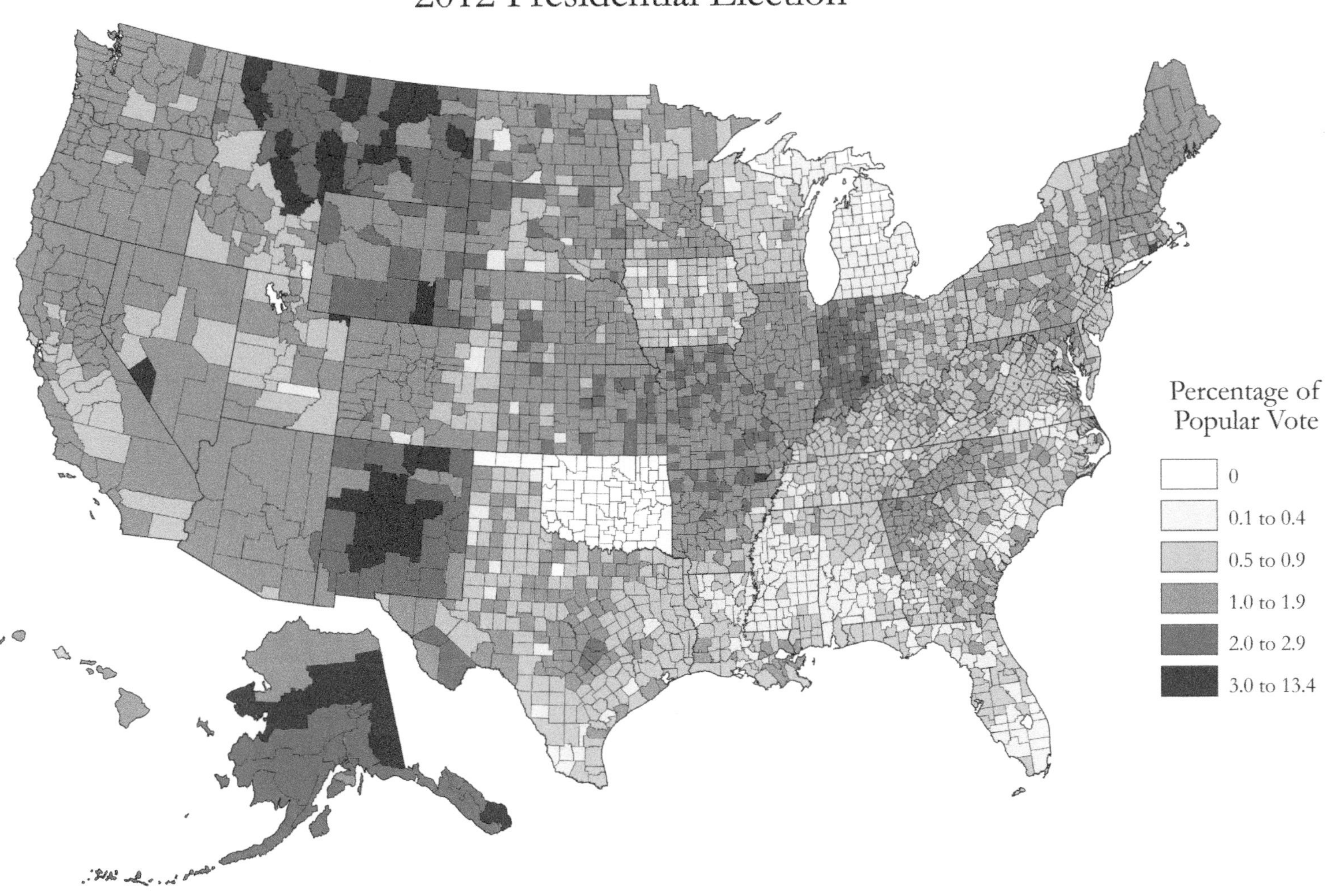
Gary Johnson, Libertarian Party Popular Vote
2012 Presidential Election
Percentage of
Popular Vote
0
0.1 to 0.4
0.5 to 0.9
1.0 to 1.9
2.0 to 2.9
3.0 to 13.4

FIGURE 5.13

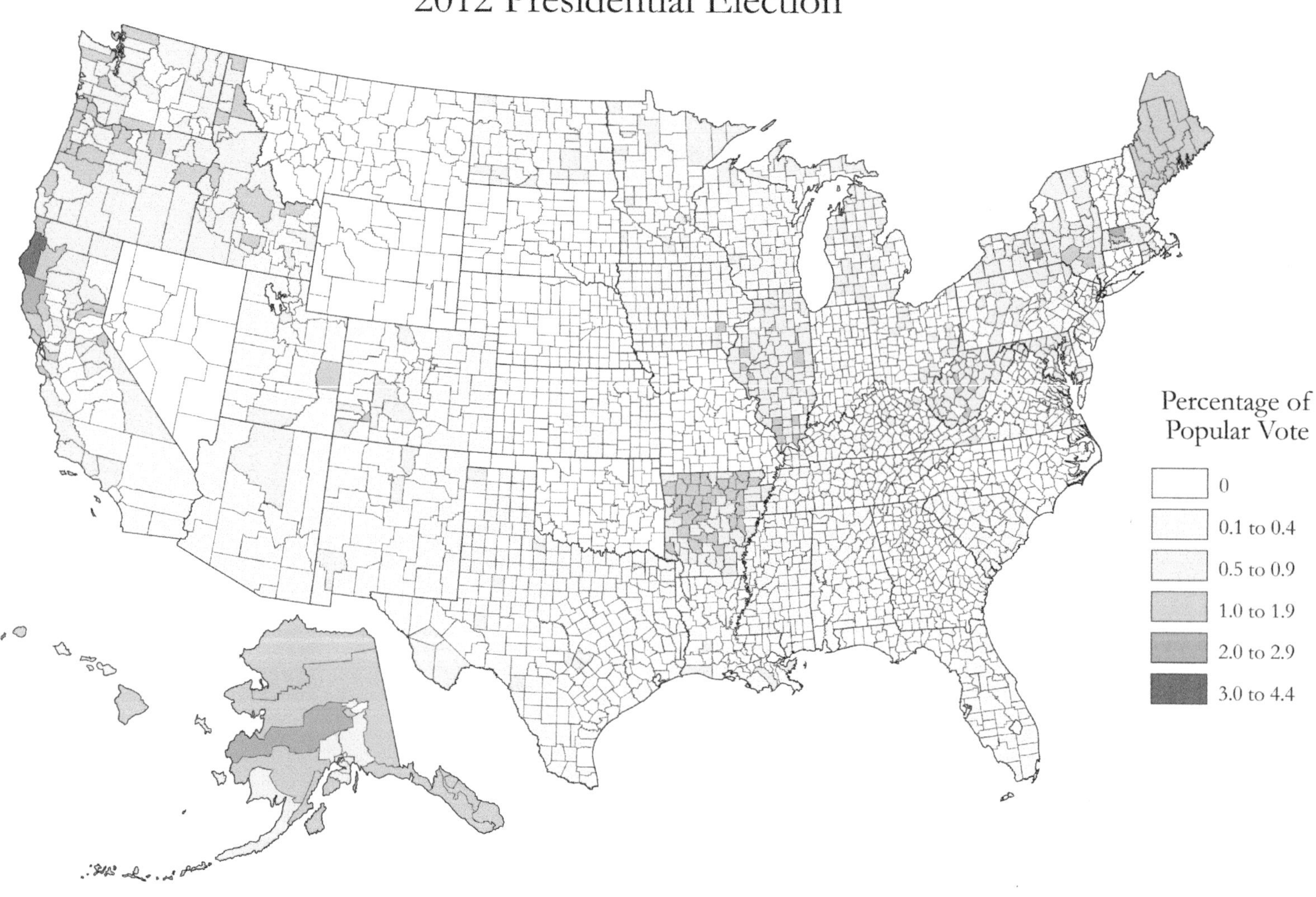

Jill Stein, Green Party Popular Vote
2012 Presidential Election
Percentage of
Popular Vote
0
0.1 to 0.4
0.5 to 0.9
1.0 to 1.9
2.0 to 2.9
3.0 to 4.4

Change in the Democratic Vote
From the 2008 Election to the 2012 Election
Change in Percentage
From 2008 to 2012
Increase in the
Democratic Vote
0 to 4.9
5.0 or More
Decrease in the
Democratic Vote
-0.1 to -4.9
-5.0 or more

of voters belong to the Church of Jesus Christ of Latter-day Saints, or the Mormon Church, and Romney was the first Mormon to be nominated for president by a major party. Romney may have been remembered also by many Utah voters for spearheading the organization of the successful Winter Olympic Games in Salt Lake City in 2002.

After Utah, Romney's greatest increases in percentage statewide relative to McCain in 2008 were found in West Virginia and North Dakota. Both of these states have economies heavily dependent on fossil fuels, and many in these and other states whose economies are based on extraction of nonrenewable energy criticized the Obama administration for opposing efforts to increase fossil-fuel production. The relationship between increased Romney support and the fossil-fuel industry extends into counties in neighboring states, notably central Pennsylvania, eastern Kentucky, and eastern Montana.

Another perspective on changes between 2008 and 2012 can be seen in figure 5.16, which shows counties that shifted from one major party to the other party between the two elections. In this map, the counties are grouped into four categories: those that gave popular-vote majorities to Obama in both elections, those that gave popular-vote majorities to McCain in 2008 and Romney in 2012, those that supported Obama in 2008 but Romney in 2012, and those that supported McCain in 2008 but Obama in 2012. As is consistent with the observation that the 2012 election was a maintaining election, the very large majority of counties supported the same party in both elections.

Not surprisingly, more counties shifted to the Republicans than shifted to the Democrats. The largest concentration of counties that shifted toward the Republicans is located in the Upper Midwest, including Minnesota, Iowa, Wisconsin, Illinois, and Michigan. Most of these counties are rural counties, and the fact that they shifted did not make any difference in the Electoral College in that Obama carried all five of these states. Only a few places shifted in the other direction, most notably in Alaska, where Obama did better statewide in 2012 than he had in 2008.

Change in the Republican Vote
From the 2008 Election to the 2012 Election
Change in Percentage
From 2008 to 2012
Increase in the
Republican Vote
0 to 4.9
5.0 or More
Decrease in the
Republican Vote
-0.1 to -4.9
-5.0 or more

FIGURE 5.16

Persistence and Change
2008 and 2012 Presidential Elections
Persistence
Democratic in 2008 and 2012 (680)
Republican in 2008 and 2012 (2,244)
Change
Republican in 2008 to Democratic in 2012 (21)
Democratic in 2008 to Republican in 2012 (190)

THE 2012 PRESIDENTIAL ELECTION IN HISTORICAL PERSPECTIVE

J. CLARK ARCHER, ROBERT H. WATREL, AND FRED M. SHELLEY

The 2012 presidential election was what political scientists have called a maintaining election, with few changes occurring between this election and other elections in the recent past. However, an examination of the geography of the 2012 election relative to previous elections over the longer sweep of history shows major changes. States that have historically been Democratic, such as the South, are now reliably Republican. On the other hand, states that historically supported Republicans are now reliably Democratic. A notable example is Vermont, which gave its electoral votes to the Democrats for the first time in history in 1964 but today is one of the most reliably Democratic states in the country.

The changes over time can be identified by examining maps of election outcomes at various times in history. If one were to look at a county-level map of each election from the past to the present, what changes could one observe over time? The Democratic and Republican parties have dominated US politics since the 1860s. Of course, some of the elections that have occurred during this period have resulted in landslides for one of the two major parties, while others have been contested very closely between them. This is evident from figure 5.17, which shows the percentage of the vote won by the Democratic Party nationwide in each presidential election between 1872 and 2012. As is indicated in the figure, the elections of 1932, 1936, and 1964 were landslide victories for Democrats Franklin D. Roosevelt and Lyndon Johnson. On the other hand, the Democrats lost by landslide margins in 1920, 1924, 1972, and 1984. Many other elections, including those of 1884, 1916, 1960, and 2000 were contested very closely.

In a few elections, third-party candidates got significant numbers of popular votes. In 1912, for example, third-party candidate Theodore Roosevelt actually outpolled the Republican nominee, William Howard Taft. Hence the Democratic nominee, Woodrow Wilson, won a comfortable margin in the Electoral College despite earning only a minority of the popular vote. Similarly, Democrat Bill Clinton won a solid Electoral College majority over Republican George H. W. Bush in 1992, although Clinton got only about 43 percent of the popular vote, because third-party candidate Ross Perot won nearly 19 percent of the popular vote against his two opponents. However, for the most part, a graph showing Republican popular vote percentage over time would be a mirror image of figure 5.17. In general, Republicans did well when Democrats did badly, and vice versa.

Although graphs such as figure 5.17 are valuable in tracking a political party's performance over time, they tell us little about how the geography of the vote has changed. In other words, the fact that two Democratic nominees in different years earned the same voting percentage masks the possibility that the two candidates' popular-vote percentages in different states may have been quite different. Thus, statistical techniques are important in helping to examine these geographical differences systematically.

One way to examine this question from a geographical point of view is through looking at statistical correlations between pairs of elections. A correlation coefficient measures the degree to which two variables are associated with each other. The value of the correlation coefficient varies from +1.00 to −1.00. A correlation of +1.00 implies that the value of one variable can be predicted exactly by knowing the value of the other variable such

FIGURE 5.17

Percent Democratic Vote, 1872 to 2012 Elections

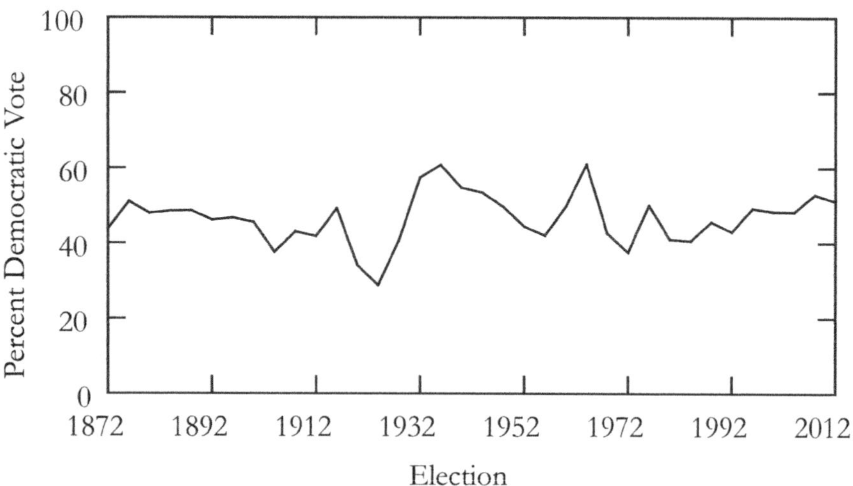

that as one increases, the other also increases. A negative correlation implies an inverse relationship such that as the value of one variable increases, the other decreases. A value of zero implies that there is no observed relationship between the two variables. In other words, it is impossible to predict the value of one variable based on knowing the value of the other variable. Applied to elections, this implies that if the same states are heavily Democratic in two separate elections and if other states are heavily Republican in the same two elections, then the correlation between them will be high and will approach 1.00.

Figure 5.18 is a graph showing these correlations between the percentage of Democratic vote in each county in the 2012 presidential election with the percentage of the Democratic vote in each county in previous elections. Illustrating the fact that the presidential election of 2012 was a maintaining election, the county-level correlation between these two elections was about 0.95. Thus, knowing the percentage of votes that a county gave to Obama in 2008 enables one to estimate the percentage of votes that Obama received in 2012 with a very high degree of accuracy. Going further back in time, we find that correlations between the 2012 election and previous elections were above .50 in each election since 1976. However, correlations between the 2012 election and elections prior to the 1960s are very low. In other words, there is no relationship between the results of these elections and the 2012 election. Thus the geographical patterns in these elections were very different. In fact, most of the elections prior to 1900 are negatively correlated with the 2012 election. Places that were more Republican in the nineteenth century were more Democratic in 2012, and vice versa.

In analyzing how voting patterns change over time, political scientists have developed the concept of a normal vote. This concept is based on observations that in most elections, a large majority of voters cast ballots for candidates of the same party as they had in previous elections. Thus, the best predictor of how someone will vote in an election is how that person has voted in past elections. In campaigning, parties and their candidates target the relatively small number of voters who may be likely to change their minds relative to previous elections. This implies that political parties and their candidates target places where there are enough such voters who can affect the outcomes in their states if they switch their votes from one party to the other in a given election. This is evident in examining the geographies of campaign expenditures and campaign spending in 2012, as illustrated elsewhere in this atlas.

As was the case in 2012, the majority of elections are maintaining elections. However, some elections or sequences of elections are associated with more substantial changes in the distributions of voting percentages. These elections are known as realigning elections.

FIGURE 5.18

Correlation of 2012 Percent Democratic Popular Presidential Vote by County with Percent Democratic Popular Presidential Vote by County in Previous Elections, 1872 to 2008

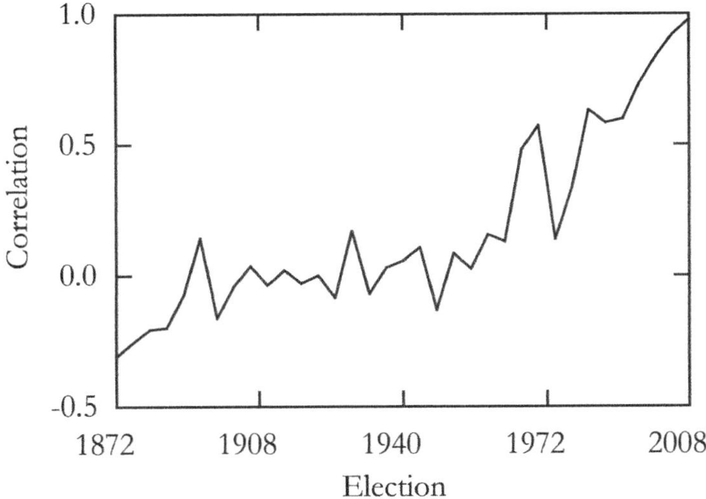

How can we examine the long-run pattern of maintaining and realigning elections? To do so, it is important to recognize that since the Civil War, the two major political parties in the United States have competed for the presidency. At any given time, some places are solidly supportive of one party, whereas others are divided relatively equally between the two parties. For example, the Pacific Coast states and the Northeast are solidly Democratic regions, whereas the Great Plains, most of the South, and most of the Rocky Mountain states are heavily Republican. "Purple" states such as Ohio, Florida, Virginia, and Colorado thus determine the outcome of the election. If they cast their electoral votes for the Republican candidate, as in 2004, the Republicans are likely to win the election. On the other hand, if they cast their electoral votes for the Democratic candidate, as in 2008 and 2012, the Democrats are likely to win the election.

Throughout history, various regions of the country have been long-term keys to election outcomes. Between the 1880s and the 1940s, the key region of the country included Illinois, Indiana, Ohio, Pennsylvania, New York, and New Jersey. The "Solid South" was strongly Democratic, and the northern tier of states from northern New England to the Upper Midwest was strongly Republican. In today's parlance, the North was red, the Deep South was blue, and the states in between were purple states. Both parties recognized this geography, and both realized that they had to win the states in between in order to win an Electoral College majority. Typically, both parties selected nominees from these key states. In fact, in all but one of the presidential elections between 1860 and 1964, at least one of the major-party nominees for president or vice president came from one of these six states.

Today, the South has emerged as a key swing region. No president has been elected without electoral votes in the South since Calvin Coolidge in 1924. In 2012, Obama lost most of the South but won the electoral voters of Virginia and Florida. Of the "purple" states in the late nineteenth and early twentieth centuries, however, Ohio has remained a swing state. In fact, no Republican has ever won the presidency without carrying Ohio.

The electoral pattern typical of most elections between 1880 and 1944 has been termed the sectional normal vote. The sectional normal vote is characterized by strong geographic polarization between the heavily Republican northern states and the heavily Democratic South. Both parties assumed that the "Solid South" would go Democratic, and both worked from this assumption in identifying candidates and campaign issues.

In the 1880s and 1890s, the Populist revolt occurred, nearly upsetting this pattern. The Populists were disaffected farmers and advocates for farmers in the West, Midwest, and South. They believed that ordinary, common people were being repressed by the elite (government and big business). Industrialization resulted in declining farm prices and reduced purchasing power for farmers.

The Populists tried unsuccessfully to unite the South and the West against the much more industrialized Northeast. Although the Populists were unsuccessful in winning presidential elections, many of the reforms they advocated, including increasing the money supply, the direct election of US senators by the voters of their states, increased government regulation of banks and securities, and the progressive income tax, were enacted into law by the early twentieth century. The direct election of US senators, who had originally been selected by their states' legislatures, and the progressive income tax were the subjects of constitutional amendments. As these and other Populist-backed measures went into effect, the Populist revolt lost momentum, and the sectional normal vote pattern resumed.

The sectional normal vote disappeared during the middle of the twentieth century. Several factors were associated with the end of the sectional normal vote. Large numbers of Americans began moving to the Sunbelt. Since World War II, most areas in the Sunbelt have grown in population much more rapidly than places in the Northeast and Midwest. By the end of 2013, in fact, the three largest states by population—California, Texas, and Florida—were located in the Sunbelt. Second, many Americans began moving to suburbs. Suburbs have grown much faster than either central cities or rural areas since World War II. Today, well over half of Americans live in suburbs. Finally, the civil rights movement enfranchised African Americans and other minorities whose right to vote had not previously been enforced by the federal government. All of these shifts affected the geography of US presidential elections.

In part because of these changes, the sectional normal vote pattern collapsed after World War II. At that time, each party began to make inroads into areas traditionally associated with the other party. The Republicans became competitive and eventually became dominant in the South. On the other hand, the Democrats made inroads in the North. States such as Vermont and Minnesota, once reliably Republican, are now dependably Democratic. The electoral pattern typified by the 2012 election has been termed the contemporary normal vote pattern.

Even within these very broad patterns, however, there are more subtle variations. How can these variations be identified? This can be done using a statistical method known as T-mode factor analysis. The process of T-mode factor analysis begins with the creation of a matrix containing the percentage of vote won by the candidate of one of the major parties at each presidential election by county in each state. Thus, each column of the matrix contains the percentage of vote won by that party's candidate in a given election by county in each state.

From this matrix, correlations between each column, or each pair of elections, are calculated. This yields a second matrix consisting of correlation coefficients between each pair of elections. T-mode factor analysis identifies groups of elections characterized by high correlation coefficients among one another. Each of these groups is identified as a factor. The factor can be conceptualized as a composite of each spatial unit's percentage on each election relative to the overall pattern. Because most of the factors are associated with sets of consecutive elections, each factor can be considered as an electoral era within the time span considered in the analysis.

For each election, another correlation coefficient can be calculated with each of the factors. These correlation coefficients are known as factor loadings. The higher the factor loading, the more representative that election is of the factor, or the electoral era identified. These factor loadings can be graphed in order to examine their trajectory over time.

In this analysis, all of the thirty-six presidential elections between 1872 and 2012 were analyzed using this method. The analysis yielded nine factors, which represent collectively most of the geographical variation within the entire set of election returns. The graphs shown in figure 5.19 represent the loadings on each factor for each of the elections, and the graphs are shown in chronological order. In each case, the election with the highest loading on that factor is identified. The remaining maps in this section show the distribution of votes for the elections that load highest on each of the factors (for more on T-mode factor analysis see chapter 11).

Figure 5.20 shows the county-level popular vote for the election of 1876, at the dawn of the sectional normal vote era. The 1876 election was disputed between Republican Rutherford B. Hayes and Democrat Samuel Tilden until a commission consisting of members of Congress and the Supreme Court decided it in favor of Hayes. In response, the Republicans agreed to hasten the withdrawal of Union troops who had occupied parts of the South since the Civil War, ending the Reconstruction era. As the Northerners withdrew, the antebellum elites of the old Confederacy assumed power, and the South became firmly Democratic. This process was in progress in 1876, by which time the Democrats had regained control of some, but not all, of the South. Meanwhile, the North was gravitating toward the Republicans.

The election of 1896 (figure 5.21) is representative of the Populist era. The Republican candidate, William McKinley, defeated his Democratic opponent, William Jennings Bryan, who had won the nominations of both the Democratic and the People's (Populist) Party. By this time, the Republicans had solid control of most of the North, particularly New England. Bryan's unsuccessful attempt to unite the South and the West was evident in that he won large majorities in the mining-oriented Rocky Mountain states, the Great Plains, and much of the agrarian South. Despite Bryan's success in these regions, McKinley swept the industrializing and more heavily populated North to win the election comfortably.

The elections of 1912 and 1940 represent the sectional normal vote during the first half of the twentieth century. The 1912 election (figure 5.22) is notable in that it is the only election in US history in which three men who served as president during their lifetimes competed for the office. It is also noteworthy in that for the only time since the Civil War a third-party candidate, Theodore Roosevelt, outpolled a major-party candidate, Republican incumbent William Howard Taft, in the Electoral College. In a manner reminiscent of the old Populist Party, Roosevelt carried a large number of counties in the Great Plains, the Rocky Mountain states, and the Pacific Coast states. However, Democrat Woodrow Wilson carried the entire South, which by this time was controlled firmly by the Democratic Party. Wilson won more than 65 percent of the popular vote in the large majority of the counties in the southern states, whose electoral votes helped to propel him to a comfortable victory in the Electoral College.

The sectional normal vote period remained in place until after World War II, although some elections during this period, such as 1920 and 1924, were Republican landslides, and others, such as 1932 and 1936, were Democratic landslides. The election of 1940 (figure 5.23) typifies this period. The North, especially in rural areas, remained solidly Republican. All of the ten states carried by Republican nominee Wendell Willkie are in the Northern Plains, the Midwest, and New England. Of these, all but Michigan and Willkie's native state of Indiana were predominantly rural states. On the other hand, Democratic incumbent Franklin Delano Roosevelt carried the entire South along with the West and the urban states of the Northeast.

The period between World War II and the 1980s was transitional between the sectional normal vote period and the contemporary normal vote period. In 1960, Democrat John F. Kennedy narrowly defeated his Republican opponent, Richard Nixon, in one of the closest presidential elections in US history (figure 5.24). By this time, the Democrats had begun to make significant inroads into the Northeast, particularly in urban areas. Although Nixon carried the large majority of northeastern and midwestern counties, he lost these regions' large cities to Kennedy. Kennedy's success in these urban areas allowed him to carry New York, Pennsylvania, Maryland, Michigan, Illinois, and Minnesota, thereby giving him his needed margin in the Electoral College. The urban-rural divide would become very significant by the 1990s and has intensified to the present day. Meanwhile, Nixon's percentage improved over most previous Republican nominees in the South, especially on the geographic margins of this region. He won the electoral votes of Virginia, Tennessee, and Florida and narrowly lost Texas.

The North-South reversal became much more evident in 1964. In this election, President

FIGURE 5.19

T-Mode Oblimin Factor Pattern Loadings Profiles: Percent Democratic Vote by County, 1872 to 2012 Presidential Elections

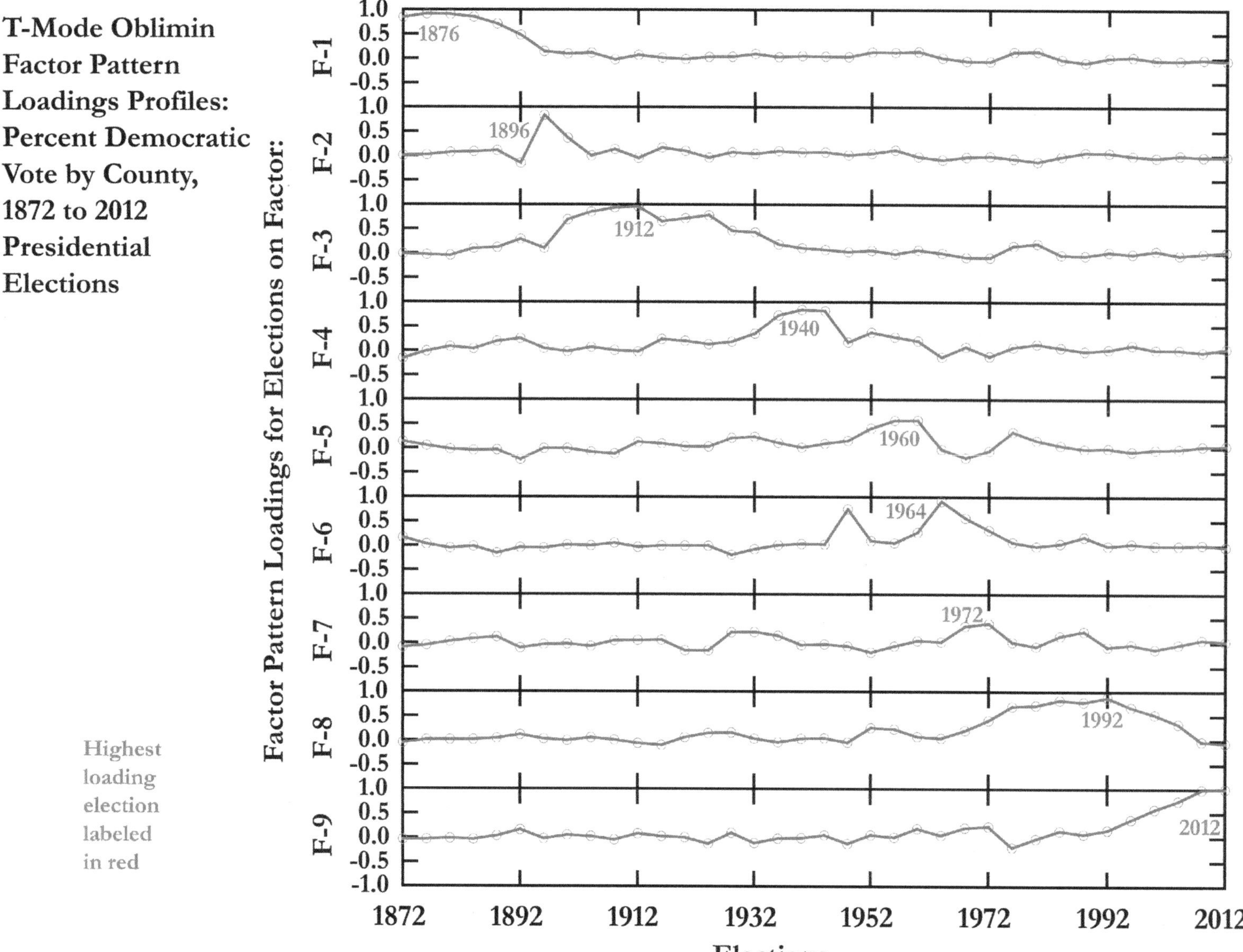

Highest loading election labeled in red

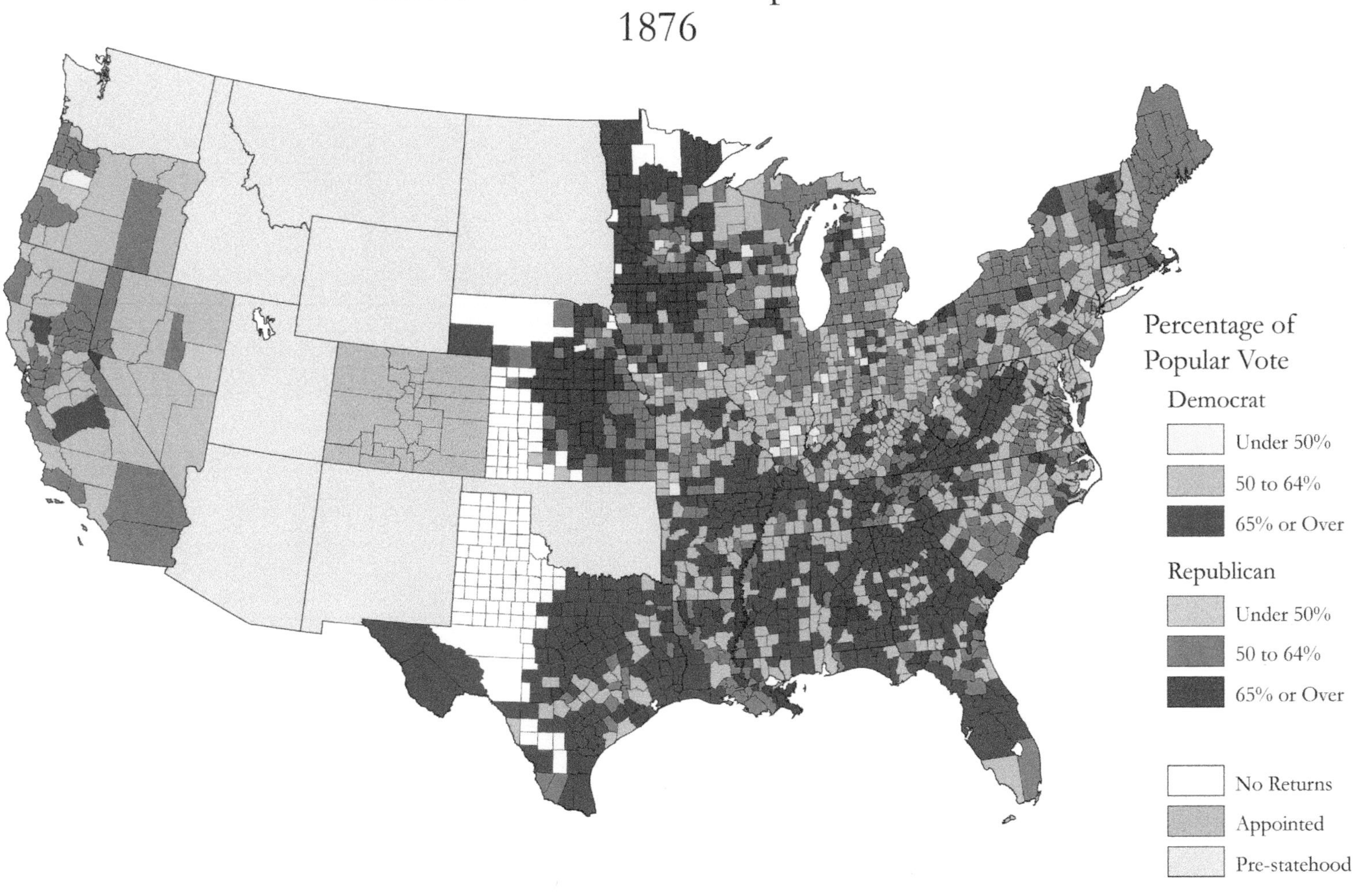
Presidential Election Popular Vote
1876
Percentage of
Popular Vote
Democrat
Under 50%
50 to 64%
65% or Over
Republican
Under 50%
50 to 64%
65% or Over
No Returns
Appointed
Pre-statehood

FIGURE 5.21

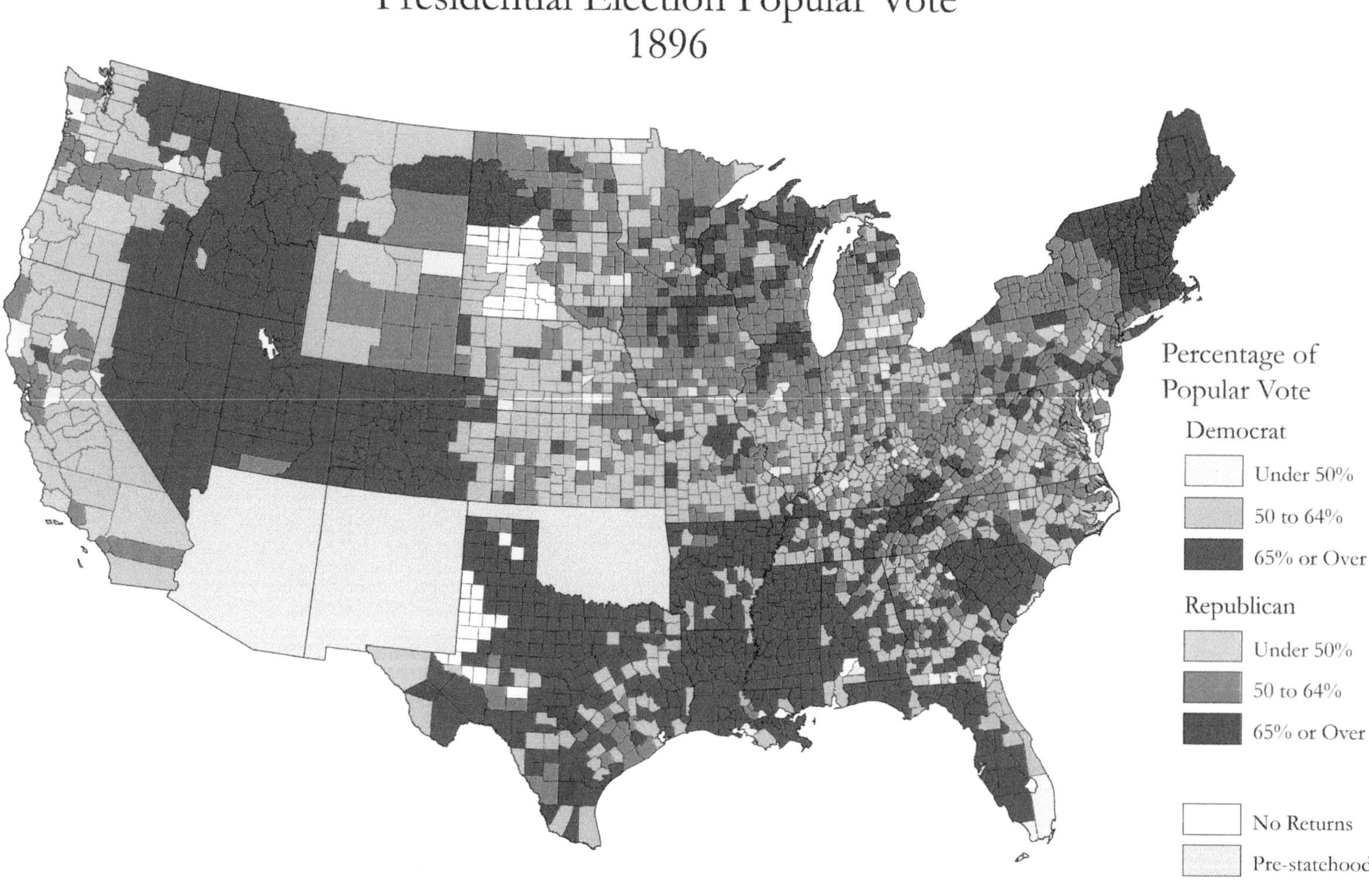
Presidential Election Popular Vote
1896
Percentage of
Popular Vote
Democrat
Under 50%
50 to 64%
65% or Over
Republican
Under 50%
50 to 64%
65% or Over
No Returns
Pre-statehood

FIGURE 5.22

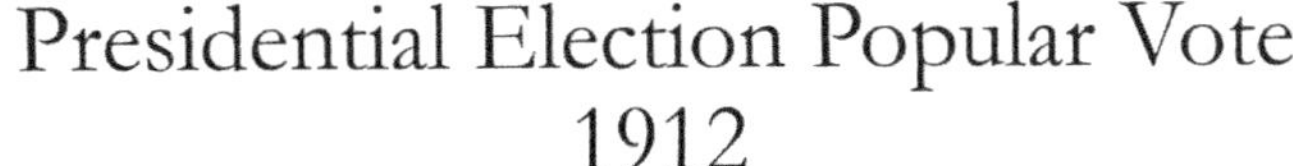

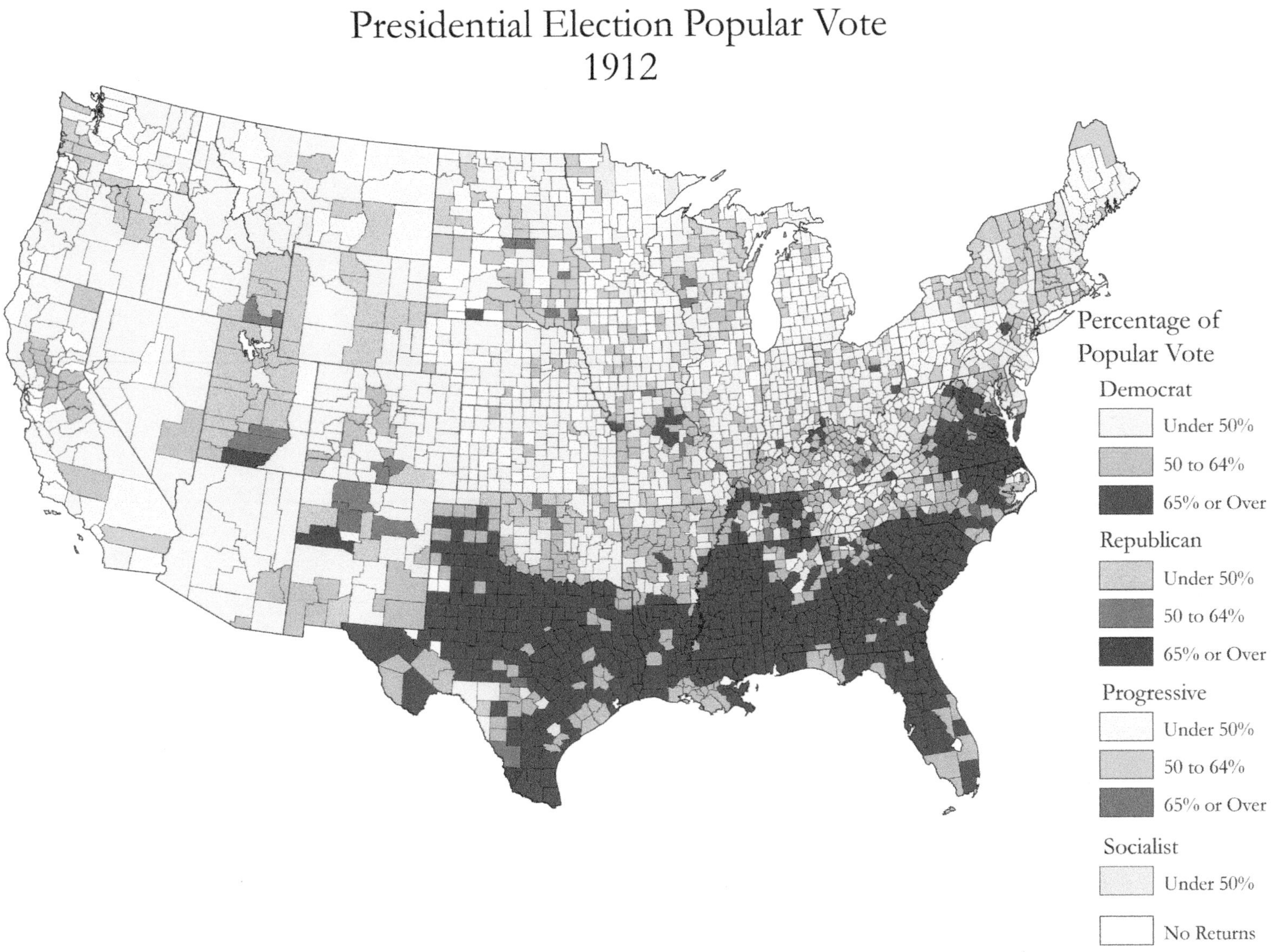
Presidential Election Popular Vote
1912
Percentage of
Popular Vote
Democrat
Under 50%
50 to 64%
65% or Over
Republican
Under 50%
50 to 64%
65% or Over
Progressive
Under 50%
50 to 64%
65% or Over
Socialist
Under 50%
No Returns

FIGURE 5.23

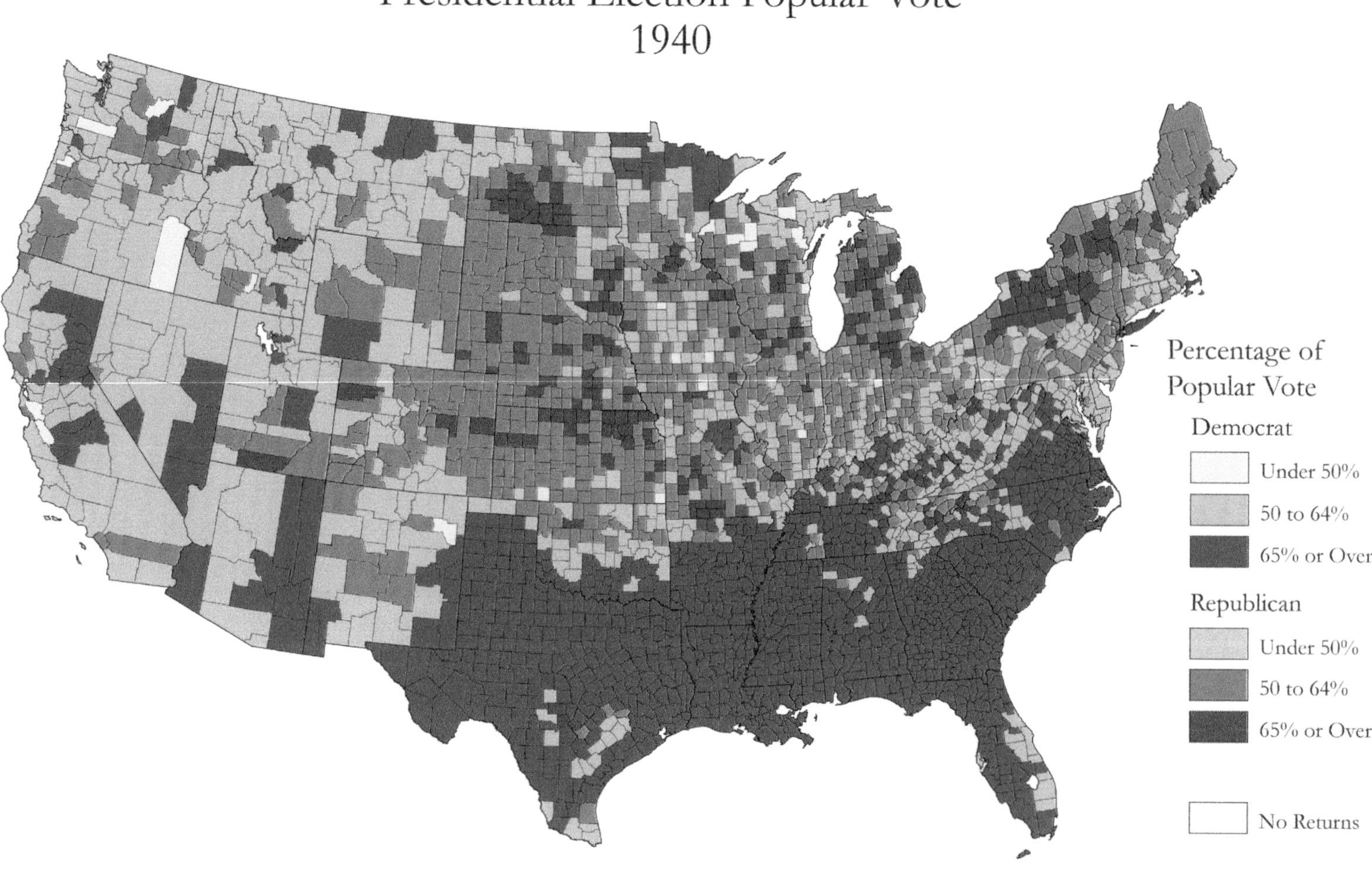
Presidential Election Popular Vote
1940
Percentage of
Popular Vote
Democrat
Under 50%
50 to 64%
65% or Over
Republican
Under 50%
50 to 64%
65% or Over
No Returns

Lyndon Johnson, who took office when Kennedy was assassinated in 1963, defeated Republican Barry Goldwater in a landslide comparable to Franklin Roosevelt's easy victories between 1932 and 1944 (figure 5.25). However, while Roosevelt lost most rural areas of the Northeast, Johnson won large majorities throughout the region. Johnson carried every county in New York and all but one county in New England. Goldwater amassed large majorities in the Deep South, where his opposition to the Civil Rights Act resonated with white voters, who continued to dominate the electorate prior to the passage of the Voting Rights Act of 1965. Goldwater also did fairly well in the rural West, initiating a pattern that has continued to the present day.

Eight years later, the national tide reversed as President Richard Nixon defeated his Democratic opponent, George McGovern, in an equally strong landslide (figure 5.26). Nixon won forty-nine of the fifty states in 1972, losing only Massachusetts along with the District of Columbia to McGovern. Nixon's largest margins were in the South, the Great Plains, and the Rocky Mountain states. In addition to Massachusetts, McGovern's few bright spots included several major cities, including Washington, San Francisco, and Detroit.

By 1992, the contemporary normal vote had come to dominate the presidential electoral geography of the United States (figure 5.27). In this election, Democrat Bill Clinton ousted Republican president George H. W. Bush. An independent candidate, Ross Perot, carried no states and only a few mostly rural counties, but by winning nearly 19 percent of the popular vote he became the most successful third-party candidate since Theodore Roosevelt in 1912. Clinton swept the Northeast, carrying every state's electoral votes and a large majority of the counties. He broke nearly even with Bush in the South and the West. Clinton was especially successful in large metropolitan areas, in counties with large nonwhite populations, and in academic communities such as Madison, Ann Arbor, Iowa City, and Boulder.

The distinction between counties with large nonwhite populations and other counties is evident in those parts of the South with large rural African American populations, in heavily Hispanic South Texas, and in counties with American Indian reservations in the Dakotas, Arizona, and New Mexico. These trends have persisted ever since. Meanwhile, the Republicans did best in rural areas, especially outside the Northeast, Midwest, and Pacific Coast states. They did well also in counties with large military installations, for example, near Pensacola, Florida, and Charleston, South Carolina, reflecting the Republicans' support for larger military budgets. Thus, the 1992 election presages that of 2012, in which all of these trends have intensified, as illustrated by figures 5.5, 5.6, 5.7, and 5.8, which completes a composite picture of the sweep of electoral geography over the 140-year period between 1872 and 2012.

FIGURE 5.24

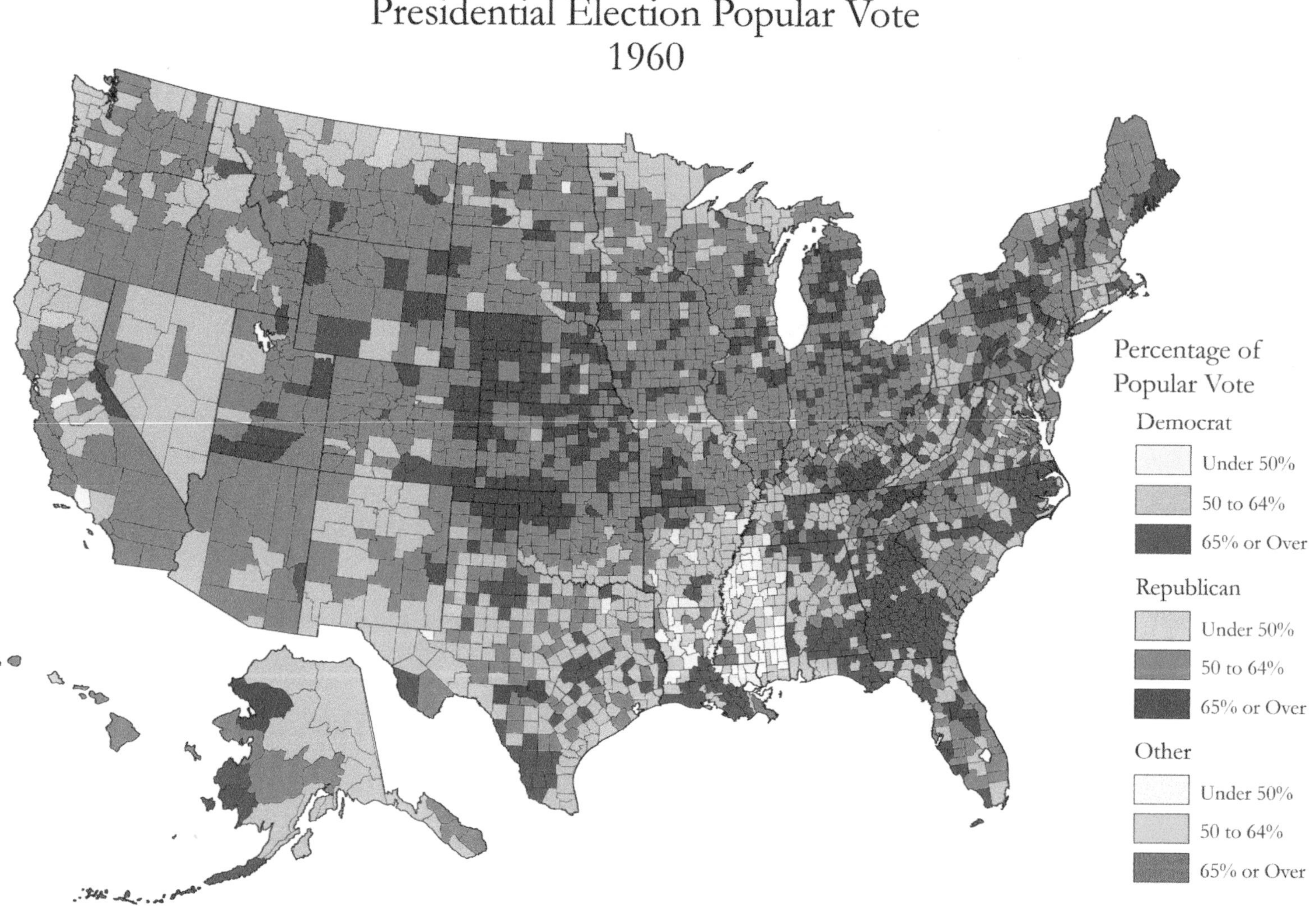
Presidential Election Popular Vote
1960
Percentage of
Popular Vote
Democrat
Under 50%
50 to 64%
65% or Over
Republican
Under 50%
50 to 64%
65% or Over
Other
Under 50%
50 to 64%
65% or Over

FIGURE 5.25

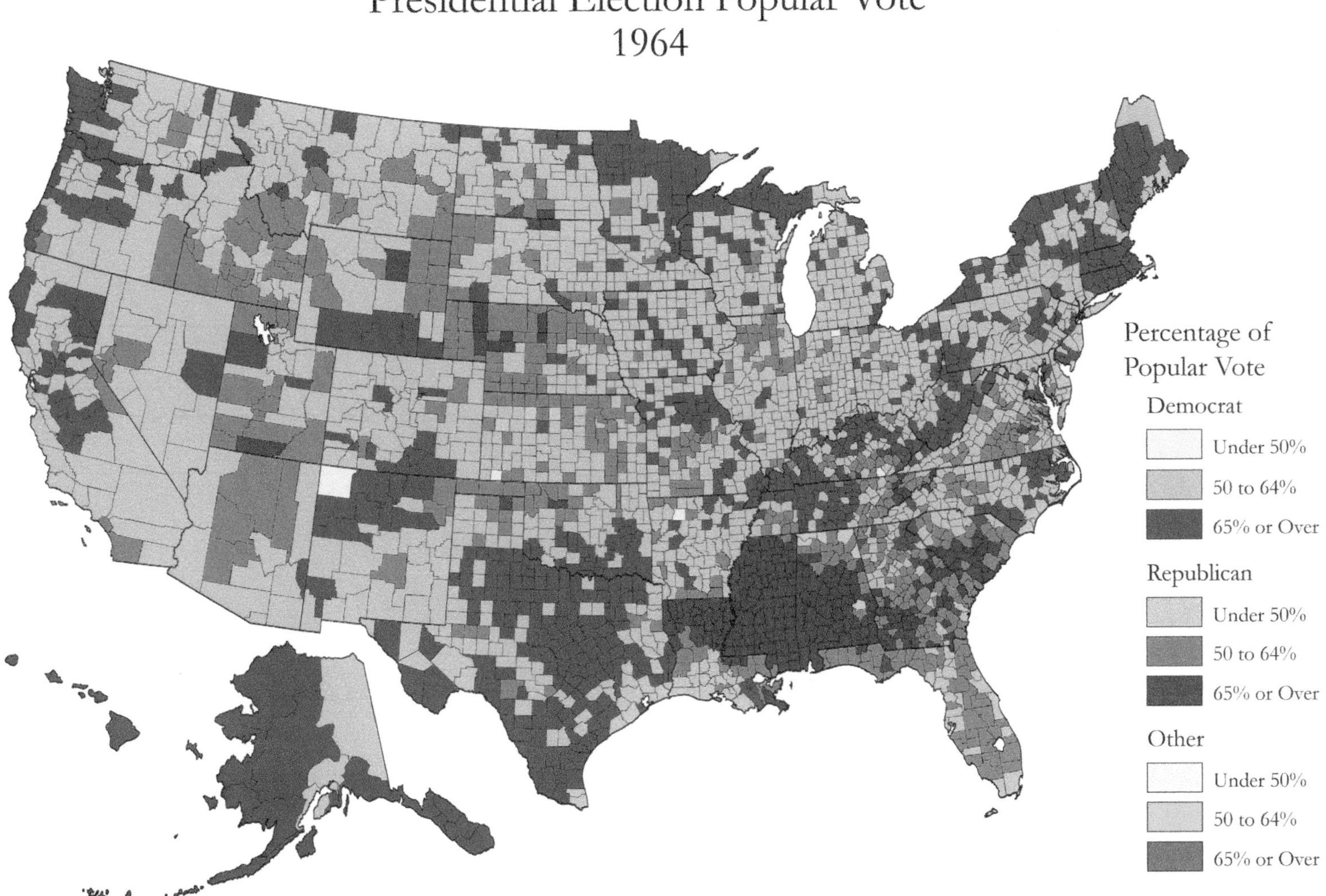

Presidential Election Popular Vote
1964
Percentage of
Popular Vote
Democrat
Under 50%
50 to 64%
65% or Over
Republican
Under 50%
50 to 64%
65% or Over
Other
Under 50%
50 to 64%
65% or Over

FIGURE 5.26

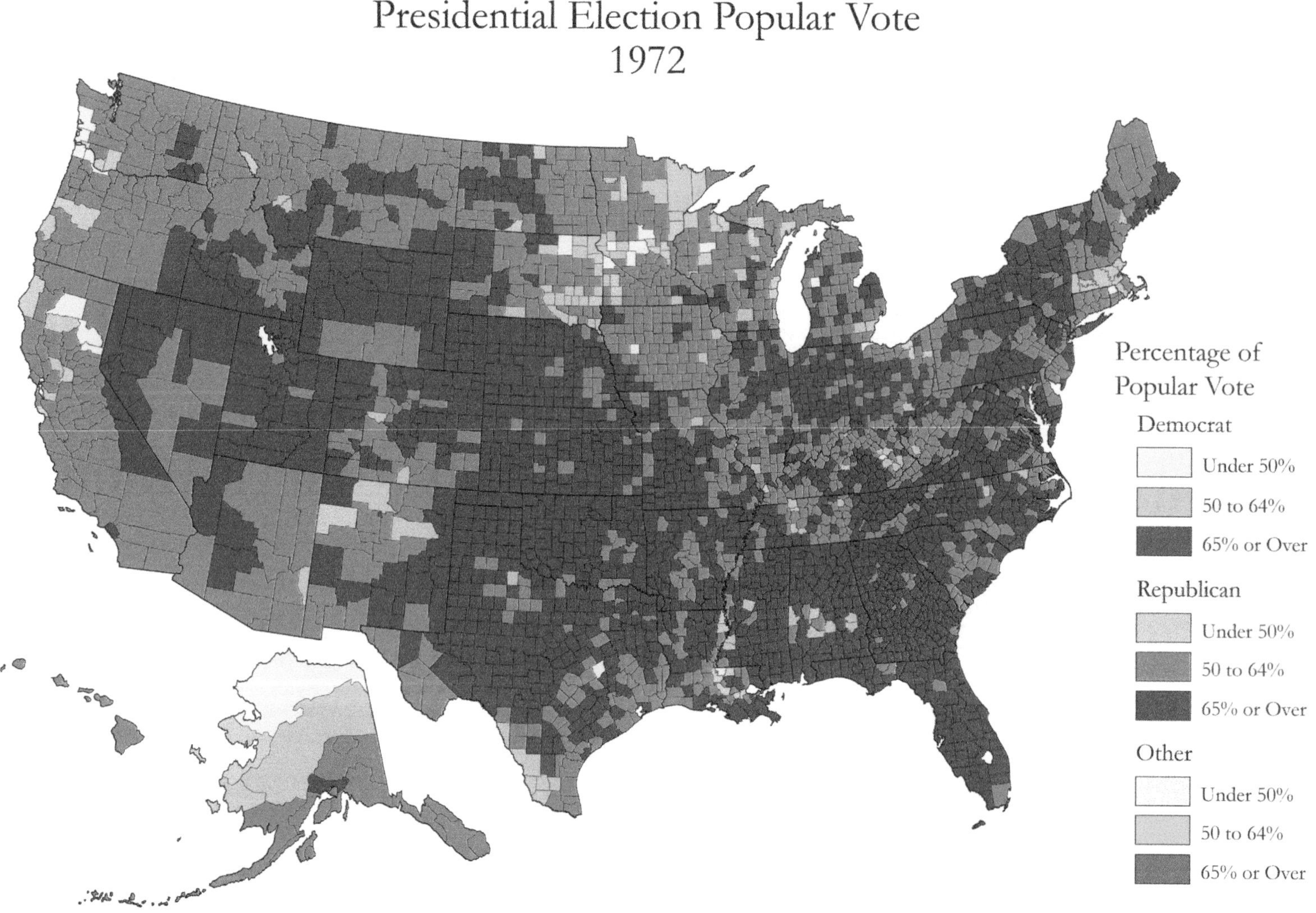
Presidential Election Popular Vote
1972
Percentage of
Popular Vote
Democrat
Under 50%
50 to 64%
65% or Over
Republican
Under 50%
50 to 64%
65% or Over
Other
Under 50%
50 to 64%
65% or Over

FIGURE 5.27

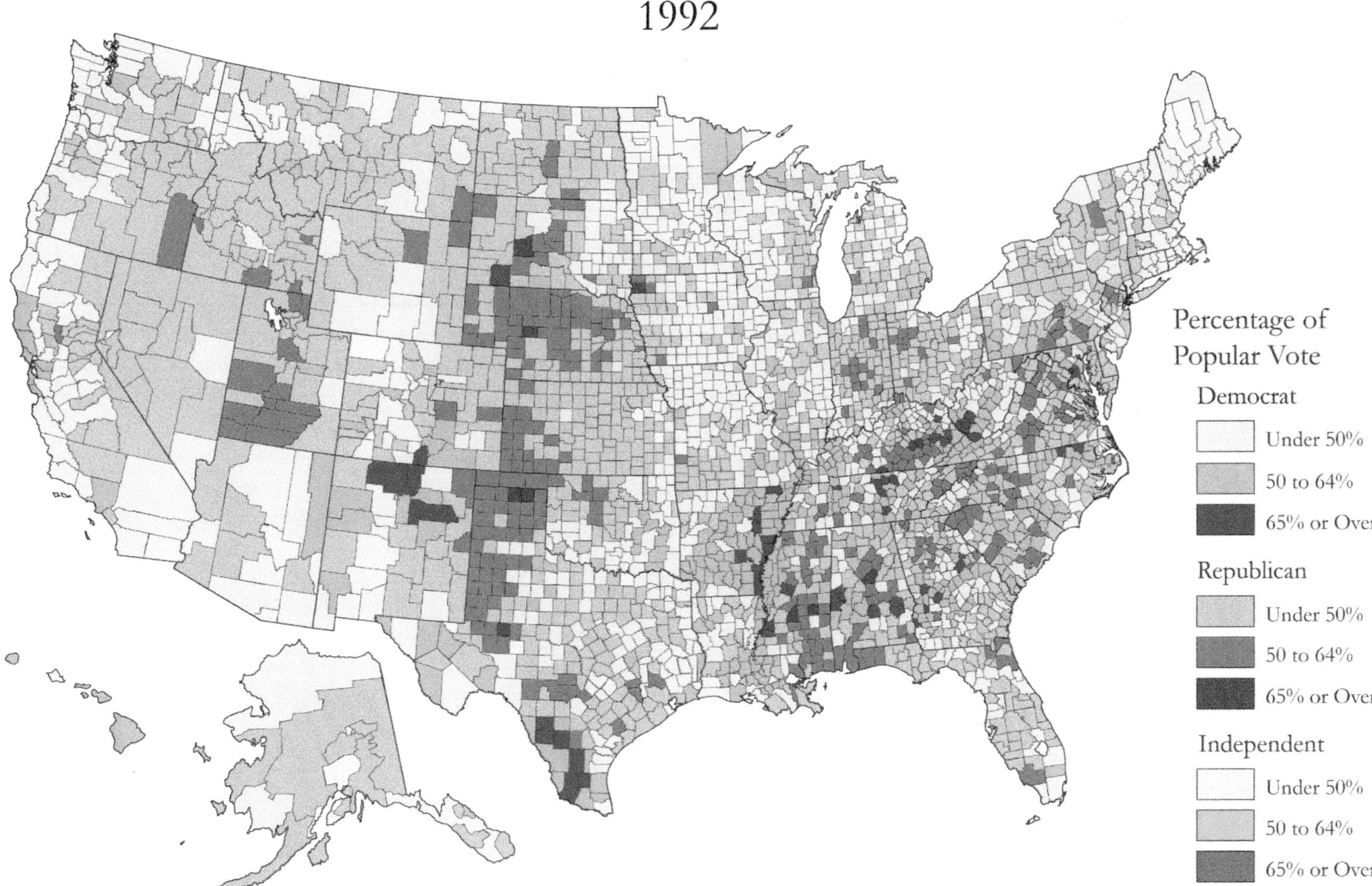
Presidential Election Popular Vote
1992
Percentage of
Popular Vote
Democrat
Under 50%
50 to 64%
65% or Over
Republican
Under 50%
50 to 64%
65% or Over
Independent
Under 50%
50 to 64%
65% or Over

FIGURE 5.28

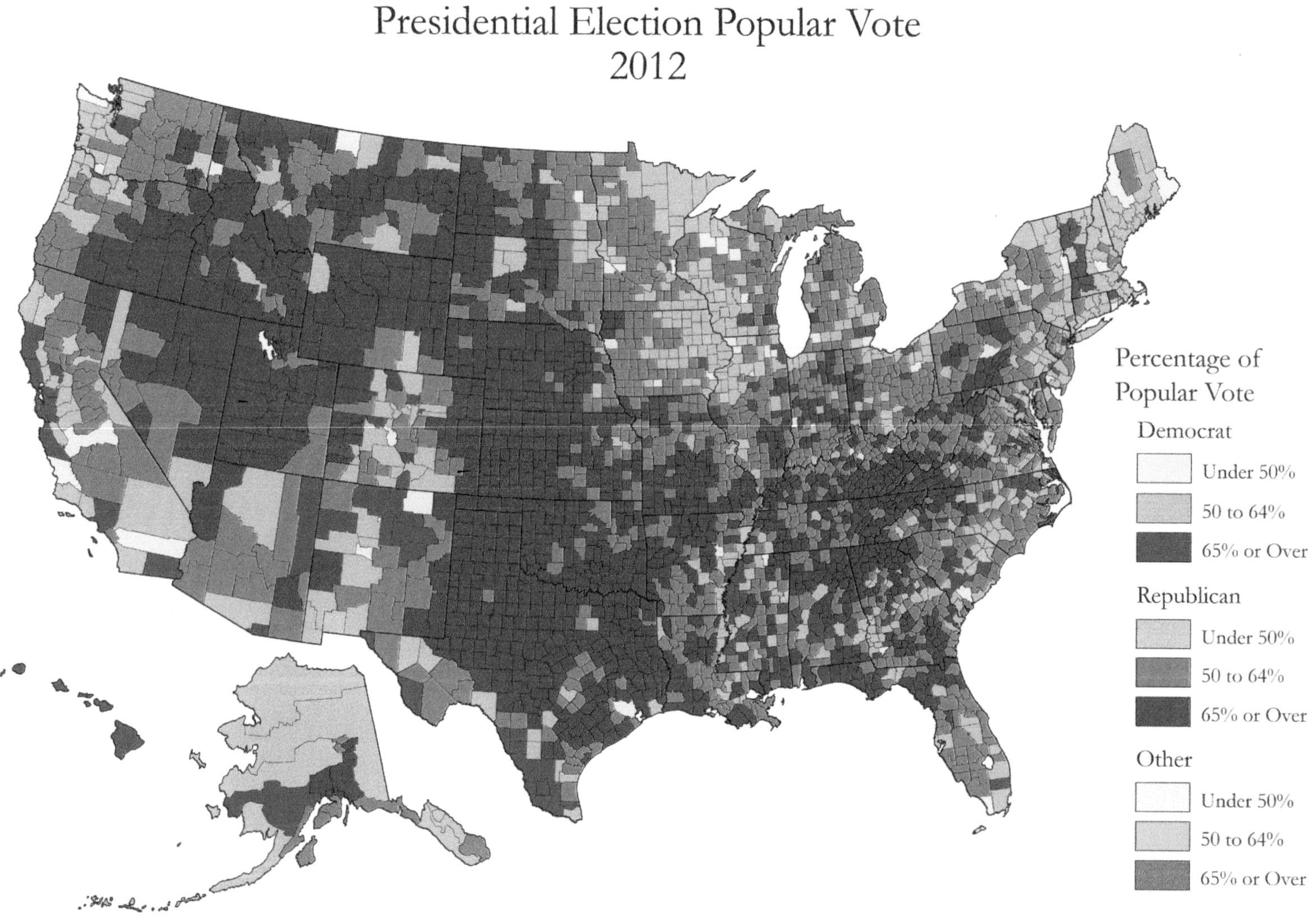
Presidential Election Popular Vote
2012
Percentage of
Popular Vote
Democrat
Under 50%
50 to 64%
65% or Over
Republican
Under 50%
50 to 64%
65% or Over
Other
Under 50%
50 to 64%
65% or Over

METROPOLITAN CONCENTRATION OF THE DEMOCRATIC VOTE

RICHARD L. MORRILL AND JASON COMBS

Similar to the 2008 election, Barack Obama's victory in 2012 was due in large part to his support in metropolitan areas. The continuation of the urban-rural polarization is one of the most dramatic features of the 2012 election and was the basis for the Obama victory. Figures 5.6, 5.7, and 5.8 illustrate the degree of urban-rural polarization in the election.

The Democrats' metropolitan success in 2012 follows a trend that dates back several decades. In general, a polarization of the vote since the 1960s has continued, with nonmetropolitan areas and rural regions supporting Republicans and metropolitan places supporting Democrats. In recent elections, Republican candidates have geographically or spatially won a majority of the country; it is the urban centers that overwhelmingly support liberal candidates that continue to shift elections into the Democratic column.

Despite the fact that Romney polled well in smaller cities and rural counties, Obama's heavy support in America's largest cities proved to be the difference in the 2012 election. Of the fifty-two metropolitan regions with populations exceeding one million, Obama won thirty-seven. Of the two-party vote, which represents more than 98 percent of all votes, the Democrat won 57.6 percent of the votes (39,500,191) in the metropolitan areas compared with Romney's 42.4 percent (29,064,018 votes), a difference of 10,436,173 votes (figure 5.29).

The Democratic victory in 2012 was not just a matter of winning metropolitan areas; it was carrying key places in a dramatic fashion that was the difference in the outcome. The three largest metropolitan areas—New York, Los Angeles, and Chicago—alone provided an advantage of nearly five million votes, almost equal to Obama's margin for the entire nation. He amassed a margin of nearly five million additional votes in the Philadelphia, Washington, Miami, San Francisco, Boston, Detroit, and Seattle metropolitan areas, each of which he carried by more than four hundred thousand votes. His overall margin in the thirty-seven metropolitan areas that he carried was more than twelve million, or more than twice his nationwide margin of victory. These landslide metropolitan victories for Obama were decisive, often impacting the Electoral College vote.

Romney did carry fifteen metropolitan areas with populations of one million or more. The Republican candidate enjoyed success primarily in the South, West, and Upper Midwest, winning in metropolitan areas like Dallas, Houston, Jacksonville, and Nashville in the South, Salt Lake City in the West, and Cincinnati and Indianapolis in the Midwest. In comparison to Obama's dominance in the larger metropolitan areas, Romney won his fifteen metropolitan regions by a mere 1,584,358—less than Obama's margin of victory in the New York metropolitan area alone.

Voting patterns dating back to the 1960s and tensions between more conservative, rural voters and their liberal, urban counterparts are most likely to continue as demographic trends also continue. As the United States becomes more urbanized and rural areas continue decades-long population declines, the philosophical differences between the two populations will only become more acute. This shift poses concerns for the Republican Party, which, if it decides to support more moderate proposals in an attempt to attract metropolitan voters, could potentially alienate itself from its conservative base.

FIGURE 5.29

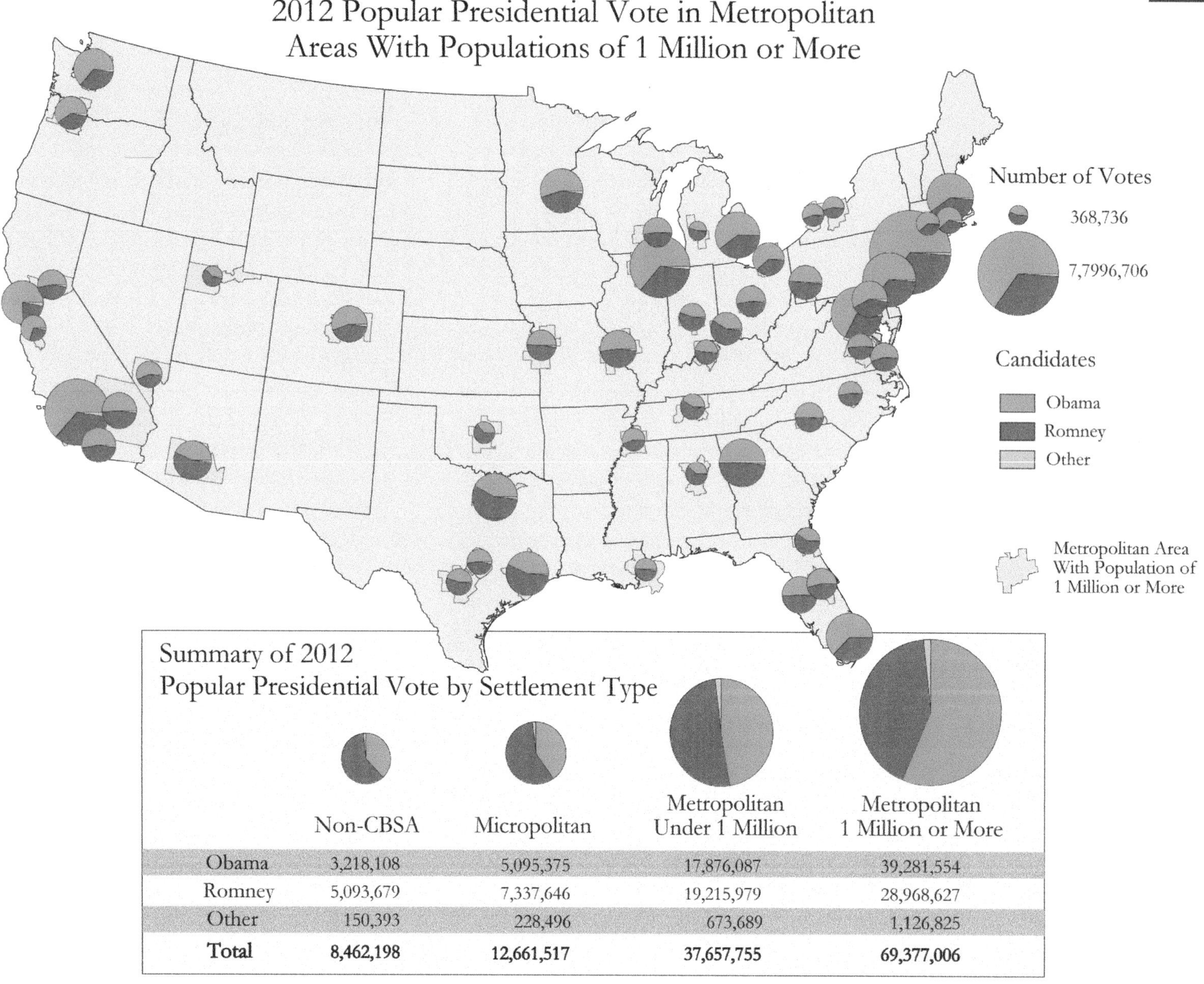

	Non-CBSA	Micropolitan	Metropolitan Under 1 Million	Metropolitan 1 Million or More
Obama	3,218,108	5,095,375	17,876,087	39,281,554
Romney	5,093,679	7,337,646	19,215,979	28,968,627
Other	150,393	228,496	673,689	1,126,825
Total	**8,462,198**	**12,661,517**	**37,657,755**	**69,377,006**

MICROPOLITAN COUNTY VOTING

JASON COMBS

The political divide between metropolitan areas, micropolitan counties, and rural regions was even more pronounced in the 2012 election cycle in comparison to 2008. Party strength became more entrenched, with Democrats enjoying continued success in the metropolitan areas and Republicans in smaller cities and rural counties. Despite the fact that the Republican candidate won an overwhelming majority of smaller cities and rural counties, President Obama carried a majority of metropolitan areas, and their tremendous population advantage was the difference in the election—metropolitan areas accounted for 83.6 percent of all votes in 2012 in comparison to only 9.9 percent for micropolitan counties and 6.4 percent for rural counties.

This section of the chapter examines voting patterns in micropolitan counties. A relatively new term, "micropolitan" areas include a central city with a population of 10,000 to 49,999 in addition to surrounding counties economically linked to the central city. There are currently 685 counties in the United States that have been classified as micropolitan (figure 5.30). In these 685 counties, Republican candidate Mitt Romney garnered 58.6 percent of the votes (7,370,122) compared with President Obama's 41.4 percent (5,197,265). Moreover, Romney carried the rural counties by an even wider margin, capturing 61.4 percent (5,014,787 votes) compared with Obama's 38.6 percent (3,149,851 votes). In both the micropolitan and rural county categories, Romney fared much better than the previous Republican presidential candidate John McCain did in 2008.

The Republican candidate won 547 micropolitan counties (80.0 percent) in comparison with the Democrat's 138 counties, a mere 20.0 percent of the total. Romney enjoyed success in micropolitan counties across the country, especially in the Great Plains, Midwest, Mountain West, and parts of the South (figure 5.27). Romney won 112 micropolitan counties with at least 70 percent of the vote and another 28 micropolitan counties with at least 80 percent of the vote, including three each in Nebraska and Utah and ten in Texas. Additionally, Romney carried two micropolitan counties with at least 90 percent of the vote—Roberts County, Texas (92.13 percent), and Madison County, Idaho (93.29 percent)—and three more counties approached that threshold, including Uintah, Utah (89.97 percent), Box Elder, Utah (88.11 percent), and Gray, Texas (87.20 percent). All of Romney's top counties have significant white populations, and there is also a Mormon influence as well.

Obama did not have widespread support at the micropolitan level but did enjoy pockets of success (figure 5.28). Several micropolitan counties along the Pacific Coast and in the Southwest backed Obama, as did counties in the fertile crescent stretching from the lower Mississippi delta through Alabama and Georgia to the Carolinas. Other pockets of support included micropolitan counties in upstate New York, New Hampshire, and Vermont as well as several counties in Illinois, Iowa, and Wisconsin. In contrast to Romney, Obama carried a mere fifteen micropolitan counties with at least 70 percent of the vote and only three with at least 80 percent of the vote, including Baldwin County, Georgia (80.92 percent), Starr County, Texas (86.34 percent), and Macon County, Alabama (87.0 percent). Other Obama counties that approached that mark include Maverick, Texas (78.60 percent), and Taos, New Mexico (78.09 percent).

FIGURE 5.30

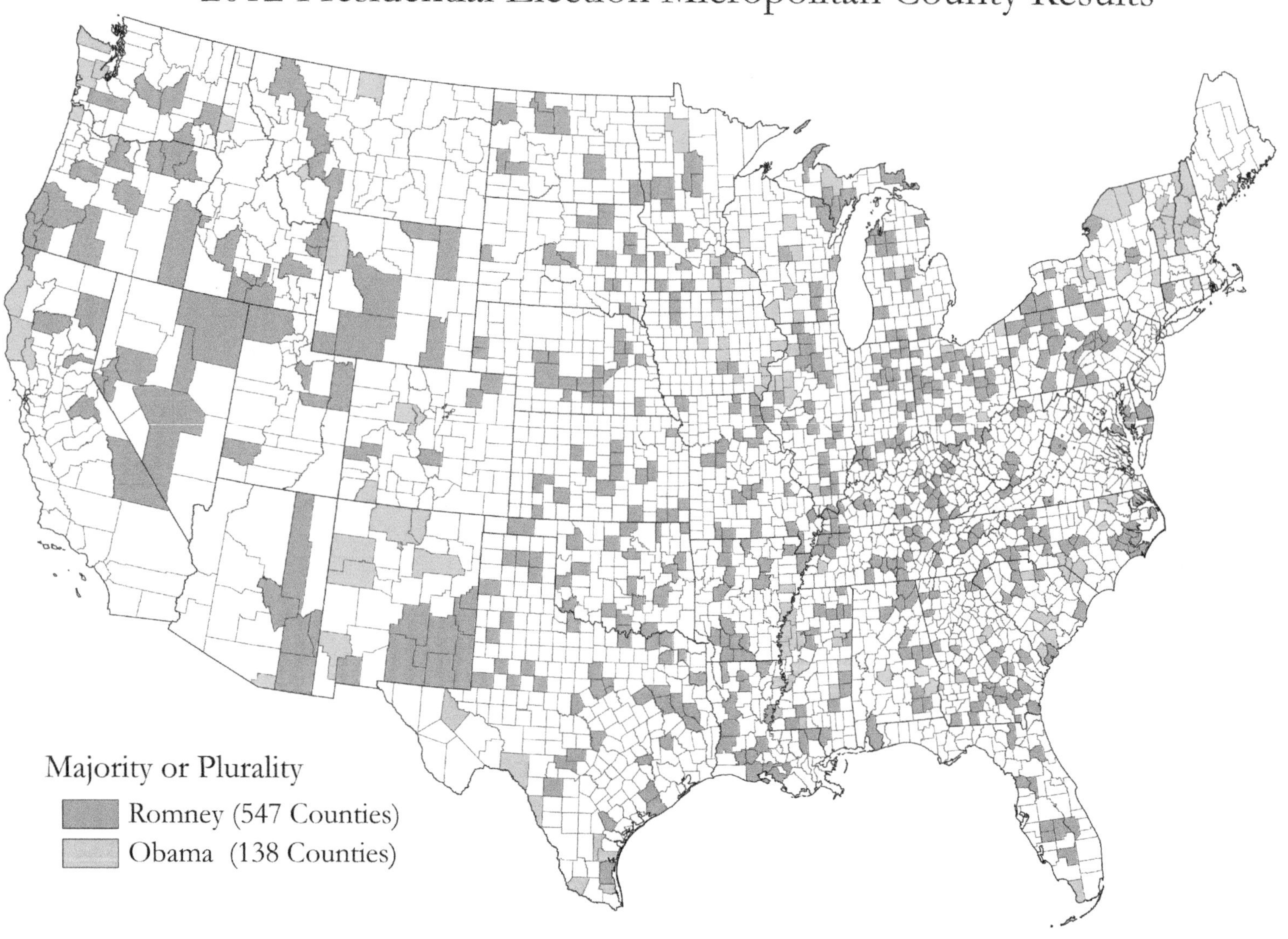
2012 Presidential Election Micropolitan County Results
Majority or Plurality
Romney (547 Counties)
Obama (138 Counties)

It is important to note that all of Obama's top counties contain majority African American or Hispanic populations.

Despite the fact that Romney dominated in micropolitan counties, the Republican's margin of victory for all 685 counties was only 2,172,857, just slightly more than President Obama's margin of victory in the New York City metropolitan area alone (2,142,327). This fact and the 2012 election in general highlight several important trends. One is that presidential candidates who carry a majority of metropolitan areas are likely to enjoy success, and the other is that voting cleavages between more liberal metropolitan areas and more conservative micropolitan and rural counties are also likely to continue. The polarization of the electorate and these voting patterns are not new, but ideological divisions in the United States are clearly becoming more pronounced.

POLITICS IN THE DIVERSIFYING SUBURBS

CHRISTOPHER NIEDT

It has been more than a decade since US census reports revealed that the suburban demographic majority had finally arrived. Reporters greeted the occasion with excitement, but social scientists were considerably more measured. The latter had technical questions about the conventional census-based definition of the suburbs and more fundamental concerns about whether the suburb-city distinction was still relevant in the present-day United States. Those who did find the distinction relevant could track a long arc of suburban cultural and economic ascendancy; the suburbs' share of the national population rose from 23 percent in 1950 to 46 percent in 1990, and in this light, the final jump to above 50 percent in 2000 was largely a symbolic milestone.

The threshold has been most significant for the study of electoral politics. The methodological challenges of isolating the suburban vote are just as challenging as those of demographic analysis. But the relevance of the city-suburb distinction and the majority itself were clearer. Jurisdictional boundaries between city and suburbs, particularly in places where annexation is difficult, have a direct influence on representation, policy, and ultimately the life chances of those living on either side of the city line. Suburban majorities may enhance the domination of legislators at the state and federal levels, freeing them from coalitions with urban and rural representatives.

Even before the suburbs became home to more than half of the US population, they had become coveted partisan territory. In the 1950s and 1960s, political scientists and sociologists had debated whether suburban life turned urban Democrats into Republicans but failed to show that location—independent of voters' other characteristics—accounted for political behavior. Nevertheless, Republican strategists and the grassroots activists of the New Right courted suburban voters, and by the late 1980s and early 1990s, as supposedly "urban" issues such as the drug war and federal spending on welfare programs came to the fore, there was an observable suburban place effect on voting patterns. The rise of the Democratic Leadership Coalition marked the beginning of a suburban drift toward the Democrats.

Yet even as the parties vied to win over suburban voters, suburbs themselves have been experiencing growing ethnic and class diversity, making the suburban electorate less uniform. This has resulted in a tension among election observers inside and outside of the academy. On the one hand, there is the continuing tendency to treat the swinging suburbs monolithically—the implicit suggestion being that suburbanites are moderate or susceptible to savvy partisan appeals; on the other hand, there is a recognition that suburban diversity—more than the shifts within the suburban white, middle-class constituencies—may account for the oscillation. This is an empirical question that has not been answered fully by the existing literature or by exit polling. The basic analysis presented here, based on census data and official vote tallies, reflects this tension. I will begin by examining the overall suburban vote and its significance for the primary and general elections before turning to the question of diversity.

In the 2012 primary season, suburban Republicans largely supported Mitt Romney and played a key role in his nomination. This pattern was inconsistent early in the year: the suburbs expanded his lead in New Hampshire and may have decided Florida but did not deliver Minnesota to Romney. But it became much more apparent in March, particularly in the pivotal midwestern contests. In Michigan, Rick Santorum led among rural and urban Republican voters, but Romney's 50,700-vote lead in the suburbs saved him from the symbolic defeat of losing his native state. Ohio's suburbs provided a similar margin, giving the margin of votes needed for Romney to win a narrow victory. Suburban Chicago almost single-handedly won Illinois for Romney on March 20, breaking a series of Santorum victories in the southern and Plains states. Two weeks later, the Milwaukee suburbs did much the same in Wisconsin, adding a disappointing defeat for Santorum that contributed to the suspension of his campaign. In several other states, the suburbs either substantially expanded Romney's margins of victory or reduced Santorum's margins considerably.

It is more difficult to establish the suburban vote's effect on the general election. In 2008, suburban voters had played a key role in moving certain states, such as Nevada and Virginia, into the Democratic column. Suburbs in other swing states were not as decisive but shifted nearly as many votes toward the Democrats as urban jurisdictions. Four years later, many of these suburbanites moved back toward the Republicans but not enough to erase earlier gains at the county or state levels. The heavily suburban Tampa and Orlando metropolitan areas along the I-4 corridor of Florida, for example, had given Barack Obama a margin of 261,000 votes in 2008, a number that exceeded the statewide margin of victory. The same areas shifted only 31,200 votes back to the Republicans in 2012, allowing the Democrats to hold Florida. On the other hand, Indiana and North Carolina's suburban areas joined the countryside in swinging back toward the Republicans, resulting in Republican pickups rather than a reprise of 2008's razor-thin Democratic victories in these states.

The suburbs are critically important in determining House control, and post-2012, suburban residents were almost evenly divided between Republican and Democratic districts. After the wave of Republican victories in 2010, the percentage of suburbanites living in Republican districts rose from 47 to 61 percent. Yet the districts that flipped from Democratic to Republican were only 54 percent suburban, even though suburban residents now account for 58 percent of the national population. By comparison, micropolitan and rural areas were overrepresented: 27 percent of those in the newly Republican districts lived in micropolitan or rural areas, far exceeding their 15 percent share of the national population. Redistricting and Democratic gains in 2012 reduced the number of suburbanites living in Republican districts from 61 to 56 percent, even as the percentage in micropolitan and rural areas continued to increase. The same shift, seen from another angle, has also slightly diminished the suburbs' share of the Republican base, which dropped from 64 to 61 percent in 2010 and again to 60 percent in 2012. For the Democrats, the suburbs' importance rose slightly, from 54 percent in 2008 and 2010 to 55 percent after the most recent election. Suburban populations still account for majorities in both parties' districts, however, and make up a full two-thirds of the population in the ninety swing districts recently identified by political analyst Charlie Cook.

The importance of suburban voters within swing districts fits the common perception that the suburbanites occupy an intermediate position between liberal urban centers and conservative rural areas. Although the generalization is often overdrawn, it has been borne out in multiple waves of the Hofstra/PSRAI National Suburban Survey (NSS). In June 2012, for example, 39 percent of suburban respondents had an unfavorable impression of the Tea Party, compared with 46 percent in the cities and 27 percent in rural areas. That October, 52 percent of suburban registered voters responded that they were leaning toward voting for Obama in the general election, compared with 62 percent in the cities and 39 percent in rural areas.

But the apparent suburban moderation obscures growing suburban political divisions often drawn along the lines of race and ethnicity. According to the most recent American Community Survey, Latino, African American, and Asian American residents account for 15, 10, and 5 percent of the suburban population, respectively. This demographic diversity has effects on politics, as reflected in the responses to the 2012 NSS. In the June survey, suburban minority respondents voiced support for a more assertive federal government. Suburban minority respondents were more likely than suburban whites to have a favorable view of health-care reform (41 percent to 26 percent) and more likely to support a broad government role in the regulation of business (49 percent to 35 percent), green job creation (73 percent vs. 47 percent), and the reduction of income disparities (73 percent vs. 50 percent). As the election approached, suburban minority respondents were more satisfied with the direction of the country than suburban whites (44 percent vs. 24 percent), more approving of Obama's performance (67 percent vs. 41 percent), more likely to vote for Obama (70 percent vs. 40 percent), and more likely to support Democratic congressional candidates (68 percent vs. 35 percent).

The Democratic-Republican congressional balance, in fact, looks quite different when seen through the lens of suburban diversity. Although 56 percent of suburbanites now live in Republican districts, the rate varies considerably by ethnic background and class: 62 percent of whites live in Republican districts, compared with 43 percent of African Americans, 41 percent of Latinos, and 40 percent of Asian Americans. Class divisions are also apparent: just over half of suburbanites who live in census tracts where median incomes are below the metropolitan level are included in Republican districts, compared with only one-third of those in tracts where median incomes are less than half the metropolitan level. These figures do not provide direct evidence for the voting behavior of these suburban groups, as these districts reflect decennial, state-level struggles over redistricting. But they do illustrate a divide between suburban constituencies and their representatives that has consequences for policy and the development of group interests.

The effect of growing suburban diversity is also apparent in metropolitan-level general election results from the red, blue, and swing states. Many metropolises, like the nation as a whole, swung their votes away from Obama in 2012, as illustrated in Figure 5.14. But the size of the shift varied considerably by region, and variations appeared at the metropolitan level as well, often corresponding with patterns of ethnic diversity. The maps below compare the percentage shift toward the Republicans to non-Hispanic whites as a percentage of total population. In the three metro areas shown here—Atlanta (figure 5.31), Los Angeles (figures 5.32 and 5.33), and Washington, DC (figure 5.34)—we see similar patterns. The Democratic vote in the central cities of all three metros was already quite high before 2012, and partisan strength remains stable. The less ethnically diverse newer suburbs and exurbs shifted strongly toward the Republicans. But suburban areas with large or growing Latino, black, and Asian populations bucked the national trend and shifted toward the Democrats. This included places like Gwinnett and Clayton Counties outside of Atlanta, Prince George's and Charles Counties near DC, and the western San Gabriel Valley and Santa Ana outside of Los Angeles. Obviously, ethnicity is only one of several factors that have been associated with support for Obama and the Democratic Party. Nevertheless, the correspondence between the vote and minority population share is striking.

Whether these trends continue in the 2014 and 2016 elections will depend on whether the parties speak to diversifying suburbs in new and creative ways rather than dusting off the outmoded city-suburb binaries of past generations. In the past two presidential elections, national groups such as Building One America and the Brookings Metropolitan Policy Program have developed policy platforms aimed particularly at aging suburban constituencies, which focused on transportation and housing investment (rather than antiurban animus). Politicians at the federal level have been slow to pick up on these approaches, so it has been difficult to judge their resonance. But the critical decisions about how to frame messages and mobilize the suburbs (during and between campaign seasons) will affect the outcomes of future contests. It will provide the real-life answer to the twenty-first-century version of the old suburban politics puzzle: whether suburban electoral behavior reflects place-independent factors, a place effect rooted in homogeneity and exclusion, or a new suburban politics that confounds our expectations.

FIGURE 5.31

Atlanta Area

Shift to Republican Party
2012 Presidential Election

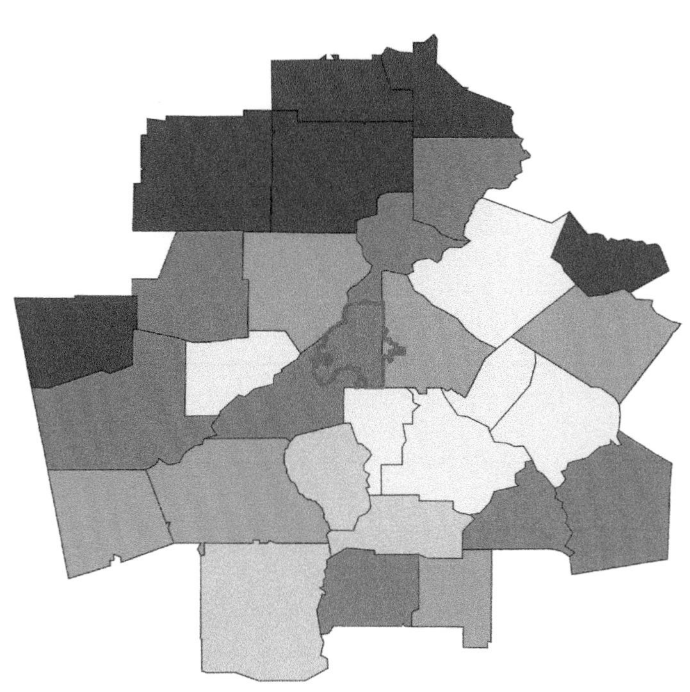

Percentage Shift
to Republican Party

- -0.42 to -3.54
- -0.41 to 0.62
- 0.63 to 1.88
- 1.89 to 2.60
- 2.61 to 4.82

Atlanta Area Shift to Republican Party
1.56 Percent of Total Popular Vote

City of Atlanta

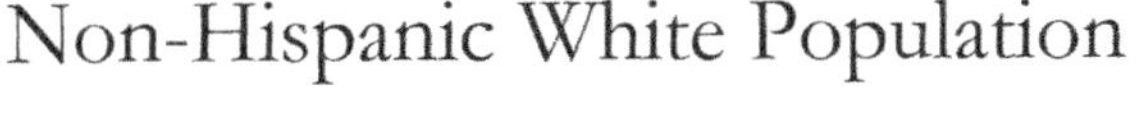

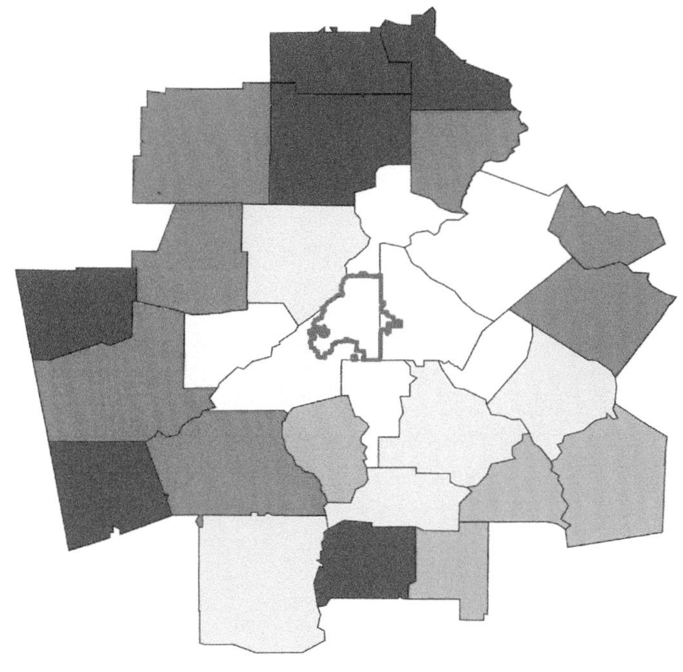

Percentage of
Total Population

- 14.35 to 49.98
- 49.99 to 61.67
- 61.68 to 73.91
- 73.92 to 81.60
- 81.61 to 95.46

Atlanta Area Non-Hispanic White Population
51.60 Percent of Total Population

FIGURE 5.32

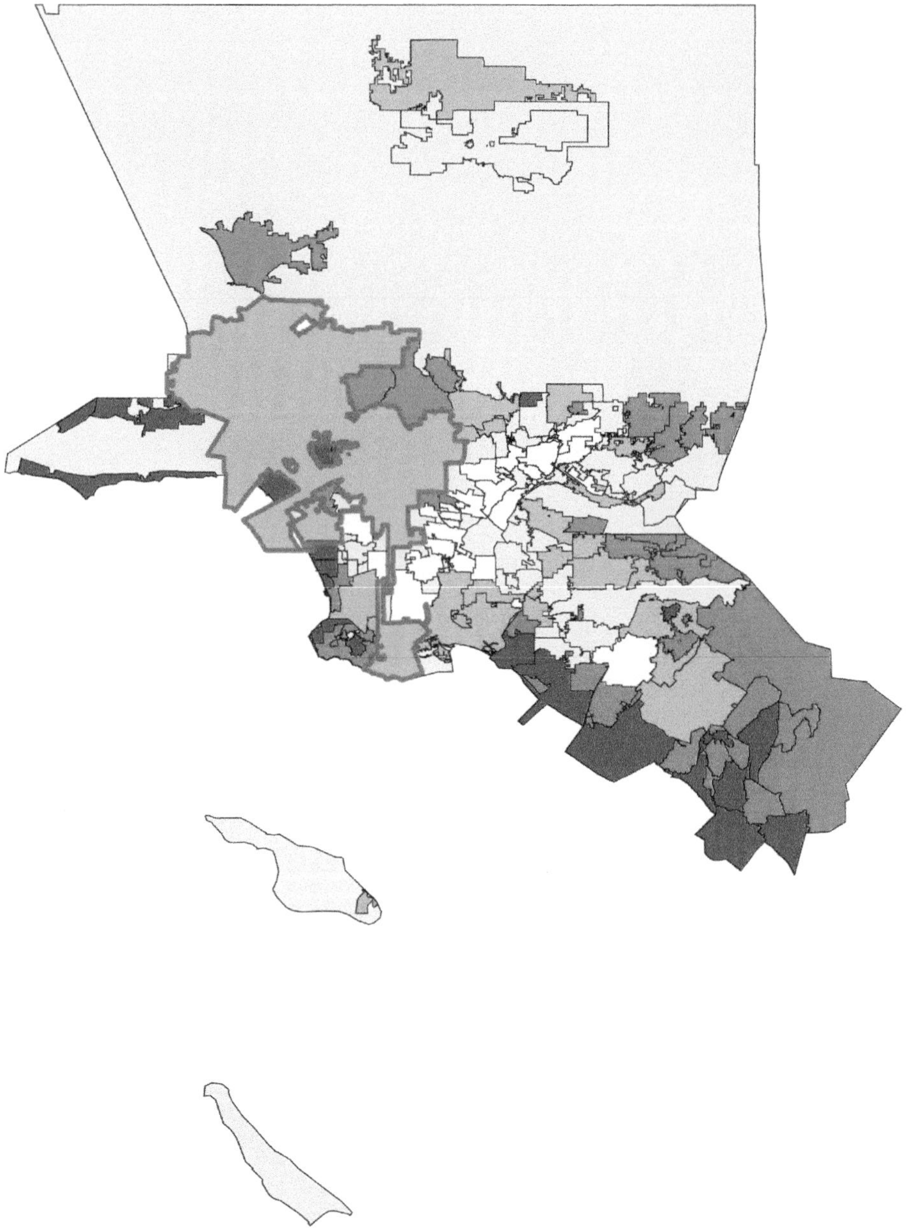

Los Angeles Area Non-Hispanic White Population

Non-Hispanic White Population Percentage of Total Population

- 69.2 to 89.6
- 47.6 to 69.1
- 28.3 to 47.5
- 9.5 to 28.2
- 0.8 to 9.4

City of Los Angeles

Los Angeles Area Non-Hispanic White Population
32.39 Percent of Total Population

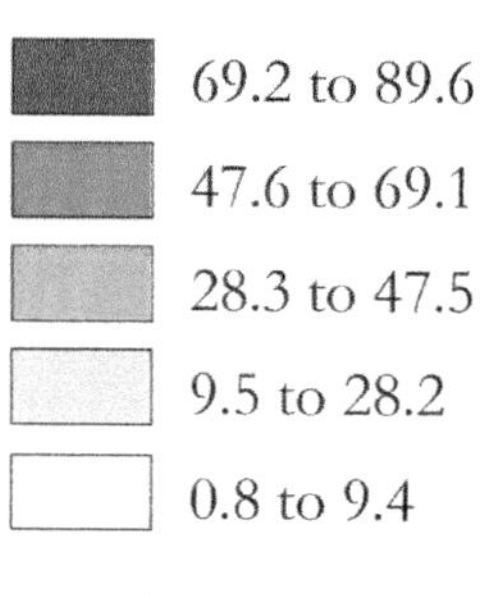

FIGURE 5.33

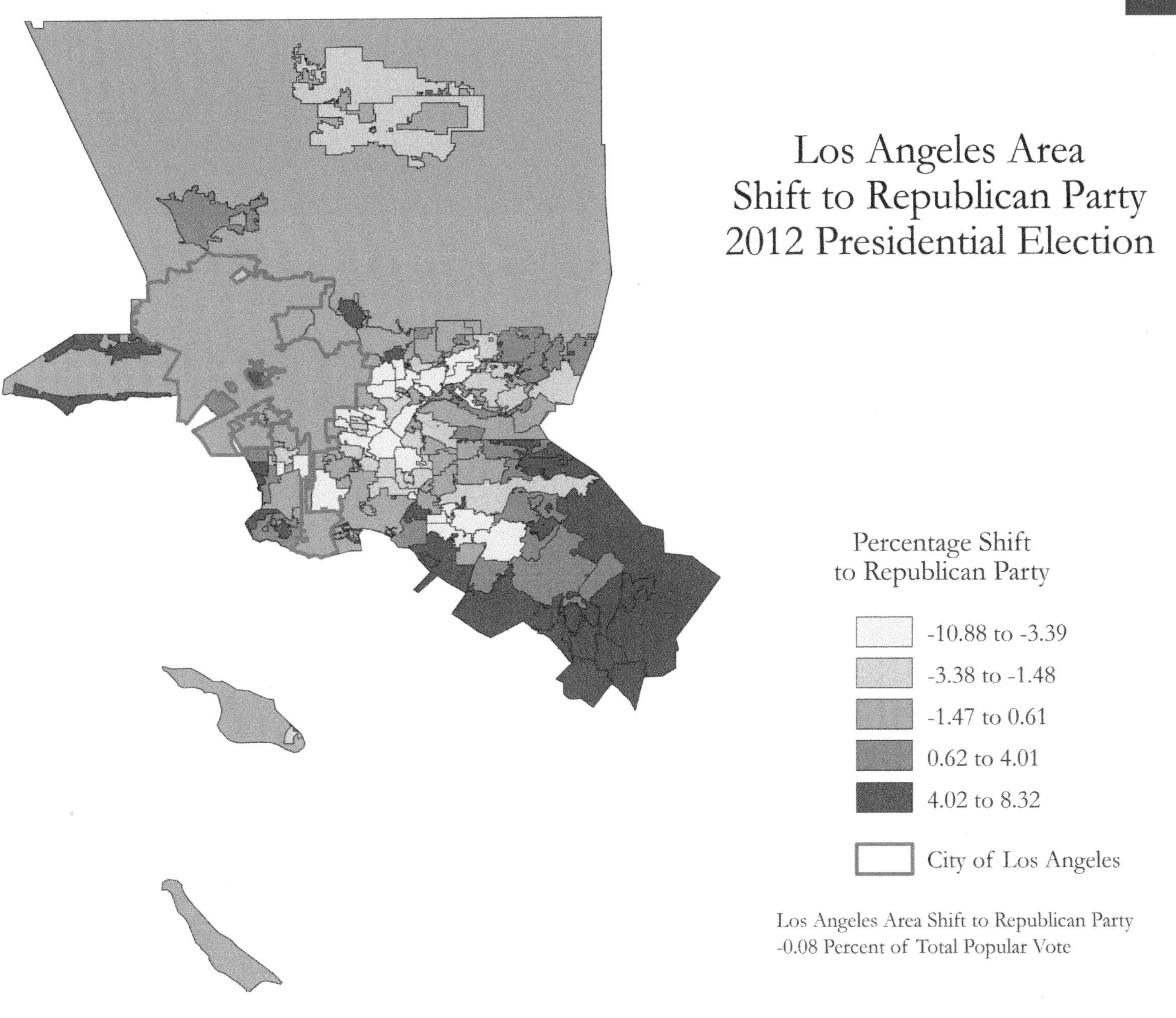
Los Angeles Area
Shift to Republican Party
2012 Presidential Election
Percentage Shift
to Republican Party
-10.88 to -3.39
-3.38 to -1.48
-1.47 to 0.61
0.62 to 4.01
4.02 to 8.32
City of Los Angeles
Los Angeles Area Shift to Republican Party
-0.08 Percent of Total Popular Vote

FIGURE 5.34

Washington Area

Shift to Republican Party 2012 Presidential Election

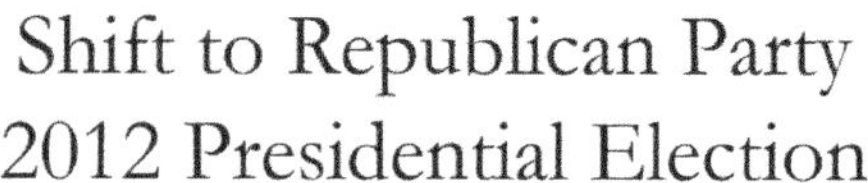

Non-Hispanic White Population

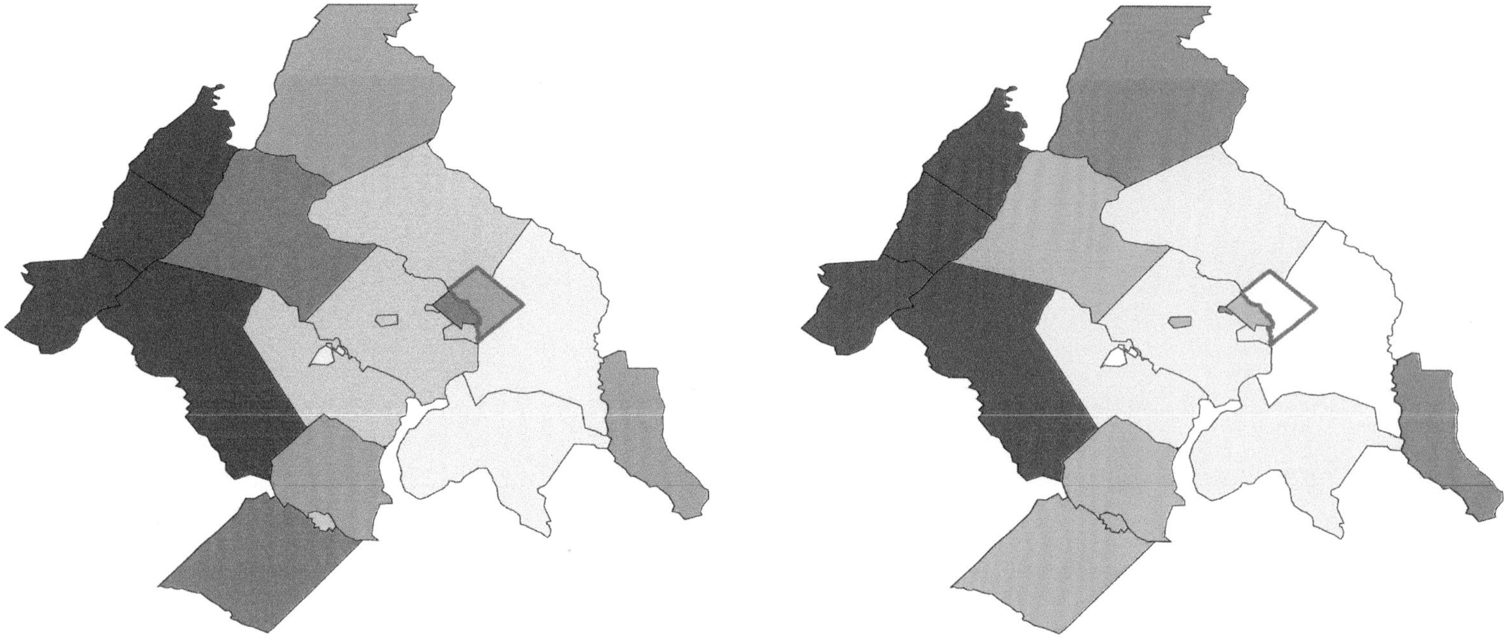

Percentage Shift to Republican Party

- -0.42 to -3.54
- -0.41 to 0.62
- 0.63 to 1.88
- 1.89 to 2.60
- 2.61 to 4.82

Washington Area Shift to Republican Party
0.41 Percent of Total Popular Vote

District of Columbia

Percentage of Total Population

- 14.35 to 49.98
- 49.99 to 61.67
- 61.68 to 73.91
- 73.92 to 81.60
- 81.61 to 95.46

Washington Area Non-Hispanic White Population
49.87 Percent of Total Population

REGIONS

NORTHEAST

WILLIAM BERENTSEN

The northeastern United States has become a dependable stronghold for the Democratic Party in presidential and congressional elections; and New England, in particular, now heavily favors Democrats in national elections, including the 2012 presidential election. Once a Republican Party stronghold, a stepwise and not always obvious trend toward the current situation began nearly a half century ago. "Almost in reverse correlation with Republican advances in the South have come Republican losses in the Northeast, which for much of the Party's history was its strongest base" (Reiter and Stonecash 2011, xiii–iv).

Around the year 1900, the Northeast, and especially New England, was completely dominated by the Republican Party. For example, in the 1894 US House election, the only New England Democrat to win a seat was the grandfather of JFK, John Francis Fitzgerald, who then joined twenty-five Republican representatives from New England in Washington, DC. In the 1896 and 1900 presidential elections, the Republican presidential candidate, William McKinley, carried all northeastern states (Reiter and Stonecash 2011); but in 2004, 2008, and 2012, Republican presidential candidates won none at all. The same outcomes also occurred in 1964, 1992, and 1996. Related to this evolving pattern of political dominance by New England Democrats in national elections, in 2013 there were no Republican US House members from New England, and the only Republican senator was the politically moderate Susan Collins (Maine).

On the other hand, as Figure 6.1 indicates, voters in the Appalachian region of the Northeast have strongly favored Republican candidates in the last two presidential elections, and in parts of the Mid-Atlantic region, notably in electoral-rich Pennsylvania, they appear likely to continue to vote Republican as long as Democratic politicians and policymakers view burning coal as a serious problem for the United States (see the following section on Appalachia in this chapter for a more in-depth discussion). In short, in recent presidential

FIGURE 6.1

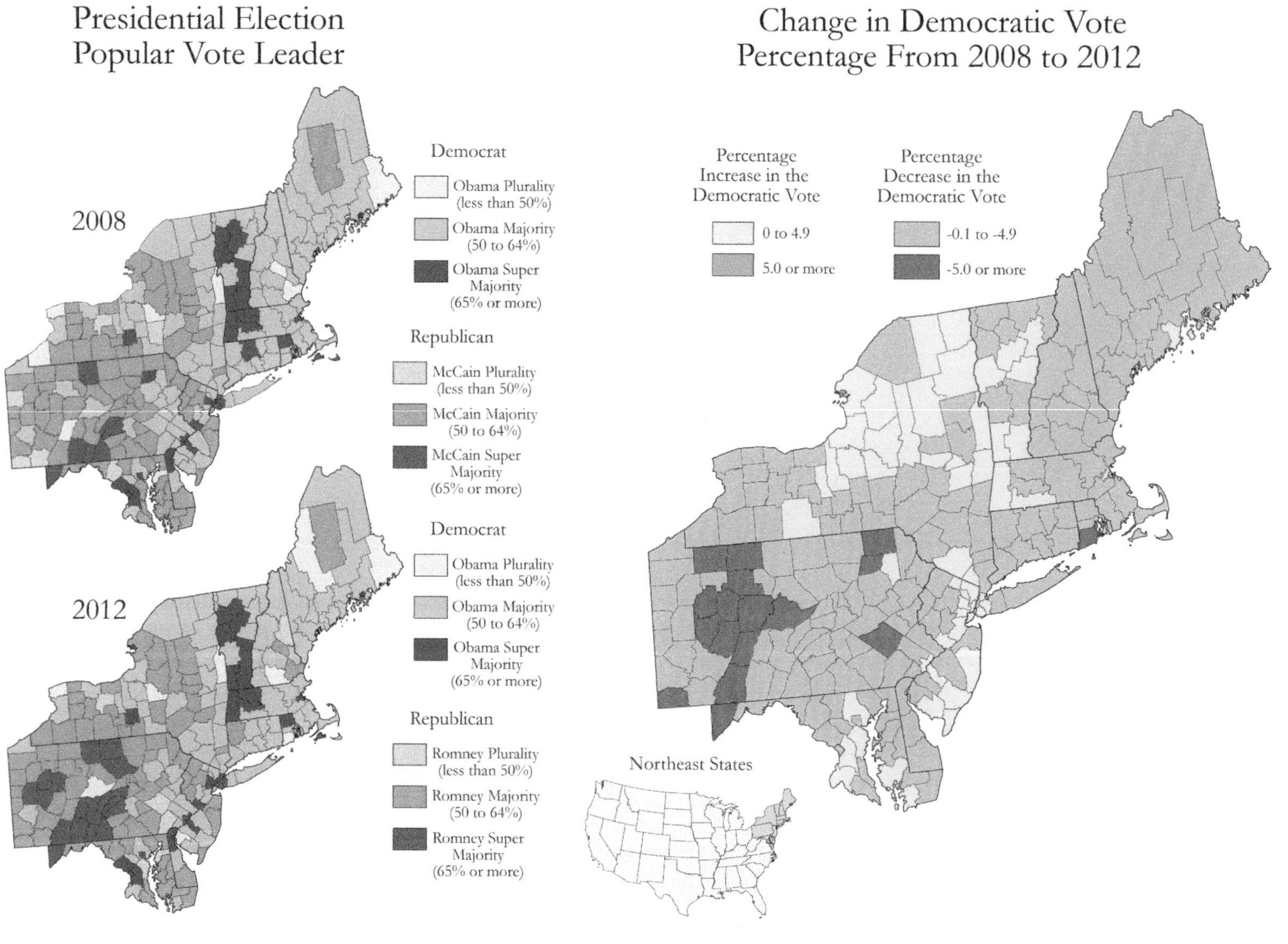

Northeast Region Presidential Elections
Presidential Election
Popular Vote Leader
2008
2012
Democrat
Obama Plurality (less than 50%)
Obama Majority (50 to 64%)
Obama Super Majority (65% or more)
Republican
McCain Plurality (less than 50%)
McCain Majority (50 to 64%)
McCain Super Majority (65% or more)
Democrat
Obama Plurality (less than 50%)
Obama Majority (50 to 64%)
Obama Super Majority (65% or more)
Republican
Romney Plurality (less than 50%)
Romney Majority (50 to 64%)
Romney Super Majority (65% or more)
Change in Democratic Vote
Percentage From 2008 to 2012
Percentage Increase in the Democratic Vote
0 to 4.9
5.0 or more
Percentage Decrease in the Democratic Vote
-0.1 to -4.9
-5.0 or more
Northeast States

elections, voters in the Appalachian Northeast most often chose Republican and in the non-Appalachian Northeast voted Democratic.

The maps depicting voting by counties in the Northeast in recent presidential elections illustrate both some of the generalizations made above and more details as well. As noted above, in presidential elections, New Englanders voted overwhelmingly Democratic in 2008 and 2012, but the geographic patterns are quite different in the Mid-Atlantic states. In the 2008 election, voters in only one New England county favored John McCain over Barack Obama—and that one was a very low-population county in Maine.

In 2012, voters in five counties in rural New England favored Mitt Romney (figure 6.1). The mapped results in the Mid-Atlantic states show larger geographic areas in which voters favored the Republican candidates over Obama in both 2008 and 2012, though the most populous areas in the region favored Obama, who won by double-digit margins in both elections in all Northeastern states except Pennsylvania and New Hampshire in 2012, where margins of victory were smaller, about half of those in 2012, dropping from about 10 to 5 percent. Obama's margins of victory in the Northeast were largely built in and/or near the region's populous urbanized counties (notably Pittsburgh, Erie, Buffalo, Rochester, Syracuse, Albany, Burlington, Portland, Boston, Providence, Hartford, Springfield, New Haven, New York, Newark, Trenton, Philadelphia, Baltimore, and Washington, DC). Republican victories in less populated rural areas and smaller towns appear prominently in the maps, notably in Appalachia, but these counties accounted for far too few votes to offset Democratic vote totals in highly urbanized regions.

There was a clear trend toward Republican presidential vote gains between 2008 and 2012 across much of the Northeast (except in and near New York City and in parts of upstate New York). While these gains in 2012 in much of the Northeast only modestly reduced still very large statewide percentage gaps between the Republican and Democratic candidates (in most cases, a gap from two to six percentage points), in Pennsylvania and New Hampshire, especially, the trend could indicate concerns for Democrats in the 2016 presidential election. In 2000, George W. Bush needed every electoral vote he got, including the four that he won in New Hampshire, the only electoral votes won thus far by a Republican presidential candidate in the Northeast during the twenty-first century.

The Republican Party will obviously seek electoral gains in the 2016 election, especially in New Hampshire and Pennsylvania, where the gaps between Obama and Romney were not large in 2012. A win by the Republican nominee in either state in 2016, and especially in Pennsylvania, could well have profound consequences for choosing the next president. However, that scenario would almost certainly be more likely with a Republican candidate who was more moderate on social issues than all recent Republican candidates, perhaps someone like Chris Christie, governor of New Jersey. In turn, though, that might also trigger Republican losses in selected southern, Great Plains, and Mountain West states, where the social conservatism of Republican Party platforms and politicians has produced impressive electoral gains for the party in recent decades (Reiter and Stonecash 2011).

While social conservatism attracts many voters to Republican candidates in other parts of the United States, in the Northeast it has led to Republican losses. The northeastern US voters, perceived as more liberal than other US voters, are, in fact, often simply more politically moderate (Berentsen 2009). Those northeasterners who do favor a limited role of government do not also, as is the case elsewhere, expect government to regulate people's social lives. Northeastern Republican voters and politicians are, for example, generally both fiscal conservatives and social moderates, the latter position frequently now causing strife between northeastern Republican office holders on the one hand and Republican officials and pundits elsewhere on the other, notably among Tea Party followers.

While there are Tea Party followers and activists in the Northeast (Cho, Gimpel, and Shaw 2012), these conservative Republicans have thus far not had the same level of electoral impact within the region as they have had elsewhere. At least two other related factors that undercut conservatives' electoral efforts in the Northeast are that voters there are less oriented toward religion than voters elsewhere, and, contrary to voting patterns in other US regions, highly educated people in the Northeast tend to vote Democratic rather than Republican (Reiter and Stonecash 2011).

The Democratic Party has achieved a high-water mark in recent presidential and congressional elections in the Northeast, and it continues to dominate in these elections in urban areas and in New England, in particular.

While in comparison to 2008 the results of the 2012 presidential election indicate a possibly worrying trend for Democrats, the size of many presidential electoral victories in most northeastern states and the underlying choices of broad swaths of the region's voters provide only limited bases for Republicans hopes for future electoral success in the region. Nomination of a moderate Republican as a presidential candidate in 2016, especially one from the Northeast, would most likely make electoral victories in Pennsylvania and New Hampshire a distinct possibility—but such a nominee has not been put forward by the Republican Party anytime recently, and nomination of a moderate would very possibly lead to electoral problems for the Republican Party in other parts of the country. In short, in the near term, the northeastern United States appears likely to remain a major presidential electoral vote generator for the Democratic Party, as it has been in all elections since 1992.

REFERENCES

Berentsen, William H. 2009. "The Northeast." In *Atlas of the 2008 Election*, edited by G. Webster, S. Brunn, F. Shelley, C. Archer, and S. Lavin, 121–25. Lanham, MD: Rowman & Littlefield.

Cho, Wendy K. Tam, James G. Gimpel, and Daron R. Shaw. 2012. "The Tea Party Movement and the Geography of Collective Action." *Quarterly Journal of Political Science* 7:105–33.

Reiter, Howard, and Jeffrey M. Stonecash. 2011. *Counter Realignment: Political Change in the Northeastern United States* (New York: Cambridge University Press).

APPALACHIA

KENNETH C. MARTIS

The Appalachian region stretches southwestward from southern New York State, inland paralleling the Atlantic coast, to northern Alabama and Georgia and northeastern Mississippi. Appalachia can be defined in three ways. First, it is a physiographic region containing the rolling hills of the Appalachian Piedmont, mountain peaks of the Appalachian Valley and Ridge, and dendritic drainage pattern and complex incised topography of the Appalachian Plateau. Appalachia is also a long-recognized cultural region characterized by a high percentage of rural white population; large areas with poor rankings in educational, social, and economic indicators; high reliance on agriculture and extractive industries such as coal, timber, and natural gas; distinctive musical and food heritage; and high adherence to fundamentalist Protestant and nonaffiliated Christian churches.

Appalachia is also a rare phenomenon in American geography in that it is a precisely politically defined region by the United States Congress. In 1965 the Appalachian Regional Commission (ARC) was created to promote economic development in this lagging region. In order to funnel the assistance, a map was created to define the Appalachian region by county. Today the expanded ARC area encompasses 420 counties in 13 states, the entire state of West Virginia, and the Appalachian portion of Alabama, Georgia, Kentucky, Maryland, Mississippi, New York, North Carolina, Ohio, Pennsylvania, South Carolina, Tennessee, and Virginia. The ARC boundary lines are used in the electoral analysis for this region.

HISTORICAL POLITICAL PARTY SUPPORT PATTERNS

The Appalachian region stretches over one thousand miles from the northern state of New York into the heart of the Deep South. Like all large regions, voting tendencies have not been uniform over time. Appalachian political similarity can be traced to before the Civil War. In many states, the so-called upcountry was distinguished from the original coastal plain settlements, and many differences and disputes existed. It was the Civil War, however, which began to define much of the politics of this region. This is especially so south of the Mason-Dixon Line. The mountainous Appalachian region was not hospitable to large plantations and slavery, and this region remained predominantly white. After secession, substantial portions of the Southern Appalachians remained Unionist, especially large areas of eastern Tennessee and southeastern Kentucky. In addition, the Appalachian portion of Virginia completely broke away from the mother state to form West Virginia.

In the post–Civil War political realignment, much of Appalachia adopted the Republican Party as the party of the Union. An examination of Appalachian county voting maps in the *Historical Atlas of U.S. Presidential Elections 1788–2004* reveals a consistent Republican support pattern in the abovementioned areas and, of course, the Appalachian portion of the northern states of Ohio, Pennsylvania, and New York. Beginning with the realignment in the 1890s, the Appalachian areas of western North Carolina and western Virginia also show Republican support.

In the late 1920s and early 1930s the Great Depression brought another significant realignment of American politics, and Appalachia was no exception. New Deal policies of government assistance to impoverished areas and programs like the Tennessee Valley Authority were welcomed in this region. In the same period, the United Mine Workers, a powerful force in many areas, aligned with the Democratic Party and its pro-union policies. For example, West Virginia voted Democratic in every election from 1932 through 1952 after having voted Republican every time from 1896 through 1928 (except for the split Republican ballot election of 1912). It is important to note that even in this era of expanded Democratic support, the core Unionist areas of eastern Tennessee and southeastern Kentucky remained loyal to the GOP.

The 1950s brought an era where electoral support in Appalachia moved back and forth between the major parties. This era of swing support lasted almost exactly a half century, until 2000. The popularity of war hero Dwight Eisenhower brought back Republican support to much of Appalachia through 1960 and the candidacy of Richard Nixon. The 1960 election was significant for Appalachia when Catholic candidate John F. Kennedy used the heavily Protestant West Virginia and its Democratic primary as a bellwether as to whether a Catholic could win the presidency. Kennedy won the primary and the presidency, carrying West Virginia while losing the majority of Appalachian counties.

In 1964 the popularity of Lyndon Johnson and his War on Poverty brought a temporary Democratic resurgence. Much of the Democrat-supported War on Poverty was aimed at Appalachia, and the creation of the ARC was part of this effort. The Nixon elections of 1968 and 1972 showed a Republican swing, like the rest of the nation. In the 1976 election, the post-Watergate atmosphere was difficult for the Republicans to overcome, and southerner and born-again Christian Jimmy Carter did well in this region. Another swing occurred again, with popular Republicans Ronald Reagan and George H. W. Bush getting heavy support in 1980, 1984, and 1988. It is important to note that even in this Republican era, unionized coal counties in southern West Virginia, northeastern Kentucky, and southwestern Pennsylvania showed loyal and consistent support for the Democrats. In 1992 and 1996, moderate southerner Bill Clinton carried most Appalachian counties.

Figure 6.2 illustrates the geography of the vote in the 1996 Clinton-Dole contest. The only large areas of Republican support again continue to be post–Civil War Unionist areas of southeastern Kentucky, eastern Tennessee, and western North Carolina. Added to this area are the northern areas of the Deep South states of Georgia, Alabama, and Mississippi, following the trend of the larger South toward the Republican Party. Although Bill Clinton won the Electoral College vote 379–159 in 1996, this was the last election in which a Democratic presidential candidate did well in Appalachia.

The 2012 election witnessed the final stage of the realignment of the Appalachian region from a swing area with pockets of staunch Democratic support to an overwhelmingly Republican area. This process began in the 2000 presidential election with a stunning turnaround in Appalachian voting patterns, which have continued and even expanded through 2004, 2008, and 2012. Therefore, to understand the 2012 voting pattern it is essential to understand the critical 2000 election. The realignment is encapsulated by the issues and stances of the two 2000 candidates and parties. The Democratic candidate, Vice President Al Gore, was an outspoken leader in citing the dangers of global warming, in which the burning of fossil fuels (practically, coal) is a major culprit. This struck to the heart of many Appalachian counties where coal was the sole economic base and states such as West Virginia, Kentucky, and Pennsylvania, where coal makes up a large portion of the economy. A second significant issue was the long-term support of candidate Gore for some sort of gun control. Gun ownership, hunting, and target shooting are a way of life in large areas of Appalachia. While gun ownership and Second Amendment rights became a prominent campaign issue, gun ownership became an example of a much wider group of traditional values and social issues separating Al Gore and Texas governor George W. Bush.

In general, in the last half of the twentieth century, the national Republican Party became more and more conservative and the national Democratic Party more and more liberal. In economic and social welfare issues, great areas of Appalachia were supportive of Democratic principles. However, in social policy, most Appalachians were supportive of traditional principles. Appalachians trend to be older, whiter, more rural, and more socially conservative than the average American voter.

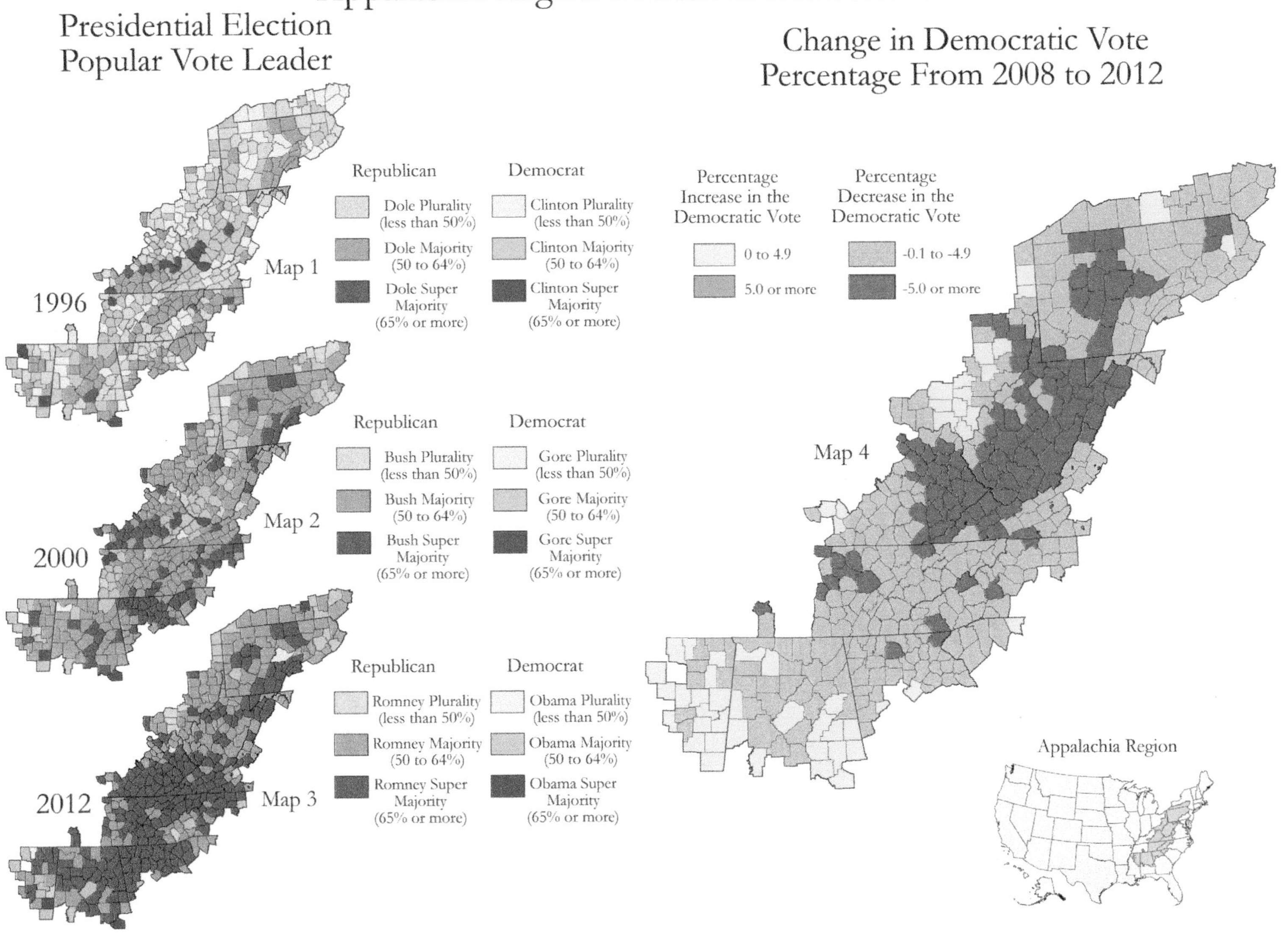
Appalachia Region Presidential Elections
Presidential Election
Popular Vote Leader
1996
Map 1
Republican
Democrat
Dole Plurality (less than 50%)
Dole Majority (50 to 64%)
Dole Super Majority (65% or more)
Clinton Plurality (less than 50%)
Clinton Majority (50 to 64%)
Clinton Super Majority (65% or more)
2000
Map 2
Republican
Democrat
Bush Plurality (less than 50%)
Bush Majority (50 to 64%)
Bush Super Majority (65% or more)
Gore Plurality (less than 50%)
Gore Majority (50 to 64%)
Gore Super Majority (65% or more)
2012
Map 3
Republican
Democrat
Romney Plurality (less than 50%)
Romney Majority (50 to 64%)
Romney Super Majority (65% or more)
Obama Plurality (less than 50%)
Obama Majority (50 to 64%)
Obama Super Majority (65% or more)
Change in Democratic Vote
Percentage From 2008 to 2012
Percentage Increase in the Democratic Vote
0 to 4.9
5.0 or more
Percentage Decrease in the Democratic Vote
-0.1 to -4.9
-5.0 or more
Map 4
Appalachia Region

Besides gun ownership, Appalachians are concerned with a variety of social issues such as pro-life/pro-choice, honoring traditional marriage/allowing gay marriage, concern for violence and sexuality portrayed in the media, belief in American exceptionalism, and freedom of religious expression (such as sympathy for school prayer and the public display of Christian religious symbols). In 2000, on virtually every one of the "family values" issues and other issues like crime, taxes, and national defense, the Republican Party in general, and George W. Bush in particular, seemed more supportive of local standards. In that election, a perfect storm of economic self-interest, coal, communal values, guns, and social issues came to the fore. Figure 6.2 shows the substantial swing of Appalachian counties to the Republicans in 2000 as compared to 1996. Only a cluster of high-poverty counties in southern West Virginia and eastern Kentucky went Democratic, along with several counties surrounding Pittsburgh in southwestern Pennsylvania and fringe counties in Al Gore's central Tennessee.

West Virginia, the only state entirely within the Appalachian region, is representative of this political realignment. In 2000, West Virginia could easily have been said to be the most Democratic state in the United States. Before the 2000 election, West Virginia had: voted Democratic in every presidential election except three since 1932; had an all Democratic US House delegation since 1982; had two Democratic senators since 1958; had a state senate 85 percent Democratic; and had a state house of delegates 75 percent Democratic. In 1996 Bill Clinton won the state by a comfortable 14.75 percent margin. Yet Republican George W. Bush won West Virginia in 2000 by a 6.3 percent margin. George W. Bush went on to win the presidency in one of the most disputed and close elections in American history, 271 to 266 in the Electoral College. If the five electoral votes of the most Democratic state in the union, West Virginia, had gone to Al Gore, the electoral count would have been exactly switched, and the vice president would have won the presidency. West Virginia and Appalachia played a critical role in this formative election.

The elections of 2004, 2008, and 2012 confirmed the 2000 Appalachia realignment. Figure 6.2 illustrates the 2012 presidential vote and the almost total transformation of Appalachia into a Republican bastion. All the above-mentioned variables and now the almost four-year Obama administration perceived "war on coal" pushed Appalachians in overwhelming numbers even more toward the Republican Party (see figure 6.3 as an example of the media campaign focused on the Appalachian coal states). Mitt Romney accentuated the differences by his famous pronouncement in the October 3, 2012, presidential debate, "And, by the way, I like coal."

In addition, exit polls indicate that the variable of race played a role in 2008 and 2012 in voter sentiment. The margin of Republican victory in West Virginia, for example, rose from 6.3 percent in 2000 to 12.9 percent in 2004, 13.1 percent in 2008, and an astounding 28.8 percent in 2012, one of the highest margins of victory for the Republicans in a losing effort. As figure 6.2 indicates, only a scattering of the 420 counties in the region voted for the reelection of President Obama, and most of these were on the fringe of Appalachia. The few odd interior Obama counties are explained by large universities in rural counties, such as Centre County in central Pennsylvania (Penn State) and Athens County in southeastern Ohio (Ohio University), and some large cities with significant African American populations such as Allegheny County (Pittsburgh) in southwestern Pennsylvania and Jefferson County (Birmingham) in north central Alabama. The change in Democratic vote percentage from 2008 to 2012 shows the final swing of "core Appalachia" (southern West Virginia, eastern Kentucky, and western Virginia) to the Republican Party. This is exemplified by five counties that gave the Democrats a supermajority in 1996 now giving the Republicans a supermajority in 2012. Because of deep historical roots, energy policy, and traditional social values, the Republican Party has turned the Appalachian region into one of its own, at least on the national level.

FIGURE 6.3

FIGURE 6.3. "War on Coal" Billboard Displayed Throughout Appalachia during the 2012 Presidential Campaign

SOUTHEAST

JONATHAN LEIB

Republican candidate Mitt Romney won more votes in the twelve-state Southeast than Democratic candidate Barack Obama in the 2012 presidential election. Romney received 54.4 percent of the two-party popular vote in the region, 8.8 percentage points higher than Barack Obama's 45.6 percent. Obama's share of the two-party vote was 1.6 percentage points less in 2012 than in 2008; however, his 2012 two-party share of the vote was higher than Democratic nominee John Kerry's percentage in 2004.

Of the region's twelve states, Romney won ten to Obama's two. However, Obama won two of the region's four largest states (Florida and Virginia), meaning that the president won 31 percent of the region's electoral votes (42 out of 135). In 2012, Obama won two of the three states he won in 2008: Florida (which had the closest result of any state in the country) and Virginia (Obama is the first Democratic presidential candidate to win Virginia since Lyndon Johnson).

The third state Obama won in the region in 2008, North Carolina, was won by Mitt Romney in 2012. Both the 2008 and 2012 elections in North Carolina were close: Obama won the state in 2008 with 50.2 percent of the two-party vote while losing the state with 49.0 percent of the vote in 2012. In fact, Obama actually won 35,000 *more* votes in North Carolina in 2012 than he did in 2008.

As figure 6.4 indicates, at the county level the 2012 general pattern of support for the Democratic and Republican candidates was similar to that of the 2008 election. Generally speaking, President Obama had his highest level of support in the urban areas of the region's Atlantic coastal states and in rural African American population majority counties in the Deep South. In Virginia, Obama carried the northern Virginia suburbs of Washington, DC, as well the I-64 corridor from metropolitan Richmond to Hampton Roads.

In North Carolina, Obama carried the I-85 conurbation from Raleigh-Durham to Greensboro-Winston Salem to Charlotte. In Georgia and Alabama, Obama carried the counties containing Atlanta (Fulton) and Birmingham (Jefferson). In Florida, Obama won key central Florida counties in metro Orlando and Tampa-St. Petersburg in addition to the South Florida conurbation from West Palm Beach to Miami. Obama's win in Tampa's Hillsborough County was considered important both because of its reputation as a key swing county as well as because the Republicans held their 2012 nominating convention in Tampa.

The second area of Obama voting strength was found in parts of the South's rural areas, especially in the region's "Black Belt," originally named after the dark, rich soil of the region. This area, stretching from the South Carolina midlands through central Georgia and Alabama and extending into northeastern Mississippi, was the center of the region's antebellum plantation economy and contained the largest number of slaves. Today, as a legacy of the South's history, this region contains the highest percentage of the rural South's African American population. A second region of Obama's rural support came from the African American–majority counties in the delta region of western Mississippi and southeastern Arkansas.

By contrast, strong support for Mitt Romney was found in a variety of areas. Within the eastern half of the Southeast, Romney's greatest level of support was generally found in white-majority rural areas, especially in Appalachian parts of the region from West Virginia, south through eastern Kentucky, western Virginia, eastern Tennessee, and western North Carolina (with the notable exception of Buncombe County, home of the increasingly liberal city of Asheville), and further south to northern Georgia and northeastern Alabama.

FIGURE 6.4

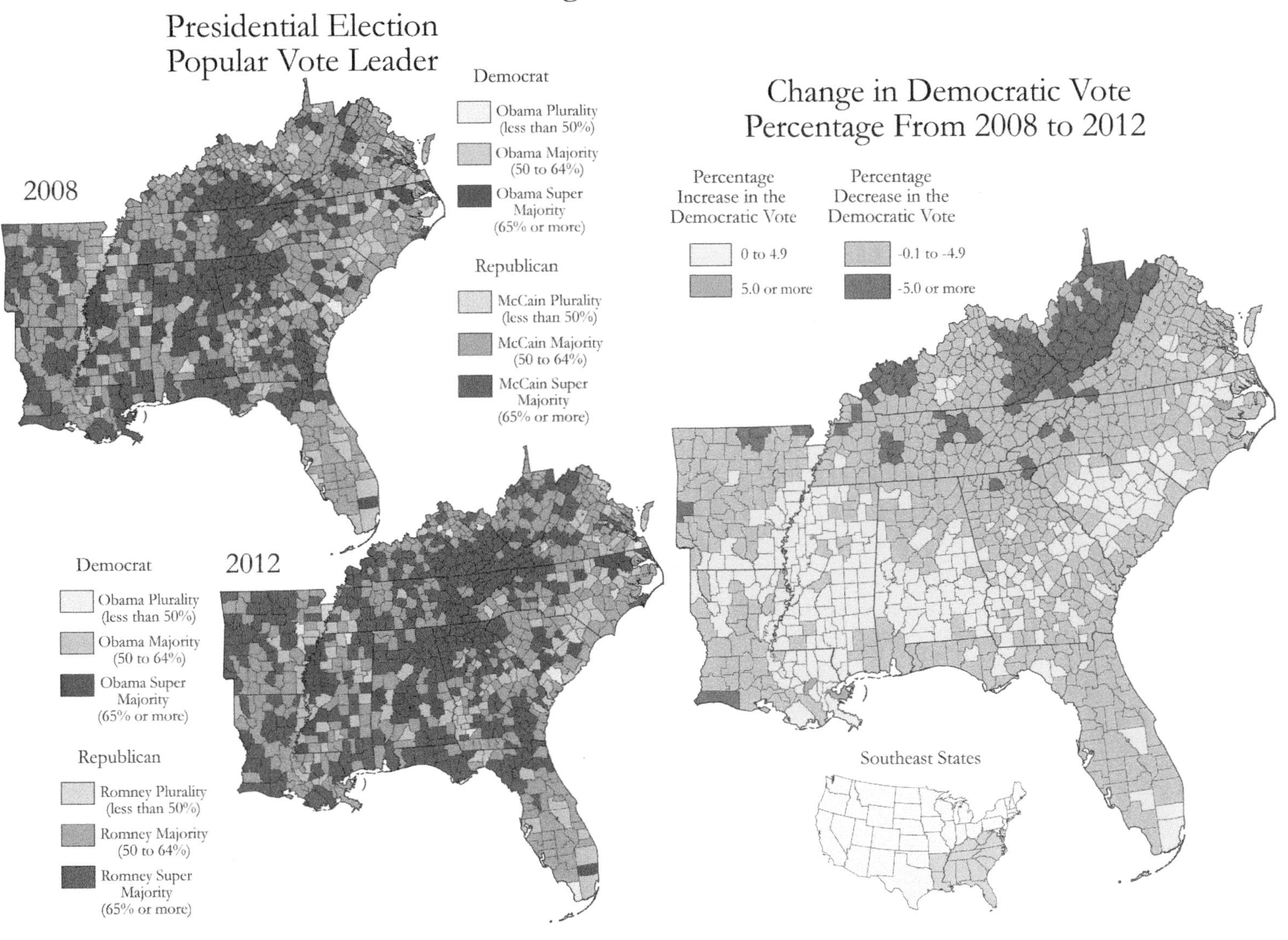

Southeast Region Presidential Elections
Presidential Election
Popular Vote Leader
2008
Democrat
Obama Plurality (less than 50%)
Obama Majority (50 to 64%)
Obama Super Majority (65% or more)
Republican
McCain Plurality (less than 50%)
McCain Majority (50 to 64%)
McCain Super Majority (65% or more)
2012
Democrat
Obama Plurality (less than 50%)
Obama Majority (50 to 64%)
Obama Super Majority (65% or more)
Republican
Romney Plurality (less than 50%)
Romney Majority (50 to 64%)
Romney Super Majority (65% or more)
Change in Democratic Vote
Percentage From 2008 to 2012
Percentage Increase in the Democratic Vote
0 to 4.9
5.0 or more
Percentage Decrease in the Democratic Vote
-0.1 to -4.9
-5.0 or more
Southeast States

Romney also dominated in the western half of the region, carrying all but four counties each in Kentucky and Tennessee as well as most of rural Arkansas and Louisiana.

While the county-level results in 2008 were significantly different from those of 2004, there was little change in the county-level results in the Southeast between the 2012 and 2008 elections. What change there was served to reinforce patterns first seen in 2008. As was noted in the previous section on Appalachia, from 2008 to 2012, Republicans significantly increased their level of support throughout West Virginia, eastern Kentucky, and southwestern Virginia. Republicans also significantly increased their level of support in western Kentucky and central Tennessee.

As shown in Figure 6.4, increases in Obama support between 2008 and 2012 also reinforced the 2008 map. The largest percentage of counties that increased their Democratic support between 2008 and 2012 is found in the rural Black Belt region, already a Democratic stronghold. One county that should be mentioned that saw an increase in Democratic support between 2008 and 2012 is Osceola County, Florida. Located just south of Orlando, Osceola County is home to a fast-growing Latino population, primarily migrants from the island of Puerto Rico (Sanchez 2009). The migration of Puerto Ricans to Osceola County has helped to swing the county toward the Democrats in presidential elections. Indeed, the growth of Latino populations in key southern swing states, such as Florida, North Carolina, and Virginia, may give a boost to Democratic candidates in presidential elections in the near future. As well, the growth of Latino populations in Georgia, combined with the in-migration of foreign immigrants and northerners to metro Atlanta, has the potential to swing Georgia toward the Democrats in future elections.

One question that arose in the 2008 elections was to what extent white voters would vote for the first major-party African American presidential candidate. While the percentage of white voters casting ballots for Obama in 2008 varied widely around the South, no state saw a percentage of its white vote equal to that of the national average. Such an assessment about the 2012 election is made more difficult as statewide exit polling was not conducted in every state. However, the five states in the region for which exit polls were conducted show a similar result to that of 2008.

Nationally, exit-polling data found that Obama won 39 percent of the white vote. Five states in the South had statewide exit polls (Alabama, Florida, Mississippi, North Carolina, and Virginia). None of these five southeastern states had a statewide white Obama vote percentage as high as the national level. However, there was great variation across the South. The white Obama vote percentage was highest in those states at the margins of the region (Virginia and Florida, each at 37 percent), whereas white voter support for Obama was virtually nonexistent in the Deep South (Alabama at 15 percent and Mississippi at 11 percent). At the same time, 2012 exit-poll data showed that the percentage of white voters in the electorate has dropped in these five southeastern states between 2004 and 2012, from a decline of one percentage point in North Carolina (71 percent in 2004, 70 percent in 2012) to five percentage points in Alabama and Mississippi.

To what extent will a growing nonwhite electorate have an effect on southern elections in the future? This is open to debate. On the one hand, Democrats have done very well with nonwhite voters in recent elections. As the region's electorate becomes more diverse, this should be a positive sign for Democrats. However, the extent to which the electorate becomes more diverse in 2016 and beyond is open to question. The US Supreme Court's 2013 ruling gutting the preclearance enforcement provision of the 1965 Voting Rights Act means that southern state legislatures, dominated by Republicans as of 2013, can rewrite their states' electoral laws to the benefit of Republicans at the expense of Democrats.

As one example, in August 2013 the Republican-majority North Carolina state legislature passed a set of sweeping bills changing the state's electoral laws, which are seen generally as benefitting white and wealthier voters at the expense of minority and poorer voters. As one example, the legislature voted to greatly reduce the ability of North Carolinians to cast their ballots before Election Day. If recent trends continue, these restrictions will harm Democrats more than Republicans as Democratic voters are more likely to participate in early voting. Toner and Trainer (2013) reported that nearly half of all early votes cast in the 2012 presidential election in North Carolina were cast by registered Democrats (47.6 percent), while registered Republicans cast only 31.5 percent of the state's early votes (the remainder, 20.9 percent, were cast by those voters with no registered partisan affiliation). It is too soon to tell the extent to which restrictions on early voting, as well as other measures, will impact the increasingly swing state of North Carolina, as well as the effect of those measures passed in other southeastern states, in 2016 and beyond.

REFERENCES

Sanchez, Luis. 2009. "The Changing Face of Florida's Hispanics." *Florida Geographer* 40:4–13.

Toner, Michael E., and Karen E. Trainer. 2013. "The Six-Billion-Dollar Election: The Impact of Federal Election Laws." In *Barack Obama and the New America: The 2012 Election and the Changing Face of Politics*, edited by Larry J. Sabato. Lanham, MD: Rowman & Littlefield.

MIDWEST

JOHN HEPPEN

The Midwest in 2012 proved to once again be a battleground region, with Ohio being the key prize for both candidates. Surprisingly, Mitt Romney's home state of Michigan was not in play going into Election Day. The state in which he was raised and where his father was president of American Motors Corporation and governor in the 1960s was discounted early by his campaign. The auto bailout helped Barack Obama, and Romney's editorial piece in the *New York Times* titled "Let Detroit Go Bankrupt" in November 2008 most likely doomed his fate among the voters of the Great Lakes State.

As figure 6.5 illustrates, once again the Detroit metropolitan area, including Wayne County, home to Detroit, suburban Washtenaw, home to the University of Michigan, Oakland, Macomb, and Monroe Counties went Democratic. One bright spot for the GOP in Michigan is that comparison of the 2008 and 2012 maps shows that Romney won more counties than McCain in northern Michigan and the Upper Peninsula and some counties in a southern band in the state, but those rural and midsized urban counties, like Jackson and Van Buren, were not enough to even make the race close in his home state. But Romney did increase the Republican vote share from 40.9 to 44.6, so perhaps his native-son status helped him a little.

The loss of Detroit typified the problem the GOP had in both 2008 and 2012 in the Midwest. Though Indiana was a pickup in 2012, it never was seriously contested by either party. The problem for Mitt Romney was the urban giants of the Midwest. Ohio and Wisconsin were seen as potential gains for Romney given the election of Republican governors in those states in 2010 and a slower-than-desired economic recovery. But Cleveland, Akron, Youngstown, Cincinnati, Dayton, Columbus, and Toledo once again proved to be Democratic strongholds. In the final days of the campaign, the Romney team thought it had a chance in Ohio and devoted resources and visits, but a campaign advertisement backfired. A television advertisement claimed that Obama policies had led to a loss of jobs for makers of the Jeep vehicle assembled in Toledo, Ohio. Mitt Romney ran an ad in Ohio stating that General Motors jobs in Ohio and Chrysler jobs in Toledo were being lost to China. The television advertisement was shown to be faulty, as both General Motors and the Chrysler Corporation denied the assertions and Lucas County, home to Toledo and a Chrysler assembly plant, was a county that showed an increase in the Obama vote from 2008 to 2012.

Like in Michigan, though, Romney did make some gains in Ohio. The share of the Republican vote increased by about one percentage point in Ohio statewide, but that was not nearly enough. In rural parts of Ohio the GOP made gains, and those gains extended into Indiana. A region of counties straddling the Ohio and Indiana border remained a stronghold of the Republican Party as counties of rural and medium-sized cities stayed mostly loyal to the Party of Lincoln.

Indiana swung away from Obama, unlike 2008, when his slim margin in the Hoosier State was one of the pleasant surprises for the Democrats. The swing from 2008 to 2012 represented a loss of six percentage points for Obama. At the state level, this represents one of the largest losses by Obama from election to election. Northwestern Indiana from Gary to South Bend remained Democratic as urban places and college-town counties appeared as islands of blue in a sea of red in Indiana. In addition, Indianapolis, Bloomington (Monroe County), home to Indiana University, and

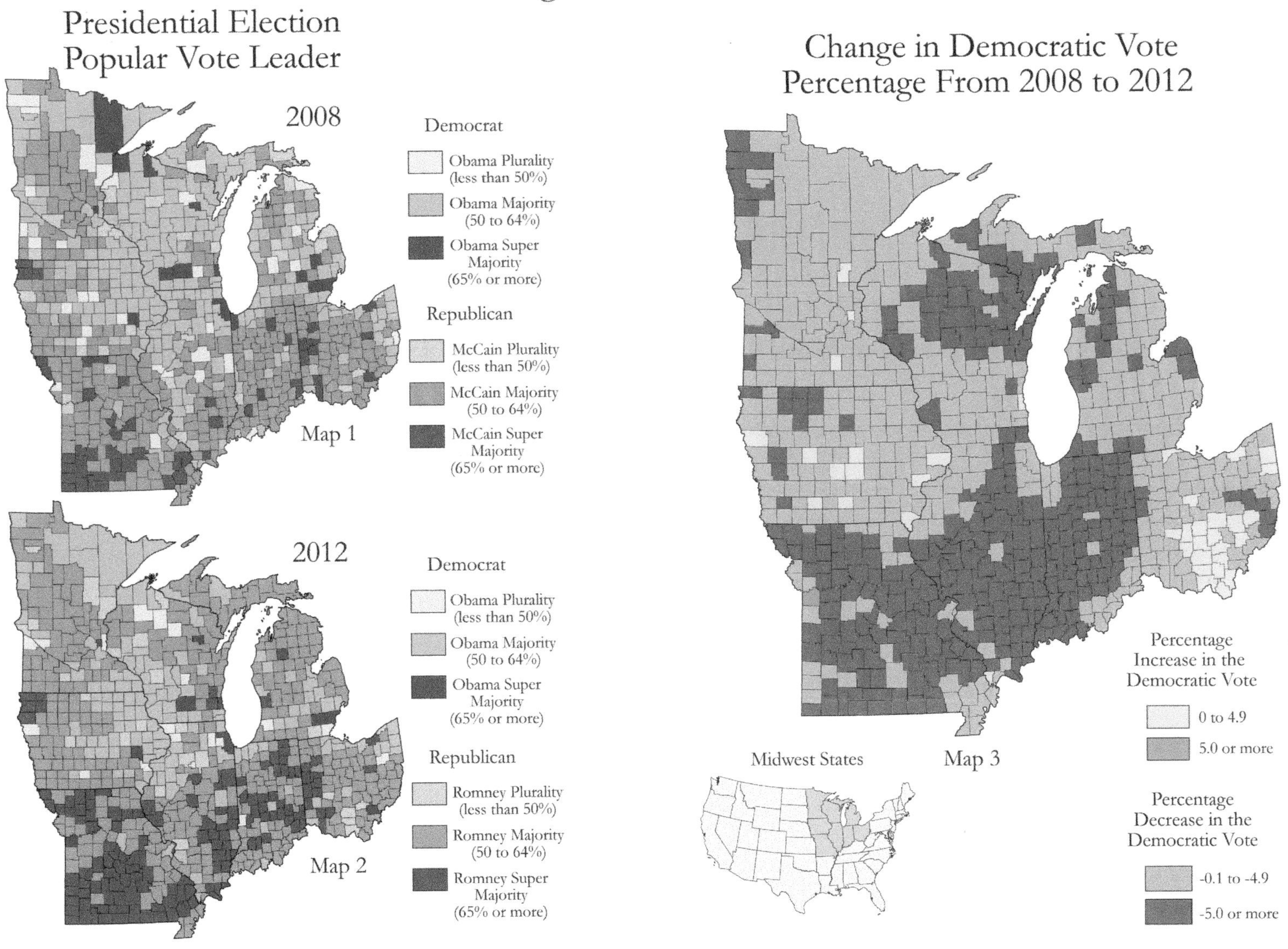
Midwest Region Presidential Elections
Presidential Election
Popular Vote Leader
2008
Democrat
Obama Plurality (less than 50%)
Obama Majority (50 to 64%)
Obama Super Majority (65% or more)
Republican
McCain Plurality (less than 50%)
McCain Majority (50 to 64%)
McCain Super Majority (65% or more)
Map 1
2012
Democrat
Obama Plurality (less than 50%)
Obama Majority (50 to 64%)
Obama Super Majority (65% or more)
Republican
Romney Plurality (less than 50%)
Romney Majority (50 to 64%)
Romney Super Majority (65% or more)
Map 2
Change in Democratic Vote
Percentage From 2008 to 2012
Midwest States
Map 3
Percentage Increase in the Democratic Vote
0 to 4.9
5.0 or more
Percentage Decrease in the Democratic Vote
-0.1 to -4.9
-5.0 or more

Delaware County, home to Ball State University, Vigo County, home to Terre Haute and Indiana State University, and rural Perry County in extreme southern Indiana along the Ohio River went for the president.

A further look at the lower Midwest from Ohio to Illinois shows that there are multiple regions of the Midwest in presidential elections: an urban Midwest supportive of Obama and a rural Midwest more skeptical of Obama's presidency. The urban Midwest included the urban giants of the urban-industrial Midwest that forms part of the great American Manufacturing Belt. These Great Lakes cities have been derided as a Rust Belt in opposition to the Sunbelt. Nevertheless, the Rust Belt still possesses enough electoral votes to make a difference. Urban centers such as Chicago, Milwaukee, Minneapolis-Saint Paul, Cleveland-Akron, Flint, and Detroit provided the raw votes to carry Obama to victory in this region. Most of the rural areas of the lower Midwest supported Romney, and, as noted and depicted in figure 6.5, many counties in Indiana switched allegiance back to the GOP, contributing to the Republican rebound in Indiana.

Rural counties in the northern tier of the Midwest were friendlier to Barack Obama in Michigan, Wisconsin, and Minnesota in 2008. The 2012 election saw a retreat of northern support for the president to just the hardiest Democratic counties along Lake Superior. Mining counties, Marquette and Gogebic in Michigan, stayed Democratic, and counties in Minnesota and Wisconsin on Lake Superior continued their Democratic leanings. In addition to mining and forestry counties in the north, counties home to large American Indian populations remained loyal to Obama. Menominee County in northeastern Wisconsin stands out as a supermajority county just like urban counties of Milwaukee and Dane, home of the state capital, Madison, and the University of Wisconsin. These old forest and mining communities have a history of union activism and radical politics. To this day, Duluth and the Iron Range is a stronghold of the Democratic Party.

Rural areas in the lower Midwest, which are more agriculturally based, saw the Republican Party prevail. It appears that in the continued shadow of Reagan's America, places of postindustrial America and the overlooked mining and forestry counties continue to hold onto New Deal–era leanings, and they remain suspicious of neoliberalism and the era of freer trade.

Agricultural areas more dependent on exports and enjoying an overall trend of rising prices tended to be more supportive of Mitt Romney. Iowa, with its economy tied more to agriculture and lacking an urban metropolis, offers a glimpse into potential electoral changes. For both elections, the state was safely in the Obama camp, but the percentage of his vote fell, and he lost counties in the central and western portions of Iowa. Eastern Iowa, though, which is more industrial and urban than western Iowa, remained a strong base for the Obama vote. In the east, Obama won the urban places of Dubuque, Waterloo, Cedar Falls, and Des Moines. One pick-up from 2008, though, was Sioux City (Woodbury County).

The overall trend in the Midwest was a loss of votes for Obama in both statewide and county percentages. Obama lost about two percentage points in Iowa, though after Ohio, Iowa had the highest number of counties with an increase in the Democratic vote. One state out of Obama's reach in the Midwest was once again Missouri, and like he did in the region as a whole, the president lost ground. His lone bright spots were in St. Louis, Kansas City (Jackson County), and Columbia (Boone County). He did lose suburban Jefferson County (St. Louis) and downriver Ste. Genevieve County, two counties he had picked up in 2008. It appears that in the future, Missouri will continue to be a Republican state.

Missouri saw a large gain in counties that are categorized as Romney supermajority, especially in the south and central portions of the state. Missouri is considered by many to be a bellwether or crossroads of the nation, with characteristics that are both northern and southern, urban and rural, eastern and western, and a historic border state/slave state that stayed loyal to the Union. Missouri has a history of supporting the eventual winner in presidential elections. It supported the winner in every presidential election since 1904 with 1956, 2008, and 2012 being the exceptions. So perhaps the last two elections signal a change in Missouri as it moves away from being a bellwether state to partisan state. One partisan state was, of course, Illinois. It's no surprise that Obama won Cook County, home to Chicago and near-ring suburbs, and every suburban county that shares a border with Cook, but Obama did lose votes and counties when one takes a glance at the 2008 and 2012 maps.

In summary, the Midwest remains a region with enough electoral votes (101) to influence greatly who becomes president of the United States. Its recent history suggests that Democrats hold the advantage, but an advantage the party must not take for granted, as there was slippage in support for Obama across the region and its subregions. A candidate hoping to take the midwestern bounty of electoral votes will have to navigate the many regions that create the Midwest.

GREAT PLAINS

ROBERT H. WATREL

With the results of the 2012 election, the Great Plains region continued its streak as one of the most Republican regions in the United States. As illustrated in figure 6.6, the Great Plains states consist of North Dakota, South Dakota, Nebraska, Kansas, Oklahoma, and Texas. These states have long been supporters of Republican presidential candidates, and the last time a state gave all of its electoral votes to a Democratic candidate was in 1976. Not only have these states been strong supporters of Republican presidential candidates, but over the past ten to fifteen years, the Republican Party has come to dominate state politics in the region. Although Barack Obama made some small inroads during the 2008 presidential election, they quickly eroded after four years in office. Indeed, the Great Plains is so reliably in the Republican column for presidential elections, that it is not surprising that Texas, the only state with a significant number of electoral votes, is the only state Barack Obama and Mitt Romney chose to visit during the 2012 campaign.

The level at which the 2012 Republican candidate, Mitt Romney, polled in all six Great Plains states was quite impressive. None of these states gave less than 57 percent of its total votes or a margin of victory of less than 15 percent to the Republican candidate, with Oklahoma leading both of these categories at 66.7 percent and 33.2 percent, respectively. The wave of Republican support was even more impressive when observed at the county level. As shown in Figure 6.6, of the 648 counties that comprise the Great Plains states, 603 counties returned majorities or pluralities for the Republican candidate Romney while only 45 counties did so for Obama.

Although Obama experienced a drubbing from voters in the Great Plains in 2012, there were pockets of counties where voters have consistently supported Democratic candidates. Counties where voters gave Obama a majority or plurality of votes are counties that have long been bastions of support for Democrats over the past several election cycles. These Democratic-majority counties can roughly be grouped into five categories: counties with large American Indian populations, counties with large Hispanic populations, several metropolitan counties mainly in Texas, a couple of counties with large universities, and several other counties that have traditionally voted Democratic.

In the northern Great Plains, almost all the counties with Democratic majorities have large American Indian populations, which have historically been strong supporters of the Democratic Party. In North Dakota, Rolette County (Turtle Mountain Indian Reservation), Benson County (Spirit Lake Indian Reservation), and Sioux County (Standing Rock Indian Reservation) all have American Indian populations of 50 percent or more. This pattern also holds true for South Dakota. Counties with large American Indian populations, such as Corson (Standing Rock Indian Reservation), Dewey and Ziebach (Cheyenne River Indian Reservation), Shannon (Pine Ridge Indian Reservation), Todd (Rosebud Indian Reservation), Buffalo (Crow Creek Indian Reservation), and Roberts (Lake Traverse Indian Reservation), have been strong supporters of the Democratic presidential candidates. In Nebraska, the only county to give Obama a majority of votes in 2012 was Thurston County, which contains the Winnebago and Omaha Indian Reservations.

Another area of traditional Democratic support is located in the southern Great Plains, close to or along the United States-Mexico border. These are counties with historically high Hispanic populations. Some of these counties have been strong supporters of the Democratic

FIGURE 6.6

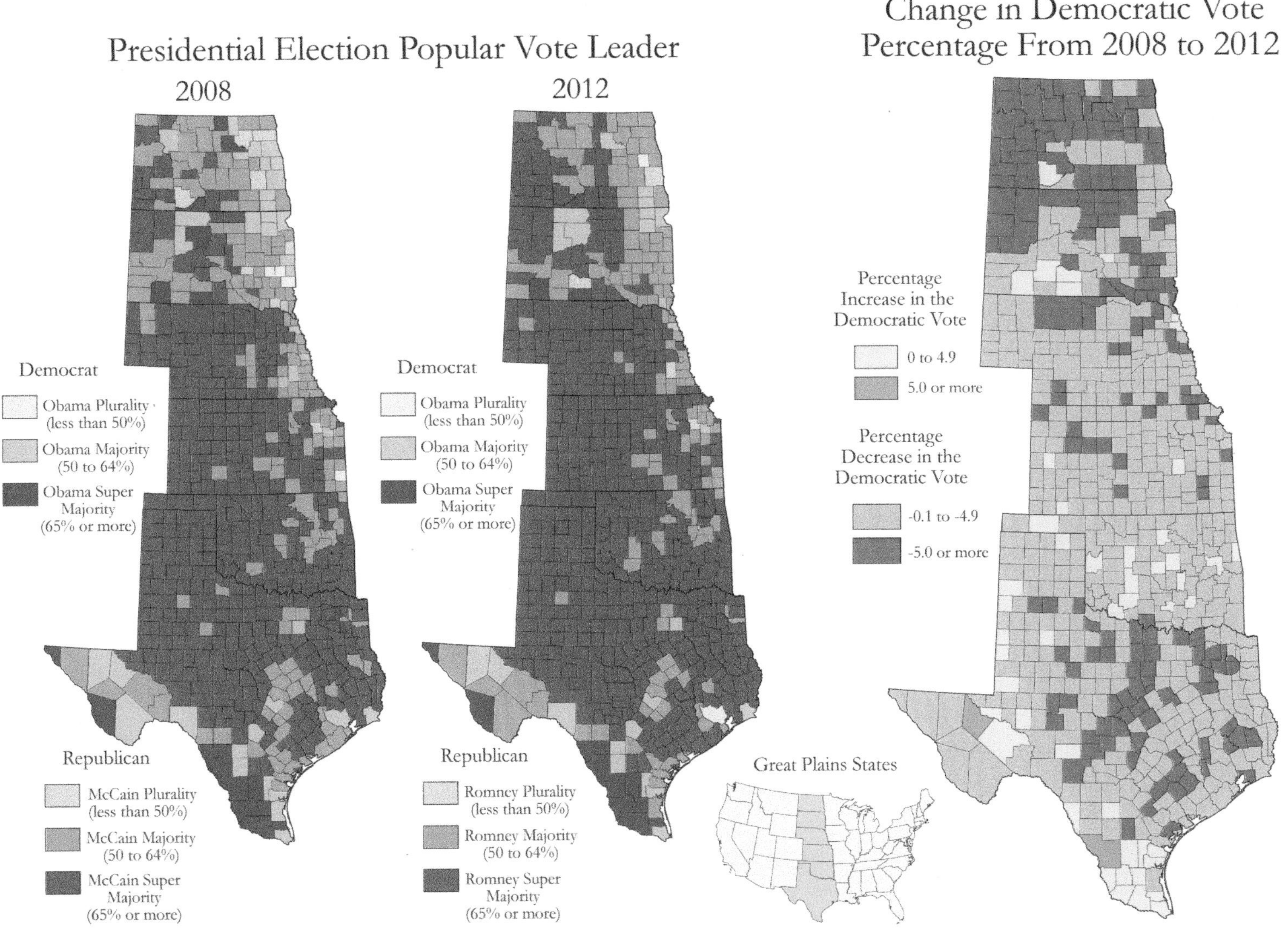
Great Plains Region Presidential Elections
Presidential Election Popular Vote Leader
2008
2012
Democrat
Obama Plurality (less than 50%)
Obama Majority (50 to 64%)
Obama Super Majority (65% or more)
Republican
McCain Plurality (less than 50%)
McCain Majority (50 to 64%)
McCain Super Majority (65% or more)
Democrat
Obama Plurality (less than 50%)
Obama Majority (50 to 64%)
Obama Super Majority (65% or more)
Republican
Romney Plurality (less than 50%)
Romney Majority (50 to 64%)
Romney Super Majority (65% or more)
Change in Democratic Vote Percentage From 2008 to 2012
Percentage Increase in the Democratic Vote
0 to 4.9
5.0 or more
Percentage Decrease in the Democratic Vote
-0.1 to -4.9
-5.0 or more
Great Plains States

Party for many decades. Brooks, Duval, Starr, and Jim Hogg Counties have never given a Republican presidential candidate a majority of their votes. All of these counties have Hispanic populations of over 75 percent. Not all counties with large Hispanic populations vote Democratic, but these counties have a long history of Democratic support. Counties such as Zavala, Dimmit, Jim Hogg, Starr, Brooks, and Duval gave supermajorities (65 percent or more) to Obama in 2008 and 2012.

Of the remaining counties in the Great Plains that gave Obama a majority of votes, three had universities: Clay County, South Dakota (University of South Dakota), Douglas County, Kansas (University of Kansas), and Travis County, Texas (University of Texas at Austin). Another eight are either rural or urban counties that tend to lean toward the Democratic Party. The rural counties include Ransom County, Steele County, and Sargent County in North Dakota and Day County and Marshall County in South Dakota, while the urban counties include Wyandotte County in Kansas (Kansas City) and Dallas County (Dallas), Harris County (Houston), Bexar County (San Antonio), and Jefferson County (Beaumont and Port Arthur) in Texas.

The loss of support for Obama among Great Plains voters is not readily apparent when comparing voting returns between the 2008 and 2012 elections. However, when looking over the change in the percentage of the Democratic vote from the 2008 to 2012 elections by county in Figure 6.6, the scale of the swing toward the Republican candidate becomes apparent. The "Change in Democratic Vote Percentage" map shows the overall dissatisfaction with President Obama's first four years in office. The most noticeable decrease in support for Obama occurred in the northern Great Plains states of North and South Dakota. Indeed, in forty of the fifty-three counties of North Dakota and in thirty-one of the sixty-six counties in South Dakota, Obama saw a decrease of 5 percent or more from 2008 to 2012. Even in counties that have traditionally supported Democratic presidential candidates, Obama's vote percentage actually decreased. All counties with larger populations of American Indians in North Dakota and several in South Dakota saw a decrease in support for the Democratic candidate from 2008 to 2012. The only real significant percentage increases for Obama came from counties in southern Texas with larger Hispanic populations.

Not only has the Republican Party dominated presidential politics in Great Plains states, but over the past ten to fifteen years the Republicans have increased their hold over state governments and delegations to the US Congress, so much so that several of these states can be considered one-party states. For example, currently, in all six of the Great Plains states, their executive offices (e.g., governor, lieutenant governor, attorney general, etc.) are all held by Republicans. In four states, North Dakota, South Dakota, Kansas, and Oklahoma, Republicans have supermajorities—more than 66 percent representation—in both houses of the legislature. Only Nebraska, which has a nonpartisan unicameral legislature, and Texas do not hold Republican supermajorities, although Republicans enjoy a little over 60 percent representation in both Texas legislative bodies.

The prospect for future Democratic presidential candidates in the Great Plains states looks bleak. Although there are a few metropolitan counties and pockets of counties with some ethnocultural diversity (e.g., American Indians, Hispanics, and African Americans) in the region, most counties are rural, lightly populated, and predominantly white with conservative political values. Whatever swing votes were garnered by Democratic candidate Obama in the 2008 election, helped by the "Great Recession" and the wars in Iraq and Afghanistan, quickly eroded by the election of 2012. A slow economic recovery, a perceived growth in government, increased government spending, congressional gridlock, and the ever-present fear of gun control all contributed to the Republican gains in 2012 over 2008. Although the Great Plains states of North Dakota, South Dakota, Nebraska, Kansas, and Oklahoma will probably not cast their electoral votes for a Democratic presidential candidate anytime soon, the state of Texas, with its changing demographics, could be another story. With increasing Hispanic, African American, and urban populations, and because it is the only Great Plains state with a significant number of electoral votes at thirty-eight, Texas could very well become a competitive state for Democratic presidential candidates in the not-too-distant future.

MOUNTAIN WEST

TONY ROBINSON

Following Barack Obama's resounding victory in the 2008 election, the political world was abuzz with talk of a transformation in American party prospects. Democrats were on the rise, it seemed, and perhaps a long-term "realignment" of party power was in the works. No region of the country seemed to be changing as fast at the Rocky Mountain West back in 2008, as that once rock-ribbed Republican region saw Democrats winning sizable presidential victories in three states (Colorado, New Mexico, and Nevada) while also winning five of the eight western governorships and a 17–11 Democratic advantage in congressional House districts seats. A tectonic shift was happening in the Rocky Mountain West, some argued, with the GOP losing its long-standing grip on regional power.

But what happened in 2012? As figure 6.7 shows, compared with 2008, the Democrats lost ground across the West. In the 2010 and 2012 elections, Democrats lost three regional governorships (controlling two of eight governor's offices after 2012) and saw a 17–11 advantage in state congressional seats turn into a 13–18 disadvantage. The "Change in Democratic Vote Percentage" map shows that in almost every county in the eight-state region, Democrats performed worse in 2012 than in 2008, with almost all Democratic gains posted only in Arizona, where 2008 candidate John McCain (an Arizonan) was no longer on the ballot for president. The sea of red in this map could lead one to conclude that the post-2008 reports of a Western realignment were greatly exaggerated: Republicans remain popular and dominant across the West.

Such a conclusion would be overstated. Yes, Obama lost ground almost everywhere across the West compared with his 2008 banner election year. But any examination of party performance across the West must include the reality that Democrats have now posted two election cycles in a row where they won three of the eight western states (Colorado, New Mexico, and Nevada, collectively worth twenty electoral votes, compared to eighteen for swing state Ohio), whereas they had previously lost *all* eight western states in *every* election since 1968 (except Colorado, Montana, and New Mexico in Clinton's 1992 victory). Between 1968 and 2004, Democrats won only three of eighty possible states in presidential elections in the region (winning just 4 percent of all possible electoral votes). In the past two presidential elections, Democrats have won six of sixteen states (and 43 percent of all electoral votes). At the lower level, Democrats continue to control three of the region's eight statehouses, two of the region's governorships, and eight of sixteen US Senate seats and are only at a 13–18 disadvantage in US House seats. Those patterns suggest significant and enduring Democratic beachheads in the Rocky Mountain West, regardless of a slight deterioration in Democratic prospects since 2008.

A comparison of the 2008 and 2012 "Presidential Election Popular Vote Leader" maps, moreover, shows that while Obama's overall percentage of the vote declined, in the end the Democrats won almost every western county in 2012 as they did in 2008, and they ultimately won the electoral votes of the same three states. Comparing absolute vote totals for the two election years also suggests that the Democratic beachhead in the region is enduring. Obama lost the entire eight-state Rocky Mountain West by 262,000 votes in 2008 and by a wider 372,000 votes in 2012. However, this loss of votes only translates into a 0.6 percent worse performance in the polls for Obama (who dropped from 48.5 percent to 47.9 percent of all regional votes). In comparison, Obama's nationwide performance dropped 1.8 percent between 2008 and 2012 (dropping from 52.9 percent of the vote to 51.1 percent). Obama's consistent performance in the West in the last two elections—even with more dramatic Democratic deterioration elsewhere in

FIGURE 6.7

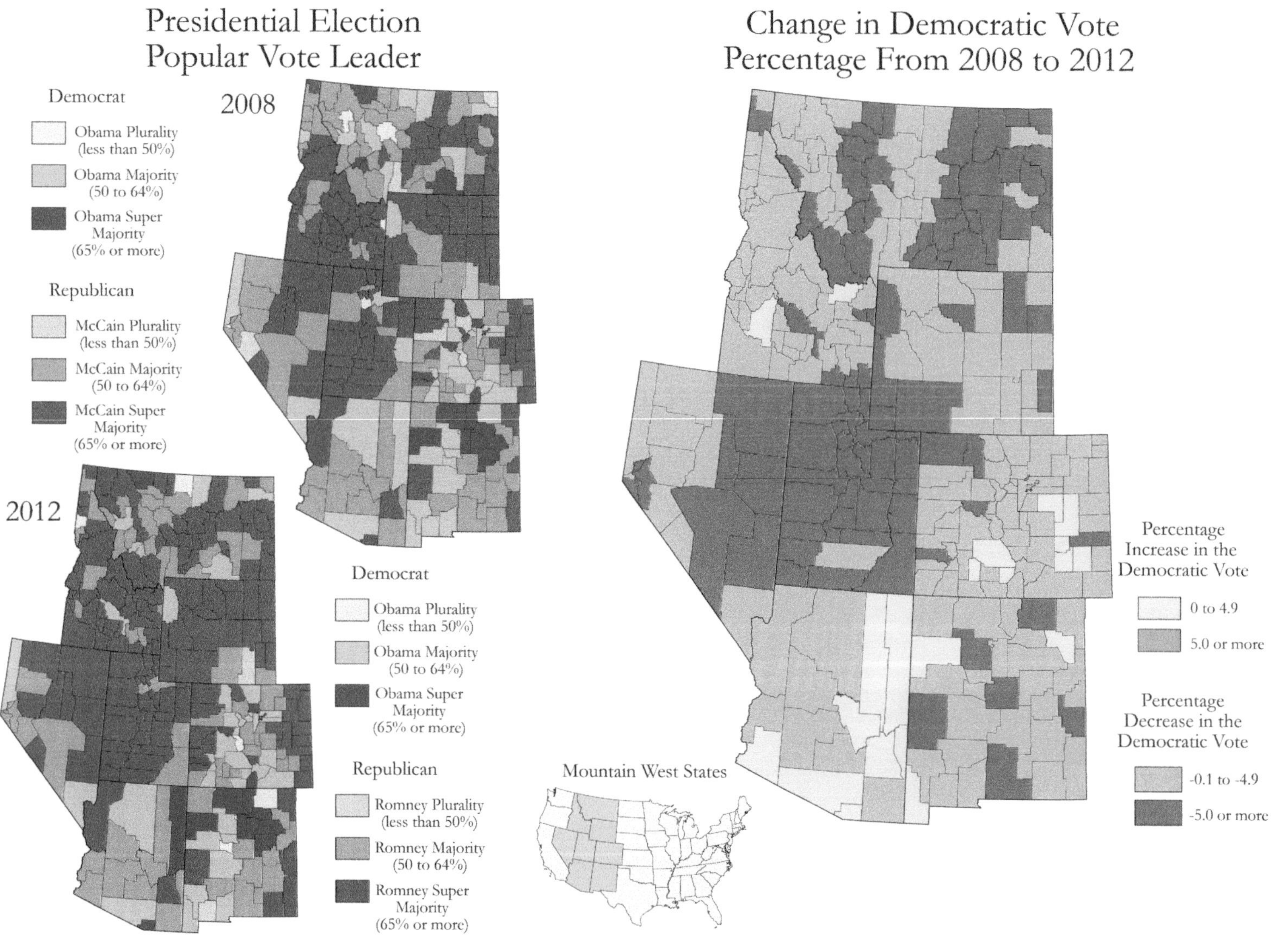

Mountain West Region Presidential Elections
Presidential Election
Popular Vote Leader
2008
Democrat
Obama Plurality (less than 50%)
Obama Majority (50 to 64%)
Obama Super Majority (65% or more)
Republican
McCain Plurality (less than 50%)
McCain Majority (50 to 64%)
McCain Super Majority (65% or more)
2012
Democrat
Obama Plurality (less than 50%)
Obama Majority (50 to 64%)
Obama Super Majority (65% or more)
Republican
Romney Plurality (less than 50%)
Romney Majority (50 to 64%)
Romney Super Majority (65% or more)
Change in Democratic Vote
Percentage From 2008 to 2012
Percentage Increase in the Democratic Vote
0 to 4.9
5.0 or more
Percentage Decrease in the Democratic Vote
-0.1 to -4.9
-5.0 or more
Mountain West States

the nation—suggests an enduring Democratic blue foundation in this once solid-red region.

What accounts for growing Democratic prospects in the region, compared to the 1968–2004 era? Democratic growth is rooted in two related developments: a changing socioeconomic structure and changing demographics. In the past decade, the Rocky Mountain West was the fastest-growing region in the country (at over 20 percent population growth). Most of this growth was concentrated in urban areas like the Colorado Front Range, and most everywhere that growth and in-migration occurred, Democrats found improved prospects. Evidence of Democratic strength in a changing West is in the region's urban-rural electoral divide. Though Nevada voted Democratic for president in both 2008 and 2012, figure 6.7 reveals that the Democratic vote was entirely driven by only two urbanized Nevada counties (Las Vegas's Clark County and Reno's Washoe County). The more rural remainder of the state voted Republican. Overall, figure 6.7 shows that Democratic-majority counties often contain an urban center (such as New Mexico's Santa Fe, the Denver-Fort Collins corridor in Colorado, or the Missoula and Butte areas of Montana).

While Democrats dominate many urban counties in the West, the brightest red Republican areas of these maps, such as in Wyoming, eastern Colorado, southern Idaho, and western Utah, are sparsely populated, rural areas. The influence of Mormonism is also revealed in the rural areas of Utah and Idaho, where bright red sweeps of Utah and southern Idaho counties correlate with large concentrations of socially conservative Mormon voters (70-plus percent and 50-plus percent Mormon in many of these counties, respectively, and, no doubt, aided by the 2012 candidacy of fellow Mormon Mitt Romney).

Unfortunately for the GOP, however, population in these rural, socially conservative counties is shrinking as a percentage of the overall Rocky Mountain West. Census data show that the urban population as a percentage of all residents has grown by about 4 percent across the Rocky Mountain West from 1990 to 2010: in Nevada, a growing Democratic stronghold in the West, the urban percentage of the population has grown by 6.8 percent over this period, to over 94 percent today. As the West continues to urbanize, we can predict that the Democratic foundation revealed in the 2008 and 2012 elections will endure.

A related dynamic is the tendency of Democratic-learning counties to have a high percentage of white-collar jobs held by educated professionals (a group some call the "creative class") or to be classified as "recreation-destination" counties, such as mountain ski towns or environmental amenity communities. As a "New West" unfolds along Colorado's Front Range, for example, "wired cities" of high-tech professionals have exploded, as have recreation-destination counties attracting a more liberal demographic than the resource-extraction and agriculture economy of old. In a phrase, the New West has more lattes and fewer lassos, and Democrats perform well with these new "latte" demographics. Figure 6.7 also shows a consistent Democratic blue peppering of recreation-destination counties across the Rocky Mountain spine, such as Jackson Hole in northwest Wyoming, Blaine County in south-central Idaho (home of the Sun Valley ski resort), and Colorado's mountain ski-town communities along the Democratic-blue summit of the Rockies. At the same time, more isolated rural counties, such as in the eastern plains of Montana, Wyoming, and Colorado, have not attracted many creative-class migrants and are not hot spots of the creative-class economy; these areas remain Republican strongholds.

A final aspect of the changing demographic and socioeconomic patterns of the New West is growing racial/ethnic diversity, which also contributes to growing Democratic strength. Blacks and American Indians vote Democratic at nearly 90 percent levels, though admittedly neither of these groups is a significant share of the Western electorate. Even though a map of western Indian reservations closely matches several county boundaries that Democrats won in both 2008 and 2012 (for example, Montana's Crow reservation to the south, Blackfoot reservation to the north, and Fort Peck reservation to the east), American Indians make up only about 2 percent of the overall Western electorate, and this population is not growing.

Latinos, however, are a different story. Latinos make up 45 percent of New Mexico's population, for example, and the swath of blue Democratic counties across that state testifies to the electoral impact of over 70 percent of those Latinos voting Democratic. Similarly, heavy Latino concentrations are present along Arizona's southern border, in Nevada's southern Clark County (Las Vegas), and in Colorado's southwest and in the metro Denver area, all areas of Democratic strength.

Census data show these already sizable Latino populations growing by 34 percent in the Rocky Mountain West, more than twice the region's overall population growth. Latinos accounted for 37 percent of New Mexico voters, 18 percent of New Mexico and Nevada voters, and 14 percent of Colorado voters in 2012. The Latino share of the electorate in these states has grown 6 percent in the past decade, and it is no mistake that Democrats won these same three states in both 2008 and 2012. In fact, if the racial composition of the western electorate in 2012 were the same as it was in 1992 (which was the only other time since 1968 when a Democratic presidential candidate won a western state), Obama would not have won a single state in the Rocky Mountain West.

All told, recent trends point to Democratic ascendance in the West. Even as the GOP regained some lost ground in 2012, these maps of enduring Democratic strength in the fastest-growing, most heavily populated, creative-class counties of the West point to a new economy and new electorate in the region. Put urbanizing, "wired" counties together with recreation-destination mountain communities, and add the heavily Latino southwestern areas, and it explains regional Democratic ascendance. Democrats remain a slight minority across the region as a whole, but they are positioned on the right side of regional demographic changes: more lattes, more Latinos, and fewer lassos.

PACIFIC REGION

JOHN AGNEW

Before the 1930s the three contiguous West Coast states (California, Oregon, and Washington) were reliably Republican in presidential elections. Since then, but particularly since the 1990s, they have become equally reliably Democratic states. Entering into US presidential elections only in 1960, following their acquisition of statehood, Alaska and Hawaii have tended in opposite directions: the former usually Republican (except for the 1964 landslide year of Lyndon Johnson) and the latter usually Democratic (except for the Richard Nixon 1972 landslide and the 1984 Ronald Reagan landslide). Republican Ronald Reagan won all of the states (including Alaska and Hawaii) in 1984, but George H. W. Bush could manage only Alaska and California in 1988.

Thereafter, only Alaska has stayed in the Republican column. The other states are now ones that Democratic candidates can more or less take for granted. These days, presidential candidates rarely put in appearances in the region except in pursuit of campaign funding, mainly in southern California. This drift toward the Democratic Party in the Pacific region is part of the national story of the geographic "flipping" of the parties as the Republican Party has pursued a "southern strategy" since the Nixon presidency and the Democrats have become the party of metropolitan areas and minority groups that were once either prone or open to supporting Republican presidential candidates but are now a reservoir of votes for the Democratic Party. The parties have become more ideologically polarized nationally, and in the Pacific region, except for Alaska, the Republicans see declining registration rates as the numbers of registered Democrats and Independents have increased. It was Mitt Romney's failure to successfully appeal much beyond this narrowing base of white, rural, and socially conservative voters that sealed his fate in the 2012 election (Jacobson 2013).

The state level, though determinant in driving the allocation of Electoral College votes and thus in deciding the overall outcome, only tells one side of the story. County-level returns show that there is, in fact, considerable variation across the region that is not well captured by the well-known stereotype since the 1990s of the region as the "left coast." For example, figure 6.8 shows California, the state of the region with easily the largest number of Electoral College votes, though as a whole it went heavily for Barack Obama in 2012 as it had in 2008, is divided in political complexion between its interior and coastal counties. Mitt Romney captured many of the same counties in the interior as had John McCain in 2008. Much of this interior-to-coastal contrast can be put down to rural-urban differences in demography and political ideology with the largely agribusiness-valley and rural-mountainous counties breaking for Republican candidates as the urban-metropolitan counties in southern California and the Bay Area go for Democrats. This is now a well-established pattern in California and in Oregon and Washington as well. The older north-south divide in California, based on issues such as the politics of water (the north has it and the south wants it) and the greater conservatism of immigrants to southern California from the Midwest and South in the 1930s and 1940s, has disappeared. Much of the geographical polarization throughout the Pacific region, though it does not seem to have increased much across recent presidential elections, can be ascribed to the rightward drift of the Republican Party, narrowing the appeal of the party in the region to very specific cultural-geographical constituencies (evangelical Christians, Mormons, farmers, small-town conservatives) and producing candidates in state and congressional elections who are so extreme, particularly on cultural issues, that they cannot appeal to moderate voters (Fiorina and Abrams 2008). Republican presidential candidates suffer the consequences, however much they try to moderate their message. Mitt Romney did better in 2012 at eating into the coastal zone of Democratic strength across the three contiguous states than did John McCain in 2008, but the swing of votes his way was nowhere enough to make a dent in the final outcome. The Republican "fortresses" are, with the exception of suburban Orange County, to the south of Los Angeles, in rural areas of low population density without the heft needed to command statewide majorities. Paradoxically, with the exception of Orange County, it is typically poorer areas that now vote predominantly Republican while the richer areas support the Democrats. At the same time, it is well known that richer individuals overall tend to vote more Republican. What seems to be at work in the three contiguous states, as in the US as a whole, is that richer people in the coastal (and more metropolitan) areas are perhaps more conflicted between economic and cultural issues than those in the interior, and in the presence of significant middle-class groups and ethnic minorities, such places tend to break more for Democratic candidates (Feller, Gelman, and Shor 2012).

If 2008 marked the consolidation of the California coastal-interior pattern to county-level voting in presidential elections, 2012 revealed several new features that could well become trends in the years ahead. In an election with general turnout decline statewide since 2008 across all party registrations and none, Los Angeles County and several historically Republican counties in its vicinity (San Bernardino, Kern, and Visalia) had moderate swings to Barack Obama. These and some traditionally Democratic-leaning counties in the outer Bay Area (e.g., San Joaquin County) with similar swings are ones in which economic hardship since the economic crash of 2008 has been well above state averages.

In 2008, counties with high rates of mortgage foreclosures, even when traditionally Republican (such as San Bernardino and Riverside Counties), went heavily for Obama. This continued in 2012. These counties are also ones with increasing numbers of Latino voters relative to the state as a whole. Though still only at 26.3 percent of the voting-age population, Latinos are, as of 2012, estimated to be 38.3 percent of the total population of California. Over the next twenty years, the former number will undoubtedly increase at a faster rate than the latter. As is well known, the Latino vote in California and other Pacific Region states tends, partly because of Republican positions on immigration and economic issues, to vote increasingly Democratic. Still only a small proportion of the electorate statewide in California and the other states in the region, its current role in increased support for Democratic candidates, including presidential ones, can be exaggerated (Fiorina and Abrams 2008). But if the "bellwether" counties such as San Bernardino are any guide, this is set to change in the not-too-distant future (UC Davis 2013). 2012 may not be the so-called last white election (Davis 2013), but in California particularly, the die is cast.

If anything, the rural-urban divide, particularly between the sparsely populated southeast of the state on the one hand and Portland and the population centers of the Willamette Valley on the other, is even starker in Oregon than in California and Washington State. In 2012, Romney did nearly as well in southeast Oregon as had Bush in 2004, and he improved in several counties over McCain in 2008. Even though it still went for Obama in 2012 as it did in 2008, Oregon remains more competitive in presidential elections than California and Washington. This perhaps reflects the fact that it is generally more rural than the other two, with only one metropolitan area of any size. If Obama could be characterized as "hanging on" in Oregon in 2012, Washington tells a less dramatic story. The basic west-east pattern there is entrenched, but the Seattle-Tacoma metropolitan area exerts such a strong overall effect on the statewide outcome that even with declining turnout by Democrats and Independents for Obama in 2012, he still managed to win the state relatively easily.

Hawaii and Alaska represent opposite ends of the political spectrum as far as the 2012 and other recent presidential elections are concerned. Ever since coming to statehood, they have been dominated respectively by the Democratic and Republican parties in just about all

FIGURE 6.8

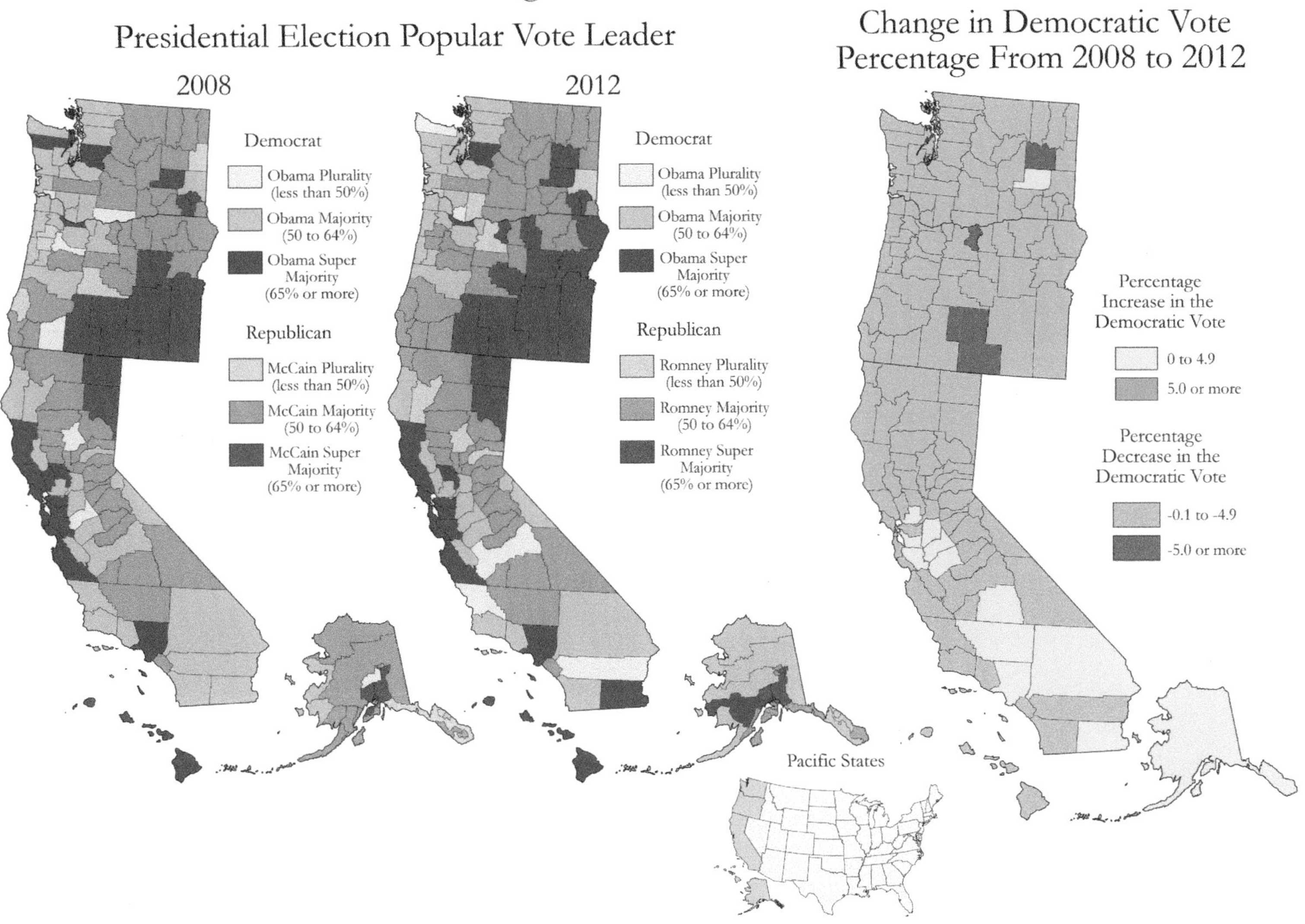
Pacific Region Presidential Elections
Presidential Election Popular Vote Leader
2008
Democrat
Obama Plurality (less than 50%)
Obama Majority (50 to 64%)
Obama Super Majority (65% or more)
Republican
McCain Plurality (less than 50%)
McCain Majority (50 to 64%)
McCain Super Majority (65% or more)
2012
Democrat
Obama Plurality (less than 50%)
Obama Majority (50 to 64%)
Obama Super Majority (65% or more)
Republican
Romney Plurality (less than 50%)
Romney Majority (50 to 64%)
Romney Super Majority (65% or more)
Change in Democratic Vote Percentage From 2008 to 2012
Percentage Increase in the Democratic Vote
0 to 4.9
5.0 or more
Percentage Decrease in the Democratic Vote
-0.1 to -4.9
-5.0 or more
Pacific States

types of election. In 2012, all across Hawaii, Obama, himself born in the state, acquired a substantial majority of the vote. This was not simply a "friends and neighbors" vote. Hawaii remains a difficult state for Republicans, irrespective of the birthplace of their adversaries. With most of the population of native Hawaiian and Asian heritage, Hawaii has a completely different ethnic profile from the other states in the region. In Alaska, Romney maintained enough core support, particularly in the more populous parts of the state, to counter a moderate overall swing from 2008 to the Democratic candidate. This surprisingly lackluster performance for the Republican reflects the fact that in 2008 the former governor of Alaska, Sarah Palin, was John McCain's running mate, and her local name recognition helped produce a larger-than-usual majority for the Republicans that would be difficult for an outsider to duplicate. But Alaska still remains the anomaly in the Pacific region: the one state where Republicans are the ticket to beat.

REFERENCES

Davis, M. 2013. "The Last White Election?" *New Left Review* 79:5–52.

Feller, A., A. Gelman, and B. Shor. 2012. "Red State/Blue State Divisions in the 2012 Presidential Election." *Forum* 10 (4): 127–31.

Fiorina, M. P., and S. J. Abrams. 2008. "Is California Really a Blue State?" In *The New Political Geography of California*, edited by F. Douzet et al. Berkeley, CA: Berkeley Public Policy Press.

Jacobson, G. C. 2013. "How the Economy and Partisanship Shaped the 2012 Presidential and Congressional Elections." *Political Science Quarterly* 128 (1): 1–38.

UC Davis. 2013. "Changing Political Tides: Demographics and the Impact of the Rising California Latino Vote." *California Civic Engagement Project*. UC Davis Center for Regional Change, Policy Brief Issue, May 6.

SUBGROUPS OF THE POPULATION

VOTE FOR PRESIDENT AND CHARACTERISTICS OF UNITED STATES COUNTIES

RICHARD L. MORRILL

America's counties differ greatly on many demographic, social, economic, and geographic characteristics. Many of these differences can be associated also with levels of support for President Obama and Governor Romney in the 2012 presidential election. Counties are admittedly problematic units of analysis, and it is risky to relate county average character to political outcomes. Nevertheless, examination of counties on the basis of various characteristics as related to levels of support for the two candidates does provide some useful insights.

As in 2008, the vote for Obama or Romney in 2012 varied greatly by the age of the voters. Obama won a large majority of voters aged eighteen to twenty-nine, a small majority of those between thirty and forty-four, and well under half of voters aged forty-five or more (table 7.1).

Thus, younger voters favored Obama and older voters, Romney on average. Maps of age distribution by county are informative in analyzing this general observation. We would expect counties with high shares of people aged eighteen to forty-four and over sixty-five to echo these same divisions. For example, places with large percentages of children under eighteen reflect large percentages of families with dependent children, a group expected to prefer Romney to Obama.

Maps of percentage of the population under eighteen (figure 7.1), aged eighteen to forty-four (figure 7.2), and aged over sixty-five (figure 7.3) illustrate this point. These maps tell us where the counties highest or lowest for the three age groups are situated and hint at related characteristics that help explain the patterns. Many counties with the highest share under eighteen are located in the Mormon realm of the Mountain West and in less obvious but important metropolitan suburbs and satellite places. Counties with highest shares of people aged eighteen to forty-four tend to be areas with colleges or universities or are at or near the centers of large, growing metropolitan areas such as Seattle and Los Angeles. However, counties with the lowest shares of younger adults tend to be regions of long-term

TABLE 7.1. Percentage Vote for Obama and Romney by Age of Voter

	Obama (%)	Romney (%)
18–29	60	37
30–44	52	45
45–65	47	51
Over 65	44	56

Source: CNN exit polls.

rural small-town decline, as in the northern Plains. These regions tended to give majorities of popular votes to Romney. Counties with high shares over sixty-five also are often areas of long-term rural decline, such as in the Plains and Appalachia, where younger people move away, leaving older residents behind.

As in 2008, there was a modest tendency for the most highly educated to vote for Obama, while there were rather small differences for lesser levels of education (table 7.2).

Again, county-level data and maps are informative. Counties with the highest shares of those completing high school only tended to support Romney (figure 7.4), whereas those counties with the highest shares of college graduates tended to support Obama (figure 7.5). This is evident also by comparing the percentage of counties with the highest and lowest levels of education on the basis of which candidate got a majority of votes in these counties. On average, 19 percent of residents of counties carried by Obama hold bachelor's degrees in comparison with 14.5 percent of those of counties carried by Obama. On the other hand, counties carried by Romney were more likely to contain higher percentages of people who never attended college (table 7.3).

From the map of counties highest and lowest in BA/BS shares, it is clear that university counties dominate along with many counties in major metropolitan areas. High shares of those with only a high school education tend to be in small-town and rural counties across the midsection from Kansas and Missouri to Indiana, Pennsylvania, Ohio, and West Virginia as well as in the South.

Again as in 2008, voting differed by kinds of household, with adult members of traditional nuclear families (husband, wife, and dependent children) more likely to vote for Romney, whereas single-parent families, members of gay or lesbian couples, and people living outside the traditional family structure tended to vote for Obama (table 7.4).

Thus, we similarly may expect counties with the highest and lowest levels of different kinds of households to echo these patterns. This expectation is borne out by comparison of counties with high and low percentages of people in these various categories, as illustrated by maps of husband-wife households (figure 7.6), unmarried partner households (figure 7.7), and lesbian, gay, bisexual, and transsexual (LGBT) households (figure 7.8).

The map of counties with the highest and lowest shares of husband-wife families with children (figure 7.6) reinforces this observation. High shares and high levels of Republican voting occurred in the Mormon realm of the Interior West, parts of the southern Plains, and exurban areas in all parts of the country. However, low shares and high Democratic voting percentages occurred in primarily African American areas of the South, areas in Florida with an old population and consequently higher numbers of widows and widowers, and the most densely populated central cities. The map of counties highest and lowest in singles is not shown but is in general the inverse of the husband-wife family map. Figures 7.7 and 7.8 also show patterns reversed from figure 7.6. The counties with the highest percentages of unmarried partners are located in urban and environmental counties of the West and environmental counties across the North, while areas with lowest shares dominate the entire Plains region, Mormon Utah, and parts of the Deep South. Counties with the highest increase in Democratic votes between 2008 and 2012 had high shares of single-parent families, whereas counties shifting most Republican had low shares.

The votes also varied by employment, income, and poverty status. As indicated

FIGURE 7.1

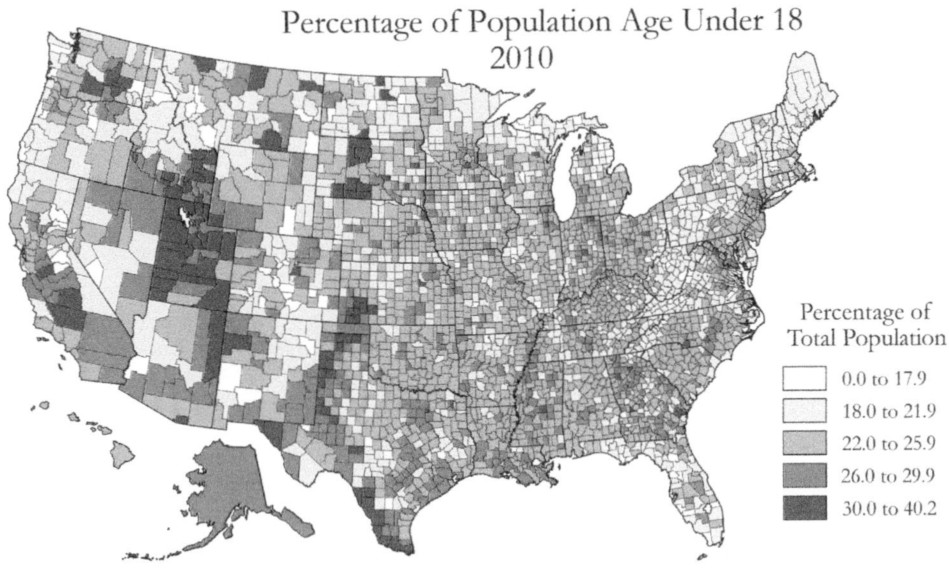
Percentage of Population Age Under 18
2010
Percentage of
Total Population
0.0 to 17.9
18.0 to 21.9
22.0 to 25.9
26.0 to 29.9
30.0 to 40.2

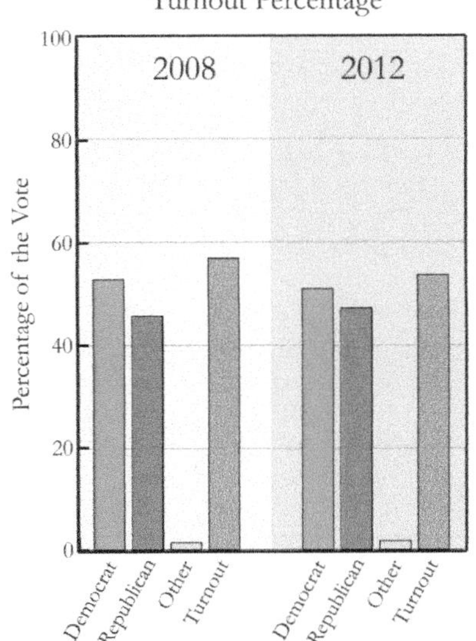
Total U.S. Popular Vote and
Turnout Percentage
2008
2012
Percentage of the Vote
100
80
60
40
20
0
Democrat
Republican
Other
Turnout
Democrat
Republican
Other
Turnout

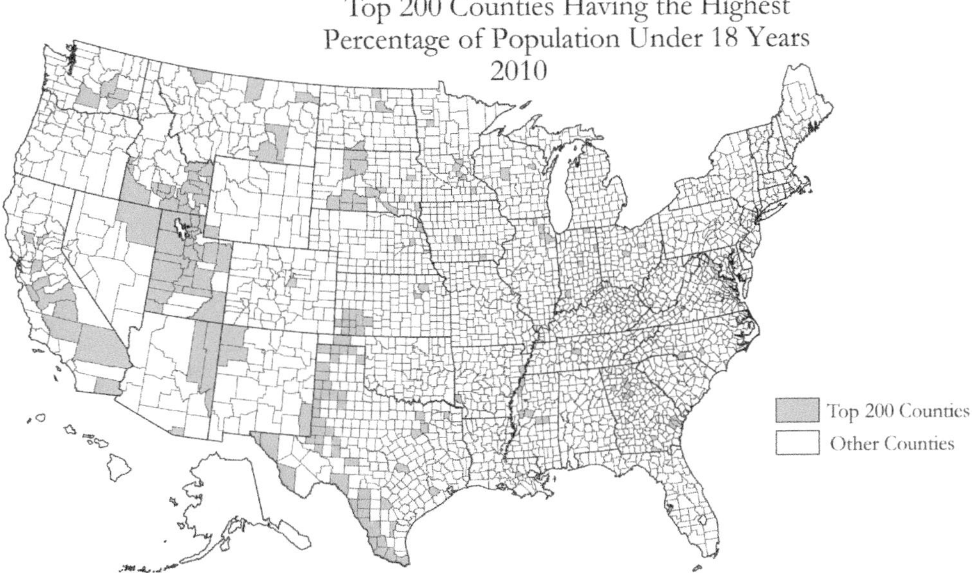
Top 200 Counties Having the Highest
Percentage of Population Under 18 Years
2010
Top 200 Counties
Other Counties

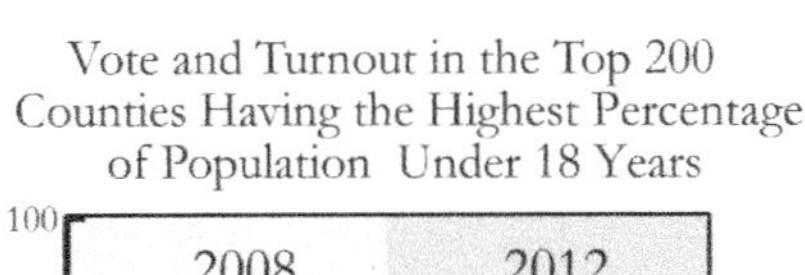
Vote and Turnout in the Top 200
Counties Having the Highest Percentage
of Population Under 18 Years

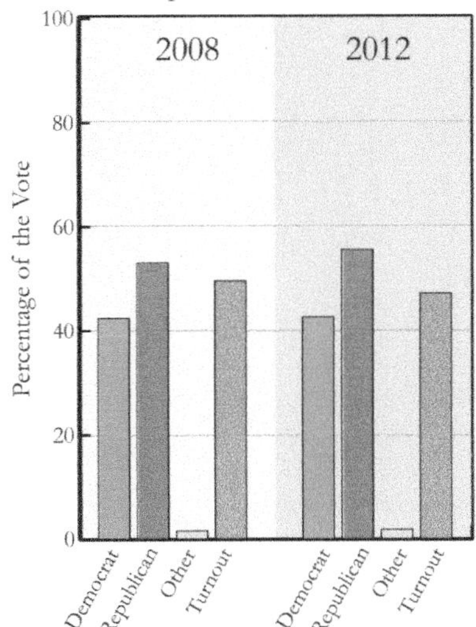
2008
2012
Percentage of the Vote
100
80
60
40
20
0
Democrat
Republican
Other
Turnout
Democrat
Republican
Other
Turnout

FIGURE 7.2

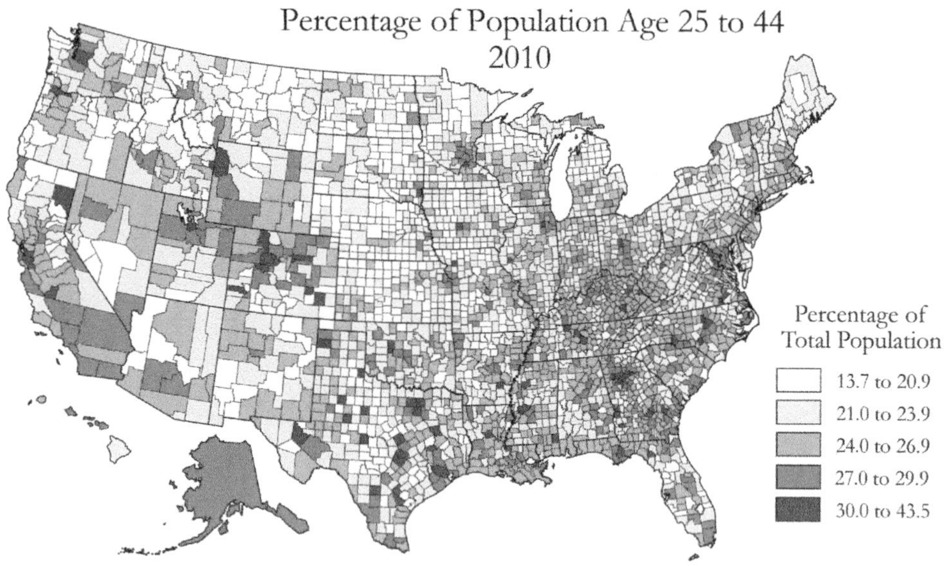

Percentage of Population Age 25 to 44
2010
Percentage of
Total Population
13.7 to 20.9
21.0 to 23.9
24.0 to 26.9
27.0 to 29.9
30.0 to 43.5

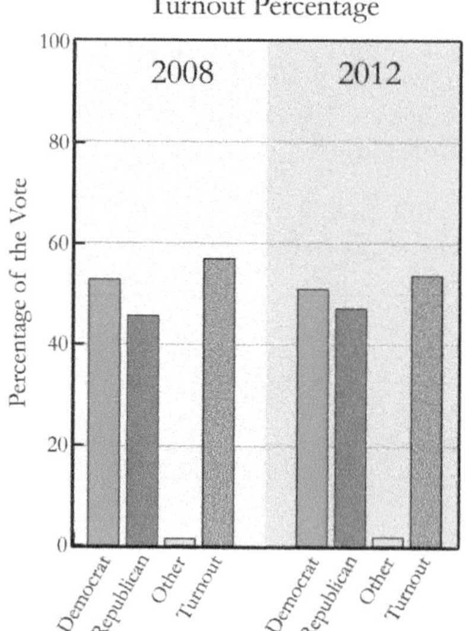

Total U.S. Popular Vote and
Turnout Percentage
2008
2012
Percentage of the Vote
100
80
60
40
20
0
Democrat
Republican
Other
Turnout
Democrat
Republican
Other
Turnout

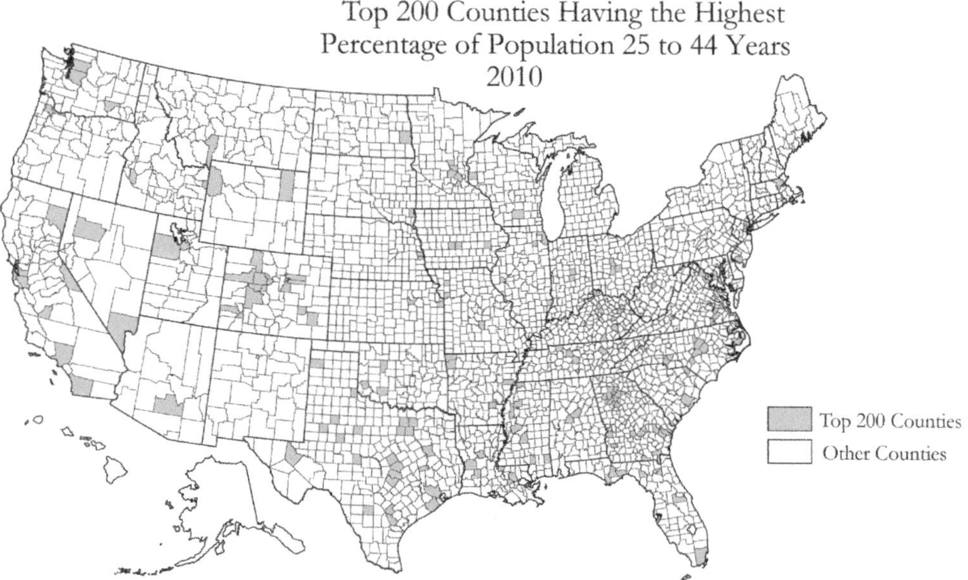

Top 200 Counties Having the Highest
Percentage of Population 25 to 44 Years
2010
Top 200 Counties
Other Counties

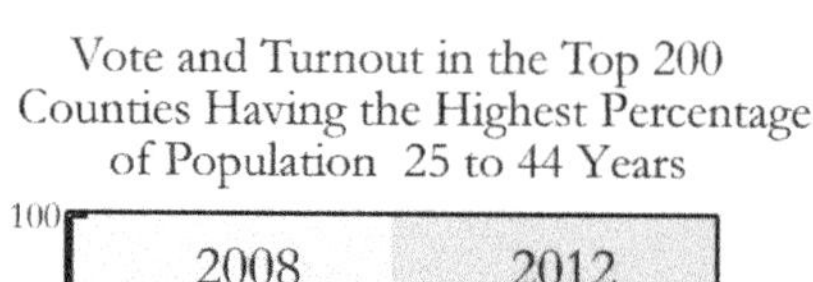

Vote and Turnout in the Top 200
Counties Having the Highest Percentage
of Population 25 to 44 Years

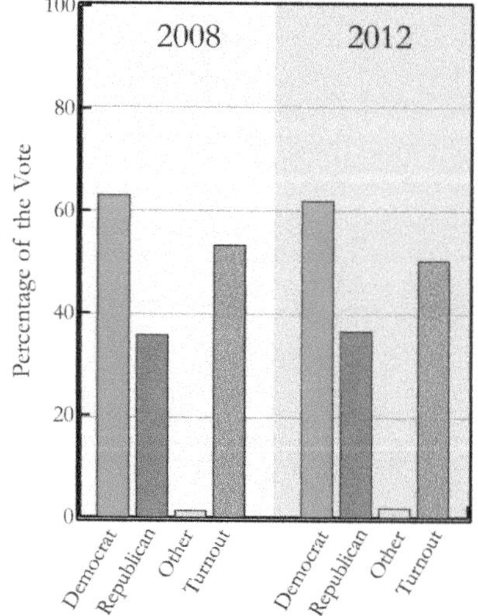

2008
2012
Percentage of the Vote
100
80
60
40
20
0
Democrat
Republican
Other
Turnout
Democrat
Republican
Other
Turnout

FIGURE 7.3

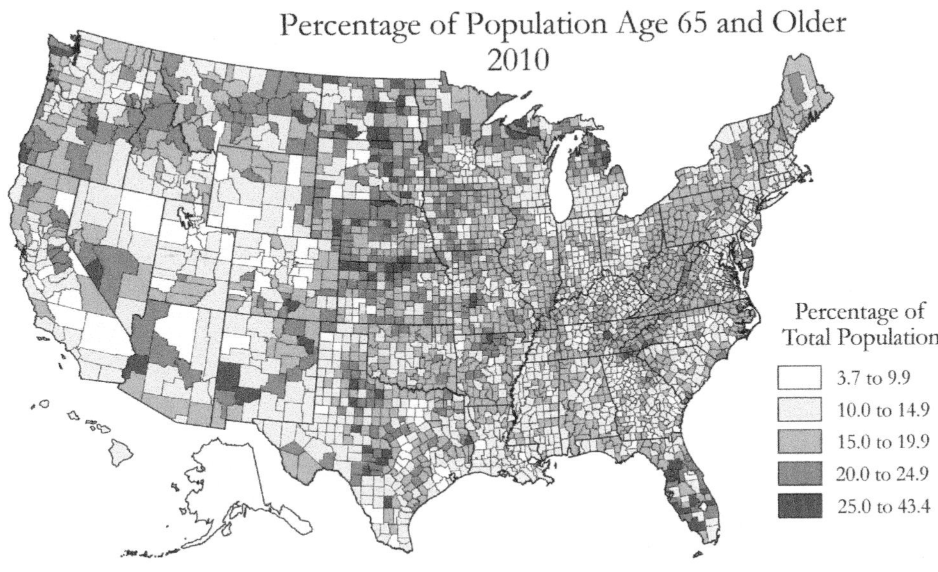

Total U.S. Popular Vote and Turnout Percentage

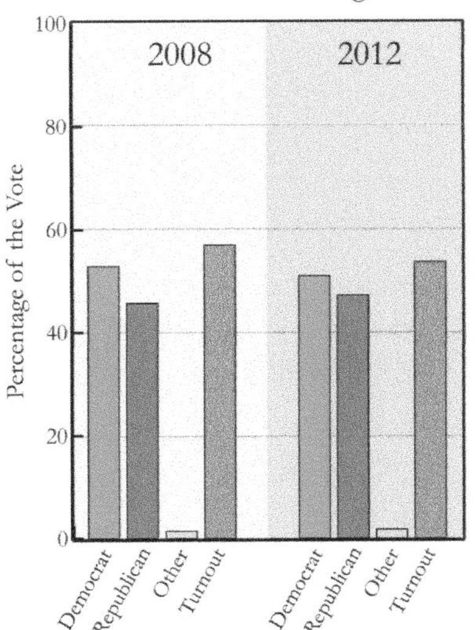

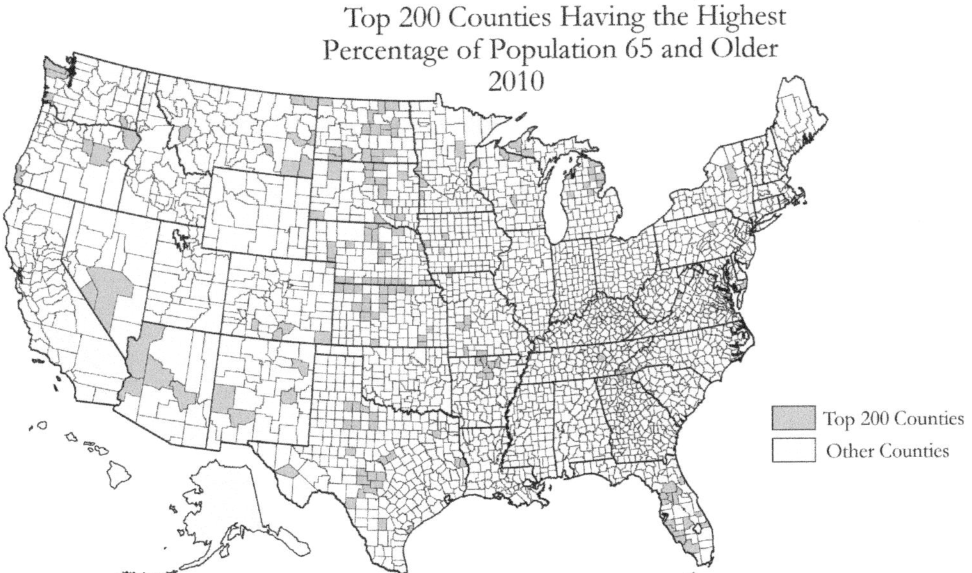

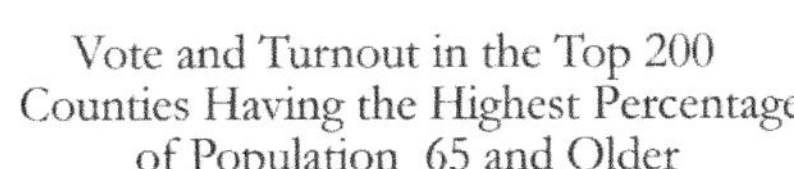

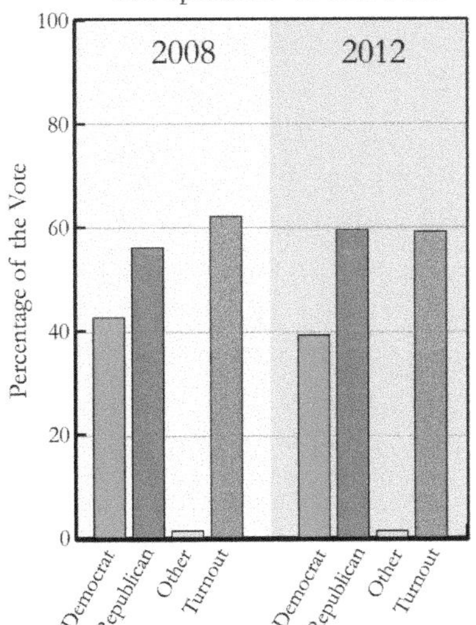

TABLE 7.2. Support for Obama and Romney by Level of Education

Level of Education	Obama (%)	Romney (%)
No college	51	48
BA, BS	47	51
Postgraduate work	55	42

Source: CNN exit polls.

below, female voters were more likely to support Obama, whereas male voters were more likely to support Romney. Support varies also on the basis of female labor force participation. The map of female labor force participation is a remarkable portrait of north and south, even today, but more subtly of the influence of metropolitan location and university and capital cities even in the South (figure 7.9). Female labor force participation rates are especially high in the areas in and around Washington, DC. The Ozark and Appalachia areas of traditional values contrast with the more "modern" rural counties of the northern Plains and Mountain West. Thus, places with relatively high rates of female labor force participation were more likely to support Obama.

Although high rates of female labor force participation were associated with support for Obama, in general income was correlated with support for Romney. According to exit polls, persons with incomes of over $50,000 gave 46 percent of their votes to Obama, whereas those with incomes of $30,000 or less gave Obama 63 percent of their votes. Those in between, with incomes between $30,000 and $50,000, gave 57 percent support to Obama. However, *places* with high levels of income and low levels of poverty tended to support Obama even though poorer *people* tended to support him, and vice versa.

How could both be true? The exit polls indicated that overall, the poor did tend to vote for Obama and the rich for Romney, but the geographic pattern is quite complex. The seeming anomaly is understandable from the income map (figure 7.10) and the poverty map (figure 7.11). Income and poverty are, of course, related to unemployment levels (figure 7.12). The highest-income counties are in fact prevalent in the largest metropolitan regions, including the cities of the northeastern megalopolis, San Francisco, Seattle, Denver, Minneapolis, and Chicago. The lowest-income counties include poor Democratic-leaning black and Latino counties, but these are outweighed by the larger number of poor, white-dominated counties in Appalachia and the Ozarks.

The map of percent poor is subtly different. Here the dominance of counties with large percentages of African Americans and those with large percentages of American Indians drives the Obama vote of poor counties overall. The counties that are lowest in median income are precisely the counties with the highest share of poverty. Areas with high percentages of American Indians, blacks, and Latinos vote Democratic, but poor white areas in the Ozarks and Appalachia vote even more strongly Republican. Overall, Obama's counties had higher median incomes but also higher poverty rates. The median annual income of Obama's counties was $46,075 as compared with $42,460 for Romney's counties. On the other hand, the poverty rate in Obama's counties was 13.7 percent as opposed to 13.1 percent in Romney's counties. These seemingly anomalous percentages can be explained by the fact that many of Obama's counties are heavily populated and include significant numbers of very wealthy people along with many poor people, including residents of low-income, inner-city neighborhoods.

Occupation was another factor associated with the outcomes of the election in different places. Not surprisingly, occupational status is associated with level of education. Persons employed in business and the professions are likely to hold college degrees, whereas many blue-collar jobs in agriculture, fishing, mining, forestry, construction, and manufacturing do not require higher education. However, these occupations have been affected disproportionately by recession and globalization and are associated with higher levels of unemployment (figure 7.12).

FIGURE 7.4

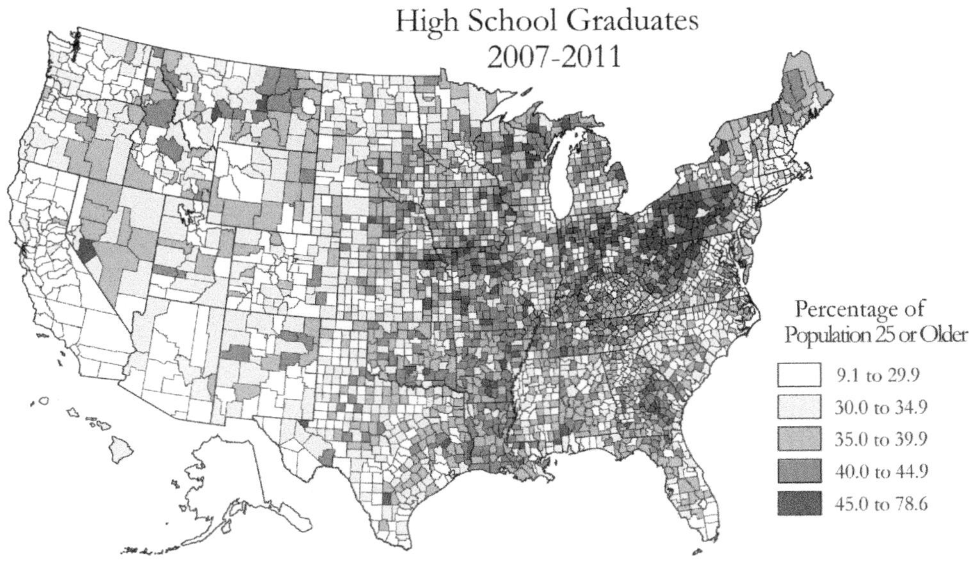
High School Graduates
2007-2011
Percentage of
Population 25 or Older
9.1 to 29.9
30.0 to 34.9
35.0 to 39.9
40.0 to 44.9
45.0 to 78.6

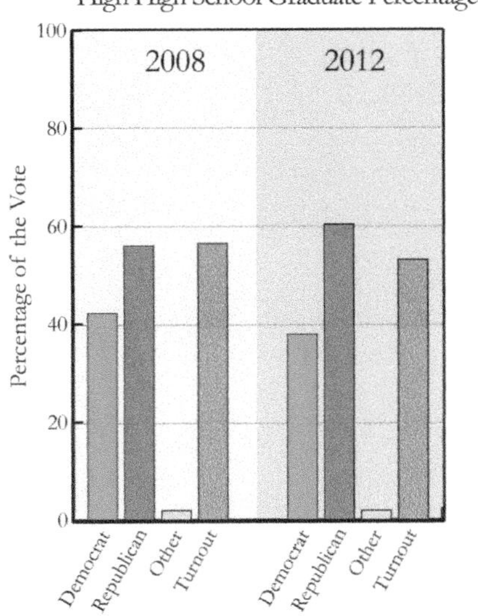
Top 200 Counties Having
High High School Graduate Percentages
2008
2012
Percentage of the Vote
100
80
60
40
20
0
Democrat
Republican
Other
Turnout
Democrat
Republican
Other
Turnout

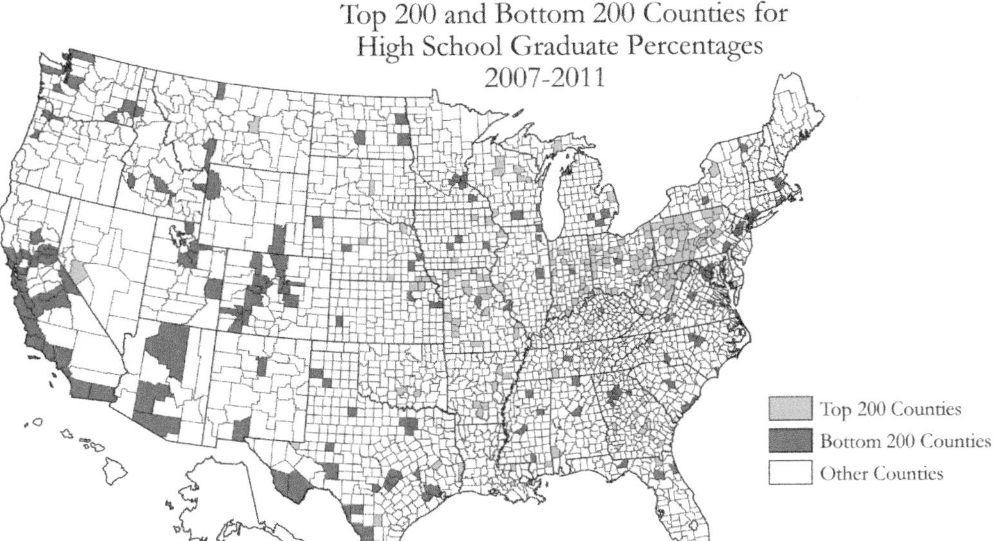
Top 200 and Bottom 200 Counties for
High School Graduate Percentages
2007-2011
Top 200 Counties
Bottom 200 Counties
Other Counties

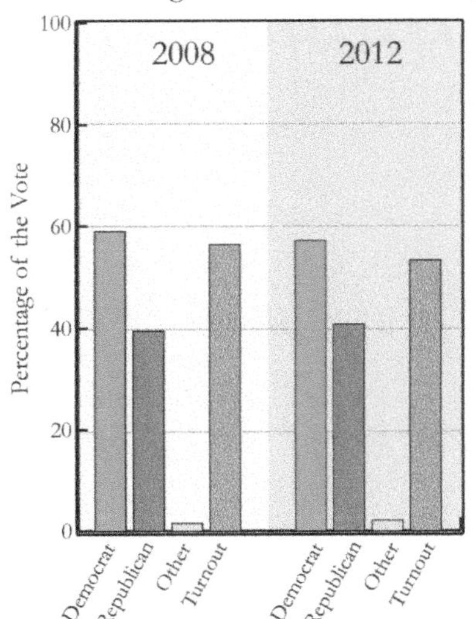
Bottom 200 Counties Having
Low High School Graduate Percentages
2008
2012
Percentage of the Vote
100
80
60
40
20
0
Democrat
Republican
Other
Turnout
Democrat
Republican
Other
Turnout

FIGURE 7.5

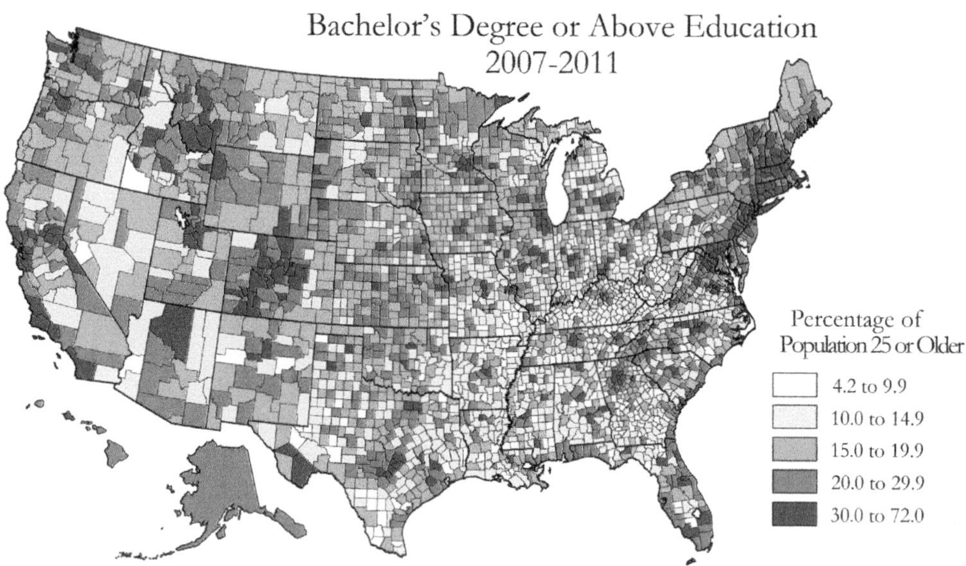

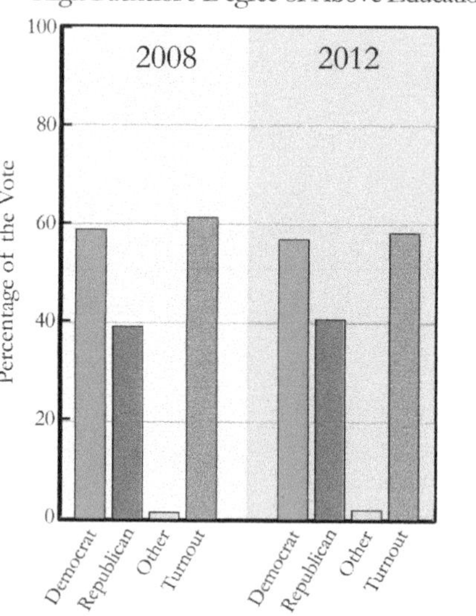

Top 200 and Bottom 206 Counties for
Bachelor's Degree or Above Education
2007-2011

Top 200 Counties
Bottom 206 Counties
Other Counties

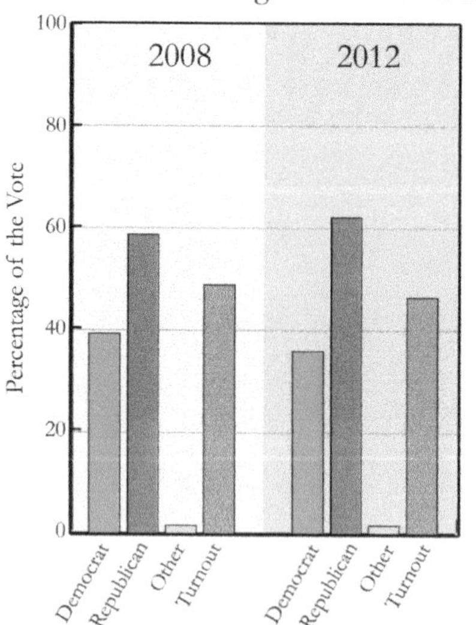

TABLE 7.3. Support for Obama and Romney in Counties with Most and Least Educated Residents

Candidate	Percentage High School Only	Percentage BA/BS
Romney	33	14.5
Obama	27	19.0

Source: Calculated by author.

Nevertheless, people in professional occupations tend to live in counties carried by Obama. This is evident from maps showing percentages of people in the primary sector, including agriculture, fishing, mining, and forestry (figure 7.13), construction (figure 7.14), manufacturing (figure 7.15), and business and professional occupations (figure 7.16).

Most primary-sector economic activity takes place in rural areas, which tended to support Romney (see chapter 5). The construction occupation map is similarly explained by the low share of these occupations in the same Democratic-leaning metropolitan cores but with high shares in the Mormon realm, in Texas, and in Appalachia. Except for Appalachia, these places are growing rapidly in population and consequently have a larger need for construction workers.

Historically, labor unions played important roles in support for Democratic nominees for president including Franklin D. Roosevelt and John F. Kennedy. However, this influence has weakened considerably. In the 1950s, nearly 30 percent of American workers were employed in manufacturing. Today, this percentage has dropped to about 12 percent, with a lower and lower percentage belonging to labor unions. Nevertheless, manufacturing-oriented counties, especially in the union-oriented Rust Belt, still tended to support Obama. The manager-professional map is dual, like many other maps, with many small counties in the Republican-leaning northern Plains, farm and ranch owners, and small business managers. However, these are outweighed by the large concentration of Democrats in the large metropolitan cores. The counties with the lowest shares are in the South, with others located in the states on the margins of the South. These observations are consistent with observations earlier about education and household types, suggesting a slight weakening of higher-class association with Obama. But Democratic-gaining counties did have the lowest shares of construction occupations.

Another factor associated with Democratic support was veteran status (figure 7.17). Over the past several decades, Republicans have been associated with more aggressive foreign policies and more support for higher military budgets. Military bases also provide substantial amounts of employment for both military personnel and their families. Veterans are more likely to support Republicans as opposed to nonveterans. This tendency may be reinforced by the fact that veterans with twenty or more years of service are prone to retire in places near military bases, where they are eligible for medical care, reduced-cost goods and services, and other benefits.

All of these observations are related to population size and urban status (see chapter 5). Places with larger populations (figure 7.18) and denser populations (figure 7.19) were likely to support Obama. On the other hand, rural places tended to support Romney, as indicated previously (figure 7.20).

Migration rates are also related to levels of Democratic and Republican support. Figure

TABLE 7.4. Support for Obama by Family Type

Family Type	Support for Obama (%)
Traditional nuclear family	45
Nonfamily	62
Lesbian, gay, bisexual, transsexual	76

Source: Calculated by author.

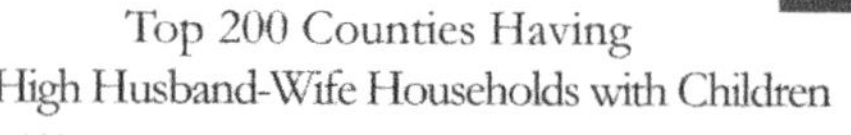
FIGURE 7.6

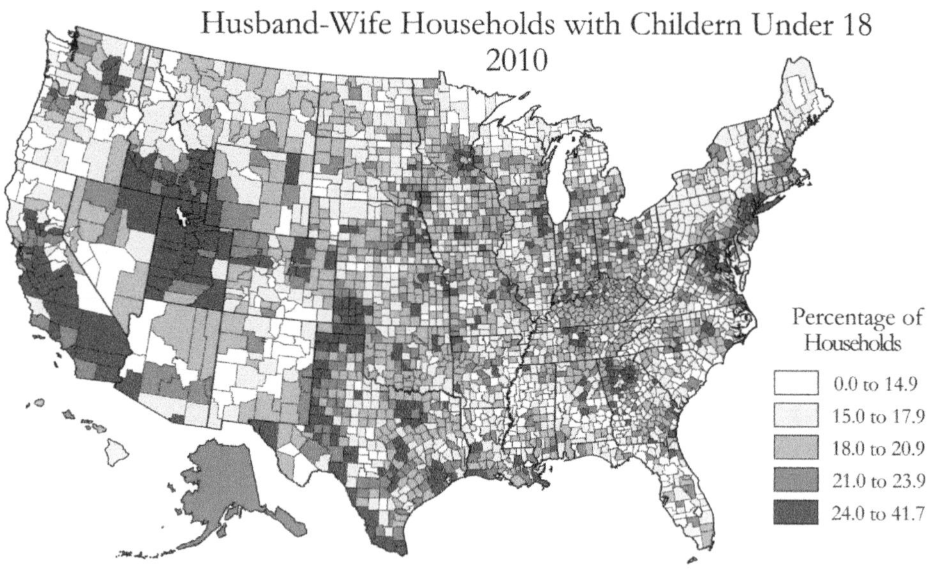
Husband-Wife Households with Childern Under 18
2010
Percentage of Households
0.0 to 14.9
15.0 to 17.9
18.0 to 20.9
21.0 to 23.9
24.0 to 41.7

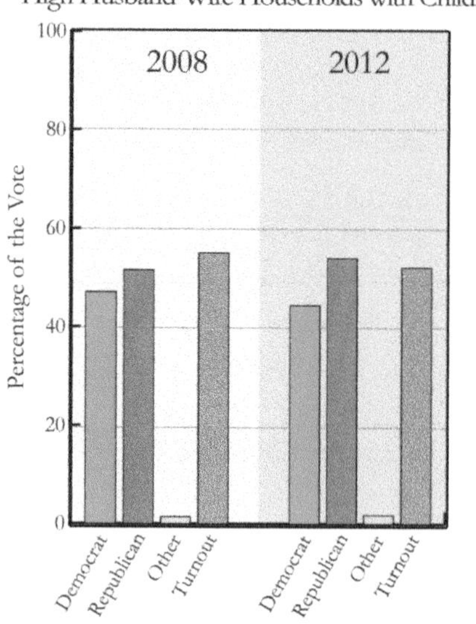
Top 200 Counties Having
High Husband-Wife Households with Children
2008
2012
Percentage of the Vote
100
80
60
40
20
0
Democrat
Republican
Other
Turnout
Democrat
Republican
Other
Turnout

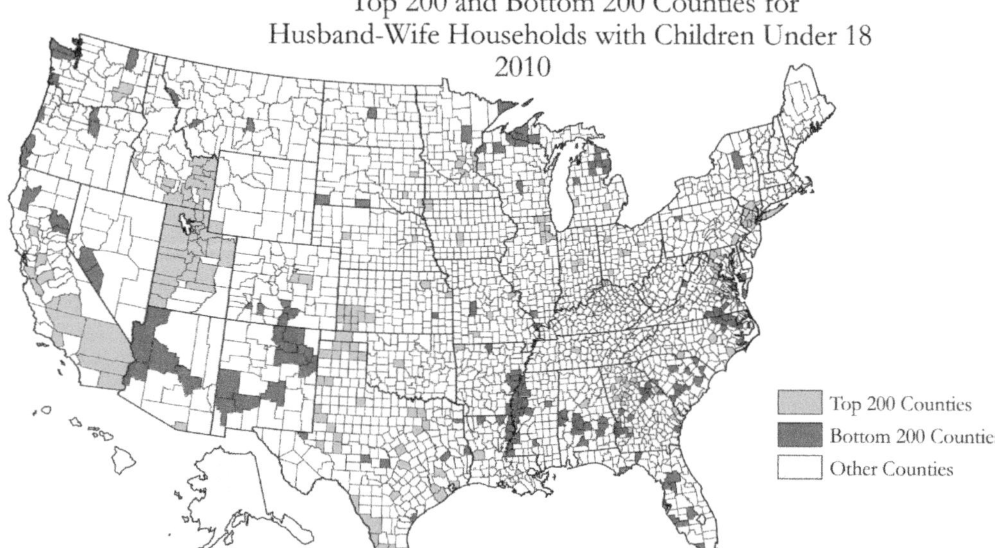
Top 200 and Bottom 200 Counties for
Husband-Wife Households with Children Under 18
2010
Top 200 Counties
Bottom 200 Counties
Other Counties

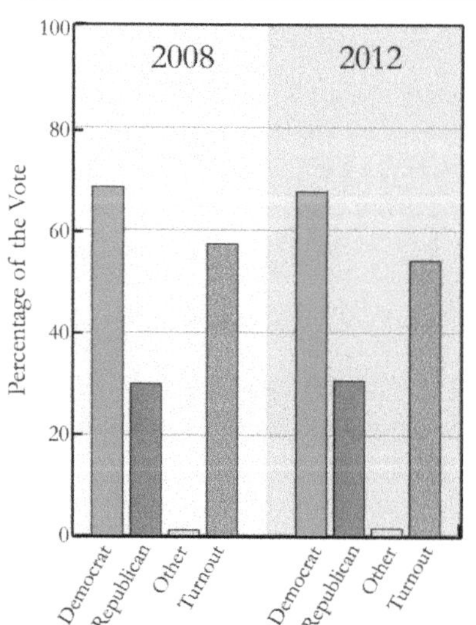
Bottom 200 Counties Having
Low Husband-Wife Households with Children
2008
2012
Percentage of the Vote
100
80
60
40
20
0
Democrat
Republican
Other
Turnout
Democrat
Republican
Other
Turnout

FIGURE 7.7

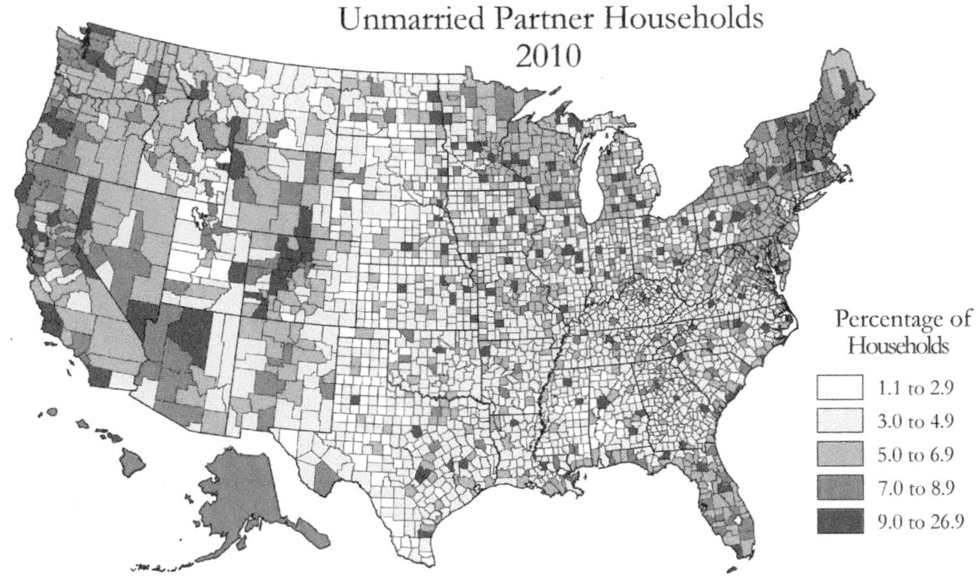
Unmarried Partner Households
2010
Percentage of Households
1.1 to 2.9
3.0 to 4.9
5.0 to 6.9
7.0 to 8.9
9.0 to 26.9

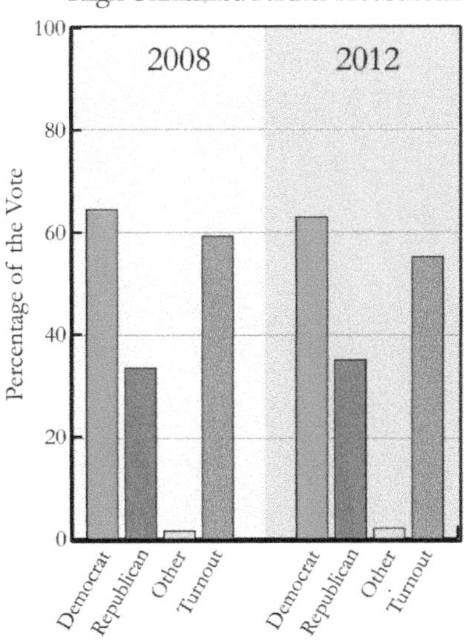
Top 200 Counties Having
High Unmarried Partner Households
2008
2012
Percentage of the Vote
0
20
40
60
80
100
Democrat
Republican
Other
Turnout
Democrat
Republican
Other
Turnout

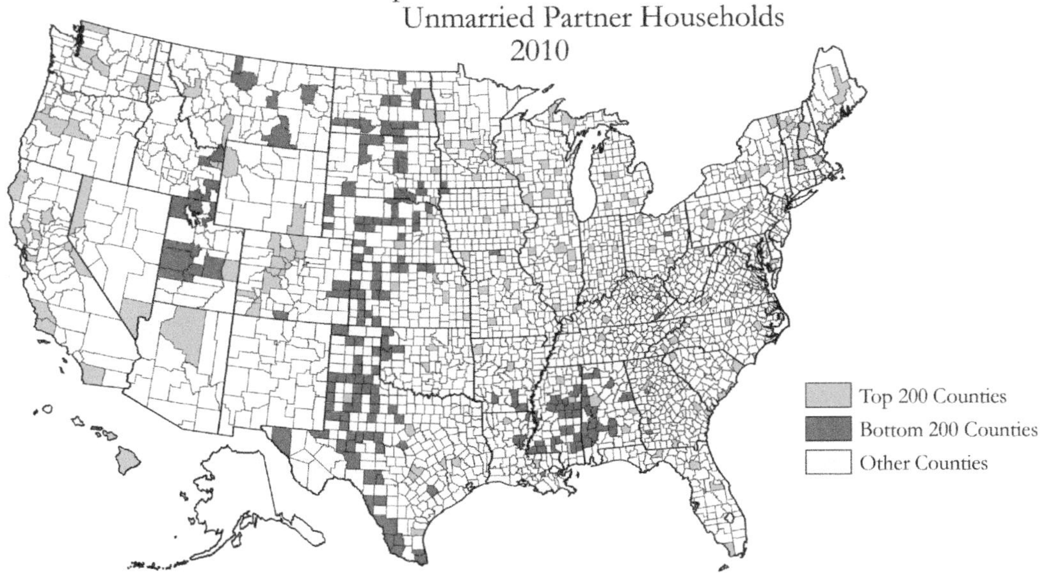
Top 200 and Bottom 200 Counties for
Unmarried Partner Households
2010
Top 200 Counties
Bottom 200 Counties
Other Counties

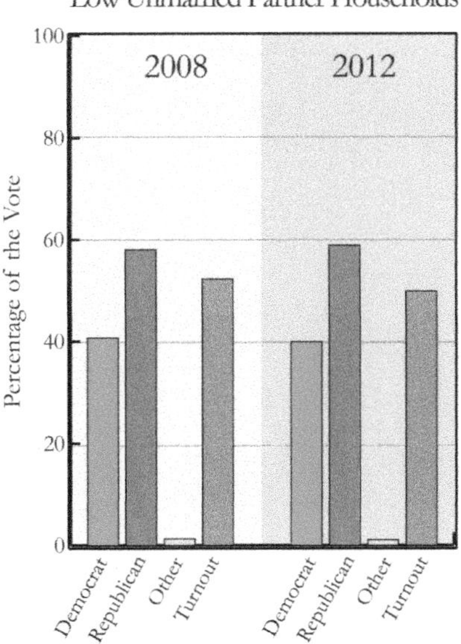
Bottom 200 Counties Having
Low Unmarried Partner Households
2008
2012
Percentage of the Vote
0
20
40
60
80
100
Democrat
Republican
Other
Turnout
Democrat
Republican
Other
Turnout

FIGURE 7.8

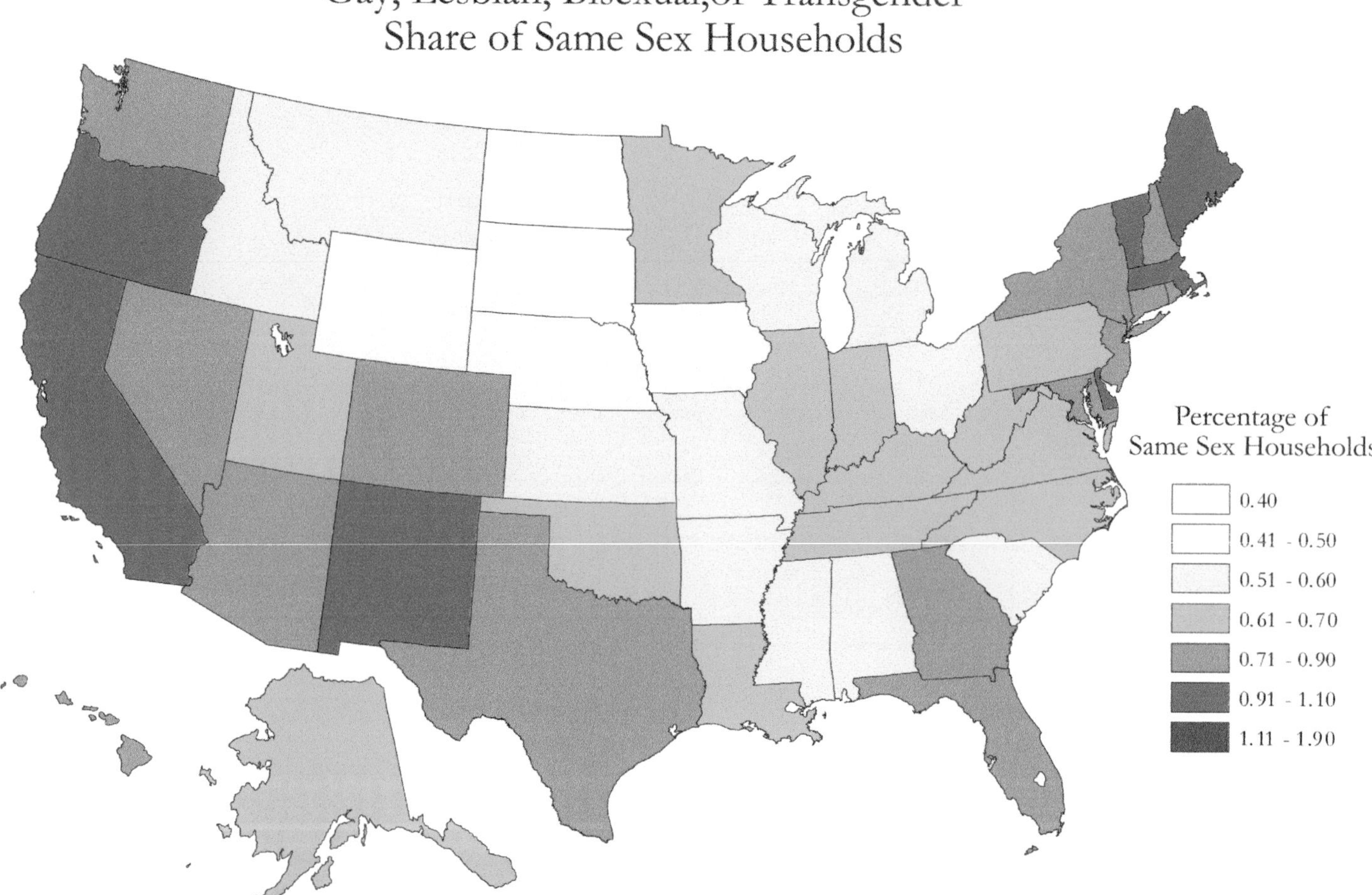
Gay, Lesbian, Bisexual,or Transgender
Share of Same Sex Households
Percentage of
Same Sex Households
0.40
0.41 - 0.50
0.51 - 0.60
0.61 - 0.70
0.71 - 0.90
0.91 - 1.10
1.11 - 1.90

FIGURE 7.9

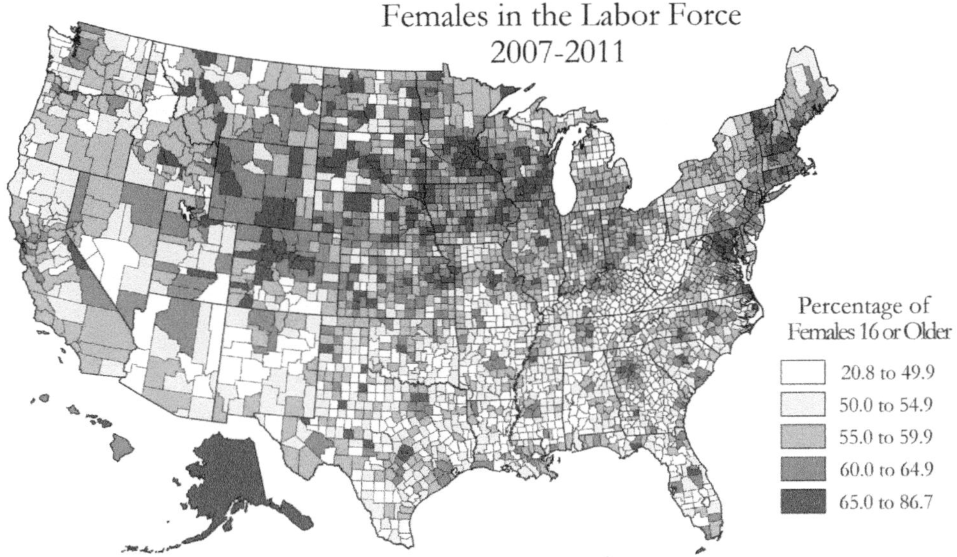

Top 199 Counties Having
High Females in the Labnor Force

2008 | 2012

Percentage of the Vote: 0, 20, 40, 60, 80, 100

Democrat, Republican, Other, Turnout | Democrat, Republican, Other, Turnout

Top 199 and Bottom 200 Counties for
Females in the Labor Force
2007-2011

Top 199 Counties
Bottom 200 Counties
Other Counties

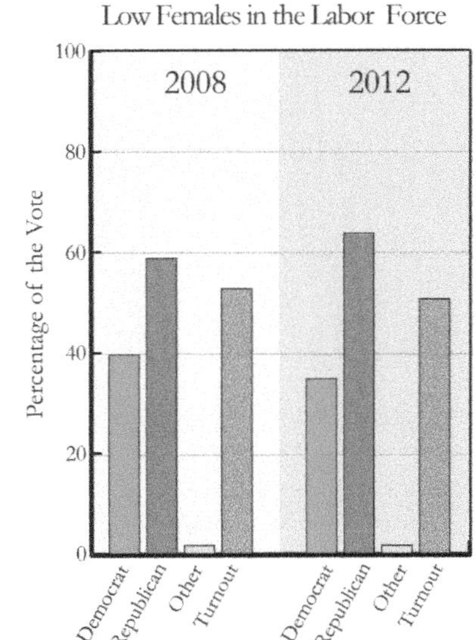

FIGURE 7.10

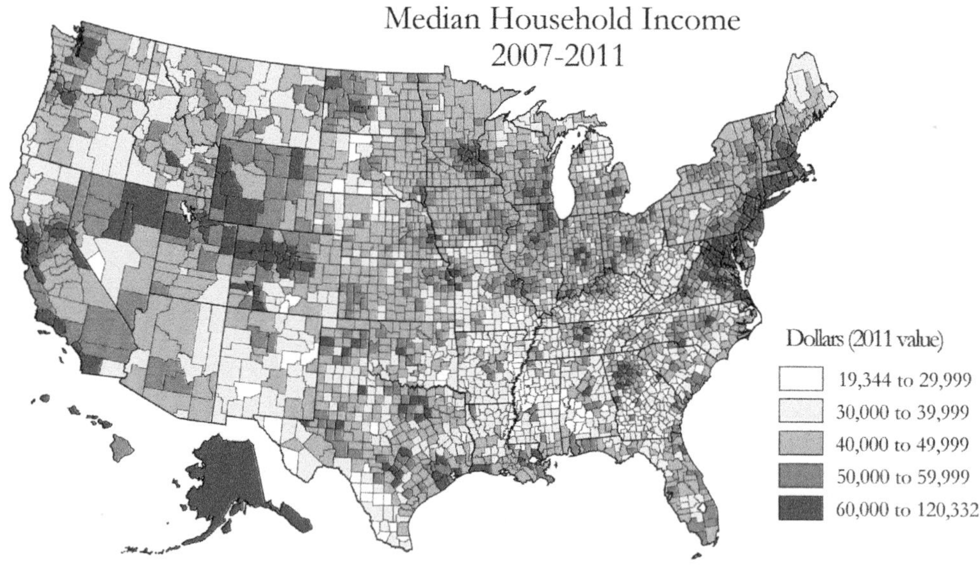

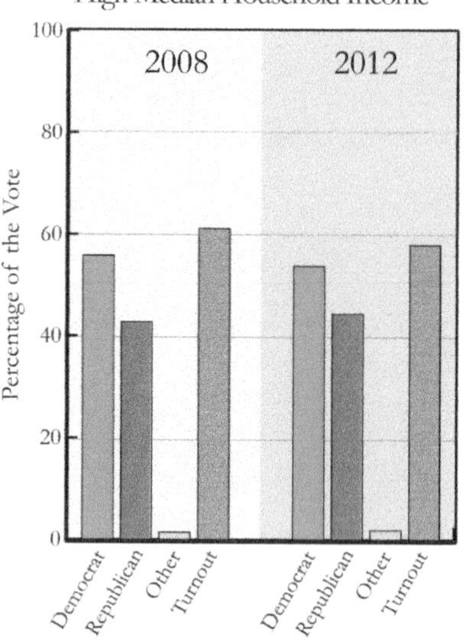

Top 200 and Bottom 200 Counties for
Median Household Income
2007-2011

Top 200 Counties
Bottom 200 Counties
Other Counties

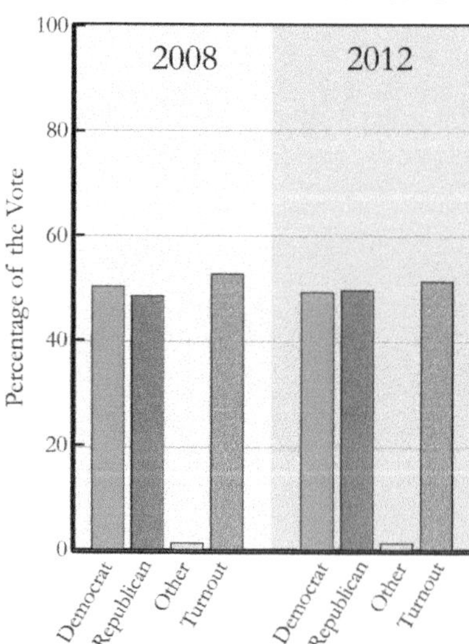

FIGURE 7.11

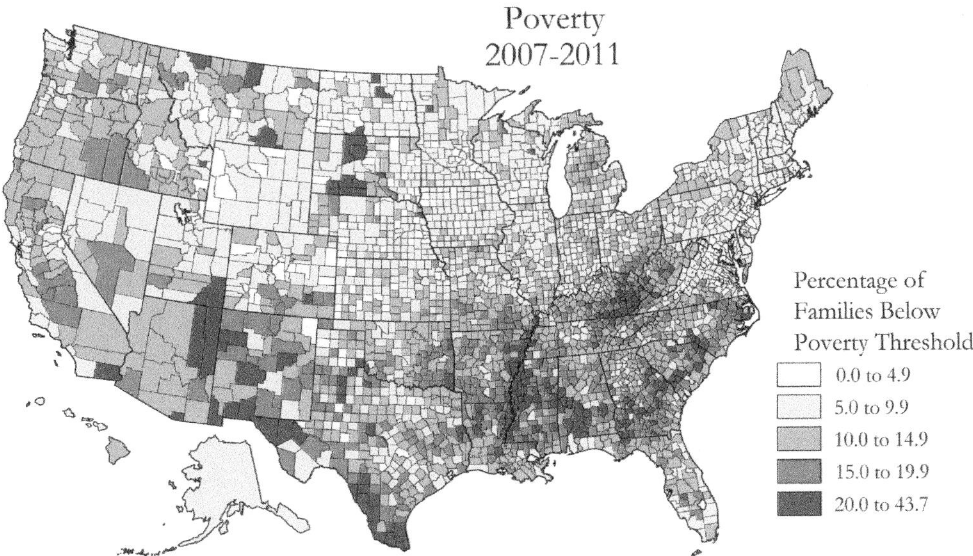

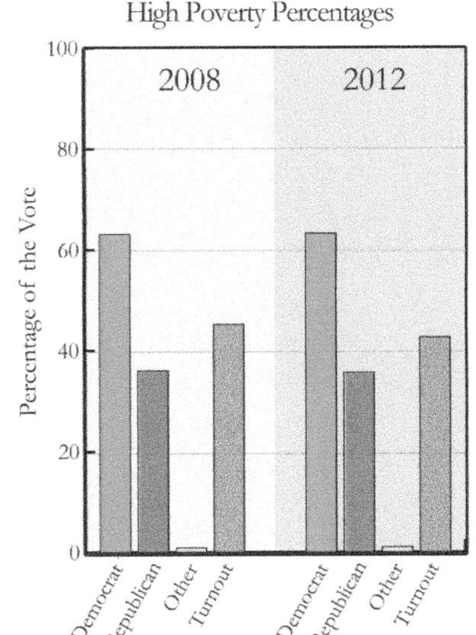

Top 205 and Bottom 202 Counties for
High and Low Poverty Percentages
2007-2011

Top 205 Counties
Bottom 202 Counties
Other Counties

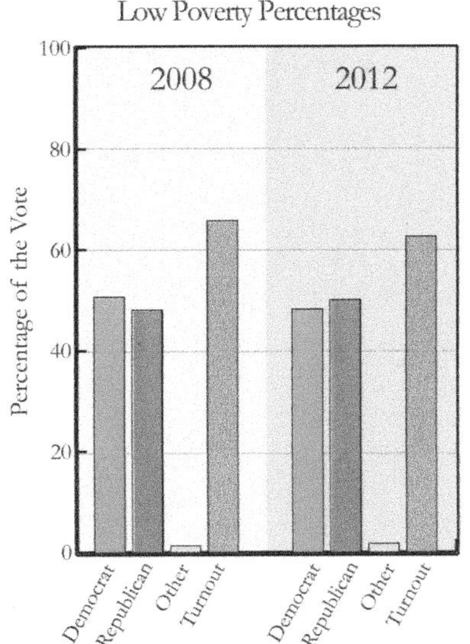

FIGURE 7.12

Unemployment
2012
Percentage of
Workers
Unemployed
0.8 to 4.9
5.0 to 6.9
7.0 to 8.9
9.0 to 10.9
11.0 to 28.3

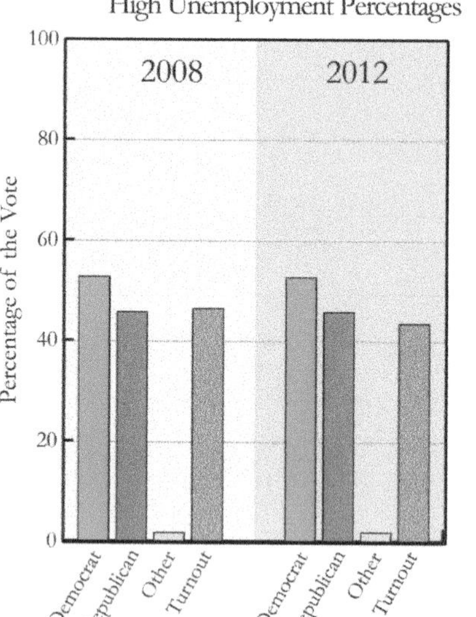
Top 201 Counties Having
High Unemployment Percentages
2008
2012
Percentage of the Vote
100
80
60
40
20
0
Democrat
Republican
Other
Turnout
Democrat
Republican
Other
Turnout

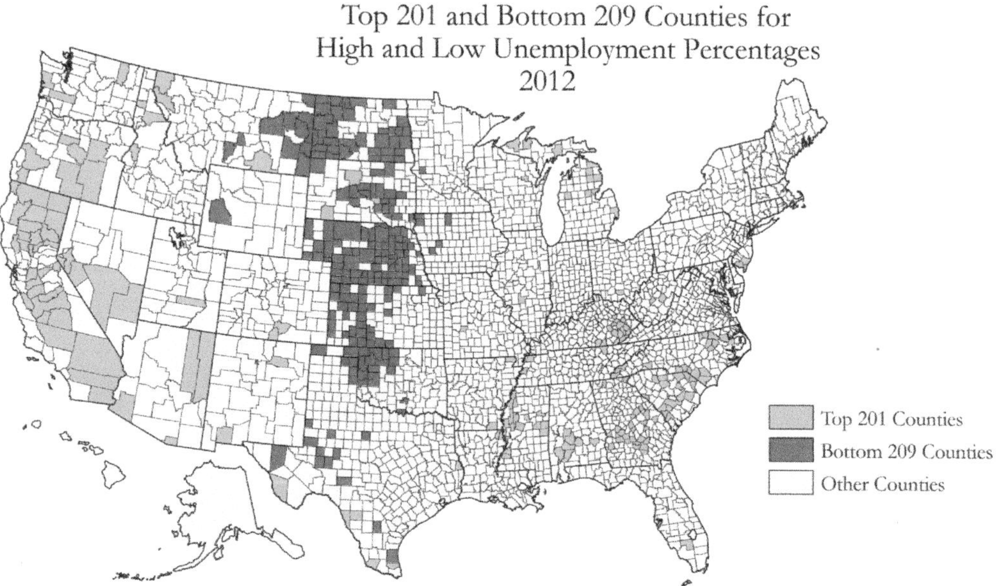
Top 201 and Bottom 209 Counties for
High and Low Unemployment Percentages
2012
Top 201 Counties
Bottom 209 Counties
Other Counties

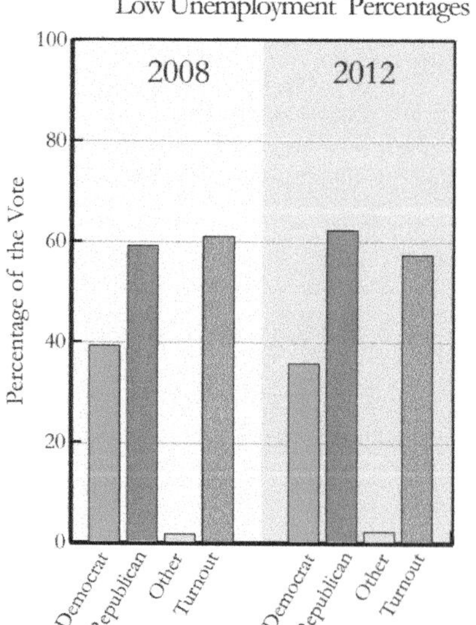
Bottom 209 Counties Having
Low Unemployment Percentages
2008
2012
Percentage of the Vote
100
80
60
40
20
0
Democrat
Republican
Other
Turnout
Democrat
Republican
Other
Turnout

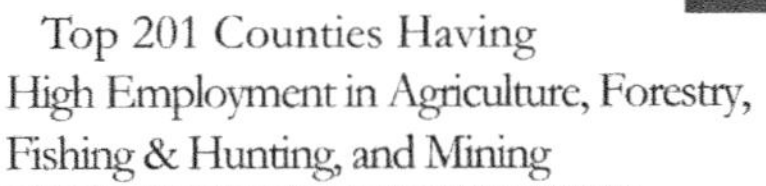
FIGURE 7.13

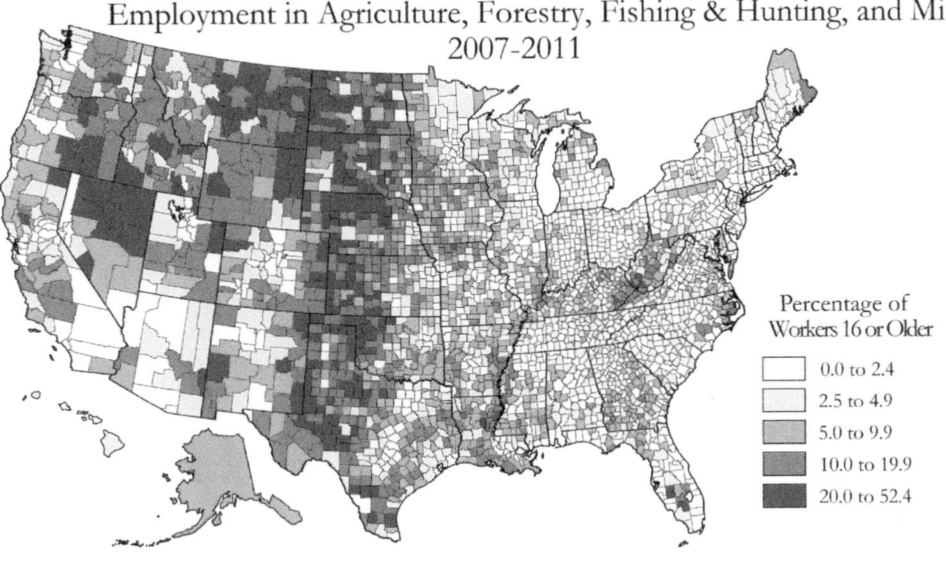
Employment in Agriculture, Forestry, Fishing & Hunting, and Mining
2007-2011
Percentage of
Workers 16 or Older
0.0 to 2.4
2.5 to 4.9
5.0 to 9.9
10.0 to 19.9
20.0 to 52.4

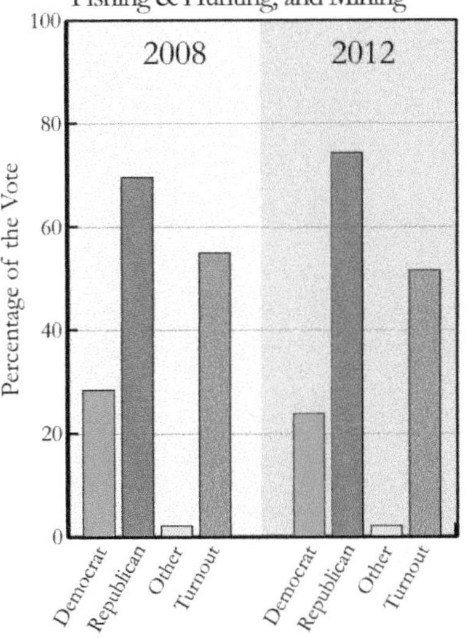
Top 201 Counties Having
High Employment in Agriculture, Forestry,
Fishing & Hunting, and Mining
2008
2012
Percentage of the Vote
100
80
60
40
20
0
Democrat
Republican
Other
Turnout
Democrat
Republican
Other
Turnout

Top 201 and Bottom 212 Counties for Employment in
Agriculture, Forestry, Fishing & Hunting, and Mining
2007-2011
Top 201 Counties
Bottom 212 Counties
Other Counties

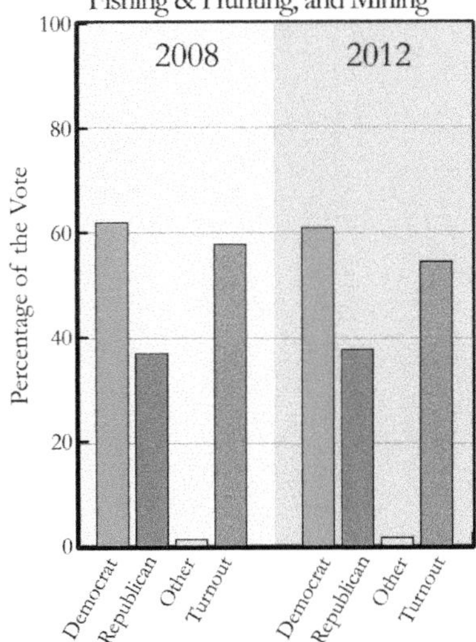
Bottom 212 Counties Having
Low Employment in Agriculture, Forestry,
Fishing & Hunting, and Mining
2008
2012
Percentage of the Vote
100
80
60
40
20
0
Democrat
Republican
Other
Turnout
Democrat
Republican
Other
Turnout

FIGURE 7.14

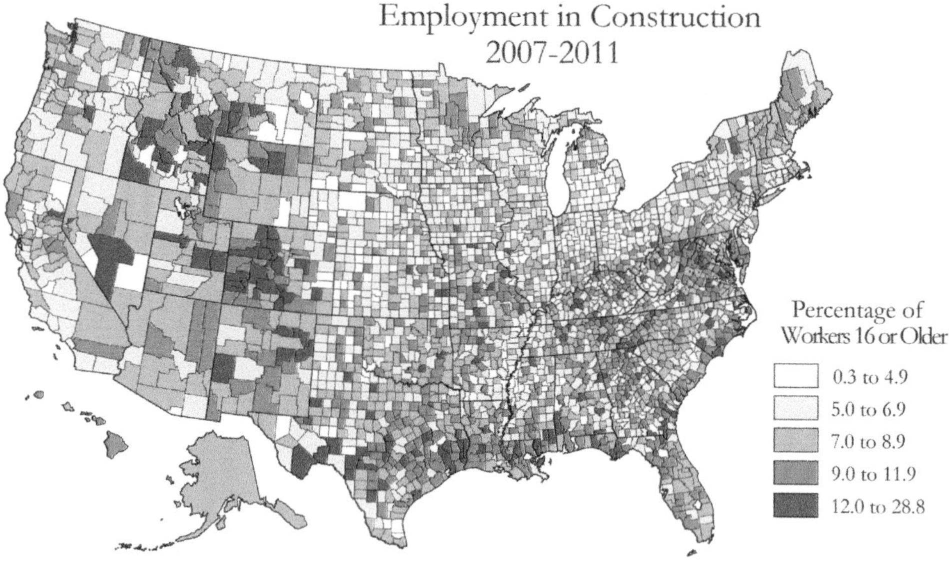
Employment in Construction
2007-2011
Percentage of
Workers 16 or Older
0.3 to 4.9
5.0 to 6.9
7.0 to 8.9
9.0 to 11.9
12.0 to 28.8

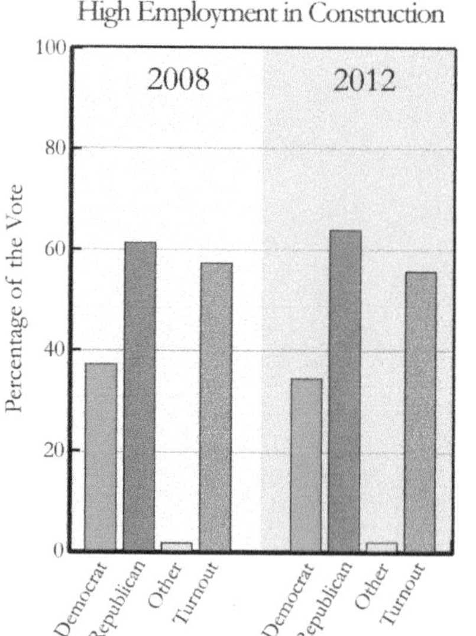
Top 199 Counties Having
High Employment in Construction
2008
2012
Percentage of the Vote
100
80
60
40
20
0
Democrat
Republican
Other
Turnout
Democrat
Republican
Other
Turnout

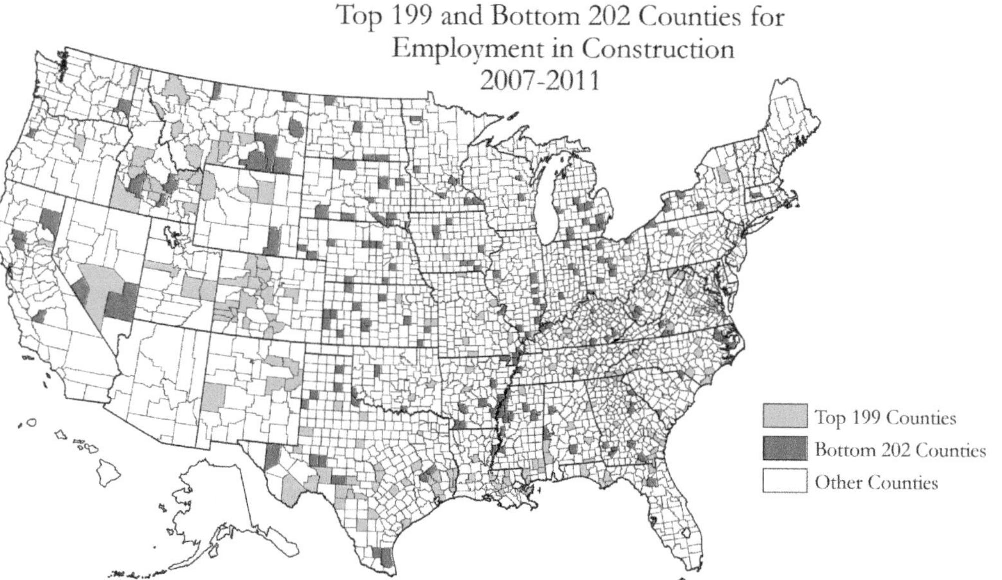
Top 199 and Bottom 202 Counties for
Employment in Construction
2007-2011
Top 199 Counties
Bottom 202 Counties
Other Counties

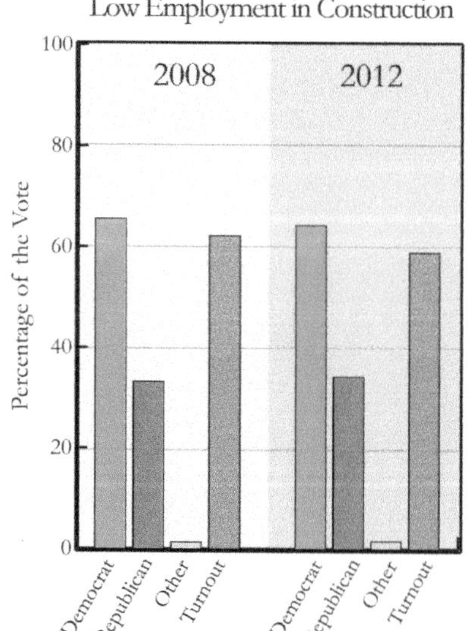
Bottom 202 Counties Having
Low Employment in Construction
2008
2012
Percentage of the Vote
100
80
60
40
20
0
Democrat
Republican
Other
Turnout
Democrat
Republican
Other
Turnout

FIGURE 7.15

Employment in Manufacturing
2007-2011
Percentage of
Workers 16 or Older
0.0 to 4.9
5.0 to 9.9
10.0 to 14.9
15.0 to 19.9
20.0 to 41.9

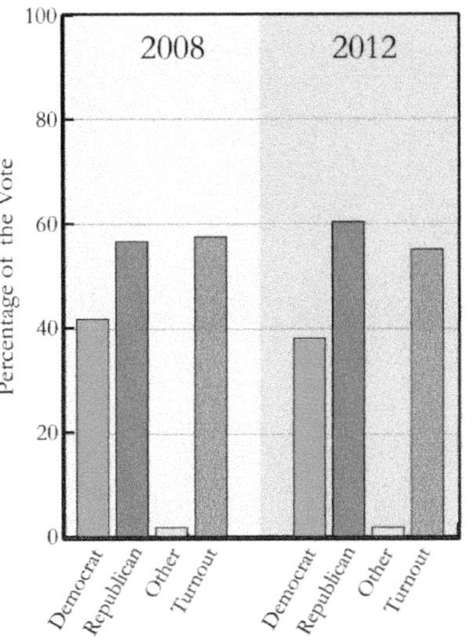
Top 204 Counties Having
High Employment in Manufacturing
2008
2012
Percentage of the Vote
100
80
60
40
20
0
Democrat
Republican
Other
Turnout
Democrat
Republican
Other
Turnout

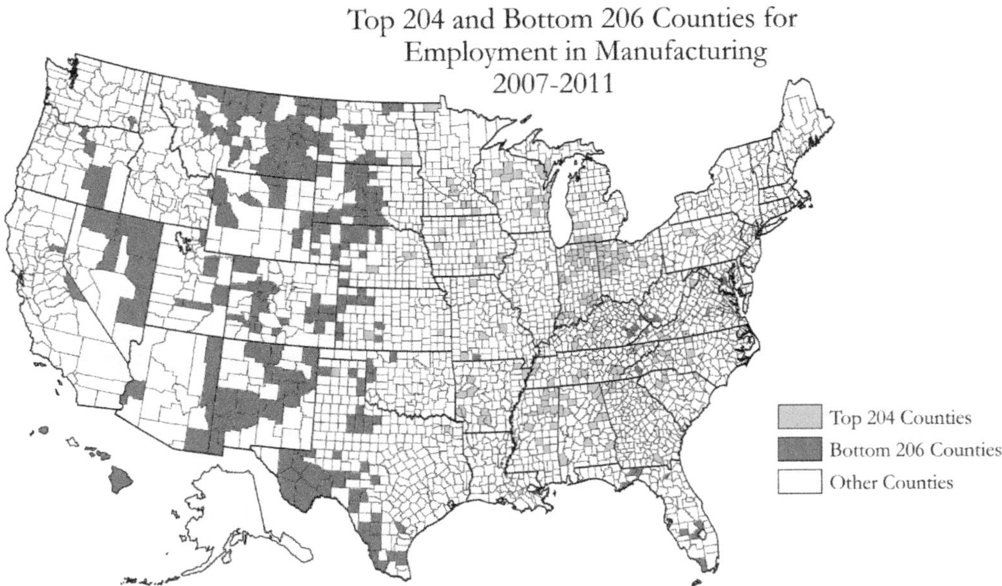
Top 204 and Bottom 206 Counties for
Employment in Manufacturing
2007-2011
Top 204 Counties
Bottom 206 Counties
Other Counties

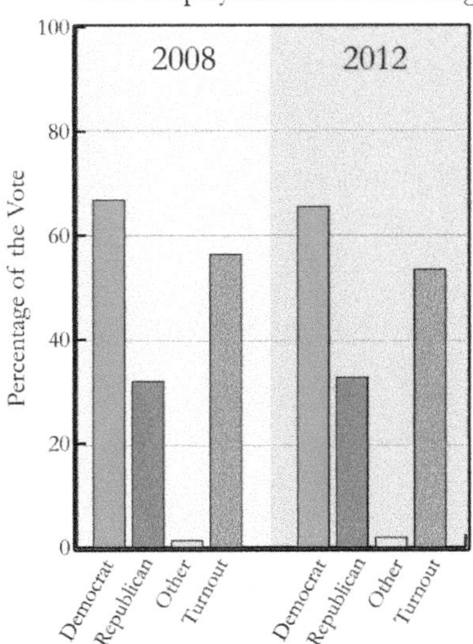
Bottom 206 Counties Having
Low Employment in Manufacturing
2008
2012
Percentage of the Vote
100
80
60
40
20
0
Democrat
Republican
Other
Turnout
Democrat
Republican
Other
Turnout

FIGURE 7.16

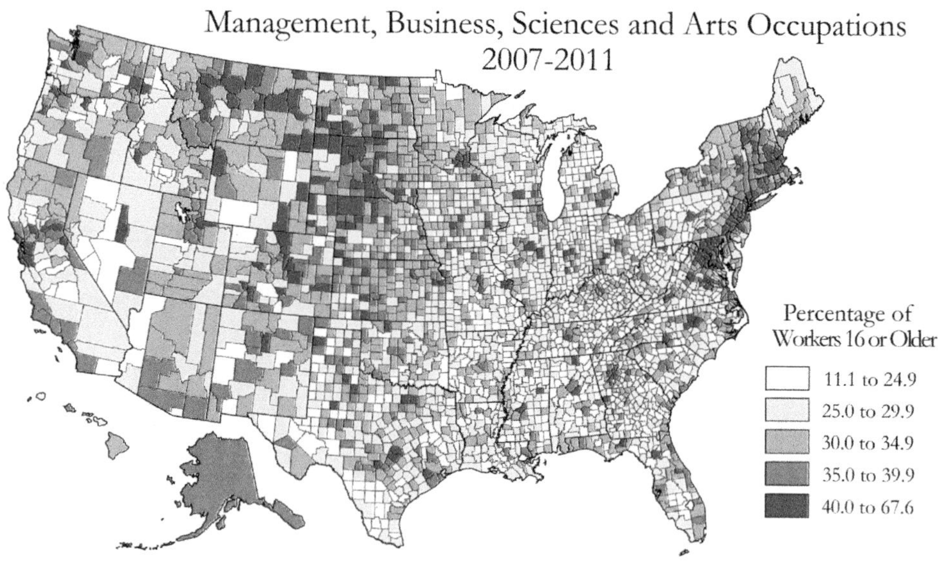
Management, Business, Sciences and Arts Occupations
2007-2011
Percentage of
Workers 16 or Older
11.1 to 24.9
25.0 to 29.9
30.0 to 34.9
35.0 to 39.9
40.0 to 67.6

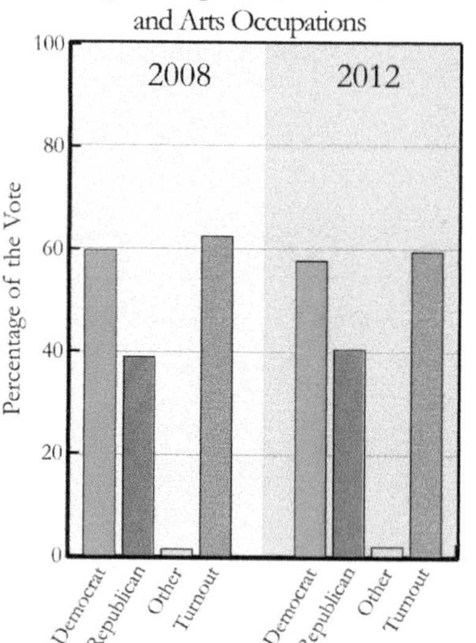
Top 199 Counties Having
High Management, Business, Sciences
and Arts Occupations
2008
2012
Percentage of the Vote
100
80
60
40
20
0
Democrat
Republican
Other
Turnout
Democrat
Republican
Other
Turnout

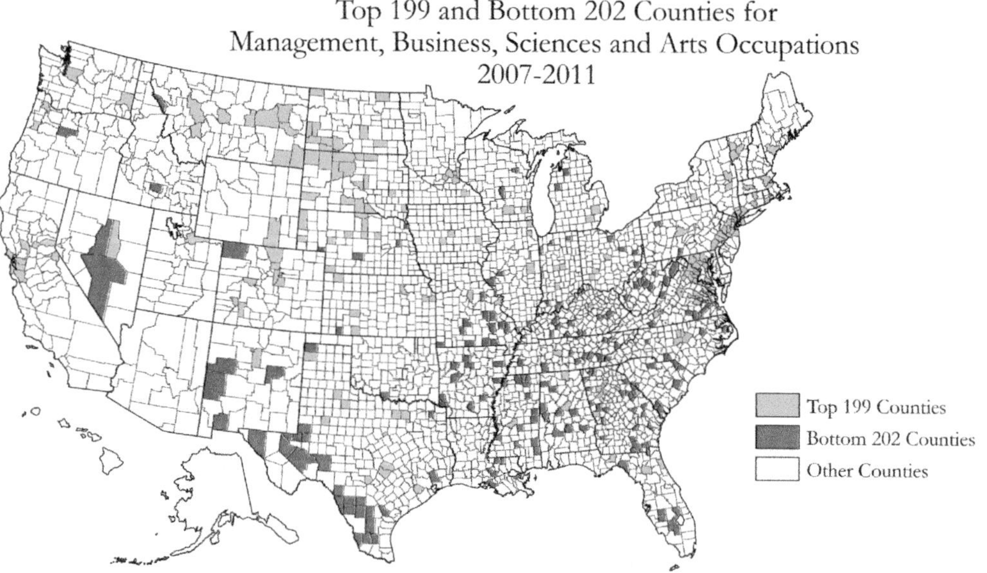
Top 199 and Bottom 202 Counties for
Management, Business, Sciences and Arts Occupations
2007-2011
Top 199 Counties
Bottom 202 Counties
Other Counties

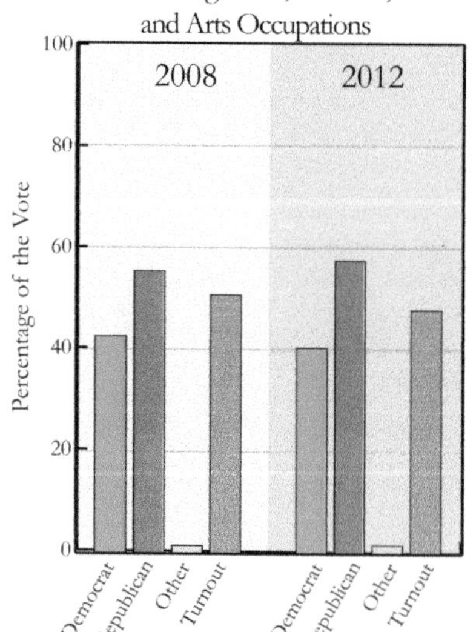
Bottom 202 Counties Having
Low Management, Business, Sciences
and Arts Occupations
2008
2012
Percentage of the Vote
100
80
60
40
20
0
Democrat
Republican
Other
Turnout
Democrat
Republican
Other
Turnout

FIGURE 7.17

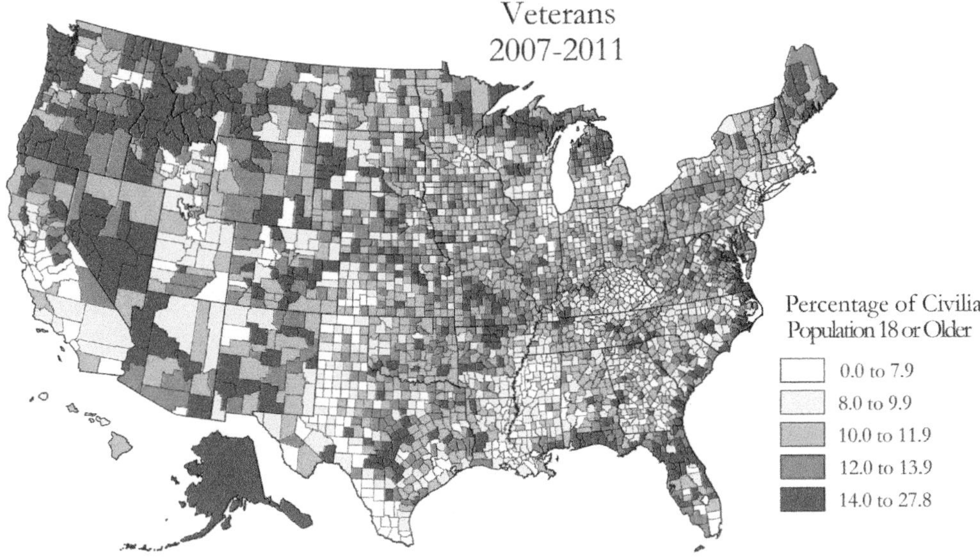
Veterans
2007-2011
Percentage of Civilian
Population 18 or Older
0.0 to 7.9
8.0 to 9.9
10.0 to 11.9
12.0 to 13.9
14.0 to 27.8

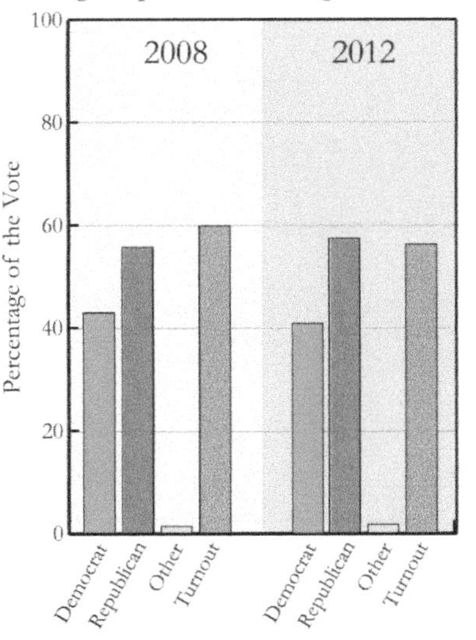
Top 206 Counties Having
High Population Percentage of Veterans
2008
2012
Percentage of the Vote
100
80
60
40
20
0
Democrat
Republican
Other
Turnout
Democrat
Republican
Other
Turnout

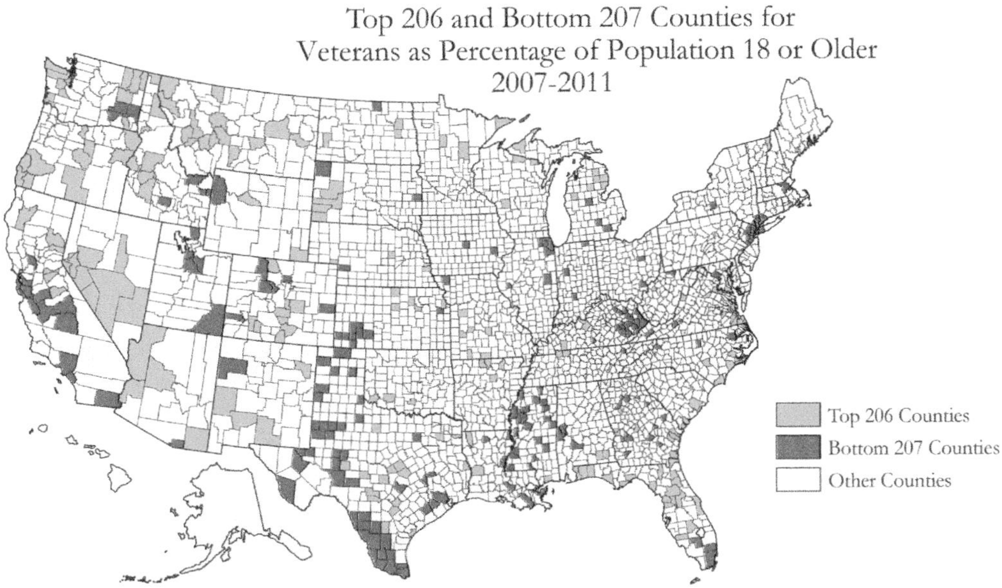
Top 206 and Bottom 207 Counties for
Veterans as Percentage of Population 18 or Older
2007-2011
Top 206 Counties
Bottom 207 Counties
Other Counties

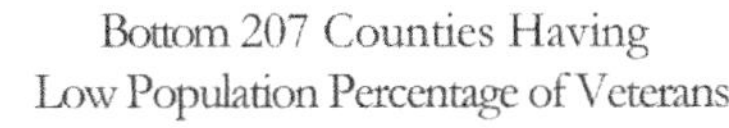
Bottom 207 Counties Having
Low Population Percentage of Veterans

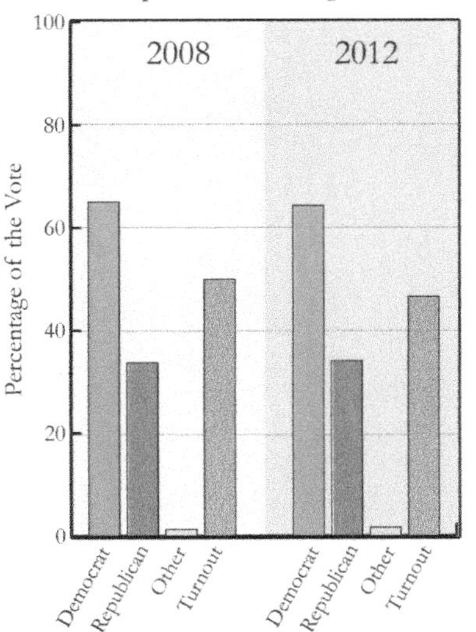
2008
2012
Percentage of the Vote
100
80
60
40
20
0
Democrat
Republican
Other
Turnout
Democrat
Republican
Other
Turnout

FIGURE 7.18

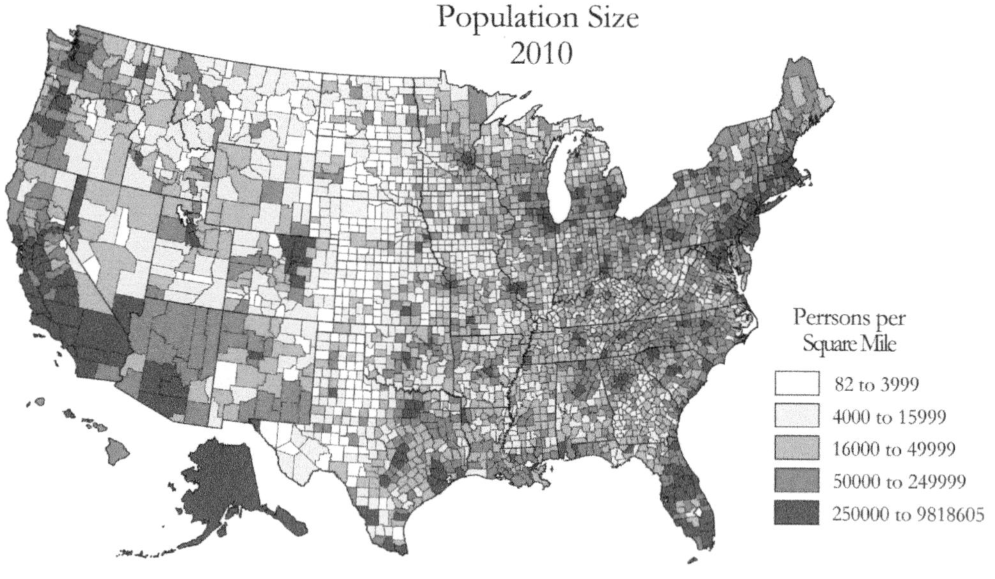
Population Size
2010
Perrsons per
Square Mile
82 to 3999
4000 to 15999
16000 to 49999
50000 to 249999
250000 to 9818605

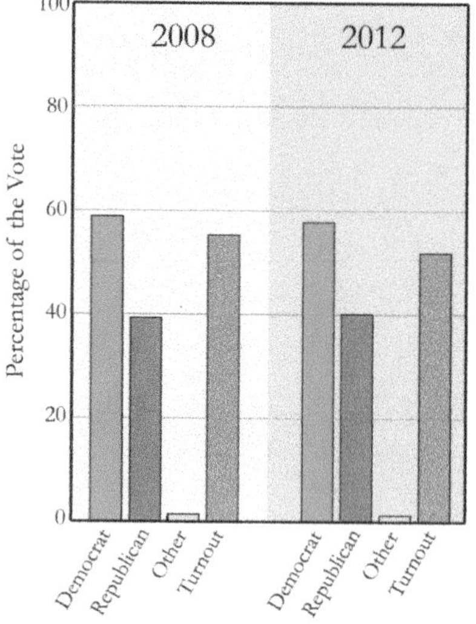
Top 200 Counties Having
Largest Population Size
2008
2012
Percentage of the Vote
0
20
40
60
80
100
Democrat
Republican
Other
Turnout
Democrat
Republican
Other
Turnout

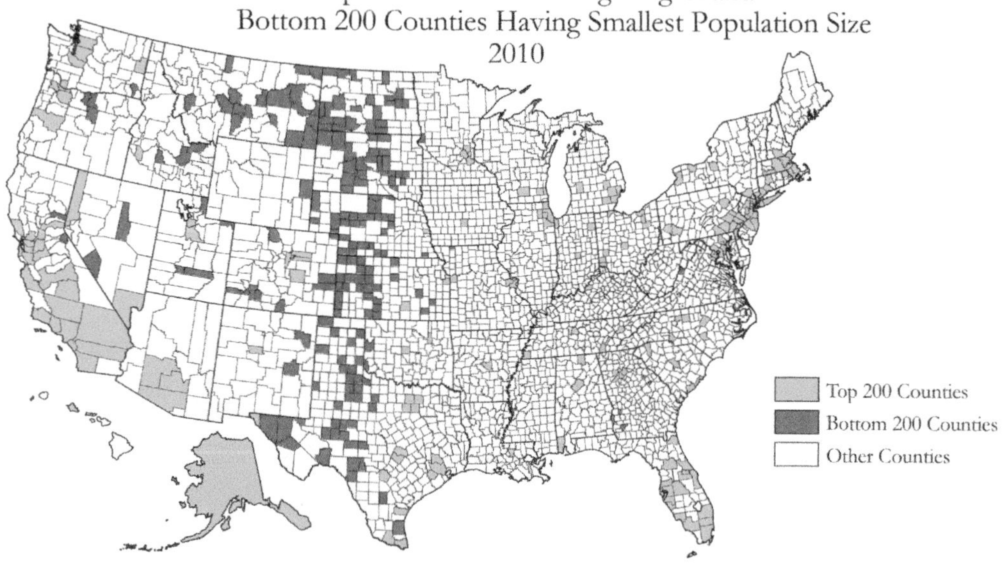
Top 200 Counties Having Largest and
Bottom 200 Counties Having Smallest Population Size
2010
Top 200 Counties
Bottom 200 Counties
Other Counties

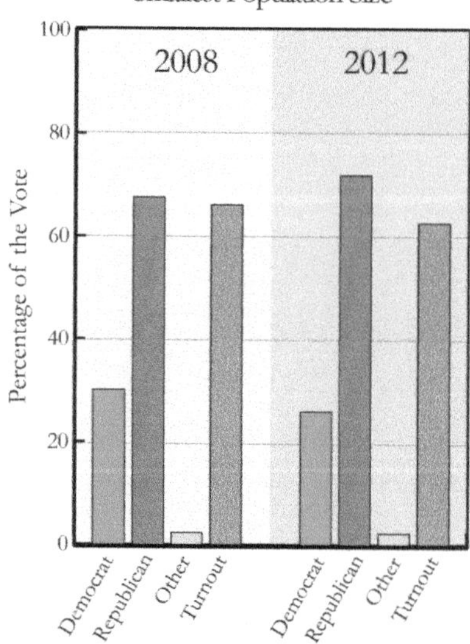
Bottom 200 Counties Having
Smallest Population Size
2008
2012
Percentage of the Vote
0
20
40
60
80
100
Democrat
Republican
Other
Turnout
Democrat
Republican
Other
Turnout

FIGURE 7.19

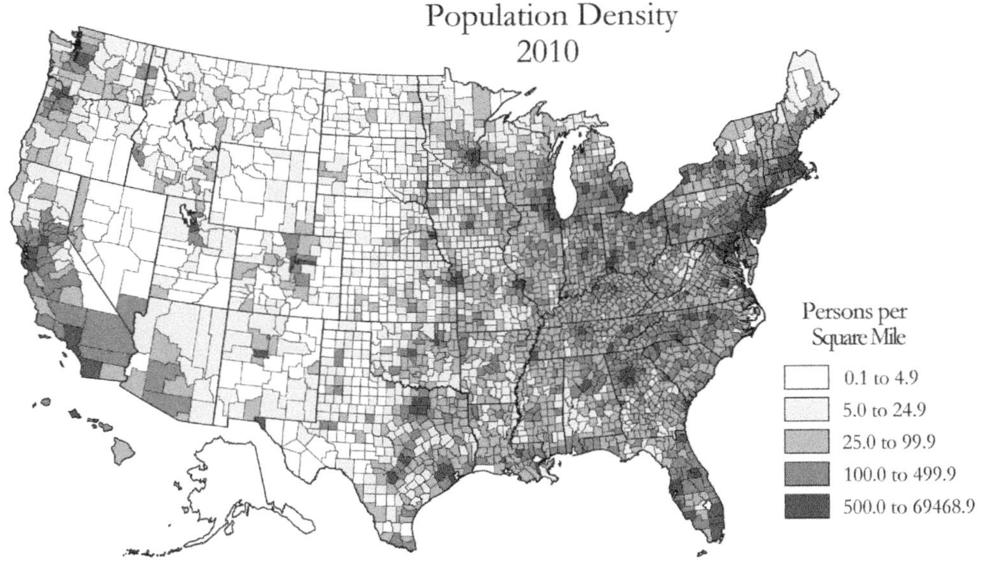

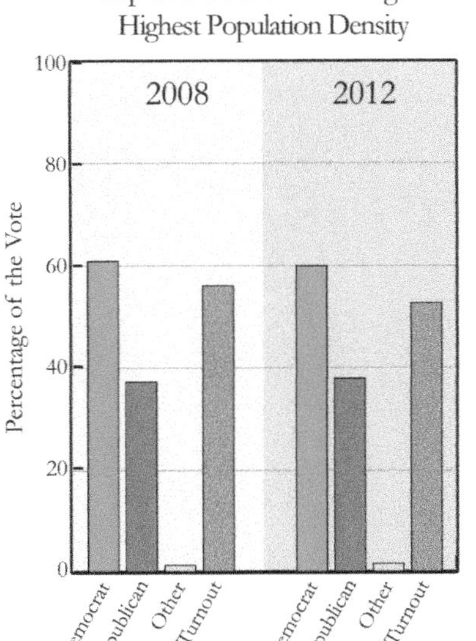

Top 200 Counties Having Highest and
Bottom 200 Counties Having Lowest Population Density
2010

Top 200 Counties
Bottom 200 Counties
Other Counties

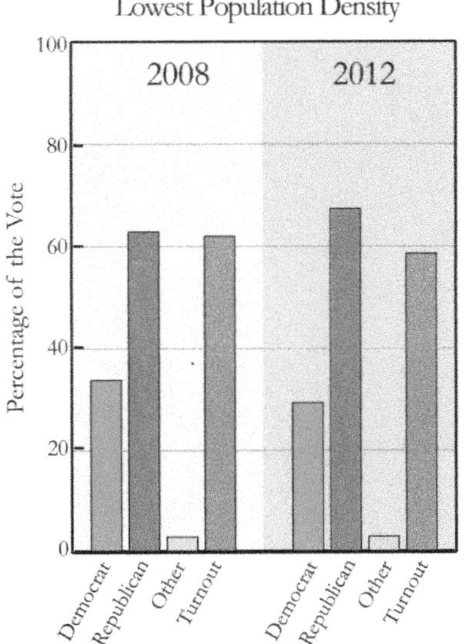

FIGURE 7.20

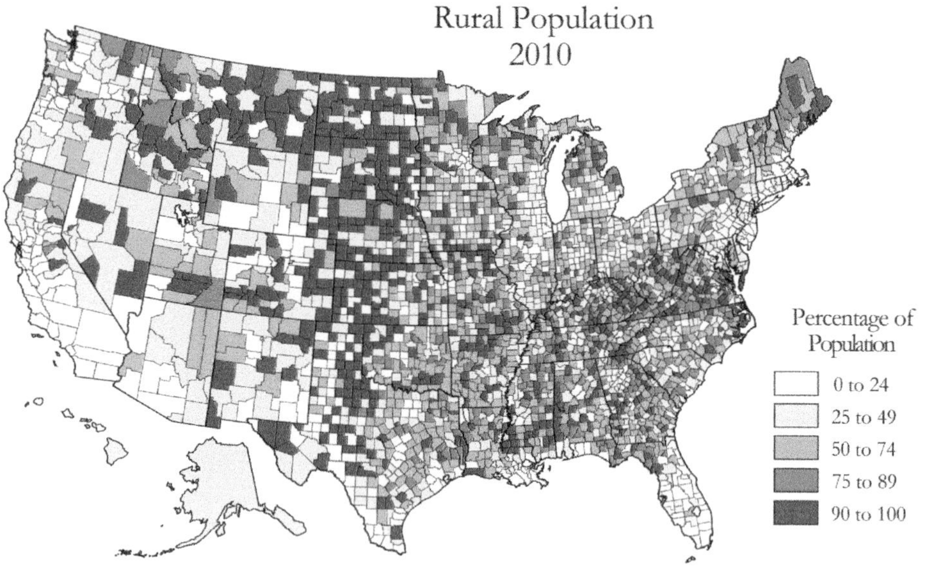

Top 686 Counties Having Entirely Rural Population

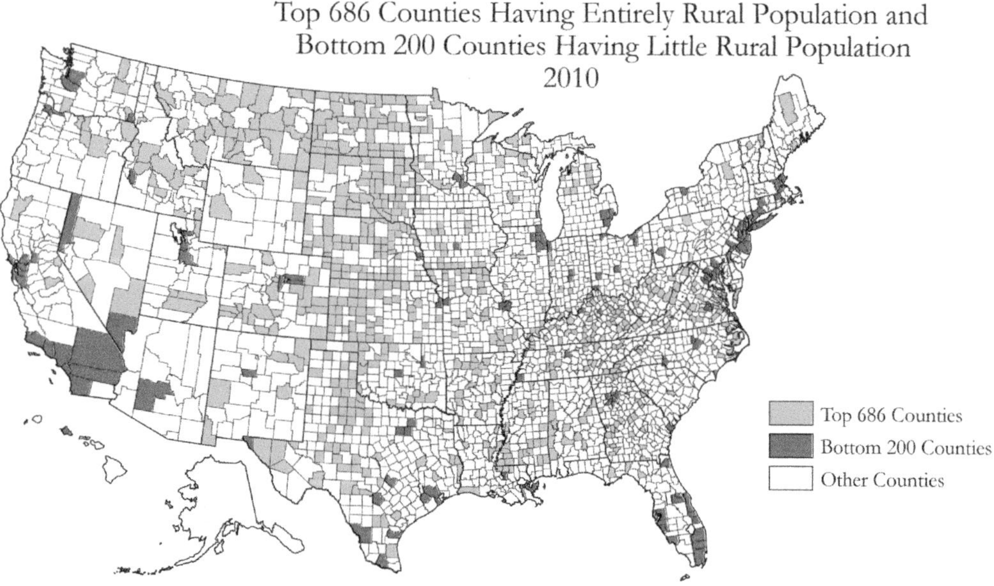

Bottom 200 Counties Having Little Rural Population

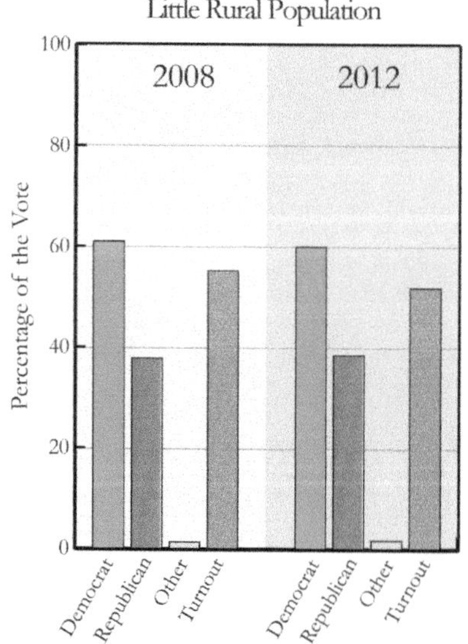

FIGURE 7.21

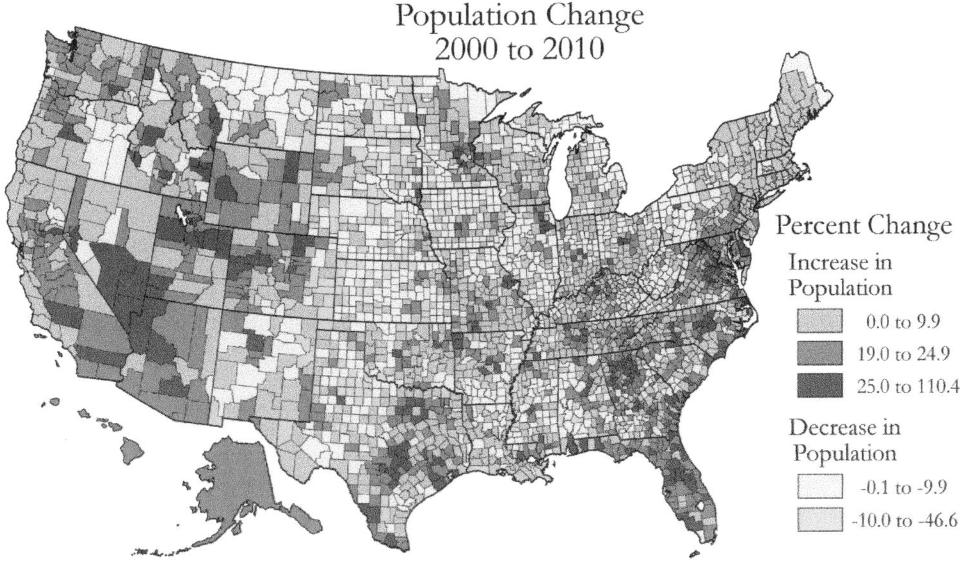

Population Change
2000 to 2010
Percent Change
Increase in Population
0.0 to 9.9
19.0 to 24.9
25.0 to 110.4
Decrease in Population
-0.1 to -9.9
-10.0 to -46.6

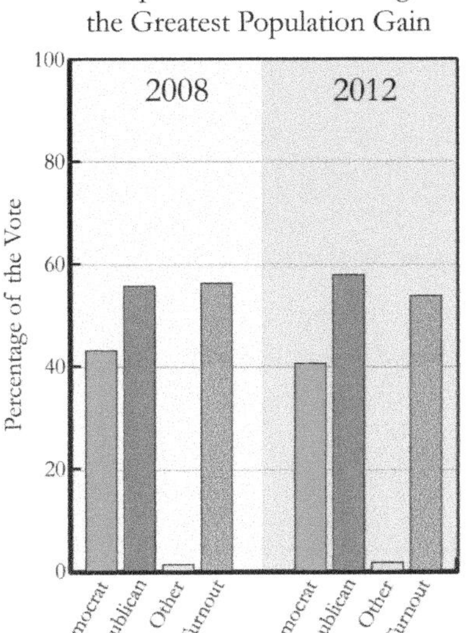

Top 200 Counties Having the Greatest Population Gain
2008
2012
Percentage of the Vote
0
20
40
60
80
100
Democrat
Republican
Other
Turnout
Democrat
Republican
Other
Turnout

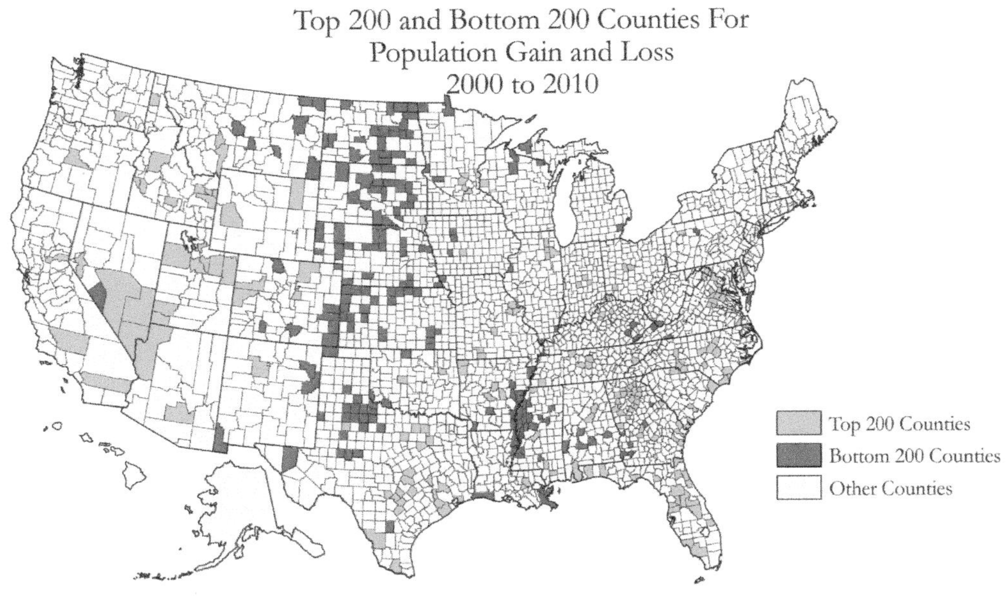

Top 200 and Bottom 200 Counties For Population Gain and Loss
2000 to 2010
Top 200 Counties
Bottom 200 Counties
Other Counties

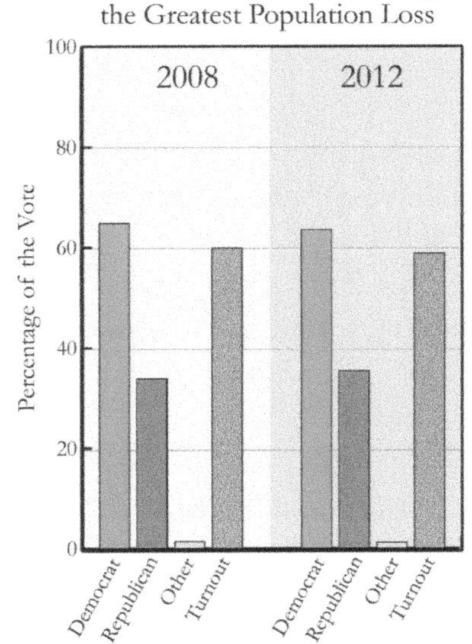

Bottom 200 Counties Having the Greatest Population Loss
2008
2012
Percentage of the Vote
0
20
40
60
80
100
Democrat
Republican
Other
Turnout
Democrat
Republican
Other
Turnout

7.21 shows the counties with the highest and lowest rates of population change between 2000 and 2010. The two hundred counties with the highest percentage increases grew by 27 percent or more, while those with the biggest losses declined in population by 10.5 percent or more. This map of population change reveals the large areas of population decline in Republican-leaning areas of the Plains, but their small numbers were exceeded by the large absolute losses in Democratic Detroit, New Orleans, and Democratic-voting, African American–dominated rural counties in the South.

Many of the growing areas of the country are indeed Republican leaning. However, some of these places, such as Phoenix, may be becoming less Republican in part because many of their new residents are young voters and/or immigrants. Perhaps more importantly, Republican gains in these growing regions may not be able to overcome Democratic margins in metropolitan cores and inner suburbs. These data underscore concern among Republicans that they will need to make more inroads among urban residents and suburbanites in order to recapture the presidency in 2016 and beyond.

Short-term trends may obscure longer-term trends, however, as is illustrated by figure 7.22. This map shows population change during 2011–2012, a period including the 2012 election itself. Although the general trend of population declines in isolated rural areas and in inner cities and gains in suburbs and exurbs is continuing, North Dakota experienced the most population growth on a population basis in 2011–2012. Most of this growth occurred in western North Dakota and is driven by the energy industry; the Bakken Formation under the surface of this area is now one of the largest oil-producing regions in the United States. This region remains heavily Republican, and perceived hostility to the fossil fuel industry on the part of Democrats made North Dakota the second most Republican-shifting state in the country (following Utah). Energy production may also be driving population growth in heavily Republican West Texas. However, in both cases it should be recognized that these counties are small in population, and therefore, even a small number of new residents means a significant percentage increase.

Figures 7.23 and 7.24 focus on nonmovers. Although the United States is a highly mobile society, the majority of Americans today reside in the state in which they were born and/or raised. Nonmovers often live in rural areas and small towns, which have tended to support Republicans, including Romney, for the presidency. Demography is also related to migration status. Young adults, who are more likely to have voted for Obama, are more likely to move than are older adults, who are more likely to have been Romney supporters. However, many people who do relocate move to suburban and exurban places near large metropolitan areas. In general, these people are moving to places that are intermediate politically between conservative rural areas and liberal metropolitan cores. Interpretation of figure 7.23 in particular must also consider the fact that areas near state boundaries are more likely to have larger percentages of people who move across state boundaries. Many movers from these counties move short distances but across these boundaries into different states. Large metropolitan areas such as New York, Philadelphia, Washington, Charlotte, Kansas City, and Portland, among others, straddle state lines.

While all of these factors are related to differences within the US electorate, gender and ethnicity remain very important predictors. The gender gap, defined as the difference between the percentage of women who vote for Democrats and the percentage of men who vote for Democrats, has been a significant predictor of presidential voting for several decades. Beginning in 1980, exit polls have confirmed that women are more likely than men to have voted for Democratic nominees. 2012 was no exception: nationwide, the gender gap was about 7 percent. In fact, men were more likely to vote for Romney than for Obama, and hence Obama owes his margin of victory to the votes of women. However, there are significant differences in the gender gap among the states (figure 7.25). Although it is impossible to ascertain this with complete accuracy, it is likely that the votes of women swung the states of Florida, Iowa, Minnesota, Nevada, New Hampshire, Ohio, Oregon, Pennsylvania, Virginia, Washington, and Wisconsin into the Democratic column. Without these states, of course, Obama would have lost the election.

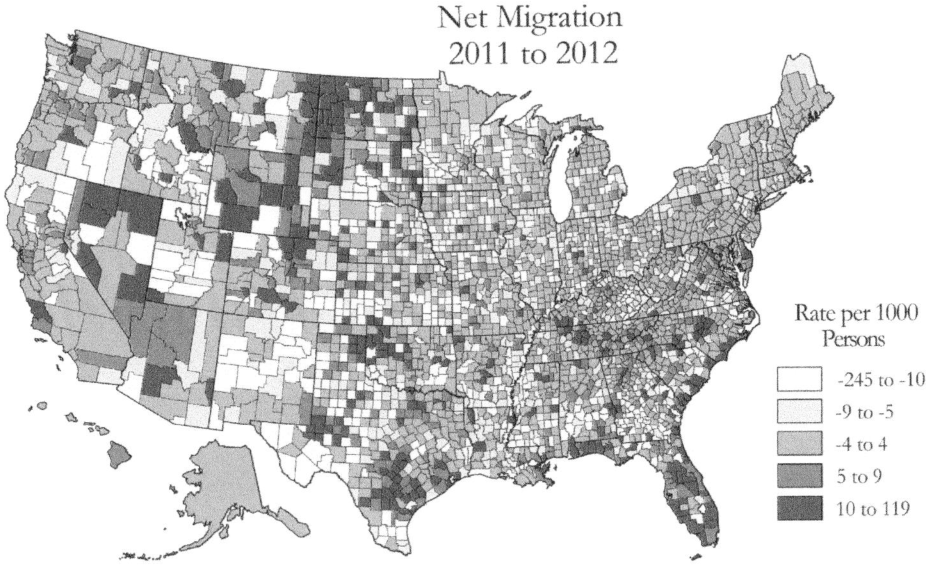
Net Migration
2011 to 2012
Rate per 1000
Persons
-245 to -10
-9 to -5
-4 to 4
5 to 9
10 to 119

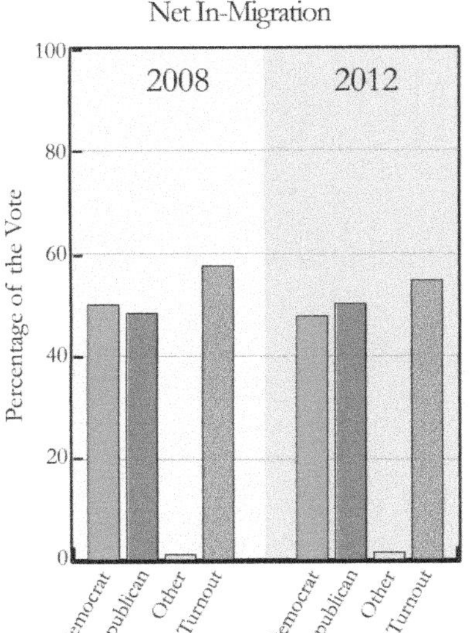
Top 200 Counties Having
Net In-Migration
2008
2012
Percentage of the Vote
100
80
60
40
20
0
Democrat
Republican
Other
Turnout
Democrat
Republican
Other
Turnout

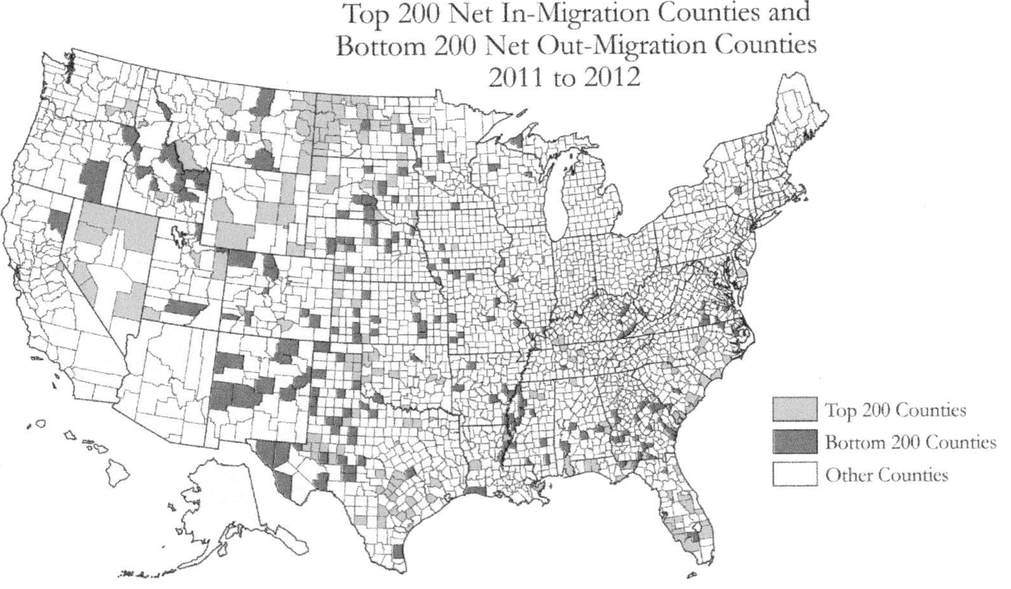
Top 200 Net In-Migration Counties and
Bottom 200 Net Out-Migration Counties
2011 to 2012
Top 200 Counties
Bottom 200 Counties
Other Counties

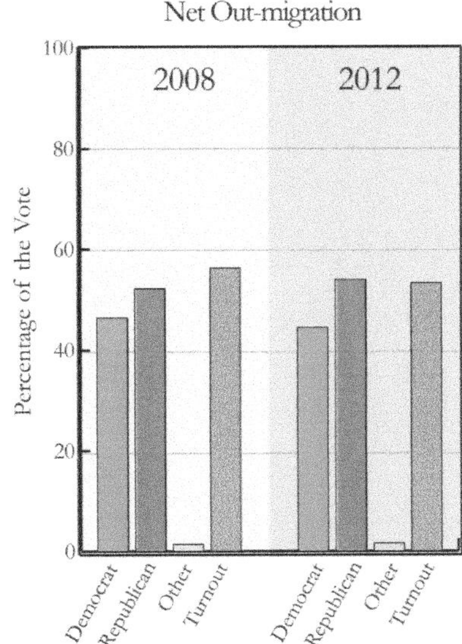
Bottom 200 Counties Having
Net Out-migration
2008
2012
Percentage of the Vote
100
80
60
40
20
0
Democrat
Republican
Other
Turnout
Democrat
Republican
Other
Turnout

FIGURE 7.23

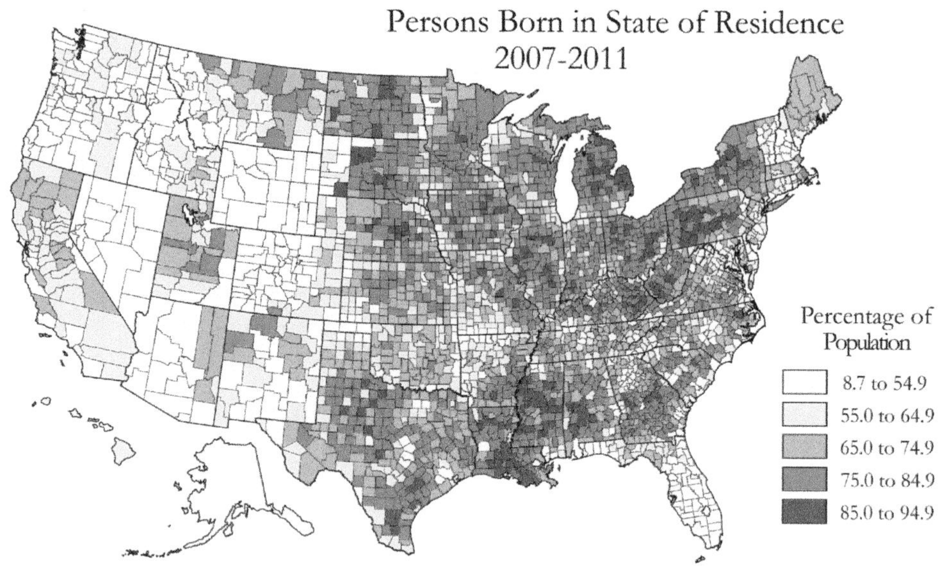

Top 201 Counties Having
High Percentage Born in State of Residence

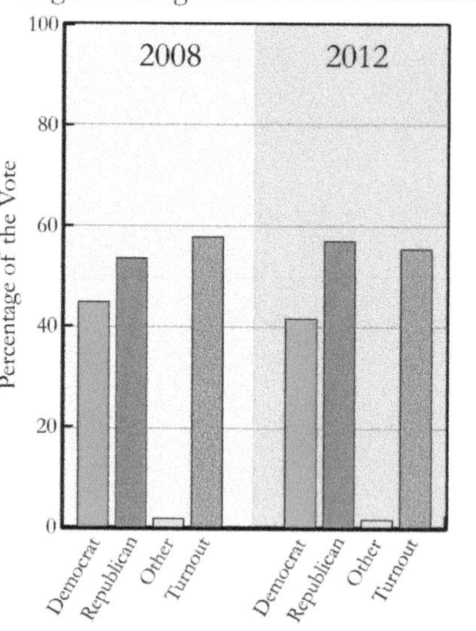

Top 201 and Bottom 200 Counties for
Percentage of Population Born in State of Residence
2007-2011

Top 201 Counties
Bottom 200 Counties
Other Counties

Bottom 200 Counties Having
Low Percentage Born in State of Residence

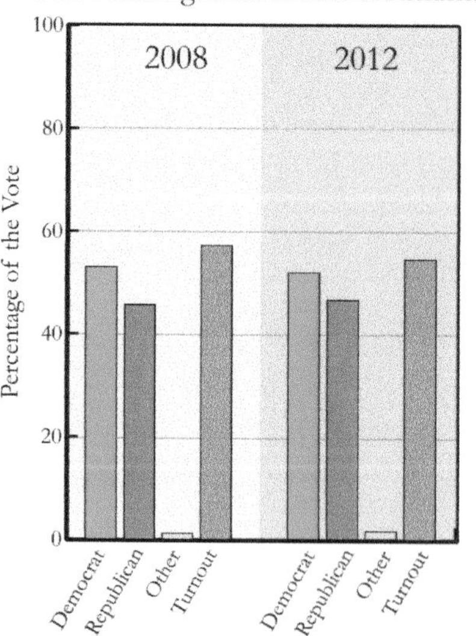

FIGURE 7.24

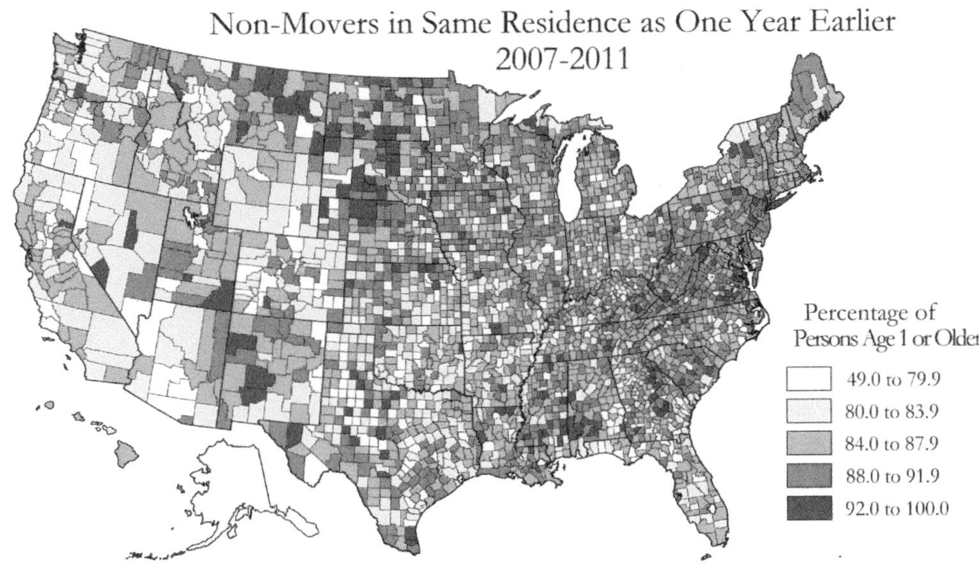
Non-Movers in Same Residence as One Year Earlier
2007-2011
Percentage of
Persons Age 1 or Older
49.0 to 79.9
80.0 to 83.9
84.0 to 87.9
88.0 to 91.9
92.0 to 100.0

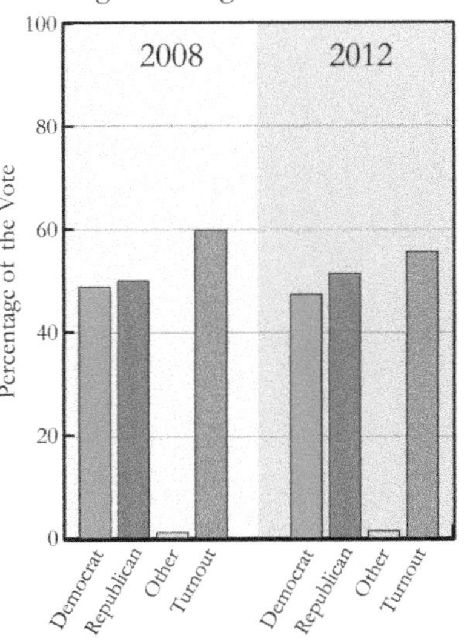
Top 209 Counties Having
High Percentage of Non-Movers
2008
2012
Percentage of the Vote
0
20
40
60
80
100
Democrat
Republican
Other
Turnout
Democrat
Republican
Other
Turnout

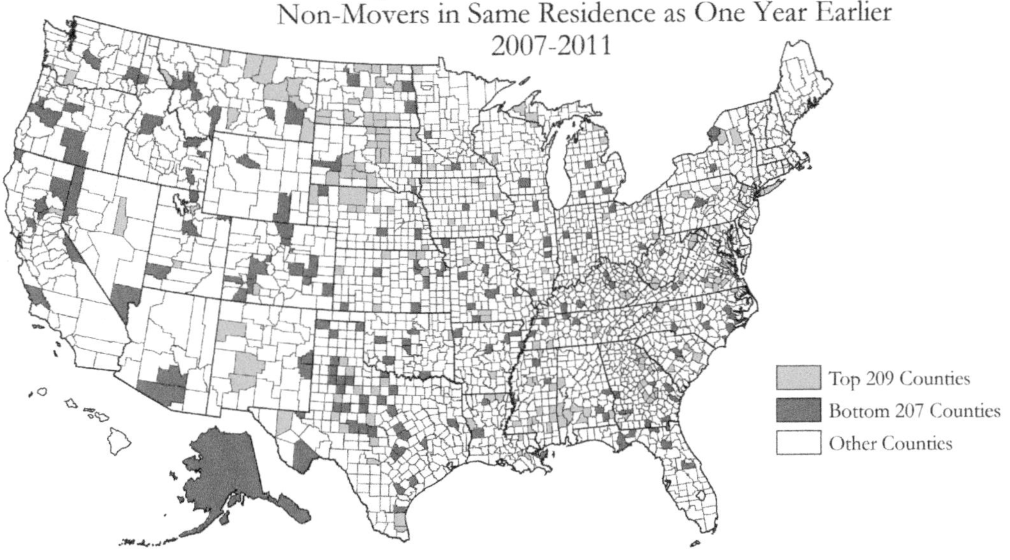
Top 209 and Bottom 207 Counties for
Non-Movers in Same Residence as One Year Earlier
2007-2011
Top 209 Counties
Bottom 207 Counties
Other Counties

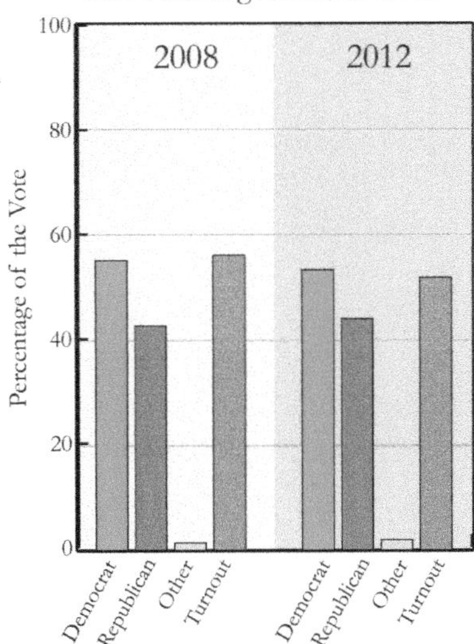
Bottom 207 Counties Having
Low Percentage of Non-Movers
2008
2012
Percentage of the Vote
0
20
40
60
80
100
Democrat
Republican
Other
Turnout
Democrat
Republican
Other
Turnout

FIGURE 7.25

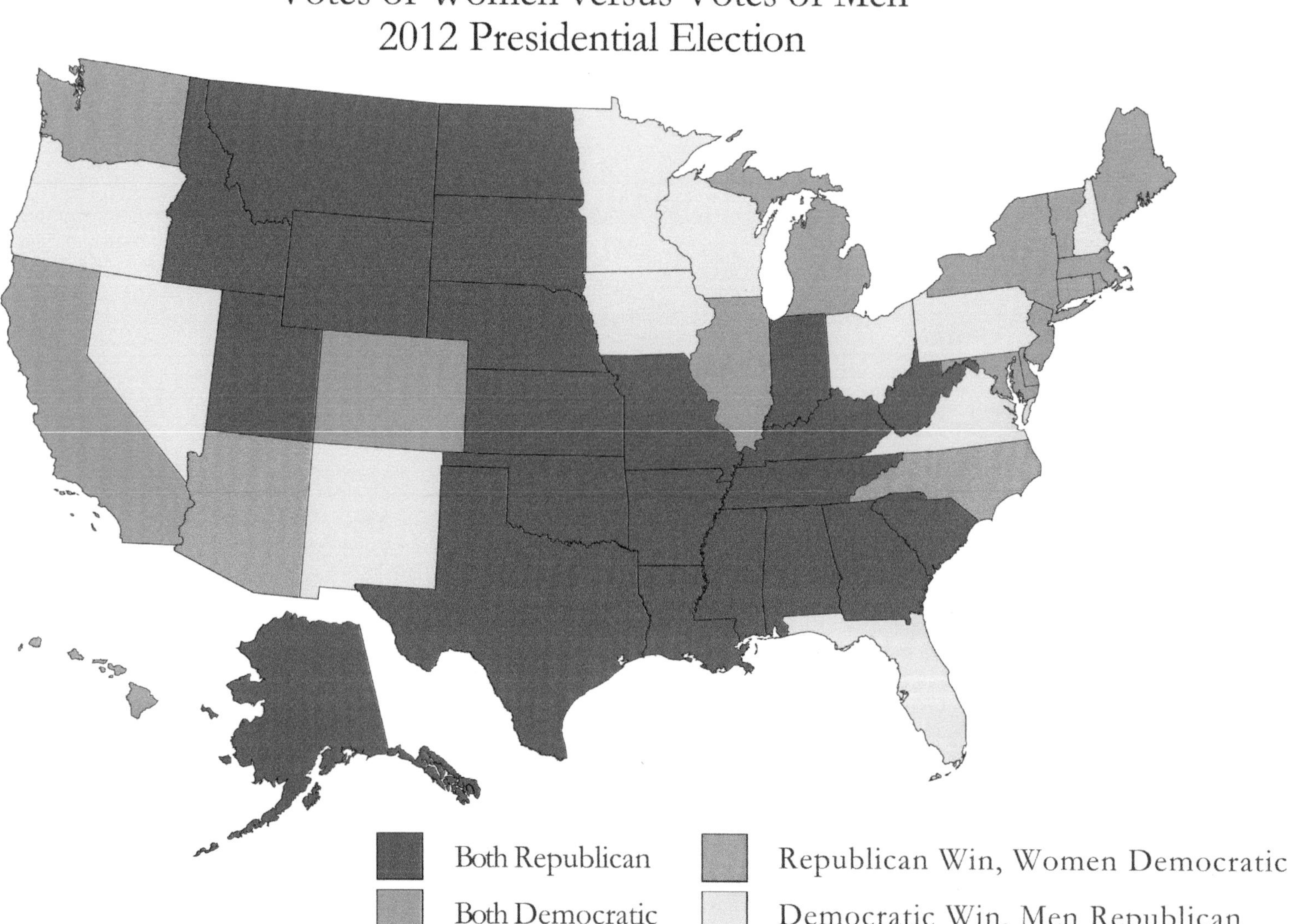
Votes of Women versus Votes of Men
2012 Presidential Election
Both Republican
Republican Win, Women Democratic
Both Democratic
Democratic Win, Men Republican

Even greater differences are evident when looking at race and ethnicity. While white non-Latino Americans gave Obama only a minority of their votes, Obama won large majorities among African Americans, Latinos, and Asian Americans. According to exit polls, Obama won only 41 percent of the white non-Latino vote, but he won 93 percent of the African American vote, 71 percent of the Latino vote, and 73 percent of the Asian American vote. Immigrants and American Indians also gave large majorities to Obama. Nearly all of the counties with large minority percentages in their populations gave Obama majorities of their votes, and in many cases these margins were very large. Because some of these counties themselves have large populations, their votes were critical to the outcome in the Electoral College. Indeed, the majority of the white non-Latino population is in areas Romney carried, compared to great disparities toward minority groups in counties carried by Obama.

In addition, it is consistent that Democratic-gaining counties had the highest share of all minority groups in combination, while counties that switched from Democratic to Republican had the lowest percentages of minority groups in combination. In other words, the gap between white and nonwhite votes increased between 2008 and 2012, implying the increased importance of race in the 2012 elections. Interpretation of exit-poll data suggests that Obama won more than half of the white non-Latino vote in only nine states: the New England states of Maine, Massachusetts, New Hampshire, Rhode Island, and Vermont, along with Hawaii, Iowa, Oregon, and Washington.

Figures 7.26 through 7.31 provide useful comparisons with the overall distribution of votes for the two candidates. They include maps of the foreign-born population (figure 7.26), non-Hispanic whites (figure 7.27), African Americans (figure 7.28), American Indians (figure 7.29), Hispanics (figure 7.30), and Asian Americans (figure 7.31). The essays in this chapter by Ryan Weichelt and Wanjing Chen discuss the Hispanic and Asian American vote, respectively, in more detail.

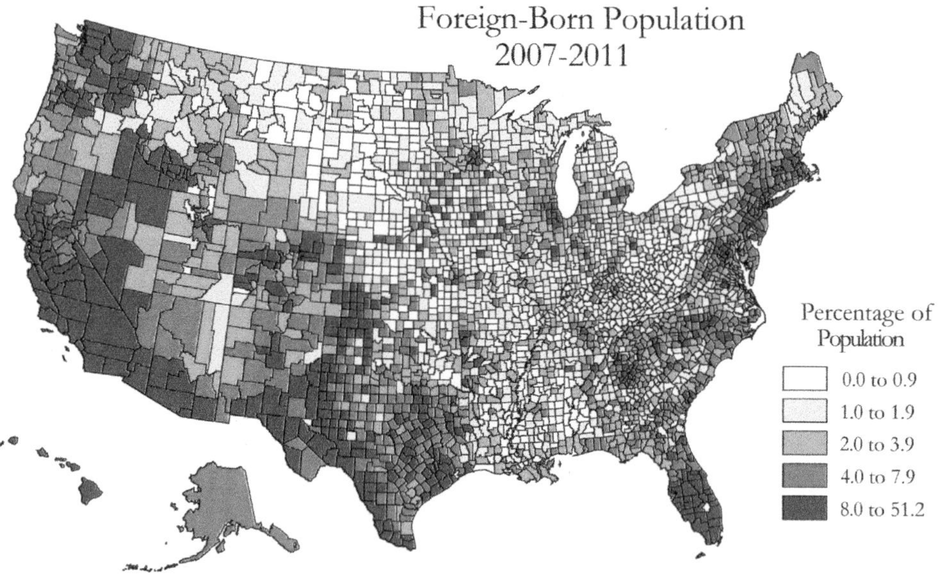
Foreign-Born Population
2007-2011
Percentage of
Population
0.0 to 0.9
1.0 to 1.9
2.0 to 3.9
4.0 to 7.9
8.0 to 51.2

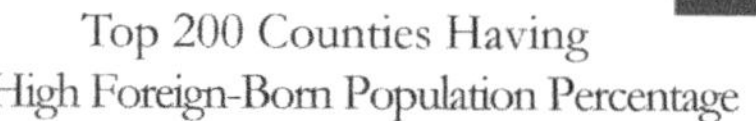
FIGURE 7.26

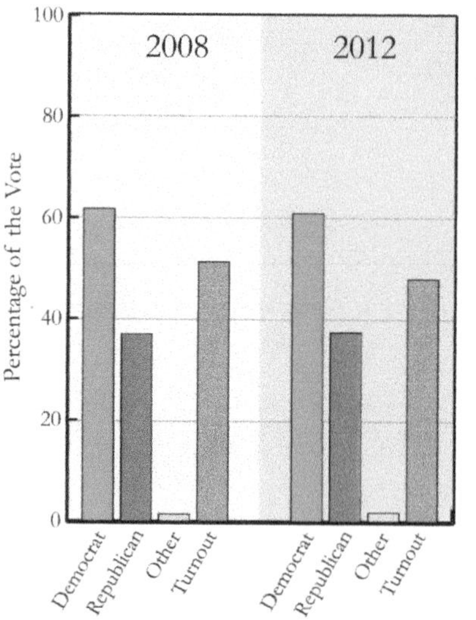
Top 200 Counties Having
High Foreign-Born Population Percentage
2008
2012
Percentage of the Vote
100
80
60
40
20
0
Democrat
Republican
Other
Turnout
Democrat
Republican
Other
Turnout

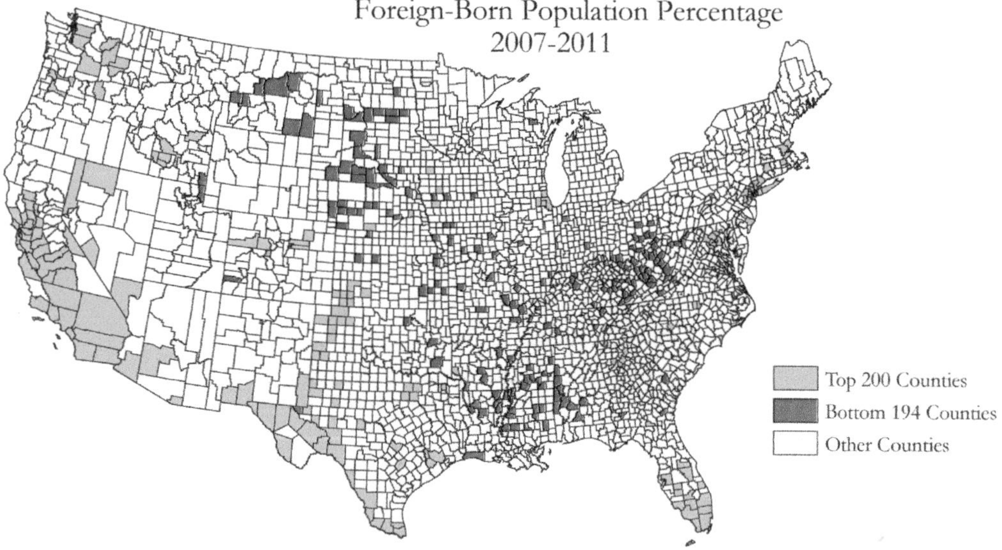
Top 200 and Bottom 194 Counties for
Foreign-Born Population Percentage
2007-2011
Top 200 Counties
Bottom 194 Counties
Other Counties

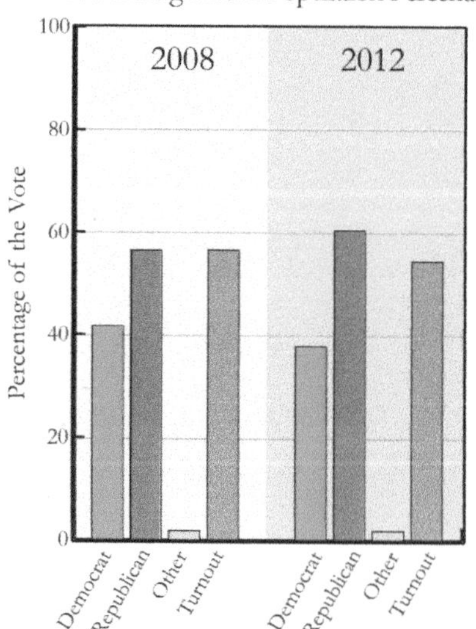
Bottom 194 Counties Having
Low Foreign-Born Population Percentage
2008
2012
Percentage of the Vote
100
80
60
40
20
0
Democrat
Republican
Other
Turnout
Democrat
Republican
Other
Turnout

FIGURE 7.27

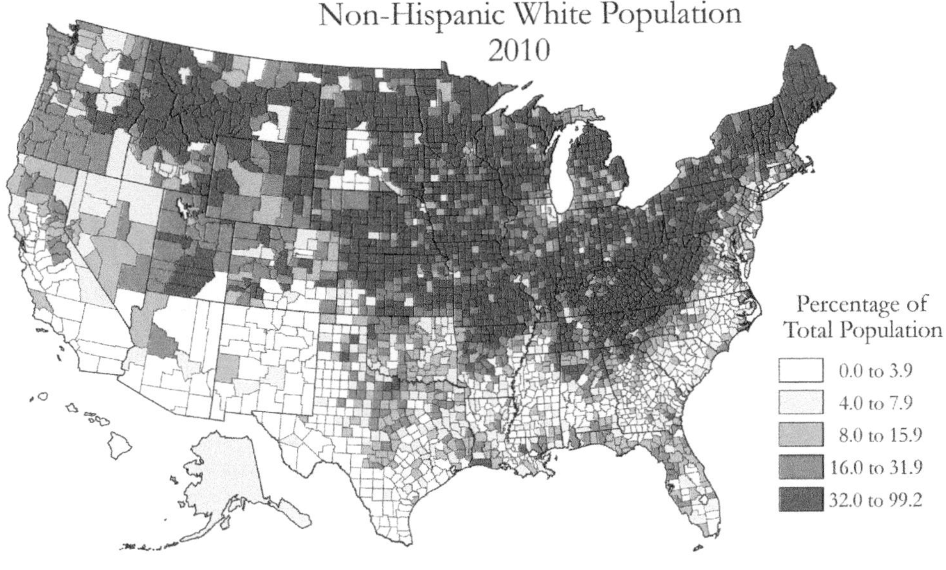
Non-Hispanic White Population
2010
Percentage of
Total Population
0.0 to 3.9
4.0 to 7.9
8.0 to 15.9
16.0 to 31.9
32.0 to 99.2

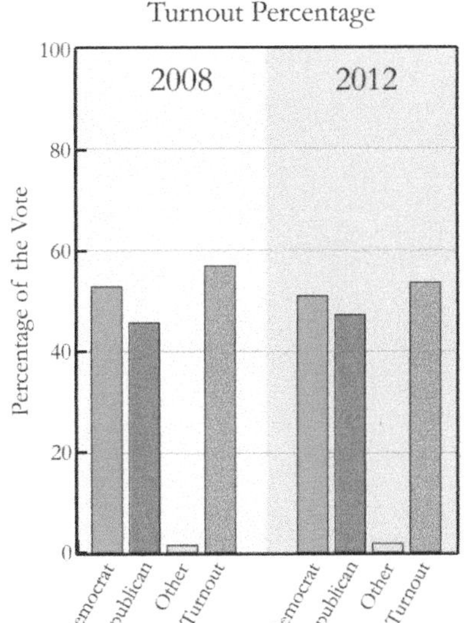
Total U.S. Popular Vote and
Turnout Percentage
2008
2012
Percentage of the Vote
100
80
60
40
20
0
Democrat
Republican
Other
Turnout
Democrat
Republican
Other
Turnout

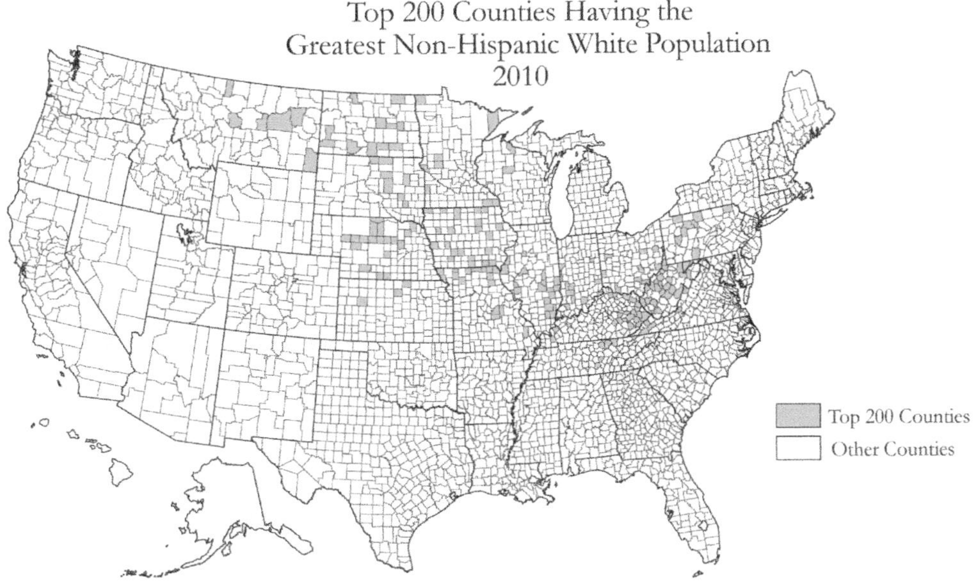
Top 200 Counties Having the
Greatest Non-Hispanic White Population
2010
Top 200 Counties
Other Counties

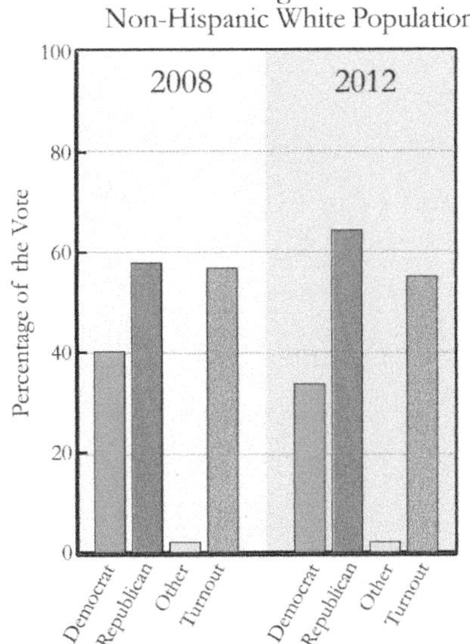
Vote and Turnout in the Top 200
Counties Having the Greatest
Non-Hispanic White Population
2008
2012
Percentage of the Vote
100
80
60
40
20
0
Democrat
Republican
Other
Turnout
Democrat
Republican
Other
Turnout

FIGURE 7.28

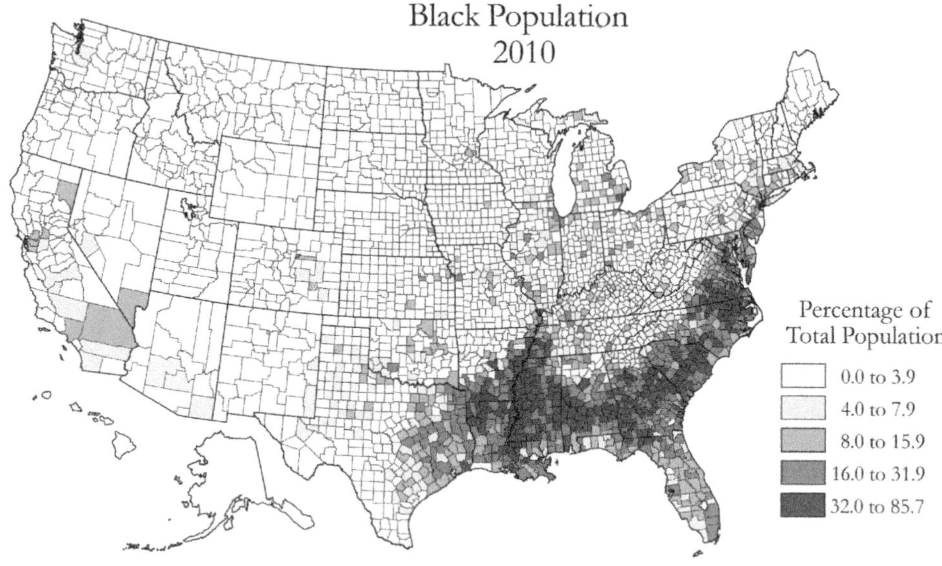

Black Population
2010
Percentage of
Total Population
0.0 to 3.9
4.0 to 7.9
8.0 to 15.9
16.0 to 31.9
32.0 to 85.7

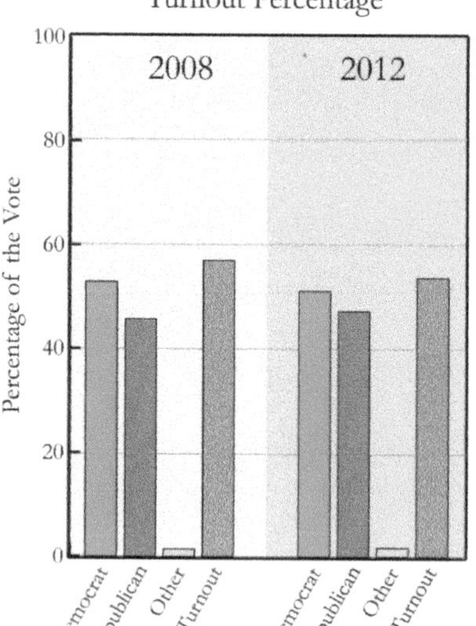

Total U.S. Popular Vote and
Turnout Percentage
2008
2012
Percentage of the Vote
100
80
60
40
20
0
Democrat
Republican
Other
Turnout
Democrat
Republican
Other
Turnout

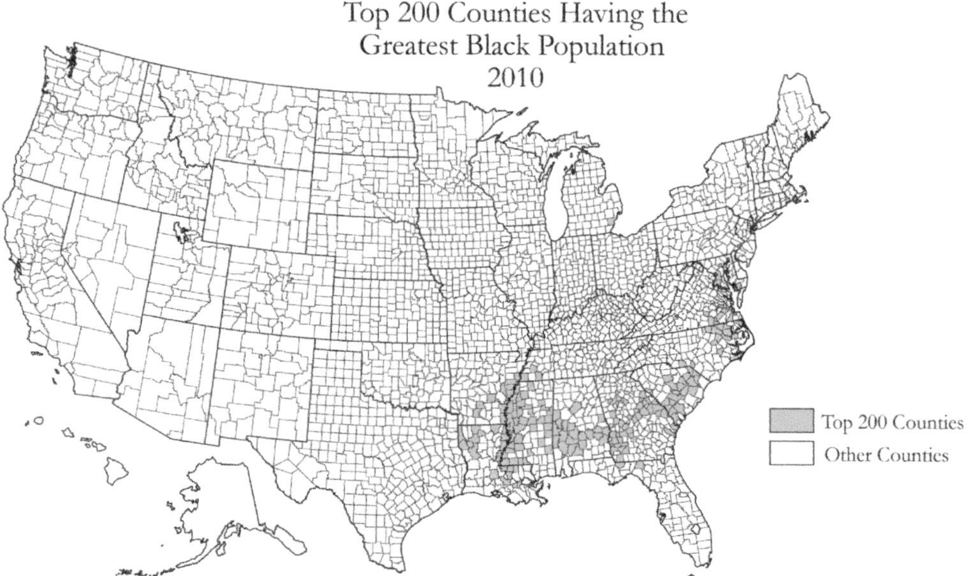

Top 200 Counties Having the
Greatest Black Population
2010
Top 200 Counties
Other Counties

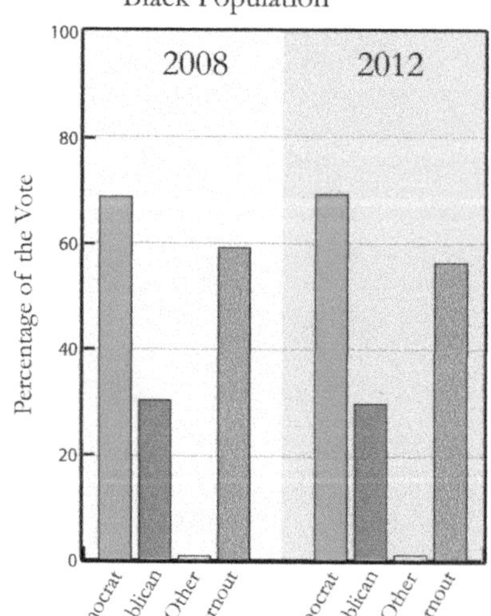

Vote and Turnout in the Top 200
Counties Having the Greatest
Black Population
2008
2012
Percentage of the Vote
100
80
60
40
20
0
Democrat
Republican
Other
Turnout
Democrat
Republican
Other
Turnout

FIGURE 7.29

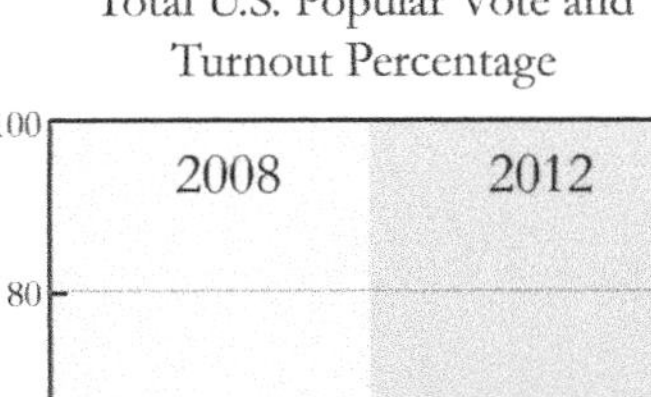

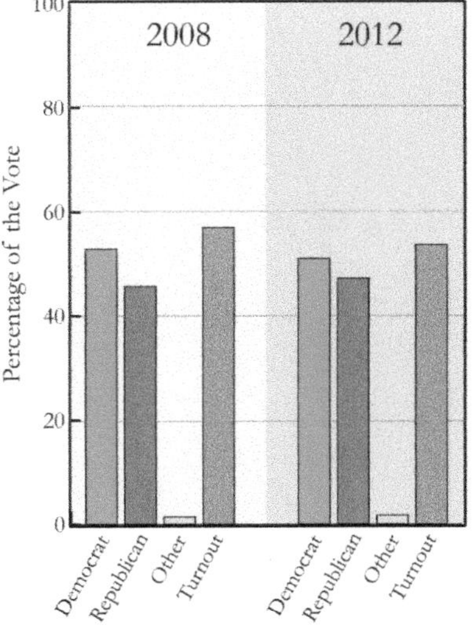

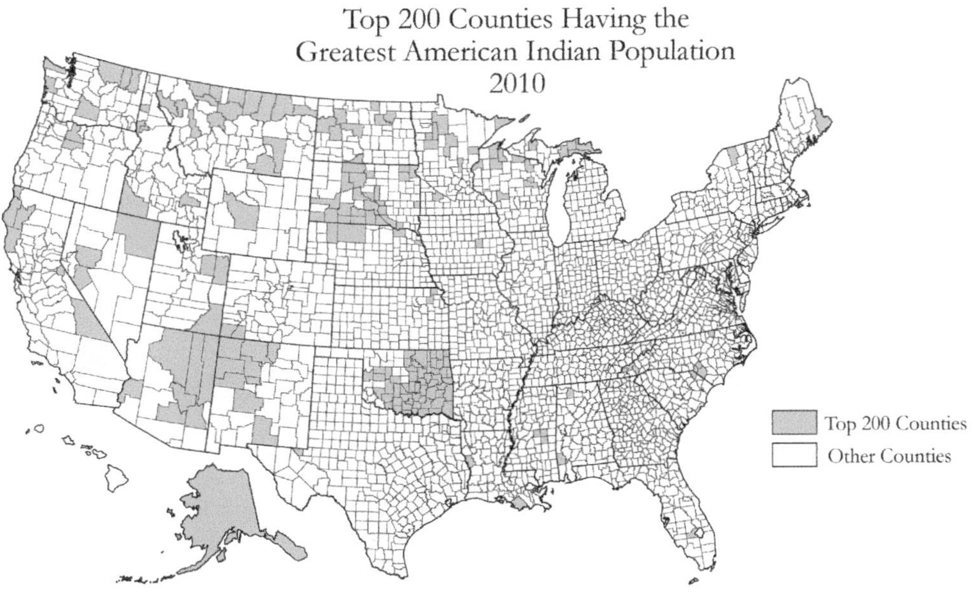

Vote and Turnout in the Top 200
Counties Having the Greatest
American Indian Population

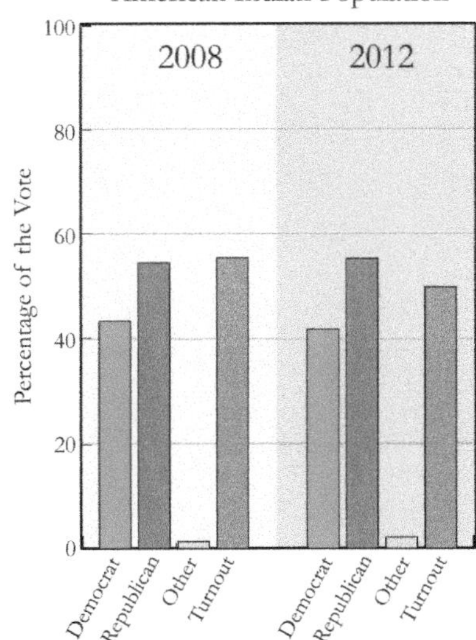

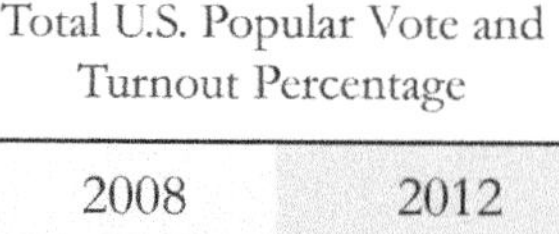
FIGURE 7.30

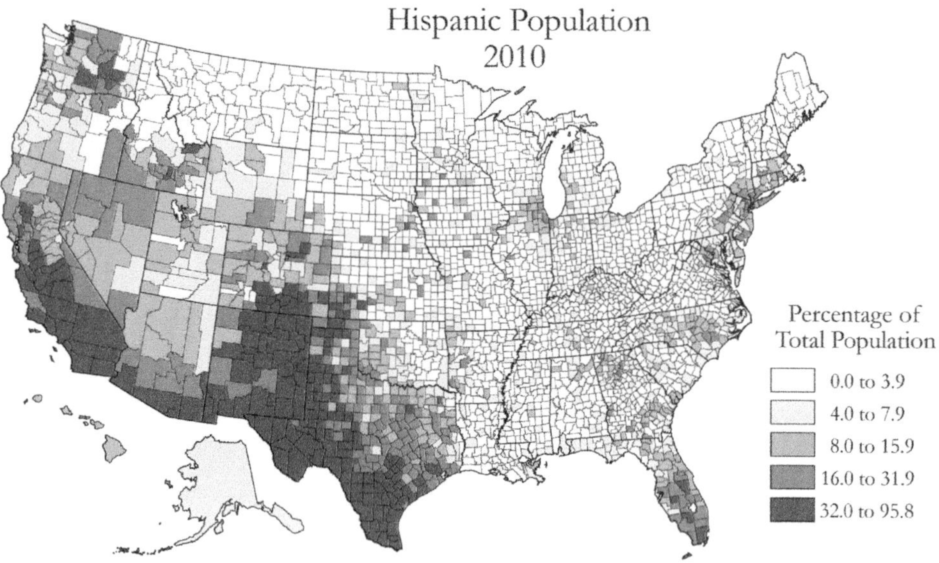
Hispanic Population
2010
Percentage of
Total Population
0.0 to 3.9
4.0 to 7.9
8.0 to 15.9
16.0 to 31.9
32.0 to 95.8

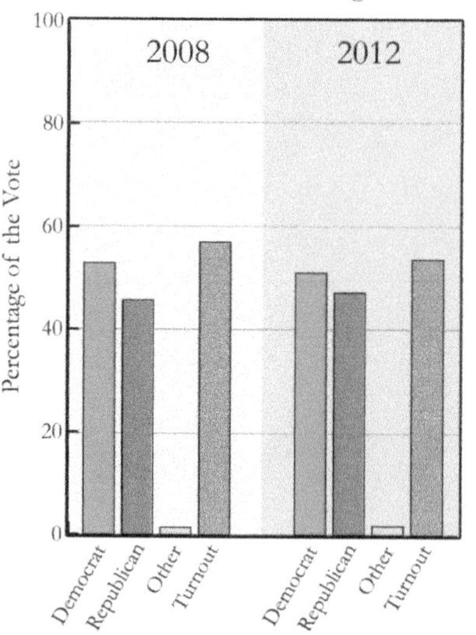
Total U.S. Popular Vote and
Turnout Percentage
2008
2012
Percentage of the Vote
100
80
60
40
20
0
Democrat
Republican
Other
Turnout
Democrat
Republican
Other
Turnout

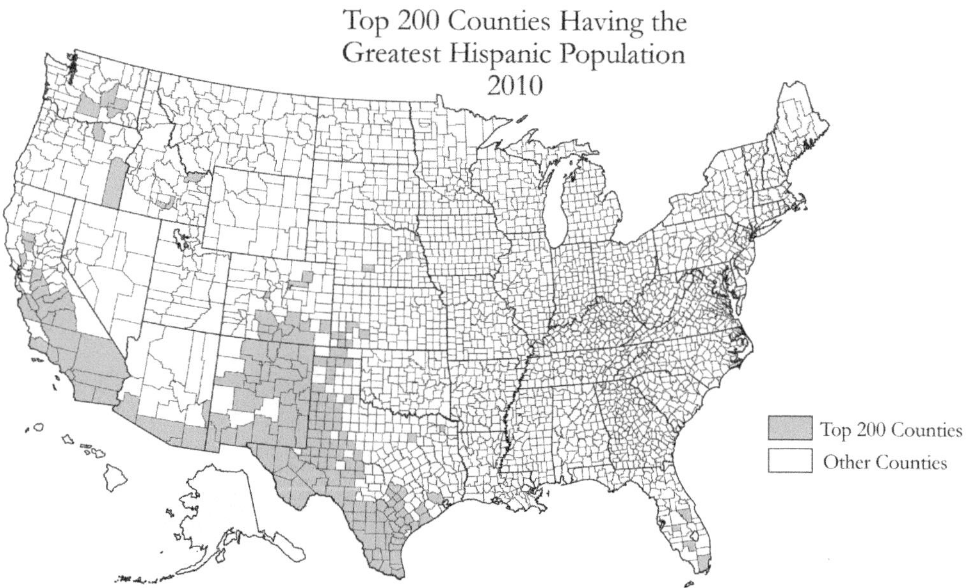
Top 200 Counties Having the
Greatest Hispanic Population
2010
Top 200 Counties
Other Counties

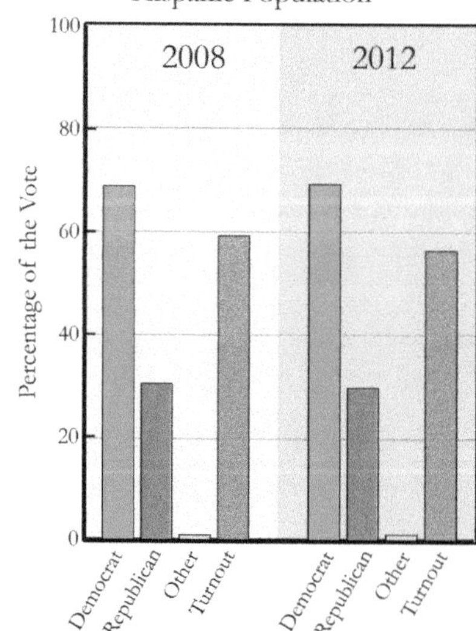
Vote and Turnout in the Top 200
Counties Having the Greatest
Hispanic Population
2008
2012
Percentage of the Vote
100
80
60
40
20
0
Democrat
Republican
Other
Turnout
Democrat
Republican
Other
Turnout

FIGURE 7.31

Asian Population
2010
Percentage of
Total Population
0.0 to 3.9
4.0 to 7.9
8.0 to 15.9
16.0 to 31.9
32.0 to 43.9

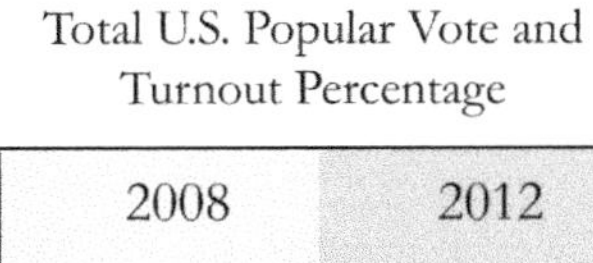
Total U.S. Popular Vote and
Turnout Percentage

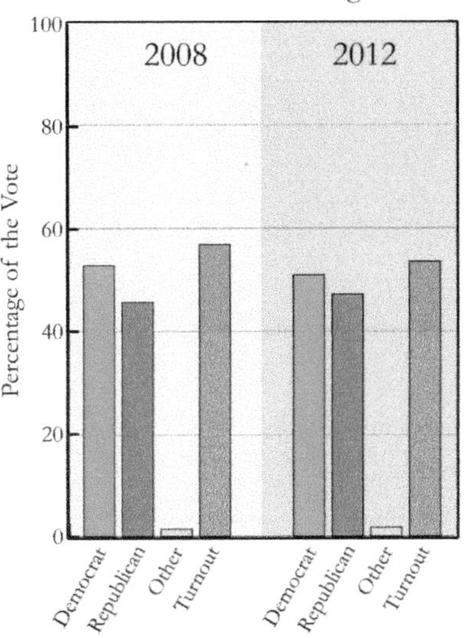
2008
2012
Percentage of the Vote
100
80
60
40
20
0
Democrat
Republican
Other
Turnout
Democrat
Republican
Other
Turnout

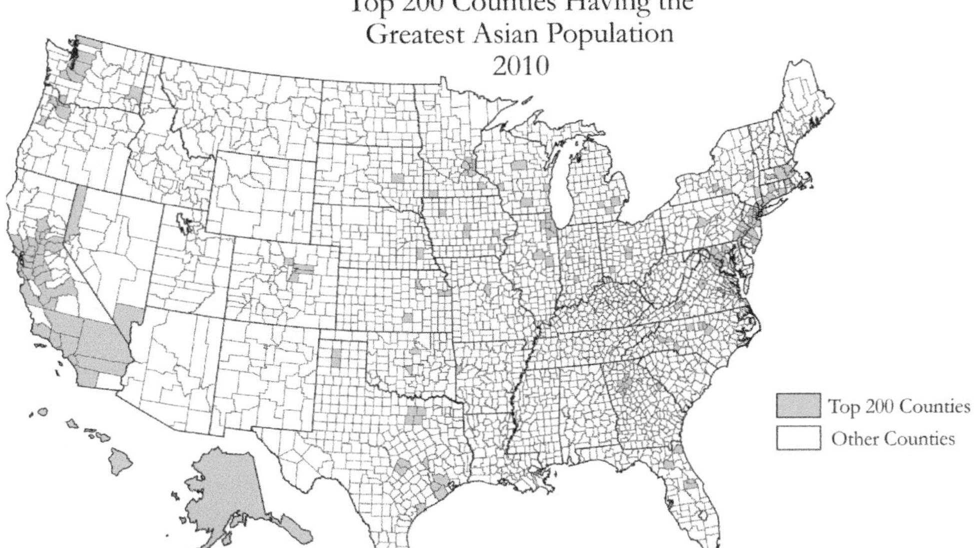
Top 200 Counties Having the
Greatest Asian Population
2010
Top 200 Counties
Other Counties

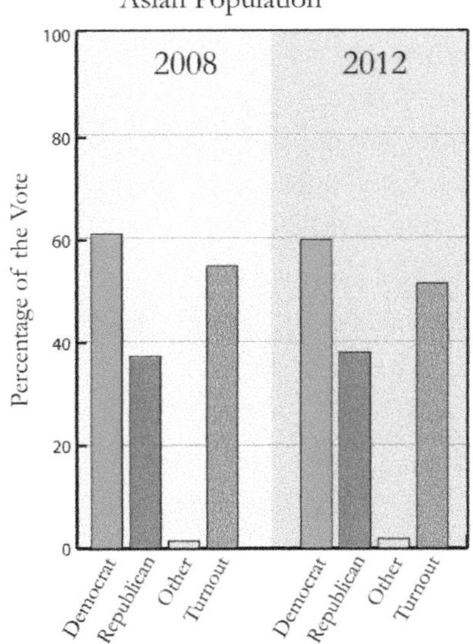
Vote and Turnout in the Top 200
Counties Having the Greatest
Asian Population
2008
2012
Percentage of the Vote
100
80
60
40
20
0
Democrat
Republican
Other
Turnout
Democrat
Republican
Other
Turnout

HISPANIC VOTING IN THE 2012 PRESIDENTIAL ELECTION

RYAN WEICHELT

The study of Hispanic voting behavior has been neglected compared to the study of other minority groups in the United States. Much of the early literature concerning this topic attached uniform expressions of common political beliefs to an otherwise heterogeneous population (DeSipio 1996). Arvizu and Garcia (1996) suggest this problem has arisen due to Hispanics' wide geographic distribution. In effect, this distribution reduces their collective impact on electoral outcomes. This lack of a collective impact has weakened the perception of Hispanics' role in the political system. However, Hispanics are a highly diverse population that is growing very rapidly, and their impact on American elections continues to increase.

The 2010 census revealed that 63 percent of all Hispanics claim Mexican origin. These populations tend to be clustered along the Mexican American border from California to Texas. The second-largest group was Puerto Ricans (9 percent), who are concentrated in New York City and other metropolitan areas of the Northeast. Cuban populations, the third-largest group (3.5 percent), are found in South Florida, mainly in the Miami area. The cultural and geographic differences among these and other ethnic groups of Latin American origin translate into differing political attitudes about major policy questions involving immigration, foreign policy, and social services. Thus, Claassen (2004) suggests that there is no unitary "Hispanic" experience—there are only "Mexican" experiences, "Cuban" experiences, "Puerto Rican" experiences, and so on (2004).

Claassen's argument was bolstered by the results of the Latino National Political–Survey (LNPS). The LNPS was conducted in the 1980s to gauge the political perceptions of Hispanic national origin groups. Hailed as the largest survey of Hispanic political beliefs, those studying the LNPS report concluded that enough differences existed among Mexicans, Puerto Ricans, and Cubans to study them separately (Uhlaner, Cain, and Kiewiet 1989). The report questioned respondents about ideology, party affiliation, and political cooperation among groups, to name a few issues.

Concerning ideology, Mexican respondents were more likely to call themselves liberal, followed by Puerto Ricans and then Cubans. In terms of voting, Mexicans favored Democrats more than Puerto Ricans or Cubans, with the least support for Democrats coming from Cubans. However, a majority of all groups believed the federal government should do more, even if that meant raising taxes (Rodriguez 2002).

Perhaps recognizing the growing numbers and political importance of Hispanic voters, in 2012 the mass media placed greater emphasis on the role of Hispanic voters in the presidential election than had been the case in the past. The political parties themselves also recognized the increased importance of Hispanic voters. Both parties used key Hispanic political figures in their respective conventions to inspire voters. Republicans placed Cuban American senator Marco Rubio of Florida on center stage at their convention, while Democrats highlighted Julian Castro, the mayor of San Antonio, and his twin brother Joaquin Castro, a representative from Texas. The Castro brothers are Mexican Americans. Democrats pushed for improving the economy and immigration reform as main topics intended for Latino ears. Republicans provided similar pleas but were less specific as how to address immigration reform. An analysis of exit polls among Latino voters identified immigration and the economy as key issues. A Pew report stated that 77 percent of Hispanic voters felt undocumented immigrants should be given the chance to apply for legal status, compared with 65 percent among all voters polled (Lopez 2008).

Further analysis of exit polls provides additional evidence of Hispanic leanings. CNN exit polls showed Latino men favored Obama over Romney 65 percent to 33 percent, and this increased among Latino women to 76 percent for Obama and 23 percent for the Republican (CNN 2012). This trend continued for young Hispanic voters aged 18–29, who gave Obama a 74–23 edge. Nationwide, according to exit polls, 71 percent of Hispanics voted for Obama in 2012 as compared to 67 percent in 2008. Obama's support among Hispanics was greatest among low-income voters and those lacking college degrees.

As in 2008, Hispanic votes coupled with African American votes bolstered Obama's victory nationally, but demographic changes at the state level provided vital Hispanic votes in the key swing states of Florida, Nevada, New Mexico, and Colorado. With the exception of New Mexico, the percentage of all voters in these states who are Hispanic increased from 2008 to 2012. The largest increases occurred in Nevada and Florida at 3 percent compared to 2008. In Florida, Hispanic populations increased from 2.6 million in 2000 to more than 4.2 million by 2010. Nearly 13.9 percent of registered voters in Florida identify themselves as Democrats, and it has been estimated that there are about 476,000 registered as Republicans and 645,000 as Democrats (Vogel 2013). The article indicates that Latino Democratic voter registration in Florida increased by 26 percent between 2008 and 2012, as compared to 7 percent for Republicans. Hispanic support probably provided votes needed for Obama to win the state by a narrow margin of 74,309 votes. In Nevada, 18 percent of voters are Hispanic. Although according to exit polls Obama's support among Latinos in Nevada dropped from 76 percent in 2008 to 70 percent in 2012, their votes likely gave Obama the margin that he needed to win the state, which he carried with 52.4 percent of the overall vote.

In Colorado, Hispanic populations increased by 303,086 persons, an increase of 41 percent, from 2000 to 2010 (US Census 2011). Latino support for Obama in Colorado increased from 61 percent in 2008 to 75 percent in 2012. Obama secured a smaller statewide percentage in 2012 than in 2008, but he nevertheless won the state by 137,858 total votes (Lopez and Taylor 2012). As with Florida and Nevada, the increase in Latino populations throughout the state certainly helped Obama secure Colorado.

The patterns witnessed in Florida and Colorado were replicated throughout the United States on November 6. With Obama weakened by a poor first debate and fledgling economy, pundits predicted accurately that Obama's victory would be tighter than in 2008. Though voter turnout was lower in 2012 than in 2008, increases in Hispanic populations nationally provided key voters to help push Obama to an electoral victory. While Latinos generally have been supportive of Democrats in the past, the challenge for both parties is to find a way to appeal to all by not alienating particular groups. As more Latinos gain further education, exit polls indicate that Democratic support begins to drop. Republicans may gain further votes in the Hispanic communities as socioeconomic status increases among successive generations. This is exemplified by Republican senators Ted Cruz and Marco Rubio, who have both gained national attention as "models" for young, upwardly mobile Latinos.

Additionally, the 2012 congressional elections further signify the growing strength of Hispanics in both parties. Thirty-one Latinos were elected November 3 to the US House and Senate (see chapter 8). This record number of elected officials signifies the growth of Hispanics, yet, as the LNPS indicated, subgroups of Latinos adhere to differing ideologies. Immigration reform and other issues will test Latino allegiances in coming elections, but as Hispanic populations continue to grow, both parties will have to adapt their strategies to garner these votes in key battleground areas to take the White House.

REFERENCES

Arvizu, J. R., and F. Chris Garcia. 1996. "Latino Voting Participation: Explaining and Differentiating Latino Voting Turnout." *Hispanic Journal of Behavioral Sciences* 18:104–28.

Claassen, R. L. 2004. "Political Opinion and Distinctiveness: The Case of Hispanic Ethnicity." *Political Research Quarterly* 57 (4): 609–20.

CNN Presidential Election Exit Polls. 2012. http://www.cnn.com/election/2012/results/race/president.

DeSipio, L. 1996. *Counting on the Latino Vote*. Charlottesville: University of Virginia Press.

Lopez, Mark Hugo. 2008. "The Hispanic Vote in the 2008 Election." Pew Hispanic Trust. Accessed March 12, 2010. http://pewhispanic.org/files/reports/98.pdf.

Lopez, Mark Hugo, and Paul Taylor. 2012. "Latino Voters in the 2012 Election, Pew Research Hispanic Trends Project, November 7, http://www.pewhispanic.org/2012/11/07/latino-voters-in-the-2012-election.

Rodriguez, D. 2002. *Latino National Political Coalitions: Struggles and Challenges*. New York: Routledge.

Uhlaner, C. J., B. E. Cain, and D. R. Kiewiet. 1989. "Political Participation of Ethnic Minorities in the 1980s." *Political Behavior* 11 (3): 195–231.

Vogel, Mark. "Florida's Hispanic Population." *Florida Trend*, April 30, 2013, http://www.floridatrend.com/article/15528/floridas-hispanic-population.

ASIAN AMERICAN VOTING

WANJING CHEN

Asian Americans are the third-largest minority group in the United States, after African Americans and Latino Americans. In national polls, they are often overlooked or categorized with other minority groups. However, some ongoing demographic changes in this group may have increased their political influence in elections. The Asian American population grew by 46 percent between 2000 and 2012. US Census Bureau data show that by the end of 2012, Asian Americans made up 6 percent of the total US population and accounted for 3 percent of the votes cast in the presidential election of 2012. Asian Americans voted heavily for Democratic candidates in the 2012 election. For example, they gave 73 percent support to President Obama, which was second only to African Americans among major racial and ethnic groups.

What made Asian Americans favor the Democratic Party so decisively? The question is even more intriguing when we look at the exit poll data over the past two decades. When Bill Clinton ran for president in 1992, he carried only 31 percent of the Asian American vote. Thus, this ethnic group has demonstrated a bigger shift in presidential voting than has any other ethnic group over the past twenty years.

One possible reason underlying this huge shift is that the Democrats' stands in the past several elections on major political issues, including immigration reform, the Iraq war, and health care, fit better with Asian American voters' viewpoints, while the Republicans often took the opposite positions. Meanwhile, the Democratic Party is more supportive of government, promoting a big government getting involved actively in social and economic issues. Its political philosophy is more collectivism oriented compared with that of the Republican Party and also more consistent with Asian American voters' political and cultural backgrounds. Moreover, the Democrats have also been more oriented to ethnic and racial diversity.

Another downside of the Republicans is their emphasis on Christianity and that they are perceived to be opposed to science, for example, by lobbying for creationism in schools, denouncing global warming as a hoax, and restricting stem-cell research. These positions may have cost them considerable support among Asian Americans, who hold the highest level of educational attainment of all American minority groups. Fourteen percent of Asian Americans hold jobs in the fields of science and engineering, significantly higher than the 5 percent of the US general public who work as scientists and engineers. These characteristics suggest that they would not be pleased with the Republicans' positions on religion and science.

In addition, demographic changes within this ethnic group may have contributed to the shift. In the 1990s, streams of refugees from Vietnam, Laos, and Cambodia, whose political attitudes were based heavily on anti-Communism, strongly supported the Republicans. Today, more and more Asian Americans are native born or are immigrants who came to the United States via other means, including employment opportunity or family reunification programs. Yet these factors still cannot fully explain why as much as 73 percent of the Asian vote went to President Obama in the 2012 election.

Fortunately, several detailed surveys of Asian Americans taken before and after the election shed some light on this question. A preelection survey carried out by the National Asian American Survey (NAAS) revealed that Asian American voters favored the Democratic Party's positions on almost all the key issues in this election, including women's rights, health care, education, immigration, jobs, and foreign policy. Only on the budget deficit issue did the Republican candidate Mitt Romney have a slight edge (42 percent vs. 39 percent). Preelection surveys also showed that 59 percent of Asian Americans approved of Obama's job performance, as compared to a 49 percent approval rating among all Americans.

Asian American voters showed strong support for the Affordable Health Care Act ("Obamacare") law. Asian Americans' support for the health-care act is consistent with their emphasis on family. A recent report by the Pew Research Center showed that 54 percent of Asian Americans believe having a successful marriage is one of the most important things in life, 67 percent say that being a good parent is one of the most important things in life, and 28 percent live in a multigenerational household, as compared to 34 percent, 50 percent, and 14 percent, respectively, for the US public overall.

Affordable health care is likely attractive to Asian Americans, who are more likely to take responsibility for taking care of their family members. What does not fit in with Asian voters' family values is that they are less likely than the general public to support increasing expenses on economic assistance for needy people. This is likely a result from their perspective that the US population is not hard working enough, and they are not willing to pay for others' "laziness." Survey data also demonstrated that 93 percent of Asian Americans think people from their countries of origin are very hard working, while only 57 percent agree that Americans as a whole are hard working.

Obama's campaign strategy also worked better than did Romney's campaign strategy. His campaign demonstrated a clear understanding of Asian Americans' attitudes and used social media to present this message effectively. For example, Obama's Asian American Facebook page was managed by the same team that managed other campaign pages on Facebook. The contents of this page were highly related to Asian Americans voters' unique characteristics and political views. Many posts by the campaign emphasized what Asian voters like about Obama, including health care, education, hardworking background, and family values. In contrast, the Republicans did not even have an official team running a Facebook campaign. Romney's campaign page directed at Asian American voters reposted long daily news stories in English from other major media websites, with no content directed specifically at Asian Americans. As approximately 40 percent of Asian Americans do not speak English as their primary language and around 50 percent mainly get news on political and community issues from ethnic media instead of mainstream media, it is highly doubtful that as many Asian American voters got the messages that the Republicans tried to convey.

The Asian Americans' voting trend by age was partly consistent with the general trend. Obama drew a disproportionate share of support among young Asian American adults (86 percent of voters aged eighteen to thirty-four) and sizable leads in all other age categories, including the elderly. Asian American voters over age seventy leaned to Democrats more than middle-aged voters, which is a pattern not found among the overall voters. Though Asian Americans as a whole are well educated and enjoy above-average income, senior citizens in this group do not fit with these characteristics. One in three Asian Americans above age sixty-five live in poverty, without social security. Many of them came to the United States as refugees, and many worked at low-wage jobs before retiring. They have to rely heavily on social security to cover their basic living expenses. Thus, Obama's refusal to cut social security and Medicare may have been attractive to this age group. The gender gap between Democrats and Republicans that prevailed among American voters in general was absent among Asian Americans. Preelection survey data released by the NAAS showed that Asian American men split 42 percent for Obama, 24 percent for Romney, and 33 percent undecided. The split among Asian American women was almost identical, with 43 percent for Obama, 23 percent for Romney, and 34 percent undecided. This survey result is consistent with exit poll data as well.

The absence of a gender gap among Asian American voters could be attributed partly to

Asian Americans' strong family orientation. Asian American voters are thus more likely to have been exposed to the opinions of family members in shaping their own opinions. Perceived interest of the family may take precedence over individual preferences. Limited English skills and reliance on ethnic media as opposed to mainstream media may also indicate that family members play a very important role in determining the voting preferences of individual Asian Americans.

The public opinion surveys referenced above include data for Asian Americans as a whole. However, Asian Americans come from more than a dozen countries. Each Asian American population has a unique history and culture. According to 2010 census data, the largest number of Asian Americans trace their roots to China, the Philippines, the Indian subcontinent, Vietnam, Korea, and Japan. Of these, Vietnamese Americans stand out as the only Asian American subgroup that leaned toward Romney, providing him with 54 percent of their vote. This may reflect the history that several hundred thousand refugees from South Vietnam moved to the United States in the 1970s, and many of these refugees supported the strong anti-Communist positions of the Republican Party. However, as the percentage of second-generation immigrants increases through time, the influence of anti-Communist policy may be declining. All of the other Asian American subgroups gave strong support to the Democrats, especially descendants of migrants from the Indian Peninsula, including India, Pakistan, and Bangladesh. Exit poll data indicate that over 85 percent of Indian Americans voted for Obama.

How did the Asian American vote vary geographically? And how much influence did Asian American voters have on election outcomes? Recent demographic changes in this ethnic group, increasing numbers, and their active civic participation have increased their influence considerably. Though California, New York, Texas, New Jersey, and Hawaii are still the states with the largest Asian American populations, as shown in Figure 7.31, some other states, including several important swing states like Nevada, Florida, Virginia, North Carolina, and New Hampshire, are experiencing substantial growth in their Asian American populations. For example, Nevada's Asian American population doubled between 2000 and 2010.

Exit poll data from CNN and the Asian American Legal Defense and Education Fund (AALDEF) break down Asian American voting by state in mainland states with significant numbers of Asian Americans (table 7.5). Of these twelve states, Louisiana is the only one in which the majority of the Asian American vote went to Romney. This seeming anomaly could be explained by the fact that many Asian Americans in Louisiana are Vietnamese Americans, who are mostly Republican and who dominate the fishing and shrimping industry in southern Louisiana. Table 7.5 also illustrates that Asian Americans tended to shift their votes toward Obama in 2012 relative to 2008, whereas voters nationwide shifted away from Obama. This shift was especially pronounced in California, which contains the largest number of Asian Americans in the United States. In all the surveyed states except Texas and Michigan, in 2012 Asian votes shifted toward the Democrats relative to 2008.

Using data on Asian Americans' share of the vote from the 2008 presidential election, we can estimate their actual influence on the result in the 2012 election. In Nevada, for example, if Asian Americans had not cast ballots, President Obama would have carried the state by only a 4 percent margin, significantly less than the actual 6 percent margin. The same was true in Virginia, where Obama would have carried the state by a tiny 2 percent margin instead of by 4 percent. As the Asian American population increases, especially in purple states, both parties should take a closer look at the Asian American vote in the years ahead. The good news for both parties is that nearly half of Asian American registered voters remain independent or undecided with respect to their party identification, suggesting that many are still open to persuasion and outreach in future elections.

TABLE 7.5. Asian American Vote by State in Presidential Elections of 2008 and 2012 in Selected States

State	Democratic Vote Percentage			
	Asian Americans, 2012 (%)	Asian Americans, 2008 (%)	All Voters, 2012 (%)	All Voters, 2008 (%)
California	79	64	60	61
Georgia	61	n/a	46	47
Louisiana	16	12	40	40
Maryland	71	71	62	62
Massachusetts	82	81	61	62
Michigan	86	88	54	57
Nevada	81	57	52	55
New Jersey	77	77	58	57
New York	86	78	62	63
Pennsylvania	89	79	52	55
Texas	57	61	41	44
Virginia	72	66	51	53

Sources: Exit polls from CNN and Asian American Legal Defense and Education Fund.

THE BIBLE BELT AND THE 2012 ELECTIONS

DANIEL A. McGOWIN AND GERALD R. WEBSTER

The term "Bible Belt" was coined by journalist H. L. Mencken following his coverage of the Scopes "monkey trial" in Dayton, Tennessee, in 1925 (Heatwole 1978). Though ill defined geographically by Mencken, the term has been used regularly ever since to refer to a religiously conservative region in the southeastern quarter of the United States. Despite the label's repeated use and attempts to tie it to other similar "belts" (e.g., "Beauty Pageant Belt" or "Divorce Belt"), the Bible Belt's location has been defined in contrasting fashions by different authors (Brunn, Webster, and Archer 2011).

We utilize the methodology employed by Brunn, Webster, and Archer (2011), who incorporated and updated a geographic definition of the Bible Belt by Charles Heatwole first published in the *Journal of Geography* in 1978. Heatwole delineated the geographic extent of the Bible Belt based on the distribution of twenty-four Protestant denominations that believe in the literal interpretation of the Bible. Here we use 2010 data from the Glenmary Research Center to examine the top two hundred counties in terms of their proportion of adherents (with a threshold of 43.3 percent) belonging to such denominations. In total, there were 29 million members of Bible Belt denominations in 2010, with nearly 20 million being members of the Southern Baptist Convention. The other large denominations included the Lutheran Church-Missouri Synod (2.2 million), Christian Churches and Churches of Christ (1.4 million), Seventh-day Adventists (1.2 million), and Church of God (Cleveland, TN) (1.1 million). While counties with high proportions of members of Bible Belt denominations are located from western North Carolina south to northern Florida and west to the Texas panhandle, the Bible Belt's core would today appear centered on the Oklahoma-Texas borderlands (Webster et al. forthcoming).

How do residents of the Bible Belt vote? The past few decades have witnessed the Republican Party highlighting its positions on so-called cultural issues, including abortion, same-sex marriage, school prayer, and immigration, among others, to attract religious conservatives. The Republican Party's positions on these issues tend to resonate well with voters in the Bible Belt. Therefore, it should come as no surprise that during the 2012 election, the two hundred counties with the highest proportion of members of Bible Belt denominations displayed overwhelming support for Republican Party presidential nominee Mitt Romney. At the national level, incumbent Democrat Barack Obama received 51.1 percent of the vote. However, Romney received 69.23 percent of votes in the top two hundred Bible Belt counties while Obama garnered only 29.4 percent in these counties (figure 7.32).

An examination of individual counties reveals a pattern that reflects the findings of the Brunn, Webster, and Archer 2011 article on the Bible Belt. According to their research, the core or "buckle" of the Bible Belt is now located in southwestern Oklahoma and North Central Texas. Of the ten Bible Belt counties with the highest percentage of 2012 votes for Mr. Romney (above 87 percent in each), nine are located in this "buckle." Four of these counties—Motley, Shackelford, and Borden in Texas, and Cimarron in Oklahoma—saw Mr. Obama receive less than 10 percent of the vote, with Borden County providing the Democratic candidate with only 8.82 percent of the county's votes. In total, there were thirty-one counties where the Republican candidate

FIGURE 7.32

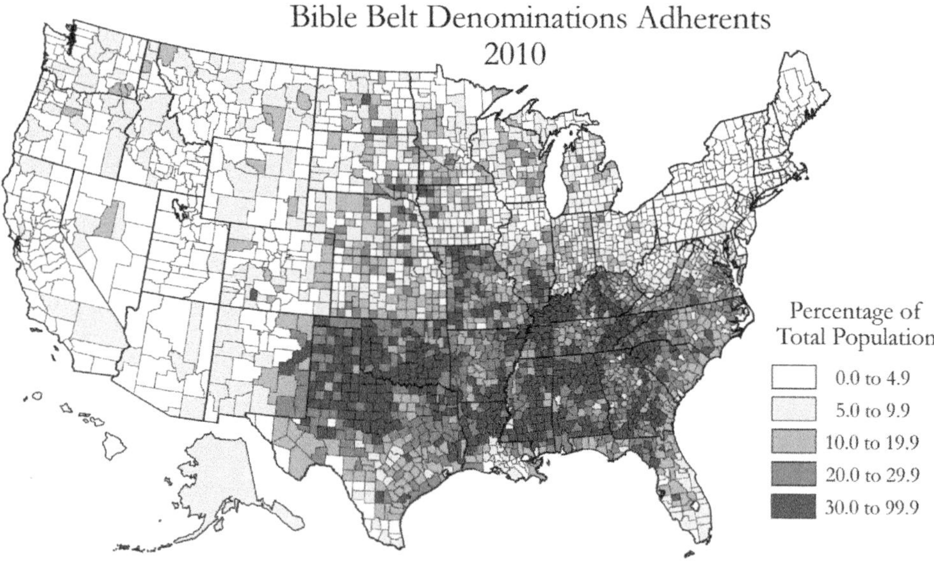

Total U.S. Popular Vote and
Turnout Percentage

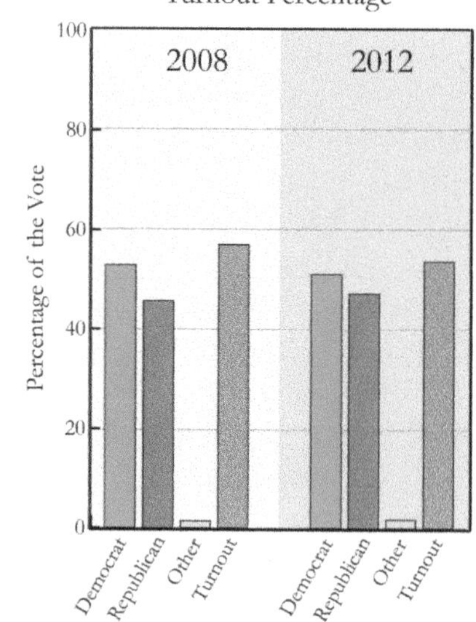

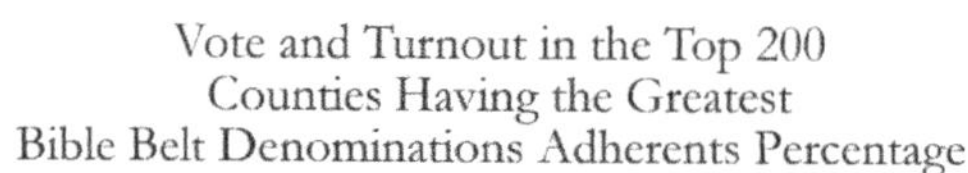

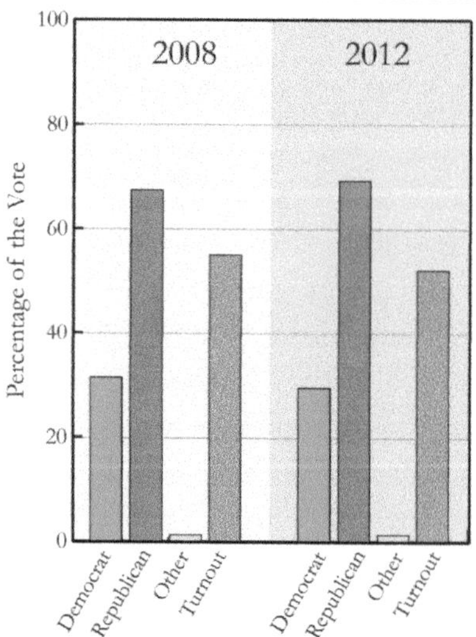

received at least 80 percent of the vote, and more than half of all Bible Belt counties (109) supported Mr. Romney with over 70 percent of the vote. However, not every Bible Belt county overwhelmingly supported the 2012 Republican Party nominee, and there were five wins by President Obama. Fredericksburg, Virginia, for example, provided Mr. Obama with 62.35 percent of its votes. These Democratic-leaning Bible Belt counties tend to be exceptions to the general profile of Bible Belt counties, particularly in terms of their ethnic composition.

Bible Belt counties display several demographic tendencies. For example, the top two hundred Bible Belt counties have an average population of just over twenty-five thousand people compared with approximately one hundred thousand residents for the average county in the United States. Bible Belt counties also tend to be less densely populated versus the rest of the United States—forty people per square mile versus the national average of eighty per square mile. In terms of voting, counties with a higher percentage of votes for the Republican Party's nominee tend to have small populations. Indeed, eight of the ten Bible Belt counties with the highest percentage of 2012 votes for Mr. Romney have populations of less than 10,000 people each. The populations of Bible Belt counties also tend to include fewer minority groups. Sixty-six percent of the US population is non-Hispanic white, but non-Hispanic whites constitute over 80 percent of the population in Bible Belt counties. Finally, education levels lag in the top two hundred Bible Belt counties, with less than 15 percent of the adult population having a college degree, compared with more than 25 percent nationally. Thus, these religiously conservative counties tend to be sparsely populated, largely composed of white residents with lesser levels of educational attainment, and they strongly support the Republican Party in presidential elections.

REFERENCES

Brunn, S. D., G. R. Webster, and J. C. Archer. 2011. "The Bible Belt in a Changing South: Shrinking, Relocating, and Multiple Buckles." *Southeastern Geographer* 51 (4): 513–49.

Heatwole, C. 1978. "The Bible Belt: A Problem in Regional Definition." *Journal of Geography* 77:50–55.

Webster, G. R., R. Watrel, J. C. Archer, and S. D. Brunn. Forthcoming. "Bible Belt Membership Patterns, Correlates and Landscapes." In *The Changing World Religious Map: Sacred Places, Identities, Practices and Politics*, edited by Stanley D. Brunn. New York: Springer.

RELIGION AND THE 2012 PRESIDENTIAL ELECTION

FRED M. SHELLEY

Voter preferences in the 2012 election were related significantly to their religious views. As a general rule, people who claim to be religious are more likely to have voted for Republican candidates, including Mitt Romney, in recent elections. According to 2012 exit polls, 39 percent of voters who attend religious services at least once a week voted for Barack Obama, whereas 59 percent voted for Romney. However, Obama won majorities among voters who said that they do not attend religious services regularly. He won 55 percent among those who attend services "occasionally" and 62 percent among those who never attend services.

Support for Obama also varied by denomination. Roman Catholics gave Obama a 50 percent–48 percent majority, roughly equivalent to his national margin of victory. However, Protestants gave Obama only 42 percent of their votes. White born-again Christians were much less likely to support Obama, with only 21 percent. On the other hand, non-Christians gave Obama 74 percent of their votes, and those with no religious affiliation gave him 70 percent of their votes.

Choice of denomination and frequency of religious service attendance together was also related to the likelihood that voters would support Obama and Romney. Among Roman Catholics, 42 percent of those attending Mass regularly voted for Obama, as opposed to 56 percent among those who do not. Twenty-nine percent of Protestants who attend church regularly supported Obama, as opposed to 44 percent who attend church less than once a week. However, this trend is strongest among whites. Eighty percent of nonwhites who attend religious services regularly supported Obama, only slightly less than the percentage given to Obama by the overall nonwhite population.

The relationships between religious identification and electoral outcomes vary, however, both geographically and by denomination. This is illustrated by comparison of Roman Catholics, mainline and evangelical Protestants, Mormons, and non-Christians. Each of the figures in this section includes two maps: the percentage of people belonging to the denomination in question, and the two hundred counties with the highest percentages belonging to that denomination.

Nationwide, the distribution of Roman Catholics (figure 7.33) parallels the immigration history of the United States. Numerous Roman Catholics live in and near northeastern cities, particularly the New York, Philadelphia, and Boston metropolitan areas. Many of these Roman Catholics are descended from Irish, Italian, Polish, and other Roman Catholic immigrants. In recent years, these large Roman Catholic populations have been augmented by an influx of Latino Catholics, including Puerto Ricans and Mexican Americans. Cook County, Illinois (Chicago), is also among the two hundred counties with the highest Roman Catholic percentages. All of these places were heavily Democratic in 2012.

Elsewhere, high Roman Catholic percentages are associated with other migration streams. In South Texas and in California, many Roman Catholics are Mexican Americans. Many Roman Catholics in northern New Mexico and southern Colorado identify themselves as Spanish Americans in that their ancestors moved to the present-day United States before Mexico became independent from Spain in 1821. Nearly all of the heavily Hispanic places in these areas supported Obama in 2012. On the other hand, most Roman Catholics in South Louisiana are Cajuns of French Canadian ancestry. These voters in the Cajun-dominated parishes supported Romney very heavily. For example, Lafayette Parish contains the city of Lafayette and is often considered the center of

FIGURE 7.33

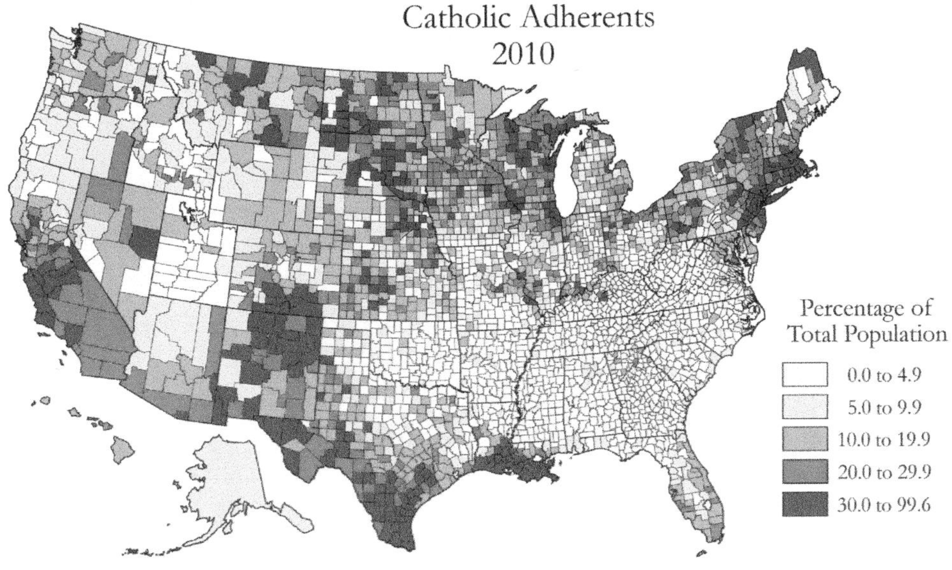

Catholic Adherents
2010
Percentage of
Total Population
0.0 to 4.9
5.0 to 9.9
10.0 to 19.9
20.0 to 29.9
30.0 to 99.6

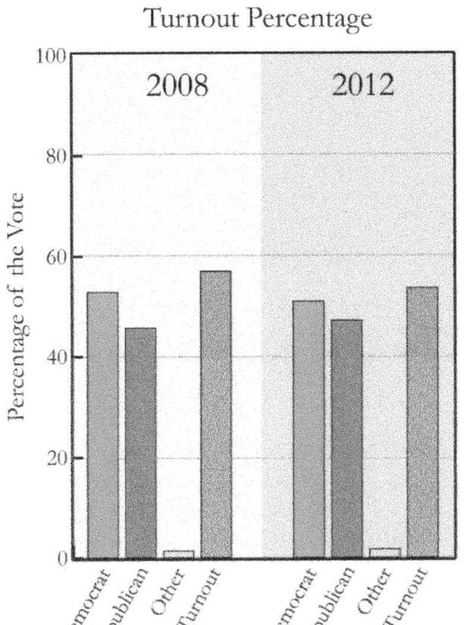

Total U.S. Popular Vote and
Turnout Percentage
2008
2012
Percentage of the Vote
0
20
40
60
80
100
Democrat
Republican
Other
Turnout
Democrat
Republican
Other
Turnout

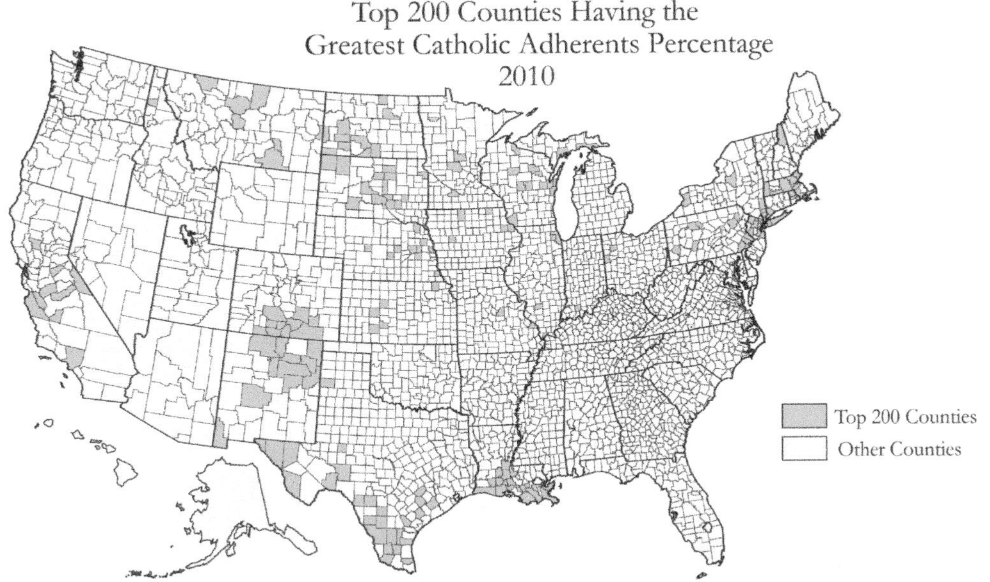

Top 200 Counties Having the
Greatest Catholic Adherents Percentage
2010
Top 200 Counties
Other Counties

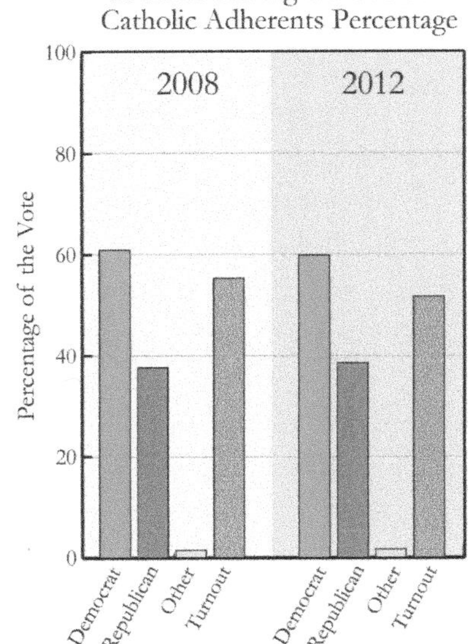

Vote and Turnout in the Top 200
Counties Having the Greatest
Catholic Adherents Percentage
2008
2012
Percentage of the Vote
0
20
40
60
80
100
Democrat
Republican
Other
Turnout
Democrat
Republican
Other
Turnout

Cajun culture. Romney won Lafayette Parish by a 66–32 margin. More generally, differences between Roman Catholics and the general population appeared to decrease outside strongly pro-Obama areas, including suburbs, and in purple and red states.

Mainline Protestants generally fall between Roman Catholics and evangelical Protestants in levels of Democratic support. Methodists are most common in the Great Plains, the Midwest, Appalachia, and the South Atlantic region (figure 7.34). Relative to Roman Catholics, relatively few Methodists are descended from immigrants of European or Latin American origin. Romney carried most places with large Methodist percentages throughout the country. The exception is Iowa and neighboring areas of the Corn Belt. Iowa, along with neighboring Wisconsin and Minnesota, is the only area in the United States in which rural white Protestants are as likely to be Democrats as Republicans.

Lutherans are much more concentrated geographically in the Upper Midwest (figure 7.35). Many American Lutherans are descended from Scandinavian or German immigrants. Historically, Scandinavian Americans are more likely to be Democrats as opposed to German Americans. Nevertheless, those counties with the largest Lutheran percentages generally gave majorities to Romney, notably in the Dakotas, Nebraska, and western Minnesota.

Romney did even better among evangelical Protestants including Baptists, Pentecostals, and nondenominational Christians. Evangelicals are most heavily concentrated in the South and Southwest from West Texas eastward to Kentucky, Tennessee, and the Carolinas (figure 7.36). Baptists are especially dominant in smaller towns and rural areas because these areas have not experienced in-migration from the North in contrast to larger metropolitan areas such as Dallas-Fort Worth, Memphis, Atlanta, and Charlotte. Given Republican dominance of the South, especially in rural areas, it is not surprising that Romney carried nearly all of the most heavily Baptist areas of the country.

The same applies to Pentecostals (figure 7.37). The largest populations of Pentecostals in the United States are found in heavily Republican Oklahoma and Arkansas, along with central Appalachia. All of these places are heavily Republican. Most of these places have predominantly white populations, although Pentecostals in the South are seen as more welcoming to minorities relative to non-Pentecostal evangelical denominations.

Nondenominational Christians are more spread out around the United States and are less concentrated in the South (figure 7.38). Most nondenominational Christian churches are evangelical in orientation and theology, and they tend to espouse beliefs similar to those of organized denominations such as the Baptists. In contrast to Baptists and Pentecostals, however, many nondenominational churches are located in metropolitan areas and particularly in suburbs. This is evident from the fact that suburbs of Atlanta, Dallas-Fort Worth, and Indianapolis have large nondenominational percentages. As with other evangelicals, most of these counties gave majorities to Romney. However, Romney's margins of victory tended to be lower in these counties than they were in counties dominated by other evangelical Christians. This is probably due to the fact that members of nondenominational churches are more likely than other conservative Christians to be well educated, residents of suburbs, relatively young, and nonwhite relative to traditional evangelical denominations.

The Church of Jesus Christ of Latter-day Saints, or the Mormon Church, is the United States' most heavily concentrated denomination geographically (figure 7.39). The large majority of Mormons live in the Interior West, especially in Utah, where the church is headquartered. Utah was Romney's strongest state, and Romney also did very well in neighboring Idaho and Wyoming. Romney's strong support among Mormons is not surprising given that the Mormons hold conservative beliefs on social issues and the fact that Romney himself is a Latter-day Saint and was the first Mormon in history to be nominated for the presidency by a major political party.

FIGURE 7.34

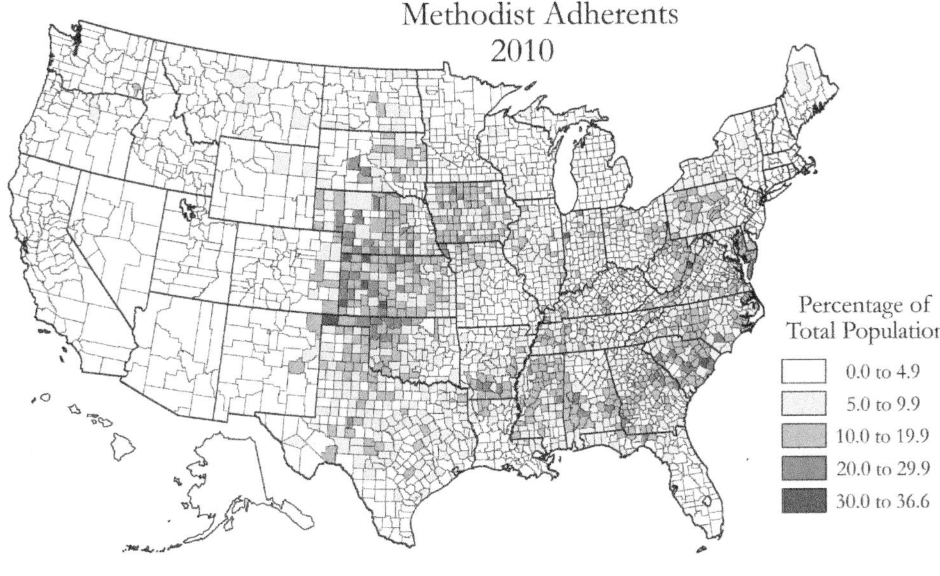

Methodist Adherents
2010
Percentage of
Total Population
0.0 to 4.9
5.0 to 9.9
10.0 to 19.9
20.0 to 29.9
30.0 to 36.6

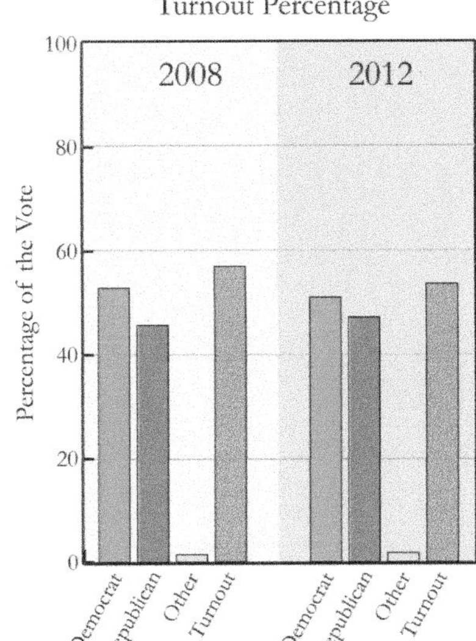

Total U.S. Popular Vote and
Turnout Percentage
2008
2012
Percentage of the Vote
0
20
40
60
80
100
Democrat
Republican
Other
Turnout
Democrat
Republican
Other
Turnout

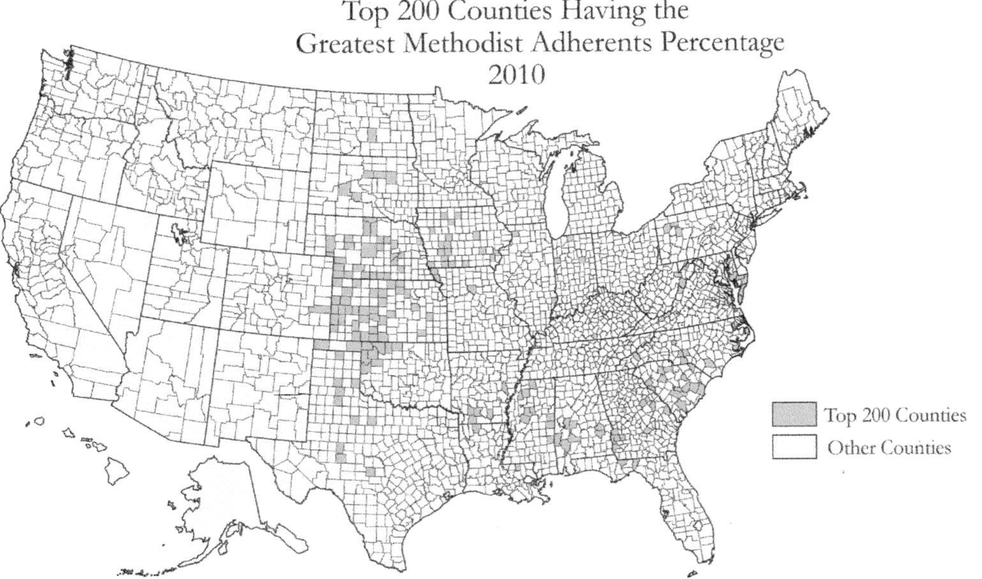

Top 200 Counties Having the
Greatest Methodist Adherents Percentage
2010
Top 200 Counties
Other Counties

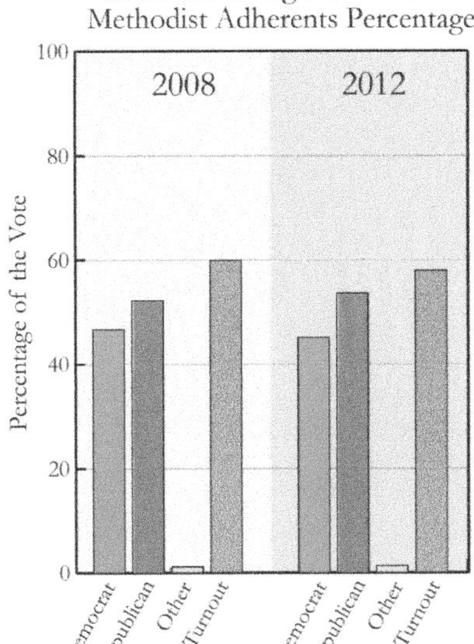

Vote and Turnout in the Top 200
Counties Having the Greatest
Methodist Adherents Percentage
2008
2012
Percentage of the Vote
0
20
40
60
80
100
Democrat
Republican
Other
Turnout
Democrat
Republican
Other
Turnout

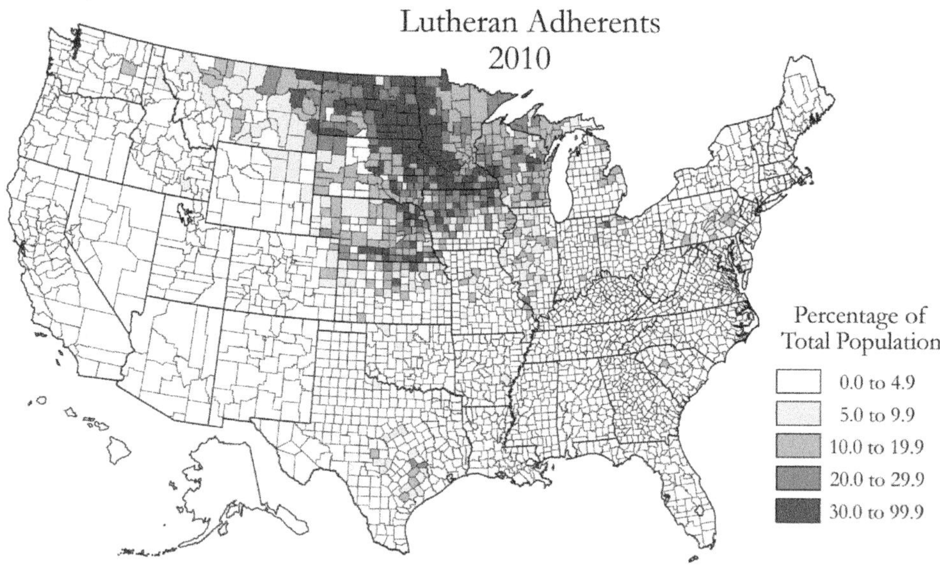
Lutheran Adherents
2010
Percentage of
Total Population
0.0 to 4.9
5.0 to 9.9
10.0 to 19.9
20.0 to 29.9
30.0 to 99.9

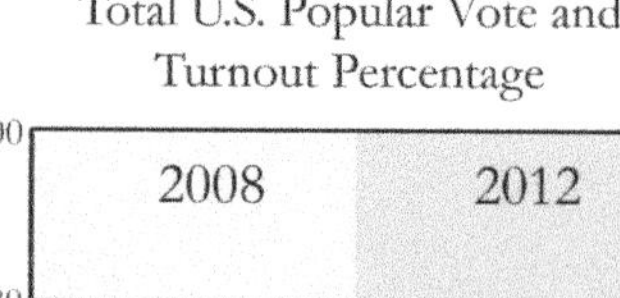
FIGURE 7.35

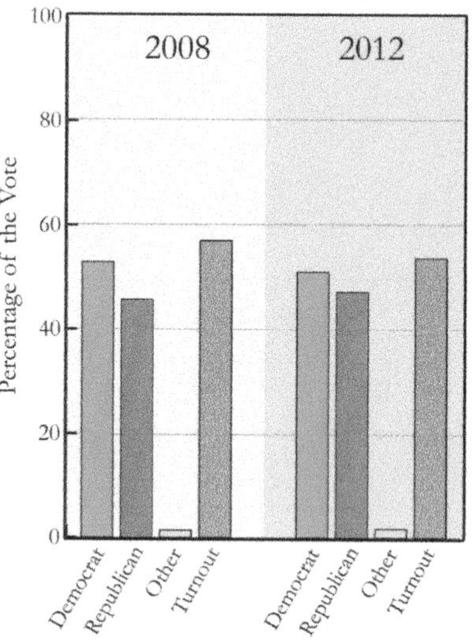
Total U.S. Popular Vote and
Turnout Percentage
2008
2012
Percentage of the Vote
0
20
40
60
80
100
Democrat
Republican
Other
Turnout
Democrat
Republican
Other
Turnout

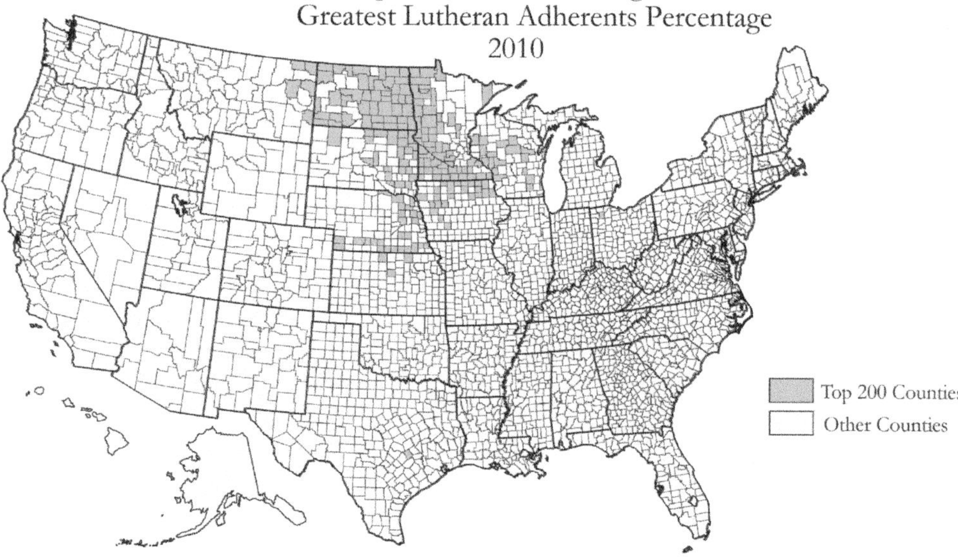
Top 200 Counties Having the
Greatest Lutheran Adherents Percentage
2010
Top 200 Counties
Other Counties

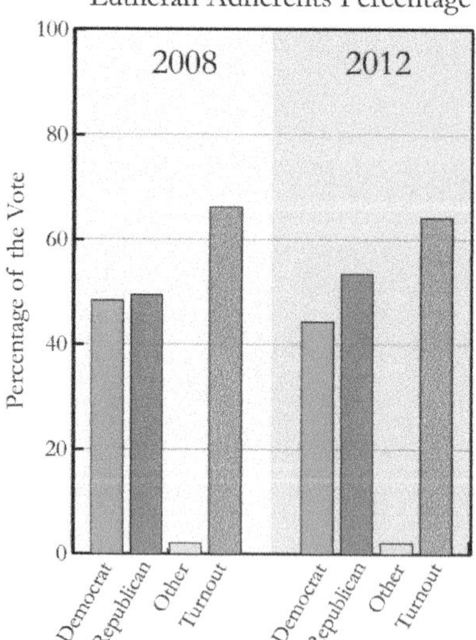
Vote and Turnout in the Top 200
Counties Having the Greatest
Lutheran Adherents Percentage
2008
2012
Percentage of the Vote
0
20
40
60
80
100
Democrat
Republican
Other
Turnout
Democrat
Republican
Other
Turnout

FIGURE 7.36

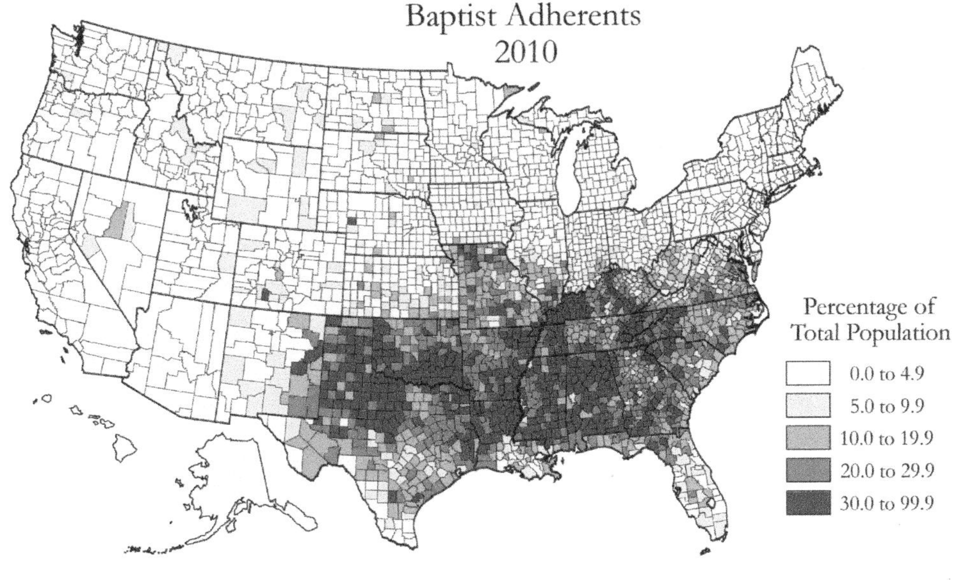

Baptist Adherents
2010
Percentage of
Total Population
0.0 to 4.9
5.0 to 9.9
10.0 to 19.9
20.0 to 29.9
30.0 to 99.9

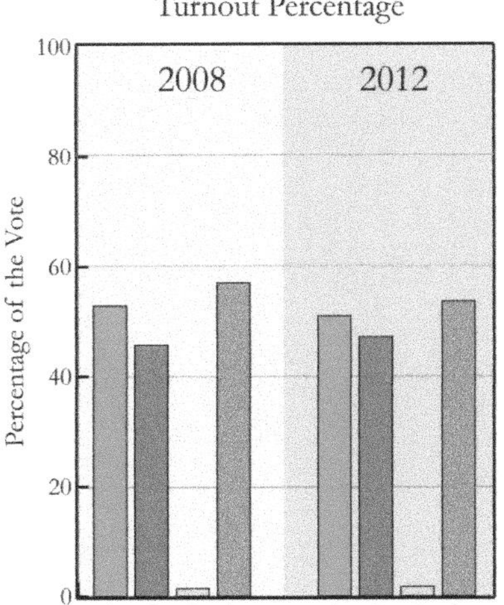

Total U.S. Popular Vote and
Turnout Percentage
2008
2012
Percentage of the Vote
0
20
40
60
80
100
Democrat
Republican
Other
Turnout
Democrat
Republican
Other
Turnout

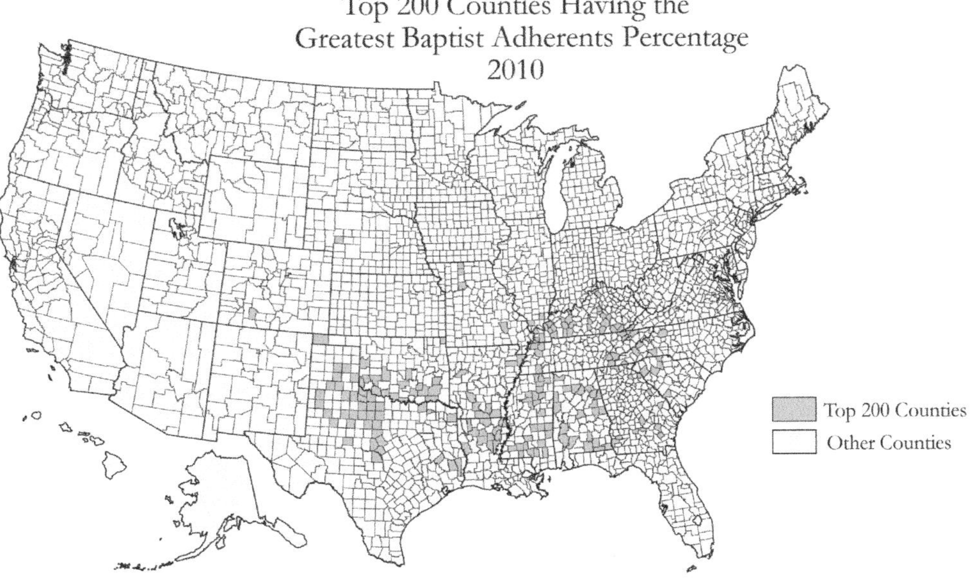

Top 200 Counties Having the
Greatest Baptist Adherents Percentage
2010
Top 200 Counties
Other Counties

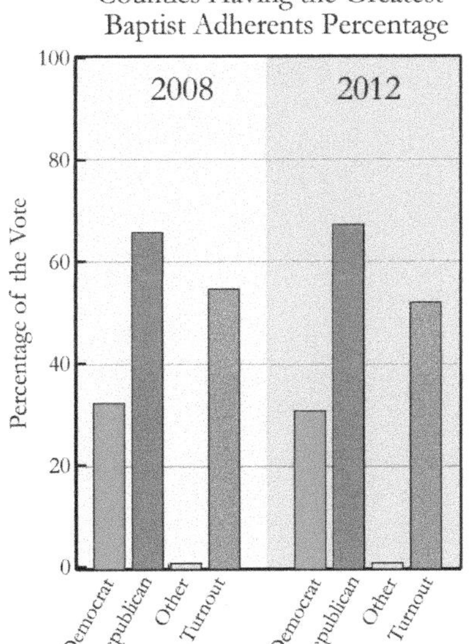

Vote and Turnout in the Top 200
Counties Having the Greatest
Baptist Adherents Percentage
2008
2012
Percentage of the Vote
0
20
40
60
80
100
Democrat
Republican
Other
Turnout
Democrat
Republican
Other
Turnout

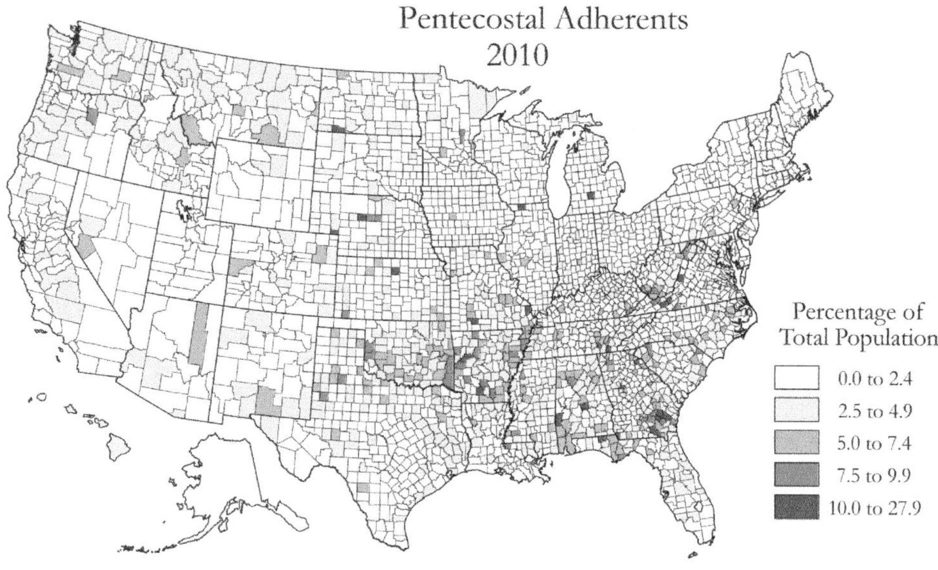
Pentecostal Adherents
2010
Percentage of
Total Population
0.0 to 2.4
2.5 to 4.9
5.0 to 7.4
7.5 to 9.9
10.0 to 27.9

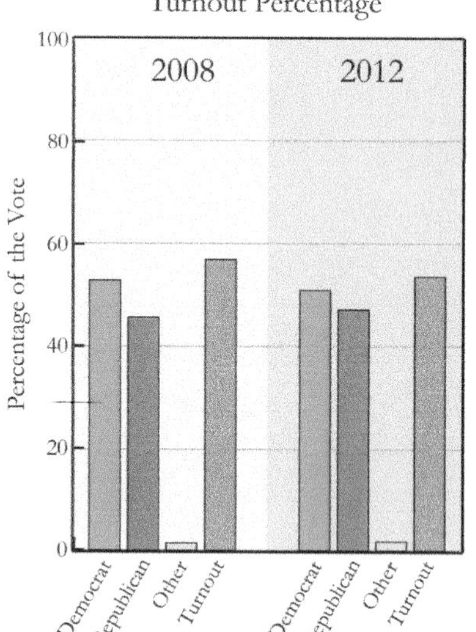
Total U.S. Popular Vote and
Turnout Percentage
2008
2012
Percentage of the Vote
0
20
40
60
80
100
Democrat
Republican
Other
Turnout
Democrat
Republican
Other
Turnout

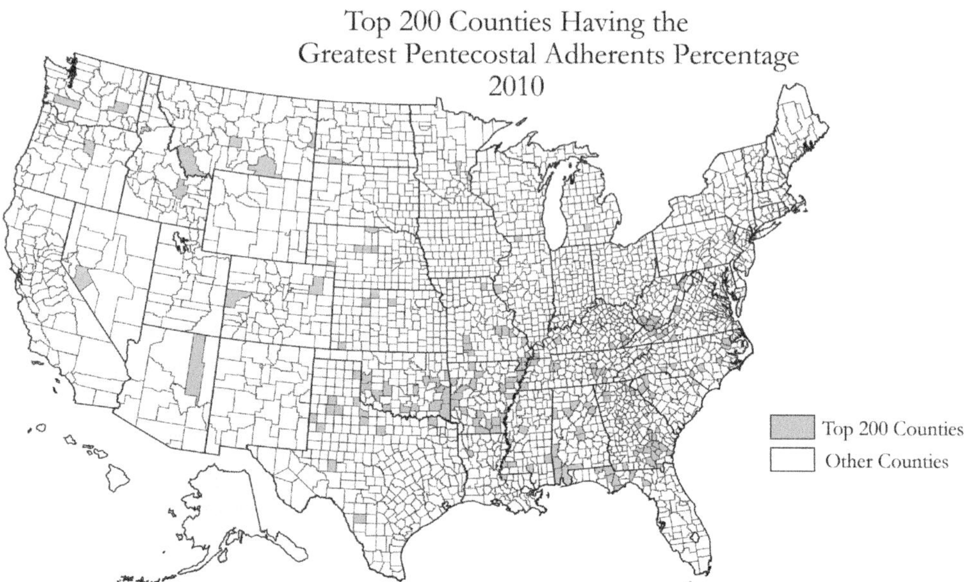
Top 200 Counties Having the
Greatest Pentecostal Adherents Percentage
2010
Top 200 Counties
Other Counties

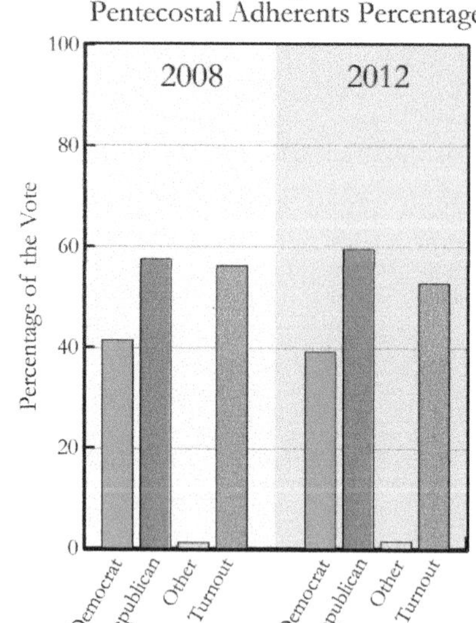
Vote and Turnout in the Top 200
Counties Having the Greatest
Pentecostal Adherents Percentage
2008
2012
Percentage of the Vote
0
20
40
60
80
100
Democrat
Republican
Other
Turnout
Democrat
Republican
Other
Turnout

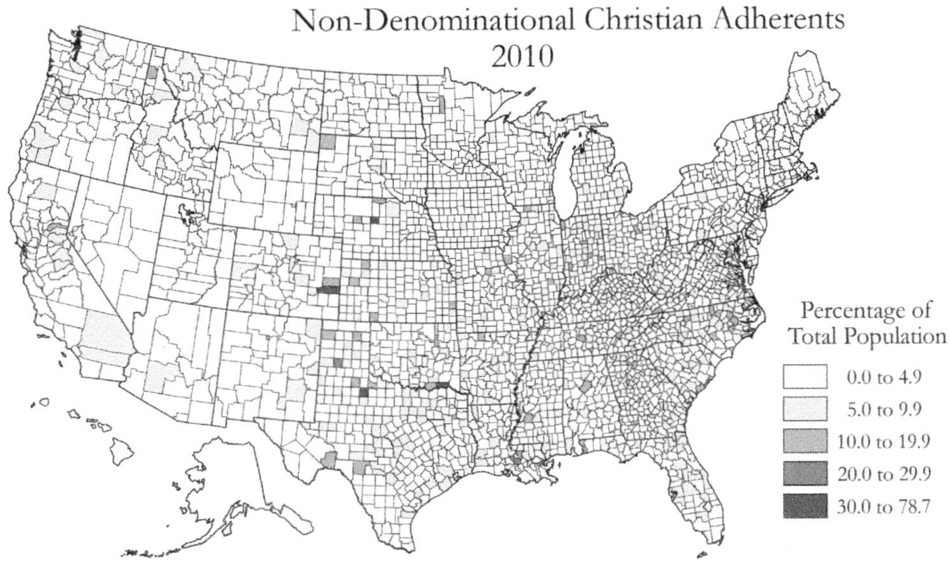

Non-Denominational Christian Adherents
2010
Percentage of
Total Population
0.0 to 4.9
5.0 to 9.9
10.0 to 19.9
20.0 to 29.9
30.0 to 78.7

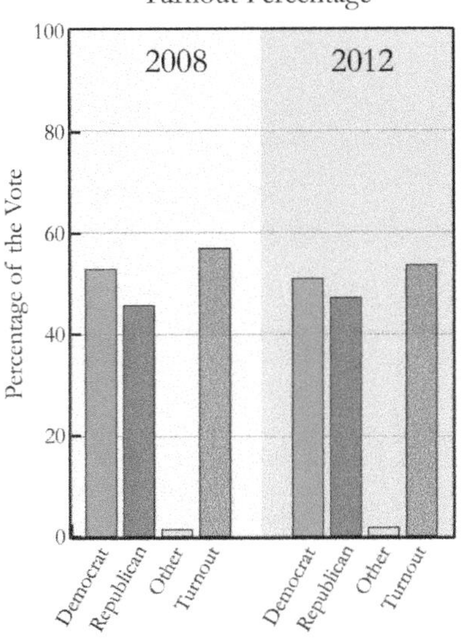

Total U.S. Popular Vote and
Turnout Percentage
2008
2012
Percentage of the Vote
0
20
40
60
80
100
Democrat
Republican
Other
Turnout
Democrat
Republican
Other
Turnout

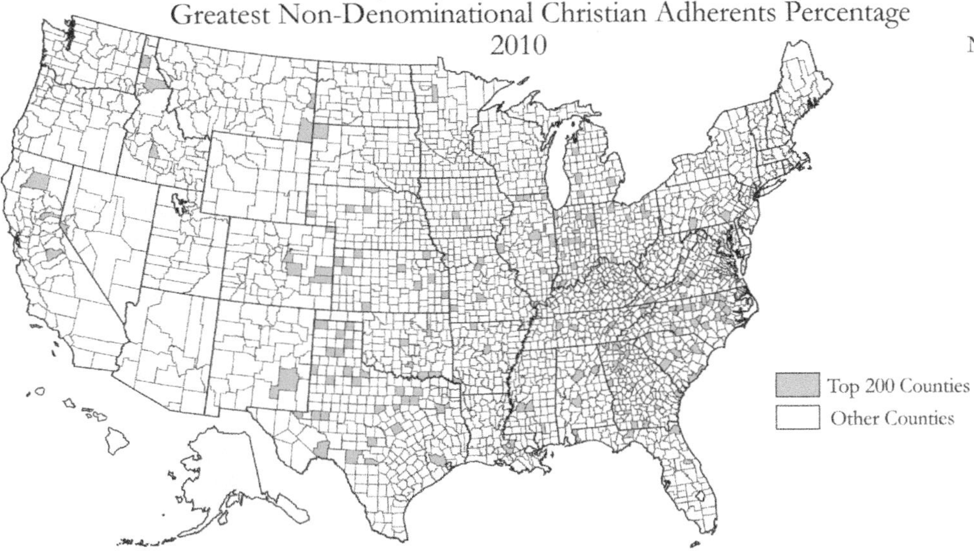

Top 200 Counties Having the
Greatest Non-Denominational Christian Adherents Percentage
2010
Top 200 Counties
Other Counties

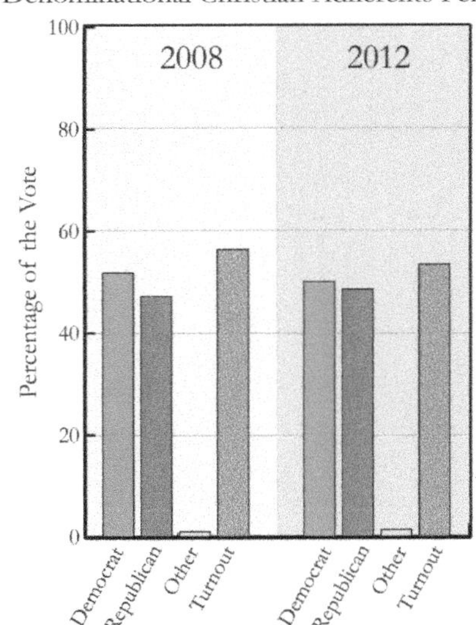

Vote and Turnout in the Top 200
Counties Having the Greatest
Non-Denominational Christian Adherents Percentage
2008
2012
Percentage of the Vote
0
20
40
60
80
100
Democrat
Republican
Other
Turnout
Democrat
Republican
Other
Turnout

FIGURE 7.39

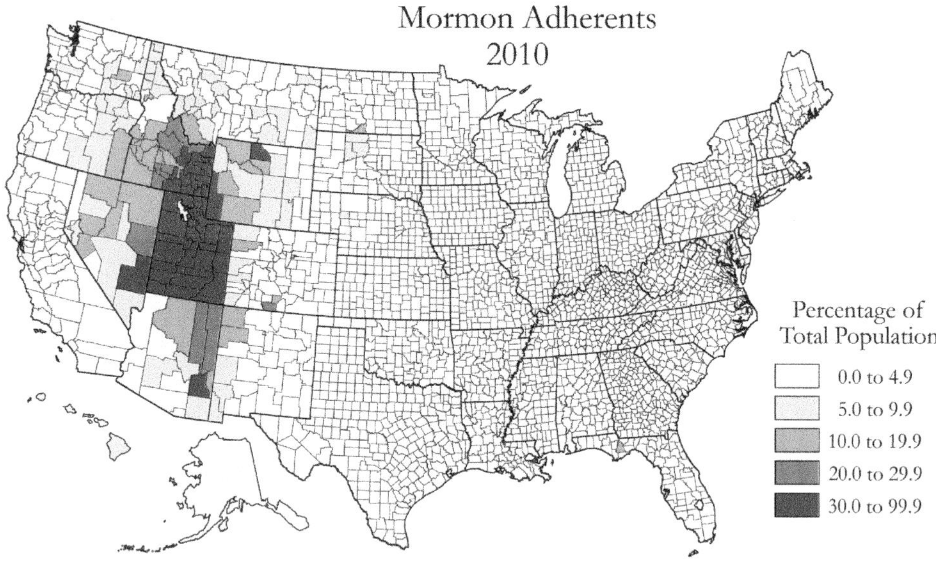
Mormon Adherents
2010
Percentage of
Total Population
0.0 to 4.9
5.0 to 9.9
10.0 to 19.9
20.0 to 29.9
30.0 to 99.9

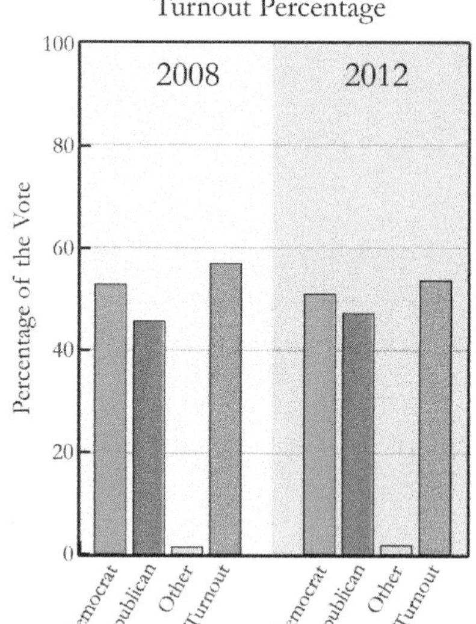
Total U.S. Popular Vote and
Turnout Percentage
2008
2012
Percentage of the Vote
100
80
60
40
20
0
Democrat
Republican
Other
Turnout
Democrat
Republican
Other
Turnout

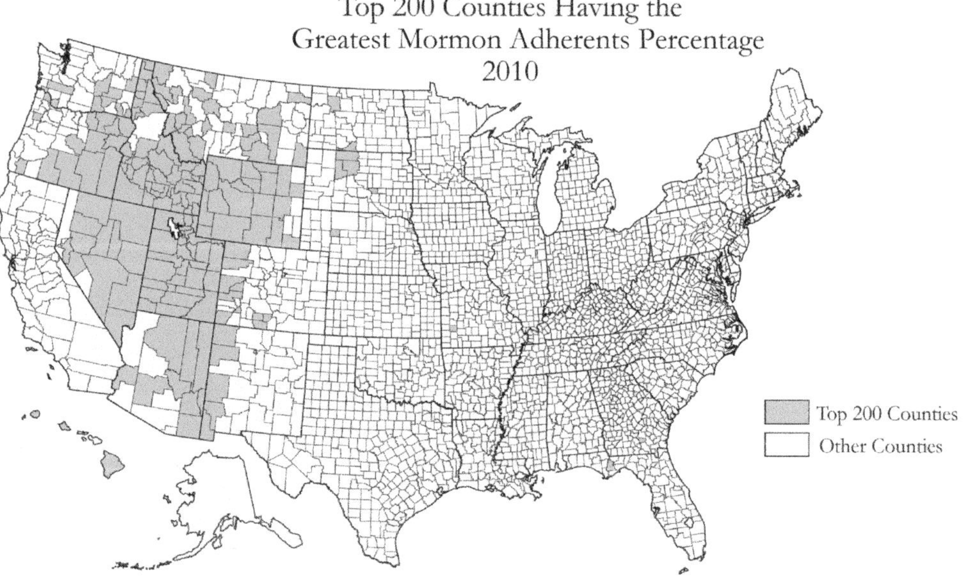
Top 200 Counties Having the
Greatest Mormon Adherents Percentage
2010
Top 200 Counties
Other Counties

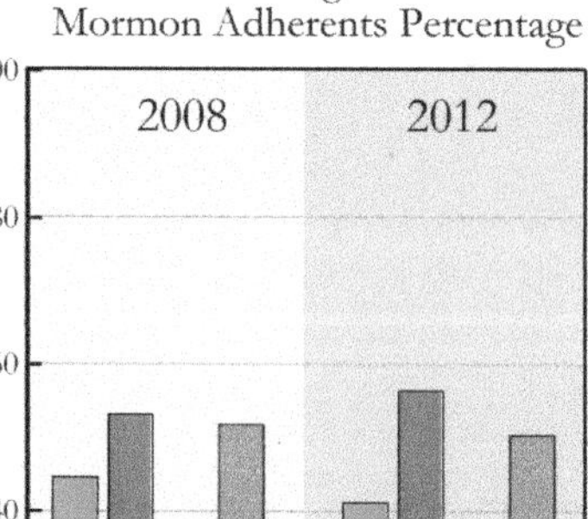
Vote and Turnout in the Top 200
Counties Having the Greatest
Mormon Adherents Percentage
2008
2012
Percentage of the Vote
100
80
60
40
20
0
Democrat
Republican
Other
Turnout
Democrat
Republican
Other
Turnout

While Christians gave solid majorities to Romney, people adhering to non-Christian religions supported Obama in large numbers. In contrast to many Christian denominations, Jews in the United States are heavily urbanized (figure 7.40). Especially large concentrations of Jews are found in the New York, Boston, and Washington, DC, metropolitan areas, with other concentrations in Chicago, the San Francisco Bay Area, and southern California. For many years, America's Jewish population has been heavily Democratic, and Obama carried most of the two hundred counties around the country with the largest Jewish populations.

Muslims in the United States are also a highly urbanized religious group (figure 7.41). Significant concentrations of Muslims are found in the Washington, DC, New York, Detroit, Chicago, and San Francisco metropolitan areas. Their Democratic votes helped to deliver these counties to Obama. It is ironic that while Jews and Muslims have a long history of animosity to each other in the Middle East and elsewhere, both groups share similar residential patterns and political preferences in the United States.

FIGURE 7.40

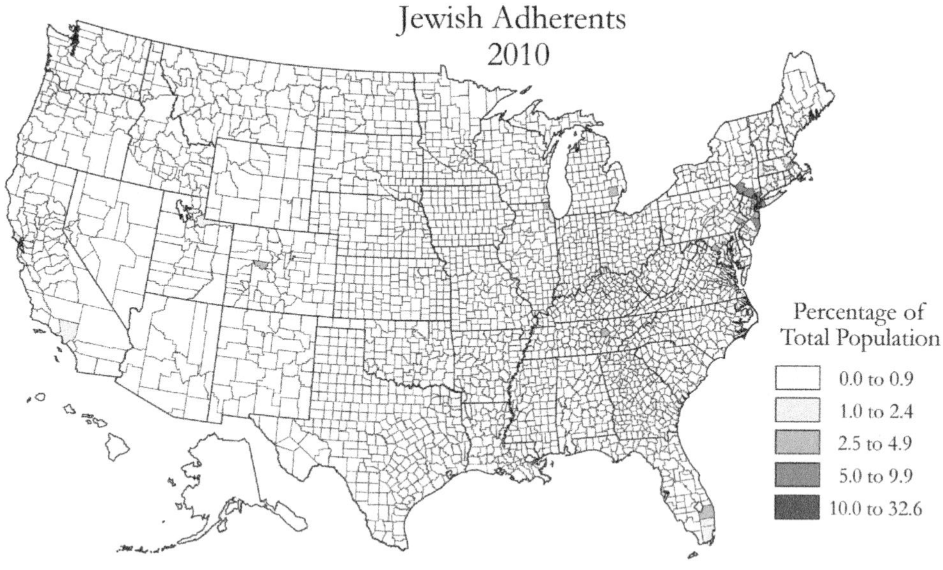
Jewish Adherents
2010
Percentage of
Total Population
0.0 to 0.9
1.0 to 2.4
2.5 to 4.9
5.0 to 9.9
10.0 to 32.6

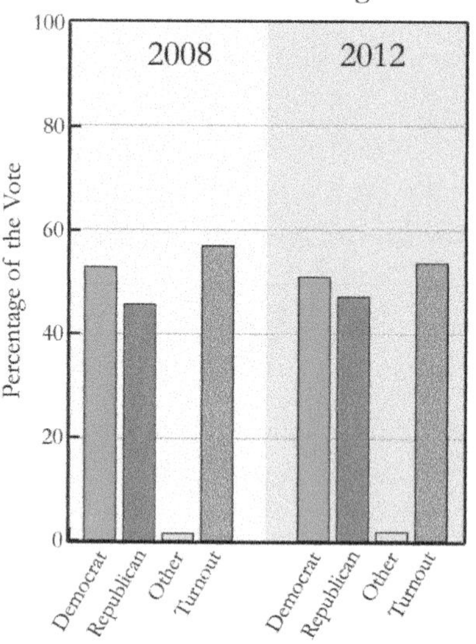
Total U.S. Popular Vote and
Turnout Percentage
2008
2012
Percentage of the Vote
100
80
60
40
20
0
Democrat
Republican
Other
Turnout
Democrat
Republican
Other
Turnout

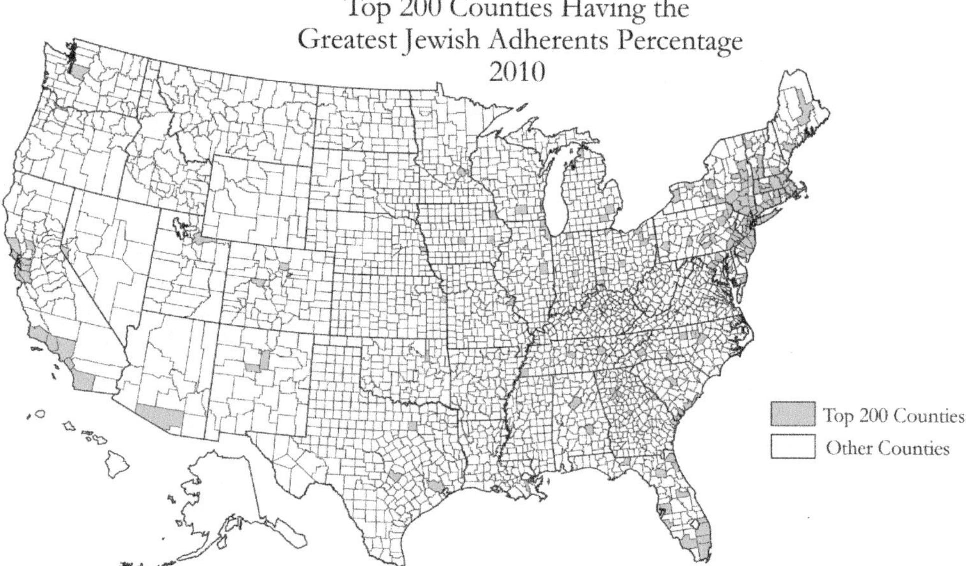
Top 200 Counties Having the
Greatest Jewish Adherents Percentage
2010
Top 200 Counties
Other Counties

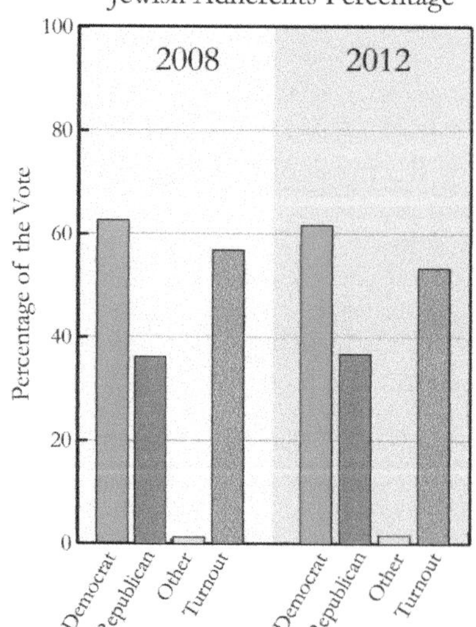
Vote and Turnout in the Top 200
Counties Having the Greatest
Jewish Adherents Percentage
2008
2012
Percentage of the Vote
100
80
60
40
20
0
Democrat
Republican
Other
Turnout
Democrat
Republican
Other
Turnout

FIGURE 7.41

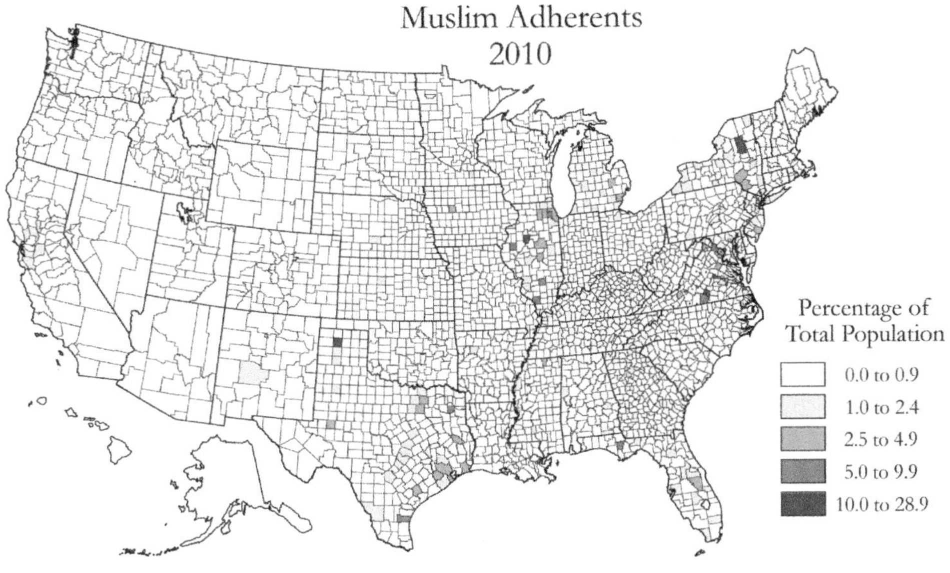
Muslim Adherents
2010
Percentage of
Total Population
0.0 to 0.9
1.0 to 2.4
2.5 to 4.9
5.0 to 9.9
10.0 to 28.9

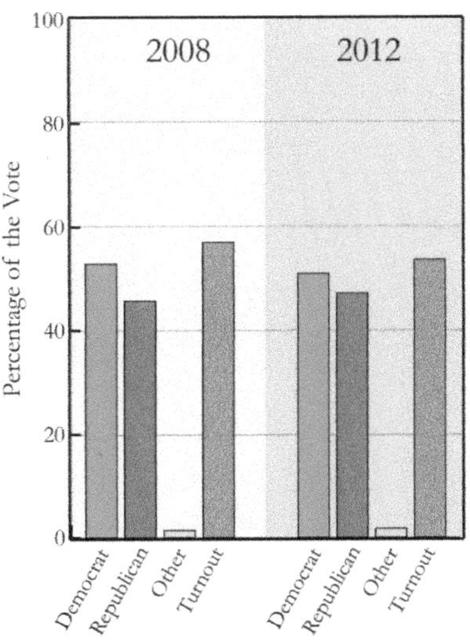
Total U.S. Popular Vote and
Turnout Percentage
2008
2012
Percentage of the Vote
0
20
40
60
80
100
Democrat
Republican
Other
Turnout
Democrat
Republican
Other
Turnout

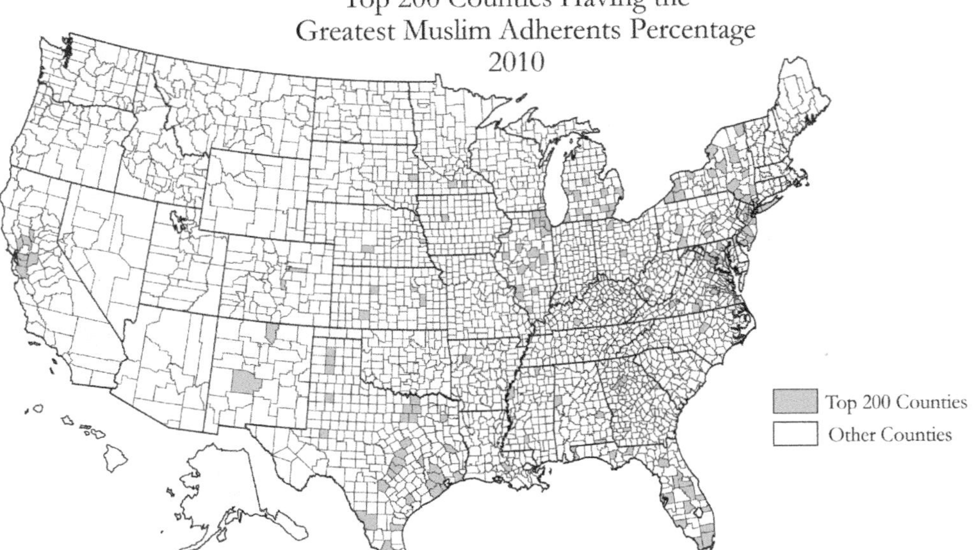
Top 200 Counties Having the
Greatest Muslim Adherents Percentage
2010
Top 200 Counties
Other Counties

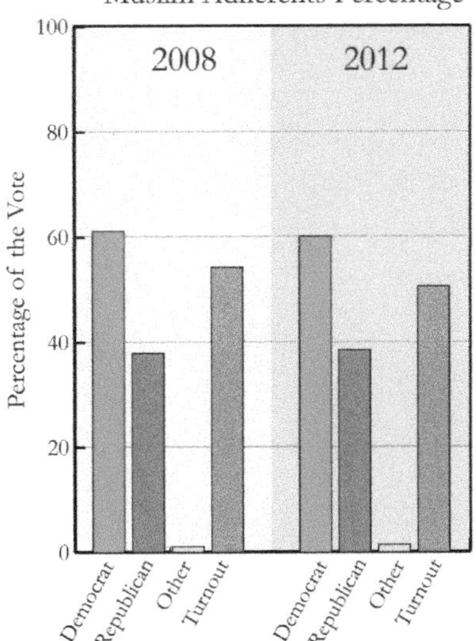
Vote and Turnout in the Top 200
Counties Having the Greatest
Muslim Adherents Percentage
2008
2012
Percentage of the Vote
0
20
40
60
80
100
Democrat
Republican
Other
Turnout
Democrat
Republican
Other
Turnout

ISSUES AND CONGRESSIONAL VOTES

HEALTH CARE IN THE 2012 ELECTIONS

SARA McLAFFERTY

Persistent health inequalities and soaring health-care costs have made health care one of the most important domestic policy issues in the United States in recent decades. The United States currently devotes more than 17 percent of its gross domestic product (GDP) to health-care expenditures yet ranks below many economically developed countries on a wide variety of health-outcome measures. The divergence between health-care spending and outcomes created a compelling backdrop for the enactment in 2010 of the Patient Protection and Affordable Care Act, also known as "Obamacare." The act was one of President Obama's signature, and most controversial, accomplishments of his first term. Debate over the Act spilled into the 2012 presidential election campaign, and health care emerged as a key point of disagreement between the candidates and parties.

Access to health care is shaped strongly by the uneven geographical availability of health services as well as an array of economic, social, and cultural factors that intersect to limit people's ability to obtain health care when needed. One of the key factors is health insurance coverage. Lacking insurance, people potentially face huge out-of-pocket costs for medical care and may forgo needed preventive and treatment services. In 2010, an estimated 49 million Americans, 17.4 percent of the population, had no health insurance, while the remainder relied on either private insurance or public programs such as Medicare and Medicaid. The uninsured population is geographically concentrated at the state scale. In Texas, almost a quarter of the population lacks health insurance, as does one out of every five residents in Nevada and Florida. In contrast, only 4 percent of the population in Massachusetts is uninsured.

Geographic disparities in insurance coverage reflect both differences in population composition among states and differences in state-level health-care policies. Immigrants, young adults, and the working poor are heavily represented in the uninsured population, and in many states that have high concentrations of uninsured, these population groups are large. Although insurance data are available for only a subset of counties (60 percent), we can observe important patterns at the county level. The map of percentage uninsured by county reveals areas of concentration along the US-Mexico border and in south Florida, places where immigrants predominate. Hot spots of uninsured population also occur in places with a large temporary or seasonal workforce, including agricultural counties in California and Washington as well as tourist destination counties in the South and West such as Orange County, Florida (Orlando), and Clark County, Nevada (Las Vegas).

In contrast, high rates of health insurance coverage exist in the northeastern and midwestern states. Many of these states have adopted policies that raise the income eligibility limit for Medicaid so that a large fraction of the low-income population has access to this publicly funded health insurance program. Massachusetts even has its own public health insurance program, MassHealth, for low- to medium-income residents of the state.

The Patient Protection and Affordable Care Act aims to improve access to health care while controlling costs and protecting the rights of vulnerable populations. The focal point of the law is to expand health insurance coverage and thus reduce the number of uninsured through a two-pronged strategy that involves expanding eligibility for Medicaid and requiring people without insurance to purchase insurance or pay a tax penalty. During the 2012 election campaign, Obama strongly embraced the law, whereas Mitt Romney vowed to repeal it. Given the law's emphasis on expanding insurance coverage, one might expect an association between high rates of uninsurance and Democratic voting.

State and county-level election results for 2012 reveal a complex relationship between voting and the uninsured population. Texas, the state with the largest uninsured population, voted solidly for Romney, as did five of the other top ten states with the highest percent uninsured (Alaska, Georgia, Oklahoma, Mississippi, and Montana). At the county scale, only 49 of the 200 counties with the highest percent uninsured voted for Obama. Interestingly, the top six counties, all located in the US-Mexico border region and with very high percentages of uninsured (> 35 percent), voted solidly Democratic, suggesting the possibility that the large uninsured population may have swayed the vote in favor of Obama. However, other counties with high percentages of uninsured frequently supported the Republican candidate.

Although a large majority of the counties with the highest percentage of uninsured voted for Romney, Obama captured a strong majority (54 percent) of the total votes from those counties. A majority of voters supported the Democratic candidate in many of the most heavily populated counties, including Dallas County and Harris County (Houston) in Texas, Miami-Dade County, Florida, and Los Angeles County, California. Still, some urban counties with large uninsured populations, such as Tarrant County, Texas (Fort Worth), and Oklahoma County, Oklahoma (Oklahoma City), favored the Republican candidate.

The lack of consistent geographical correlation between uninsured population and outcomes of the 2012 presidential election has several possible explanations. Although health care received vigorous attention during the election campaign, exit polls indicate that it ranked below economic concerns such as jobs and incomes in influencing voters' decisions. Also, some of the uninsured were not eligible to vote or may have been deterred from voting by stringent local- or state-level voter eligibility rules such as requiring a driver's license or birth certificate. In these cases, the large size of the uninsured population would not translate into an equivalent election impact. At the other end of the spectrum, the strong support for the Democratic candidate in states with low rates of uninsurance such as Massachusetts, Vermont, and Hawaii suggests that voters may have valued the commitment to publicly funded health insurance in their states and supported the candidate who expressed a similar commitment to the Affordable Care Act. In this sense, attitudes toward health care reflected broader attitudes about government's role in ensuring a strong social safety net.

FOREIGN POLICY IN THE 2012 PRESIDENTIAL ELECTION

STEVEN RADIL

To an extent, the election of Barack Obama in 2008 was a referendum on the foreign policies of the Bush administration. The perceived need to chart a new course in foreign affairs was symbolized by Obama's campaign slogan of "Change," and much of the 2008 campaign and postelection transition focused on foreign policy issues regarding the conduct of the Bush administration's "global war on terror." These issues included the wars in Afghanistan and Iraq, the indefinite detention of foreign nationals at Guantanamo Bay, the use of rendition and torture by the Central Intelligence Agency, continued killings by US drone aircraft, and, above all, the failure of US intelligence agencies and armed forces to capture or kill Osama bin Laden. The clearly militarized geopolitics of war and antiterrorism played an important role in the 2008 election.

Four years later, foreign policy issues were largely secondary to the state of the US economy. Frequently, foreign policy issues were discussed as rationales to improve the economy in order to preserve and enhance the ability of the United States to continue to prosecute its global war on terror. This was a marked departure from not only the 2008 election but the 2004 election as well, in which terrorism, national security, and the ongoing wars in Afghanistan and Iraq dominated the campaigns. Despite moderate concern and occasional discussion of policies regarding Iran's nuclear program, the civil war in Syria, and the Arab Spring revolutions, the economy was the central theme of the 2012 contest. In fact, foreign policy issues such as immigration and trade were consistently framed as domestic economic concerns.

In a CNN exit poll associated with the 2012 election, only 4 percent of respondents identified foreign policy as the most important factor in the election while 60 percent identified the economy as the top issue (CNN 2012). However, foreign policy did make noticeable impacts on the 2012 election as well, often in subtle ways. A notable example is found in the issue of immigration, a heated and oft-discussed topic during the Republican primaries. Although often treated by the candidates as a domestic and economic issue, a geographic perspective on immigration (movement of people across international boundaries) suggests its appropriateness for inclusion in a discussion of foreign policy.

During the Republican primaries, candidates used their stances on immigration reform and questions about legalizing the citizenship of immigrants already in the United States in an attempt to differentiate themselves from a crowded field and to solidify their bona fides with the conservative voters who vote in the Republican primaries. For instance, Mitt Romney harkened to the law-and-order tradition of the GOP when he advocated for fencing the entire southern boundary with Mexico, suggested the "self-deportation" of undocumented immigrants, and declared any path to citizenship as "amnesty."

Romney's hard stance was critiqued as potentially damaging to Republicans during the general election, but it left little opportunity for other candidates to run further to the right on the issue without risk of further alienating general-election voters. The strategy may have served Romney well during the primary but may have hurt him in the general election. Hispanic support for Romney has been estimated at only 27 percent nationally, a decline of 13 percent in Hispanic support for Republican presidential candidates in 2004, when George W. Bush got 40 percent of the Hispanic vote, and from 2008, when John McCain got 31 percent of the Hispanic vote.

The Romney campaign tended to avoid consistent engagement on the foreign policy issues that had been important in the two previous presidential elections, particularly regarding the geopolitics of the war on terror. Romney's approach to such topics rarely went beyond vague critiques that Obama's policies had left the United States less secure and that Obama was ambivalent about using American military power.

Romney's relatively restrained campaign approach to foreign policy issues was the likely result of the killing of Osama bin Laden in Pakistan in 2011. The Obama administration's willingness to violate the territorial sovereignty of an allied, nuclear-armed state unilaterally in order to kill bin Laden stripped Republican challengers of the ability to apply their traditional argument that Democrats are weak on national security. Thus, Romney was left with little to work with to mount a coherent challenge to Obama's prosecution of the war on terror that would also satisfy the core of the Republican voting base.

Romney was presented with an opportunity late in the campaign to press Obama on his policies regarding the numerous Arab Spring movements when the US ambassador to Libya, Chris Stevens, and three other Americans were killed in an attack on a US diplomatic mission in Benghazi, Libya, by militants. However, Romney's criticisms about the process of security at a specific mission in a specific place were largely aimed at the bureaucracy of the State Department and had little impact on the course of the election.

However, one geopolitical relationship that Romney assertively campaigned on in both the Republican primary and the general election was the relationship between the United States and China. In keeping with his business-based credentials for seeking the presidency and with experience in global finance, Romney consistently argued that a significant part of the economic problem in the United States was that China was a "currency manipulator" and that manufacturing jobs would return to the United States if the Chinese government allowed its currency exchange rates to fluctuate rather than be set by fiat.

This argument, long a staple of US trade organizations and interests, was combined by Romney with narratives of Chinese government-backed corporate espionage to suggest that the economic challenges facing the United States were partly the responsibility of a foreign geopolitical foe and that, as president, Romney would "crack down on cheaters like China" and prevent the Chinese from "stealing our jobs." This narrative overlooked and excused the actions of bankers, corporations, and financial firms in producing a global economic crisis but did suggest that foreign policy was part of the Republican approach to the election as long as the specific issues could also be folded into the emphasis on the domestic economic concerns of the electorate.

The Republican approach to sublimate foreign policy issues to domestic economic concerns may have been something of a missed opportunity as it failed to produce any sustained national discussion of the Obama administration's prosecution of the war on terror. As a candidate in 2008, Obama was highly critical of the foreign policies and practices of the Bush administration, including the status of foreign prisoners held at Guantanamo Bay, the use of torture, and the failure to kill or capture bin Laden. A constant refrain from the Obama campaign at the time was that the United States should reemphasize other aspects of American power beyond the use of military force. More plainly, then-candidate Obama felt the prosecution of the war on terror had become too militarized. The sovereign states of Afghanistan and Iraq had been invaded and occupied for years on end, and the conflict against Al Qaeda and its various affiliates had begun to diffuse to other states, notably Yemen and Pakistan. Arguing against a militarized US foreign policy during the 2008 campaign, Obama was warmly embraced beyond the United States and was even awarded the 2009 Nobel Peace Prize for "his extraordinary efforts to strengthen international diplomacy and cooperation between peoples."

Since receiving the Nobel Peace Prize, Obama's prosecution of the war on terror has been at least as militarized as his predecessor's as he committed more troops to the war in Afghanistan, increased the use of drones to kill suspected militants, and gave the order for the raid that killed bin Laden. If the killing of Osama bin Laden seemed to make the geopolitics of a militarized war on terrorism largely invisible during the campaign, the impacts of over a decade of still-ongoing war have been directly felt within places economically reliant on military spending. Counties with major military installations or bases have historically been Republican strongholds, although they leaned slightly Democratic in 2008. However, the top two hundred counties with the largest military expenditures demonstrated surprisingly strong support for Obama in 2012.

Military expenditures by county were calculated using the Consolidated Federal Funds Report (CCFR). The CCFR program, which was ended by Congress in 2011, reported federal government expenditures annually by state, county, and subcounty area, and expenditures were reported by the responsible department or agency. Using the CCFR data for the last available year (2010), the two hundred counties with the most military expenditures were identified. In these counties, 57.5 percent supported Obama in the election as opposed to the overall 51 percent that voted for Obama nationally. Although this strong support for Obama in military-reliant counties seems in contrast with the rhetoric of a demilitarized foreign policy from his first presidential campaign, it also likely reflects a place-specific recognition by voters within those counties that Obama has prosecuted the war on terror quite similarly to his predecessor.

The relatively high percentage of Obama support in these counties may also reflect the fact that some are large central-city counties in which Obama was highly popular in general, including Los Angeles County, California, Cook County, Illinois (Chicago), and King County, Washington (Seattle). Also, relatively high levels of support for Obama in smaller counties that host major military installations may have occurred because of strong support for Obama among African American and Latino enlisted personnel stationed on these bases. About 20 percent of the Army's enlisted personnel are African Americans.

The cause of the strong support for Obama within military-reliant counties is not likely to be due to a single event, even one as significant as the killing of bin Laden. Whatever the source of such strong support, it is clear that it undoubtedly helped Obama during his reelection campaign and removed a key foreign-policy campaign tool from the Republican challenger. In sum, foreign policy and foreign affairs clearly mattered in important ways to the 2012 election outcomes despite the election being dominated by the discussion of other issues.

REFERENCE

CNN Presidential Election Exit Polls. 2012. http://www.cnn.com/election/2012/results/race/president.

ENVIRONMENTAL AND ENERGY BALLOT MEASURES IN THE 2012 ELECTIONS

BARRY D. SOLOMON AND ADAM M. WELLSTEAD

Marijuana legalization and same-sex marriage ballot propositions took the national center stage on election night. However, there were many other initiatives contested across thirty-eight states, including several legislative referenda. Of the other 169 propositions addressing a myriad of issues, 18 energy- and environmental-specific ballot measures were prominent in 15 states (an additional measure on coastal zone management in Alaska was rejected by voters in August). Water, sewer, and land conservation bonds addressing large-scale infrastructure projects were contested in four states. Energy-based propositions focusing on clean energy policies made up the second category. Property rights concerning hunting, fishing, and farming/ranching activities formed the third set of propositions. The final proposition grouping was land and water conservation and state sovereignty measures.

A series of bond issues that addressed water, sewerage, and land conservation were voted on by electorates in mostly blue states (with one exception). All but one of these passed. Oklahoma's measure was the largest, at $300 million. Question 764 was a legislatively referred constitutional measure approved by voters to allow the Oklahoma Water Resources Board to issue bonds for a reserve fund to finance water and sewage treatment projects. The board will create the Water Infrastructure Credit Enhancement Reserve Fund that would be used only in cases where a city or municipality defaulted on a loan and other reserve funds were depleted.

All of the other similar bond issues on state ballots were also approved, with the exception of Hawaii. Rhode Island and Maine each had a pair of somewhat similarly worded measures presented to voters. One of these was for drinking water and wastewater projects, while the other focused on land conservation, recreation, and water access. The larger of these twin measures was approved in Rhode Island, which also passed it by larger margins. The final natural resource measure was a legislatively referred constitutional amendment in Hawaii that would have authorized special-purpose revenue bonds to assist dam and reservoir owners with safety projects. While this measure received more yes than no votes, it was defeated because it received slightly less than 50 percent of the total votes cast.

The 2012 presidential election was quiet on energy and climate issues, and few such issues were considered in ballot measures. The exceptions occurred in California, Washington, and Michigan. The sole victory for clean energy advocates occurred in California, where voters approved Proposition 39. This was a complex measure that changed the rules for determining the state sales tax obligations of multistate businesses that operate in the state. Based on the default single sales factor method, increased revenues from these businesses are projected to amount to $1 billion per year. Up to $550 million of the increased revenues will be dedicated each year over five years to be spent on clean energy projects, primarily for energy efficiency retrofits in public schools, colleges, universities, and other public facilities. Most of the rest of the funds will also be spent on schools.

In Washington, Advisory Vote 2 was approved by voters following passage of H.B. 2590 by the state legislature. This was a nonbinding vote that concurred with the extension of a tax on the possession of petroleum products until July 1, 2020. The tax proceeds are used to clean up oil spills and other pollution and to provide liability insurance.

The only other energy ballot initiative was voted on in Michigan, where Proposal 12-3 was soundly defeated. This measure was introduced by a coalition called Michigan Energy Michigan Jobs. If it had been approved, the measure would have expanded the existing state renewable portfolio standard (RPS) to require electric utilities in the state to derive 25 percent of their energy from specified renewable energy sources such as wind, solar, biomass, and hydroelectricity by 2025. The current requirement in Michigan is for 10 percent by 2015, and passage of the measure would have matched the RPSs in Minnesota, Illinois, and several other states. While the reasons for defeat of the proposal are not fully clear given the strong public support for renewable energy, many voters may have opposed the mechanism of a constitutional amendment, and opponents of the measure (primarily the two largest electric utilities in Michigan) outspent proponents by a 2–1 margin.

Not surprising was the prominence of ballot measures in red states reaffirming hunting, fishing, and farming/ranching rights. The only such measure in a blue state was Oregon's proposed Measure 81, banning Columbia River commercial salmon fishing with gill nets by nontribal persons. The sports-fishing industry and conservationists who got the measure on the ballot were pitted against the commercial fishing industry. The measure failed by a 2–1 margin.

The hunting and fishing rights propositions in Idaho, Kentucky, Nebraska, and Wyoming were similar and promoted by hunting organizations to preclude future legislators from infringing on hunting and fishing activities largely due to the potential threat of animal rights lobbying. In all cases, they passed by large margins (70–85 percent). Except for the one in Idaho, these measures were constitutional amendments. In North Dakota, Constitutional Measure 3 declared the right to farm using "modern methods," employing agricultural technology and modern livestock production and ranching practices, and it was approved by 67 percent of the ballots cast. The campaign in support of the measure was led by the North Dakota Feeding Families Committee and the North Dakota Farm Bureau.

Land and water conservation and natural resources sovereignty-related initiatives were on the ballot in Alabama, Arizona, and Alaska. The Alabama Forever Wild Land Trust Amendment, which was sponsored by Republican representative Randy Davis, was extended for another twenty years by three quarters of Alabamans. This measure, largely supported by environmental and hunting groups, would allow Forever Wild Land Trust to use the proceeds from the state's oil and gas revenues (up to a maximum of $15 million per year) and preserve land for public recreational and environmental use.

In Arizona, there were two environmental and land use issues on the ballot. Proposal 119, known as the Arizona State Trust Land Amendment, would allow the state to exchange public lands to manage development, specifically if it is related to protecting military facilities or developing lands for sale or public use. This constitutional amendment was strongly supported by the business lobby and its concern for the state's $9 billion defense and aerospace manufacturing industries. Environmental groups also supported this initiative because it was seen as safeguarding at-risk lands and ecosystems from commercialization. This proposal, unlike previous land-exchange ballot initiatives, was approved by 62 percent of voters. Proposal 120 was a proposed constitutional amendment that would "grant the state exclusive control over air, water, public lands, minerals, wildlife and other natural resources within the state's boundaries." This measure was brought to fruition because of the often-raised concern during the 2012 campaign about states' rights and federal government infringement of those rights. In contrast to Proposal 119, Proposal 120 was defeated soundly, with 68 percent voting no.

Finally, during the August 28 primary election, 62 percent of Alaskan voters rejected Ballot Measure 2. This measure would resurrect Alaska's coastal zone management program. Its supporters argued that Alaska was the only coastal state in the union without a management program. Without such a program, effective decision making, particularly from American Indian groups and small communities, would be hindered. Nearly $1 million was raised by the "Vote No on 2" group.

MEMBERSHIP, PARTY, AND CAUCUSES IN THE 113TH CONGRESS

ERIN H. FOUBERG

The 2012 elections affected Congress in many ways, as seen in the maps in this section and throughout the atlas. Although Republicans picked up some seats in Congress, partisan control of the two chambers remained unchanged. The Republicans retained control of the House of Representatives while the Democrats retained control of the Senate. Of course, determining partisan control depends on the outcomes of individual elections in the various states, and each individual election has its own unique characteristics, as described in detail in chapter 9. Yet the overall pattern of congressional representation after the election is also significant. It affected the membership in various House of Representatives caucuses as well as the outcomes of important votes in the House after the new Congress convened after the election.

This is illustrated in figures 8.1 through 8.4. Figure 8.1 provides a perspective on the relationships between seats and votes in the House. In many states, one party or the other received a disproportionate share of the vote for House candidates relative to the number of seats won by that party. As sections by Richard Engstrom and Kenneth C. Martis in chapter 2 illustrate, this discrepancy in some states may be the result of gerrymandering.

Figures 8.2 and Figure 8.3 show partisan control of each district in the House of Representatives following the election. For the most part, the pattern of House district victories follows the general pattern nationwide in that Democrats tended to control urban districts while Republicans tended to control exurban and rural districts. Thus, although the Republicans won only a narrow majority of the 435 seats in the House, in combination the Republican districts encompass a much larger proportion of the country's land area relative to the districts controlled by the Democrats. Thus, the House results reinforce the general observation of the degree to which American politics has become polarized on the basis of urban status, with metropolitan districts continuing to tend toward the Democrats while Republicans continued to increase strength outside central cities and their suburbs.

Figure 8.4 examines the distribution of House seats on the basis of seniority. Although seniority is less important in determining power in Congress than it was before the 1970s, it remains an important measure of political power. Representatives with long tenures in office often wield a disproportionate amount of power, for example, by serving as chairs of important congressional committees. Frequently, seniority is associated with safe districts. In many states, districts are drawn in such a way as to protect senior incumbents and minimize the chance that these incumbents will be defeated by opponents either in primary or general elections.

One impact of the 2012 election was the change in membership of the 113th Congress, which was seated in 2013, as compared to the 112th Congress that met in 2011 and 2012. As a result of this change, membership in various caucuses within the House of Representatives also changed.

Caucuses consist of members who associate voluntarily on the basis of common interests and/or political philosophies. Some, including the black and Hispanic caucuses, are organized along ethnic lines, including African American and Latino members, respectively. Others include the Blue Dog Democrats, which consists of moderate, fiscally conservative Democrats who are elected primarily from red states, and the Tea Party caucus. Most caucuses consist primarily or exclusively of members of one of the two major parties. The black caucus, Hispanic caucus, and Blue Dog Democrats exist within the Democratic Party, while members of the Tea Party caucus are Republicans. Figure 8.5 shows the distribution

FIGURE 8.1

Imbalances of Popular Votes Received and U.S. Congressional Seats Won, by State, for the 2012 Elections

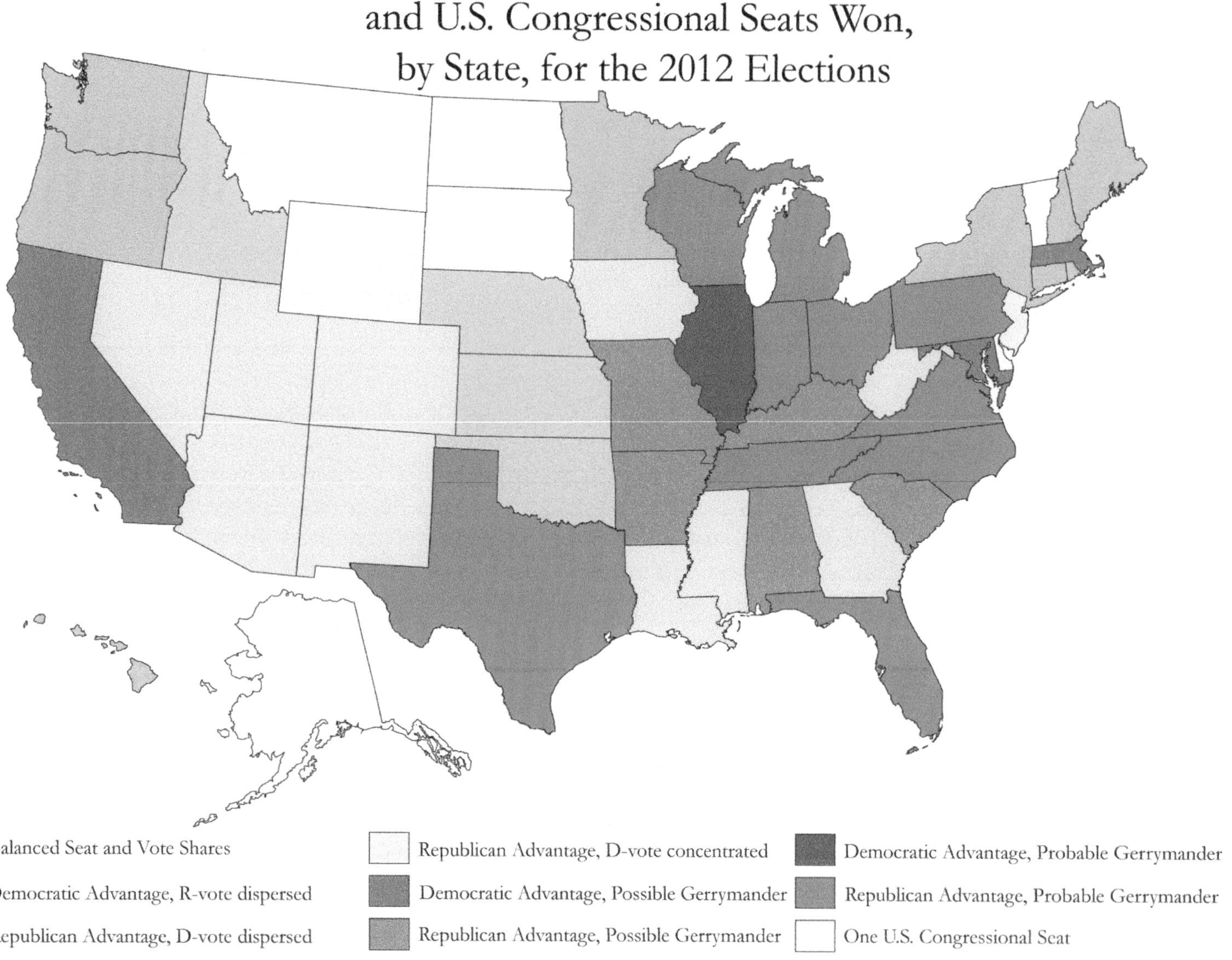

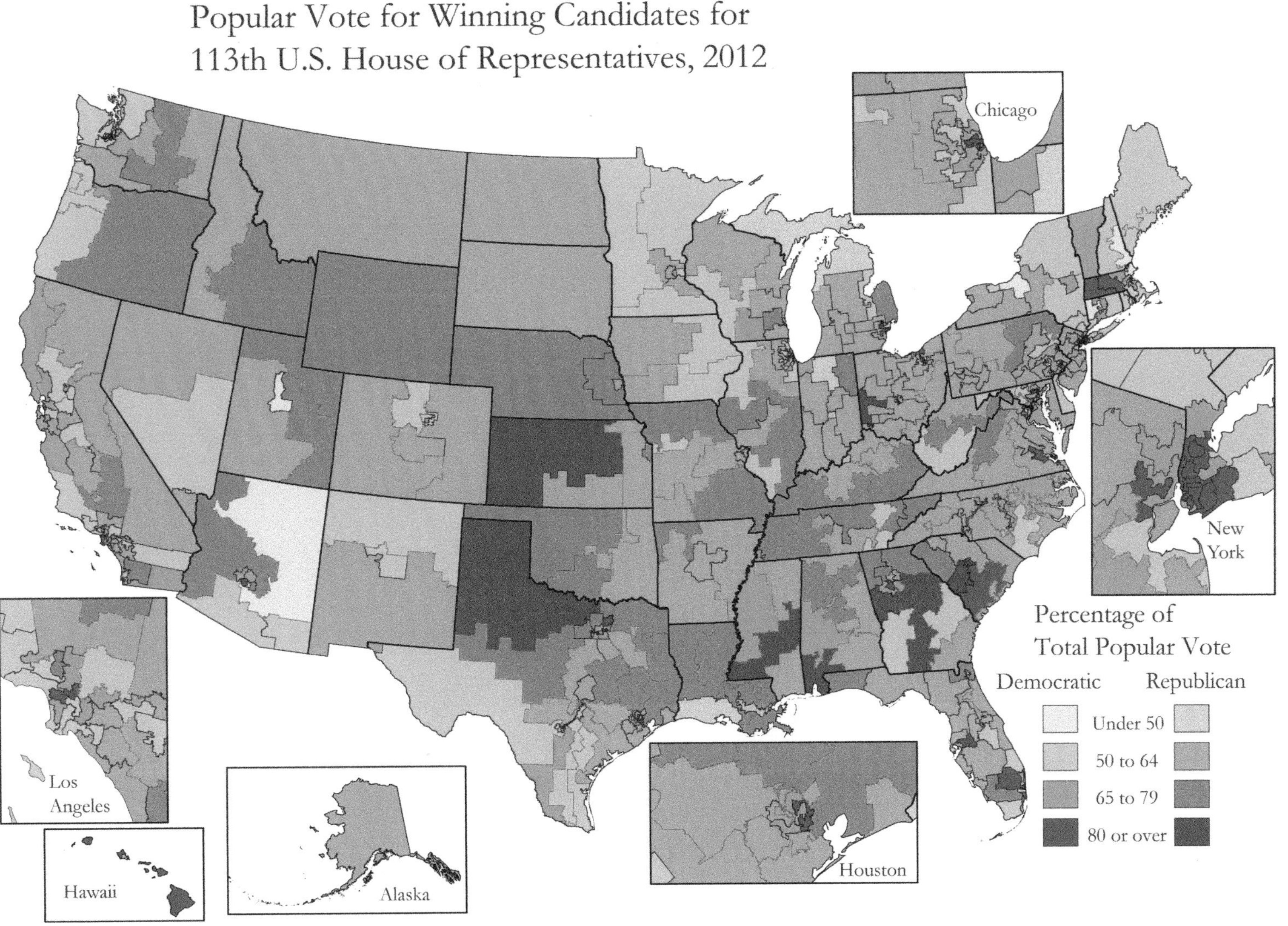
Popular Vote for Winning Candidates for
113th U.S. House of Representatives, 2012
Chicago
New
York
Los
Angeles
Hawaii
Alaska
Houston
Percentage of
Total Popular Vote
Democratic
Republican
Under 50
50 to 64
65 to 79
80 or over

FIGURE 8.3

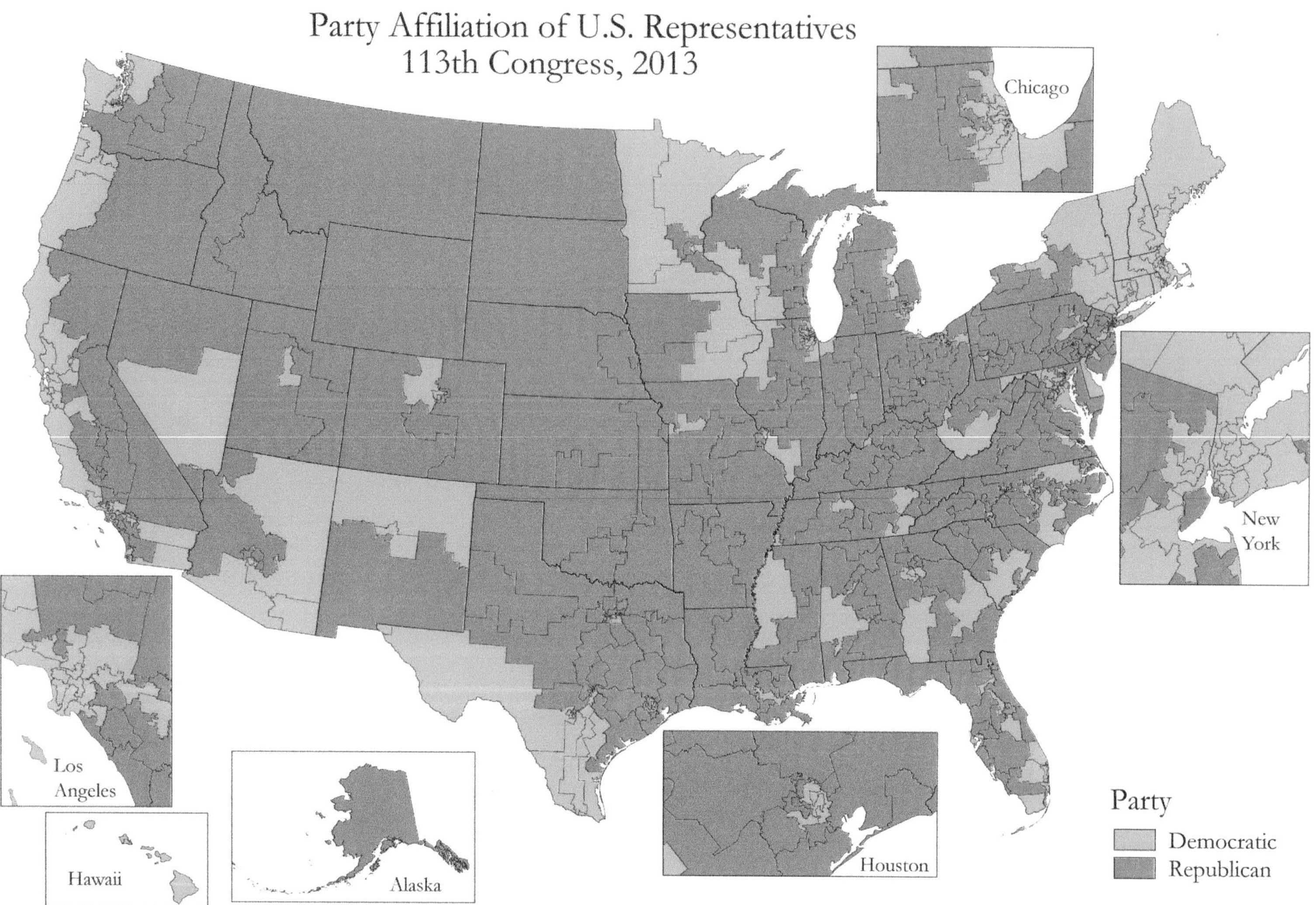
Party Affiliation of U.S. Representatives
113th Congress, 2013
Chicago
New
York
Los
Angeles
Hawaii
Alaska
Houston
Party
Democratic
Republican

FIGURE 8.4

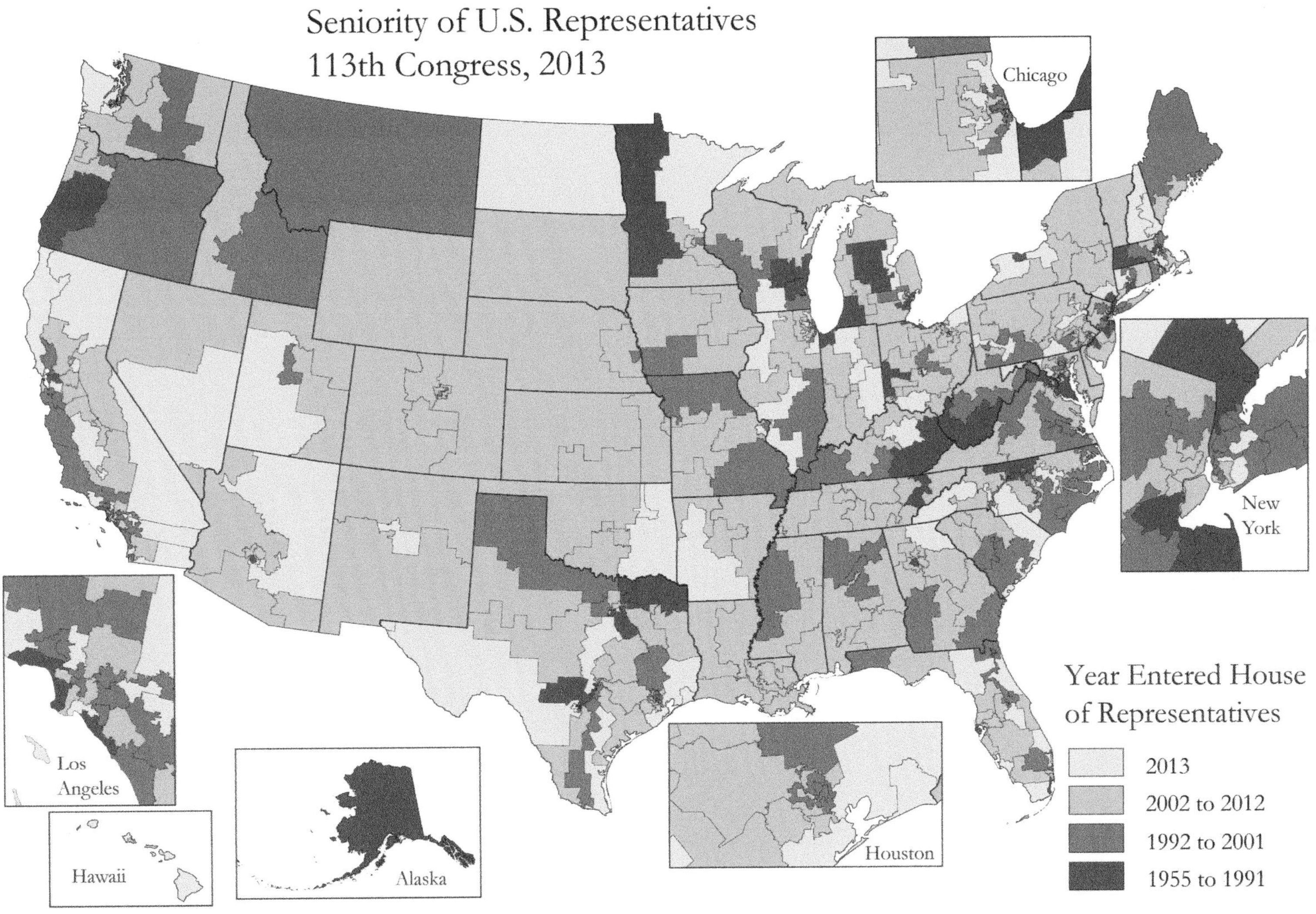

Seniority of U.S. Representatives
113th Congress, 2013
Chicago
New
York
Los
Angeles
Hawaii
Alaska
Houston
Year Entered House
of Representatives
2013
2002 to 2012
1992 to 2001
1955 to 1991

of white, non-Hispanic voters by House district, and figure 8.6 shows the distribution of membership in the black, Hispanic, and Tea Party caucuses in the House of Representatives in the 113th Congress.

In the 113th Congress, the Blue Dog Democrats lost strength while the Tea Party caucus grew. These changes occurred in part because of reapportionment and redistricting following the 2010 US census (see chapter 2). After the 2010 census results were released and states began their redistricting efforts, the Tea Party entered redistricting debates at first to undermine gerrymandering efforts that protect incumbents. A district drawn specifically to protect an incumbent can protect the House member from competitive elections, and members of the Tea Party saw these plans as undermining democracy and in some cases entrenching the strength of the Democratic Party.

The Tea Party primarily employed lobbying campaigns to effect change in redistricting plans in key states. Republicans controlled eighteen states as they went through redistricting, and Democrats controlled six states (see figure 2.2). The Tea Party focused its lobbying efforts in these states along with those states in which legislative control of their two houses was split between the two parties, because some of the other states elect only one member of the House and other states entrust redistricting partly or fully to nonpartisan commissions. In states with Republican-dominated legislatures, Tea Party lobbying helped influence the districting process such that moderate Democrats were placed in more conservative, Republican-leaning districts. For example, in Pennsylvania the Tea Party lobbied during the redistricting process, and in 2012 the state had thirteen Republican seats won by an average of twenty-two points and five Democratic seats won by an average of fifty-three points. Thus, more than two-thirds of Pennsylvania's representatives elected in 2012 were Republicans, although Barack Obama carried the state easily at the presidential level.

The impact of this process is seen by examining the fate of the Blue Dogs. In the 111th Congress, elected in 2008, the Blue Dog Democrats had fifty-four members, after the 2010 election it had twenty-six, and in the 113th Congress it has fifteen members. Several Blue Dogs were defeated in the 2012 election, and others retired rather than face stiff Republican competition for their seats. With Tea Party–influenced redistricting leading up to the 2012 elections and a change in political climate in 2010, Blue Dogs lost members through competitive elections. It is difficult for moderate Democrats to win in states where redistricting packed Democrats into a few districts. The Democratic Congressional Campaign Committee recruited moderate candidates to run in 2006 and 2008, but in 2012 they focused on more liberal candidates for the few sure seats they had.

Another challenge for Blue Dog Democrats is the rise of the New Democrat Coalition, which has more than forty members and is fiscally conservative but socially liberal. Founded in 1997, two years after the Blue Dog Democrats, the New Democrat Coalition focuses on growing the American economy with particular attention to new technologies. New Democrats are geographically concentrated in the North and West, whereas remaining Blue Dog Democrats are primarily in the South.

Ten years prior, following the 2000 census, districts were reshaped to accommodate the Supreme Court's directives concerning the creation of majority-minority districts (that is, districts in which more than half of the population belongs to a minority group). The result has been an increase in the number of African American and Latino representatives. Many of these representatives represent urban areas, and many have been elected by large majorities with little or no major-party opposition. However, the concentration of urban Democrats in majority-minority districts provided opportunities for legislatures to spread their conservative and nonminority populations out in such a way as to win other, less urbanized districts by smaller margins, as in the case of Pennsylvania. In the case of the black and Hispanic caucuses, this is evident especially in the New York, Chicago, and Los Angeles metropolitan areas. On the other hand, most members of the Tea Party caucus represent rural or exurban areas, primarily in red states. Thus Figure 8.6 illustrates also that Tea Party activists were successful in electing their own supporters to the House, often at the expense of Blue Dog Democrats.

FIGURE 8.5

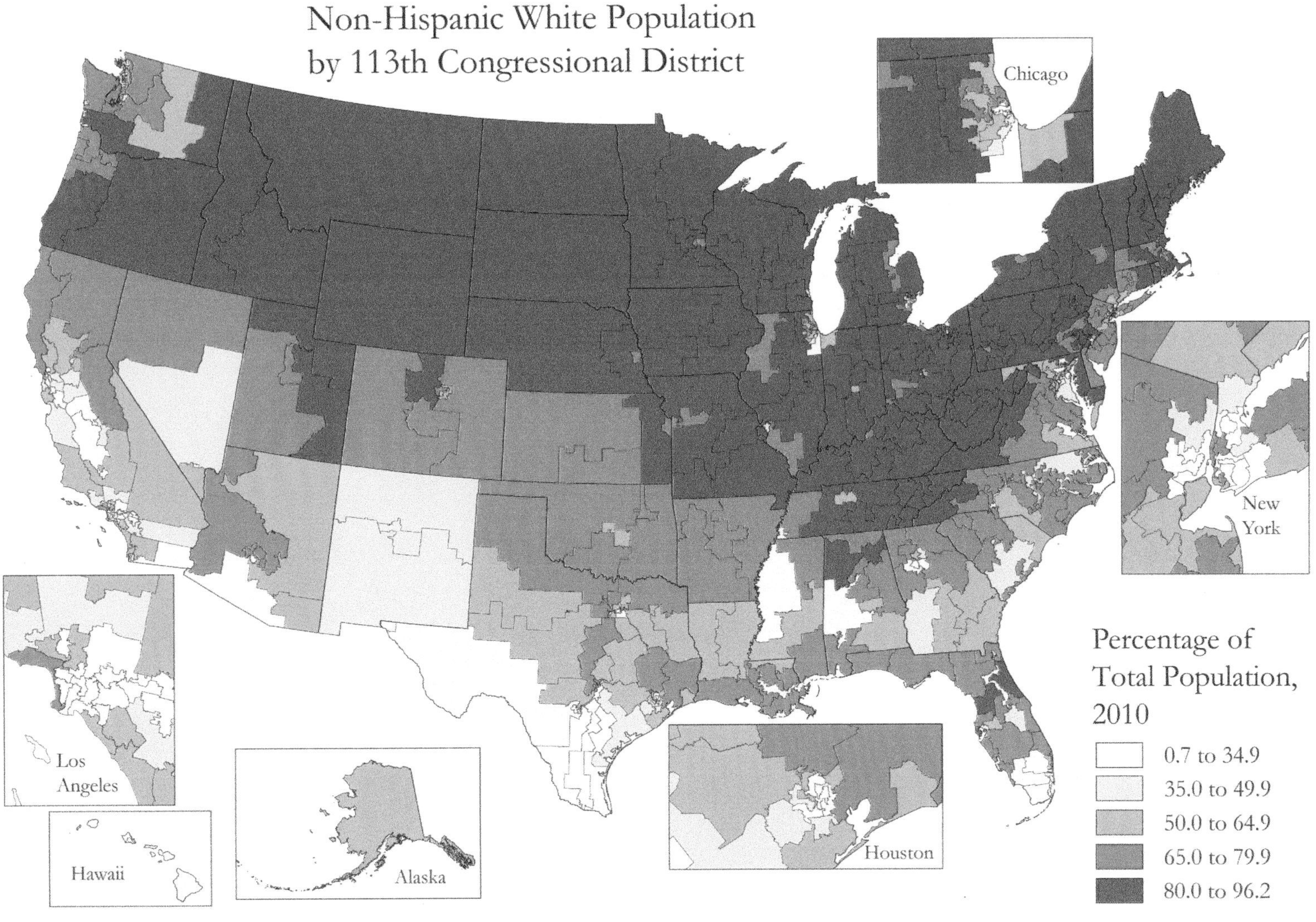
Non-Hispanic White Population
by 113th Congressional District
Chicago
New York
Los Angeles
Hawaii
Alaska
Houston
Percentage of
Total Population,
2010
0.7 to 34.9
35.0 to 49.9
50.0 to 64.9
65.0 to 79.9
80.0 to 96.2

FIGURE 8.6

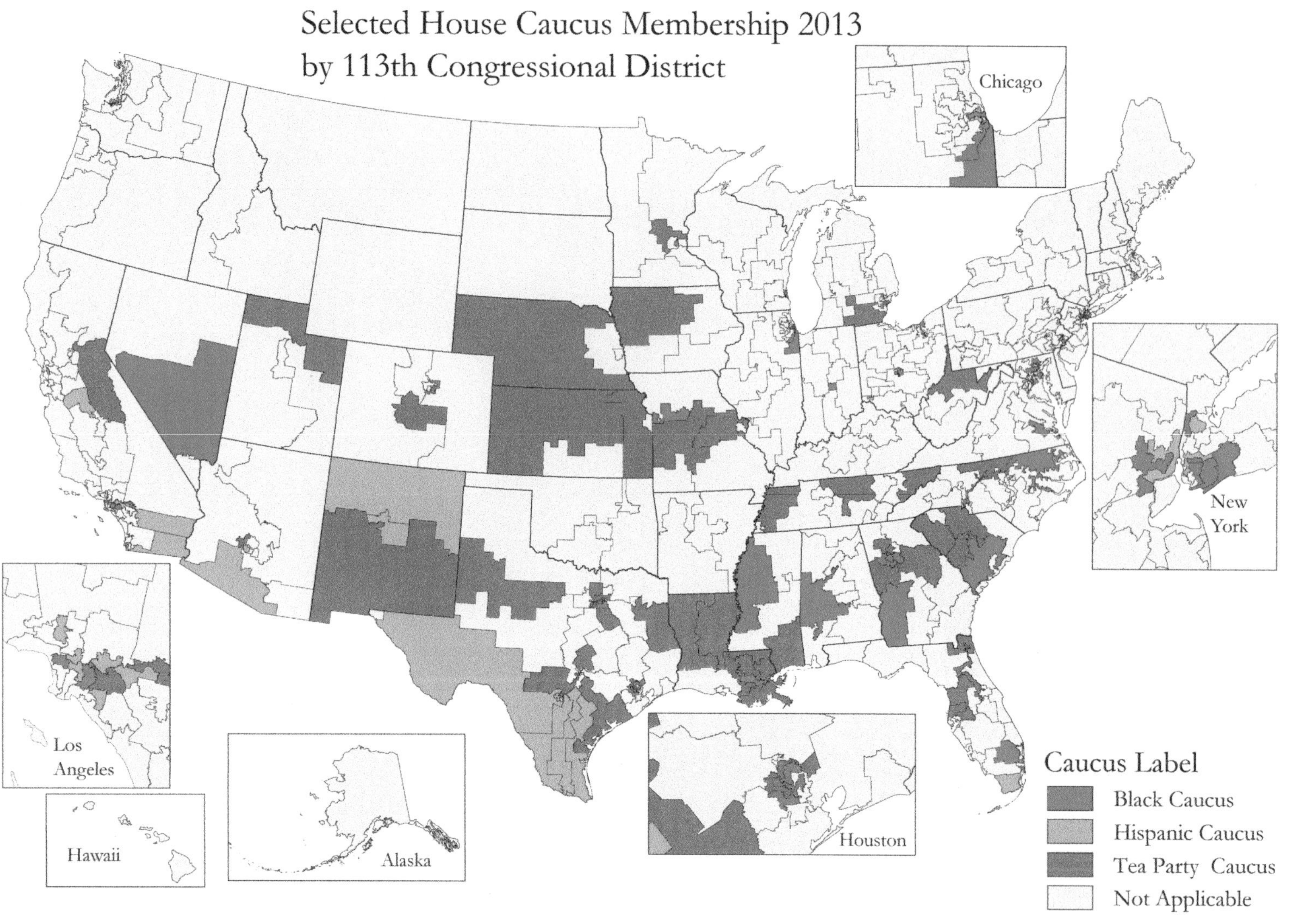

Selected House Caucus Membership 2013
by 113th Congressional District
Chicago
New
York
Los
Angeles
Hawaii
Alaska
Houston
Caucus Label
Black Caucus
Hispanic Caucus
Tea Party Caucus
Not Applicable

THE 2013 FARM BILL CONTROVERSY

ERIN H. FOUBERG

Every five years, Congress considers a farm bill that establishes policies regarding agriculture in the United States, including agricultural subsidies and government aid to provide food to poor and indigent persons. In 2008, Congress enacted a farm bill that was signed into law by President George W. Bush and that had a life span of five years. Thus, the provisions of the 2008 farm bill were set to expire in September 2013. Hence, a priority for the 113th Congress, which convened in January 2013, was to draft and enact a new farm bill.

However, the 113th Congress failed to pass a farm bill during its 2013 session. Fiscally conservative Republicans, including Tea Party members, sought to cut spending to support the Supplemental Nutrition Assistance Program (formerly known as food stamps) by $40 billion over a ten-year period. The House Agriculture Committee passed H.R. 1947, which incorporated $20.5 billion in cuts. However, the House voted 195 to 234 to reject the Agricultural Committee's bill, which by that time included additional spending reductions from floor amendments.

Focus on the Supplemental Nutrition Assistance Program (SNAP) is aimed at curbing state extension of assistance to able-bodied adults who qualify for aid. Some states allow able-bodied adults between the ages of eighteen and fifty to receive SNAP aid for only three months during a thirty-six-month period, but forty-five states and the District of Columbia employ full or partial waivers on these limitations. Supporters of H.R. 1947 were seeking to save money on SNAP by imposing limits on the length of time able-bodied adults can qualify by eliminating state waivers. H.R. 1947 also included provisions to allow states to drug test and to impose work requirements on people who do qualify for supplemental nutrition.

Another approach to cutting costs in the farm bill is to means-test farmers who receive federal support. Means tests either limit the total support to a per capita amount or limit federal support for farmers with annual incomes over a certain amount. Democratic representative Ron Kind (Wisconsin) proposed legislation requiring the means-testing of farmers in order to receive federal crop insurance and subsidies. The package of proposals did not make it past the House, with a close vote of 208 to 217.

The distribution of votes in favor of H.R. 1947 tends to be agricultural versus urban regions of the country (figure 8.7). In urban areas, the vote against the farm bill was likely based on opposition to cuts in the Supplemental Nutrition Assistance Program. In agricultural areas, the vote in favor of the farm bill was in response to importance of crop and livestock producers' knowledge of what to expect from the government in order to plan production.

After H.R. 1947 failed, another bill was submitted for consideration. This new bill, H.R. 2642, included eleven of the twelve titles in H.R. 1947 along with sixty floor amendments made to H.R. 1947 but removed the nutrition title. Unlike H.R. 1947, H.R. 2642 was passed by the House (figure 8.8). Many of the differences between the two votes involved representatives who represent districts associated with the major controversies associated with the first bill. This legislation moved forward to a conference committee with the US Senate, which passed a farm bill in June 2013 with bipartisan support by a vote of 66 to 27. The conference committee reconciles the House and Senate bills and moves a farm bill forward to both bodies once an agreement is reached.

FIGURE 8.7

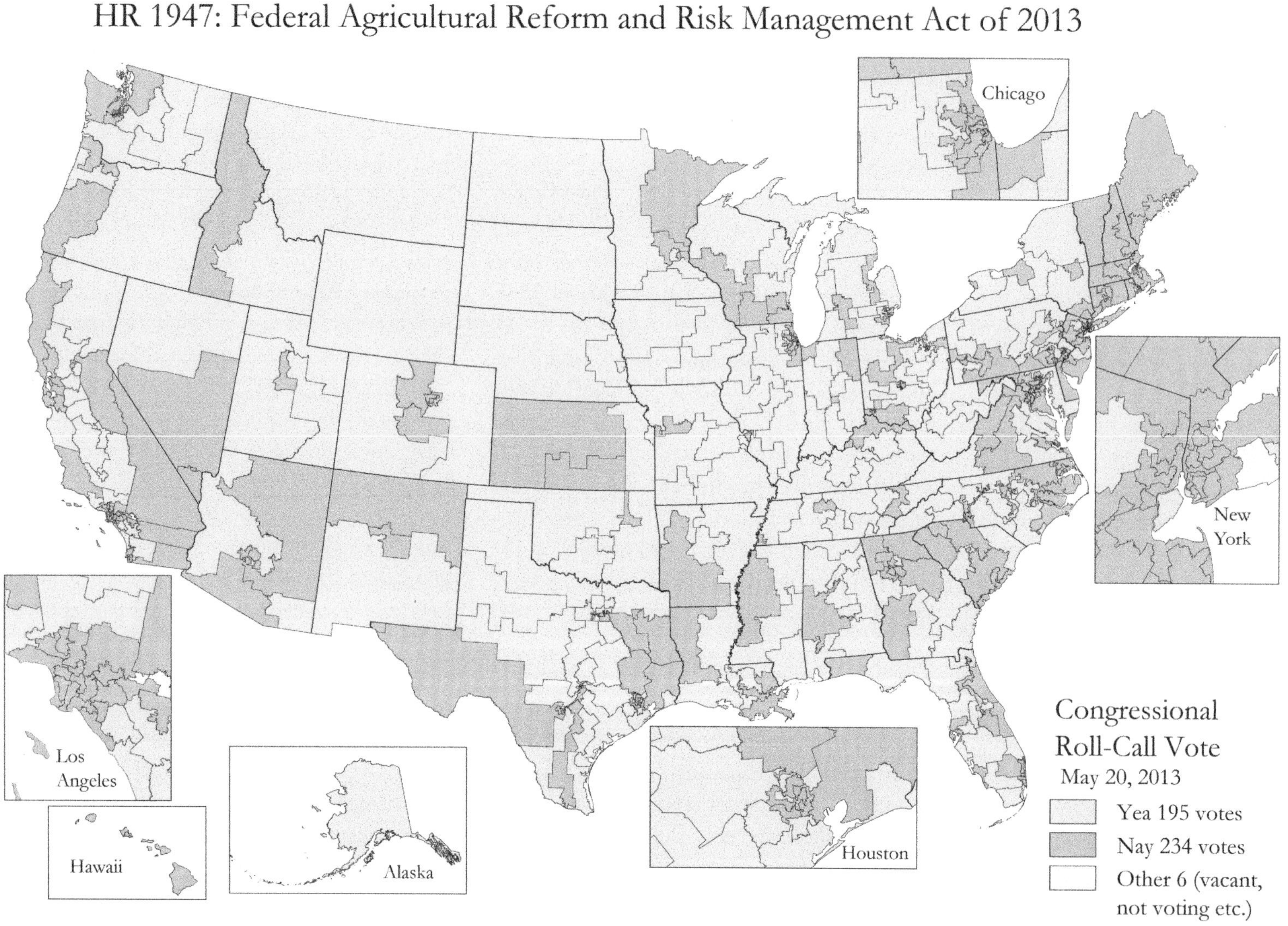

HR 1947: Federal Agricultural Reform and Risk Management Act of 2013

Chicago

New York

Los Angeles

Hawaii

Alaska

Houston

Congressional Roll-Call Vote

May 20, 2013

Yea 195 votes

Nay 234 votes

Other 6 (vacant, not voting etc.)

FIGURE 8.8

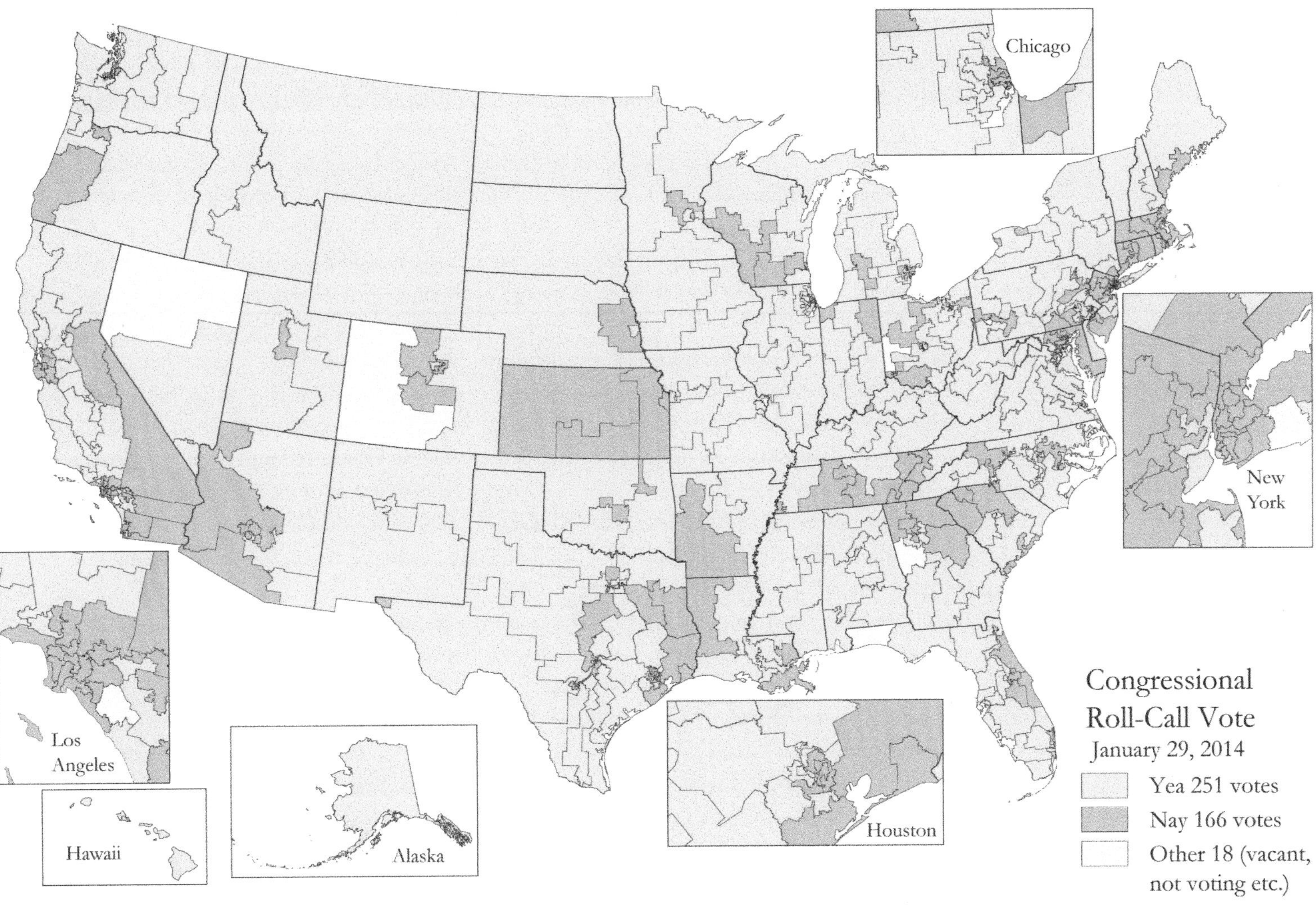
HR 2642: Agricultural Act of 2014
Chicago
New
York
Los
Angeles
Hawaii
Alaska
Houston
Congressional
Roll-Call Vote
January 29, 2014
Yea 251 votes
Nay 166 votes
Other 18 (vacant,
not voting etc.)

OTHER VOTES IN THE 113TH HOUSE OF REPRESENTATIVES

ERIN H. FOUBERG

In addition to the farm bill controversy, the House of Representatives considered several other bills of great national importance. Many of these bills are associated with the various issues described in the other sections of this chapter.

On June 14, 2013, the House passed the National Defense Authorization Act (H.R. 1960) with 315 voting yes and 108 voting no. The National Defense Authorization Act authorized $552.1 billion for defense and $80.7 billion for operations overseas and includes a 1 percent pay raise for troops, provisions regarding Guantanamo Bay, and provisions aimed at curbing sexual assault and rape within the armed services. An overwhelming majority of Republicans, 212 of 230 voting, voted for the bill, while the Democratic Party was more evenly split. 103 Democrats voted for the act, and 90 voted against it (figure 8.9). Opposition shown on this map likely reflected a "protest" against this version of the bill and a desire for certain amendments important to their constituencies to be passed.

The final act, H.R. 3304, was based on H.R. 1960 and a Senate bill that did not receive a full vote of the Senate. H.R. 3304 passed the House by a voice vote in October 2013 and passed the Senate by unanimous consent in November 2013. The legislative bodies agreed to amendments, and the final National Defense Authorization Act for fiscal year 2014 was signed into law by President Obama on December 26, 2013.

As the earlier section of this chapter by Sara McLafferty makes clear, health care was a major issue in the election. Congress passed the Affordable Health Care Act in 2010 over the near-unanimous objection of Republicans in the House. Republicans made this a campaign issue, and the 113th Congress focused on delaying, repealing, or defunding the act before it took effect in 2014.

Every member of the Tea Party caucus voted yes on House Resolution 300, a "Resolution to Delay Individual Health Insurance Mandate," on July 17, 2013. Not only did every Tea Party member vote to delay the implementation of the Affordable Health Care Act, so, too, did all 228 Republicans who voted on the measure. On the other hand, 183 of 187 Democrats who voted cast a "no" ballot. Note the relationship between figure 8.10, which shows the distribution of votes on House Resolution 300, and figures 8.2 and 8.3 that show the partisan distribution of seats.

At the time of the government shutdown, Congress had not passed a budget since April 2009 (Khimm 2011), and as a result had to pass continuing resolutions to fund the federal government and programs. Conservative Republicans in the House sought to have the 2010 Affordable Health Care Act defunded before the law rolled out in 2014. To accomplish their goal, House Republicans made passage of continuing resolutions contingent on defunding the Affordable Health Care Act. Although the House voted several times in September on continuing resolutions, the Republican-controlled House did not pass the necessary continuing resolutions, and the federal government shut down on October 1, 2013.

On October 16, 2013, members of the House of Representatives voted on the Continuing Appropriations Act of 2014, which reopened the federal government after brinkmanship led to its closure on October 1, 2013. The distribution of the votes correlates well with the distribution of Republican and Democratic members of the House. The vote was partisan. All 198 Democrats present voted in favor of the act. The Republicans, on the other hand, were split, with 87 voting yes and 144 voting no. The distribution of votes is shown

FIGURE 8.9

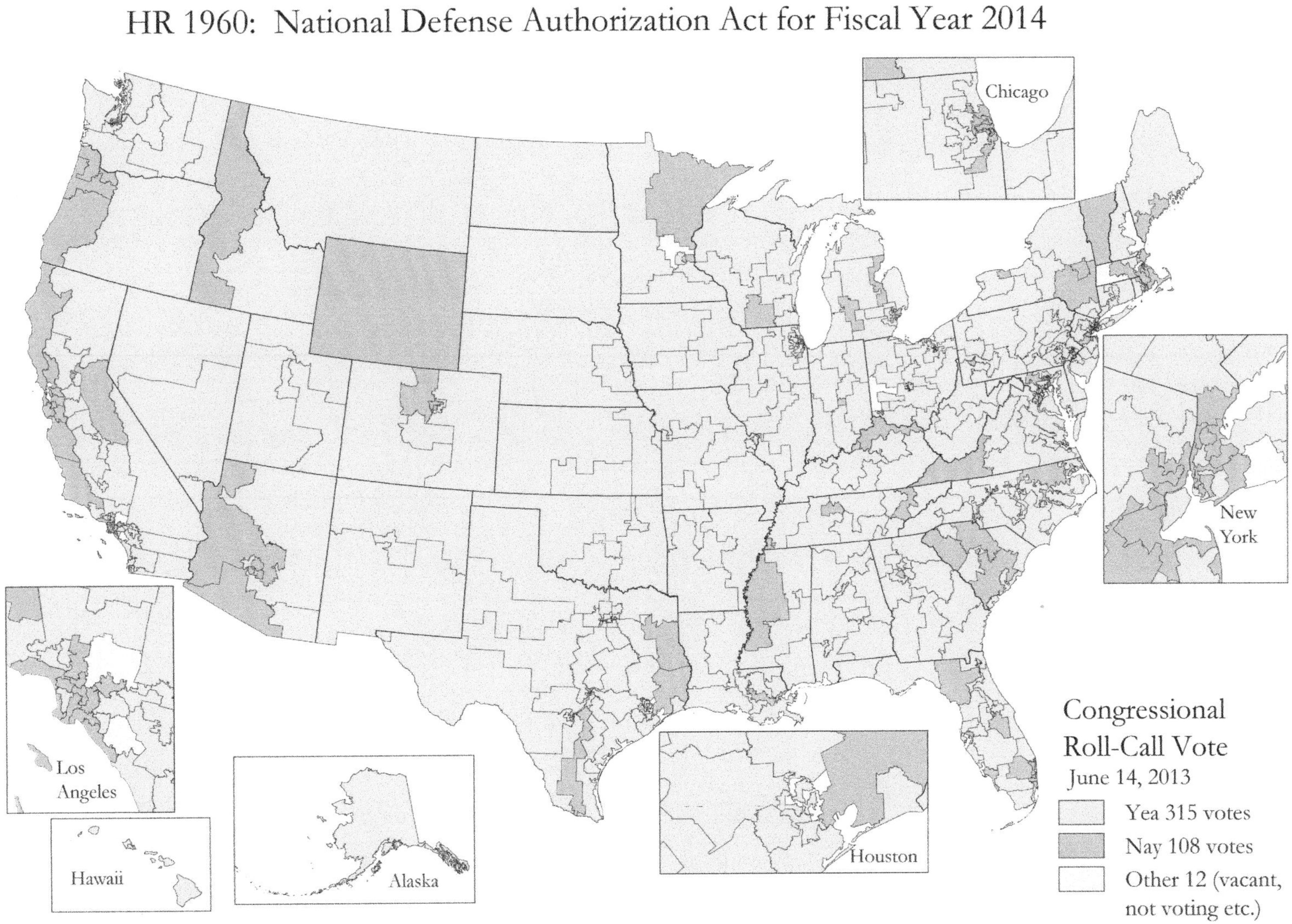

HR 1960: National Defense Authorization Act for Fiscal Year 2014

Chicago

New York

Los Angeles

Hawaii

Alaska

Houston

Congressional Roll-Call Vote
June 14, 2013

Yea 315 votes

Nay 108 votes

Other 12 (vacant, not voting etc.)

FIGURE 8.10

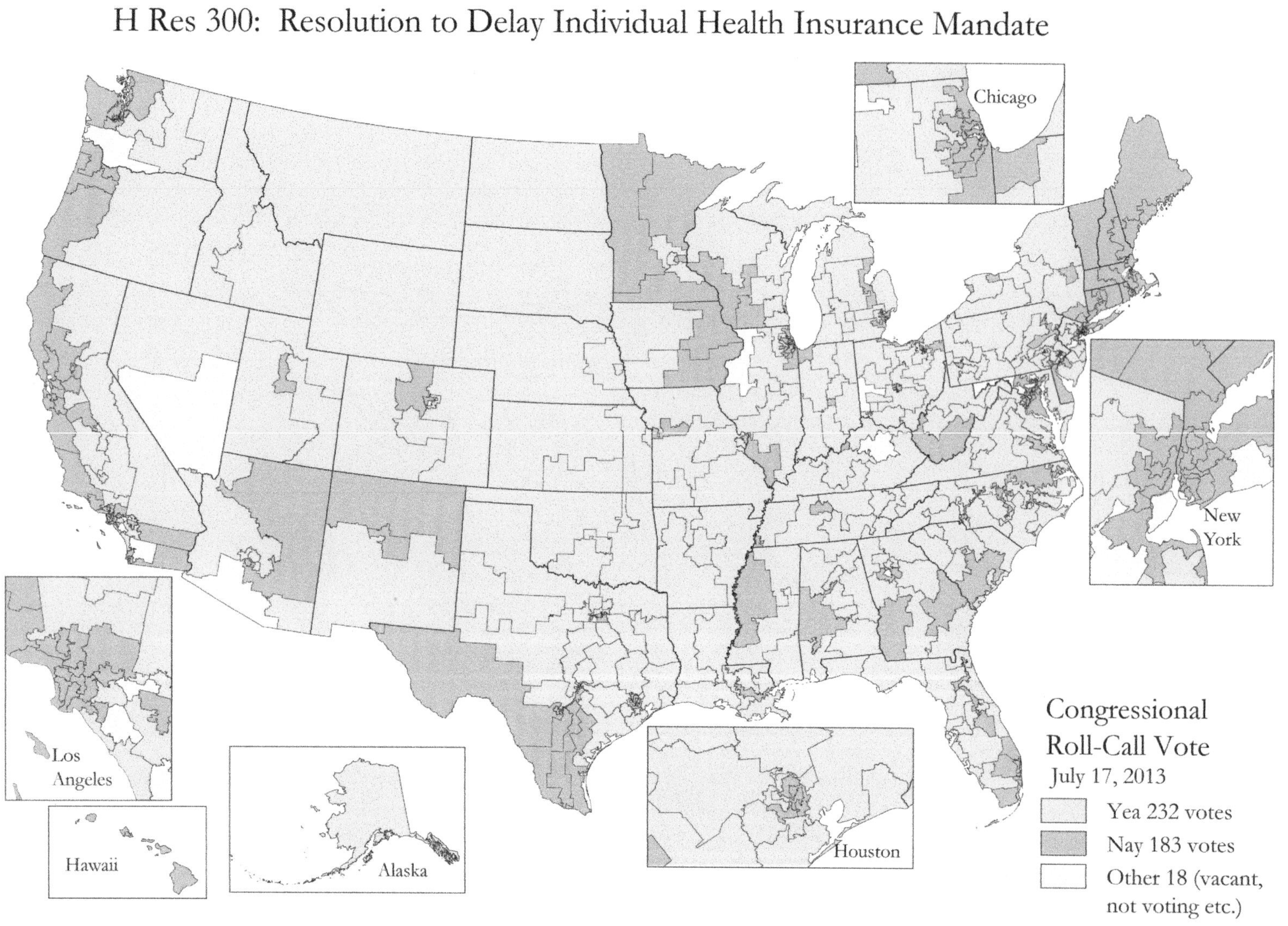

H Res 300: Resolution to Delay Individual Health Insurance Mandate

in figure 8.11. In effect, it can be viewed as a map of splits within the Republican caucus analogous to splits within the Democratic caucus on the National Defense Authorization Act, as shown in figure 8.9. The vast majority of Tea Party caucus members voted against the Continuing Appropriations Act, but more moderate Republicans, especially many representing more urban and suburban districts with higher percentages of votes for Obama at the presidential level, supported the Continuing Appropriations Act.

REFERENCE

Khimm, Suzy. 2011. "Will Republicans' Budget-Cutting Mania Hurt Them in 2012?" *Mother Jones*, March 22, 2011, http://www.motherjones.com/2011/03/will-republicans-budget-cutting-mania-hurt-them-2012.

FIGURE 8.11

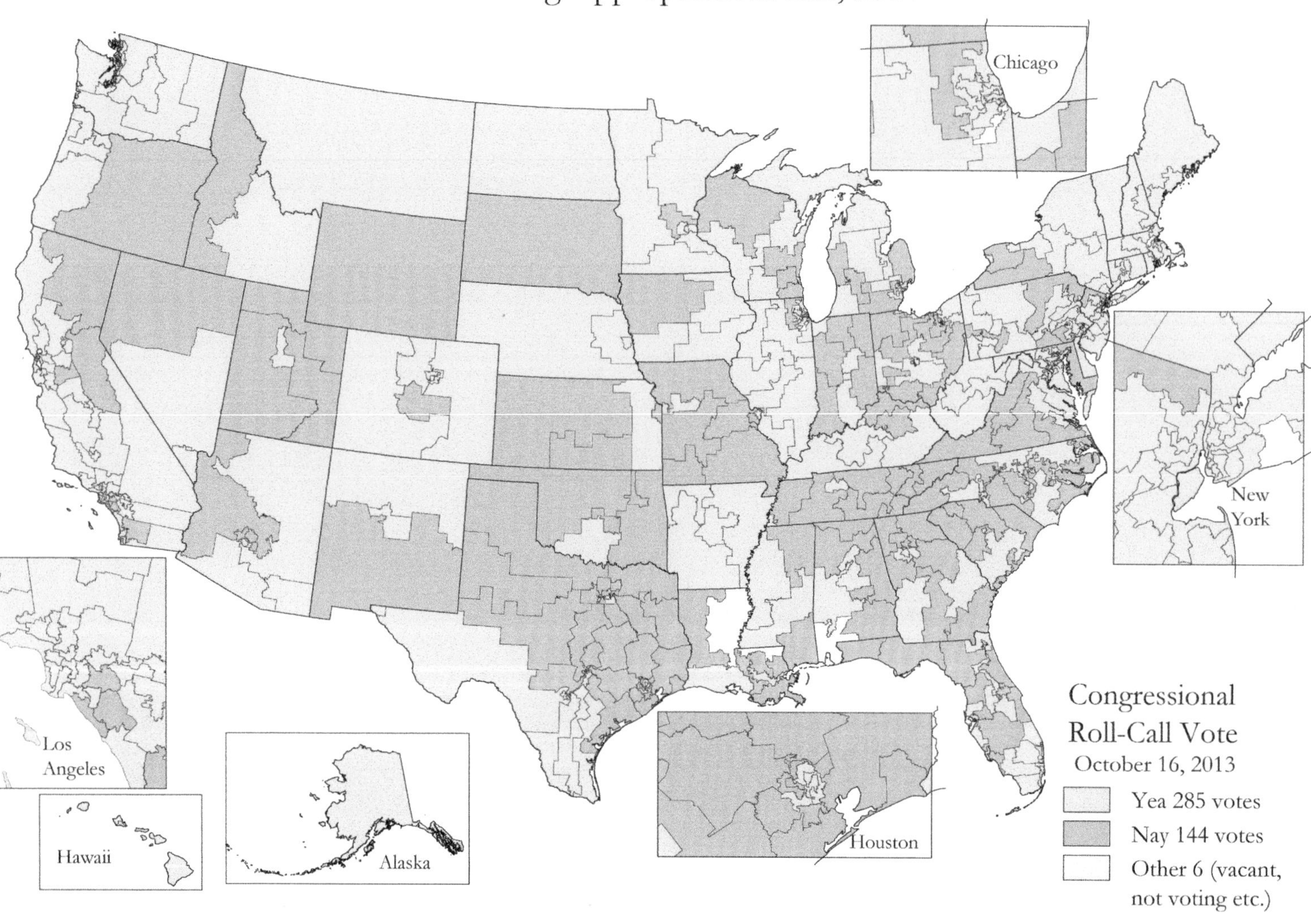
HR 2775: Continuing Appropriations Act, 2014
Chicago
New
York
Los
Angeles
Hawaii
Alaska
Houston
Congressional
Roll-Call Vote
October 16, 2013
Yea 285 votes
Nay 144 votes
Other 6 (vacant,
not voting etc.)

CHAPTER NINE

STATE AND LOCAL ELECTIONS

PERSISTENCE AND CHANGE IN STATE AND LOCAL ELECTIONS

RICHARD L. MORRILL

Although most of the media and voter attention in the 2012 campaign focused on the presidential election, ballots throughout the country included contests for the US Senate and House of Representatives, state governors, and other state and local officials. Some of these elections had very important impacts on the national political landscape and may be significant in the future of American politics. In this section we look at the outcomes of some important and closely contested races for these state and local offices.

In the Senate, thirty-three seats were at stake, twenty-one held by Democrats, ten by Republicans, and two by independents. Although the Democrats had to defend two-thirds of the contested seats because of their success in the off-year 2006 election, the Senate results proved to be more favorable to them than did governorships or the House of Representatives. Democratic incumbents were reelected in fifteen states, and they held onto five seats from which incumbent Democratic senators retired. One Democratic seat shifted to the Republicans when Ben Nelson of Nebraska was replaced by Deb Fischer.

Five Republican incumbents were reelected, and two retiring Republicans were replaced by new Republican senators. Republican seats shifted to the Democrats in Indiana and Massachusetts. The tenth Republican, Olympia Snowe of Maine, retired and was replaced by independent Angus King. Of the two independents, Bernie Sanders of Vermont was reelected while Joseph Lieberman of Connecticut retired and was replaced by Democrat Chris Murphy. Thus, the Democrats experienced a net gain of two Senate seats, while King and Sanders caucus with the Democrats. Very likely, Democrats won seats in Indiana and Missouri that they might otherwise have lost when the Republicans nominated very conservative candidates who held extreme views on rape and pregnancy. The sections by Annika Hagley and Joshua Dyck on Massachusetts, John Wertman on Virginia, Steven Radil on Indiana, Kenneth French on Wisconsin, and Richard Morrill and Larry Knopp on Montana provide more details about some of the most significant Senate races in 2012.

The large majority of states hold gubernatorial elections in nonpresidential election years. In 2012, only twelve states held gubernatorial elections. Of these, New Hampshire and Vermont elected governors for two-year terms, and the others elected them for four-year terms (figure 9.1) Eight Democratic governorships and four Republican governorships were at stake. Of the eight Democratic seats, incumbent Democratic governors were reelected in Delaware, Missouri, Vermont, and West Virginia, and three other Democrats who left office were replaced by other Democrats in Montana, New Hampshire, and Washington. Only in North Carolina, in which Patrick McCrory defeated incumbent Beverly Perdue, did the Republicans win a governorship held previously by a Democrat. Republican governors were reelected in North Dakota and Utah, and in Indiana, Republican Mike Spence won the seat held by retiring Republican Mitch Daniels. In Wisconsin, an effort to recall Republican governor Scott Walker was unsuccessful, as discussed in detail in the section by Ryan Weichelt. Thus, overall, Republicans picked up one governorship.

Forty-nine of the fifty states (all but Nebraska) have bicameral legislatures. Of these, after the 2012 election Republicans control both houses in twenty-six states and Democrats control both houses in nineteen states. Each party controls one house in Iowa, Kentucky, New Hampshire, and Virginia. Generally, Republicans do as well at the state legislative level as they do at the House of Representatives level, and for the same reasons: concentration of Democrats in central cities and other small areas and gerrymandered redistricting. However, the pattern of change before and after the 2012 elections was somewhat favorable to the Democrats.

Figure 9.2 shows the somewhat complex pattern of change. States shaded in gray had little or no change or did not have legislative elections in 2012. Red and blue shadings represent Republican and Democratic gains, respectively. West Virginia was the only state with a Democratic legislature but large Republican gain. However, Arizona, Florida, and Montana had Republican legislatures but sizable Democratic gains. Republican-controlled Kansas, Michigan, Pennsylvania, and Texas had experienced small Democratic gains. In Texas, Democratic state senator Wendy Davis contributed to her party's gain by holding onto a Republican-leaning seat in the Fort Worth area in which President Obama won only about 45 percent of the popular vote. In 2013, Davis became a national figure by filibustering against an attempt by the Republican leadership to pass a bill imposing severe restrictions on abortion in the state. Davis's reelection victory is described in more detail in the section by Brooks Heitmeier.

States with Republican legislatures and higher Republican gains were Indiana, North Carolina, and Tennessee, with smaller gains in eight other states. States with Democratic legislatures and larger Democratic gains were in Illinois, Colorado, Maine, Massachusetts, Minnesota, and Oregon, with smaller gains in five more states. Missouri and South Dakota were Republican states, and New Mexico, a Democratic state with mixed results (gain in one, loss in the other) in legislative outcomes. Kentucky had a divided legislature with Republican gains, and New Hampshire has a divided legislature with moderately higher Democratic gains.

The region of most consistent change appears to be Appalachia and states bordering this region, including Indiana, West Virginia, Kentucky, Tennessee, and North Carolina. Here Republicans gained legislative seats consistently. In the southern borderlines from California through Arizona, New Mexico, Texas, and skipping over to Florida, Democrats gained consistently. These gains coincided with Democrats' share of the increasing Hispanic vote.

FIGURE 9.1

Persistence and Change for Gubernatorial and U.S. Senatorial Elections by State, 2012

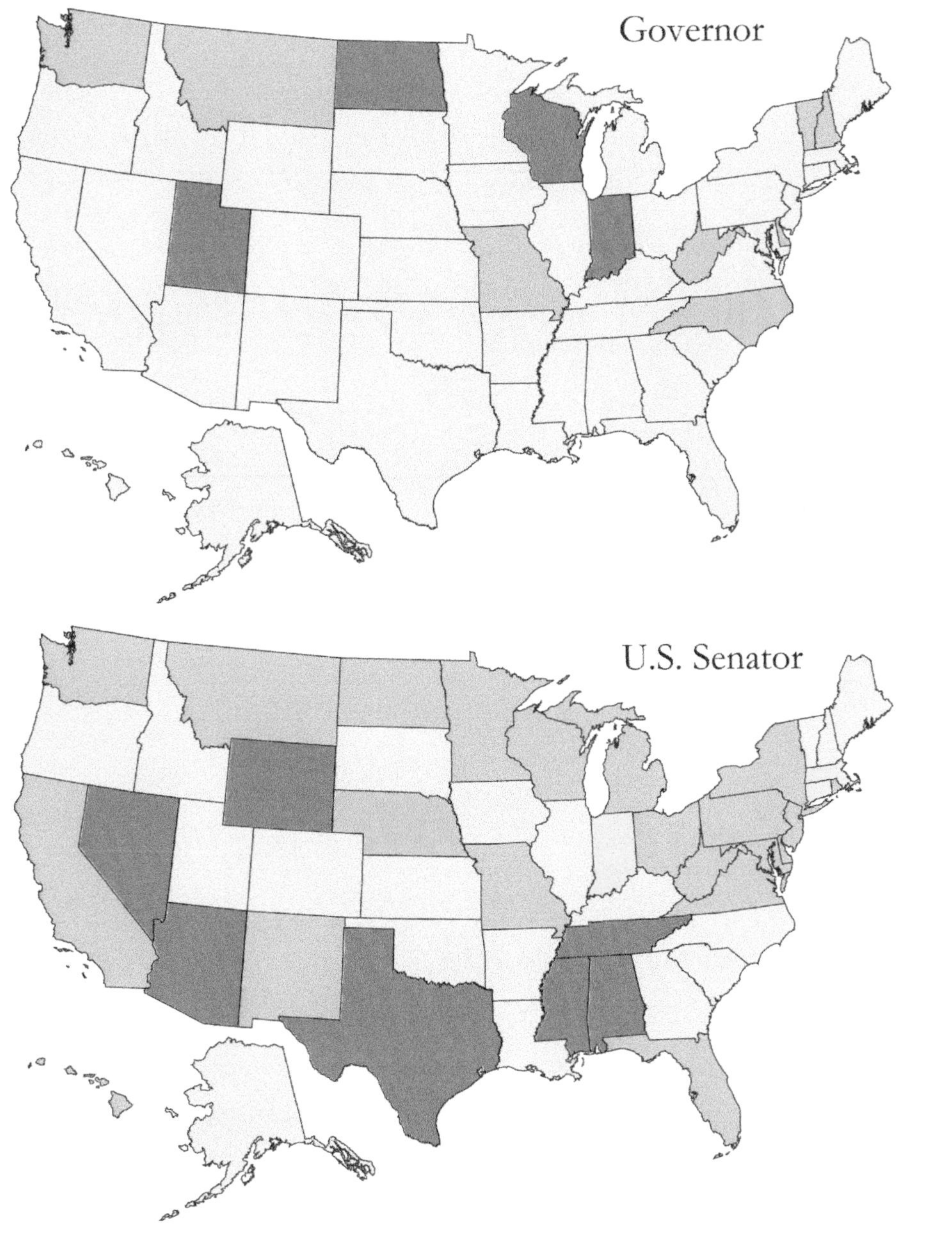

Democrat Continues
Republican Continues
Change from Republican to Democrat
Change from Democrat to Republiican
No Election

FIGURE 9.2

Persistence and Change for State Legislative Elections, by State, 2012

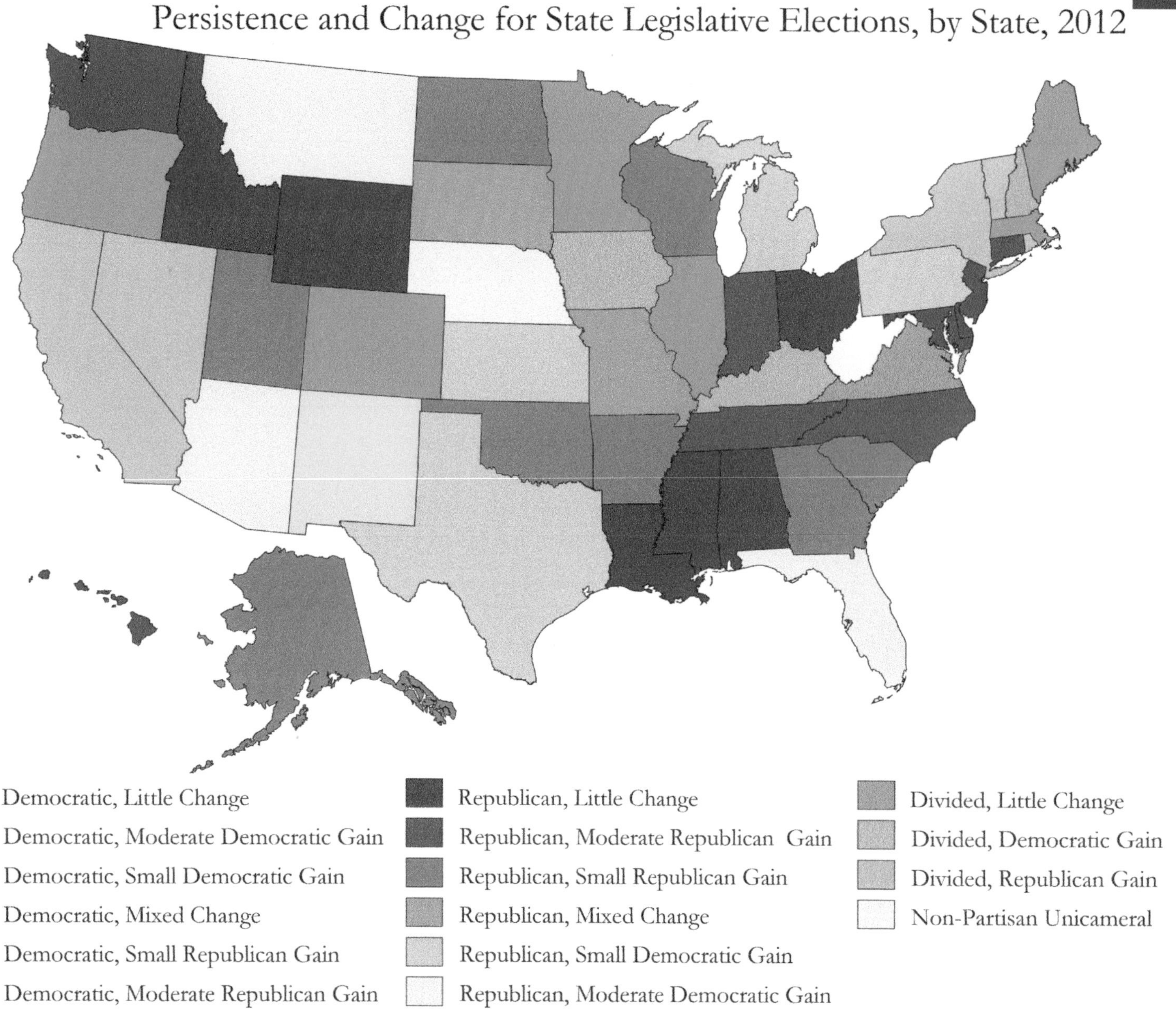

A TALE OF TURNOUT: THE RISE AND FALL OF SCOTT BROWN IN MASSACHUSETTS

ANNIKA HAGLEY AND JOSHUA J. DYCK

Senator Ted Kennedy of Massachusetts died on August 25, 2009, after having served in the US Senate for nearly forty-seven years. After Kennedy's death, Governor Deval Patrick appointed Paul Kirk, a former chair of the Democratic National Committee, to replace Kennedy until a special election could be held to fill the remaining two years of Kennedy's term. Patrick then called the special election for January 19, 2010.

At the start of the Massachusetts Senate special election campaign, nobody expected the shock victory of little-known Republican state senator Scott Brown. The result was one of the biggest political upsets that the Democratic Party had ever faced and evidence that Massachusetts voters had somewhat bought into the anti-Washington fervor that was sweeping the country. The Tea Party Patriots were early to recognize and tap into the dissatisfaction that voters were feeling over the lackluster performance of the economy and President Obama's Affordable Health Care Act and quickly announced their support for several unlikely outsiders in key races across the country.

So, in the midst of what Ted Kennedy might have considered the greatest policy accomplishment of his life (the passage of the Affordable Care Act), how did a Republican win the seat he vacated when he passed away on August 25, 2009? Scott Brown undoubtedly capitalized on the support of the Tea Party as well as the several missteps in campaigning made by his Democratic opponent, State Attorney General Martha Coakley. The Democrats were also complacent and resting their laurels on a misplaced sense of security they felt about easily retaining the seat of one of the longest-serving and most liberal members of the Senate. That Brown managed to pull off such a seemingly unbelievable victory was a body blow to the Democrats, the president himself, and Massachusetts Democrats, who, in the following days and weeks, retreated to lick their wounds as Senator-elect Brown garnered national media attention and Republicans demanded he be seated in time to vote on the Affordable Health Care Act.

In the aftermath of the election, the media and Massachusetts voters had plenty to say about how Brown had managed to pull off his stunning upset, and the focus narrowed to three main explanations: (1) that Coakley had been an ineffective campaigner—distant from the "masses" and engaged in backroom politics as opposed to campaigning; (2) the influence of the Tea Party—its support had allowed Brown to capitalize financially, in terms of both name recognition, and, in the weeks running up to the final vote, his ability to amass millions in donations from within the commonwealth of Massachusetts and the rest of the country; (3) that the special election had in some way been a referendum on the first months of the Obama presidency, specifically with regard to his Affordable Health Care Act. The common interpretation in play suggested that the president's mandate did not have the popular support of the nation that had voted him easily into office fourteen months previously. It was assumed to be the culmination of these three factors that allowed Brown to walk away with 52 percent of the vote, five percentage points clear of his rival Coakley, in one of the most reliably Democratic states in the country.

Two years after his election victory, Brown ran for election to a full six-year term. However, he was defeated by Democrat Elizabeth Warren in the 2012 general election, despite most polls showing him with an approval rating of well over 50 percent. Warren was a much more popular and effective campaigner than Coakley had been. As a Harvard professor and consumer advocate, she had become a beacon of hope for the Democrats who was supported by the liberal intellectual community in Massachusetts as well as liberals around the country.

To add to Brown's problems, the influence of the Tea Party machine had died down in national politics and the antigovernment feelings of voters had tempered over time. Finally, President Obama was reelected at the same time, increasing the coattail effect in the traditionally blue state of Massachusetts and restoring the balance in turnout that allowed Warren to prevail. Warren defeated Brown by eight percentage points, cruising to an easy victory and restoring an ideological liberal to a Senate seat that, before Brown, had been occupied exclusively by Democrats since 1952. Much of the punditry following the election focused on the failings of Brown and the organized nature and effectiveness of Warren's ground operation. The media sought to compare 2010 to 2012 and tell the story of Warren's win through the same analytical lens that they had applied to the race in 2010. Despite the anecdotal evidence coming from the media and both sides of the campaign, it is true that much of the story of this election can be understood through the theory of surge and decline, articulated originally by Angus Campbell (1960) and by examining some telling geographic trends.

James E. Campbell's 1987 "Revised Theory of Surge and Decline" posits that on-year election surges tend to be disproportionately made up of a one-sided partisan surge; whichever candidate the political environment favors. We now know that the political environment in 2012 favored President Obama's reelection over Republican challenger Mitt Romney. An electoral environment stacked toward the Democratic Party presented a complicated challenge for a Republican candidate in the state of Massachusetts, where registered Democrats outnumber registered Republicans more than two to one.

The maps that accompany this article show two frames of town-by-town voting trends in Massachusetts. In figure 9.3, we present a choropleth map of where Brown's support was strongest in 2012, looking simply at the percentage of votes for Scott Brown. Figure 9.4 shows the change in turnout by town between the 2010 special election and the 2012 general election. The towns where Brown was the weakest in 2010 showed the greatest gains in turnout in 2012, pointing toward two voting trends.

Brown's 2010 campaign was helped by an unexpected Republican turnout surge in support of his candidacy in the special election of 2010; this trend outpaced any gains in Democratic strongholds. However, in 2012, the top-of-the-ticket effects, along with the nationalization of the Senate campaign, appear to have pushed turnout higher in places with fewer Brown voters. Brown did not lose because he lost the support of voters who supported him in 2010; he lost because of a fundamentally different electorate. The theory of surge and decline means we normally expect a surge of partisans who turn out to support the winning presidential candidate; in Massachusetts in 2012, this turnout surge was exacerbated to such an extent that a moderate senator, who campaigned as an independent voice for Massachusetts voters and had won by a considerable margin two years previously, was unable to even make his reelection race marginal. The maps clearly show that Scott Brown was a victim of the surge.

REFERENCES

Campbell, Angus. 1960. "Surge and Decline: A Study of Electoral Change." *Public Opinion Quarterly* 24:397–418.

Campbell, James E. 1987. "The Revised Theory of Surge and Decline." *American Journal of Political Science* 34:965–79.

FIGURE 9.3

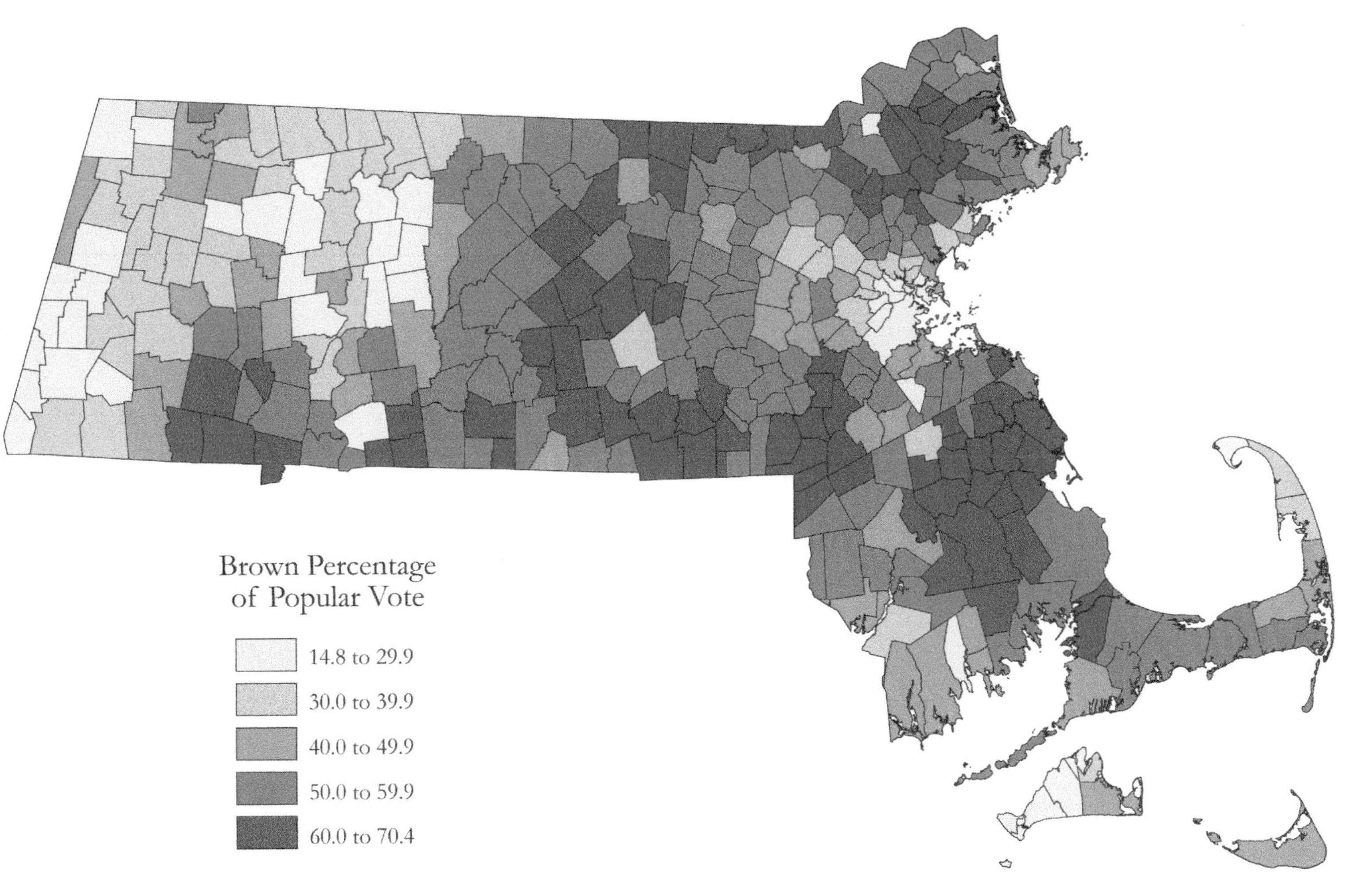
Republican Popular Vote
Massachusetts US Senate Election 2012
Brown Percentage
of Popular Vote
14.8 to 29.9
30.0 to 39.9
40.0 to 49.9
50.0 to 59.9
60.0 to 70.4

FIGURE 9.4

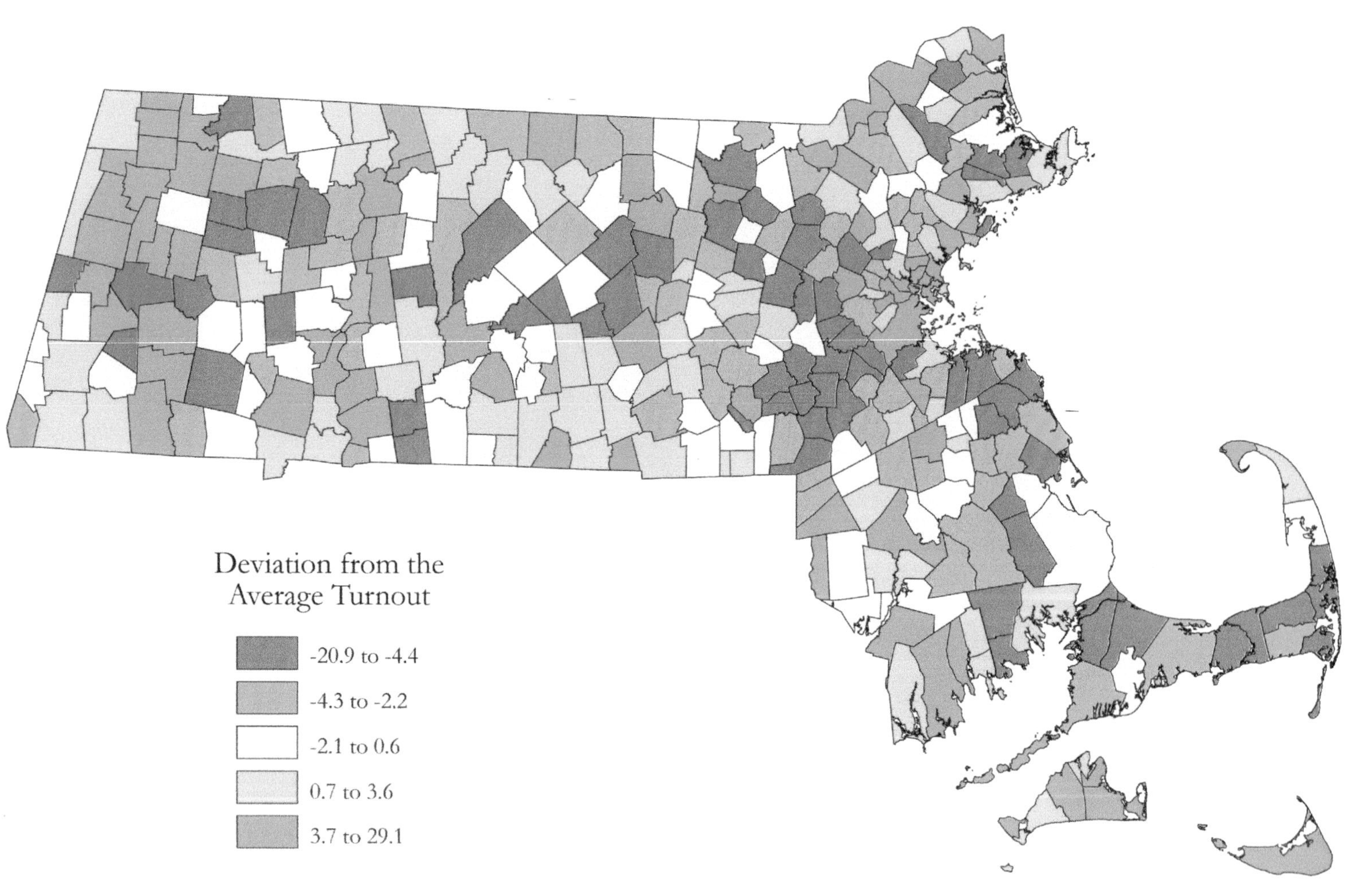

Deviation from the Average Turnout:
Massachusetts US Senate Election 2012
Deviation from the Average Turnout
-20.9 to -4.4
-4.3 to -2.2
-2.1 to 0.6
0.7 to 3.6
3.7 to 29.1

2012 VIRGINIA SENATE ELECTION

JOHN A. WERTMAN

The 2012 US Senate election in Virginia between Democrat Tim Kaine and Republican George Allen was one of the nation's most closely watched down-ballot races. Allen, a former senator and governor, was attempting to retake the seat that he had held from 2001 to 2007 and that he lost to Democrat James Webb in 2006 due in part to a racially insensitive remark he made during the campaign. Webb retired after just one term in office, and so the seat was open. Kaine, a former governor of the commonwealth, was aiming to follow his close friend Mark Warner as Democrats who held the governor's mansion in Richmond and then won election to the US Senate.

The contest was one of the most expensive Senate elections in the nation in 2012. Between them, Kaine and Allen spent over $12 million on the race, but that was just a fraction of the amount expended on the campaign by outside groups. According to the Center for Responsive Politics, more than $52 million in outside expenditures was aimed at the Kaine-Allen race, $28 million of which was used for negative campaigning against former governor Kaine. The race was also notable in that it played out in swing state Virginia, which was closely contested in the race for the White House.

The Kaine-Allen election was a perfect demonstration of how Virginia's politics have changed over the past dozen years. The battle between the two well-known political heavyweights shared many similarities with the state's 2000 Senate contest between Allen and then-senator Chuck Robb, a Democrat. Both races featured well-funded candidates with national political support on each side. Both races occurred down ballot from hotly contested presidential elections. And both races featured popular Virginians with near-universal name recognition who had won multiple elections prior to the Senate campaigns in question. But demographic changes that have occurred in Virginia, especially in the Washington suburbs, since Robb lost to Allen in 2000 were critical as Kaine won the hard-fought contest and was sworn in as senator in January 2013 (figure 9.5).

Virginia had been a reliable GOP state in federal elections going back several decades, and after Lyndon Johnson won the commonwealth's electoral votes in 1964, forty-four years passed until another Democrat won Virginia's electoral votes in 2008. In US Senate races in the state held during the 1978–2002 period, Republicans won seven of the nine contests. So what changed between 2000 and 2012 that shifted the political winds toward the Democratic Party?

A look at Virginia's demographics, particularly in suburban Washington, DC, counties, provides some answers. According to census data and estimates, Virginia's population grew from 7,078,515 in 2000 to 8,185,867 in 2012—growth of just over 1.1 million, or 15.64 percent. During this same time period, the population growth in Fairfax, Prince William, and Loudoun Counties alone was 456,751, or 32.16 percent.

The change in racial makeup in the three counties paints an even clearer picture. In 2000, Fairfax County was 64.4 percent white (not of Hispanic or Latino origin). By 2012, this figure had dropped by 11 percent. The comparable changes during the same time period are even more striking in Prince William (17.2 percent) and Loudoun (18.7 percent). In all three counties, whites have seen their share of the population decrease far more rapidly than in Virginia as a whole (6.1 percent decrease from 2000 to 2012). The key context to this demographic shift—as is widely accepted by now—is, of course, that minorities are much more likely to vote for Democrats than whites are.

So how, specifically, did these demographic changes affect Virginia balloting in

FIGURE 9.5

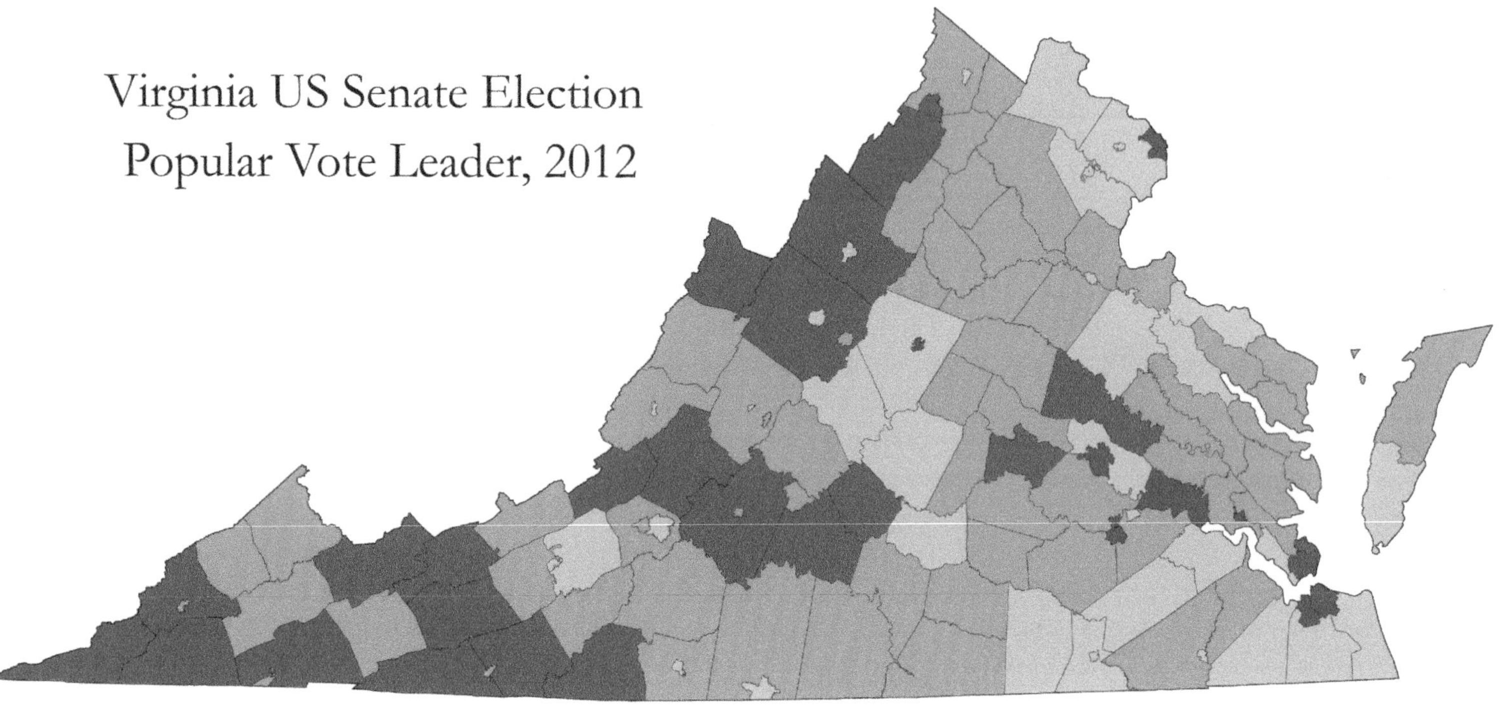

Virginia US Senate Election
Popular Vote Leader, 2012

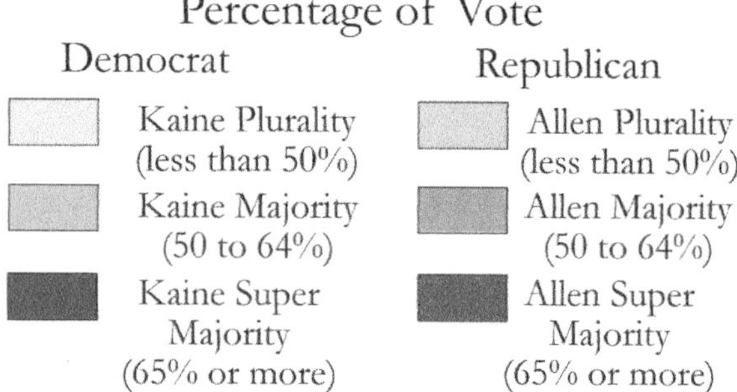

Percentage of Vote
Democrat
Republican
Kaine Plurality (less than 50%)
Allen Plurality (less than 50%)
Kaine Majority (50 to 64%)
Allen Majority (50 to 64%)
Kaine Super Majority (65% or more)
Allen Super Majority (65% or more)

2012 versus 2000? In comparing the two Senate races, the Democratic share of the two-party vote increased by 9.34 percent in Fairfax, 10.31 percent in Loudoun, and 11.86 percent in Prince William. All told, Tim Kaine received 215,794 more votes in the three counties in 2012 than Chuck Robb did in 2000. That figure was a huge factor in turning Robb's statewide loss by 124,367 votes in 2000 into Kaine's win by 224,536 votes in 2012. The Democrat also benefitted from an increased share of the vote in farther-out Stafford and Fauquier Counties, but the numbers in Fairfax, Prince William, and Loudoun were much more critical to Kaine's win.

Despite Kaine's victory and the changing demographics in Virginia it highlights, the commonwealth is by no means a solidly Democratic state as of 2013. Republican Bob McDonnell won the 2009 gubernatorial election by 17.36 percent, and the GOP controls the hundred-member House of Delegates by an overwhelming 67–31 margin (with one GOP-leaning Independent and one vacancy). The 2013 gubernatorial race featured Republican Ken Cuccinelli against Democrat Terry McAuliffe, and McAuliffe's victory provided additional clues about the state's electoral trends. Regardless, however, Virginia figures to remain a swing state for at least the next several election cycles, with the two major parties fighting for each opportunity for a win.

2012 INDIANA SENATE ELECTION

STEVEN RADIL

Unlike 2008, Indiana was not a swing state in the 2012 presidential election. Barack Obama managed to carry Indiana by a narrow 1 percent margin in 2008, but Indiana's voters returned to their historical form in 2012 as Mitt Romney carried the state by just over 10 percent of the total popular vote. This return to form made Indiana notable as it was one of only two states (along with North Carolina) that were won by Obama in 2008 but returned to the GOP in 2012.

Although Indiana was not contested seriously by the Obama campaign, the state was nonetheless seen as important by both parties as Democrats strove to maintain control of the Senate. Senator Richard Lugar, a Republican who had represented Indiana in the US Senate since 1977, had been upset in a primary contest with State Treasurer Richard Mourdock. Lugar, widely regarded as a foreign policy expert and as a moderate on social issues, faced a withering critique by Mourdock as too worldly to be concerned with the plight of Hoosiers and as far too moderate on social issues. Mourdock contrasted himself as a committed social and fiscal conservative. With the support of numerous state and national Tea Party–affiliated groups, he managed to secure the nomination with 60 percent of the primary vote. What had been seen as a secure seat for the Republicans was now up for grabs after Lugar's primary defeat. The contest became a focal point for both parties and various political action groups. Millions of dollars in outside money poured into the state, and the race was closely followed given the Democrats' narrow majority in the Senate.

In the general election, Mourdock faced Representative Joseph Donnelly. Donnelly, who had announced his intention to run for the seat before Lugar's primary defeat, was polling behind Mourdock until a debate between the candidates held just two weeks before the election. During the debate, Mourdock responded to a series of questions about abortion by stating that "even when life begins in that horrible situation of rape, that it is something God intended to happen." Mourdock's comments drew immediate and sustained attention from national media and were roundly criticized from all sides, including by the Romney campaign, which issued a statement repudiating the comments. Despite efforts at damage control, Mourdock's lead vanished nearly overnight. He lost to Donnelly by nearly 6 percent. Mourdock's last-minute gaffe and subsequent loss played a significant role in the Democrats' maintaining control over the Senate.

As noted by Heppen (2008), Indiana's many sparsely populated counties that are still largely economically dependent on agriculture have historically voted Republican while more populous counties with medium-sized urban areas and more diversified economies have electorates that, at times, lean Democratic. Although the most populous counties (such as Marion County, home to Indianapolis, and Lake County, home to Gary) are as reliably Democratic as are other highly urbanized areas in neighboring states, Heppen also frames the numerous counties in Indiana with older middle-sized cities once heavily dependent on manufacturing (such as Allen County, home to Ft. Wayne, and Vanderburgh County, home to Evansville) as comprising possible swing regions of the state that can push the state Democratic under the right *economic* circumstances. For instance, a combination of a sustained decline in manufacturing jobs followed by the 2007 financial crisis helped deliver Indiana for Obama during the 2008 presidential election. However, Mourdock's loss suggests that factors other than economics also matter in determining Indiana's status as a swing state.

Comparing the results of the 2010 and 2012 Senate elections in Indiana helps to illustrate the point (figure 9.6). In 2010, the Republican Senate candidate Dan Coats decisively defeated his Democratic challenger and garnered over 50 percent of the vote in seventy-six out of Indiana's ninety-two counties. Two years later and under similar economic circumstances, Mourdock managed to carry only fifty counties. Many of the counties that flipped to support the Democrat Donnelly were those very counties with middle-sized cities that were so instrumental in delivering Indiana for Obama in the 2008 presidential election, including Allen and Vanderburgh Counties.

Taken together, the 2008 and 2012 elections demonstrate the role of Indiana's swing counties that can shift elections in favor of Democrats. Perhaps more importantly, the 2012 election illustrates how the electorate in these swing counties can clearly be mobilized by social issues as well as by economic concerns. Mourdock's gaffe during his debate with Donnelly was especially damaging to his campaign in these counties. The two elections have not only clarified the geography that constitutes the swing regions of Indiana but clarified that Republican candidates cannot take these regions for granted on either social or economic issues.

REFERENCE

Heppen, John. 2008. "Indiana." In *Atlas of the 2008 Elections*, edited by Stanley D. Brunn et al., 152–54. Lanham, MD: Rowman & Littlefield.

FIGURE 9.6

Indiana US Senate Election Popular Vote Leader, 2012

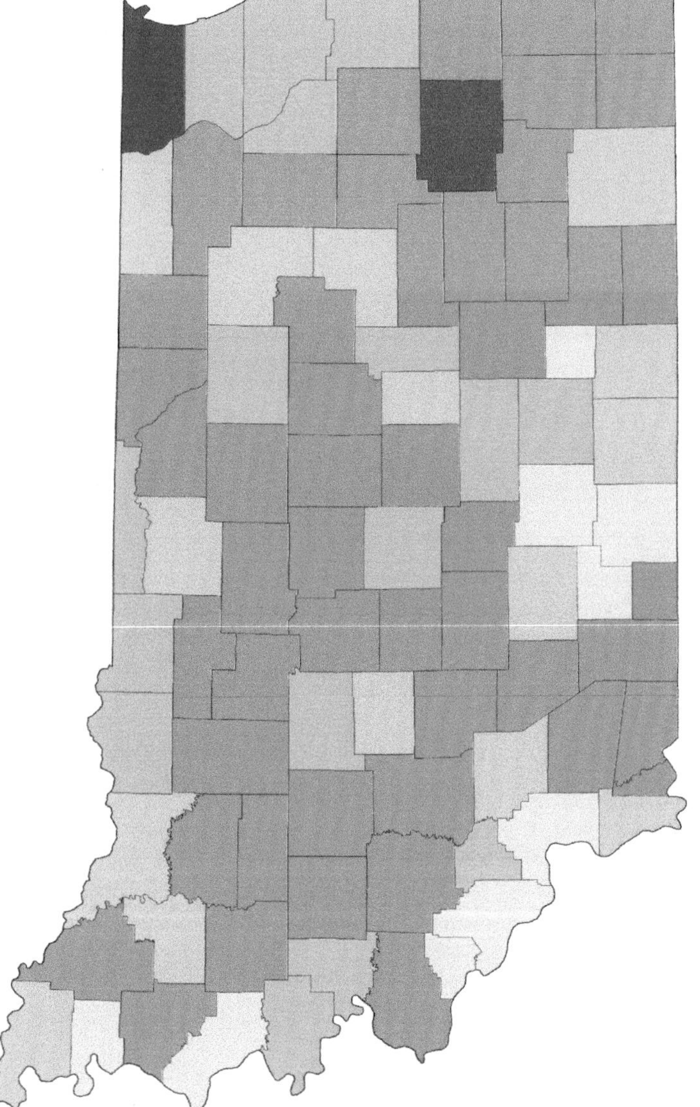

Percentage of Vote

Democrat

- Donnelly Plurality (less than 50%)
- Donnelly Majority (50 to 64%)
- Donnelly Super Majority (65% or more)

Republican

- Mourdock Plurality (less than 50%)
- Mourdock Majority (50 to 64%)
- Mourdock Super Majority (65% or more)

2012 WISCONSIN SENATE ELECTION

KENNETH FRENCH

The tensely contested 2012 Wisconsin senatorial race was for the seat vacated by four-term Democratic senator Herb Kohl, who decided to retire rather than seek reelection. The two main candidates for the Senate seat were experienced politicians. The Republican Party nominee was Tommy Thompson, a former four-term governor (1987 to 2001) and former secretary of health and human services (2001 to 2005) under President George W. Bush. The Democratic Party nominee was Tammy Baldwin, a former Wisconsin assembly member (1993 to 1999) and US congresswoman (1999 to 2012) from the Second District, which includes Madison and surrounding counties. In a state that has become more politically polarized in recent years, the two candidates represented the opposite ends of the political spectrum. The outcome of the 2012 Senate election was historically significant for Wisconsin and for the nation as a whole.

Political tensions were high in Wisconsin leading up to the November 6, 2012, senatorial election. Republican governor Scott Walker drew some criticism when signing a law that removed collective bargaining rights, which led to several protests in Madison and an eventual recall election. Governor Walker won the recall vote by a wide margin on June 5, 2012; however, the political climate of the state was still on edge during the senatorial race. Negative campaign advertisements, funded by state and national organizations, added to the vitriolic climate by portraying Thompson as a Washington lobbyist tied to special interest groups and Baldwin as an angry, extreme leftist liberal. In three public debates, both candidates had predictably different opinions on universal health care, the economy, and government spending. Thompson led in the opinion polls early in the campaign. However, Baldwin moved slightly ahead in the polls near the election date. The presidential election also focused the national spotlight on Wisconsin, which generally leans toward Democratic presidential nominees. Some political pundits viewed Wisconsin as a possible swing state due to the recent gubernatorial recall vote and for having a native son, Congressman Paul Ryan of Janesville, as the Republican vice presidential candidate. In fact, the voting outcome and geographic distribution for both the senatorial and presidential races were similar.

In the 2012 Wisconsin senatorial general election, Baldwin received 51.5 percent of the popular vote, Thompson had 45.9 percent, and Libertarian candidate Joseph Kexel had 2.1 percent of the vote (figure 9.7). The race was close in several counties, as the winning candidate in seventeen of Wisconsin's seventy-two counties won less than 50 percent of the popular vote. Baldwin did well in the major cities, including the southeastern urban corridor along Lake Michigan (Milwaukee, Racine, and Kenosha), Madison, Eau Claire, and La Crosse. Also, historically progressive strongholds in the north and southwest voted for the Democratic candidate. Thompson fared well in Green Bay (Brown County), rural areas, and the suburban counties surrounding Milwaukee.

The stark urban-suburban political divide was evident when investigating the Milwaukee metropolitan area. Baldwin won 65.5 percent of the 476,318 total votes in Milwaukee County, while Thompson received 32.6 percent of the votes. In contrast, Thompson won the western suburban communities in Waukesha County with 66.5 percent of the 238,054 total votes, while Baldwin received 31.4 percent of the votes. Spatial comparisons of the 2012 senatorial and presidential election results indicate that both

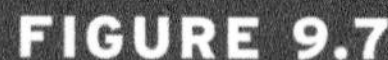

FIGURE 9.7

Wisconsin US Senate Election Popular Vote Leader, 2012

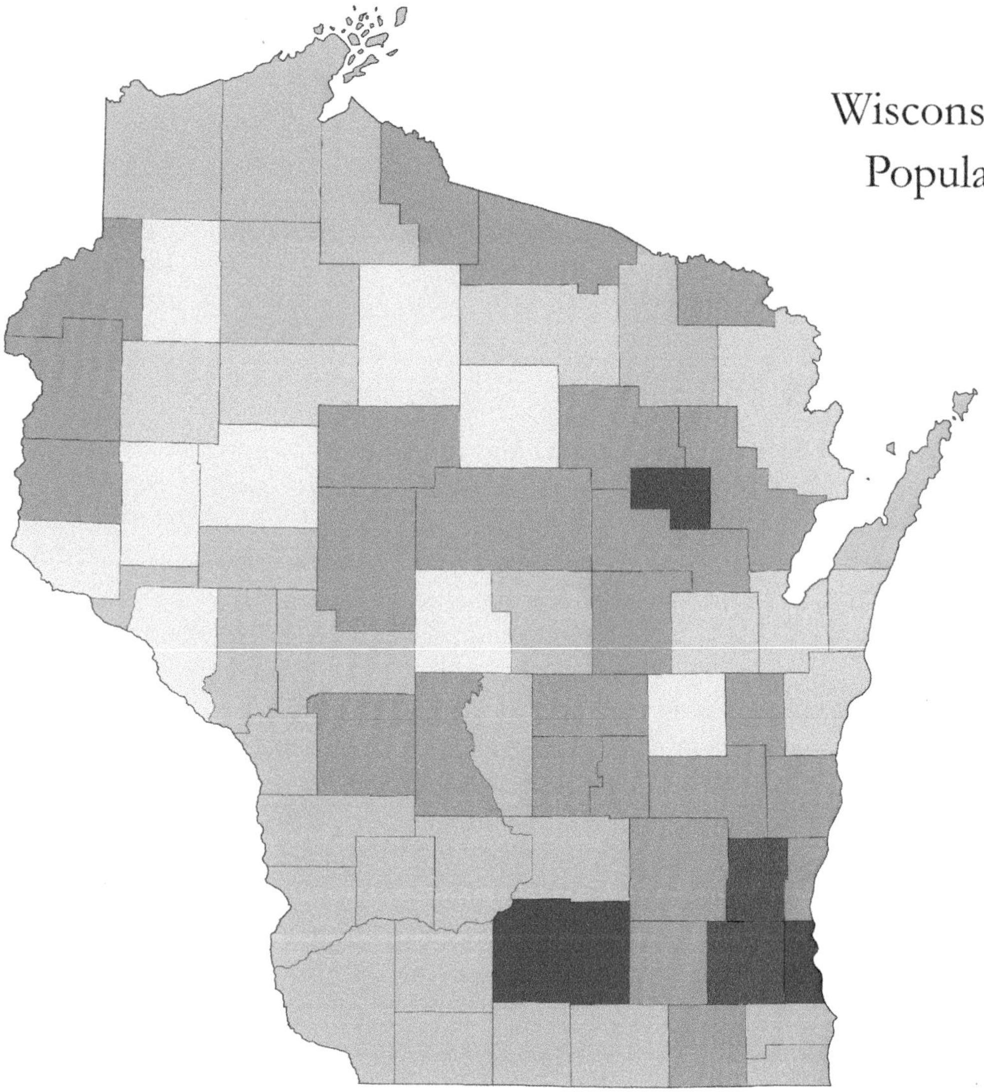

Percentage of Vote

Democrat

- Baldwin Plurality (less than 50%)
- Baldwin Majority (50 to 64%)
- Baldwin Super Majority (65% or more)

Republican

- Thompson Plurality (less than 50%)
- Thompson Majority (50 to 64%)
- Thompson Super Majority (65% or more)

Democratic candidates, Tammy Baldwin and Barack Obama, had similar patterns. Only five counties split their votes between political parties for their senatorial and presidential choices. Voters in Pierce, Chippewa, and Wood Counties favored Baldwin for Senate and Mitt Romney for president. Juneau and Marquette Counties were the opposite, as these voters preferred Thompson for the Senate seat and Barack Obama for president. Overall, with nearly three million Wisconsinites voting, Baldwin defeated Thompson by approximately 170,000 votes.

The often contentious senatorial campaign between ideologically opposing candidates added to the growing political divide and tension within the state. Nonetheless, the election of Baldwin to the US Senate was historically significant in many ways. Baldwin became the first woman to represent Wisconsin in the US Senate and the first openly lesbian senator ever elected in American history. Baldwin's sexual orientation was not a major political issue during the campaign or debates. In reference to changing history, Baldwin noted in her victory speech that she "didn't run to make history, I ran to make a difference."

2012 NORTH DAKOTA SENATE ELECTION

ROBERT H. WATREL

With Democratic senator Kent Conrad announcing his retirement in January of 2011 after twenty-six years in office, the 2012 senatorial election in North Dakota became part of the battle for control of the US Senate. In a close, surprising upset victory, Democratic candidate Heidi Heitkamp defeated former Republican representative Rick Berg by the narrow margin of 2,881 votes and became the first woman ever elected to Congress from North Dakota. Her victory was no small feat in a state where voters have continued to gravitate toward the Republican Party and during a presidential election year where Republican Mitt Romney won the state with 58.3 percent of the vote. At the state level, Republican Kevin Cramer won the House seat vacated by Berg with 55 percent of the vote, and Republican governor Jack Dalrymple won reelection with 63 percent.

Both candidates are familiar faces in North Dakota state politics. Heitkamp was elected as the state tax commissioner from 1986 to 1992 and state attorney general from 1992 to 2000, and in 2000 she made an unsuccessful bid for the governorship. From 2001 to 2011 Heitkamp worked in the energy sector as director of the Great Plains Synfuel plant. Berg was elected to the North Dakota House of Representatives from 1984 to 2010 and served as majority leader from 2003 to 2009. In 2010 he was elected to the US House of Representatives, beating the Democratic incumbent, and after one term in office decided to run for the US Senate.

During the campaign, Berg followed a more national Republican Party line and seemed less interested in local issues. He tried to ride the anti-Obama wave by criticizing the Affordable Care Act, the Obama administration's anti-energy policies, the size of the deficit, government spending, and regulation of businesses. Heitkamp, on the other hand, campaigned as an independent who would not follow the national Democratic Party and would vote for what was best for North Dakota and, if necessary, in a bipartisan manner. She distanced herself from Obama by coming out against gun control, Obama's energy policy, and parts of the Affordable Care Act. In the end, her strategy worked.

The pattern shown in figure 9.8 is typical for a competitive congressional race at the state level in North Dakota. Heitkamp received majorities in the more populous counties in the eastern third of the state, including the cities of Fargo and Grand Forks, plus counties with large American Indian populations. It may well have been the reliably Democratic American Indian voters who helped get Heitkamp elected. The voters in Sioux County (Standing Rock) and Rollette County (Fort Berthold) cast over 80 percent of their votes for Heitkamp, and those in Benson County (Spirit Lake), over 65 percent for Heitkamp. Berg received majorities from the more conservative counties of western North Dakota, which include the cities of Bismarck, Mandan, Dickinson, and Williston. Many believed the so-called oil patch vote in the western part of the state, with the influx of new people associated with the oil boom, would help turn the vote in Berg's favor, but it did not materialize. Thus Heitkamp was able to eke out a narrow victory, providing the Democrats a key seat in their efforts to retain control of the Senate.

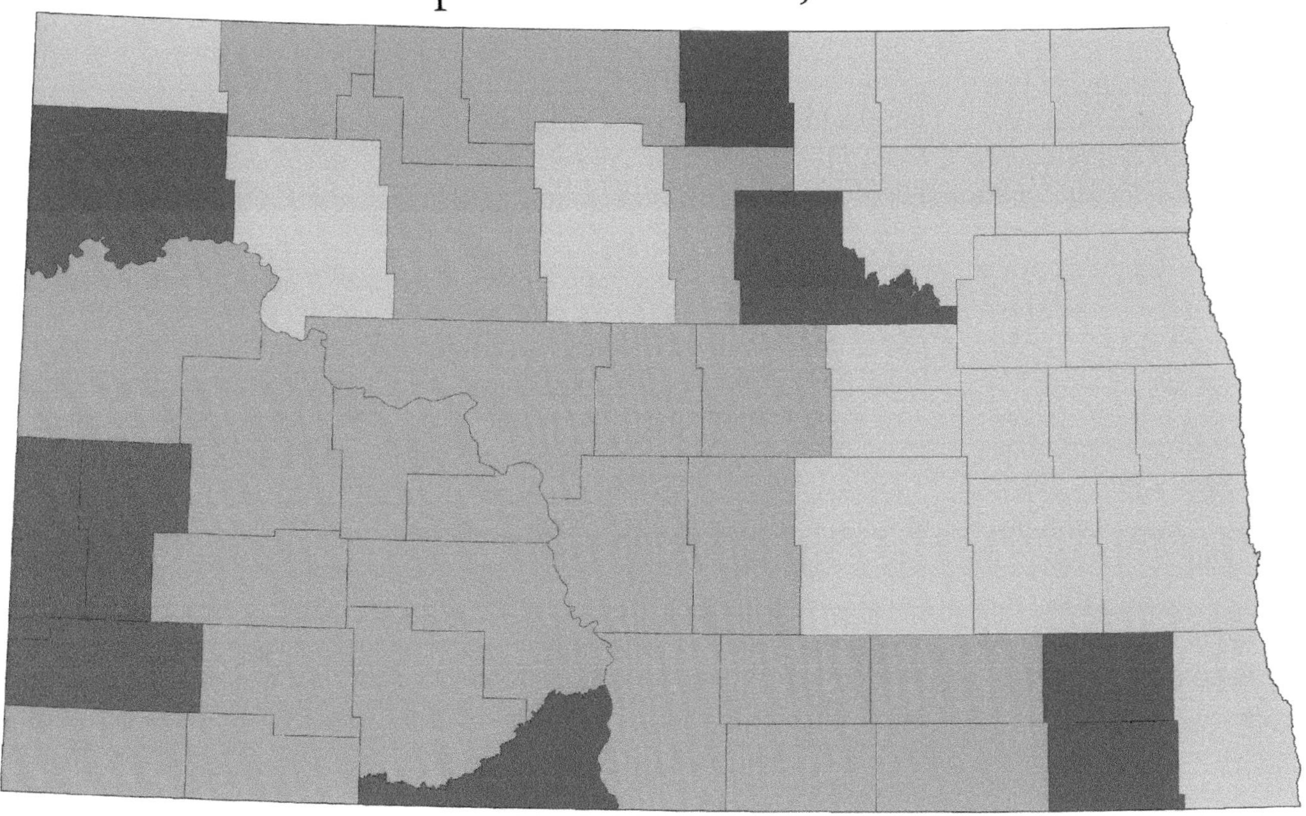
North Dakota US Senate Election
Popular Vote Leader, 2012

FIGURE 9.8

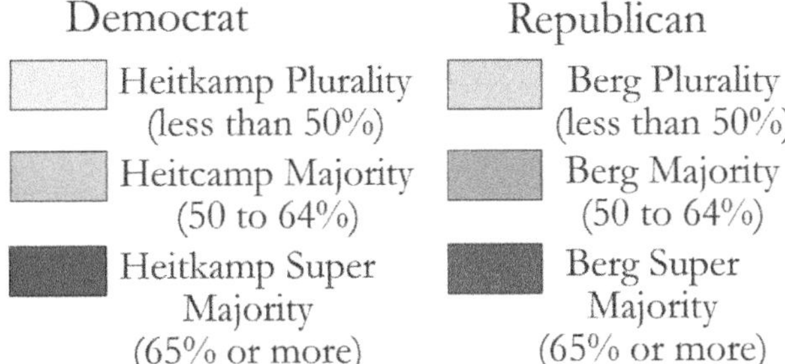
Percentage of Vote
Democrat
Republican
Heitkamp Plurality (less than 50%)
Heitcamp Majority (50 to 64%)
Heitkamp Super Majority (65% or more)
Berg Plurality (less than 50%)
Berg Majority (50 to 64%)
Berg Super Majority (65% or more)

2012 MONTANA SENATE ELECTION

RICHARD L. MORRILL AND LARRY KNOPP

Montana's US Senate race was one of the most critical and hardest-fought US Senate elections in 2012. The Democratic incumbent, Senator Jon Tester, was viewed by Republicans, in the state and nationally, as vulnerable and an opportunity for a Republican gain in that Mitt Romney easily carried Montana over Barack Obama, by a 57 percent to 43 percent margin. The race attracted some $21 million in outside money in a race costing a giant $51 million, or more than $1,000 per voter. Tester's challenger, Representative Denny Rehberg, had served six terms in the House of Representatives. Thus Tester's victory by 236,000 to 218,000 over Rehberg was quite remarkable.

Rehberg's campaign to unseat Tester really began two years earlier, in early 2011, and brought in many outside advocates. Tester ran a campaign touting his work for Montana (including public projects) and attacked Rehberg as a career politician with little to show for it. Rehberg relentlessly attacked Tester as a blind supporter of unpopular Obama policies and said his top priorities would be repeal of the Obama health-care act and extension of the Bush tax cuts.

Given the issues, Rehberg would seem to have had the upper hand. However, Montana is not a conservative state in the sense understood in the South and Midwest but more libertarian and often supportive of independent thinking and action. Many Montanans resented the US Supreme Court's 2012 decision to overturn Montana's long-standing constraints on outside money in *American Tradition Partnership v. Bullock*. Although the majority of campaign funds were in support of Rehberg, Democrats raised significant funds for Tester. Many of these funds were in so-called dark money, for which names of donors were not known.

One of the bizarre but effective ad campaigns was run by a group called Montana Hunters and Anglers, whose ads urged voters to support the Libertarian candidate, Dan Cox, as the "true conservative." But Montana Hunters and Anglers was actually an environmentalist front allied with the League of Conservation Voters, who spent $500,000 for one TV ad (Barker 2012). Presumably Cox's candidacy took votes away from Rehberg. It is plausible and even probable that this ploy made the difference, since Tester won with a plurality of 48.6 percent, with 44.8 percent for Rehberg and 6.6 percent for Cox.

As Obama did in the country as a whole, Tester won large margins in a few counties, overcoming Rehberg's smaller margins in more counties (figure 9.9). Tester won fourteen of the fifty-six counties and lost the other forty-two to Rehberg. Tester won the most urban counties and counties with major universities, while Rehberg dominated rural, small-town Montana. In a final similarity, Tester did extremely well in counties with sizable minority populations, all of which have major American Indian reservations.

Tester carried five counties with 65 percent or more of the two-party vote. These included Missoula County, home of the University of Montana, which by itself provided the margin by which he won the entire state. The others were Silver Bow County (Butte), which still follows its historic leftist voting bent (74 percent), and three reservation counties, Glacier County (Blackfeet), Blaine (Gros Ventre and Assiniboine), and Big Horn (Crow). He strongly carried another reservation county, Roosevelt County, along with Lewis and Clark County (the state capital of Helena) and Cascade County (Great Falls). He also won his home Chouteau County and adjacent Havre County, both of which have about 14 percent American Indian populations. Tester enjoyed much smaller margins in two more counties with reservations,

FIGURE 9.9

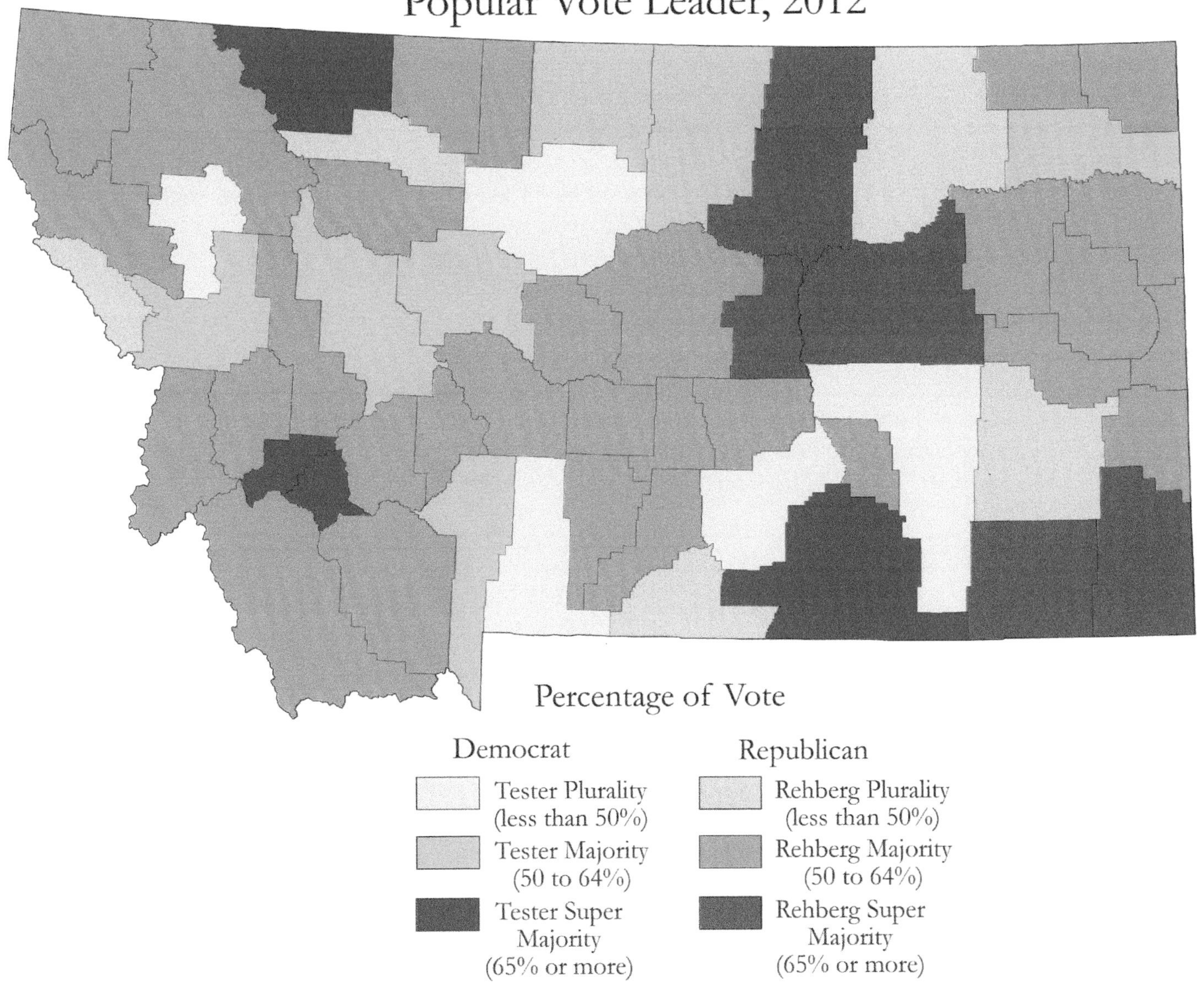

Montana US Senate Election
Popular Vote Leader, 2012
Percentage of Vote
Democrat
Tester Plurality (less than 50%)
Tester Majority (50 to 64%)
Tester Super Majority (65% or more)
Republican
Rehberg Plurality (less than 50%)
Rehberg Majority (50 to 64%)
Rehberg Super Majority (65% or more)

Rosebud County (Northern Cheyenne) and Lake County (Flathead). He also carried Gallatin County (Bozeman and Montana State University) and adjacent Park County (Livingston). He carried Yellowstone County (Billings), whose Billings *Gazette* supported him for reelection, by a very narrow margin. Yellowstone County is Montana's largest county by population.

At the opposite extreme, Tester lost another fourteen counties, receiving less than 35 percent of the two-party vote, and Carter and Garfield Counties at under 17 percent. Most of the counties that Rehberg won are quite small in population, with the interesting exception of Flathead (Kalispell), which provided by far the highest margin for Rehberg with a difference of eight thousand votes.

Tester's support exceeded that for Obama in every Montana county. This is a testament to the principle that "all politics is local," with people preferring a homeboy who happens to be a rancher, not an urban "egghead," and perhaps even more because Obama is not only African American but from too-big Chicago. The difference was greatest in Tester's home Chouteau County and tiny Wibaux County. It was lowest in the more urban, education-rich counties and especially in counties with Indian reservations. Thus, the difference was least in those areas in which Obama did relatively well. Nevertheless, the county-level correlation between the Tester vote and the Obama vote was a very high .97.

Correlations between the Tester vote and other variables illustrate a consistent pattern. Tester did best in counties with substantial minority populations and young voters, who are generally concentrated in urban areas and college towns. He also did well in high-poverty counties, including the Indian reservation counties that have the lowest per capita income in the state. Rehberg's vote was higher in rural counties with relatively more farmers and ranchers and with older populations.

REFERENCE

Barker, Kim. 2012. "In Montana, Dark Money Helped Democrats Hold a Key Senate Seat." *ProPublica*, December 27, 2012, http://www.propublica.org/article/in-montana-dark-money-helped-democrats-hold-a-key-senate-seat.

WISCONSIN GOVERNOR ELECTION AND RECALL

RYAN WEICHELT

As the 2012 elections approached, political observers throughout the United States focused on the state of Wisconsin. Wisconsin's voters elected a conservative Republican governor, Scott Walker, in 2010. After Walker spearheaded enactment of controversial legislation, he was recalled by the voters but survived a recall election and continued his term. The 2010 midterm elections were marked by an impressive Republican wave of support. Nationally, the GOP took back control of the House of Representatives and narrowed its gap in the Senate. Similar gains occurred at the state and local level. Generally Democratic leaning, Wisconsin was the only state in 2010 to completely switch party control of all statewide political offices. What seemed to be the most significant defeat was that of longtime progressive Democratic incumbent Russ Feingold, who lost to the relatively unknown Tea Party candidate Ron Johnson.

Wisconsin's electoral patterns have been relatively stable since 1992. Democratic support had long been bolstered by major urban areas, including the industrial cities of Milwaukee, Racine, and Kenosha along Lake Michigan, and the state capital of Madison in Dane County. American Indian areas, like Menominee County, the Black River Falls area, and the northern counties of Douglas, Bayfield, and Ashland, have long been Democratic strongholds. Furthermore, Democrats always fared well in the rural counties north of Highway 29 due to sparse populations and the higher number of public lands and workers. Republican support was highest in the suburban counties of southeastern Wisconsin and through the Fox River Valley stretching from Fond du Lac to Green Bay.

In 2010, Republican Milwaukee County executive Scott Walker was elected governor. Walker capitalized on the Tea Party agendas of balancing a Wisconsin budget that had expanded to over $2 billion under former Democratic governor James Doyle. He was elected over Tom Barrett, the mayor of Milwaukee, with 52.3 percent of the statewide vote to 46.5 percent for Barrett (figure 9.10).

Walker was vague in his campaign about cutting the budget, but with Republicans gaining control of the state assembly and state senate, Walker was able to push through controversial legislation and thrust Wisconsin into the national spotlight. On taking office in January 2011, Walker began unveiling his plans to balance the budget. The bulk of Walker's budget plan required massive cuts to public education, corrections, and the University of Wisconsin system. Republican efforts to curtail statewide unions and their ability to collectively bargain gained the most attention.

At the center of the debate was Act 10. This act was intended to cut back on Wisconsin's debt by requiring state employees to contribute higher amounts of their pay to health insurance and their pensions. Act 10 also limited the collective bargaining rights of public employee unions. As a result, unions would no longer be able to put these issues on the bargaining table and could bargain only for increases in wages. Further, unions could not require employees to pay union dues. This large victory over unions in a state with a long history of industry and labor ties energized Tea Party Republicans throughout the United States and vaunted Scott Walker as a major Republican figure.

During the controversy over Act 10 and other controversial laws enacted during the Walker administration, cries to recall Walker surfaced. Adopted by the Wisconsin Constitution in 1926, Wisconsin recall law states that a recall election can be held if the petitioner can obtain the number of signatures equivalent to 25 percent of the number of voters in the previous election. All signatures must be collected

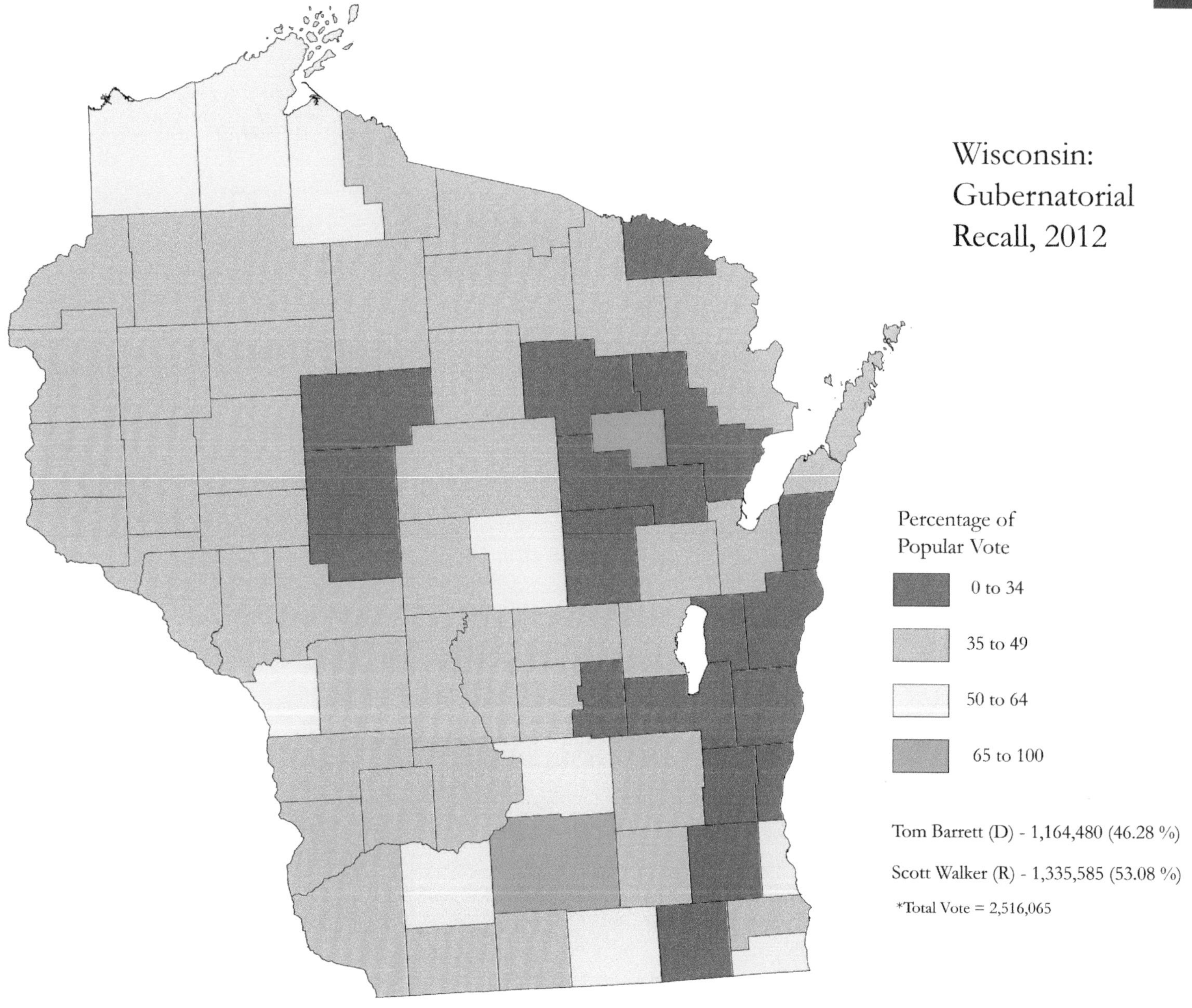
FIGURE 9.10
Wisconsin:
Gubernatorial
Recall, 2012
Percentage of
Popular Vote
0 to 34
35 to 49
50 to 64
65 to 100
Tom Barrett (D) - 1,164,480 (46.28 %)
Scott Walker (R) - 1,335,585 (53.08 %)
*Total Vote = 2,516,065

within sixty days once the intention to start the procedure is filed, and the process cannot be certified less than one year from the day the elected official took office. In this case, recall signatures could not be turned in before January 3, 2012, and signatures could be collected as early as November 3. Over 540,000 certifiable signatures were needed to meet the 25 percent margin. By March 29, 2012, 900,938 signatures were certified, and the General Accountability Board (GAB), which oversees elections in the state, announced that a recall election would be held on June 5, 2012.

Before 2011, in the history of Wisconsin only two elected officials had ever been successfully recalled, including state senator George Petak in 1996 and state senator Gary George in 2003. On August 9, 2011, six state senators faced recall elections. Democrats were able to successfully defeat two Republican state senators, dropping the Republican majority to one, seventeen Republicans to sixteen Democrats. The results provided energy for Democrats as the collection of signatures began in late November, and Democrats hoped to capitalize on this energy and remove Walker from office. By Wisconsin law, an elected official who is subject to recall is opposed by another candidate who usually comes from the other political party. Three main candidates came to the forefront: 2010 candidate Tom Barrett, Dane County executive Kathleen Falk, and state senator Kathleen Vinehout. Barrett easily won the May 8 primary with 58 percent.

Bolstered by the *Citizens United* ruling, spending for the recall broke the previous election record of $37 million spent during the 2010 gubernatorial election. By the end, estimates put total spending for the governor's race alone at over $80 million. Due to Walker's ability to raise funds during 2011 and 2012 and Barrett's late entry into the race, Walker and his supporters outspent Barrett $58.7 million to $21.9 million. Further estimates show that nearly 64 percent of Walker's contributions came from donors outside of Wisconsin. Twenty-six of the top thirty-seven individual donors, representing construction, manufacturing, financing, and other special interest groups, came from out of state and in total gave over $4.7 million (Associated Press 2012).

Through all the spending and turmoil, most polls had Walker winning with a similar margin as in 2010. Walker defeated Barrett 53 percent to 46 percent, becoming the first governor to survive a recall election in US history. Compared with voter turnout in the 2010 election, 355,353 more voters cast ballots for the 2012 recall (figures 9.10 and 9.11). Exit polling conducted by the *New York Times* on June 5 indicated clearly that the election was decided by the small percentage of undecided voters. The poll identified 94 percent of Barrett voters and 94 percent of Walker voters from 2010 would vote for the same candidate (*New York Times* 2012). Spatially, Walker saw his greatest percentage increases in the north-central counties of the state by gaining between two to six percentage points compared to 2010.

Walker's relatively easy victory in 2012 can be attributed to a variety of factors. As the turmoil unfolded in Madison during the first two months of his governorship, Walker and his allies knew a recall election was almost certain. Having nearly a year to prepare and raise funds allowed him to outspend Democrats by a nearly three to one advantage. Though political advertising flooded the airwaves from February 2011 up to the June 5, 2012, election, with only about two months to campaign, Barrett and Democrats were simply too late and were outspent.

Another contributing factor to Walker's victory relates to the Republican control of the state legislature. GOP leaders used their power to fashion a brilliant strategic legislative agenda to help Walker retain the governorship. The early issue of the collective bargaining created a strong schism across the state. By painting public employees as the "haves" and the rest as the "have nots," Democrats were pushed to defend unions and public spending in the midst of a national economic crisis and a ballooning state budget. Republicans formed a unified voting bloc and with Democrats lacking in numbers, state Republicans were able to easily pass several pieces of legislation during the 2011 legislative sessions.

Walker courted northern voters by focusing on deer management by creating a "deer czar," controlling gray wolf populations with a

FIGURE 9.11

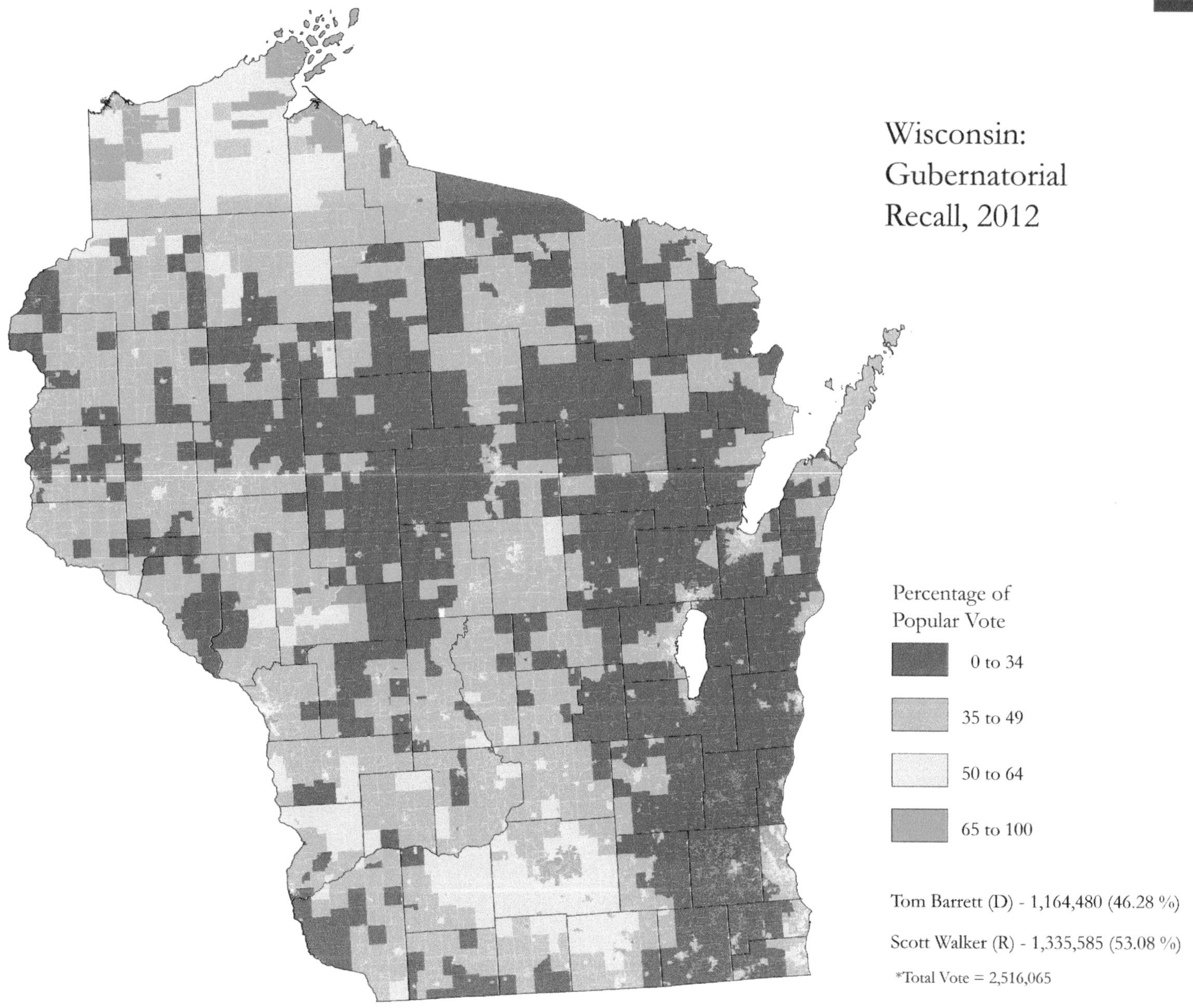

Wisconsin:
Gubernatorial
Recall, 2012
Percentage of
Popular Vote
0 to 34
35 to 49
50 to 64
65 to 100
Tom Barrett (D) - 1,164,480 (46.28 %)
Scott Walker (R) - 1,335,585 (53.08 %)
*Total Vote = 2,516,065

public hunt, and relaxing environmental regulation to open taconite mining in Ashland and Iron Counties. These efforts may have contributed to Walker's relative success in northern Wisconsin. Socially, Walker appealed to both moderate and conservative voters throughout the state by passing a conceal and carry law, enacting voter identification regulations, cutting back state welfare funds, and opening discussion about abortion control. Finally, political fatigue among enough Wisconsin voters may have contributed to Walker's June 5 success. In a CBS exit poll taken during the recall election, only 27 percent of voters felt a recall election was justified for no reason, with 60 percent believing a recall election should be used only if there was political misconduct (Burns 2012). This divide was evident in a CNN exit poll that showed 90 percent of Barrett voters believed recall elections should be used for "any reason" while 95 percent of Walker supporters said they should never be used (CNN 2012). Therefore, the perceptions of the entire recall process as a whole may explain why some voters voted against Barrett simply because they believed the process was flawed.

Overall, these factors helped to explain Walker's reelection despite the controversies associated with his administration. They also contribute to explaining why there was little geographical change in the outcome of the vote and why both gubernatorial elections can be regarded as maintaining elections in which voting patterns followed a status quo that had been in place for the previous two decades.

REFERENCES

Associated Press. 2012. "Nearly $81 Million Spent on Walker Recall." *Dailyreporter.com*, July 25, http://dailyreporter.com/2012/07/25/nearly-81-million-spent-on-walker-recall.

Burns, Alexander. 2012. "Wisconsin Recall: Scott Walker Wins." *Politico.com*, June 5, http://www.politico.com/news/stories/0612/77085.html.

CNN. 2012. "Wisconsin Governor Recall Exit Polls." http://www.cnn.com/interactive/2012/06/politics/table.wisc.exitpolls.

New York Times. 2012. "Wisconsin Recall Exit Polls: How Different Groups Voted." http://www.nytimes.com/interactive/2012/06/05/us/politics/wisconsin-recall-exit-polls.html?_r=0.

TEXAS STATE SENATE DISTRICT 10: WENDY DAVIS IS REELECTED

BROOKS HEITMEIER

Capitalizing on the national attention that she received for her filibuster against a proposal to impose dramatic restrictions on abortion in Texas, in mid-2013, state senator Wendy Davis opted to run as the Democratic candidate for governor of Texas in November 2014. In the aftermath of her entrance, Davis has largely ignored the abortion politics that granted her notoriety, prioritizing the economy and education in her campaign against her Republican opponent, Attorney General Greg Abbott. Davis's focus on more generic issues here is not too unexpected; prior to her pro-choice filibuster on the floor of the state legislature, Davis was mostly notable in that she was a Democrat representing a swing district in the Dallas-Fort Worth metropolitan area. Senate District 10 (SD-10) is located wholly within Tarrant County. It contains much of Fort Worth proper, but it also includes suburban territory to the east (Southlake and Colleyville in the northeast, Arlington and Mansfield in the southeast) and relatively undeveloped, exurban, and still rural areas in the southwest. The district was drawn so that the heavily Democratic areas of Fort Worth are offset by the heavily Republican suburban territory of Tarrant County. Thus SD-10 represents a microcosm of Texas as a whole. This is borne out by the fact that President Obama got 45 percent of the vote in SD-10 and 41 percent of the vote statewide in 2012.

The electoral polarization of the district is borne out by the results of Davis's initial victory in 2008 and her reelection in 2012; her margin of victory in each race was less than three percentage points. Perhaps she can credit her victories in part to careful issue prioritization; as a candidate for the state legislature, Davis avoided the national Democratic Party and emphasized local concerns, earning the official endorsements of city- and county-level organizations. In 2012 at least, this seemed to prove crucial to her reelection. Davis won 51 percent of the vote against Republican Mark Shelton, but Barack Obama lost the district by a substantial margin in the presidential election, capturing only 45 percent. Thus, SD-10 simultaneously voted for the Democratic Davis by two points and against the Democratic Obama by close to eight points, implying that a significant portion of the electorate voting for Romney split the ticket to vote for Davis in the state senate race. Clearly, Davis held an appeal to her district that the president did not possess.

Mapping Davis's totals against Obama's precinct by precinct further confirms the effect; Obama (in orange) earned a higher percentage of the vote than Davis (in blue) did in only thirteen of a few precincts, most of which are located in central Fort Worth. Precincts in which Davis performed better than Obama but by less than the overall margin of the entire district are shown in light blue, and those where Davis outperformed Obama by more than the overall margin are shown in dark blue. The areas generally corresponding to the latter class—the half of Arlington in SD-10, southwest Fort Worth, the unincorporated southwest corner of the county—are largely white and range from middle- to upper-middle class in terms of median household income. Notably, a number of precincts in this class simultaneously went for Romney and for Davis. The margins that Davis recorded over Obama in the dark blue precincts were significant enough to secure her reelection; if she had not done so well relative to Obama there, she would have lost to Shelton (figure 9.12).

Other areas on the map deserve consideration. The cluster of precincts where Obama outperformed Davis are located in areas with higher proportions of African American and

FIGURE 9.12

Texas State Senate District 10

2012 Presidential Election Results

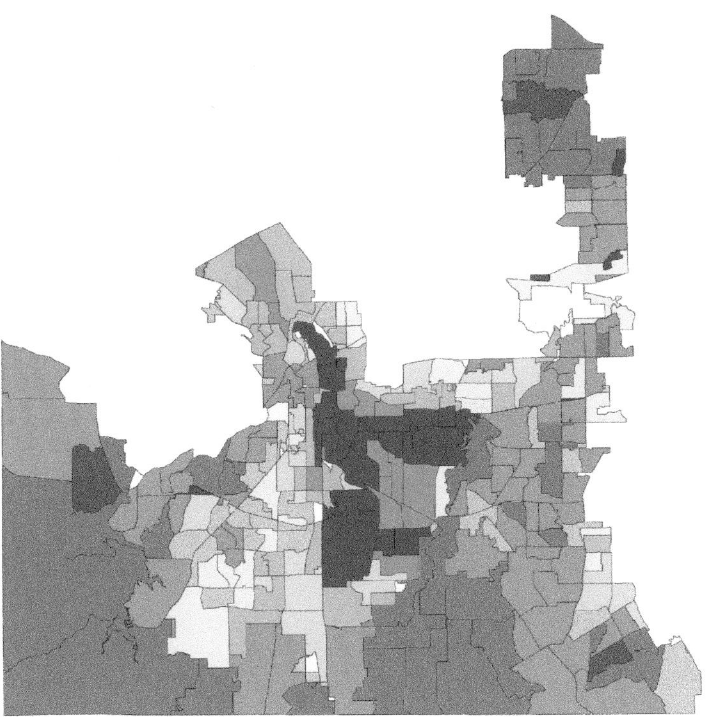

Percentage of Vote

Obama		Romney
	Under 50	
	50 to 59	
	60 to 69	
	70 to 79	
	80 to 89	
	90 or more	
Tie		No Vote

Percentage of Vote Margin: Wendy Davis Minus Barack Obama

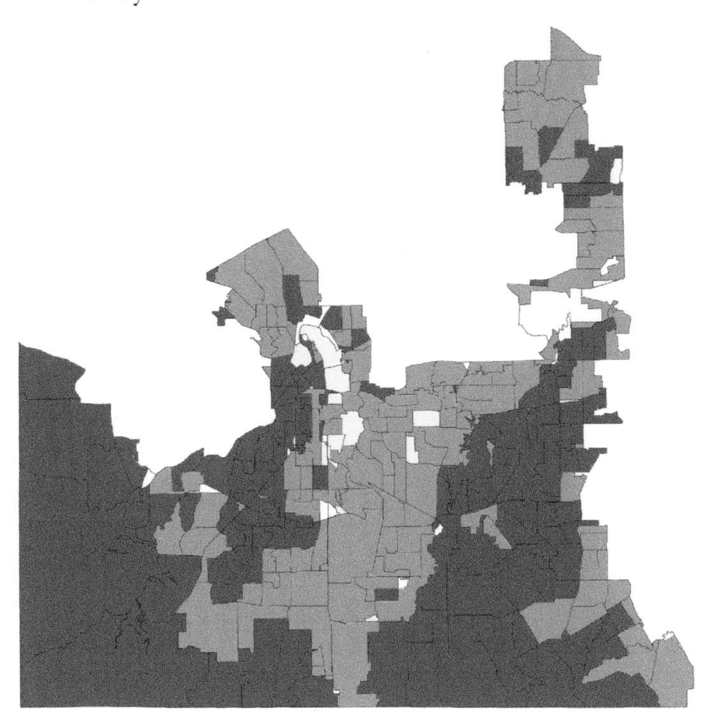

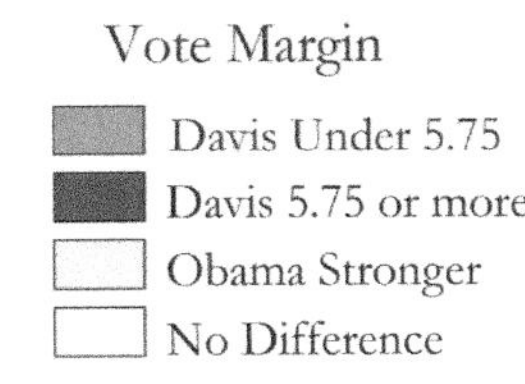

Latino voters. As these demographic groups vote reliably Democratic, it is likely that Obama's strength here was due more to leaving Davis's race blank on the ballot rather than the presence of Obama/Shelton voting. The rest of the district with high minority populations tends to be covered by the light blue shade, indicating that Davis outperformed Obama with these voters but by less than the margin of the overall district. Still, this is impressive because many of these precincts—particularly in Fort Worth—voted over 95 percent Democratic.

Interestingly, the light blue also largely accounts for precincts with some of the highest incomes in the district: Southlake, at the northeastern tip, as well as Mansfield, in the southeastern corner. An explanation for this could possibly be a function of wealth and partisan loyalty, meaning that the most affluent voters would be more inclined to vote straight-ticket Republican. Indeed, Obama and Davis both performed rather poorly against their Republican opponents in these cities. Thus, the key to Davis's victory over Shelton seems to be attributed not so much to the most affluent white areas but to the more middle-class white areas, where voters more frequently split the ticket for Romney and Davis.

For Davis to be successful in November 2014 in the gubernatorial race, she needs to see something to this effect writ large. To be sure, outperforming typical Democratic performance may not sound like too difficult of a task; Texas Democrats are facing the longest active losing streak in the country, failing to win any statewide office since 1994. However, the primary question concerning Davis's potential to enhance electoral credibility for Texas Democrats is how she will conduct her candidacy in light of her now-nationwide reputation. Regardless of how much she tries to keep the focus of her campaign on issues like jobs and education, Davis's pro-choice stance is widely known in this socially conservative state, so this one issue could further impede the possibility for Davis to make substantial inroads throughout Texas.

Speculation aside, Davis's ability in 2012 to win a district in which Obama pulled only 45 percent speaks to an appeal she captured with white, middle-class voters who are open to voting Democratic. In SD-10, Obama performed slightly better than he did statewide in Texas (41 percent), so Davis's margin over Obama statewide needs to be even higher for her to be elected governor.

CHAPTER TEN

REFERENDA

A REFERENDUM ON THE INITIATIVE PROCESS? BALLOT INITIATIVE USAGE AND CONTENT IN THE 2012 ELECTION

JOSHUA R. MEDDAUGH AND JOSHUA J. DYCK

The history of "direct democracy" in the United States has its roots in the New England town meeting, a method of decision making that predates the Constitution. While a pure participatory deliberative assembly is practicable at the local level, as the country grew in size and scope, the town meeting model became impractical and cumbersome. American democracy is built on the representative or republican ideal; representatives are chosen in frequent elections, and the legislative and executive branches come together to form policy in a system that has federalism, a separation of powers, and checks and balances.

During the late nineteenth century, reformers proposed institutions of mass direct democracy in the American states including the initiative, which allows citizens to propose, qualify, and vote on measures without input from the legislative branch, the referendum, which allows legislators to defer important policy questions to a popular vote, and the recall, which allows citizens to remove corrupt politicians from office before their terms expire. Oregon became the first state to have a direct election in 1904 and has been one of the states leading in initiative usage since its adoption. Including Oregon, twenty-four states have some form of the ballot initiative. The initiative has become the standard way in which salient and controversial issues are arbitrated in the states. However, 2012 saw a sizable decrease in initiative usage from previous years.

The 2012 general election not only witnessed marginally lower turnout in the presidential contest compared with 2008 but also witnessed a decrease in the number of initiatives that qualified for the ballot. Forty-two initiatives were voted on in 2012, which is fewer in comparison with the elections of 2008, 2004, and 2000, where sixty-eight, sixty-four, and seventy-two were contested, respectively. Seventeen measures, or 41 percent, were passed, matching the historical approval average. Of the forty-two initiatives, the most controversial measures dealt with social issues—the legalization of both marijuana usage and same-sex marriage. Unlike 2008, when social conservatives won big with marriage definition measures, social liberals celebrated the passage of Question 1 in Maine and Question 6 in Maryland, endeavors that legalized same-sex marriage in both states. Combined with the passage of Referendum 74 in Washington, same-sex marriage proponents witnessed the affirmation of their view after a string of marriage definition measures passed in the previous decade. Also of note were Colorado's Amendment 64 and Washington's Initiative 502, both of which decriminalized the production and consumption of marijuana for all persons over the age of twenty-one in both states. The total number of initiatives and historic usage are presented by state in figure 10.1 (historical initiative usage).

Legislative referenda, where the state legislature refers a measure for a public vote, tend to be less controversial than initiatives and therefore have a higher historic passage rate. There were sixteen bond measures in 2012 that dealt with the approval of state funds for capital projects. Alabama, Alaska, Arkansas, Hawaii, Maine, New Jersey, New Mexico, Oklahoma, and Rhode Island asked residents to approve funds for projects that included new roads and highways, transportation, and repaying state debt. Fourteen of the sixteen passed easily, including New Jersey Bonds A–C that appropriated $750 million for college and university spending. Even though voters in Hawaii and Maine rejected H.B. 2594 and Question 2, respectively, the national trend was for voters to approve funds for state projects.

California regained the distinction in the 2012 election of having the longest ballot, with eleven measures. Ten of the eleven measures were citizen-sponsored initiatives, accounting for approximately 24 percent of all initiatives proposed nationwide. The ten measures covered a wide range of topics, including taxes to fund education, an amendment to the "three strikes" law, and auto insurance policies. The four measures that passed (Propositions 30, 35, 36, and 39) made some significant changes to California's tax and legal codes. Proposition 30 increased the tax rates on those who earn more than $250,000 per year and raised the sales tax by 1/4 cent for four years to fund education. Proposition 39 allows multistate business owners to pay taxes based on a percentage of their sales in California. Propositions 35 and 36 concerned the legal system by increasing the penalty for human trafficking and limiting the third "strikeable" offense to felonies that are serious and/or violent to reduce the size of California's overflowing prison population. Of the measures that failed (Propositions 31, 32, 33, 34, 37, and 38), the most salient and controversial was Proposition 34, which would have repealed the death penalty; 47 percent of voters supported the repeal, while 53 percent opposed it.

One of the most interesting trends in regards to ballot measures in 2012 was the mixed messages voters across the nation sent on the issue of immigration and the power of labor unions. These messages tended to reflect the partisan and ideological disposition of the states and also their geography. Maryland's SB 167, passed by the legislature in 2011, allowed illegal immigrants the right to pay in-state college tuition rates if they graduated from a Maryland high school and their parents paid taxes. Just a year later, voters considered Question 4 by popular referendum; voters affirmed the legislature's decision to pass the Dream Act with 58 percent supporting the law. In Montana, however, 80 percent of voters supported LR-121, which denies state-sponsored services to immigrants without proof of citizenship.

On labor, we see a similar trend. In California, labor unions kept the right to endorse political campaigns with the failure of Proposition 32. However, in Michigan, collective bargaining rights failed to gain the support of voters and be added to the state constitution. As seen, the messages on immigration and labor are murky at best.

While 2012 was a down year in terms of the total number of proposals under consideration, a number of consequential, influential, salient, and conflictual ballot measures were presented to voters, and mirroring historic averages, about two of every five initiatives passed. We are reminded that it takes only a single passed ballot measure to create significant policy change. The changes in same-sex marriage, immigration, drug, and tax policies are very real and are likely to have lasting effects in the states that passed them as well as ripple effects as policies diffuse to other states in subsequent years. Justice Brandeis famously noted that the states are the *laboratories of democracy*; as 2012 shows us, the initiative is perhaps the most prominent experimental technique that states have to execute policy experimentation.

FIGURE 10.1

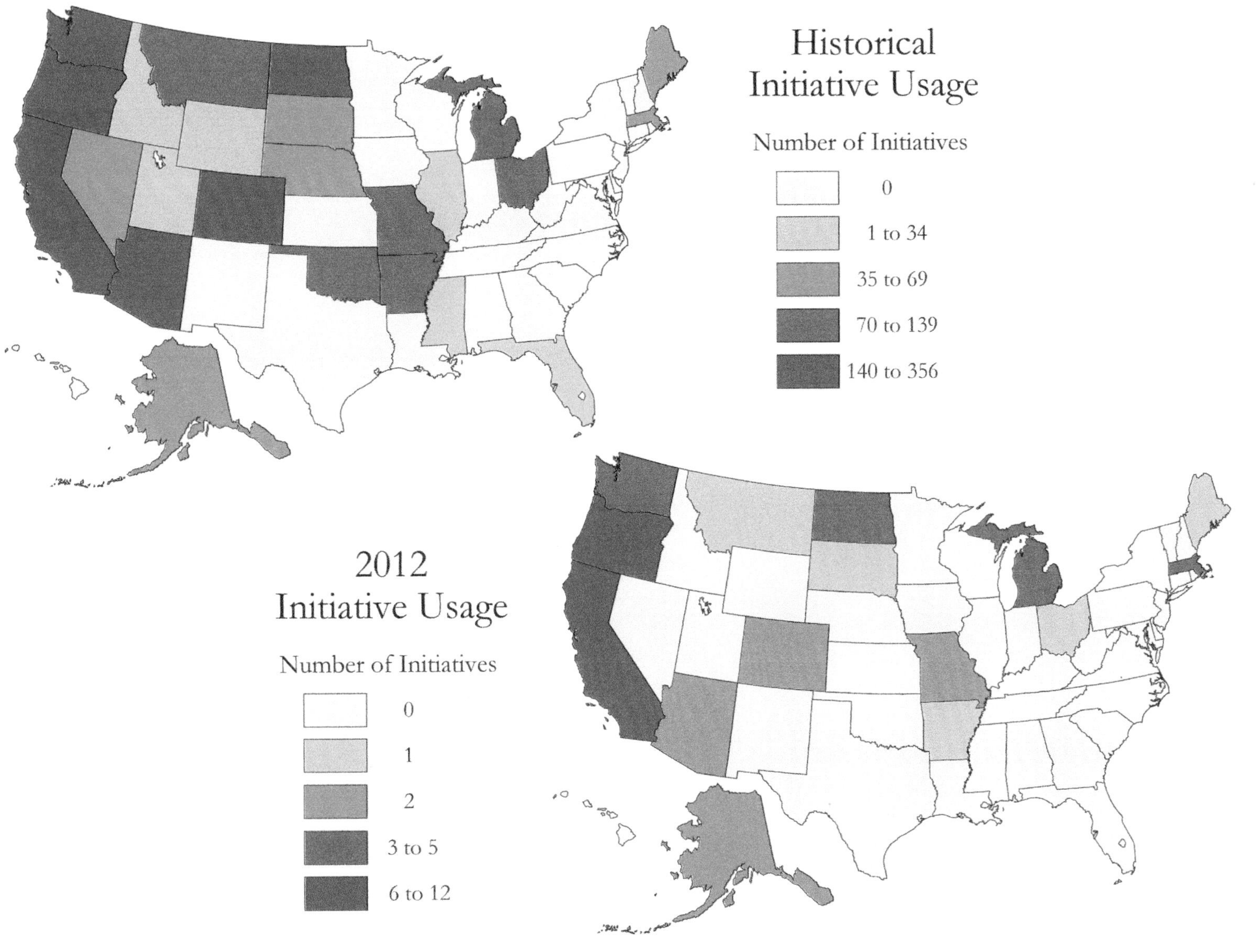
Historical
Initiative Usage
Number of Initiatives
0
1 to 34
35 to 69
70 to 139
140 to 356
2012
Initiative Usage
Number of Initiatives
0
1
2
3 to 5
6 to 12

VOTES ON SAME-SEX MARRIAGE IN MAINE, MINNESOTA, MARYLAND, AND WASHINGTON

RICHARD L. MORRILL, LARRY KNOPP, AND MICHAEL BROWN

In 2012, referenda on same-sex marriage took place in four states—Maine, Maryland, Minnesota, and Washington. Voters in Maine, Maryland, and Washington confirmed the right of same-sex marriage, and those in Minnesota defeated a measure that would have defined marriage as only between a man and a woman. Figure 10.2 shows the results for Maine, figure 10.3 those for Minnesota, figure 10.4 for Maryland, and figure 10.5 for Washington.

The results in Maine (figure 10.2) exhibited polarization associated with differences between urban and rural areas. All of the counties from York County on the New Hampshire border northeastward to Hancock County, which includes Bar Harbor, supported same-sex marriage. This region includes the state's largest city of Portland. In contrast, all of the interior counties voted no, and the farther away from the coast, the less support for the measure.

In Minnesota, the pattern similarly reflects the metropolitan and rural polarization, as with the vote for president (figure 10.3). The highest percentages of "no" votes were found in the core Twin Cities counties of Hennepin and Ramsey, which contain Minneapolis and St. Paul, respectively. In both counties, 65 percent of the voters opposed the measure, for which a no vote implies support for same-sex marriage. The measure was also defeated in three suburban counties, in Rice County, which contains Carleton and St. Olaf Colleges, and in the Mankato, Duluth, and Rochester metropolitan areas. A majority in remote, environmentally rich Cook County in the extreme northeastern corner of Minnesota also voted no. However, the entire western part of the state and almost all rural and small-town counties supported the ban.

Maryland clearly confirms the pattern of metropolitan support and rural opposition (figure 10.4). The highest levels of support were found in suburban Montgomery and Howard Counties and in Baltimore City, with weaker support in Frederick and Anne Arundel (Annapolis) Counties. In contrast, the Appalachian counties and most counties along the Eastern Shore east of Chesapeake Bay were highly opposed. A majority of voters in Prince Georges County, south and east of Washington, DC, voted against the measure, although Prince Georges County is second among Maryland's counties in population behind Montgomery County. The anomaly may be explained by the fact that Prince George's County has a very large African American population, and many African Americans throughout the country do not support legalizing same-sex marriage.

Washington's results mirrored those for the other states (figure 10.5). Polarization was extreme, with very high support in King County (Seattle) plus suburban Kitsap and Snohomish and exurban and environmental San Juan and Jefferson Counties, the latter including the state capital of Olympia. Whatcom County, the home of Western Washington University, and Whitman County in eastern Washington, which contains Washington State University, also gave majorities to the measure. However, King County was the key to the outcome. King County provided a margin of 324,000 votes in support of the measure, overcoming a deficit of 86,000 votes across the rest of the state! Areas of extreme opposition include the rural and small-town farming and forestry areas of eastern Washington and one very conservative county in western Washington.

FIGURE 10.2

Maine: Same Sex Marriage Referendum 2012 Election

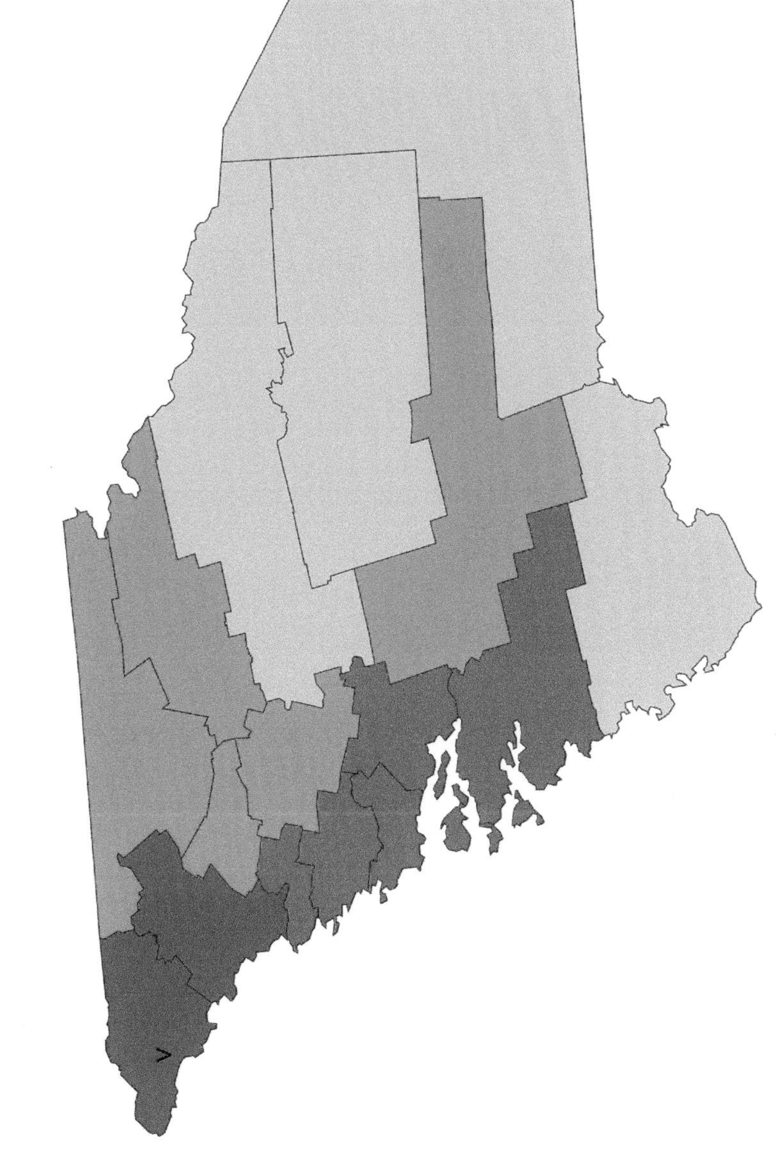

Percentage Voting "Yes"

- 0
- 1 to 41
- 42 to 49
- 50 to 56
- 57 to 65

FIGURE 10.3

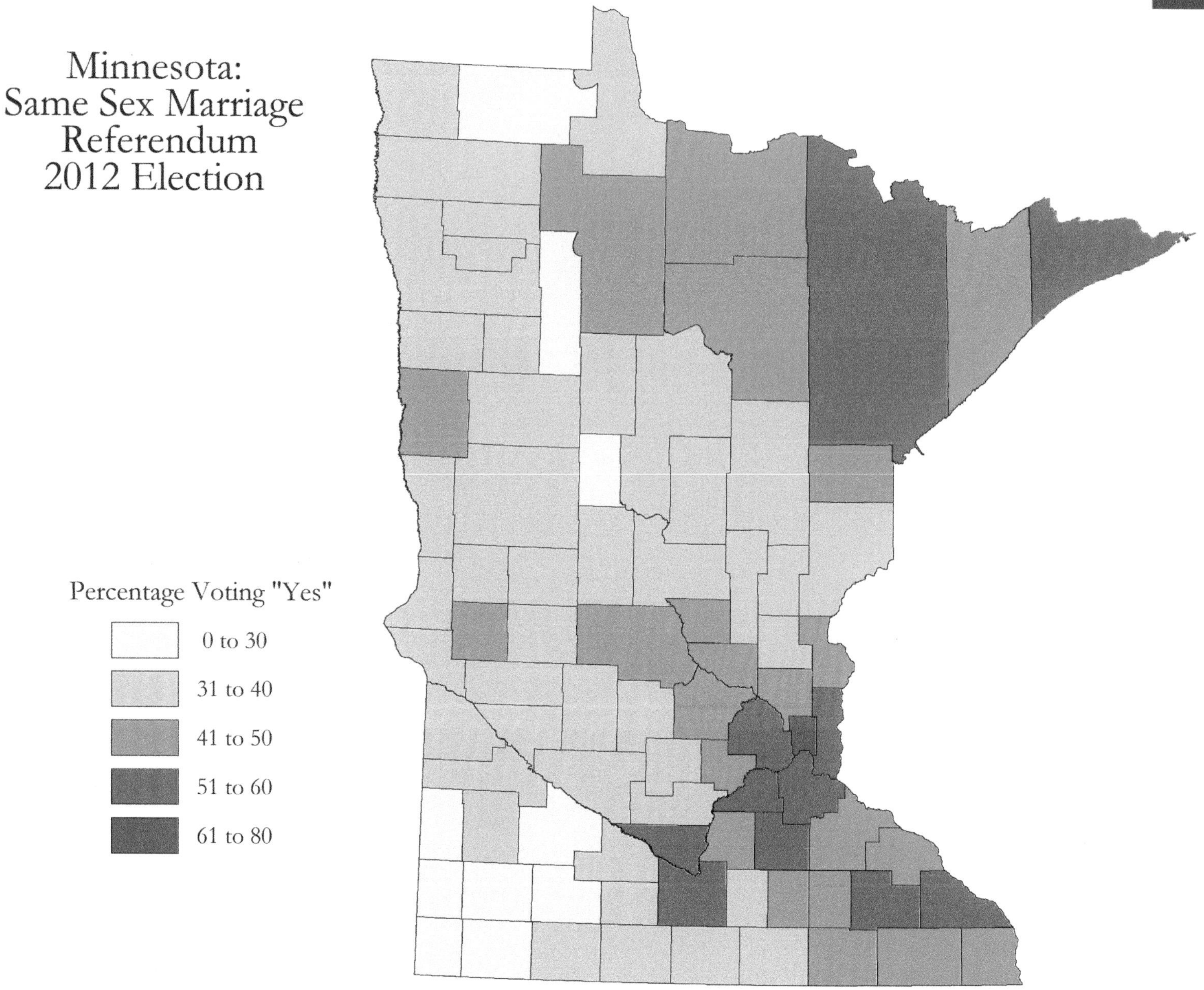

Minnesota:
Same Sex Marriage
Referendum
2012 Election

Percentage Voting "Yes"

0 to 30

31 to 40

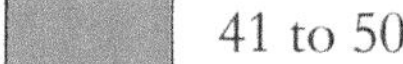
41 to 50

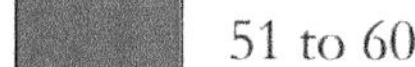
51 to 60

61 to 80

FIGURE 10.4

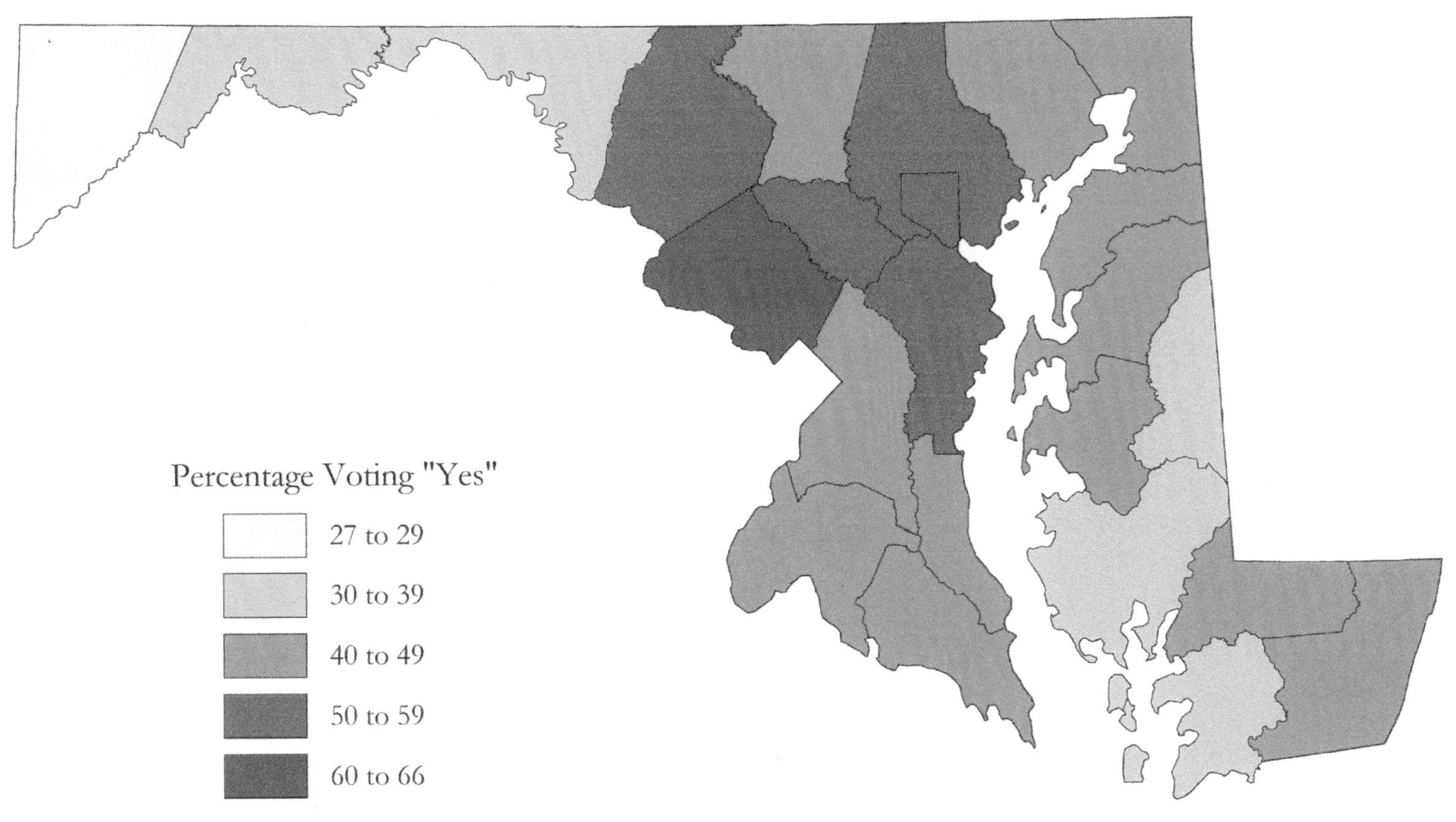
Maryland: Same Sex Marriage Referendum
2012 Election
Percentage Voting "Yes"
27 to 29
30 to 39
40 to 49
50 to 59
60 to 66

FIGURE 10.5

Washington: Same Sex Marriage Referendum 74 2012 Election

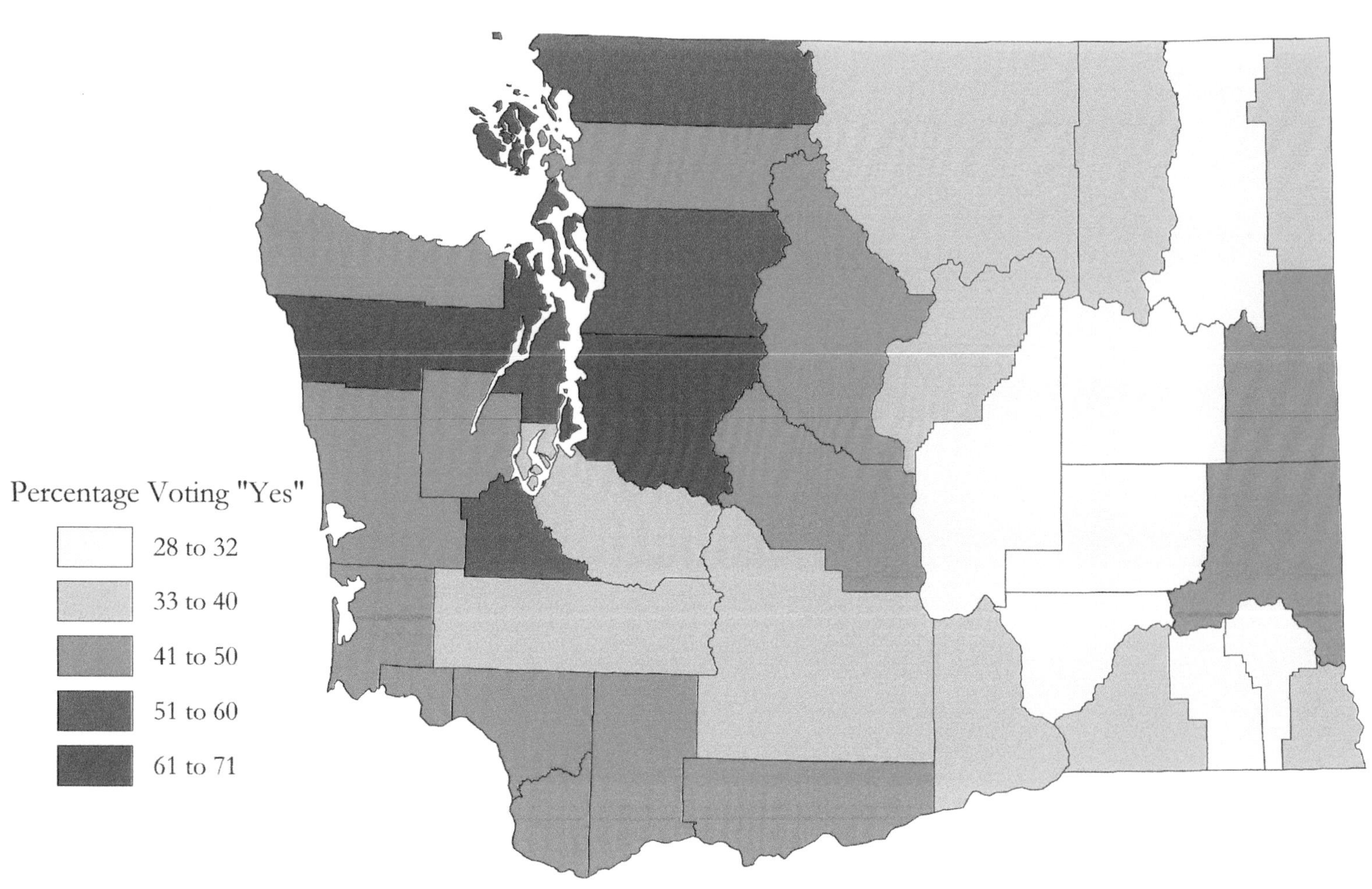

Overall, the results in these four states were quite similar. This is confirmed further by a look at the county-level correlations between support levels and various social and economic variables. Correlations for each state are consistent with one another. In all four states, support for same-sex marriage is related to education, professional status, and income with highly educated, high-income, professional people most likely to be supportive. Not surprisingly, the correlation of the same-sex measure and the vote for Obama is generally very high. The foreign-born share is consistently positive, although this might be explained by the fact that most foreign-born residents live in urban areas that supported same-sex marriage in all of the states. On the other hand, opposition to same-sex marriage was highest in places with large numbers of churchgoers, the elderly, and residents of rural areas.

LEGALIZATION OF MARIJUANA USE IN COLORADO AND WASHINGTON

RICHARD L. MORRILL AND BEN ANDERSTONE

Perhaps as a harbinger of things to come, Colorado and Washington voters approved limited recreational use of marijuana, still proscribed by federal regulation. We look here at the geographic pattern of support for and opposition to legalization, using data for counties, and compare the vote for "pot" to that for Obama in 2012. For Washington, we also compare the marijuana vote with the vote on same-sex marriage.

Colorado and Washington are both western states with large metropolitan areas, sizable agricultural areas, and also prominent recreational areas. These recreational areas include national forests that are alleged to be sites of illicit marijuana production already. We anticipated that patterns of support and opposition to recreational use of marijuana would be similar in the two states.

Figures 10.6 and 10.7 show the county-level percentages of voter support for Amendment 64 in Colorado and Initiative 502 in Washington, respectively. In both states, the highest levels of support in both numbers and percentages were in the urban cores—Denver and Boulder Counties in Colorado and King County (Seattle) in Washington. High levels of support, especially in Colorado, were in areas of high environmental amenities, such as the ski resort counties in the Rockies and Puget Sound, the Cascades, and the Olympics in Washington. The most supportive counties in Colorado were San Miguel (Telluride), Pitkin (Aspen), Gunnison (Crested Butte), Eagle (Vail), Denver, and Boulder Counties.

In Washington, the highest support levels were in environmental amenity-rich San Juan, Jefferson, King, and Whatcom (Bellingham) Counties. San Juan and Jefferson Counties are both amenity areas on Puget Sound. All of these counties in both states are highly urbanized or contain significant environmental amenities. Most of these counties, urban or environmental, gave strong support to President Obama. Thus, there were high county-level correlations between support for the referenda and support for Obama, with correlations of .89 in each state.

At the other extreme, areas of strong opposition to legalization in Colorado are thirteen contiguous agriculture-dependent counties along and near the eastern border, with nine counties voting less than 40 percent. Four counties in far western Colorado with irrigated agriculture and a strong Mormon presence were moderately negative. In Washington, areas of strongest opposition were the Columbia Basin plus Yakima and Walla Walla. These are areas of intense irrigation agriculture and a heavy Mormon and Catholic population. In western Washington, the lone county with strong opposition was Lewis County in the southwestern part of the state. Politically, Lewis County is similar to the counties of eastern Washington rather than to its neighboring counties.

Many counties in both states gave moderate approval to legalization. In Colorado, these counties included those containing most of the state's smaller cities except for conservative Colorado Springs and Grand Junction. Colorado Springs is home to the US Air Force Academy and a large fundamentalist and evangelical Christian community, including James Dobson's Focus on the Family headquarters. Other moderately supportive counties in Colorado included those in exurban Denver and some predominantly Hispanic counties. In Washington, counties with moderate support included those containing the Tacoma and Spokane metropolitan areas and Whitman

FIGURE 10.6

Colorado: Marijuana Referendum
2012 Election

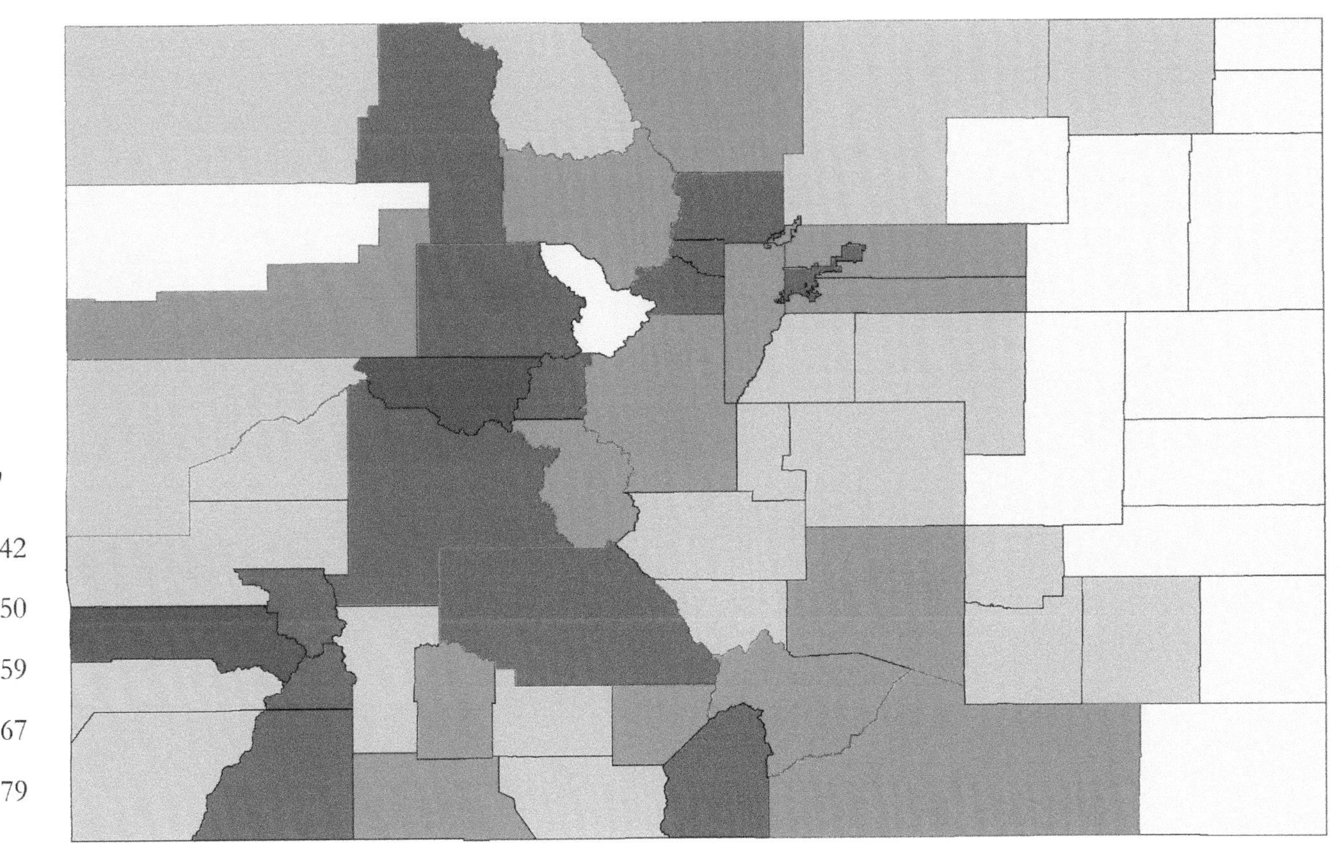

Percentage Voting "Yes"

- 32 to 42
- 43 to 50
- 51 to 59
- 60 to 67
- 68 to 79

FIGURE 10.7

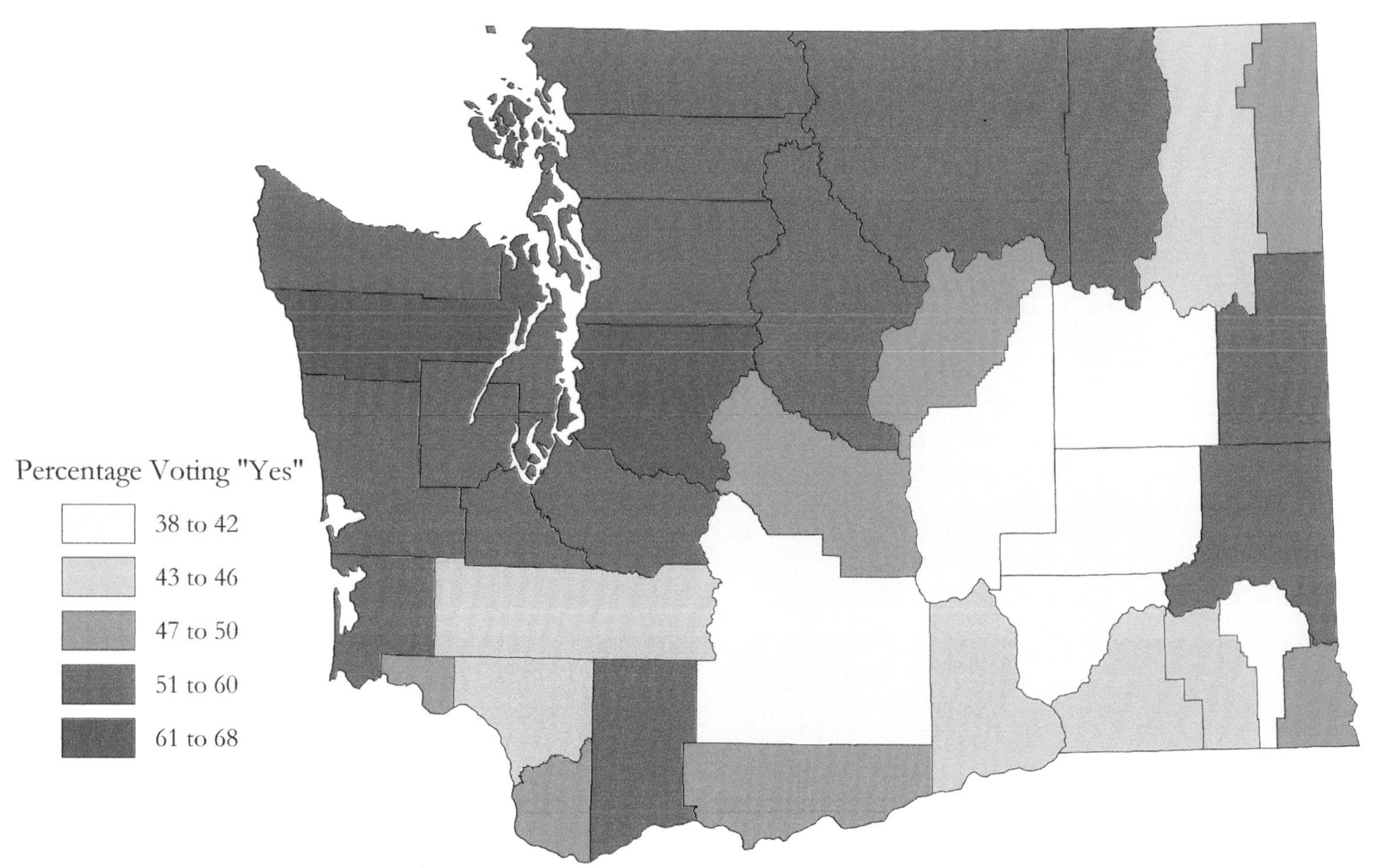
Washington: Marijuana Iniative 502
2012 Election
Percentage Voting "Yes"
38 to 42
43 to 46
47 to 50
51 to 60
61 to 68

County in eastern Washington, home of Pullman and Washington State University.

At the county level, the correlations between county-level percentages for Obama and for the two referenda were a high .89 in each state. However, there are some interesting differences in geography. In Colorado, Obama did better than would be expected on the basis of the referendum in the metropolitan core of Denver, Boulder, and Arapahoe Counties. He also did better than would be expected in Pueblo County, which has a large Hispanic population, and in rural, predominantly Hispanic counties in the southern part of the state. But in most of the state, pot was much more popular than the president. It won in eight counties that Obama lost and did better by 15 percent or more in fifteen counties. Included are many counties along the Rocky Mountain Front Range from New Mexico to Wyoming as well as many central and western Colorado counties. Even El Paso County (Colorado Springs) almost supported pot (49 percent) while rejecting Obama by a margin of more than two to one.

In Washington, Obama outpolled marijuana in the urban and industrial areas of Seattle, Tacoma, Everett, Bremerton, and Olympia on Puget Sound, and to the south in Longview and Vancouver. However, marijuana support was much higher in much of eastern Washington, including in many strongly Republican counties. It is interesting, too, that in Washington counties with major military bases all supported legalization.

In Washington, we can also compare the vote for Resolution 74, same-sex marriage. Support for legalizing marijuana was higher in thirty-seven counties, while Resolution 74 was higher only in King County and its recreation and retirement satellite, San Juan County. The preference for pot over same-sex marriage was greatest in far northeastern Washington (13 to 16 percent).

How did the two referenda correlate with other characteristics of Colorado and Washington? The data illustrate that support for legalizing marijuana was highest in places with large numbers of well-educated young adults. It was lower among the elderly, families with young children, and people with less formal education. These ecological associations should be viewed with caution. Still, the positive effect of education, urbanization, and income is consistent, and the negative relation with high shares of children or the elderly and the less educated is strong.

VOTES AT THE LOCAL LEVEL: AN EXAMPLE FROM SEATTLE

RICHARD L. MORRILL

Washington may be a left coast "blue" state, and Seattle is the most liberal Democratic city in the state. However, polarization among the electorate can be found even within heavily Democratic cities such as Seattle. People in Seattle and other cities are sufficiently segregated that smaller areas like precincts and census tracts' aggregations of precincts exhibit profound polarization. The 2012 elections in Washington illustrate this level of polarization. The votes for president, the vote to reaffirm the right to same-sex marriage, and the vote to legalize marijuana are analyzed for the state of Washington as a whole, the greater Seattle area, and the most pro-Obama tracts in the Seattle area.

Analysis of the census-tract electoral data for the entire state shows three overlapping dimensions. The dominant one is the urban-rural division. The strongest division is between center cities and small towns and rural areas, with smaller cities and metropolitan suburbs in between and less polarized geographically. The second dimension is of social liberalism and is characterized by variables on household relationships, unmarried partners, gay and lesbian, education, and occupation. The third dimension is race, contrasting areas dominated by minority racial groups and those with predominantly white populations.

In the presidential election, President Barack Obama carried Washington by a margin of 464,000 votes, winning 53 percent of the vote to 47 percent for Mitt Romney. However, Romney won most, although not all, of Washington east of the Cascade Mountains, with a strong wedge into southwestern Washington (see figures 5.6, 5.7, 5.8, and 5.9). Most of the rural areas in this portion of Washington that gave majorities for Obama are in American Indian reservations or have large Latino populations. Obama also did well in traditional logging areas of western Washington, a continuation of a long history of their identification with Democratic voting. Rural to smaller-city areas voting for Obama include university towns, notably Pullman (Washington State in eastern Washington), Bellingham (Western Washington University), Olympia, the state capitol, and many areas of "spillover" of more highly educated and professionals out of the Seattle core to water and mountain environments for retirement and second homes. At the other extreme are two areas in western Washington that are extremely "red," the Centralia area in southwestern Washington, and the city of Lynden near the Canadian border, which is still dominated by Dutch Reformed Church adherents.

Turning to the equivalent maps for Obama for the greater Seattle area, Obama's support dominates with "red" areas pushed to the rural edge. Obama's highest percentages were within the city of Seattle itself, with an inner suburban belt of moderate Obama domination (60 to 75 percent) and an outer suburban and exurban ring with lower levels of Obama support. This is repeated for the city of Tacoma to the south. To the west, however, are two islands of very high Obama support, Vashon and Bainbridge, where many residents commute to work in the Seattle core. Areas of support for Romney include a few fairly close-in affluent areas and more rural areas, including actual farming areas to the southeast.

The final map is of the tracts with the highest support for Obama, most of which are confined to the city of Seattle (figure 10.8). The areas of over 90 percent support are, first, the historic CD, or Central District, which defined the Seattle black population as of 1970–1980. This area is not much gentrified at the north end, but it also includes the core of Seattle's LGBT community (the westward extension over 90 percent). The second area is in north Seattle, extending from west of the University of Washington westward and including areas dominated by young singles and unmarried couples, including many students. Clearly, the three dimensions of polarization by settlement type, by social values and education, and by race all are exemplified by the map results.

Referendum 74, or R74, was a referendum on reaffirming the right to same-sex marriage in Washington. Maps for the Seattle area (figure 10.9) and for the state as a whole (see figure 10.5) illustrate the three overlapping dimensions: urban-rural, racial, and social. The latter is most relevant to the vote on R74. The dimension of social liberalism is characterized by variables on household relationships, including the percentage of people living with unmarried partners and the percentage of lesbians, gay persons, bisexuals, and transsexuals (LGBT). Places with high percentages of people in managerial and professional occupations and with a high percentage of people holding college degrees tended also to show strong levels of support for R74. The social divide also shows difference by age; those twenty to thirty-four years old were more likely to support R74, and those with high shares under age eighteen more likely to oppose it.

R74 won by some 229,000 votes, 52 to 48 percent. However, as seen in figure 10.5, opposition to R74 is very pervasive not only in eastern Washington but also in most of western Washington, more obviously isolating the Seattle metropolitan core. Turning to the equivalent maps for R74 for the greater Seattle area, with two-thirds of the state population, the picture is broadly the opposite of that for the state. Here blue (support for R74) dominates, with "red" areas pushed to the rural edge. The area of strongest support is reduced to the city of Seattle, plus the commuter islands, but while still majority, support for R74 is quite a bit weaker in less affluent and educated black and Latino areas. Likewise, the majority of inner suburban areas were still supportive, but only weakly. These are mainly family areas, while the areas of highest support in the city are dominated by singles and childless couples, including unmarried partners. Conversely, moderately higher support extends somewhat farther east to affluent educated suburbs, for example, the Microsoft workshed, which is also high in Asian American population. The final map (figure 10.10) is of the tracts with the highest support for R74, most of which are confined to the city of Seattle. The map for R74 shows no areas of extreme support to the south of the core LGBT area but strong support in the highly affluent and professional areas just north of the LGBT core. Thus, the vote for R74 was extremely concentrated in the metropolitan core, as the margin in the central city of Seattle, 217,000, was essentially the margin for the state.

Washington voters approved the legalization of the recreational use of marijuana (Initiative 502) by a margin of 53 to 47 percent. This compares to 55 percent for Obama and 52 percent for R74, the equally contentious referendum on same-sex marriage. The votes and the maps in fact look and are similar (figure 5.10). It is tempting and easy to describe politics in Washington as greater Seattle (weird and left) versus the rest of Washington. But the story is a little more complex than that. The correlation between R74 and Initiative 502 at the tract level is an astoundingly high .92. For Initiative 502 and percent for Obama, it was .82, and for R74 and Obama, .84. So the R74, Initiative 502 nexus is one of social liberalism, while the vote for Obama was more complex because of the added racial dimension.

Areas of strong support for 502 for the state included mountain and coastal recreation and retirement areas, Indian reservations, college and university areas everywhere, and the downtown, nonfamily cores of most cities, including Seattle, Spokane, Yakima, Vancouver, Olympia, Tacoma, and Bellingham, but not the strongly Mormon Tri-Cities (Kennewick-Richland) area. Areas of strongest opposition to 502 were the Mormon and Hispanic Catholic areas of eastern Washington, farming community areas generally, and the seemingly anomalous, more blue-collar areas of southwestern Washington, especially ultraconservative Lewis County. Areas of moderate support included most of rural small-town western Washington, especially forested areas, and moderate opposition was found in the rest of eastern Washington's open spaces.

But the main and most interesting story is greater Seattle—truly a phenomenon. Almost as if one lived in Seattle and its ferry commuter islands to the west, one feels compelled to lean socially liberal, so extreme is the demarcation. Tracts of over 70 percent support almost coincide with the Seattle city limits. The city zone of over 70 percent is surrounded by an inner suburban belt of fairly high support and then bordered by an exurban zone of moderate support, with rather few tracts of even moderate opposition.

Within the inner zone of over 70 percent support, the core of over 80 percent support is concentrated in then-nonfamily, young, and professional, often LGBT-dominated tracts to the north and east of downtown Seattle, that is, Capitol Hill, and the student and staff areas near the University of Washington campus. All of the nine precincts that reported a "yes" vote of over 90 percent are located in the area of Capitol Hill, immediately northeast of downtown.

Comparing the vote for 502 with those for R74 and Obama, 502 was more popular than Obama in rural forested areas of western Washington, including metropolitan exurban areas, but less popular than Obama in racial minority areas. The geographic patterns for R74 and 502 are very close, but with an average support for Initiative 502 several points higher and with fairly large areas of moderate opposition to R74 giving way to modest support for 502.

FIGURE 10.8

Seattle Area

Democratic Popular Vote
2012 Presidential Election

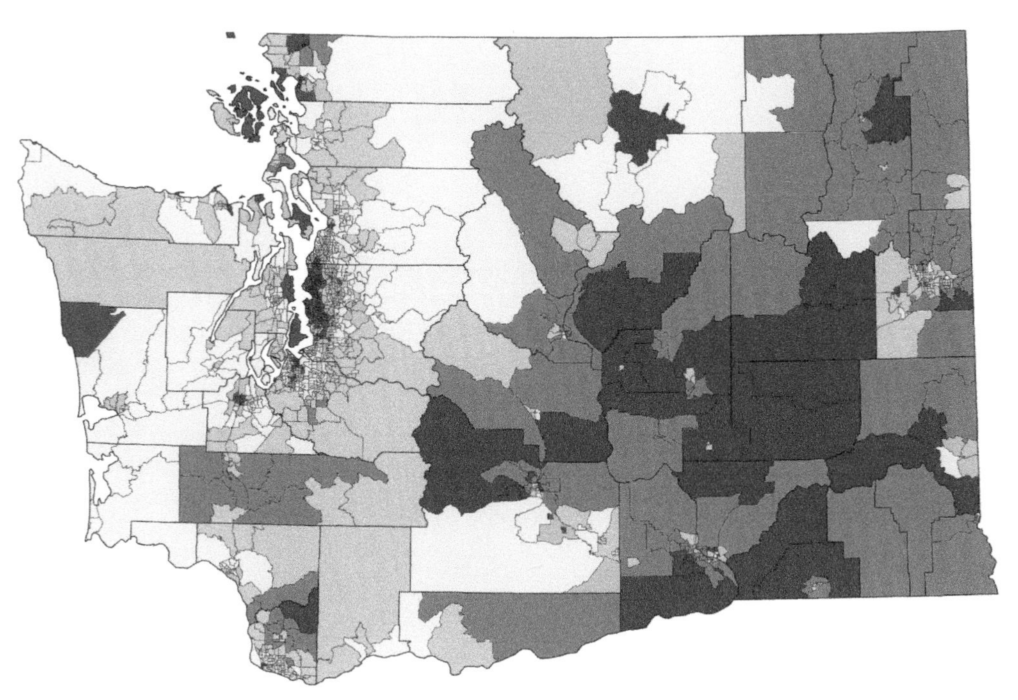

Democratic Percentage of Popular Vote

FIGURE 10.9

Seattle Area

Referendum 74: Same Sex Marriage
Washington 2012 Election

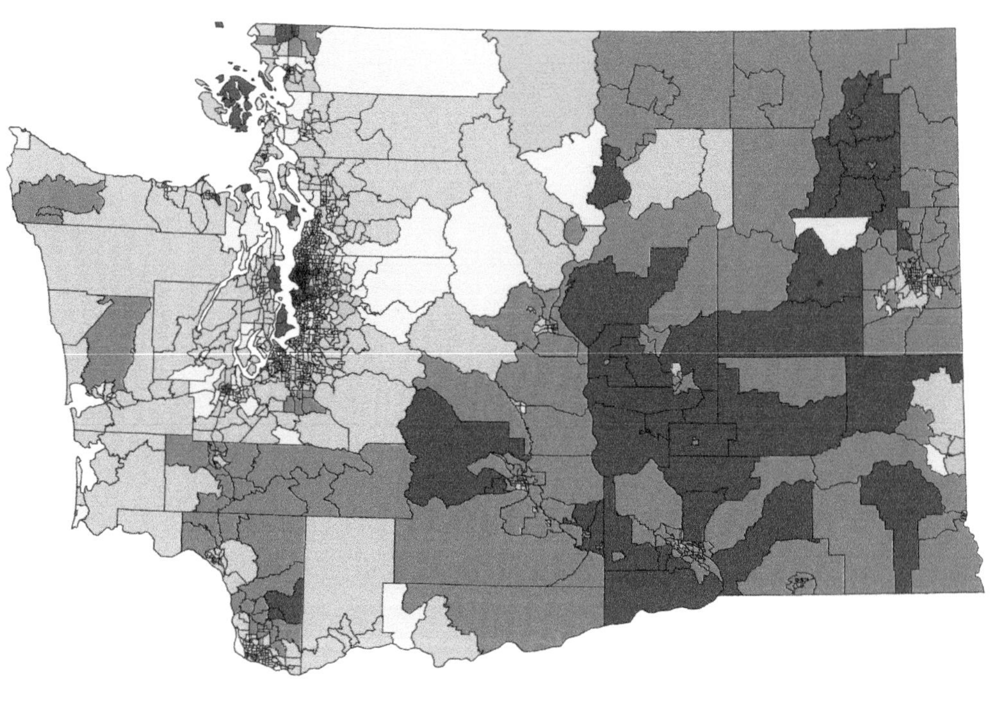

FIGURE 10.10

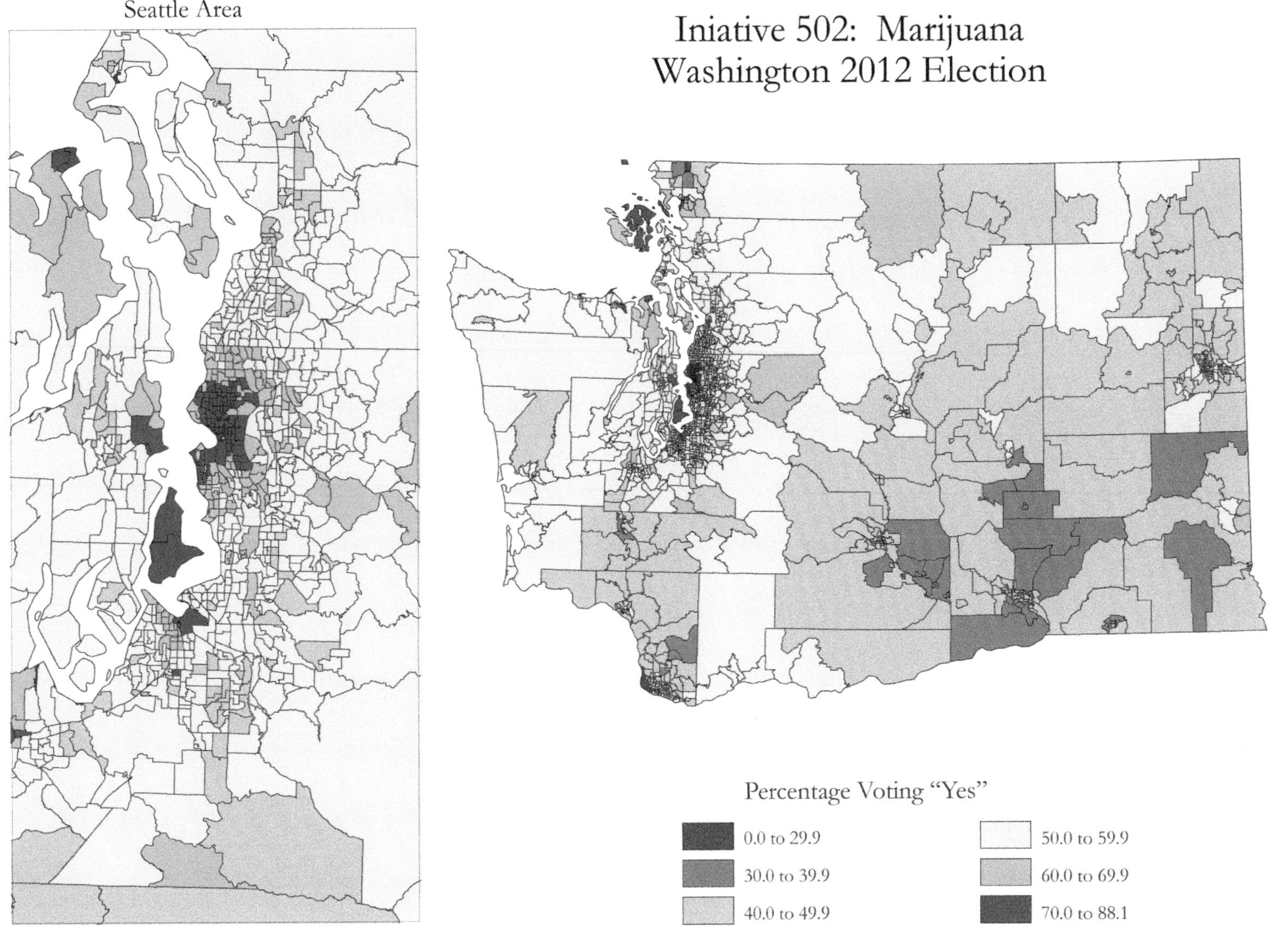
Seattle Area
Iniative 502: Marijuana
Washington 2012 Election
Percentage Voting "Yes"
0.0 to 29.9
30.0 to 39.9
40.0 to 49.9
50.0 to 59.9
60.0 to 69.9
70.0 to 88.1

TECHNICAL ISSUES, DATA, AND MAPPING

ROBERT H. WATREL AND J. CLARK ARCHER

Creation of the *Atlas of the 2012 Elections* involved the assembly and refinement of election data and other geocodable data from numerous sources, the analysis of election data using statistical and analytical software, the drafting of geographically and thematically accurate maps using geographic information systems (GIS) software, and the graphical refinement of these draft maps and other graphics using professional illustration software capable of producing publication-quality graphics.

Thematic maps such as those included in this atlas require the assemblage of data of two kinds: first, what cartographers refer to as "attribute" data needed to answer "what" or "how much" questions; second, what cartographers refer to as "locational" data needed to answer "where" questions. Attribute data indicate the existence and values of features to be mapped, such as numbers of registered voters, votes cast by party, income levels, religious affiliations, and so on. Locational data identify the geographical positions or areas where the features to be mapped were observed to be located. To map the outcome of an election, for example, it is necessary to assemble both an accurate tabular listing of votes cast by candidate or party for every relevant election subdivision such as precincts or counties and also an accurate base map that shows the geographical boundaries for each of the relevant election subdivisions.

Moreover, it is imperative that both the tabular data and the locational data be accurately geocoded or geographically referenced in relation to one another. Geographical election analysts must also take care to avoid mistakes due to changed or inaccurately depicted election district boundaries. In other words, geographical election analysts must be careful to map correct data values in their correct geographical locations. On one hand, simple checks such as summations of votes over precincts within constituencies will not guarantee avoiding mixed-up maps. But on the other hand, careful inspection of mapped patterns can uncover data or coding errors that escaped detection in tabular or statistical representations.

Although the US Constitution requires electoral votes from each state in each presidential election to be certified, it does not stipulate that records of popular votes cast in general elections held to select presidential electors also must be sent to the president of the Senate. Although electors have been chosen through the popular vote in each state since the early nineteenth century, there is no requirement that states select their members of the Electoral College by popular vote. Consequently, there is no official complete historical nationwide record of general election returns for elective federal offices in the United States as a whole. Recent presidential elections have been held under federal statutes that require the governor of each state to send "a certificate of ascertainment" showing popular votes for each elector to the archivist of the United States, and the Office of the Clerk of the US House of Representatives has compiled and published popular returns at state level (for president and US senators) and congressional district level (for US representatives), "Statistics of the Congressional and Presidential Election," for federal elections from 1920 to the present. Facsimile copies of this biennial series can be obtained at http://history.house.gov/Institution/Election-Statistics/Election-Statistics/ from the Office of the Clerk of the US House of Representatives.

In the absence of any single federal government source of popular presidential or other election returns at a county level for the nation as a whole, the authors collected "final" or "certified" election results for the November 6, 2012, general election from the Internet website of the responsible agency in each of the fifty states and the District of Columbia. But it is relevant to point out that quite directly reflecting the compound republic features of federal elections, there is very little uniformity from one state to another in how election results are presented on each state's website. The websites of some states provide election data in the form of flat ASCII text files, and others offer PDF documents or even in some cases Excel spreadsheet files. An important and necessary step in assembling the 2012 election data needed for this atlas was the data reformatting and editing step needed to bring all of the variously structured data sets collected from each state into one single common and consistent format so that mapping and analysis could be conducted for the United States as a whole.

It is also relevant that while federal regulations in place for the 2012 US presidential election required that any controversies and/or recounts involving the presidential election be resolved by December 10, 2012, in order for certification of popular presidential votes at a state level, controversies and/or recounts involving other contests continued for several weeks beyond this deadline in several states. These controversies and recounts delayed those states' release of "final" or "certified" votes at the county level for the presidential contest as well. It is worth noting that the "final" or "certified" results assembled from each state revealed roughly one or two percentage points more popular support for the Democratic Obama-Biden presidential ticket in many states relative to the earlier "preliminary" results presented in television and press coverage of the election. Upon reflection, this is perhaps not too surprising, since the Obama-Biden ticket usually received more support from voters in large metropolitan areas, where polling wait times were sometimes longer and vote tallies tended to lag behind those of less populous and more rural settings.

Thus, the maps of the 2012 presidential election and also of other 2012 elections shown in this atlas sometimes exhibit patterns that differ from those shown on maps published shortly after the election that were based on preliminary rather than on later released "final," "official," or "certified" results for the counties in each state. Large metropolitan areas throughout the country are often settings for such discrepancies. And so are some rural sections of New England, in which it appears that the preliminary county-level tallies used for maps published shortly after the election perhaps failed to incorporate sufficient returns from rural towns. Several New England states do not publish election returns by county, so the final "certified" results for townships in these states had to be aggregated to a county level by the authors for the maps and analyses in this atlas. Other election maps produced using data for smaller areas, such as the congressional district–level maps of the United States as a whole, or the census tract, or voting district–level maps for Pennsylvania or Washington State, also use final rather than preliminary voting returns. To reemphasize, all of the maps of 2012 elections shown in this atlas are based on "final" or "certified" results that were assembled by the authors from the official election reporting website of each state.

The "locational" data needed to create 2012 election maps for this atlas were mostly obtained from the US Bureau of the Census (www.census.gov). The US Census Bureau is responsible for maintaining and distributing Topologically Integrated Geographic Encoding and Referencing (TIGER) files, which encode the current boundaries of many varieties of administrative and political entities, including counties, municipalities, census blocks, census tracts, school districts, voting districts, and constituency districts for state and federal legislatures. Great care was taken to ensure that proper Federal Information Processing System (FIPS) codes were contained in the voting and other thematic data files used and that proper "joins" were established with TIGER and other polygon or GIS geographical location and topological description files pertaining to the locations and areas mapped. Considerable caution is needed to avoid creating mixed-up maps, because there are roughly 3,100 counties and county-equivalent units in the United States and many thousands of smaller areas such as townships, census tracts, or voting districts.

"GIS" is an acronym for geographic information system, a term referring to "an integrated collection of computer software and data used to view and manage information about geographic places, analyze spatial relationships, and model spatial processes" (Wade and Sommer 2006, 90). Roughly half of the maps presented in this atlas were initially created using the ArcMap component of recent or current versions of ESRI's ArcGIS software (ESRI 2012a). Most of the other maps presented in this atlas were initially created using Strategic Mapping's AtlasGIS or AtlasGIS for Windows (Strategic Mapping 1992, 1994). Both ArcGIS and AtlasGIS are mainly "vector-based" GIS systems, which permit maps to be rescaled or "zoomed" without "jaggies" or loss of line fidelity.

Both of these packages allow maps to be created using an Albers equal-area map projection, that was chosen as the standard projection for maps in this atlas. The Albers projection is a conical equal-area projection that was specifically designed to represent areas within the latitude range of the continental United States with minimum distortion (Dent, Torguson, and Hodder 2009). The Albers projection is the standard projection for thematic maps of the continental United States published by the US Census Bureau, so it renders a good cartographic depiction of the United States that is consistent with mapping of US census data and that is familiar to many map readers.

Draft maps were exported from ArcMap or AtlasGIS in various vector-graphics formats in order to be graphically improved using Adobe Illustrator CS5 or CS6 (Adobe Systems Incorporated 2010, 2013). Graphical refinements were made to line weights and styles, colors, fonts, text placement, legend placement, and other graphic aspects using Adobe's illustration software, which is generally regarded as "state of the art" in the publishing industry. These graphical refinements were made in part by following guidelines for superior map design that have been promoted by several well-known and accomplished cartographers in recent cartography textbooks (Brewer 2005; Dent, Torguson, and Hodler 2009; Slocum, McMaster, Kessler, and Howard 2009). Map design selections also were made in ways intended to promote cartographic consistency with maps in the previously published *Atlas of the 2008 Elections* (Brunn, Webster, Morrill, Shelley, Lavin, and Archer 2011), so that interested readers might most effectively compare the geographical patterns of the 2012 elections with those of the preceding 2008 elections visually by looking at both atlases at the same time.

The historical maps and analysis presented in chapter 5 of this atlas are intended to help readers interpret the geographical outcome of the 2012 US presidential election from an even longer-term temporal perspective than that of only the two early-twenty-first-century elections that were won by Barack Obama. Over the course of US political history, electorally relevant matters regarding candidates, issues, party labels, and, of course, geographical constituency boundaries have changed markedly (Martis 1989; Shelley, Archer, Davidson, and Brunn 1996; Archer, Lavin, Martis, and Shelley 2002, 2006; Brunn, Webster, Morrill, Shelley, Lavin, and Archer 2011). Many of the historical election data used in chapter 5 were derived from several computer-readable election data sets available from the Inter-university Consortium for Political and Social Research (ICPSR 1986, 1993, 1999). Many other sources too numerous to cite here were used to cross-check or supplement data from the ICPSR (see Archer, Lavin, Martis, and Shelley 2006, esp. 25–28). For presidential elections from 1976 onward, most of the county-level presidential election data used were collected by the authors for previous research (Archer, Lavin, Martis, and Shelley 2002, 2006; Brunn, Webster, Morrill, Shelley, Lavin, and Archer 2011).

The maps of the previous presidential elections that were selected for cartographic presentation based on the T-mode factor analysis results summarized in chapter 5 were drawn using state and county boundaries as these existed at the time of each of the historical elections displayed. Considerable historical geographical research underlay the identification and GIS geocoding of historical county boundaries as they existed at the time of each election (see Archer, Lavin, Martis, and Shelley 2006, esp. 28–30). The historical election maps shown in chapter 5 were created especially for this atlas to depict the levels of popular support for the leading presidential candidate in each county at each of the selected elections. Multiple maps for each of the candidates who received at least 2 percent of the national popular vote at a given election using different choropleth classification criteria, published in a previous atlas by the authors, can be examined for more specific geographical detail than that displayed by the summary maps presented here (Archer, Lavin, Martis, and Shelley 2006).

Technical aspects of the T-mode factor analysis procedures used here in chapter 5 to select historically salient presidential elections for cartographic display have been addressed at length in some previous publications by several of this atlas's authors (Archer and Taylor 1981; Archer and Shelley 1986; Archer, Shelley, Taylor, and White 1988; Shelley and Archer 1989; Shelley, Archer, Davidson, and Brunn 1996) and so will be discussed here only in outline. The basic idea is to use multivariate factor analysis methods to identify sets of elections that exhibited similar geographical patterns.

The first step in the analysis was to use GIS methods to match and, where necessary, resample historical election returns to modern county boundaries in order to create a matrix of Pearson product-moment correlation coefficients between all of the elections from 1872 to 2012 using one uniform set of areal units. The number of states participating in presidential elections during the entire time increased from thirty-seven in 1872 to fifty in 1960, with the District of Columbia added for the first time in 1964. The number of counties analyzed increased from 2,359 in 1872 to 3,079 by 1964. Alaska, which has no county subdivisions, was treated as one area in the statistical analysis, although the changing Alaska election districts are correctly shown on the maps of elections from 1960 onward.

The 36 × 36 matrix of correlation coefficients between all thirty-six presidential elections observed at county level from 1872 to 2012 was calculated in SPSS-PC, version 4.0 (SPSS 1990) using pairwise deletion of missing data in order to retain as much of the original variance as possible at each stage in the statistical analysis. The variables used in calculating these correlation coefficients were the Democratic percentage of the total popular votes in each county at each election. Counties in later-admitted states not yet participating in presidential elections were excluded from these calculations under the pairwise deletion of missing data criterion used. The next statistical step was to use principal components extraction followed by oblique oblimin factor rotation to obtain a statistically concise summary of the correlation matrix in nine rather than the original thirty-six mathematical dimensions of the input correlation matrix. Each of the nine reduced dimensions or factors thus summarizes the main geographical pattern of popular support at county level for the Democratic candidates who contested for the presidency during the elections that was most similar to the patterns identified by each factor.

The factor pattern loadings, which are graphed in figure 5.19, summarize how these patterns have varied through time. If each of the thirty-six elections studied had exhibited an entirely unique geographical pattern with no features in common with those of any of the other thirty-five elections, then no successful reduction from the original thirty-six mathematical dimensions of the input correlation matrix would have been possible. But each of the elections was not unique, so that nine varying factor pattern profiles—rather than thirty-six very uninterestingly flat profiles—present a statistically succinct and historically interesting geographical summary of more than a century of US presidential elections. The election with the highest factor pattern loading on each of the nine oblimin T-mode factors is the most representative of that factor and has been highlighted on the graph and represented by one of the historical presidential election maps. In other words, most of the most important geographical variations associated with US presidential elections from 1872 to 2012 can be visually studied by looking at the maps of these nine elections: 1876, 1896, 1912, 1940, 1960, 1964, 1972, 1992, and 2012. But as a caution, it probably should be acknowledged that a similar analysis based on Republican rather than on Democratic percentages of total popular vote by county might lead to somewhat different statistical results and hence yield a somewhat different set of most representative elections. This is the kind of matter that sustains the fascination of electoral geographers with the ongoing and ever-changing geographical patterns of the American democracy.

Many other types and sources of data were used in creating maps shown in this atlas. Information on reapportionment of the US House of Representatives and the Electoral College and then redistricting of the US House of Representatives following the 2010 census of population was gathered from several sources, including the official apportionment population count and numbers of representatives for each state from the US Census Bureau (www.census.gov) and also the new 2012 US congressional districts boundary file, also from the US Census Bureau. And a wealth of relevant information was found at the official US Electoral College website at the National Archives (www.archives.gov). Information on membership in the US House of Representatives, including the district represented, party affiliation, and seniority of each member was obtained from the Office of the Clerk of the United States House of Representatives (www.clerk.house.gov). The website of the Office of the Clerk of the US House of Representatives is also the source of data on the selected House roll-call votes mapped by House of Representatives district for display and discussion in chapter 8 of this atlas.

Data in chapters 2 and 3 involve events and processes leading up to the general election on November 6, 2012, were assembled from several sources. Data on primary elections and presidential and vice presidential candidate nominating conventions were collected from both printed and online editions of daily newspapers, such as *USA Today*, the *Washington Post*, the *New York Times*, and the *Lincoln Journal-Star*. Primary election returns for selected states were obtained from the official election websites of those states, as were the final general election returns, as was noted in the discussion above.

Campaign finance data were obtained from the Federal Election Commission website for all Democratic and Republican candidates who campaigned for office (www.fec.gov). These data were downloaded using the FEC's Campaign and Committee Viewer and summarized statistically at the state level for the period from January 1, 2011, to December 31, 2012. Total campaign contributions were summarized for Barack Obama and Mitt Romney and for the all Democratic and Republican candidates. Campaign expenditures were totaled for the Obama and Romney campaigns for the primary and general elections.

Published editorial endorsements by newspapers are sought eagerly by presidential candidates in order to increase their visibility to potential voters. Several sources were used to identify which newspapers endorsed which candidate in the general election campaign. Major sources include the websites of the American Presidency Project at the University of California Santa Barbara (www.presidency.ucsb.edu; Peters and Woolley, 2012), *Wikipedia* (www.en.wikipedia.org), and *Editor and Publisher* (www.editorandpublisher.com). Geographical latitude and longitude coordinates for the city where the central office of each endorsing newspaper is located were obtained using information from ESRI's Data and Maps for ArcGIS (2012b) and Microsoft's Streets & Trips 2011 (2010) in order that endorsements could be mapped accurately using ArcGIS Version 10.1 (ESRI 2012a).

Another important aspect of presidential election campaigns is travel, the campaign trips and local appearances made by presidential and vice presidential candidates. The locations of campaign stops made during the general election campaign from September 1 to November 6 were traced using daily reports collected from both printed and online editions of daily newspapers, such as *USA Today*, the *Washington*

Post, the *New York Times*, and the *Lincoln Journal-Star*. The most consistently useful source of campaign stop information, however, was the Politico website (www.politico.com), which provided a daily calendar of campaign activities by Obama and Biden on the Democratic side and by Romney and Ryan on the Republican side. Overall patterns of campaign stops were tallied and then mapped by state for the entire September 1 to November 6 period using AtlasGIS (Strategic Mapping Inc. 1992). And because campaign activity during the last week of the campaign can be especially revealing about campaign dynamics, the geographical coordinates for the location of each of the campaign stops made by Obama, Biden, Romney, and Ryan during the last week of the campaign were determined. Maps of the movements of the candidates were then created using MicroCAM version 2.03 (Loomer 2000) and refined for publication using Adobe Illustrator CS5 (Adobe 2010).

Many of the county-level maps of election-relevant demographic, economic, and social population characteristics in chapter 7 are based on information from the US Census Bureau website (www.census.gov). Census-based data used include material from the 2010 US census of population (US Census Bureau 2010) and from the 2007–2011 American Community Survey (US Census Bureau 2013c). 2010 census data were used to identify age group and racial and ethnic patterns by county, while 2007–2011 American community survey data were used for educational attainment, employment by industry, and income and poverty. In addition, US Census Population Division population estimates were used as a basis for estimating voting age population by county at the time of the 2012 election (US Census 2012) and for estimating net migration to and from counties for the 2011 to 2012 period (US Census 2013a). County-level labor force unemployment percentages at about the time of the 2012 election were obtained from the Bureau of Labor Statistics (2013). Religion data have not been collected or reported by the US Census Bureau since early in the twentieth century. Instead, data on religious affiliation by county in the United States were obtained from the enumeration of religious bodies compiled by the Association of Statisticians of American Religous Bodies for the *2010 U.S. Religion Census* (Grammich et al. 2012; www.USReligionCensus.org).

Most of the maps showing various population characteristics by county in chapter 6 were drafted using AtlasGIS (Strategic Mapping Inc. 1992) and then refined for publication using Adobe Illustrator CS5 (Adobe 2010). Although the older AtlasGIS software's GIS system lacks numerous refinements that have been included in the more modern ArcGIS (ESRI 2012a) system, the use of AtlasGIS in combination with data sorting and ranking features of the Microsoft Office 2007 Excel spreadsheet program facilitated the determination of appropriate choropleth map classes for each overall county-level feature distribution map and also the break-point values needed to identify and separate the top and/or bottom two hundred counties for each of the population characteristics examined. In some cases, tied ranks made it impossible to select exactly the two hundred highest and/or lowest ranked counties for a particular characteristic, but these difficulties were relatively uncommon. Once the top or bottom two hundred counties for a particular characteristic had been identified, then an especially convenient GIS selection and summation tool in AtlasGIS was used to find the sums of the total votes and of the votes for Democratic, Republican, and other party candidates cast in all the top or bottom two hundred counties shown on the lower county selection maps in chapter 7. The vote percentage values shown on the right-hand graphs that accompany each page layout consisting of an upper map of the overall county-level pattern of a feature and a lower map showing the two hundred top and/or two hundred bottom counties for that feature are thus based on calculations that involve aggregates for all included counties selected together rather than county-level averages. In other words, the graphs represent the overall political dispositions of geographical collectivities or groupings of counties that are especially high or low on a given population characteristic.

Chapter 10 information and data regarding referenda and initiatives were obtained from the websites of the Initiative and Referenda Institute at the University of Southern California (www.iandrinstitute.org) and the National Conference of State Legislatures (www.ncsl.org). In addition, locationally specific data regarding voter support for or opposition to several specific ballot propositions at county level or election district level, along with senatorial vote returns, were obtained from the official election websites of several states, including Colorado, Indiana, Maine, Maryland, Massachusetts, Minnesota, Missouri, North Dakota, Virginia, Washington, and Wisconsin. Data for congressional votes were obtained from the Office of the Clerk of the U.S. House of Representatives.

REFERENCES

Adobe Systems Incorporated. 2010. *Adobe Illustrator CS5*. San Jose, CA: Adobe Systems.

Adobe Systems Incorporated. 2013. *Adobe Illustrator CS6*. San Jose, CA: Adobe Systems.

Archer, J. Clark, Stephen J. Lavin, Kenneth C. Martis, and Fred M. Shelley. 2002. *Atlas of American Politics, 1960–2000*. Washington, DC: CQ Press.

Archer, J. Clark, Stephen J. Lavin, Kenneth C. Martis, and Fred M. Shelley. 2006. *Historical Atlas of U.S. Presidential Elections, 1788–2004*. Washington, DC: CQ Press.

Archer, J. Clark, and Fred M. Shelley. 1986. *American Electoral Mosaics*. Washington, DC: Association of American Geographers.

Archer, J. Clark, Fred M. Shelley, Peter J. Taylor, and Ellen R. White. 1988. "The Geography of U.S. Presidential Elections." *Scientific American* 259 (1) (July): 44–51.

Archer, J. Clark, and Peter J. Taylor. 1981. *Section and Party*. New York: Wiley.

Brewer, Cynthia A. *Designing Better Maps: A Guide for GIS Users*. Redlands, CA: ESRI Press.

Brunn, Stanley D., Gerald R. Webster, Richard L. Morrill, Fred M. Shelley, Stephen J. Lavin, and J. Clark Archer. 2011. *Atlas of the 2008 Elections*. Lanham, MD: Rowman & Littlefield.

Bureau of Labor Statistics. 2013. *Local Area Unemployment Statistics: Labor Force Data by County, 2012 Annual Averages*. Last accessed January 21, 2014. www.bls.gov/lau/laucnty12.txt.

Burnham, Walter Dean. 1970. *Critical Elections and the Mainsprings of American Politics*. New York: Norton.

Clerk of the House of the United States House of Representatives (Karen L. Haas). 2014. "Official List of Members, One Hundred Thirteenth Congress, January 8, 2014." Last accessed January 21, 2014. www.clerk.house.gov/member_info/olm-113.pdf.

Clerk of the House of the United States House of Representatives (Karen L. Haas). 2013. "Roll Call Votes: 113th House, 1st Session." Last accessed January 21, 2014. www.clerk.house.gov.

Dent, Borden D., Jeffrey S. Torguson, and Thomas W. Hodler. 2009. *Cartography: Thematic Map Design*. 6th ed. New York: McGraw-Hill Higher Education.

Editor and Publisher. 2013. "2012 Presidential Endorsements." Last accessed January 21, 2014. www.editorandpublisher.com/election.

ESRI. 2012a. *ArcGIS 10.1 for Desktop*. Redlands, CA: ESRI.

ESRI. 2012b. *Data and Maps for ArcGIS (2012)*. Redlands, CA: ESRI.

Federal Election Commission. 2013. "Campaign and Committee Viewer: Campaign Finance Reports and Filings." Accessed February 26, 2013 through March 8, 2013. http://www.fec.gov/finance/disclosure/candcmte_info.shtml.

Grammich, Clifford, Kirk Hadaway, Richard Houseal, Dale E. Jones, Alexei Krindatch, Richie Stanley, and Richard H. Taylor. 2012. *2010 U.S. Religion Census: Religions Congregations and Membership Study*. Kansas City, MO: Nazarene Publishing House, for the Association of Statisticians of American Religous Bodies.

Hewes, Fletcher W. 1888. *Citizen's Atlas of American Politics, 1789–1888*. New York: Scribner's.

ICPSR (Inter-university Consortium for Political and Social Research). 1986. *Electoral Data for Counties in the United States: Presidential and Congressional Races, 1840–1972 (ICPSR 8611)*. Ann Arbor, MI: ICPSR.

ICPSR. 1999. *United States Historical Election Returns, 1824–1968 (ICPSR 001)*. Updated April 26, 1999. Ann Arbor, MI: ICPSR.

ICPSR. 2013. *General Election Data for the United States, 1950–1990 (ICPSR 13)*. Updated November 22, 2013. Ann Arbor, MI: ICPSR.

Initiative and Referendum Institute at the University of Southern California. 2012. "Initiative and Referendum Institute: Ballot Watch 2012: Breakthrough Wins for Marijuana and Same-Sex Marriage." Last accessed January 21, 2014. www.iandrinstitute.org/BW%202012-3%20Election%20Results%20v1.pdf.

Loomer, Scott A. 2000. *MicroCAM for Windows Version 2.03*. West Point, NY: Geographical Sciences Laboratory, US Military Academy.

Martis, Kenneth C. 1989. *The Historical Atlas of Political Parties in the United States Congress, 1789–1989*. New York: Macmillan.

Microsoft. 2010. *Streets & Trips 2011*. Redmond, WA: Microsoft.

National Conference of State Legislatures. 2012. "Initiative and Referendum." Last accessed January 21, 2014. www.ncsl.org/research/elections-and-campaigns/initiative-and-referendum.aspx.

Paullin, Charles O., and John K. Wright. 1932. *Atlas of the Historical Geography of the United States*. New York: American Geographical Society.

Peters, Gerhard, and John T. Woolley. 2012. "2012 General Election Editorial Endorsements by Major Newspapers." Santa Barbara, CA: American Presidency Project at University of California, Santa Barbara. Retrieved March 3, 2013. Last accessed January 21, 2014. www.presidency.ucsb.edu/data/2012_newspaper_endorsements.php.

Plumbe, George E., ed. *The Daily News Almanac and Political Register for 1894*. Chicago: Chicago Daily News.

Politico. 2012. "Elections: Full 2012 Calendar." Last accessed January 21, 2014. www.politico.com/2012-election/calendar.

Shelley, Fred M., and J. Clark Archer. 1989. "Sectionalism and Presidential Politics in America: A Twentieth-Century Reinvestigation of Voting Patterns in Illinois, Indiana and Ohio." *Journal of Interdisciplinary History* 20 (2): 227–55.

Shelley, Fred M., J. Clark Archer, Fiona M. Davidson, and Stanley D. Brunn. 1996. *Political Geography of the United States*. New York: Guilford.

Slocum, Terry A., Robert B. McMaster, Fritz C. Kessler, and Hugh H. Howard. 2009. *Thematic Cartography and Geovisualization*. 3rd ed. Upper Saddle River, NJ: Pearson Prentice Hall.

SPSS Inc. 1990. *SPSS PC+ Version 4.0*. Chicago: SPSS.

Strategic Mapping, Inc. 1992. *AtlasGIS Version 2.1*. Santa Clara, CA: Strategic Mapping.

Strategic Mapping, Inc. 1994. *AtlasGIS for Windows, Version 3.0*. Santa Clara, CA: Strategic Mapping.

Turner, Frederick Jackson. 1932. *The Significance of Sections in American History*. New York: Holt.

US Census Bureau. 2010. "Apportionment Population and Number of Representatives, by State, 2010 Census." Last accessed January 21, 2014. www.census.gov/population/apportionment/files/Apportionment Population 2010.pdf.

US Census Bureau. 2010. *2010 Census of Population*, file County_2010Census_DP1.zip. Access checked January 21, 2014. www.census.gov.

US Census Bureau. 2012. *Annual Estimates of the Resident Population by Selected Age Groups and Sex for Counties, April 1, 2010 to July 1, 2011* file CC-EST2011-AGESEX. Accessed February 9, 2013. www.census.gov.

US Census Bureau. 2013a. *Annual Resident Population, Estimates, Estimated Components of Resident Population Change, and Rates of the Components of Resident Population Change for States and Counties: April 1, 2010 to July 1, 2012* file CC-EST2012-alldata. Accessed May 30, 2013. www.census.gov.

US Census Bureau. 2013b. *2007–2011 American Community Survey: DP02 Selected Social Characteristics in the United States*, file ACS_11_5YR_DP02_with_ann.csv. Last accessed January 21, 2014. www.census.gov.

US Census Bureau. 2013c. *2007–2011 American Community Survey: DP03 Selected Economic Characteristics in the United States*, file ACS_11_5YR_DP03_with_ann.csv. Last accessed January 21, 2014. www.census.gov.

US Census Bureau. 2013. "TIGER/LINE Shapefiles: 113th Congressional District Shapefiles," file tl.rd13_us_cd113.shp. Accessed date May 23, 2013. www.census.gov.

US National Archives. 2012. "Official U.S. Electoral College Website." www.archives.gov/federal-register/electoral-college/index.html.

Wade, Tasha, and Shelly Sommer. 2006. *A to Z GIS: An illustrated Dictionary of Geographic Information Systems*. Redlands, CA: ESRI Press.

Wikipedia. 2012. "Newspaper Endorsements in the United States Presidential Election, 2012." Accessed May 11, 2013. www.en.wikipedia.org/wiki/Newspaper_endorsements_in_the_United_States_presidential_election,_2012.

WEB ADDRESSES:

www.archives.gov. United States National Archives and Records Administration, Washington, DC

www.bls.gov. Bureau of Labor Statistics, United States Department of Labor, Washington, DC

www.census.gov. United States Bureau of the Census, United States Department of Commerce, Washington, DC

www.clerk.house.gov. Office of the Clerk of the United States House of Representatives, Washington, DC

www.editorandpublisher.com. *Editor and Publisher* magazine website

www.fec.gov. Federal Election Commission, Washington, DC

www.iandrinstitute.org. Initiative and Referendum Institute at the University of Southern California

www.ncsl.org. National Conference of State Legislatures

www.politico.com. *Politico* online magazine website

www.presidency.ucsb.edu. American Presidency Project at the University of California, Santa Barbara

www.USReligionCensus.org. Association of Statisticians of American Religious Bodies, 2010 US Religion Census

www.en.wikipedia.org. Wikipedia open encyclopedia project

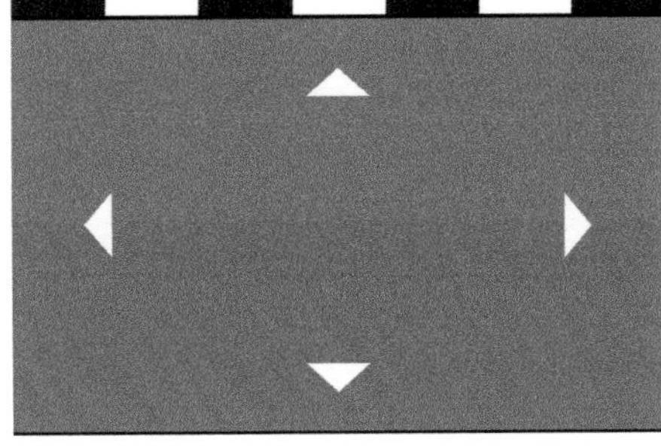

INDEX

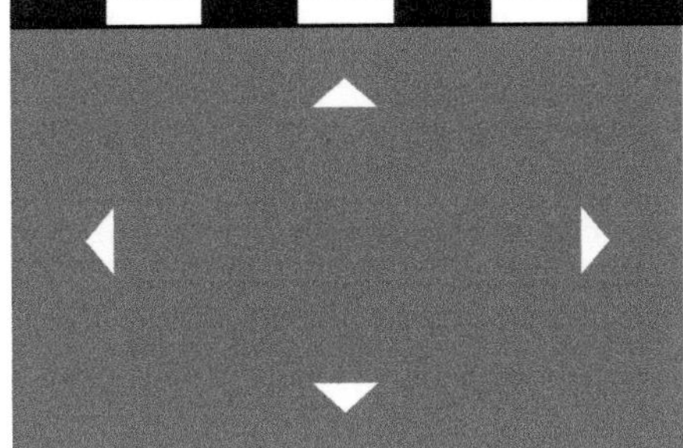

ABOUT THE CONTRIBUTORS

John Agnew is professor of geography at the University of California, Los Angeles.

Ben Anderstone is a political consultant based in Seattle, Washington.

J. Clark Archer is professor of geography at the University of Nebraska, Lincoln.

Matt Balentine is a PhD student in the Department of Geography at the University of North Carolina, Greensboro.

William Berentsen is professor of geography at the University of Connecticut.

Michael Brown is professor of geography at the University of Washington, Seattle.

Wanjing Chen is a PhD student in the Department of Geography at the University of Wisconsin, Madison.

Jason Combs is associate professor of geography at the University of Nebraska, Kearney.

Carl Dahlman is professor of geography and director of International Studies at Miami University.

Fiona Davidson is associate professor of geography at the University of Arkansas.

Joshua J. Dyck is associate professor of political science at the University of Massachusetts, Lowell.

Richard L. Engstrom is university research professor emeritus of political science at the University of New Orleans and a visiting research fellow with the Center for the Study of Race, Ethnicity, and Gender in the Social Sciences at Duke University.

Erin H. Fouberg is professor of geography at Northern State University.

Justin Frazier is an MA candidate in geography at the University of Wyoming.

Kenneth French is assistant professor of geography at the University of Wisconsin, Parkside.

Annika Hagley is assistant professor of politics and international relations at Roger Williams University.

Brooks Heitmeier is a senior majoring in geography at the University of Oklahoma.

John Heppen is professor of geography at the University of Wisconsin, River Falls.

Larry Knopp is professor of interdisciplinary arts and sciences at the University of Washington, Tacoma.

Jonathan Leib is associate professor of geography at Old Dominion University.

Chris Maier is an MA candidate in geography at South Dakota State University.

Kenneth C. Martis is professor emeritus of geography at West Virginia University.

Daniel McGowin is assistant professor of geography at Auburn University.

Sara McLafferty is professor of geography at the University of Illinois at Urbana-Champaign.

Joshua R. Meddaugh is assistant professor of political science at Clayton State University.

Richard L. Morrill is professor emeritus of geography at the University of Washington, Seattle.

Christopher Niedt is assistant professor of applied social research at Hofstra University.

Steven Radil is assistant professor of geography at Ball State University.

Edward Heath Robinson is clinical assistant professor of geography at the University of Illinois at Urbana-Champaign.

Tony Robinson is associate professor of political science at the University of Colorado, Denver.

Leah Sakala is a policy analyst with the Prison Policy Initiative.

Fred M. Shelley is professor of geography at the University of Oklahoma.

Barry D. Solomon is professor of geography and environmental policy at Michigan Technological University.

Peter Wagner is executive director of the Prison Policy Initiative.

Barney Warf is professor of geography at the University of Kansas.

Robert H. Watrel is associate professor of geography at South Dakota State University.

Gerald R. Webster is professor of geography at the University of Wyoming.

Ryan Weichelt is assistant professor of geography at the University of Wisconsin, Eau Claire.

Adam M. Wellstead is assistant professor of environmental and energy policy at Michigan Technological University.

John A. Wertman is senior program manager for government relations with the Association of American Geographers.